Programming the 80386

Quick Reference to the 80386/87 Instruction Set

Programming the 80386

John H. Crawford
Patrick P. Gelsinger

SYBEX®   San Francisco • Paris • Dusseldorf • Soest

Cover design by Thomas Ingalls + Associates
Cover photography by Casey Cartwright

Library of Congress Card Number: 87-61199
ISBN 0-89588-381-3
Manufactured in the United States of America
10 9 8 7 6 5

To our wives, Norma and Linda, who were first chip widows and then book widows.

— John Crawford
— Patrick Gelsinger
Santa Clara, 1987

Acknowledgments

CREATING A BOOK LIKE THIS ONE IS A COMPLEX AND EXACTING PROJECT. We would like to thank Intel Corporation for producing the 80386 and their customers for making the 80386 a success. Thanks to Norma Crawford for word processing of early drafts. Thanks to David Perlmutter for educating us in the operation of the 80387.

We would also like to thank the people at SYBEX who helped bring *Programming the 80386* from the early stages of development to the finished work you see. Our thanks to Dr. R.S. Langer, editor-in-chief, for his enthusiastic support and his choice of fine restaurants; David Kolodney, developmental and project editor; Tanya Kucak, editor, for her fine word chiseling by her red pen that never ran dry; Dan Tauber, technical editor; Olivia Shinomoto, word processor; Charles Cowens, typesetter; Jeff Green, proofreader; Jeffrey James Giese, technical illustrator; Suzy Anger, production coordinator; Evelyn Ong Sy and Jenny Wong, paste-up artists; and Paula Alston, indexer. We would also like to acknowledge the work of Skillful Means, typesetters for Chapter 3.

Contents

Chapter 2 33

Machine State and Memory Addressing

Chapter 3 91

Instruction Set

Chapter 4 **401**

Instruction Set Examples

Chapter 5 **431**

Memory Management, Protection, and Tasks

Introduction

THIS BOOK PRESENTS THE ASSEMBLY LANGUAGE PROGRAMMER'S VIEW OF the 80386, the latest member of the popular Intel 86 family of microcomputers. Throughout the book we focus on the 32-bit features of the chip. The 80386 is entirely compatible with the 8086 and 80286, and we summarize these features in Chapter 9. In addition to complete coverage of the 80386, we also cover the 80387, the numerics coprocessor of the 80386. Rather than presenting the 80387 in an appendix or in a separate chapter, as many books do, we present it in an integrated fashion.

Having spent years developing the chip itself, we are pleased to present the *insider's view* of how to program and use the 80386. Throughout the book, we have strived to be accurate and authoritative, as only the chip designers could be.

An important question to answer is: why should you be reading this book? Why will your understanding and programming of the 80386 benefit you for the next decade or two of your programming career? The answer is in the tremendous cumulative investment in the 86 family. To design and use a computer, investments are continually made. These investments are by those designing computers (IBM PC, PC/AT, PS/2), operating systems (UNIX, MS-DOS), programming languages (C, FORTRAN), application programs (Lotus 1-2-3, MultiMate, dBASE III), and additional hardware (graphics, extra disks, network connections, add-on memory). The investments also include programs you may write yourself and, of course, your time to learn. Thus, computer families, such as the 86, evolve and share compatibility from one generation to the next. This compatibility allows the use and leverage of massive investments already made into a computer family.

We assume you have experience in the basic theory of computer operations. We also assume this is not your first assembly language experience. We thus purposely avoid these introductory topics and recommend the less experienced reader in these areas to first read an introductory text. The book is divided into roughly three parts. Chapters 1-4 present the applications programmer's view of the 80386. Applications programmers can limit their reading to these chapters with little loss in completeness. Chapters 5-7 present the operating-system programmer's view of the 80386. These chapters are less tutorial than Chapters 1-4 and conclude with reference material on the detailed operation of the operating-system facilities. Chapters 5-7 are required reading for the operating-system programmer. Chapters 8 and 9 pick up the loose ends: debugging and 80386 compatibility with the 8086 and 80286. A more detailed description of each chapter follows.

In **Chapter 1,** we give a brief introduction to the 8086 family of processors. We also present other introductory items, such as memory organization and number representations. The bulk of the chapter is dedicated to the data types supported by the 80386 and 80387.

In **Chapter 2,** we present the internal machine state, general registers, processor control registers, and segment registers of the 80386. This is followed by an introduction to memory addressing. Instruction encodings and I/O space addressing are next presented. The chapter concludes with the 80387 internal machine state, general registers, and control registers.

Chapter 3, the most voluminous of the book, presents every instruction of the 80386 and 80387. The instruction presentation is broken into four sections: integer instructions, multiple-segment instructions, instructions for the operating-system writer, and instructions that operate on floating-point data.

Chapter 4 presents several examples of the applications programmer's instructions and machine state. It summarizes the applications programmer's view of the 80386 and 80387.

Chapter 5 presents the memory-management, protection, and multitasking facilities of the 80386. Several registers and system segments used by these facilities are introduced here rather than in Chapter 2. The chapter includes the exact semantics of all segmentation, memory access, control-transfer, and task-switching operations.

Chapter 6 presents the interrupts and exceptions of the 80386 and how they are processed. This includes the priorities of interrupts, how they are masked, and details of control transfers during interrupt processing. As in Chapter 5, an authoritative presentation of the interrupt and exception processing details is given. The chapter concludes with the 80387 exception causes and methods of processing.

Chapter 7 presents examples of the operating-system facilities of the 80386. These examples demonstrate many of the segmentation, paging, and exception facilities discussed in Chapters 5 and 6, and the operating-system and multiple-segment instructions of Chapter 3.

Chapter 8 presents the facilities included in the 80386 specifically to support debugging.

Chapter 9 takes a step backward and discusses executing 16-bit code on the 80386. This includes descriptions of real (8086), virtual-8086, and protected 16-bit modes of operation.

The following references provide additional material on the 80386 and 80387. Since we make no mention of the hardware aspects of the 80386, items 2 and 3 below are particularly useful, as they cover this area.

1. *80386 Programmer's Reference Manual,* Intel Corporation, Order No. 230985.
2. *80386 Hardware Reference Manual,* Intel Corporation, Order No. 231732.
3. *80386 Data Sheet,* Intel Corporation, Order No. 231630.
4. *80386 Assembly Language Reference Manual,* Intel Corporation, Order No. 122332.
5. *80387 Data Sheet,* Intel Corporation, Order No. 231920.

With this brief introduction, let's begin our study of the 80386. It will be challenging, but not without reward, as you make an investment in a very popular microcomputer family.

Basic Concepts

Chapter 1

THIS CHAPTER BEGINS WITH A BRIEF HISTORICAL background of the 86 family of processors developed and manufactured by Intel Corporation. The 80386 is the latest and most powerful member of this 86 family of processors. Following the history lesson, we describe the data types supported by the 80386. The chapter concludes with a description of the floating-point data types supported by the 80387.

► History of Intel Microprocessors

The first microprocessor, the 4004, was developed in 1971 by Intel. The 4004 was quickly enhanced to the 8008. These devices, very trivial by today's standards, were novel but hardly taken seriously as computers of any worth. In 1974 Intel's second-generation microprocessor, the 8080, was introduced. This was the first general-purpose microprocessor and was quite important to the microprocessor industry. In 1978 the third generation was introduced—the 8086. This marked the beginning of microprocessors as "real" computers. This is where the 86 family began.

The 8086 is a 16-bit processor, the 8080 is 8 bits, and the 4004 is 4 bits. The 8088, the little brother of the 8086, was used in the IBM Personal Computer (introduced in 1981) and this launched the personal computer revolution. With this and many other designs using the 8086 and 8088, the 8086 architecture became the most important microprocessor architecture then and now.

But the family did not stop with the 8086. In 1982 Intel introduced the 80186. This component is architecturally identical to the 8086 but includes several other common system devices on the same component. Also in 1982, the 80286 was introduced. The 80286 is an *architectural superset* of the 8086. This means that it can operate exactly as an 8086 but can also do much more. In particular, it added support for multitasking, which is the ability to execute more than one application program, or task, at a time. Multitasking requires the 80286 to support protection between each task and each task's memory area. Both the 80186 and 80286 are 16-bit components.

Finally, the 80386 was introduced in 1985. The 80386 provides two major and many minor enhancements over the 80286 and the 8086. These enhancements are summarized in Appendix A. The two most important enhancements are 32-bit operations and data types, and paging as a memory-management technique in addition to the segmentation technique found in all members of the 86 family. Both paging and segmentation will be discussed in great detail in Chapters 5, 6, and 7. In addition, the 80386 extends the multitasking capabilities of the 80286. The 80386 allows simultaneous execution of 8086, 80286, and 80386 tasks and operating systems.

A final historical point deals with numerics coprocessors. A numerics coprocessor has been associated with each major generation of the 86 family. The major 86 family components are the 8086, 80286, and 80386, and their associated numerics coprocessors are the 8087, 80287, and 80387, respectively. These coprocessors are tightly coupled with the processor to provide a computer architecture that supports floating-point operations and their data types. The minor differences among these generations of floating-point components are listed in Appendix B.

Compatibility with the 8086 and 80286

Each generation of the 86 family has maintained compatibility with each prior member. Thus, the 80386 can execute any programs that execute on the 80286 or 8086. Chapter 9 describes how to run 8086 and 80286 programs on the 80386. But aside from issues of backward compatibility, this book focuses on the full-scale 32-bit facilities available on the 386, and describes how to program the 386 as a 32-bit machine. This book does not discuss how to program either the 8086 or the 80286. (If you wanted to learn how to program the 8086 or 80286, you would be reading another book!)

However, since many readers do have experience programming the 8086 or 80286, we do, where appropriate, point out differences between these members of the family and the 80386. Appendix A summarizes the differences between the 8086, the 80286, and the 80386.

► Data Formats

The primary purpose of a computer is to store, retrieve, and operate upon data. Thus, understanding the data types supported by the machine is a good place to start when learning to program a new computer. The kinds of data types are signed and unsigned integers, BCD (packed and unpacked binary-coded decimal), strings, bits, and floating point. Most of these data types can be found in most computers. Therefore, we emphasize the differences of the 80386 data types from most other computers or, more importantly, from the 8086 or the 80286.

Memory

Before beginning a detailed discussion of data types, you need to understand the organization of memory. Memory, as in all traditional computers, is the prime source and destination of all information. Memory can be considered simply a sequential array of bytes with each byte having a unique address. Addresses normally begin with 0 and increment upward to the maximum address supported by the computer. The 80386 is a 32-bit machine and has a total *physical* address range of 2^{32} bytes or 4G bytes of physical memory. Notice the emphasis on physical address range. In Chapters 2, 5, and 7, you will learn about segmented and paged virtual memory. You will find the maximum virtual memory address to be much larger than 2^{32}.

If more than 8 bits are needed to represent the values in a data type, multiple contiguous bytes are used. A *word* is two contiguous bytes, and can store 2^{16} different values. A *dword,* or *double-word,* is four contiguous bytes, and can store 2^{32} different values.

A simple but important issue with multibyte data is whether the low-order byte is at the lowest address (numerically smaller) or at the highest address. Figure 1.1 illustrates the two possible ways to store a word

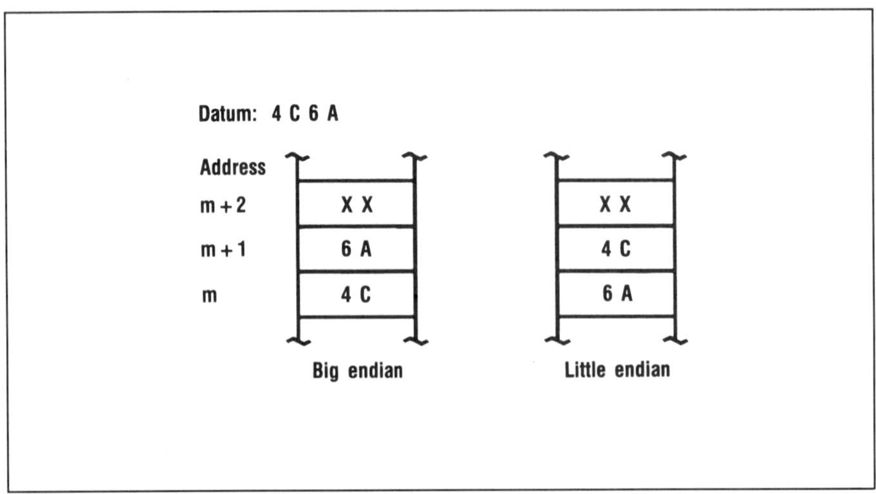

► **Figure 1.1:** Big endian vs. little endian

datum in two bytes of memory. The "big endian" method, on the left, puts the high-order 8 bits in the lowest addressed byte of the word, and the low-order 8 bits in the highest addressed byte. If this seems backward from what you are already familiar with, that is because the 80386 uses the "little endian" method shown on the right. On the 80386, the low-order 8 bits of a word are in the byte with the lowest address (m), which is also the address of the word. The high-order 8 bits of the word are stored at the highest address (m + 1).

We will not try to settle this sometimes religious debate and always heated discussion of big vs. little endian, but you might guess our opinion. Figure 1.2 shows how the bytes are stored for a dword in memory for big and little endian. Again, the 80386 is a little-endian computer.

Notation

Throughout this book, we will introduce notational conveniences that allow concise and unambiguous specifications. One convenience is the specification of numbers. A number followed by *h* will denote a hexadecimal (base 16) number. A number followed by *b* will denote a binary (base 2) number. If the number has neither the h nor the b suffix, it is assumed to be decimal. Thus, 100 is decimal, 100b is binary (with value 4 decimal) and 100h is hexadecimal (with value 256 decimal). Appendix C gives a complete list of the binary to hexadecimal and decimal conversions.

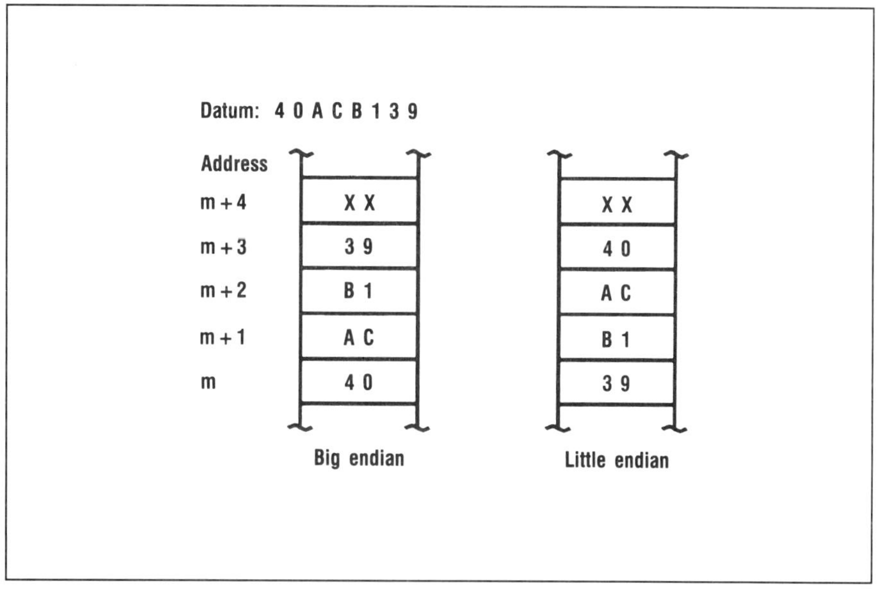

► **Figure 1.2:** Big endian vs. little endian for dwords

Unsigned Numbers

As is normally the case for conventional computers, the 80386 supports the basic unsigned number data type in byte, word, and dword lengths (8, 16, and 32 bits). Dwords are an addition to the 80386 not found in prior 86 family members. Appendix D gives a complete list of the powers of two up to 2^{32}.

Table 1.1 defines a few common abbreviations that we use throughout this book. Thus, the unsigned data types can represent numbers in the range of 0 to 256, 0 to 64K, and 0 to 4G for byte, word, and dword, respectively.

Figure 1.3 shows the organization of the bits in the unsigned data format. Above the three data formats is the memory address beginning at address m as was presented earlier. Bit 0 is the least significant bit (LSB). The most significant bit (MSB) of the unsigned number is bit 7, 15, and 31 for byte, word, and dword representations, respectively.

Signed Integers

The previous section presented the basic unsigned number data types. They have one major deficiency, however: they cannot represent negative

ABBREVIATION	POWER OF TWO	DECIMAL VALUE
1K	2^{10}	1024
4K	2^{12}	4096
16K	2^{14}	16,384
32K	2^{15}	32,768
64K	2^{16}	65,536
2G	2^{31}	2,147,483,648
4G	2^{32}	4,294,967,296

► **Table 1.1:** Abbreviations for powers of two

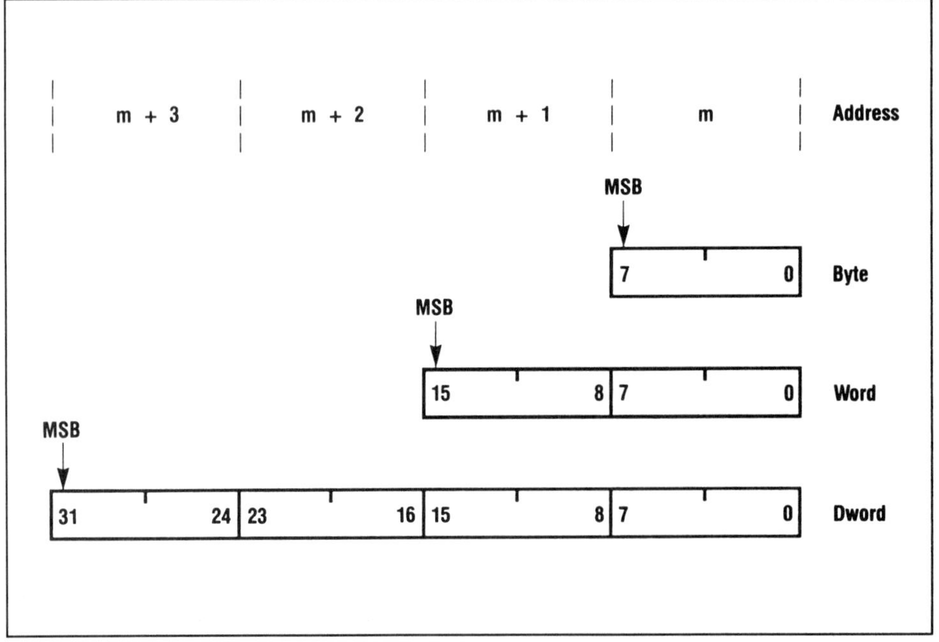

► **Figure 1.3:** Unsigned byte, word, and dword

numbers. If you try to keep track of your checking account balance, you know that signed numbers are essential.

Thus, as is normally the case, negative numbers can be represented in the 80386. There are several ways to represent negative numbers. These include biased numbers, sign magnitude, one's complement, and two's complement. Two's complement is used in the 80386 and all other 86 family members to represent signed integers. Two's complement notation will be described after a brief digression to describe the alternate methods for representing negative numbers. You will see some of these alternate notations later when we present the floating-point data types, so it is worth describing them here.

Table 1.2 gives a list of several numbers in each of these forms. This

DECIMAL	TWO'S COMPLEMENT	ONE'S COMPLEMENT	BIAS (BIAS = 127)	SIGN MAGNITUDE
128	NR	NR	11111111b	NR
127	01111111b	01111111b	11111110b	01111111b
126	01111110b	01111110b	11111101b	01111110b
⋮	⋮	⋮	⋮	⋮
2	00000010b	00000010b	10000001b	00000010b
1	00000001b	00000001b	10000000b	00000001b
0	00000000b	00000000b	01111111b	00000000b
−0	NR	11111111b	NR	10000000b
−1	11111111b	11111110b	01111110b	10000001b
−2	11111110b	11111101b	01111101b	10000010b
⋮	⋮	⋮	⋮	⋮
−126	10000010b	10000001b	00000001b	11111110b
−127	10000001b	10000000b	00000000b	11111111b
−128	10000000b	NR	NR	NR

Note: NR indicates not representable in this format.

► **Table 1.2:** Negative number formats

is not a comprehensive list of representations, but it covers all the formats you will need in this book. The table assumes an 8-bit datum.

Biased Numbers

Biased numbers are used for expressing the *exponent* of a floating-point number, because they make numeric comparison (such as less than or greater than) easy. A biased number is computed by taking the initial positive or negative number and adding a bias value to it. The bias is usually such that the most negative number allowed in the representation becomes 0 and the most positive number becomes the largest value of the representation. Table 1.2 demonstrates this with −127 being the most negative number, and a bias of 127 making 0 the biased representation of −127.

Sign Magnitude

Sign magnitude has a bit representing the sign (0 if positive and 1 if negative), with the remainder of the bits giving an unsigned integer representing the magnitude, or absolute value, of the number. The significand of a floating-point number is expressed in a magnitude notation with a sign bit giving the sign of the entire floating-point number.

One's Complement

In a one's complement number, the MSB indicates the sign of the number (0 if positive and 1 if negative). A negative one's complement number is computed by simply inverting every bit (including the MSB) of the positive number. One's complement notation was common in earlier computers because it is so easy to compute (a simple inversion of each bit). It is not, however, commonly used today.

Two's Complement

Two's complement notation is described below. It is commonly chosen to represent signed integers because it has the pleasant property that the simple binary adder used for unsigned numbers will also add two numbers in two's complement format with no additional transformations. This is important in a computer such as the 80386, which supports both unsigned and two's complement data. Two's complement is formed by computing the one's complement of the number and adding 1 to the result. As was the case for one's complement, the MSB is the sign bit. MSB = 0 indicates a positive number, and MSB = 1 indicates a negative number. Figure 1.4 displays the two's complement forms of the 80386.

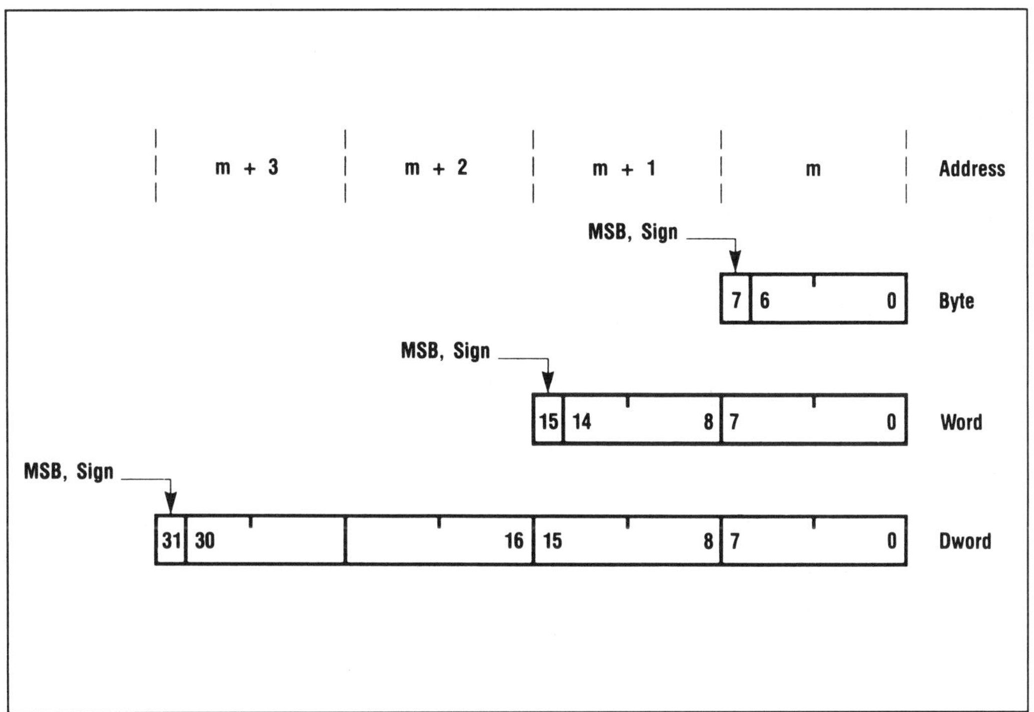

► **Figure 1.4:** Two's complement byte, word, and dword

The 80386 can perform various arithmetic computations upon two's complement numbers. The exact operations that can be performed are discussed in Chapter 3. Also, as is usually the case with two's complement, arithmetic operations (addition, for instance) can cause overflows indicating the result is in error. This is the case when two large positive numbers are added and the result is a small negative number. Chapter 2 discusses how errors such as this are recorded. These conditions are similar to those encountered on other 86 family members.

The 80386 can have 8-, 16-, and 32-bit two's complement data types. These can represent numbers in the ranges −128 to 127, −32K to 32K−1, and −2G to 2G−1, for byte, word, and dword, respectively.

Strings

As was the case in prior 86 family members, the 80386 supports operations on strings of data. A string is a contiguous sequence of bytes, words, or dwords. Support of dword strings is new to the 80386. The length of a string is from 1 to 2^{32} (4G) elements. Figure 1.5 shows the three kinds of strings.

The 80386 has instructions to move strings from one area of memory to another, to compare two strings, to fill a string with a fixed element, to read or write strings from input/output ports, and to search strings for specific data values.

ASCII

One of the most common forms of strings are ASCII strings. ASCII data is quite common in an 80386 system, since most data originating from a terminal is in ASCII (American Standard Code for Information Interchange). Thus, as was the case in other 86 family members, it is important for the 80386 to support ASCII. Appendix E gives the complete ASCII table. This includes integers, alphabetic characters, special characters, and control characters.

The 80386 supports arithmetic operations such as addition and division on ASCII numbers. These operations are described in more detail in Chapter 3.

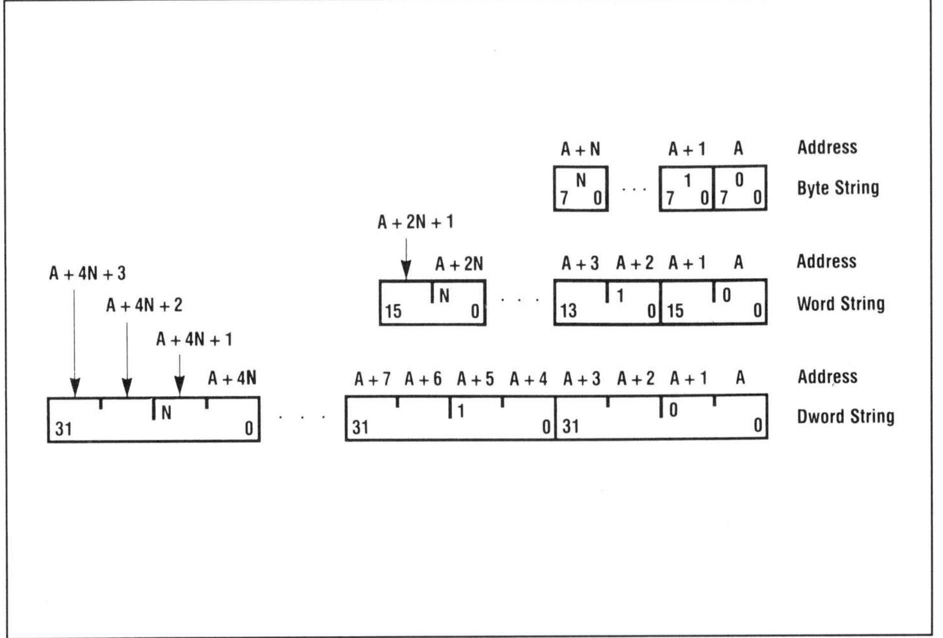

► **Figure 1.5:** Byte, word, and dword strings

Bits

Everything we have discussed so far has shown the 80386 operating on data that is at least 8 bits wide and often larger. The support of operations on bit strings is new to the 80386, as no other 86 family member supports it.

Bit support is important, since data can often be represented by a single bit. A common example is a bitmap display. In a bitmap display, each *pixel,* a single dot on the display, is mapped to a single bit in memory, which is either 1 (the dot or phosphor is lit) or 0 (the dot is dark). Another example is a semaphore where a single bit indicates whether the semaphore is free (0) or busy (1). It is possible to dedicate an entire byte to each pixel or semaphore, but this would waste much storage. In fact, you would waste 7 bits per data element, or 87.5 percent of memory. For this reason the 80386 also supports operations on bit data.

The 80386 supports bit strings that contain up to 2^{32} bits indexed by a signed dword. The actual operations are given in Chapter 3.

Figure 1.6 shows the layout of a bit string in memory. Notice that the bit index is a signed number. Thus, a bit string need not have the least significant bit referenced as 0. Within a byte, the low-order bit is bit 0 and the high-order bit is bit 7. This bit numbering is consistent with the 80386 as a little-endian machine.

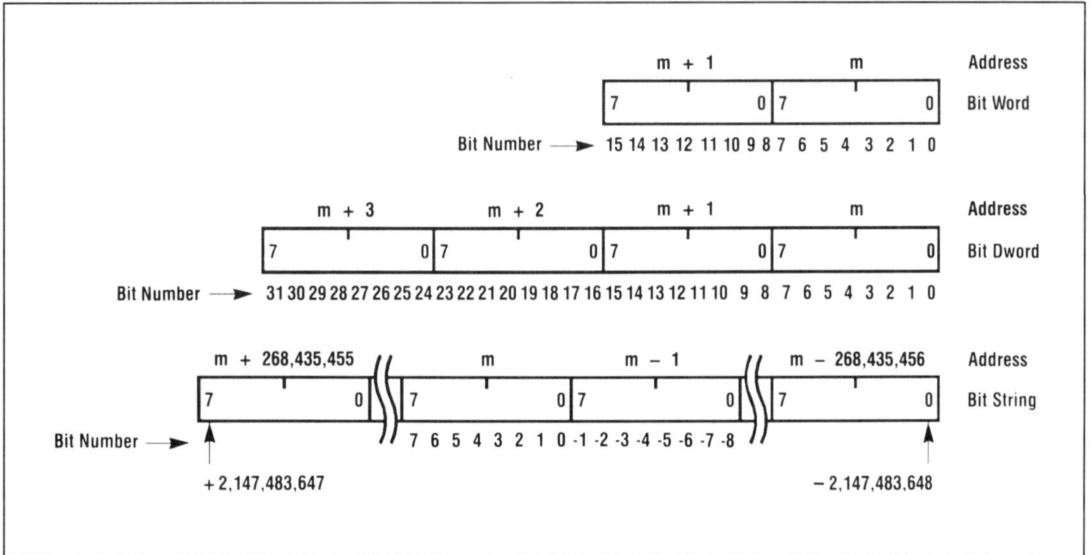

► **Figure 1.6:** Bit data types

A 32-bit signed integer is used to address a particular bit within a bit string. This 32-bit signed integer is called a *bit offset* and can have a value from −2G to 2G−1. The bit offset is divided into a byte address and a bit remainder. The byte address is the specified bit offset divided by 8, and the desired bit is within this byte. The bit of interest within this byte is determined by the bit offset modulo 8. Figure 1.7 gives two bit examples: bit offset 23 and bit offset −18 within a bit string at address N. In Chapter 4, Listings 4.5, 4.7, and 4.8 give more extensive examples of operating with bit data.

BCD

As in other 86 family members, the 80386 supports operations on BCD (binary-coded decimal) data types. The 80386 contains instructions

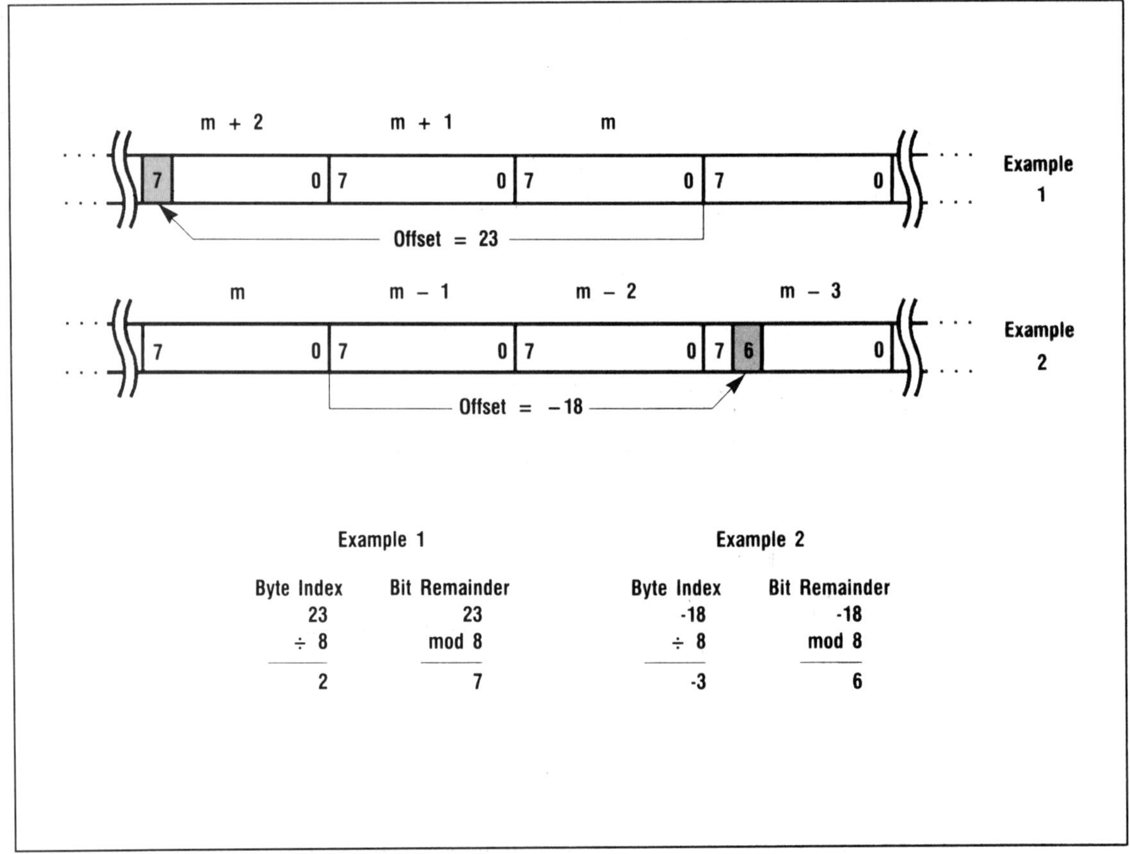

► **Figure 1.7:** Bit string offset examples

(discussed in Chapter 3) that allow the 80386 to add and subtract BCD data. Table 1.3 summarizes the BCD encodings.

BINARY	DECIMAL
0000 0000b	00
0000 0001b	01
0000 0010b	02
0000 0011b	03
0000 0100b	04
0000 0101b	05
0000 0110b	06
0000 0111b	07
0000 1000b	08
0000 1001b	09
0000 1010b	0X
0000 1011b	0X
0000 1100b	0X
0000 1101b	0X
0000 1110b	0X
0000 1111b	0X
0001 0000b	10
0001 0001b	11
⋮	⋮

Note: X indicates an illegal value for BCD representation.

► **Table 1.3:** Binary-coded decimal representations

The 80386 deals only with byte BCD quantities directly. In Chapter 3, we will show how multibyte BCD numbers are handled. Two BCD digits fit in a byte, with the low-order digit in bits 0 to 3, and the high-order digit in bits 4 to 7. Unpacked BCD stores one BCD digit per byte, in bits 0 to 3.

► Floating-Point Data Types

Floating-point data types are supported by the 80386's numerics coprocessor, the 80387. They are very similar to the 8087 and the 80287, and their differences are noted in Appendix B.

Introduction to Floating Point

So far, we have discussed various data types: signed and unsigned integers, strings, bit strings, ASCII, and BCD. None of these can represent numbers with fractional amounts—for instance, decimal fractions such as $1.21. Nor can such important physical constants as 3.1416, $8.854*10^{-14}$, $6.02*10^{23}$, 9.81, $9.11*10^{-31}$, or $1.38*10^{-23}$ be represented. Numbers with both an integer portion and a fractional portion, as in the examples above, are mathematically referred to as real numbers or rational numbers. In this book we will simply refer to these as *real numbers* even though this is not mathematically precise. Thus, for our purposes, a real number is any number that can be written as an integer and a fractional portion. Note that the integer number set described in the preceding section is a subset of the real number set in which the fractional portion is zero.

A computer represents numbers with a fixed number of bits. Thus, a computer cannot accurately represent all real numbers. In fact, a computer represents a very small subset of all possible real numbers. Fortunately, however, this subset covers most of the cases of practical importance, since use of the subset entails only a small loss of precision. The computer representation of a data type for real numbers is termed *floating point*. *Real numbers* is a mathematical term describing a set of numbers, and *floating point* describes the data type for representing a subset of real numbers in a computer.

Let's consider a few alternatives to floating point to show why floating point is the way it is. One simple alternative to floating point, for example, has to do with money. You could simply multiply all your numbers by 100 and thus convert all information into a range that could be represented by integers. For example, let's say the numbers 23.41

were read from a keyboard and converted from ASCII characters into an internal representation of 2341. All operations internally would be performed with this internal form, and when the results were output, the number would have to be divided by 100 before printing the results. This has many problems, one of which is a lack of precision. For example, if you received 7 percent interest on $23.41, would you have $25.04 or $25.05? Without taking extra precautions, you would have lost .01 and have $25.04.

Another solution is to treat numbers as fixed point. Let's imagine that you dedicated the lower 3 bits of a byte to a fraction. For example

$$10110110b = 2^4 + 2^2 + 2^1 + 2^{-1} + 2^{-2} = 22.75$$

This works, but it has a small fixed range of numbers that can be represented (from 0 to 2^6), with increments of 2^{-3}.

The solution to these problems is provided by floating-point representations. This format allows the binary point to float. A portion of the data representation is dedicated to specifying the location of the binary point, and the rest of the representation specifies the significant data bits. As you will see, this allows you to significantly extend the representable range of numbers while providing good precision over this entire range.

You can represent floating-point numbers with two integers: one to hold the significant data bits, and a second to specify the location of the binary point. Floating-point operations can be performed on these integer pairs using a sequence of integer instructions such as additions, multiplications, and shifts. This software emulation of floating point can be quite slow, which motivates the use of specialized hardware for floating-point arithmetic. Intel provides a numerics coprocessor, the 80387, to support floating-point arithmetic. The rest of this chapter will discuss the data types of the 80387.

IEEE Floating-Point Standard

Before diving into the data type details of the 80387, we'll make a few comments about the IEEE floating-point standard. Before 1979, many mainframes and minicomputers incorporated floating-point data types. There were, however, no standards as to what the floating-point representation looked like. In fact, you could run a FORTRAN program on computer A and later run it on computer B and get quite different results.

While developing the 8087 (the numerics coprocessor for the 8086 and 8088), Intel also became interested in developing a floating-point standard, particularly a standard against which the 8087 would perform.

Shortly after Intel published its proposed standard, the IEEE sanctioned a committee to develop a standard for floating-point arithmetic. The result of several years of work by many members of this committee is Draft 10.0 of IEEE Task P754, "A Standard for Binary Floating-Point Arithmetic." A few purposes of this standard, as stated in the draft, are to

1. "Facilitate movement of existing programs from diverse computers to those that adhere to this standard.
2. Enhance the capabilities and safety available to programmers who, though not expert in numerical methods, may well be attempting to produce numerically sophisticated programs.
3. Encourage experts to develop and distribute robust and efficient numerical programs portable, via minor editing and recompilation, onto any computer that conforms to this standard."

The IEEE standard is gaining acceptance in the industry. Not only do Intel chips support this standard, but many other microprocessors, minicomputers, and mainframe computers support it as well. The 80387 adheres to this standard. In summary, the 80387 provides data support over a very wide range, good intermediate value support, safe results, and good performance.

What If the 80387 Is Missing?

It is, unfortunately, possible that you do not have an 80387 in your system. Remember that the 80386 and 80387 are separate silicon components. A system that has an 80386 may not contain its numeric coprocessor. As mentioned in the introduction, there are several possible solutions.

1. You could have an 80387 added to your system. If you anticipate a large amount of computations, this is probably a wise choice. Almost all computer makers have an 80387 as an option if your computer did not come with it.
2. Your computer may have a mathematics emulation package (software emulation referred to above). If you do not have an emulation package, you may be able to get one or write one yourself.

So even if you don't have a coprocessor, if you want to do floating-point arithmetic you will have to use an emulation package and pretend that you have one. In either case, you will need to use the floating-point data types and instructions designed for the 80387.

Your system may also have an 80287 (the numerics coprocessor for the 80286) rather than an 80387. The 80386 can operate with either. If it has an 80287, refer to Appendix B to see the differences between the 80287 and the 80387.

Data Formats

The 80387 supports seven data types, summarized in Table 1.4. Notice how large a number can be represented. Remember that the largest integer number supported by the 386 is 2^{32}, or $4.29*10^9$ in decimal. Thus we have *substantially* extended our range from the data types we discussed earlier.

Also notice that the 80387 supports integer data types. This may seem odd since these, except for the 64-bit long integer form, are supported by the 80386. But if a computation had both real and integer data, the entire computation could be performed using the 80387. Data transfer between the 80387 and the 80386 would not be required.

DATA TYPE	BITS	SIGNIFICANT DIGITS (DECIMAL)	APPROXIMATE RANGE (DECIMAL)
Word Integer	16	4	$-32768 \leqslant X \leqslant 32767$
Short Integer	32	9	$-2*10^9 \leqslant X \leqslant +2*10^9$
Long Integer	64	18	$-9*10^{18} \leqslant X \leqslant +9*10^{18}$
Packed Decimal (BCD)	80	18	$-99..99 \leqslant X \leqslant +99..99$ (18 digits)
Short Real	32	6–7	$-3.39*10^{-38} \leqslant X \leqslant 3.39*10^{38}$
Long Real	64	15–16	$-1.80*10^{-308} \leqslant X \leqslant 1.80*10^{308}$
Temporary Real	80	19	$-1.19*10^{-4932} \leqslant X \leqslant 1.19*10^{4932}$

► **Table 1.4:** Data types supported by the 80387

Integer Data Types

The integer data types are represented by the two's complement notation used by integer data types on the 80386. All the integer types are common to the two chips, except that the 80386 supports an 8-bit integer and the 80387 supports a 64-bit integer. The nomenclature is also different. The following table summarizes the integer data types supported by the 80386 and 80387. In the table, NR indicates not representable in this processor.

Bits	80386	80387
8	Signed Byte	NR
16	Signed Word	Word Integer
32	Signed Dword	Short Integer
64	NR	Long Integer

Figure 1.8 shows the integer data types. These three data types can represent numbers from −32768 to 32767, $-2.147*10^9$ to $2.147*10^9$, and $-9.233*10^{18}$ to $9.223*10^{18}$ in the word, short, and long integer formats, respectively.

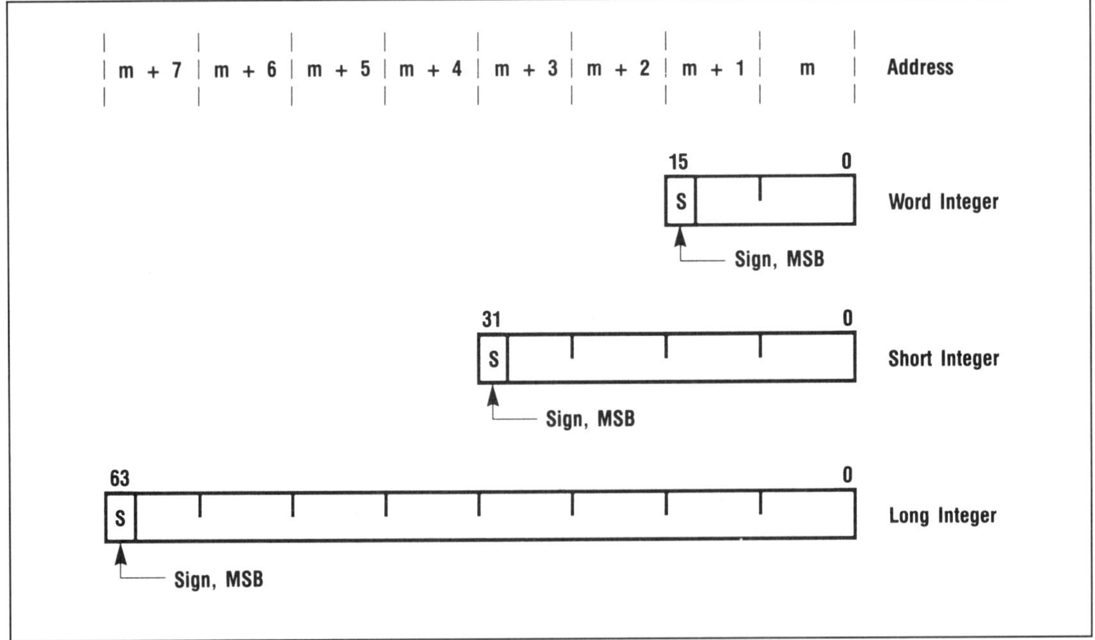

► **Figure 1.8:** Integer (two's complement) 80387 data types

BCD

Again, the 80386 supports BCD, so why should the 80387? The 80387 supports this data type for basically the same reason as the integer argument given above. The BCD type supported by the 80387 is a packed decimal type that is 80 bits, which holds 18 decimal digits and one sign bit. This is shown in Figure 1.9. Why does packed BCD stop at 18 digits and leave 7 unused bits in the representation? At 18 digits it meets the COBOL standard (one of the prime languages that uses BCD), and there was no reason to complicate the design past 18 digits.

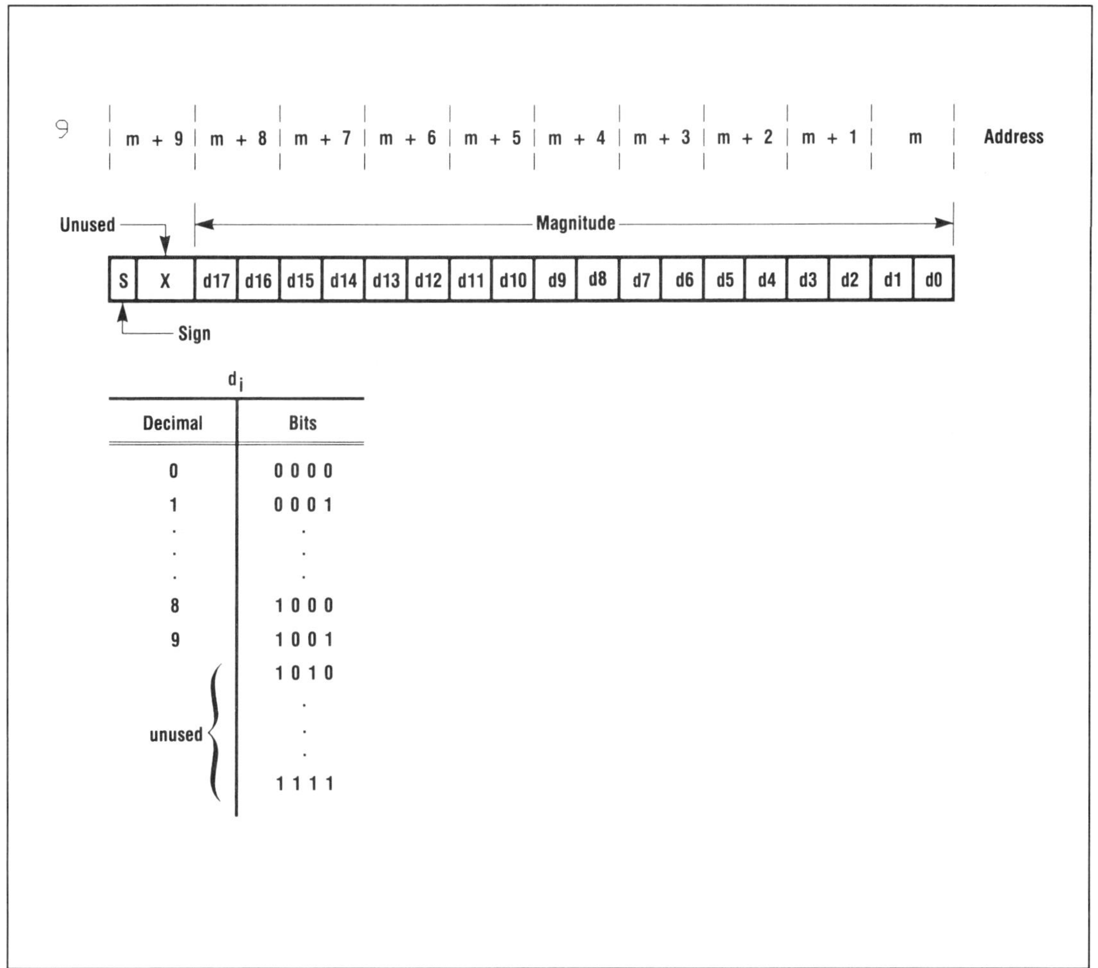

► **Figure 1.9:** 80387 BCD data type

Real Formats

The real formats are the floating-point formats mentioned above. Figure 1.10 gives the general real format. The format is composed of three parts: significand, exponent, and sign.

The following table gives the bits that are used for each part in the three real data formats.

Data Type	Total	Sign	Exponent	Significand
Short Real	32	1	8	23
Long Real	64	1	11	52
Temporary Real	80	1	15	64

Figure 1.11 gives the detailed bit locations of the three data types. Let's start with the easy one. The *sign* is simply that—a sign bit. If this bit is 1, the number is negative. If this bit is 0, the number is positive. This is the sign magnitude format that was discussed in the section on signed integers.

The *significand* gives the significant bits of the number. In some contexts the significand is referred to as the mantissa. If you consider for just a moment you can convince yourself that it is possible to store the same number in several different ways. For example (in decimal), $100.0*10^{-2}$, $10.0*10^{-1}$, $1.0*10^{0}$, $0.1*10^{1}$, $0.01*10^{2}$, and $0.001*10^{3}$ all represent 1. Now, to make computations always yield the maximum precision, the results are *normalized.* In other words, numbers always have

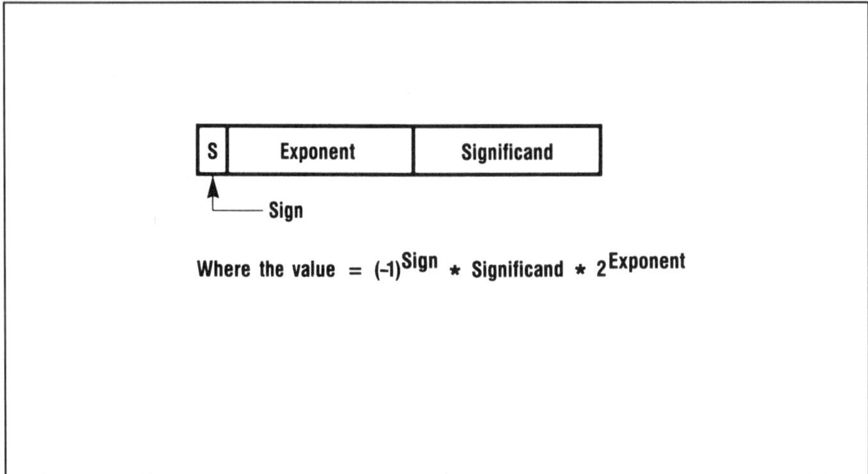

► **Figure 1.10:** General real format

their exponent adjusted such that the most significant (leftmost) bit of the binary significand is 1, with the binary point just "to the right" of this 1 bit. Thus, the correct normalized result for the example above is $1.0*10^0$.

If you always have $1.XXXXX*2^n$ (X indicates 1 or 0), you know that the bit to the left of the binary point is always 1. The 80387 eliminates this bit in its short and long real formats to give one more bit of precision. Thus, in Figure 1.11, notice the "hidden" 1 bit. A significand of 0111...010b really corresponds to 1.0111...010b in the short and long real formats.

The *exponent* field contains the power of two needed to scale the significand to achieve the final result. The exponent is stored in a biased form (discussed in the signed integers section). This is done to ease

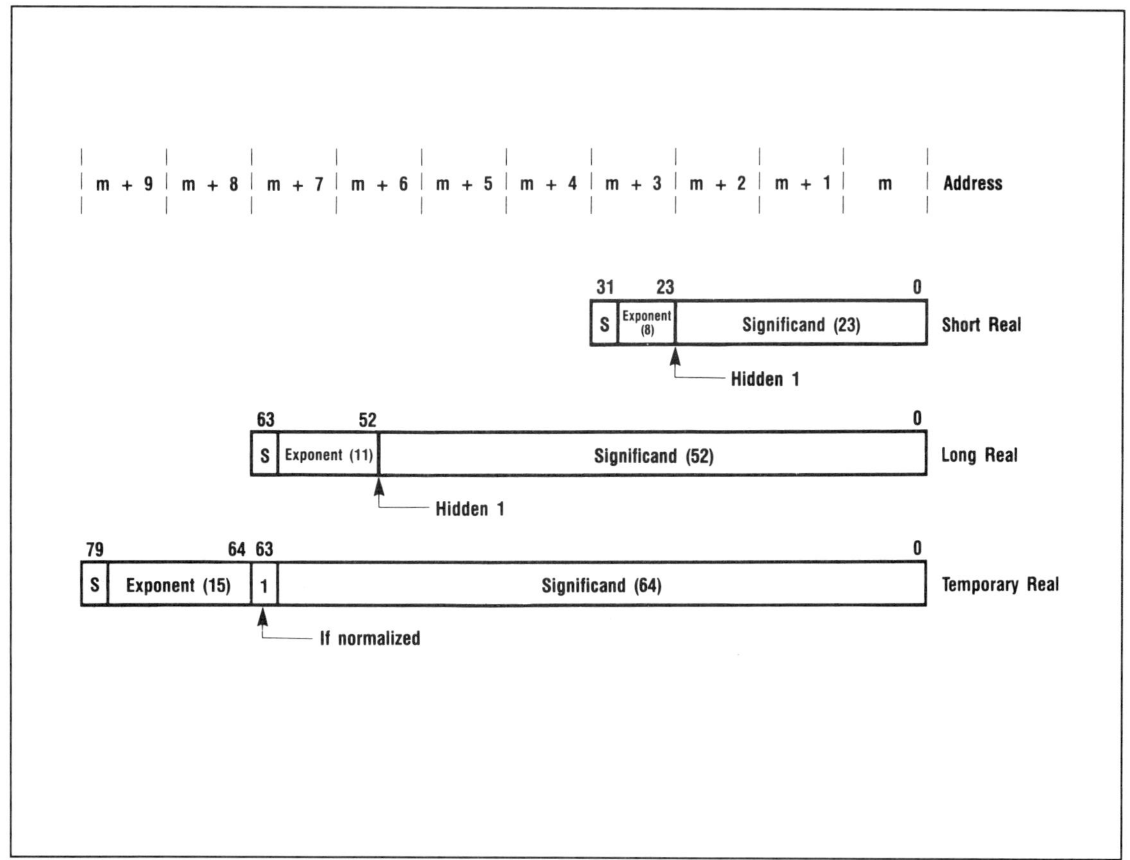

► **Figure 1.11:** 80387 real data types

numerical comparisons, since a large numerical value is always a large number—this is not the case for the other representations for signed integers. The biases are 127, 1023, and 16383 for short, long, and temporary real formats. Thus, an exponent of 10000000b (short real) is really 2^1.

Now that we have explained all three components of the floating-point formats, we are ready to summarize them with Figure 1.12 and a few examples. Compare this with Figure 1.10.

Range in Figure 1.12 gives the largest numbers, positive and negative, that can be represented by this data type. *Precision* gives the smallest possible number that can be represented by this data type. *Denormals* are discussed below and are given here for completeness. All examples will be given in short real, since short real has quite enough bits to make it difficult to comprehend.

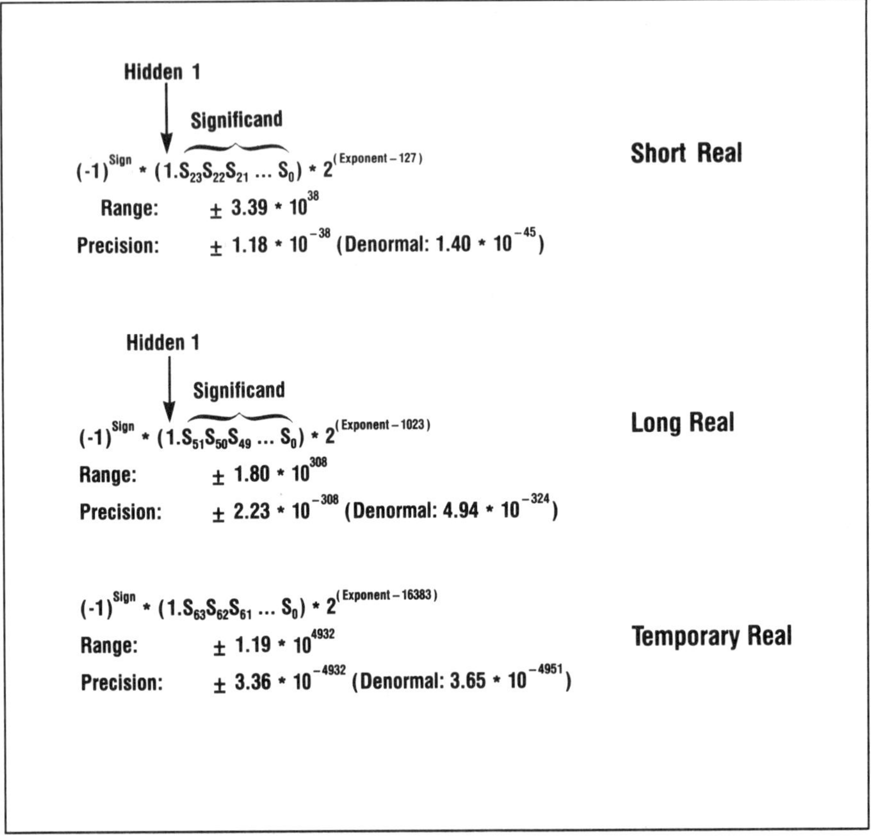

► **Figure 1.12:** Short, long, and temporary real numbers

Sign	Exponent	Significand	Sum	Value
0	10001110b	000100...0b	$(1+2^{-4})*2^{15}$	34816
1	01111100b	011000...0b	$-(1+2^{-2}+2^{-3})*2^{-3}$	-.17188
0	01111111b	000000...0b	$(1)*2^{0}$	1

Temporary Reals

We have discussed the three real formats as if they were all the same except for the number of bits in each of the three portions of the representation. This is almost true, but a few comments need to be made about the temporary real format.

1. The temporary real format is the internal form used by the 80387. No matter what data type you give (short integer, BCD, short real, and so on) the 80387 immediately converts it into temporary real.
2. The temporary real format has no hidden bit. Thus, bit 63 of the temporary real number is always 1 in a normalized number.

Why is temporary real solely used in the 80387? This is done to maximize the precision and range of computations. Even if you are performing a computation with short reals, you may have intermediate results that greatly exceed the range of a short real even though the final result may be representable in a short real.

There is no hidden bit, since the 80387 uses the temporary real format internally and the bit *is* needed to perform computations. When the short or long real given to the 80387 is converted into temporary real, an explicit 1 bit is inserted.

Special Cases

Tables 1.5 to 1.7 present all possible data representations for the three formats. We will discuss the following special cases: zeros, infinities, denormals, pseudo-denormals, and NaNs (signaling and quiet). Note that all numbers in the three tables are binary.

Zero is simply a biased exponent of 00...00b and a significand of 00...00b in all three formats. Note that a biased exponent of zero is reserved. This means that the biased exponent of zero cannot be used to represent a normal real number. Do note that both positive and negative zero can be represented. The only case where the 80387 distinguishes between the two forms of zero is when dividing by zero, as described in Chapter 3 in the description of the FDIV instruction.

Infinities are the second special case. The biased exponent value of 11...11b is reserved. As above, this indicates it cannot be used by a normal real number. If the significand is also zero, we have infinity. Again, both positive and negative infinity can be represented. Infinities will be discussed in more detail shortly.

SIGN	BIASED EXPONENT	SIGNIFICAND	CATEGORY
0/1	11...11	11...11	Quiet NaNs
0/1	11...11	⋮	
0/1	11...11	10...00	
0/1	11...11	01...11	Signaling NaNs
0/1	11...11	⋮	
0/1	11...11	00...01	
0/1	11...11	00...00	Infinities
0/1	11...10	11...11	Normals
0/1	⋮	⋮	
0/1	00...01	00...00	
0/1	00...00	11...11	Denormals
0/1	00...00	⋮	
0/1	00...00	00...01	
0/1	00...00	00...00	Zeros

► **Table 1.5:** Short and long real representations

Denormals are a special case in representing very small numbers. Denormals allow a representation of gradual underflow or a gradual loss of precision. Many computers do not gradually underflow as the 80387 does, but abruptly underflow instead. This means when they get to the

SIGN	BIASED EXPONENT	SIGNIFICAND	CATEGORY
0/1	11...11	111...11	Quiet NaNs
0/1	11...11	⋮	
0/1	11...11	110...00	
0/1	11...11	101...11	Signaling NaNs
0/1	11...11	⋮	
0/1	11...11	100...01	
0/1	11...11	100...00	Infinities
0/1	11...10	111...11	Normals
0/1	⋮	⋮	
0/1	00...01	100...00	
0/1	00...00	111...11	Pseudo-Denormals
0/1	00...00	⋮	
0/1	00...00	100...00	
0/1	00...00	011...11	Denormals
0/1	00...00	⋮	
0/1	00...00	000...01	
0/1	00...00	000...00	Zeros

► **Table 1.6:** Temporary real representations

least normalizable number, the next smaller representation used is zero. In contrast, gradual underflow uses representations that are not normalized (denormal). This results in a loss of precision, but significantly extends the range of very small numbers that can be represented. As should be obvious, gradual underflow is a far better solution than an abrupt underflow, even though some precision is lost.

Normally, numbers are required to be normalized (left shifted until the most significant significand bit is a 1). Denormals, however, do not have 1 as the most significant bit of the significand. The biased exponent of 00...00 is a special representation for an exponent with value 2^{-126}, 2^{-1022}, and 2^{-16382} for short, long, and temporary real, respectively. This is special since the normal biased exponent of 00...01 also represents exponents of 2^{126}, 2^{-1022}, and 2^{-16382}. Denormals always have a loss of precision; otherwise, a normal number would be used.

SIGN	BIASED EXPONENT	SIGNIFICAND	CATEGORY
0/1	11...11	011...11	Pseudo-NaNs
0/1	11...11	⋮	
0/1	11...11	000...01	
0/1	11...11	000...00	Pseudo-Infinities
0/1	11...10	011...11	Unnormals
0/1	⋮	⋮	
0/1	00...01	000...01	
0/1	11...10	000...00	Pseudo-Zeros
0/1	⋮	000...00	
0/1	00...01	000...00	

► **Table 1.7:** Unsupported temporary real representations

As you can see in Figure 1.12, the use of denormals allows significantly smaller numbers to be represented (sometimes referred to as *tininess*).

Pseudo-denormals are supported by the 80387 but can never be produced by the 80387. Denormals normally have 0 as the most significant bit of the significand. Pseudo-denormals, as seen from Table 1.6, have 1 for this bit. Pseudo-denormals are unusual since they can be represented in a normalized form but have not been. This is true since the special-case biased exponent of 00...00 has the same exponential value as the "normal" biased exponent of 00...01, as was pointed out above. In addition, the significand of a pseudo-denormal is normalized; that is, the MSB is a 1. Therefore, all pseudo-denormals can be represented as normals.

The next special cases are the *NaNs*. NaN stands for *Not a Number.* There are two forms of NaNs: signaling and quiet. A signaling NaN causes an invalid operation exception to be raised when used in an operation. A quiet NaN does not cause an invalid operation exception to be raised. Thus, the descriptive naming: signaling and quiet. Exceptions will be described briefly here and more completely in Chapter 6.

The signaling NaN has a 0 as the most significant significand bit. This is true except for temporary real, where the second most significant bit is a 0 and the most significant significand bit (the hidden bit) is a 1. The signaling NaN can be used, for instance, to make sure that the program initializes all variables before use. The programmer or compiler could initialize each variable in a program to a signaling NaN so that an exception is raised if an uninitialized value is used. A NaN can have anything in the remainder of its fraction portion, which can be used to store information about where or why the NaN was produced, if desired. The 80387 never produces a signaling NaN.

A quiet NaN has 1 in the most significant significand bit except for the temporary real case, where the second most significand bit is 1 and the most significant bit (the hidden bit) is also 1. A quiet NaN is produced when an invalid operation exception occurs. When this occurs, the result that is produced is the indefinite (given below). Under all circumstances (except for FCOM, FIST, and FBSTP, which are described in Chapter 3), quiet and signaling NaNs are preserved through operations. There are several special cases when dealing with NaNs:

1. Any operation that would generate an invalid operation exception but involves NaNs will yield the indefinite quiet NaN. The integer, BCD, and real indefinites are given below.
2. When operations involve signaling and quiet NaNs (SNaN and QNaN), the QNaN will be delivered as the result.

3. Operations between two SNaNs will yield the larger SNaN after it is converted to a QNaN. Converting an SNaN to a QNaN is performed by simply setting the most significant significand bit to 1.
4. Operations between two QNaNs will yield the larger QNaN.
5. Operations between an SNaN and a normal number will yield the SNaN after conversion to a QNaN.
6. Operations between a QNaN and a normal number will yield the QNaN as the result.

As this description may be a bit confusing, Table 1.8 summarizes operations involving NaNs. The table assumes an operation is occurring with operands 1 and 2 (op_1 and op_2).

Indefinites are a special case of quiet NaNs (described above). Each of the data types supported by the 80387 (word, short and long integer; packed decimal and short, long, and temporary real) have a single indefinite representation. This representation is produced by the 80387 whenever an invalid operation exception occurs and none of the input operands were NaNs. The instructions that generate invalid operation exceptions are given in Chapter 3; exactly how invalid operation exceptions can be generated is discussed in Chapter 6. Table 1.9 summarizes the indefinite encodings for each data type. The leftmost bit in the encoding is the most significant bit. For the real representations from left to right, the fields are sign, exponent, and significand.

Do note that when we were discussing BCD and integer data types, we did not tell the whole story since we did not mention indefinites. When an indefinite is to be generated for an integer data type, the most negative representation is generated. For BCD, an otherwise unused encoding is used.

Indefinites can be loaded and stored for real formats. Since the real indefinite falls within the quiet NaNs, an exception is not raised when an indefinite is loaded. For integer and BCD, indefinites cannot be loaded. For integers, the indefinites when loaded are treated as the largest negative number. For BCD, the result of loading an indefinite is undefined.

The unsupported temporary real representations given in Table 1.7 are exactly that, unsupported by the 80387 (some were, however, supported by the 80287). These formats (pseudo-zero, unnormal, pseudo-infinity, and pseudo-NaN) will cause an invalid operation exception to be raised by the 80387 if encountered.

Exceptions

Exceptions indicate that an error of some sort has been detected during the current operation. For example, when you go to start your car a bell may go off if your door is open or your seat belts are not fastened. In either case, an exception has been detected.

There are many possible exceptions. For example, we described loss of precision above. Depending upon the machine state, loss of precision could be treated as an exception. We also described signaling NaNs. Operating on a signaling NaN will generate yet another exception. There are many other possible machine exceptions, most of which we

		op_2		
		Q	**S**	**R**
	Q	>Q	Q	Q
op_1	**S**	Q	CQ(>S)	CQ(S)
	R	Q	CQ(S)	QI

KEY

Q	Quiet NaN
S	Signaling NaN
R	Regular Real (non-NaN, legal number)
>Q	The greater quiet NaN of op_1 and op_2
>S	The greater signaling NaN of op_1 and op_2
CQ(X)	Convert X to a QNaN
QI	The default quiet NaN—the indefinite real

► **Table 1.8:** Operations involving NaNs

FORMAT	BITS	ENCODING
Word Integer	16	100...000b
Short Integer	32	100...000b
Long Integer	64	100...000b
BCD	80	1 1111111 1111 1111 XX...XXb
Short Real	32	1 11...11 10...00b
Long Real	64	1 11...11 10...00b
Temporary Real	80	1 11...11 110...00b

Note: X indicates "don't care."

► **Table 1.9:** Indefinite encodings

have not yet developed the background to discuss. Detailed descriptions of the exception conditions and how they are handled is discussed in Chapter 6.

Machine State and Memory Addressing

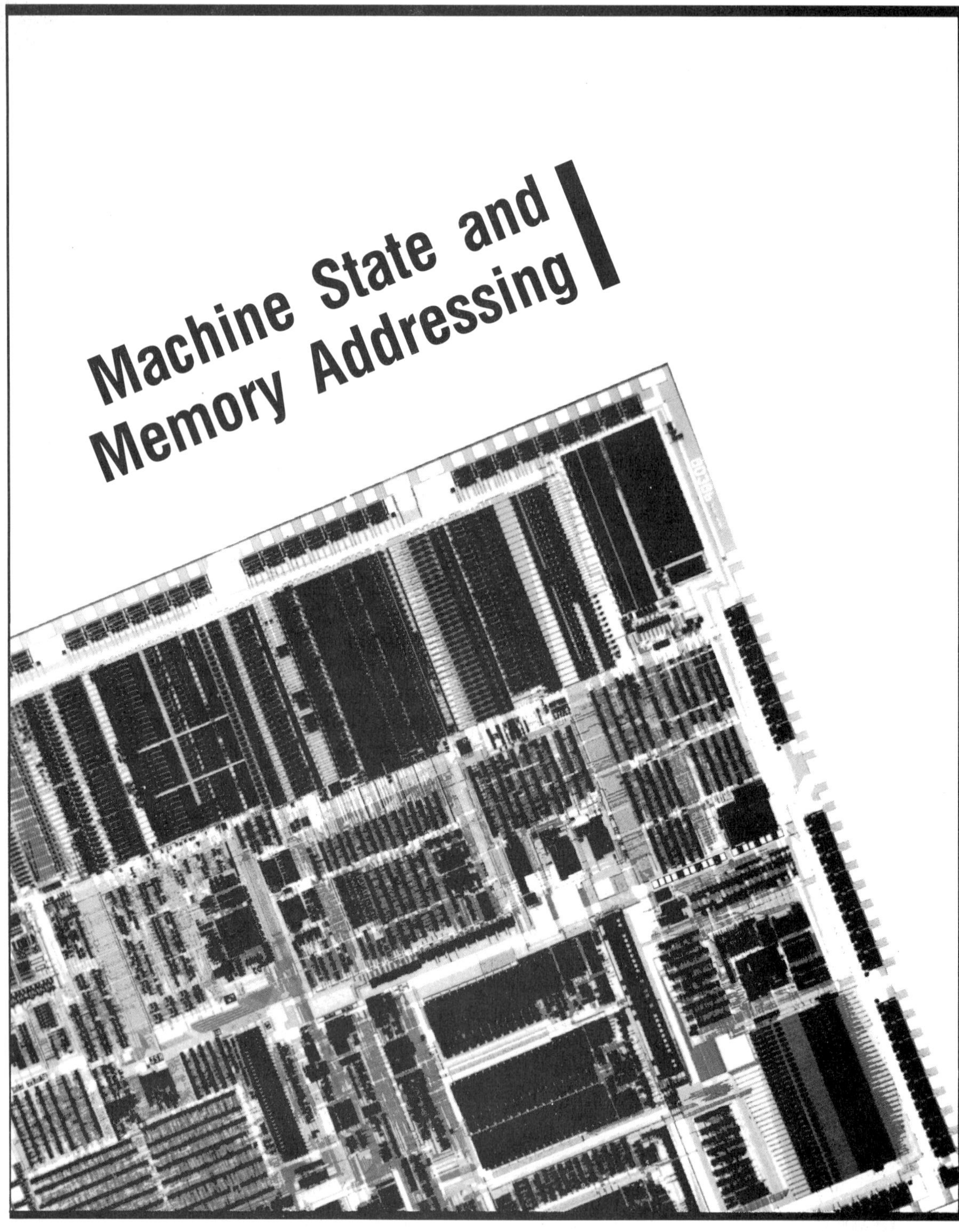

Chapter 

CHAPTER 1 DESCRIBED THE DATA TYPES REC-ognized by the 80386 and 80387, and how these data types are stored in memory. The machine instructions of the 80386 and 80387 operate directly on these basic data types. Each machine instruction specifies the *operation* to be performed, and the locations of the input and output data participating in the operation. The input/output data are called *operands*.

This chapter describes where the basic data types can be stored and accessed by the 80386 as machine instruction operands. An operand can specify data within the 80386 processor in a *register,* or outside the processor in *main memory* or *I/O memory,* or located directly in an instruction as an *immediate constant.* Main memory provides a very large space for operand storage, but access to memory is much slower than to registers or to immediate constants. Furthermore, some operations require some operands to be in registers rather than memory.

This chapter first describes the three types of registers available to the applications programmer: for storing 32-bit numbers, for controlling processor execution, and for addressing memory segments. Next, we describe the method used to form memory addresses and the binary encoding of operands in the instruction set. Then, we introduce the separate I/O memory space. Finally, we describe the registers available on the 80387 floating-point processor for storing floating-point data types, and for controlling the operation of the floating-point instructions.

► Registers

The register set available to the applications programmer consists of 16 registers divided into three categories, as shown in Figure 2.1. Additional registers are available to the systems programmer. Chapter 5 describes the registers that support memory management. Chapter 8 describes the registers that support program debugging.

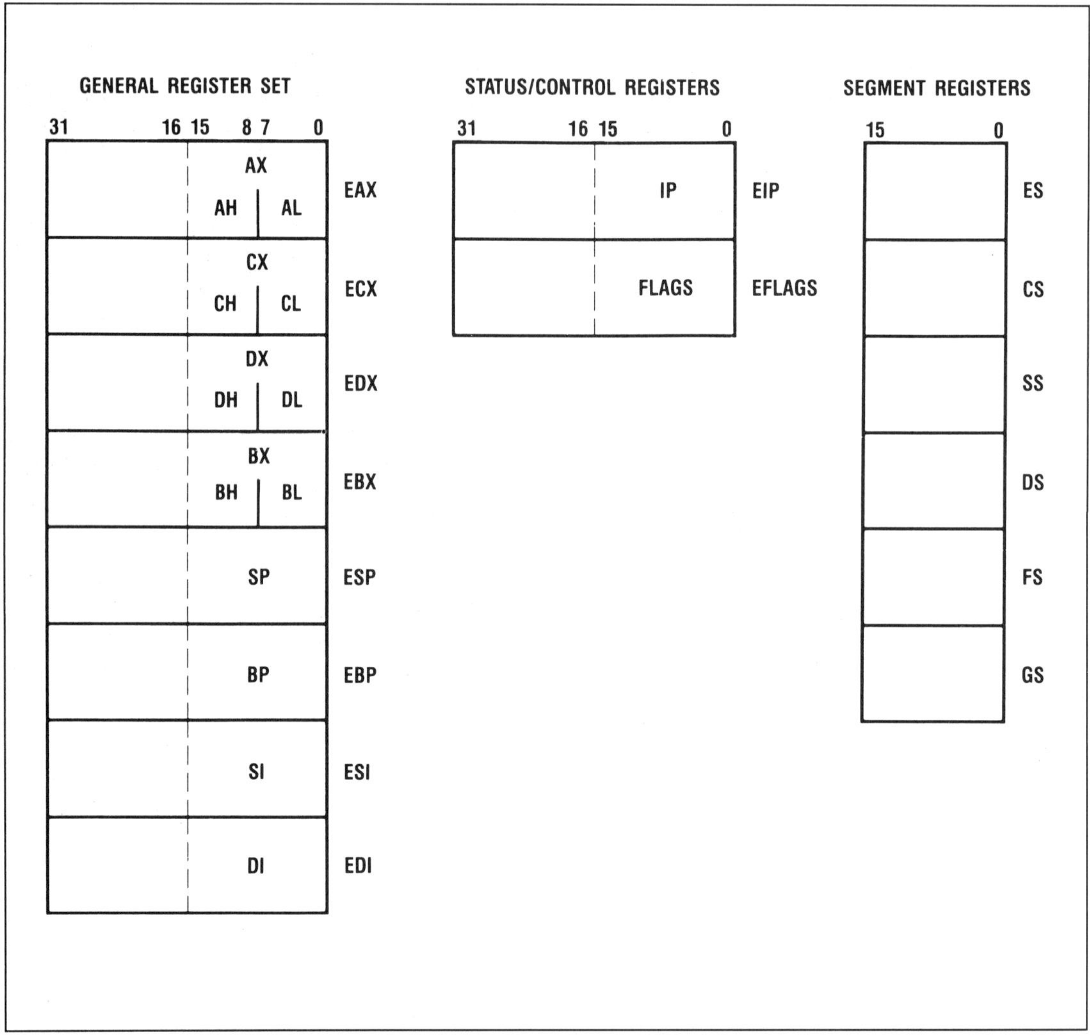

► **Figure 2.1:** 80386 registers

The three categories are as follows:

1. Eight general-purpose 32-bit registers used for arithmetic and logical operations, and for the base and index register components of memory addresses.
2. Two 32-bit processor-control registers.
3. Six 16-bit segment registers that address memory segments. Each register provides immediate access to one segment of memory at a time. Memory segments will be explained later in this chapter and in detail in Chapter 5.

The register set of the 80386 is a superset of the register set available on the previous processors in the 86 family. In cases where a 16-bit register was extended to provide a 32-bit register on the 80386, the 386 register name is simply the old 16-bit register name prefixed with an E (for *Extended*). For example, the 16-bit AX register from the 8086 was extended to form the 32-bit EAX register on the 80386, the 16-bit IP (*Instruction Pointer*) register was extended to form the 32-bit EIP register on the 386, and so on.

The General Registers

The 80386 contains eight 32-bit general registers, used for arithmetic operations such as addition, subtraction, multiplication, and division, and also to form memory addresses, as described later in this chapter. These eight registers are named EAX, ECX, EDX, EBX, ESP, EBP, ESI, and EDI, as shown in Figure 2.1.

The lower 16 bits of these registers can be accessed independently as 16-bit registers, and are named AX, CX, DX, BX, SP, BP, SI, and DI. These are the eight 16-bit general-purpose registers from the previous 86 family processors, and provide the compatible register set used for executing 8086 and 286 code, as described in Chapter 9. If one of these 16-bit registers is accessed, the upper 16 bits of the 32-bit general register are not disturbed.

The high and low halves of the X registers—AX, BX, CX, and DX—can be accessed independently as 8-bit registers. The suffix H or L is added to the first letter of the name of the 16-bit register to form the 8-bit register name for the high or low half of the register. For example, the AL register is the lowest 8 bits of the AX register, and also the lowest 8 bits of the EAX register. The AH register is the upper 8 bits of the AX register, and bits 8 through 15 of the EAX register. If one of these 8-bit registers is accessed, the remaining bits of the general register are not disturbed. You can see the overlap of the 8-bit, 16-bit, and 32-bit registers in Figure 2.1.

General Register Characterization

Operands can specify the contents of any general register for address formation and for the simple arithmetic operations such as addition and subtraction. Some of the more complex operations, such as string operations and double-precision multiplication and division, must take one or more operands from fixed registers. This technique in which an instruction requires one or more operands to be read from specific registers is called *characterization.* It is used in the 80386 to support complex operations that require more than the two operands provided in the 80386 instruction format. Since the reference to the register is built into the instruction, it does not have to be named explicitly as an operand. For example, the ECX, ESI, and EDI registers are used by the string instructions to hold the string length, the source pointer, and the destination pointer, respectively. The EAX and EDX registers are designated by the double-precision multiplication instructions to hold the double-length result. Detailed examples will be provided in connection with these instructions in Chapter 3.

With these exceptions, an operand can be any register or memory address; 80386 operand selection is symmetric.

The Processor-Control Registers

Two registers control the operation of the 80386 processor: EIP, the instruction-pointer register, and EFLAGS, the processor status and control flags register.

The Instruction-Pointer Register—EIP

The 32-bit EIP register serves only one function: to point to the next instruction the processor is to execute. As the 80386 executes a program, it fetches and executes each instruction in the program. It fetches the instruction pointed to by the EIP register, increments the EIP register by the length of this instruction, and then executes the instruction. The incrementing leaves the EIP register pointing to the next instruction in the sequence of instructions stored in memory. Thus, EIP is always pointing to the next sequential instruction to be executed. Control-transfer instructions, described in Chapter 3, can alter this sequential instruction flow by loading a new value into the EIP register.

The 16-bit IP register is contained in the lower 16 bits of the EIP register. This IP register provides the 16-bit instruction pointer used for executing 8086 and 80286 code, as described in Chapter 9.

The Processor Status and Control Flags Register—EFLAGS

The 32-bit EFLAGS register contains several status flag and control flag bits. The program sets the control bits to control the operation of certain functions of the 80386. The processor itself sets the status bits, which are tested by the program after arithmetic operations to check for special conditions. Figure 2.2 shows the individual bit fields in the EFLAGS register. Each field is briefly described below.

Bits marked as 0 or 1 in Figure 2.2 are *reserved*. The reserved bits must be loaded with 0 or 1, as indicated, and must be ignored when examining the EFLAGS register. This will ensure compatibility with future processors, in case Intel decides to use these bits to define more flags in the EFLAGS register.

One way to change bits in the EFLAGS register that is guaranteed to work with any future processor is to store the EFLAGS register, modify just the bits required, and then reload EFLAGS with the modified value. This way, only the required bits are modified, and the remaining bits (including any that are defined in future processors) are unchanged.

Arithmetic Status Flags The CF, PF, AF, ZF, SF, and OF bits are set by most arithmetic and logical instructions.

CF CF is the *Carry Flag*. It is set (CF = 1) if an arithmetic operation generates a carry or borrow out of the most significant bit, otherwise it is cleared (CF = 0). It provides an overflow indication for unsigned arithmetic, and supports multiple-precision arithmetic.

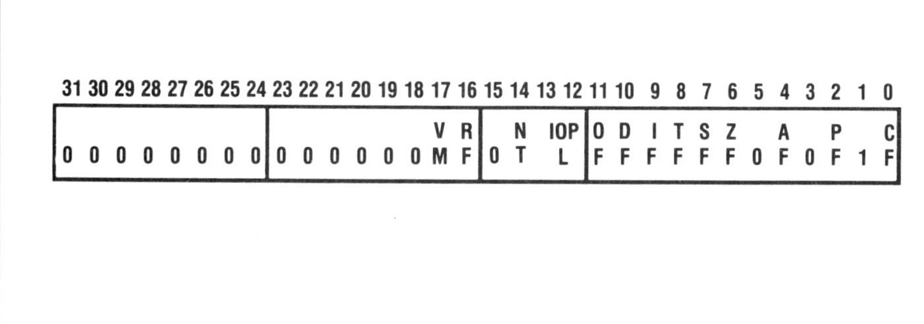

► **Figure 2.2:** EFLAGS register details

PF — PF is the *Parity Flag,* and indicates the parity of the lower 8 bits of the result. PF is 1 if there are an even number of 1s in the lower 8 bits of the result, and it is 0 if there are an odd number of 1s. This is called *odd* parity, since there are always an odd number of 1s in the data and parity bits.

AF — AF is the *Auxiliary* carry *Flag,* and is set if there is a carry or borrow out of bit 3. It is used in performing BCD arithmetic.

ZF — ZF is the *Zero Flag.* It is set if the result is 0.

SF — SF is the *Sign Flag.* It is set to the most significant bit of the result, which is the sign bit in two's complement notation.

OF — OF is the two's complement *Overflow Flag.* OF is set if the result of an arithmetic operation is too large or too small to be represented as a two's complement integer in the number of bits available to store the result. It is set by most arithmetic instructions if there is a carry into the high-order bit but no carry out, or if there is no carry into the high-order bit but there is a carry out.

This set of status flags was chosen so that a single set of arithmetic instructions could operate on unsigned binary numbers, two's complement signed binary integers, and BCD digits. Out-of-range results can be detected by looking at the CF bit after operating on unsigned numbers, at the OF bit after operating on signed integers, and at the AF bit after operating on BCD digits. A less-than relationship between two numbers can be determined by performing a subtract operation and then examining

- CF for unsigned numbers
- SF XOR OF (exclusive-or operating on SF and OF) for signed integers
- AF for BCD digits

By having exclusive-or operate on OF and SF to determine the less-than relationship for signed integers, the correct indication is obtained even if the subtract operation results in an overflow.

The following long example illustrates how these flags support unsigned numbers, two's complement signed integers, and BCD digits with a single set of instructions. Chapter 3 describes how each machine instruction affects the flags. Here we will look at the CMP instruction, which compares two numbers by subtracting one from the other, and setting the status flags accordingly. Let's suppose two 8-bit numbers are to be compared. The first has the value 85h, which has a base-10 value 133 if considered as an unsigned number, the base-10 value −123 if considered as a signed integer, or the base-10 value 5 if the low 4 bits are a BCD digit. The second number has the value 49h, which is unsigned 73, signed 73, or BCD 9. As shown in detail in Figure 2.3, subtracting 49h from 85h gives the value 3Ch as a result on the 386, and sets the flags as follows:

- CF is 0, since there is no borrow out of bit 7.
- PF is 1, since there are an even number of 1s in the 8-bit result.
- AF is 1, since there is a borrow out of bit 3.
- ZF is 0, since the result is not 0.
- SF is 0, since the most significant bit is 0.
- OF is 1, since there was a borrow out of bit 6, but not out of bit 7.

	386 Representation		True Result		
	hex	binary	unsigned	two's comp	BCD
borrow out	1	1111	1		1
	85h	10000101b	133	-123	5
subtract	− 49h	− 01001001b	− 73	− 73	− 9
result	3Ch	00111100b	60	-196	6
overflow indicator			CF = 0	OF = 1	AF = 1
less than indicator			CF = 0	(SF XOR OF) = 1	AF = 1

► **Figure 2.3:** Status flags support multiple data types

In Figure 2.3, the binary result produced by the 386 is shown on the left. The right side shows how the binary inputs and result can be interpreted either as unsigned numbers, two's complement signed integers, or BCD digits.

The correct result is produced if the inputs are unsigned numbers, since CF, the overflow indicator for unsigned numbers, is 0. CF is also the less-than indicator, so in this example you see that the 386 has correctly determined that 133 is not less than 73!

If the inputs are signed integers, the value produced (–196) is too large to fit in 8 bits. The 386 sets OF, the two's complement overflow indicator, to indicate that the result overflowed the number of bits available. In spite of the overflow, the 386 can still correctly indicate that –123 is less than 73, since the signed less-than indicator, SF XOR OF, is 1.

If the inputs are BCD numbers, the value produced by the binary subtract is an invalid decimal digit (C). This is indicated by AF, the BCD overflow indicator. AF is also the BCD less-than indicator, and here it indicates that 5 is less than 9.

The CF, ZF, SF, and OF settings depend on the size of the data used in an operation. Operations on 32-bit data set SF to bit 31 of the result, set ZF if the 32-bit result is 0, and set CF and OF according to the carry in and out of bit 31. Operations on 16-bit data set SF to bit 15 of the result, set ZF if the 16-bit result is 0, and set CF and OF according to the carry in and out of bit 15. Operations on 8-bit data set SF to bit 7 of the result, set ZF if the 8-bit result is 0, and set CF and OF according to the carry in and out of bit 7. The flag settings for 8-bit data are illustrated in Figure 2.3.

The PF and AF settings are independent of the size of the operation performed. PF is always formed as the odd parity bit over the low 8 bits of the result. AF is set if there is a carry or borrow out of bit 3 of the result.

Processor-Control Flags The TF, IF, DF, IOPL, NT, RF, and VM bits can be set by the program to control the operation of the 80386 processor. Most of these flags support features of the 80386 described in later chapters. This section summarizes these flags, and provides forward references to the chapters containing the details of how these flags are used. Most of the processor control flags are accessible by all programs, but three are not: the VM flag, the IOPL field, and the IF flag. Chapter 5 describes how these three control flags are protected.

TF The *Trap* enable *Flag* controls the generation of single-step interrupts to support program debugging (Chapter 8). A single-step interrupt will occur at the end of every instruction when TF = 1.

IF The *Interrupt* enable *Flag* enables the recognition of external interrupts (Chapter 6) signaled on a processor pin. External interrupts are accepted if IF = 1, and are held pending if IF = 0.

DF The *Direction Flag* determines whether the string instructions will post-increment (DF = 0), or post-decrement (DF = 1) the string index registers after each step. See Chapter 3 for detailed descriptions of the string instructions.

IOPL The *I/O Privilege Level* field is two bits wide, and supports the protection model described in Chapter 5. The IOPL field specifies the privilege level required to perform I/O instructions. If the current privilege level is numerically less than or equal to IOPL, I/O instructions can be executed; otherwise, a protection exception is generated.

NT The *Nested Task* bit controls the operation of the IRET instruction (Chapter 3). If NT = 0, a normal return from an interrupt is performed by restoring EFLAGS, CS, and EIP with values saved on the stack. If NT = 1, the interrupt return is through a task switch instead (Chapter 5).

RF The *Restart Flag* controls whether debug faults (Chapter 8) are accepted (RF = 0) or ignored (RF = 1). The RF bit is also cleared by the processor at the successful completion of every instruction, and it is set by the processor when a fault other than a debug fault is signaled.

VM The VM bit is the *Virtual* 8086 *Mode* bit. If set, the processor will execute in virtual 8086 mode (Chapter 9). If clear, the processor will operate in the normal protected mode (Chapter 5).

The RF, NT, DF, and TF bits can be set or cleared by a program running at any privilege level. The VM and IOPL fields can be changed only by a program executing at privilege level 0, the most privileged level. The IF bit can be changed only by a program executing with I/O privilege (Chapter 5).

The RF and VM bits can be set or cleared only by the IRET instruction or by a task switch. The other control bits can be set by the POPF instruction as well.

Segment Registers

The 80386 has six 16-bit segment registers that address memory segments. These registers are named ES, CS, SS, DS, FS, and GS, and are shown in Figure 2.1. FS and GS are new on the 80386.

To access data within a given segment, a program must load one of the segment registers with a special value that identifies that segment. This special value is called a selector, and it is described briefly later in this chapter, and in detail in Chapter 5. The six segment registers allow a program to access up to six segments at a time. As the program finishes with one segment and begins on another, it can load the selector of the new segment into the segment register used to address the old segment.

► Memory Addressing Concepts

The 80386 uses a memory addressing technique called *segmentation,* which divides the memory space into one or more separate linear regions called *segments.* A memory address consists of two parts: a segment part that identifies the containing segment, and an offset part that gives a simple byte offset within that segment. Both a segment part and an offset part must be specified for every memory reference. This chapter describes the basic memory addressing mechanisms used in every instruction that references a memory operand. The options available for specifying segments and offsets are described in detail.

Many of the memory structuring capabilities provided by segmentation are visible to the applications programmer, and so these aspects are appropriate to discuss at this point. The key structuring issue is how program units such as code procedures, data areas, and the program stack are assigned storage within one or more segments.

Chapter 1 introduced physical memory as a one-dimensional (linear) array of bytes, and described how data types that occupy more than one byte are placed in memory. In this chapter, we see that memory is divided into segments that provide a second dimension to the memory space. Chapter 5 discusses memory addressing from the operating-systems perspective, describing the memory-management mechanisms that protect segments and relocate them within the one-dimensional physical memory space. In Chapter 5, you will see how the two-dimensional virtual addresses introduced in this chapter are translated to one-dimensional addresses in physical memory.

Two-Part Addressing

Because of segmentation, a memory address on the 80386 has two parts, a segment part and an offset part. Both parts must be specified by an instruction with a memory operand. The segment part is a 16-bit segment *selector*, which contains a 14-bit field that identifies one of 16,384 possible segments. The 32-bit offset part gives a byte offset within the segment. Consecutive byte addresses within segments are obtained by incrementing the offset part from 0 up to the limit of the segment. Since the byte offset is 32 bits, the maximum offset that can be specified, and therefore the maximum size of a segment, is 4G bytes.

Notation

The notation we use for memory addresses in this chapter gives the segment part on the left, the offset part on the right, and a colon (:) separating the two parts. The segment part can be either a segment name or a segment register. If a segment register is given, the segment selector contained in that register identifies the segment. Offsets are given as numbers or register names enclosed in square brackets. Offsets can also be formed by expressions involving register names, scale factors, and constants, to reflect the addressing modes described later in this chapter.

For example, the address at offset 1234 in a segment named NEWDATA would be specified with the notation NEWDATA:[1234]. If the ES segment register contained the selector for the segment NEWDATA, and the EAX general register contained the value 1234, the same address could be specified with the notation ES:[EAX]. This notation is a subset of the assembler notation for memory addresses that we define and use in Chapter 4.

Figure 2.4 illustrates how two-part addresses are used to access memory. There are two segments in the figure, Segment A and Segment B. Segment A contains 11 bytes, so the segment offsets within A range from 0 to 10. Segment B contains 17 bytes, so its segment offsets range from 0 to 16. The byte at address A:[5]—that is, at offset 5 within Segment A—contains the value 77. The byte at address B:[12]—that is, at offset 12 within Segment B—contains the value 88.

► Memory Addressing Mechanism

Both a segment part and an offset part must be specified by an instruction that uses a memory operand. Most programs tend to work on just a few segments at a time, but generate many different offsets within these segments. The addressing mechanism on the 80386 is optimized for these program characteristics.

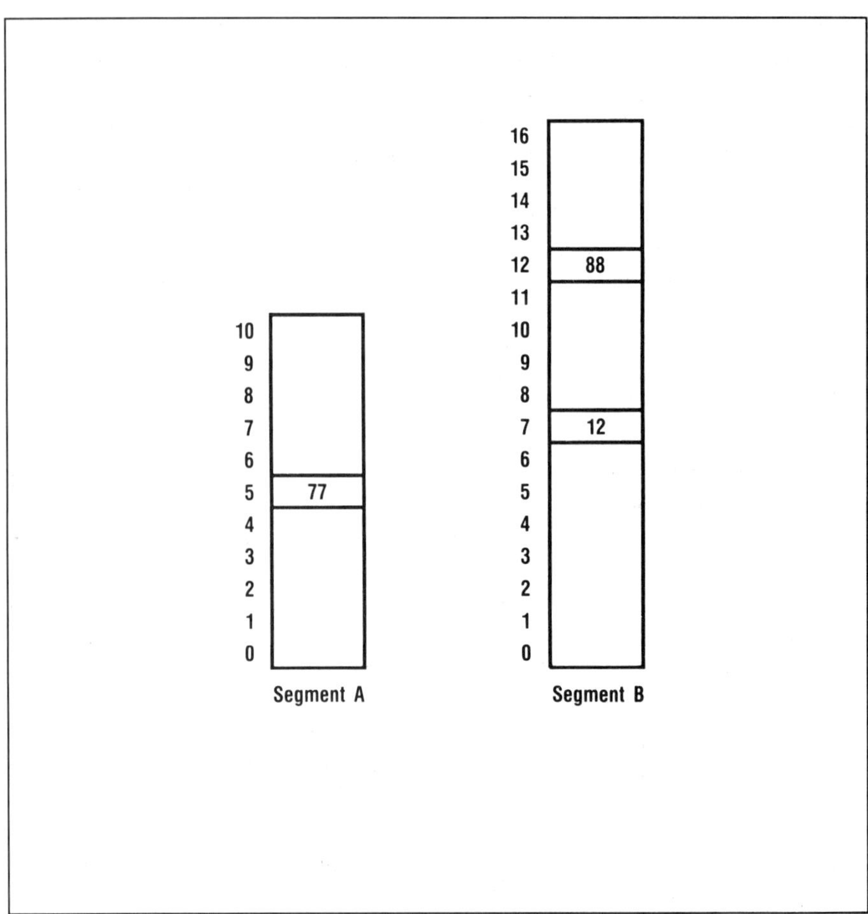

► **Figure 2.4:** Two-part addressing

The Segment Part: Segment Register

Special registers—the six segment registers introduced earlier in this chapter—are provided to hold segment selectors used as the segment parts of addresses. These registers provide access to up to six segments at any point in a program.

Every memory reference specifies implicitly, explicitly, or by default the segment register containing the selector for the segment part of the address. Code references always use the CS register, stack references always use the SS register, and certain string instructions always use the ES register for the destination operand. Any of the six segment registers can be used for all other data references. For example, if the selector for Segment B in Figure 2.4 is in the FS register, the memory reference FS:[12] would access the data stored at offset 12 in that segment, at the address B:[12]. If the selector for B is moved from the FS register to the DS register, the same data can be accessed with the address DS:[12].

The segment addressed by the CS register at any given time is called the current *Code Segment.* The EIP register contains the offset of the next instruction to execute within the segment addressed by the CS register, so the address of the next instruction to execute is CS:[EIP]. If the current code segment contains both instructions and data, the data can be referenced using the CS register as the segment part of the address. For example, a piece of data at an offset of 8 plus the value in the EAX register can be addressed as CS:[EAX + 8] from instructions in the same segment.

All code references use the CS register, so only one code segment is addressable at any time. Intersegment control-transfer instructions, described in Chapter 3, can be used to load a new value into both the CS and EIP registers to change the locus of execution to a different code segment. This provides an efficient method to transfer control between procedures that are stored in different segments. For example, the application code is typically in a different segment than operating-system code, so these intersegment control transfers provide an efficient way for applications to invoke operating-system services.

The segment addressed by the SS register is called the current *Stack Segment.* Stack operations such as PUSH, POP, CALL, and RETURN use a program stack contained within the segment addressed by SS. The top of this stack is at the offset contained in the ESP general register that is reserved for this purpose. The address of the top of the program stack is SS:[ESP]. This program stack is described in more detail later in this chapter.

The DS, ES, FS, and GS registers are available to address general data segments required by the program. The DS register is the "main" data segment register, since it is the default segment register for references other than to the stack. As you will see later in this chapter, instructions that reference data in segments addressed by CS, SS, ES, FS, and GS are one byte longer than those addressed by DS. This makes references to segments other than DS slightly more expensive in program storage and execution time, but not by much. In general, it is a good idea to arrange the data in the program so that the DS register can address the data segment most often referenced, and use the ES, FS, and GS registers to address segments that are referenced less frequently.

Figure 2.5 illustrates the use of segment registers. CS points to the

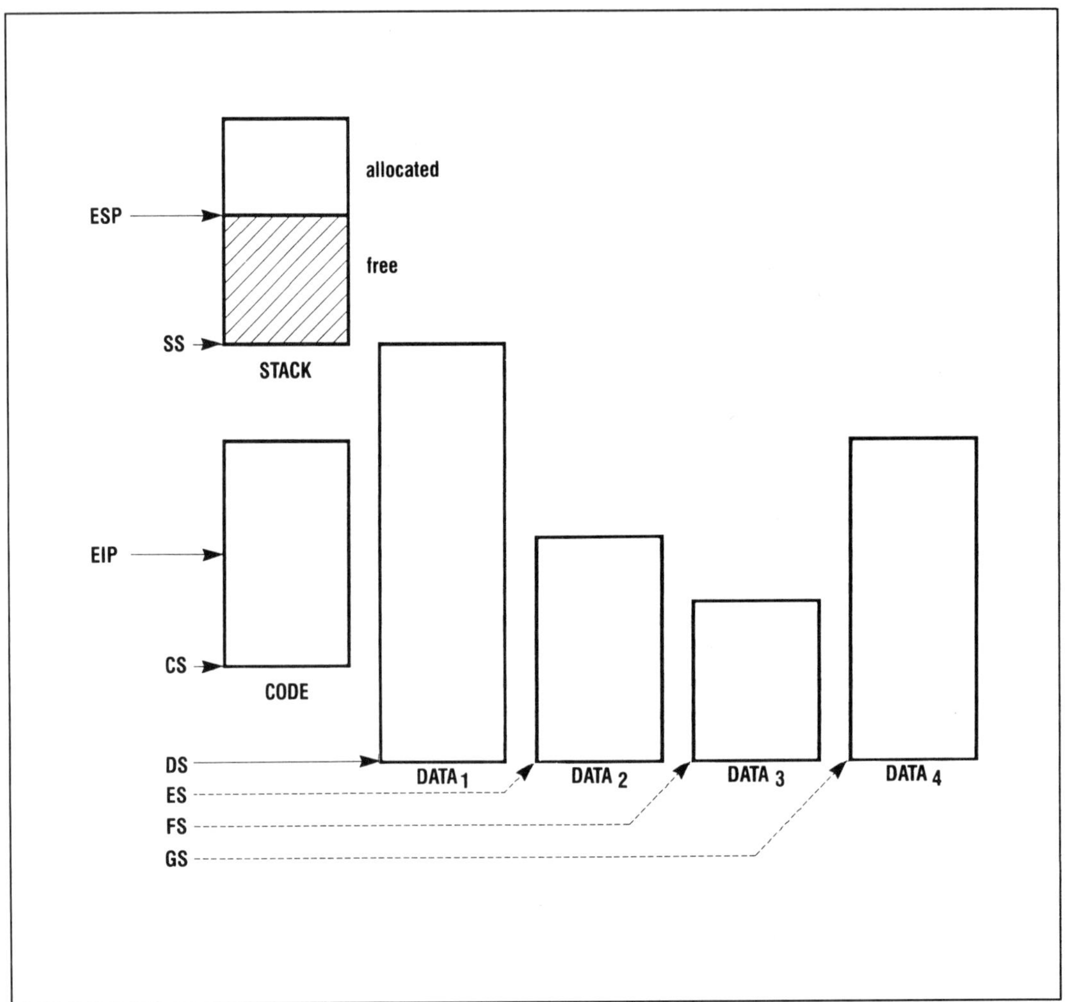

► **Figure 2.5:** Segment register usage

current code segment, and EIP gives the offset of the next instruction within this segment. SS points to the stack segment, and ESP identifies the top of the program stack within this segment. As explained in a later section, memory for the stack is allocated by moving ESP toward lower addresses, so the part of the stack segment above ESP is already allocated to the stack, and the memory below ESP is free for future allocation as needed. DS points to the primary data segment, named $DATA_1$. ES, FS, and GS are available to address other data segments, and might point to $DATA_2$, $DATA_3$, or $DATA_4$, as shown in dotted lines.

The Offset Part: Address Modes

The previous section described the mechanism for specifying the segment part of an address. Since every memory reference contains both a segment part and an offset part, we now need to describe how offset parts can be specified.

The 80386 provides a flexible mechanism for forming the offset part of an address. Each instruction that references a memory operand specifies the method by which the offset part is to be computed. This specification is called the *address mode* of the instruction. Address modes on the 80386 specify up to three components to be added to form the offset. A base register, an index register scaled (multiplied) by 1, 2, 4, or 8, and a constant displacement can be added to form the offset.

Any of the eight 32-bit general registers can be used as the *base* register, or the base component can be omitted. Any of the eight 32-bit general registers except the stack pointer register, ESP, can be used as the *index* register, or the index component can be omitted. If an index register is specified, the value contained in this register can be scaled by 1, 2, 4, or 8 before it is added into the offset. An 8- or 32-bit constant *displacement* can be specified, or the displacement can be omitted.

These base + (index * scale) + displacement address modes provide a powerful and flexible address mechanism that satisfies the addressing needs of data structures supported by high-level languages. A later section describes how data structures such as records, arrays, and even arrays of records use these addressing modes.

Use of a memory operand is faster if it is *aligned*. An operand is aligned if its offset is a multiple of its size. For example, a dword operand is aligned if its offset is a multiple of 4, and a word is aligned if its offset is a multiple of 2. Operands that are not aligned can still be accessed, but may take longer. We recommend that all operands be aligned.

The default segment register for data references is dependent on the base register selected. If the base register is ESP or EBP, the default segment register is changed from the normal DS to SS, since the ESP and EBP registers were designed to be used with the stack. For all other base register choices, including no base register, DS remains the default segment register. Accessing data in a segment addressed by a segment register other than the default requires the use of an extra instruction byte to specify the desired segment register. Use of EBP as an index register (ESP cannot be an index register) does not affect the choice of default segment register. The choice of default segment register is affected only by the base register selected.

Table 2.1 lists the variety of address modes available. Examples on the use of address modes are given in the following sections.

BASE + (INDEX * SCALE) + DISPLACEMENT

BASE	+	INDEX	*	SCALE	+	DISPLACEMENT
none		none		1		none
EAX		EAX		2		8-bit
ECX		ECX		4		32-bit
EDX		EDX		8		
EBX		EBX				
ESP[1]		---[2]				
EBP[1]		EBP				
ESI		ESI				
EDI		EDI				

Notes:
[1] SS is the default segment register if ESP or EBP is the base register.
[2] The dashes (---) signify that ESP cannot be used as an index register.

► **Table 2.1:** 80386 addressing modes

Program Stack

A *program stack* supports a LIFO (last in, first out) allocation discipline, which is well suited for nested storage required for subexpression results and subroutines. The two basic stack operations are PUSH and POP. The PUSH operation adds a new element to the stack, and the POP operation removes the last element pushed. A PUSH followed by a POP leaves the stack unchanged.

The PUSH and POP operations support use of the stack to store temporary values—for example, the intermediate parts of a complex calculation. As these intermediate parts are computed, their results can be pushed onto the stack. To compute the final expression value, the results from the intermediate computations are popped off and combined to form the final result. The nested storage provided by the stack matches the natural nesting of subexpression calculation.

The nested storage provided by the stack also supports an efficient and flexible subroutine call and return mechanism that naturally handles nested procedures. A procedure CALL instruction pushes a return address onto the stack where it remains until the matching RET instruction pops it off. A call to a nested subroutine pushes its return address, hiding an outer procedure's return address. The return from a nested subroutine pops its return address off the stack, exposing the return address of the outer procedure as the top of the stack. Use of the program stack to support a complete subroutine call mechanism is described in a later section.

The stack is in the memory segment addressed by the SS register. The ESP register contains the offset within this segment of the top of the program stack. The two-part address SS:[ESP] points to the current top of the program stack.

Temporary Storage on the Stack

On the 80386, the stack grows toward lower addresses, and each stack element is four bytes (32 bits) wide. To push an element onto the 80386 stack, first the ESP register is decremented by 4, and then the new element is written to the memory location addressed by SS:[ESP]. To pop an element off the stack, the memory location addressed by SS:[ESP] is read to retrieve the element, and then the ESP register is incremented by 4. At any time, the current top-of-stack element is addressed by SS:[ESP], and inner stack elements are addressed by positive offsets from SS:[ESP]. The second stack element is at address SS:[ESP + 4], the third is at address SS:[ESP + 8], and so on. Operands on the stack can be referenced faster if the stack is aligned. Since stack elements are four bytes in size, this is easily done by ensuring that the ESP register always contains a multiple of 4.

Figure 2.6 illustrates how PUSH and POP operate on the 80386 program stack. The leftmost stack picture shows the stack after three elements have been pushed at offsets FCh, F8h, and F4h within the stack segment that is 100h bytes in size. ESP contains the value F4h, which is the offset of the top-of-stack element. The top of the stack is at the bottom of the figure because the stack grows toward the lower addresses, which are lower in the figure. The right stack picture shows the stack after the value 12345678h has been pushed. ESP now contains the value F0h, which is 4 less than the original value. The original top-of-stack element is now the second stack element, and can be addressed at SS:[ESP + 4]. A POP operation will return the stack to the state shown in the left stack, by adjusting the value in the ESP register by 4.

Subroutines and the Stack

The 80386 program stack supports an efficient subroutine call and return mechanism. The CALL instruction pushes a return address (the address of the instruction following the CALL) onto the program stack, and jumps to the start of a subroutine. The RET instruction pops the return address from the stack, then jumps to that address to resume execution with the instruction after the matching CALL instruction. The program stack is also used to pass parameters to subroutines, and for storing variables local to the subroutine. By using a stack, the 80386 efficiently supports nested subroutines, including recursive and reentrant subroutines.

An optimization of this technique is to use the general registers for the first few parameters and for the most frequently used local variables. Since registers can be accessed more quickly than memory, this optimization can speed program execution. The stack can be used to store the remaining parameters and local variables.

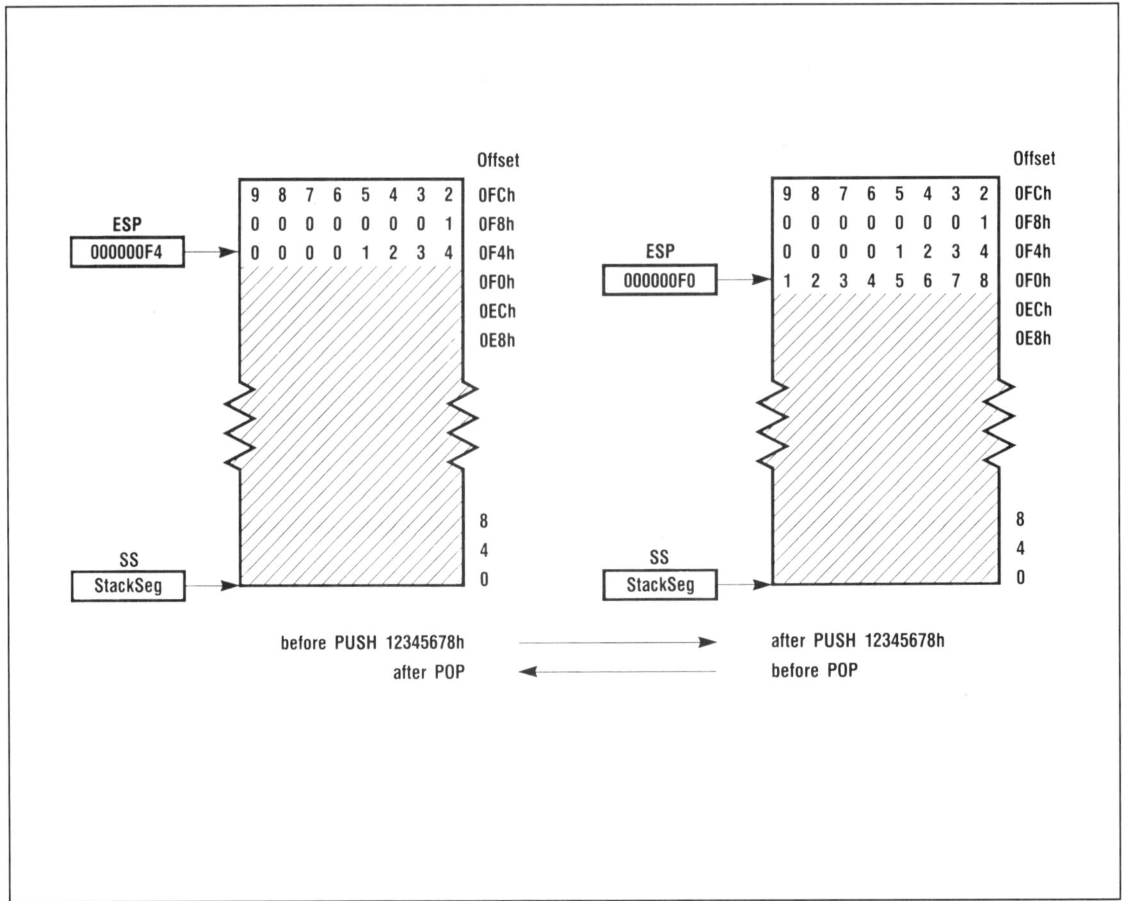

► **Figure 2.6:** Stack PUSH/POP operations

Basic Subroutine Linkage The simplest subroutine linkage supports a subroutine call with parameter passing and local variable allocation on the program stack. A subroutine call proceeds in three steps.

1. Push the parameters onto the program stack.
2. Use a CALL instruction to push the return address onto the stack and jump to the subroutine.
3. Subtract a constant from the ESP register to reserve room on the stack for local variables.

Within the subroutine, the parameters and local variables can be addressed with constant displacements from the ESP register. The address mode using ESP as a base plus a signed 8-bit displacement can be used when the size of the local variables and parameters does not exceed 127 bytes. Otherwise, a full 32-bit displacement from ESP must be used. These offsets from ESP must track any changes to ESP within the subroutine, either as temporary values are pushed and popped on the stack or as parameters are pushed to be passed to another subroutine. This tracking is easy for a language compiler to perform, but it can be confusing when writing an assembler program! An alternative is to use the EBP register as a stable base register to point to the stack area allocated to the active procedure. This allows variables and parameters to be addressed at fixed offsets from EBP, but prevents use of EBP as a general register.

The ESP and EBP registers were designed to efficiently support stack addressing, since using either ESP or EBP as a base register selects SS as the default segment register. This allows ESP or EBP to address the stack area for the current procedure without the need for an extra instruction byte to explicitly specify the stack segment.

Figure 2.7 illustrates the state of the program stack after calling a subroutine with two parameters and 32 bytes of local variables. The subroutine is in the same segment as the calling procedure, so that an intrasegment CALL (Chapter 3) is used to push a four-byte return address. The two parameters pushed onto the stack occupy eight bytes and the return address occupies four bytes. With 32 bytes of local storage, the total is 44 bytes.

Within the subroutine, the local variables are addressed by SS:[ESP + n], where n ranges from 0 to 31. The first parameter is at address SS:[ESP + 40]. The second parameter is at address SS:[ESP + 36].

To return from the subroutine, the inverse of the three parts of the CALL sequence are required.

1. Add a value to ESP to pop the local variables off the program stack.

2. Return from the subroutine by popping the return address off the stack, and jumping to that address.
3. Add a value to ESP to pop the parameters off the stack.

A form of the RET instruction described in Chapter 3 combines the last two steps.

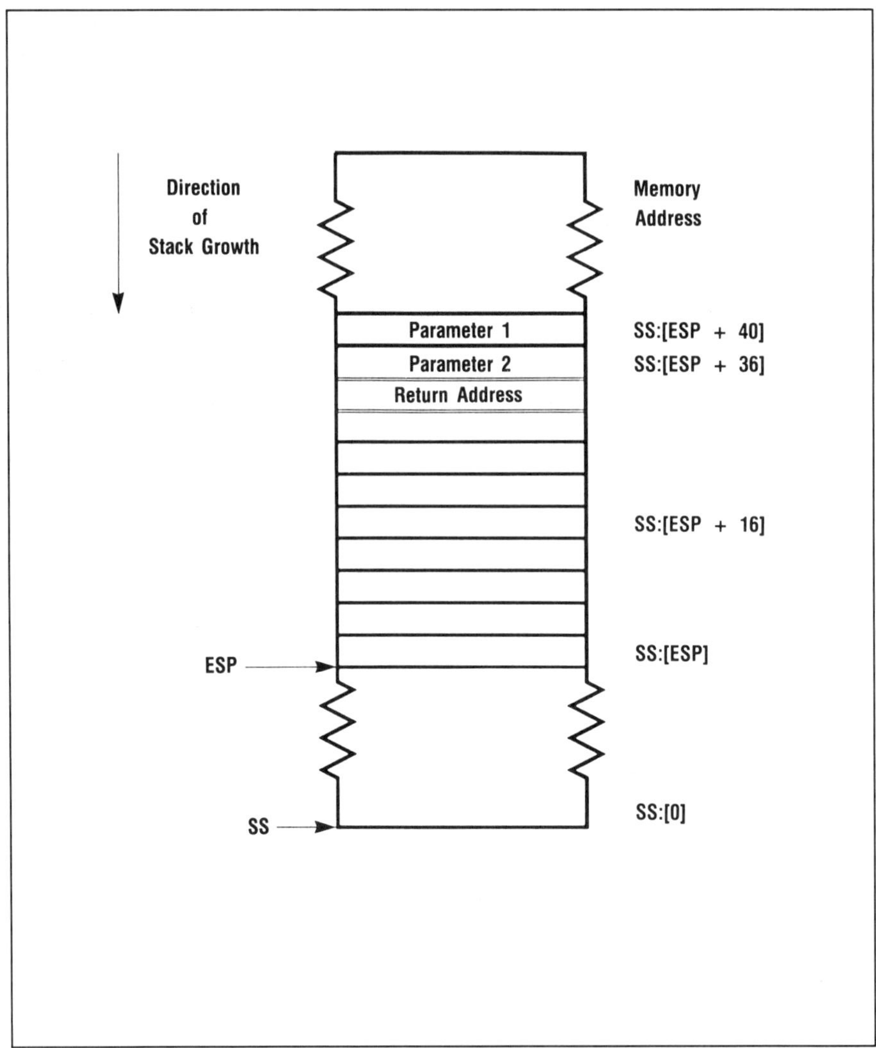

► **Figure 2.7:** Parameters, return address, and local variables stored in the program stack

Pointer Data Type

Most data types were described in Chapter 1. We deferred introduction of pointer data types until now, so we could introduce some basic addressing concepts first. A pointer data type contains a value that gives the address of a datum. Pointers are useful for building complex data structures such as lists and trees that vary dramatically in structure as a program executes. Each element in a list or tree structure contains one or more pointers to other elements, so that elements can be linked and unlinked simply by storing addresses of other elements in these pointers. Other constructs such as arrays and records are better suited for data structures that need not vary in structure, since they are usually more efficient in storage usage and execution time than structures linked by pointers.

The 80386 supports two types of pointers: a 48-bit full pointer that contains a full two-part address, and a 32-bit pointer that contains only the offset part of an address. The 48-bit pointer is used when elements from different segments are linked by pointers. The offset-only pointer is more efficient, but can only be used when all the linked elements are stored in the same segment.

A 48-bit pointer, shown in Figure 2.8, holds both parts of an address. The offset part is in the low-order 32 bits, and the segment selector is in

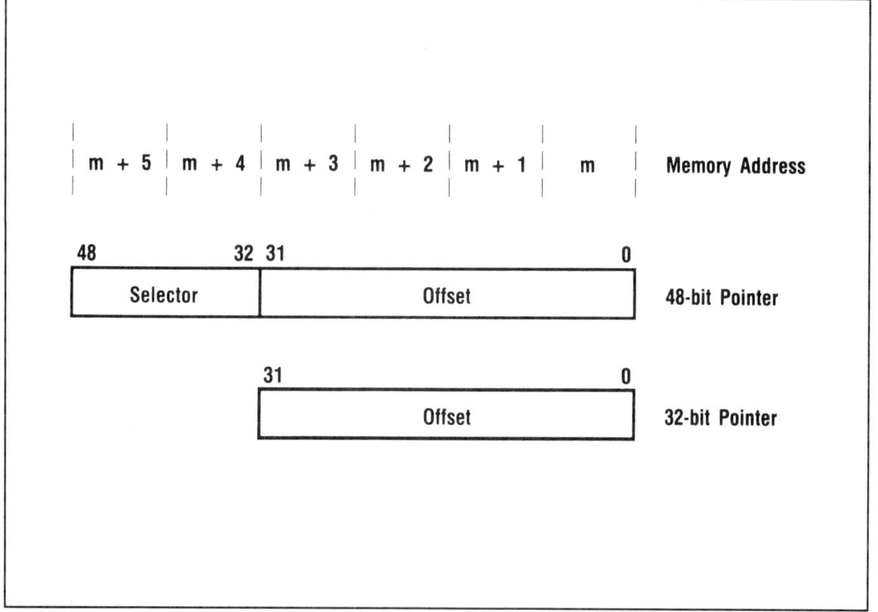

► **Figure 2.8:** 48-bit and 32-bit pointers

the high-order 16 bits. To address data with a 48-bit pointer, the two parts must be loaded into registers. The segment selector in the high-order 16 bits is loaded into one of the segment registers. The offset part in the low-order 32 bits is loaded into one of the general registers where it can be used as a base register. Chapter 3 describes the LDS, LES, LFS, and LGS instructions, which will load these 48-bit pointers into segment register/general register pairs in a single instruction.

If all the addresses to be stored in pointers have the same segment part, a useful optimization is to keep the selector for this segment in a segment register dedicated for this purpose, and store only the offset parts in 32-bit pointers, also shown in Figure 2.8. To address data with a 32-bit pointer, only the offset part needs to be loaded into one of the general registers to be used as a base register, with the segment part taken from the segment register dedicated to holding the common selector.

A 32-bit offset pointer is more efficient in both storage usage and execution time than a 48-bit pointer. If all the data for an application, including the program stack, is stored in one segment, 32-bit pointers can be used. In this model, the SS, DS, and ES segment registers are loaded with the selector for the common segment containing all the data and the program stack, so that all memory references can use the default data segment register. Note that even though there is only one segment in this model, memory addresses are still considered to have a segment part, which is implicitly the single segment containing everything.

Address Modes and Data Structures

The base + index + displacement addressing modes of the 80386 directly support the addressing needs of high-level languages. Scalar variables, records, arrays, and even arrays of records and records of arrays are directly supported by the 80386 address modes. These data structures can be located in *static* storage, as required by FORTRAN, or can be *dynamically allocated* on a program stack (and referenced relative to SS:[ESP]) or heap (and referenced indirectly through pointers) as required by Pascal or C. The base and index registers provide two dynamic components for the address mode, and the displacement supplies a static component. Statically allocated data is addressed simply by using a constant displacement within a data segment. Data allocated on the stack is addressed by using a constant displacement from either the ESP or EBP register, as discussed in a previous section. Data allocated in a heap is addressed by loading a pointer to the data into a segment register/general register pair and then using the general register as a base register. Table 2.2 correlates language needs with the address modes supplied by the 80386, and gives an example in assembler notation for each address mode.

To simplify register allocation in language translators, any of the eight general registers can be used as a base register, and any of the general registers except ESP can be used as a scaled index register. The index register value can be used directly (scaled by 1), or can be scaled by a factor of 2, 4, or 8 to support direct indexing of 16-, 32-, and 64-bit data without requiring shift instructions or use of an extra register.

STORAGE TYPE	STRUCTURE TYPE	ADDRESS MODE CATEGORY	EXAMPLE
Static	Scalar	Disp	DS:[1000]
	Array	Index + Disp	DS:[ESI*4 + 1004]
	Record	Disp	DS:[1234h]
	Array of Records	Index + Disp	DS:[EDX*8 + 1000h]
	Record of Arrays	Index + Disp	DS:[EBX*2 + 1048h]
Stack	Scalar	Base + Disp	SS:[ESP + 24]
	Array	Base + Index + Disp	SS:[ESP + ESI*4 + 120]
	Record	Base + Disp	SS:[ESP + 48]
	Array of Records	Base + Index + Disp	SS:[EBP + EDX*8 − 256]
	Record of Arrays	Base + Index + Disp	SS:[ESP + EDI*2 + 1000h]
Heap	Scalar	Base	ES:[EBX]
	Array	Base + Index	FS:[EBX + ESI*4]
	Record	Base + Disp	DS:[EAX + 12]
	Array of Records	Base + Index + Disp	ES:[EBX + EAX*8 + 6]
	Record of Arrays	Base + Index + Disp	DS:[EAX + EDI*2 + 1800h]

► **Table 2.2:** Data structures and 80386 address modes

Segmentation Strategies

The 80386 supports a wide range of segmentation strategies, which determine how program units are allocated storage in one or more memory segments. A *program unit* is an individual code procedure or data area, or the program stack. Each program unit might be contained in its own segment for the maximum flexibility in relocating, sharing, and protecting the individual units. At the other extreme, an entire application's code, data, and stack might be stored in a single segment.

There are two key characteristics that make segments a powerful mechanism for addressing, protecting, and sharing code procedures, data areas, and the program stack.

- A segment can be of any size.
- The memory-management mechanism described in Chapter 5 relocates, shares, and protects a segment as a single indivisible unit, no matter how large or small the segment may be.

Because of the variable size of segments, any program unit can be accommodated within a single segment, where it can be relocated and protected by an operating system as a single unit. A small 20-byte procedure can be stored in one segment. A large 100-megabyte data array can also be stored in a single segment. Or all the code and data for an entire application can be stored in one segment.

Figures 2.9 and 2.10 illustrate two strategies for storing program units in segments. The number of segments used to store data differentiates the two models. The model of Figure 2.10 uses only one segment for data storage, and so is called the single-segment model (even though there is a second segment to hold the code). The model of Figure 2.9 stores data for a single application in more than one segment. Alternatively, the size of pointers required differentiates the two models. The single-segment model can use 32-bit pointers, since all of the data and stack are stored in one segment. The multiple-segment model must use 48-bit pointers, since data areas are stored in several different segments, and each data pointer must explicitly specify which segment is pointed to.

Figure 2.9 shows how the code, stack, and data for two different applications can be stored in separate segments. The code for application 1 is contained in the segment named $Code_1$, its stack is in the segment $Stack_1$, and its data is in $Data_{1a}$ and $Data_{1b}$. It shares a data segment named $Data_s$ with application 2, which has its code, stack, and data in segments named $Code_2$, $Stack_2$, and $Data_2$, respectively.

In this multiple-segment strategy, the two applications are stored in eight different segments, with one segment shared between the two applications.

Each segment can have access restrictions as appropriate. For example, both code segments, $Code_1$ and $Code_2$, can be restricted to execute-only access. The shared data segment $Data_s$ can be restricted to read-only access to one

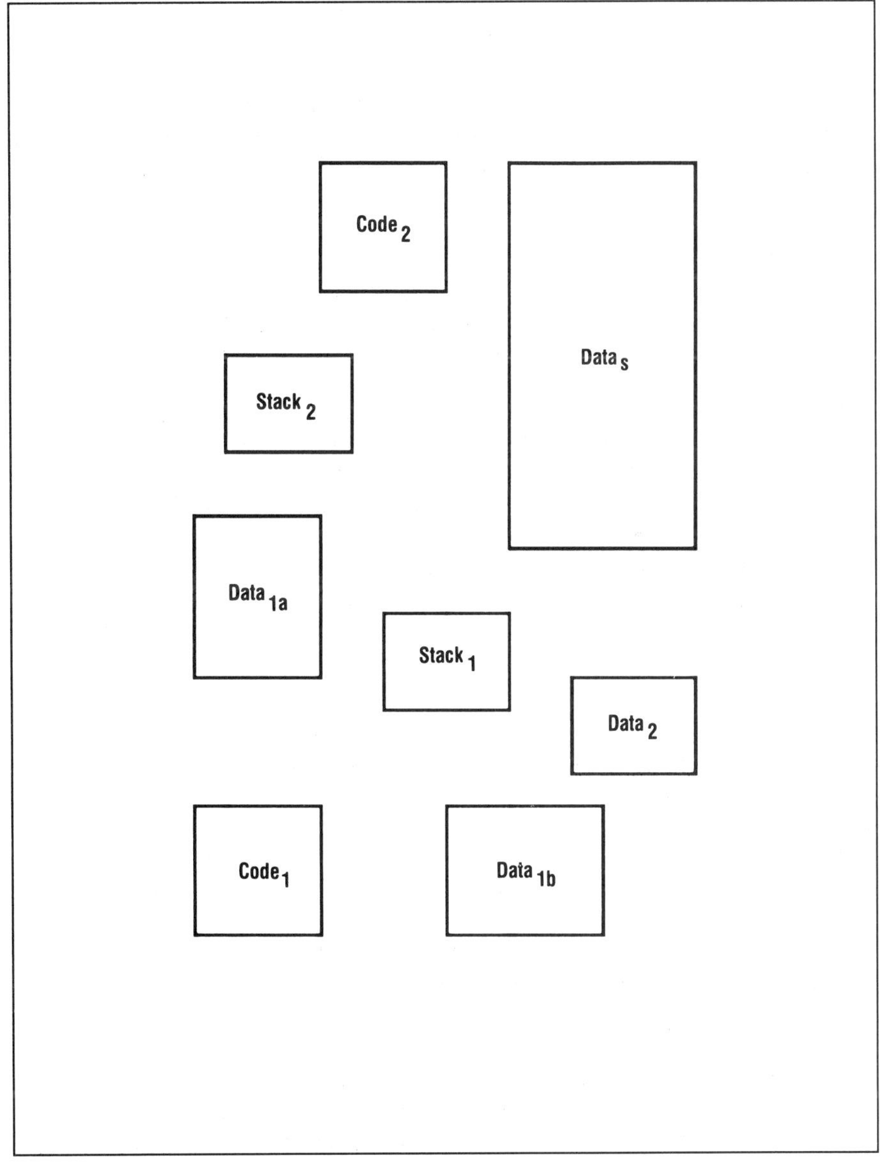

► **Figure 2.9:** Multiple-segment segmentation strategy

or both applications to prevent unauthorized changes to its data. Because there are multiple data segments, 48-bit full pointers must be used.

Balanced against the desire to put each program unit into a separate segment for flexibility in relocation and protection is the fact that storing all of the data and stack for an application in a single segment is more efficient because it allows use of 32-bit pointers. This single-segment strategy also supports the application model presented by most minicomputers and mainframe computers (which do not have segments), and so supports easy portability of applications from these environments.

Even though segmentation is not used within an individual application in this model, operating-system software can still use segmentation to separate and protect each application from other applications in a multitasking environment. In this model, each application is stored in two segments: one containing all of the code for that application, the other containing all of the data and stack. The operating system is stored in two or more other segments, and arranges the segments so that each application is insulated from all of the other applications, and so that the operating system is protected from all applications.

Figure 2.10 illustrates this single-segment segmentation strategy. $CODE_1$ holds the code for application 1, SEG_1 holds the stack and data

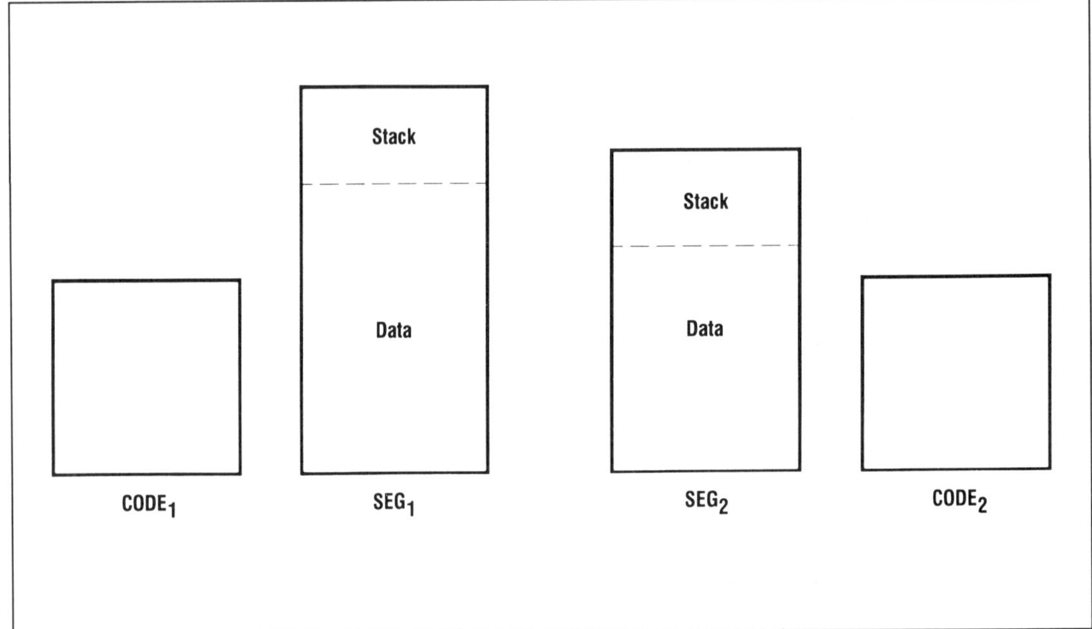

► **Figure 2.10:** Single-segment segmentation strategy

for application 1, $CODE_2$ holds the code for application 2, and SEG_2 holds the stack and data for application 2. Since there is only one data segment per application, each application can use the more efficient 32-bit offset-only pointers. One consequence of the use of 32-bit pointers is that the two applications can no longer share a data segment, as was done in Figure 2.9. Also, the common segment must permit read and write access, with no protection for read-only data as was available in the multiple-segment model.

There are advantages and disadvantages to both of the segmentation strategies illustrated above. In many cases, operating-system software dictates the use of one model or the other. If there is a choice, we recommend the single-segment model for most applications, because of its inherent simplicity. The single-segment model also offers greater efficiency because it can use simple 32-bit pointers. A few systems need the flexibility of sharing and protection provided by the multiple-segment model, but most applications are adequately served by the simpler single-segment model.

► Instruction Encoding

This section describes the instruction encoding, with an emphasis on the encoding for operands. First, the general instruction encoding is described at a high level, and then the detailed bit patterns for encoding immediate, register, and memory operands are given.

You need not understand the topics in this section to program the 80386, even at the assembly language level. The material in the previous sections described the instruction operands in terms of their symbolic representation in the assembly language. This section goes a level lower, to the actual bit patterns used to represent these symbolic operand choices in the 80386 machine instructions. If you do not need this detailed information, you can move on to the section that describes the I/O memory space later in this chapter.

The material presented in this section is aimed primarily at developers of software translators such as assemblers, compilers, and debuggers. These software translators need to know the encoding of the instructions. In fact, their main function is to hide the details of the instruction encoding from the programmer.

Instruction Fields

Figure 2.11 shows the general format of an 80386 instruction. Each instruction can have up to five fields, with the fields to the left stored at lower addresses.

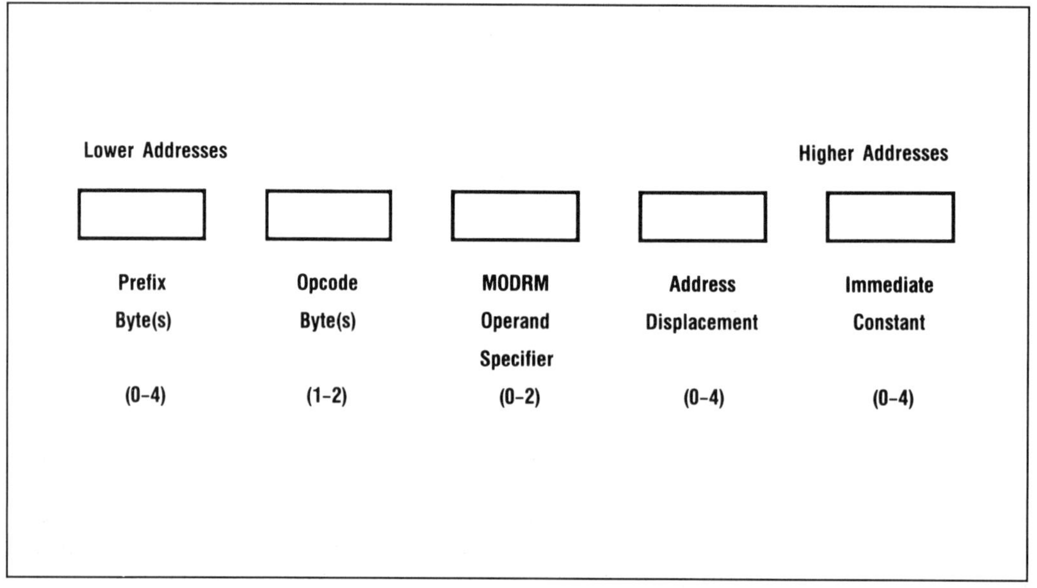

► **Figure 2.11:** General instruction format

Prefix Bytes Up to four prefix bytes may be specified, or no prefix bytes may be present in an instruction. As their name implies, if prefixes are present they are the first few bytes of an instruction. Prefixes are used to modify the interpretation of the following instruction only, and do not apply to any other instructions. Prefixes are used to specify less frequently used instruction parameters so that the instruction encoding for the usual cases can be more compact. One example of an instruction prefix is the segment register override, described later in this section. It is used to specify the segment register for a memory operand in case the default segment register is not appropriate. Other examples are the LOCK and REP prefixes described in Chapter 3.

Opcode Bytes Opcode bytes immediately follow any prefix bytes. At least one opcode byte must be present in every instruction, and some instructions require two bytes. A special one-byte instruction form combines an opcode with a 3-bit register operand specifier (refer to Figure 2.13).

MODRM Operand Specifier A MODRM operand specifier, if present, follows the opcode byte(s). The opcode determines whether this specifier is present and whether this field specifies two operands, or one operand plus extra opcode bits. This field can specify one register operand, one memory operand, two register operands, or a register operand and a memory operand. The MODRM field can be one or two bytes long.

Address Displacement An address displacement, if present, follows the MODRM field. The mod subfield of the MODRM field indicates whether the displacement is present, and its length. Displacements are present only for memory operands.

Immediate Constant An immediate constant, if present, is the last field in an instruction. That is, it is stored in the highest addressed bytes in the instruction. The opcode determines whether an immediate constant is present, and defines its length. Up to four bytes of immediate data can be present in this field.

Immediate Constants

An *immediate constant* operand is the simplest type of operand specifier, where the value of the operand is given directly in the instruction. The number of bits in the immediate constant is dependent on the operand size of the instruction and on the opcode. If present, an immediate constant is always the last field in an instruction, coming after any opcode fields or address mode fields.

Figure 2.12 illustrates the various forms of immediate constants. Constants can be 8, 16, or 32 bits long, for 8-, 16-, or 32-bit operand sizes. The 16- and 32-bit immediate forms are stored with the low-order bytes at lower addresses, and with the high-order bytes at higher addresses. Signed or unsigned bytes, signed or unsigned words, and signed or unsigned dwords can all be represented in these three forms. In addition, a small value for a 16- or 32-bit operand can be represented as a sign-extended 8-bit value to save instruction space. In this case, an 8-bit constant is given directly in the instruction, and is extended to 16 or 32 bits by replicating the sign bit, bit 7, throughout the high-order 8 or 24 bits. This saves space for the important frequent cases of signed words or signed dwords with values between −128 and 127, and also for unsigned words in one of the ranges 0 to 127 or FF80h to FFFFh, and unsigned dwords in one of the ranges 0 to 127 or FFFFFF80h to FFFFFFFFh.

Example: The instruction that pushes an immediate constant onto the stack uses an instruction form that has a one-byte opcode and one or four bytes of immediate data. This instruction is a good example at this point because it has only one operand, an immediate constant. In this example the memory addresses are indicated along the top as m, m + 1, ..., m + 4. Just below the instruction bits, an indication of their interpretation is given. Note that the opcode is at the lowest addressed byte, and the constant is stored with the low-order bytes at lower addresses.

PUSH 12345678h would be encoded as:

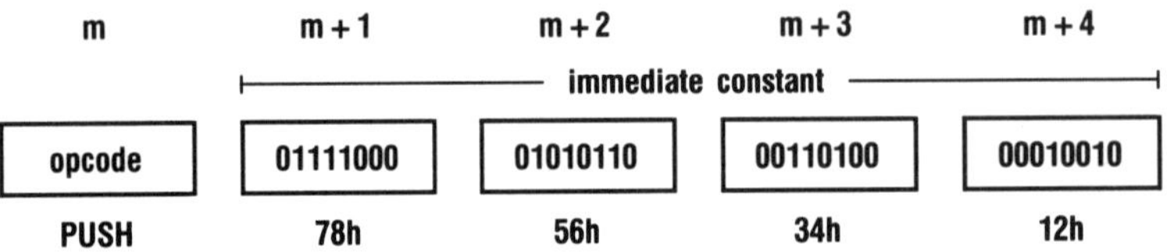

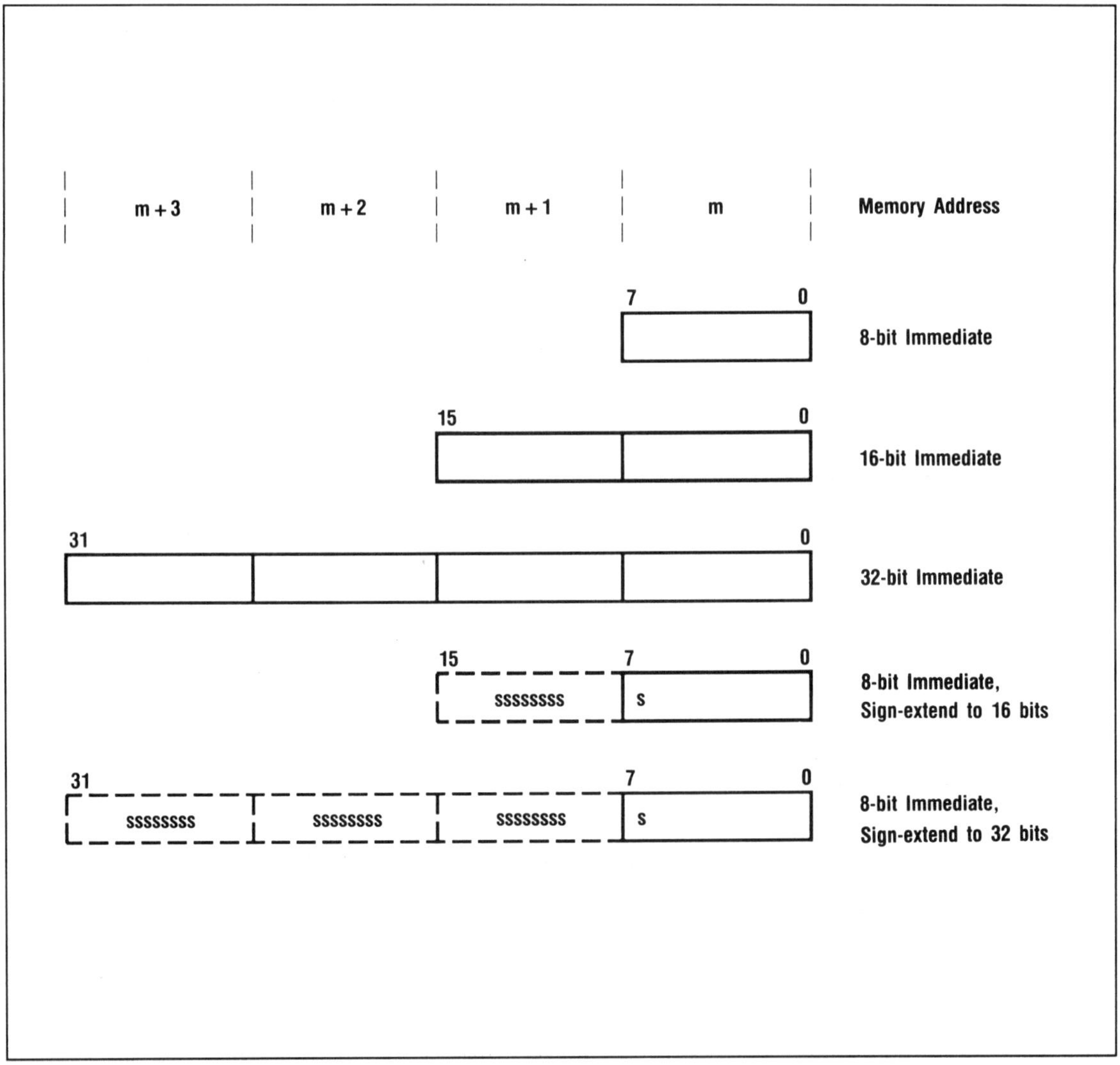

► **Figure 2.12:** Immediate operand encoding

PUSH −5 would be encoded as:

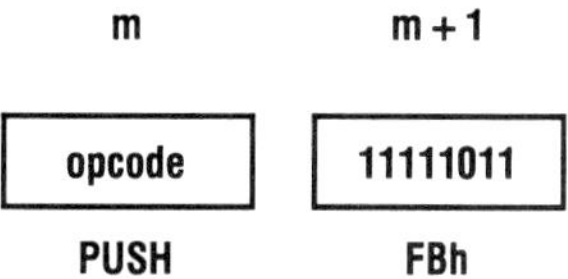

Note the use of the short one-byte immediate constant in the last example, which permits a short constant in the range −128 to 127 to be given with a single byte in the instruction. When this instruction is executed, the one-byte constant FBh is expanded to 32 bits by sign-extension to get FFFFFFFBh, the two's complement notation for −5.

Register Operands

An instruction operand can be located in a processor register. The register operand specifier selects one of the eight general-purpose registers, or one of the six segment registers, depending on the opcode. The operand size of the instruction determines whether an 8-, 16-, or 32-bit register is accessed for an operand in one of the general registers. The six segment registers are always accessed as 16-bit registers.

Figure 2.13 illustrates how the register operand specifiers are encoded

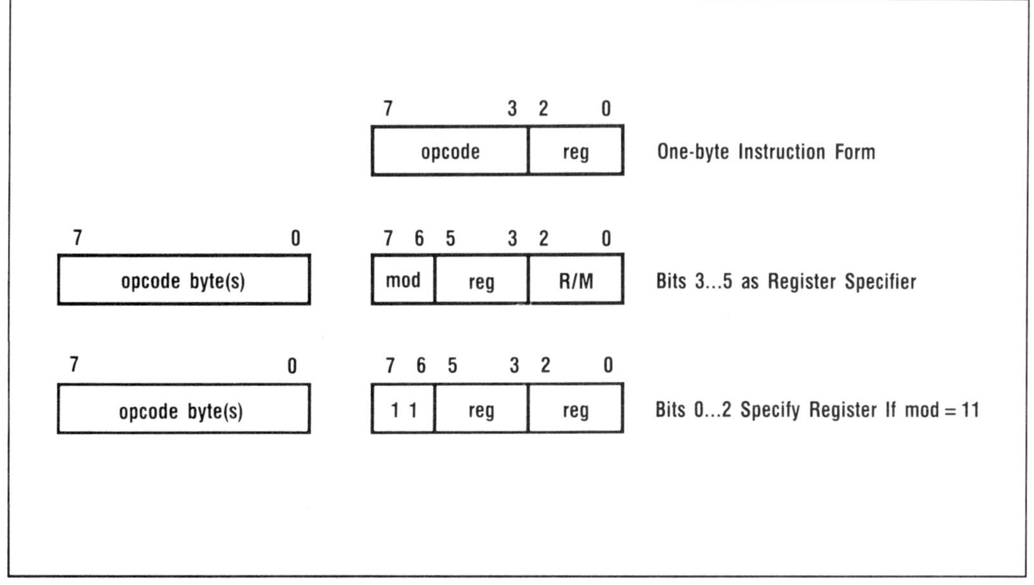

► **Figure 2.13:** Register operand encoding

in an instruction. The one-byte instruction forms use the lower 3 bits of the instruction to encode one of the eight general registers. The two- and three-byte instruction forms use a MODRM byte following the one- or two-byte opcode to encode one or two register operands. This byte contains three fields. The R/M field is in the 3 low-order bits, and specifies either a register operand or part of a memory operand, depending on the setting of the mod field. The mod field is a 2-bit field in the upper 2 bits of the byte. It specifies whether the R/M field should be interpreted as a 3-bit register name or as a memory operand. If the mod field has the value 11b (both bits are 1), the R/M field specifies a register operand, otherwise the R/M field specifies a memory operand. The R/M name comes from this dual interpretation of this field as either a *Register* or *Memory* operand based on the mod value. This byte is called the MODRM byte from the first and last field names, which are always present. The middle 3 bits of this MODRM byte can specify a register operand, or can provide 3 additional opcode bits, depending on the opcode in the first byte of the instruction.

In all of these cases, register operands are specified by a 3-bit code in the instruction. Table 2.3 gives the encoding of the 8-, 16-, and 32-bit general registers based on the operand size of the instruction and the value in one of these 3-bit register operand specifiers. Table 2.4 gives the reg field encoding for segment register operands.

REG CODE	32-BIT REGISTER	16-BIT REGISTER	8-BIT REGISTER
000b	EAX	AX	AL
001b	ECX	CX	CL
010b	EDX	DX	DL
011b	EBX	BX	BL
100b	ESP	SP	AH
101b	EBP	BP	CH
110b	ESI	SI	DH
111b	EDI	DI	BH

► **Table 2.3:** General register encoding

Example: The simplest register operand encoding uses the one-byte instruction form, which puts a register code in the lower 3 bits and the opcode in the upper 5 bits of the byte.

INC ESI would be encoded as:

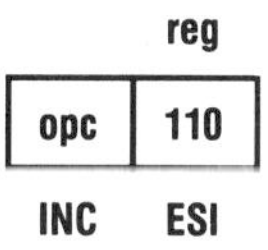

	reg
opc	110
INC	ESI

Example: Instructions that use two register operands use instruction formats that have the MODRM byte. In this case, the mod field is 11b, indicating that the R/M field contains a second register operand.

MOV DH, DL would be encoded as:

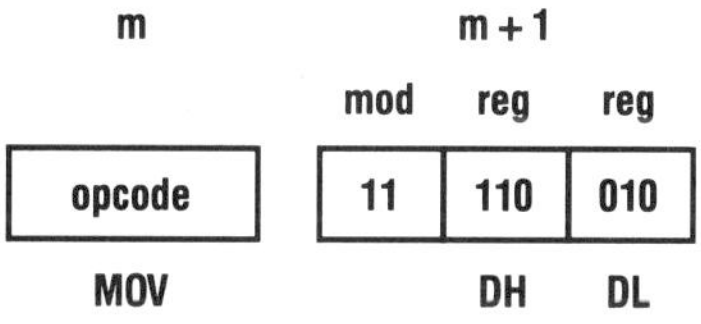

m		m + 1	
	mod	reg	reg
opcode	11	110	010
MOV		DH	DL

REG CODE	SEGMENT REGISTER
000b	ES
001b	CS
010b	SS
011b	DS
100b	FS
101b	GS
110b	Reserved
111b	Reserved

► **Table 2.4:** Segment register encoding

Example: The instruction that moves an immediate constant into a register is useful for initializing loop counters that can be allocated to registers throughout the loop. It uses the one-byte opcode form that has a register operand specifier in the lower 3 bits. In these examples, the memory addresses are indicated along the as m, m + 1, ..., m + 4. Note that the opcode is at the lowest addressed byte, and the constant is stored with the low-order bytes at lower addresses.

MOV ECX, 12345678h would be encoded as:

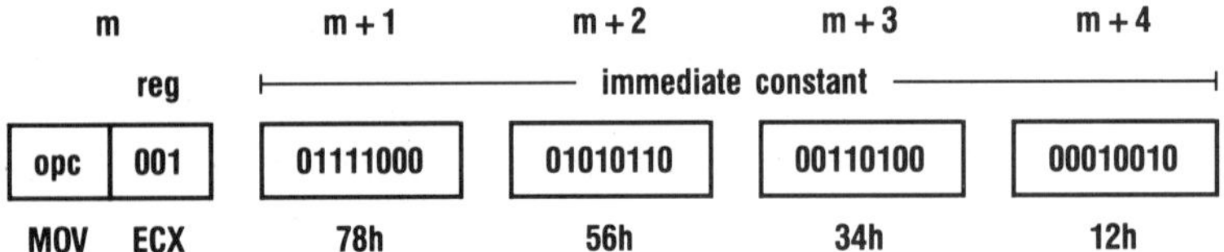

MOV AH, 37h would be encoded as:

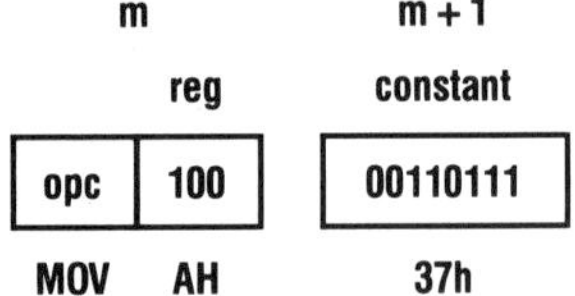

Memory Operands

An 80386 instruction can specify only one explicit memory operand. Both the segment part and the offset part of a memory address must be specified for a memory operand. The segment part is specified by giving the segment register that contains the selector for the segment containing the operand. In most cases, the default segment register can be used, so that no instruction bits are required. If a different segment register is used, an instruction prefix byte is needed.

The offset part is specified by the address mode, which indicates the base register, the index register, the scale factor for the index, and the constant displacement. The address mode is always present for instructions that specify a memory operand, and is contained in one or more bytes that follow the opcode bytes. A one- or two-byte MODRM field specifies the base register, index register, and scale factor, and indicates the size of the displacement. A one-, two-, or four-byte constant displacement, if indicated, follows the MODRM field. The low-order bytes of two- or four-byte displacements are stored at lower addresses, with the high-order bytes at higher addresses.

One-Byte Address Mode Encoding

A special short address specifier is provided for the important special cases where there is no index register given; that is, when the address mode specifies at most a base register and a displacement. This saves a byte when using the simple address modes containing just a base register, just a displacement, or both a base register and a displacement.

The format of this one-byte specifier is shown in Figure 2.14. This is the MODRM byte discussed above in the section on register operand encoding. The low-order 3 bits (R/M) specify the base register. A code of 100b in this field is a special escape code that indicates the two-byte form is being used, with the second byte of the two-byte address mode form in the following byte. Otherwise, the 3 bits encode the 32-bit base register using the same code used for specifying register operands, as given in Table 2.3. Note that only 32-bit registers can be used in addresses.

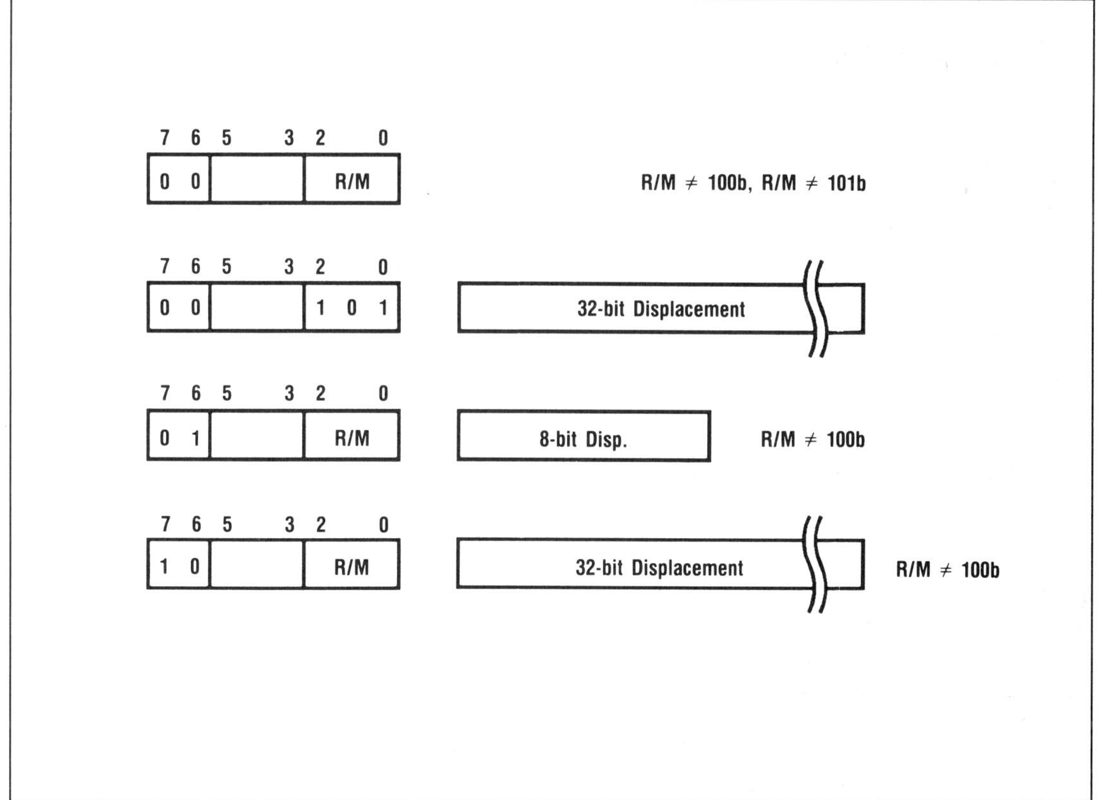

► **Figure 2.14:** One-byte address mode format

The upper 2 bits (*mod*) specify the length of the displacement. A code of 00b indicates no displacement is present. A code of 01b indicates an 8-bit displacement follows. This 8-bit displacement is extended to 32 bits by replicating the sign bit (bit 7) throughout the upper 24 bits (bits 8 through 31). A code of 10b indicates that a full 32-bit displacement follows. A code of 11b in this field indicates that the R/M field specifies a register operand rather than a memory operand, which was described in an earlier section.

Example: If mod = 00b, a register indirect addressing mode is specified, with the base register given in the R/M field.
ADD EAX, DS:[EDX] would be encoded as:

	mod	reg	R/M
opcode	00	000	010

Example: If mod = 01b, a register indirect plus displacement addressing mode is specified, with the base register given in the R/M field, and an 8-bit displacement following. The 8-bit displacement is sign-extended to form a 32-bit displacement to add to the base register value.
SUB EDI, DS:[EDI + 127] would be encoded as:

	mod	reg	R/M	displacement
opcode	01	111	111	01111111

Example: If mod = 10b, a register indirect plus displacement addressing mode is specified, with the base register given in the R/M field, and a 32-bit displacement following. Here the memory addresses are indicated as m, m + 1,..., m + 5, to indicate that the low-order bytes of the 32-bit displacement are stored at lower memory addresses.
ADD ESI, DS:[EDI + 12345678h] would be encoded as:

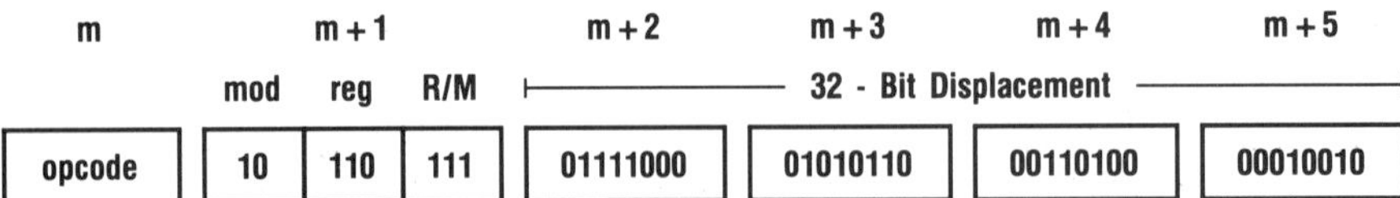

One special case requires further explanation. The combination of mod = 00b and R/M = 101b does not indicate EBP as the base register, with no displacement. Rather, it encodes the displacement-only case, that is, with no base register and no index register, but with a full 32-bit displacement.

The special cases are needed since there are really ten "base register" codes required: one each for the eight general registers, one to encode the escape to the two-byte form, and one to indicate no base register. Since there are only 3 bits available for the base register code, the code for ESP was chosen as the escape to the two-byte form (mod ≠ 11b and R/M = 100b), and some coding space was "stolen" from the mod field to permit the base field to specify "no base register" (mod = 00b and R/M = 101b). This encoding means that the address mode using EBP as a base with no displacement cannot be specified. Instead, the address mode using EBP as a base with an 8-bit displacement of 0 is used.

Example: A statically allocated variable can be addressed by using the displacement-only addressing mode, with mod = 00b and R/M = 101b.
MOV ESI, ScalarVar would be encoded as:

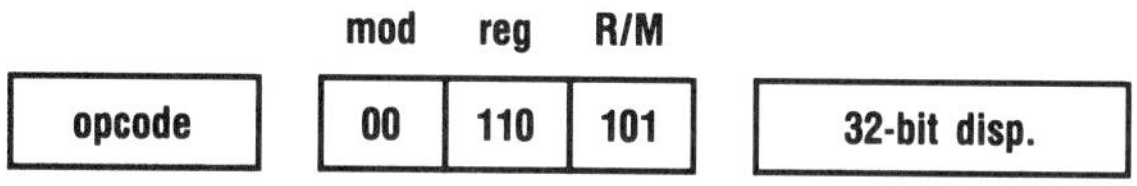

	mod	reg	R/M	
opcode	00	110	101	32-bit disp.

Example: A memory address with EBP as the base register, plus a displacement of 0, is specified with mod = 01b, R/M = 101b, and an 8-bit displacement containing 0.
MOV ESI, SS:[EBP] would be encoded as:

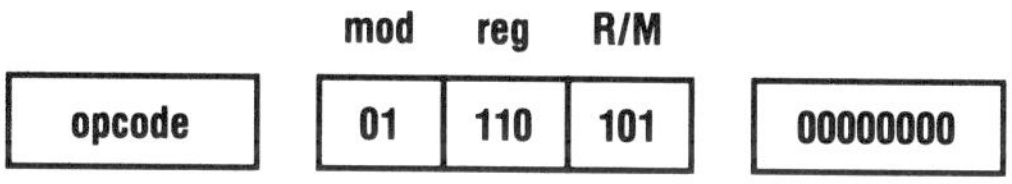

	mod	reg	R/M	
opcode	01	110	101	00000000

If an instruction requires both a displacement field and an immediate constant, the displacement comes first, as shown in the following example.

Example: A statically allocated variable can be initialized with a MOV instruction that has the displacement-only addressing mode and a 32-bit immediate field. Note that the immediate field comes after (at higher memory addresses) the displacement field.
MOV ScalarVar, BigImm ; would be encoded as:

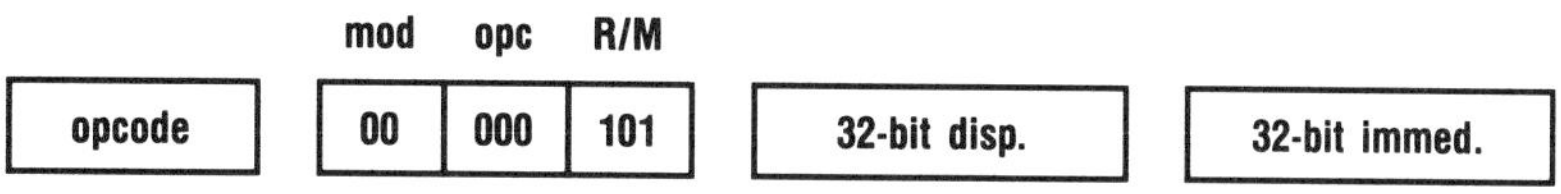

	mod	opc	R/M		
opcode	00	000	101	32-bit disp.	32-bit immed.

Table 2.5 summarizes the encoding of the one-byte address mode forms. The mod and R/M fields specify the base register and the size of the displacement, and imply the default segment register. The right-hand column gives the assembly language syntax for specifying the address mode. Since the assembler programmer normally is not aware of the

MOD	R/M	ADDRESS MODE
00b	000b	DS:[EAX]
	001b	DS:[ECX]
	010b	DS:[EDX]
	011b	DS:[EBX]
	100b	escape to 2-byte
	101b	DS:Disp32
	110b	DS:[ESI]
	111b	DS:[EDI]
01b	000b	DS:Disp8[EAX]
	001b	DS:Disp8[ECX]
	010b	DS:Disp8[EDX]
	011b	DS:Disp8[EBX]
	100b	escape to 2-byte
	101b	SS:Disp8[EBP]
	110b	DS:Disp8[ESI]
	111b	DS:Disp8[EDI]
10b	000b	DS:Disp32[EAX]
	001b	DS:Disp32[ECX]
	010b	DS:Disp32[EDX]
	011b	DS:Disp32[EBX]
	100b	escape to 2-byte
	101b	SS:Disp32[EBP]
	110b	DS:Disp32[ESI]
	111b	DS:Disp32[EDI]

► **Table 2.5:** One-byte address mode encoding

number of bits in the displacement, Disp32 is a placeholder for a variable that requires a 32-bit displacement, and Disp8 is a placeholder for a variable that requires an 8-bit displacement.

Two-Byte Address Mode Encoding

The most general address mode forms are encoded in two bytes, which provides the extra room needed to specify an index register and an index scaling factor. This two-byte form also supports the use of the ESP register as a base register for addressing relative to the top of the program stack.

The two-byte form is illustrated in Figure 2.15. As noted in the description of the one-byte address mode form, the two-byte form is indicated by the 100b escape code in the R/M field of the first byte. The mod field of the first byte is exactly the same as in the one-byte form.

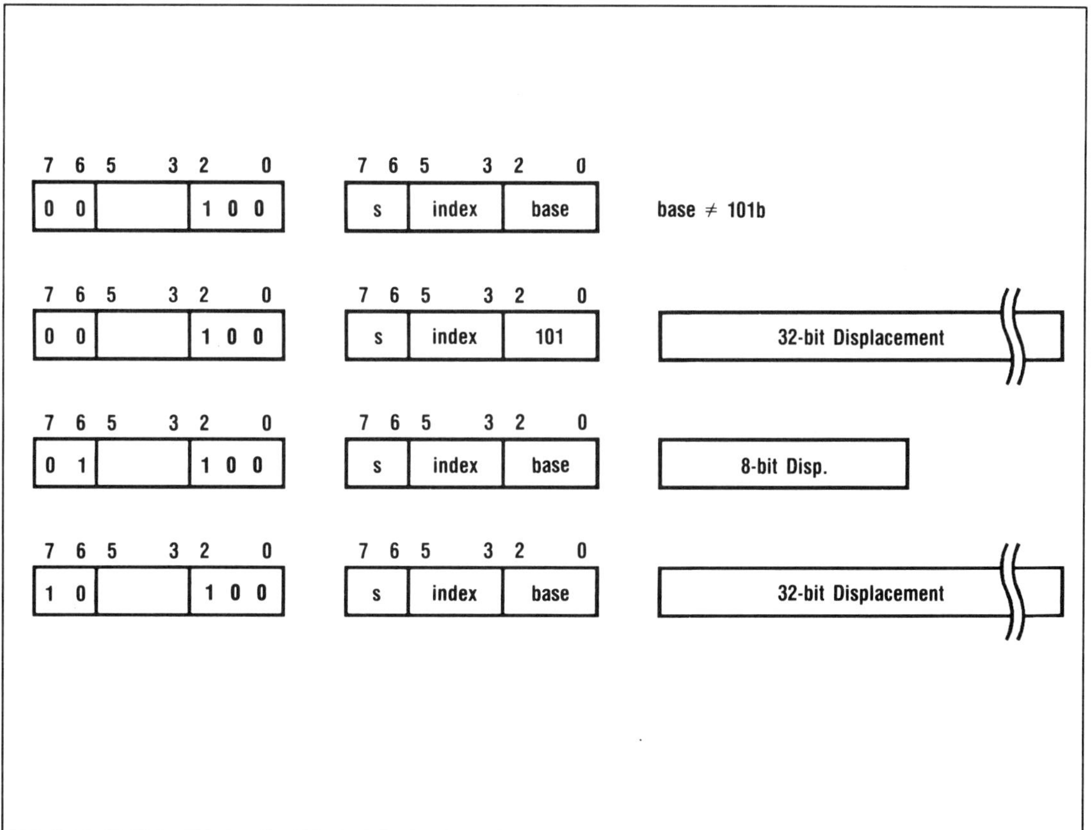

► **Figure 2.15:** Two-byte address mode format

The base field is in bits 0...2 of the second byte, and gives the code for a 32-bit base register using the same encoding as the register operands given in Table 2.3. As with the one-byte instruction form, the combination of mod = 00b and base = 101b does not indicate EBP as the base register, with no displacement. Rather, it encodes the index + displacement case, that is, with no base register, but with a full 32-bit displacement and an index register.

The "index" field is in bits 3...5, and specifies the register code for the 32-bit index register, again from Table 2.3. A code of 100b in the index field does not specify that the ESP register is an index; rather, it is used to indicate that no index register is used. The s field is in bits 6...7, and specifies the scale factor for the index register, as a shift count. If no index register is given, the scale factor must be 00b.

Table 2.6 summarizes the encoding of the two-byte address mode forms. The base and mod fields specify the base register and the size of the displacement, and determine the default segment register. The index and scale fields independently modify the address to add an index register with a scale factor. As with Table 2.5, the address mode is given as an assembly language mode. The index register modifier is just concatenated to the segment/base/displacement fraction to get the full assembler syntax. For example, a base of EDX, an 8-bit displacement, plus an index of ECX scaled by 4 would be given by the assembler syntax DS:Disp8[EDX][ECX*4]. Alternatively, the index part could be "added," with the notation DS:Disp8[EDX + ECX*4].

MOD	BASE	ADDRESS MODE
00	000	DS:[EAX]
	001	DS:[ECX]
	010	DS:[EDX]
	011	DS:[EBX]
	100	SS:[ESP]
	101	DS:Disp32
	110	DS:[ESI]
	111	DS:[EDI]

► **Table 2.6:** Two-byte address mode encoding

01	000	DS:Disp8[EAX]
	001	DS:Disp8[ECX]
	010	DS:Disp8[EDX]
	011	DS:Disp8[EBX]
	100	SS:Disp8[ESP]
	101	SS:Disp8[EBP]
	110	DS:Disp8[ESI]
	111	DS:Disp8[EDI]
10	000	DS:Disp32[EAX]
	001	DS:Disp32[ECX]
	010	DS:Disp32[EDX]
	011	DS:Disp32[EBX]
	100	SS:Disp32[ESP]
	101	SS:Disp32[EBP]
	110	DS:Disp32[ESI]
	111	DS:Disp32[EDI]

INDEX	ADDRESS MODE
000b	[EAX*s]
001b	[ECX*s]
010b	[EDX*s]
011b	[EBX*s]
100b	no index
101b	[EBP*s]
110b	[ESI*s]
111b	[EDI*s]

s	INDEX SCALE FACTOR
00b	1
01b	2
10b	4
11b	8

► **Table 2.6:** Two-byte address mode encoding (continued)

Example: A base + index addressing mode is specified with mod = 00b, and the base and index fields give the base and index registers, respectively.

MOV EAX, DS:[EBX + ESI*2] would be encoded as:

	mod	reg	2nd	s	idx	bas
opcode	00	000	100	01	110	011

Example: A full three-component base + index + displacement addressing mode is specified with mod = 01b for an 8-bit displacement, and mod = 10b for a 32-bit displacement.

MOV EAX, SS:[ESP + 24][ESI*8] would be encoded as:

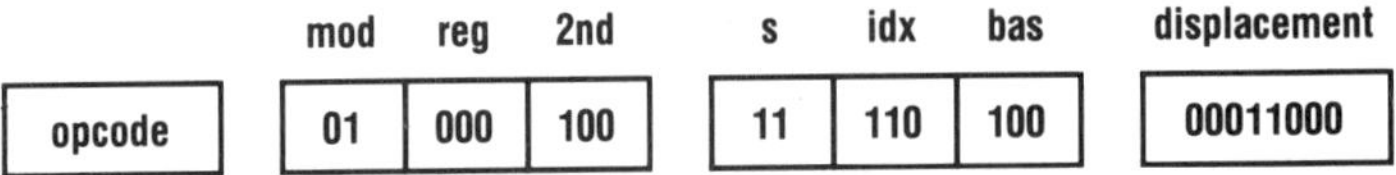

MOV EAX, DS:[9999999 + EDI + EAX*4] would be encoded as:

	mod	reg	2nd	s	idx	bas	
opcode	10	000	100	10	000	111	32-bit displacement

Example: By specifying a scaled index in combination with a displacement-only addressing mode, the important case of a single scaled index into a statically allocated array can be handled. This uses mod = 00b with base = 101b to indicate no base register with a 32-bit displacement, and the index and scale fields are used to specify the index register and scale factor, respectively.

MOV EAX, TABLE[ESI*4] would be encoded as:

	mod	reg	2nd	s	idx	bas	
opcode	00	000	100	10	110	101	32-bit displacement

Example: Stack-relative addressing is done with the two-byte form by using ESP as a base register with the null index code (100b), and a choice of 0 (stack top), 8-bit, or 32-bit (inner stack element references) displacement.

MOV EDI, 0[ESP] ; would be encoded as:

	mod	reg	2nd	s	idx	bas
opcode	00	111	100	00	100	100

MOV EDI, 24[ESP] ; would be encoded as:

	mod	reg	2nd	s	idx	bas	
opcode	01	111	100	00	100	100	00011000

Segment Override Prefix Byte

An instruction prefix byte can specify the segment register to be used to address a memory operand in case the default segment register is not appropriate. As its name implies, it is an 8-bit field that is appended to the front of the instruction. Since there are six segment registers, there are six byte codes for segment override instruction prefix bytes, given in Table 2.7.

Example: To address memory via a pointer, first the pointer is loaded into a segment register/general register pair. Then an address mode using the general register as a base, combined with a segment override prefix specifying the segment register, provides access to the data pointed to by the pointer.

MOV EDX, ES:[ESI] would be encoded as:

ES: prefix		mod	reg	base
00100110	opcode	00	010	110

CODE	SEGMENT REGISTER
26h	ES:
2Eh	CS:
36h	SS:
3Eh	DS:
64h	FS:
65h	GS:

► **Table 2.7:** Segment override prefix encoding

Example: To address data stored in a code segment, the CS override prefix can be specified. For example, a table of label offsets can be stored in the code segment and used to implement a CASE or SWITCH statement. A scaled index + displacement addressing mode, combined with the CS override prefix, forms the necessary addressing mode to be used with the indirect jump instruction (JMP) that references the table.

JMP CS:24[ESI*4] ; would be encoded as:

CS: prefix		mod	opc	2nd	s	idx	bas	
00101110	opcode	00	100	100	10	110	101	32-bit disp.

► I/O Space

The previous sections described the structure of main memory space, and how operands in main memory are referenced in instructions. A second memory space, called the I/O space, is also available. As its name implies, it is optimized for storage of control ports for input/output (I/O) devices such as keyboards, disks, CRT displays, printers, and so on. A separate space for I/O ports is appropriate, because the addressing and protection of I/O devices is quite different from the addressing and protection of program code and data. Typically, an I/O device has only a few control ports, requiring only a small number of bytes of addressable storage, and there are only a small number of devices in the system. I/O ports cannot be relocated within the I/O space, and they must be protected individually so that access to individual devices can be controlled. On the other hand, program code and data require many thousands, even millions of bytes of addressable storage, and need a different protection mechanism.

A separate I/O space is provided on the 80386. The I/O space is not segmented. It is a simple one-dimensional address space that is 64K bytes in size. Like main memory, the I/O space is byte addressable. I/O ports can be one, two, or four bytes in length. As with main memory, the little-endian method of byte ordering is used for addressing two or four byte ports. The lower addressed bytes contain the least significant bits, and the higher addressed bytes contain the most significant bits.

Special instructions, described in Chapter 3, are provided to transfer data between I/O space and the processor registers or main memory. I/O addresses are specified as follows:

- If the I/O address is less than 256, it can be given in an 8-bit immediate field in the instruction.

- Larger I/O addresses, or I/O addresses computed as the program executes, are taken from the DX register.

The 64K I/O space is protected by a mechanism, described in Chapter 5, that allows separate protection of each byte in the I/O space. This protection mechanism is totally separate from, and completely different than, the protection mechanism for main memory.

► Floating-Point Registers

As noted in Chapter 1, the 80387 coprocessor can be used with the 80386 for high-performance operations on data in one of the floating-point formats. Even if you don't have an 80387, you will have to use a software emulation of it in order to work with floating-point data. So either way—with the chip itself or with an emulator—you will need to be familiar with the 80387 architecture.

When used with the 80386, the 80387 adds the three sets of registers shown in Figure 2.16 to support floating-point computations.

1. A stack of eight 80-bit accumulators to hold up to eight floating-point operands.
2. Three 16-bit status and control registers: one for a status word, one for a control word, and one for a tag word.
3. Four 32-bit error-pointer registers (FIP, FCS, FOO, and FOS) to identify the instruction and memory operand causing an exception.

Floating-Point Accumulator Stack

Floating-point instructions treat the 80-bit registers as a stack of accumulators rather than as a simple array of eight registers. The top of the accumulator stack is named ST. Accumulators under ST are addressed relative to ST with names of the form ST(i), where i ranges from 1 to 7. ST(0) can be used as a substitute for ST to name the top of the accumulator stack.

ST acts like an accumulator because it is implicitly used as one operand of all floating-point instructions. This was done to provide 64 floating-point opcodes while taking only 8 codes from the 80386 opcode space. This trick was accomplished by dedicating what otherwise would be a 3-bit register field to extra opcode bits. In order to avoid most of the restrictions of the accumulator model, a stack of eight accumulators was provided along with operand access to "inner" accumulators.

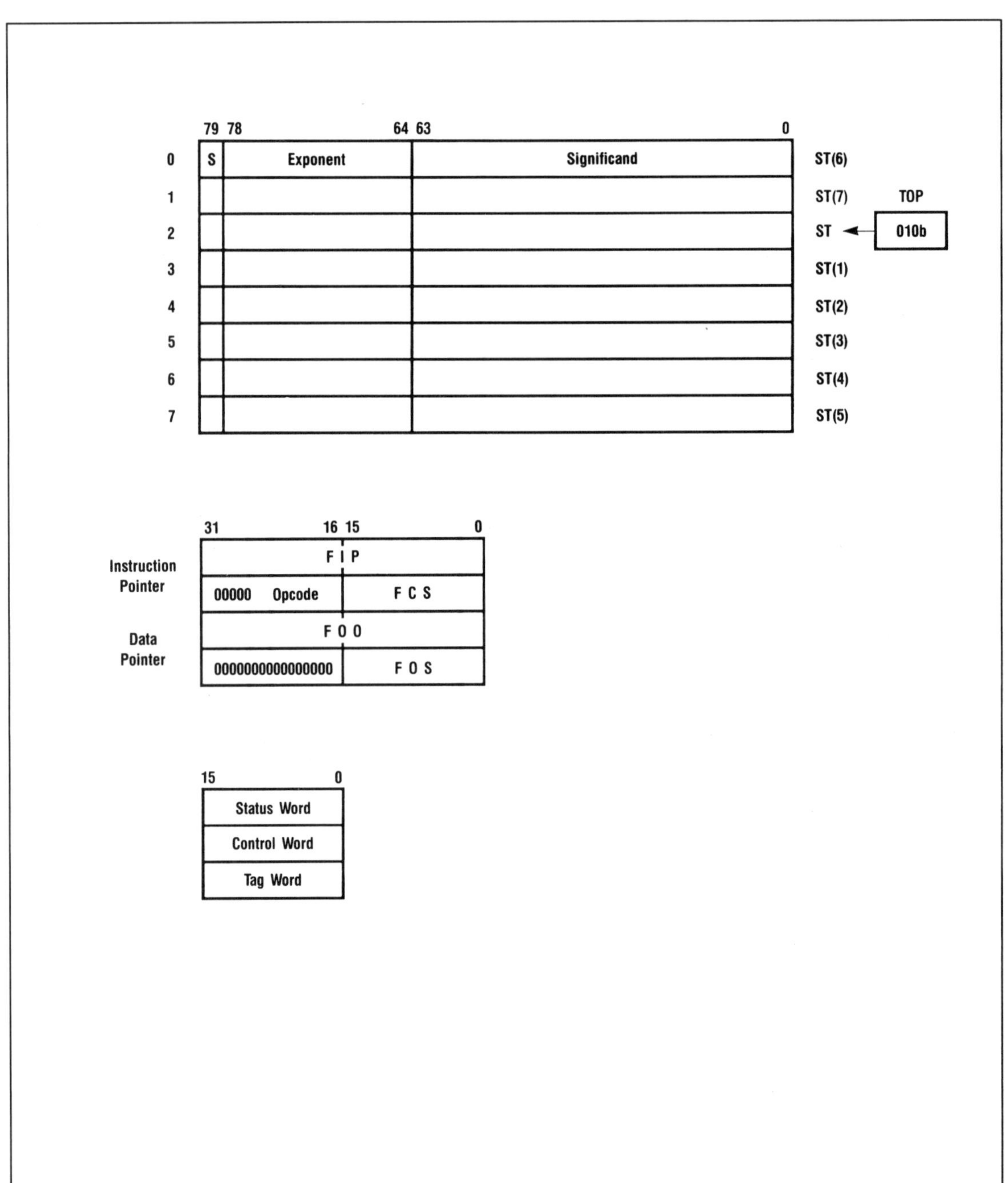

► **Figure 2.16:** 80387 registers

Although floating-point operations must use ST as one operand, they may name any floating-point accumulator or a memory operand as a second operand.

The accumulator stack is really an array of eight physical registers, with a separate 3-bit field to identify the current stack top. Careful use of the terms register and accumulator serve to distinguish between the two interpretations of these floating-point operand locations. The term *physical register* refers to the physical organization of the stack. The term *accumulator* describes a floating-point operand location. Thus, we have either an accumulator stack or a physical register array.

A 3-bit field named TOP in the status word contains the absolute register number of the current top of the accumulator stack, ST or ST(0). A push onto the stack will decrement TOP and store a new value into the new ST. After a push, the previous ST becomes ST(1), and all the stacked accumulators have their ST-relative names incremented by 1. A pop from the stack will read a value from the current ST and then increment TOP. After a pop, the accumulator named ST(1) before the pop becomes the new ST, and all the stacked accumulators have their ST-relative names decremented by 1.

Incrementing and decrementing the 3-bit TOP field ignores wraparound. If TOP = 000b, a push will decrement TOP to 111b and store the new value into register 7. If TOP = 111b, a pop will read a value from register 7 and then increment TOP to 000b.

The floating-point accumulator stack is illustrated in Figure 2.16. Assuming that the TOP field contains 010b, the ST-relative accumulator names on the right correspond to the physical register numbers on the left. The current top of the accumulator stack, ST, corresponds to physical register 2. Each 80-bit accumulator in the stack provides storage for a real number stored in the temporary real format described in Chapter 1. The high-order bit is the sign bit. Bits 64...78 provide a 15-bit exponent field. Bits 0...63 provide a 64-bit significand.

The floating-point instructions, described in Chapter 3, are designed to work well with this accumulator stack model. Load instructions read an operand from memory and push it onto the accumulator stack. Store instructions take the value from the current top of stack and write it out to memory, and may optionally pop the accumulator stack if the value is not needed immediately for another computation. Arithmetic operations such as addition or multiplication take one operand from the ST register, and the other from another register or memory, and store the result back into the ST register. A special operate-and-pop form is available that operates on the top two stack operands, ST and ST(1), pops the stack once, and puts the result into the new ST. This operate-and-pop sequence is equivalent to the classical stack machine operation, which pops two source operands off the stack, ST and ST(1), performs an operation, and pushes the result back onto the stack.

The following example illustrates the operation of the accumulator stack by showing several snapshots of the stack as a sequence of instructions executes. Another example of the operation of the accumulator stack is given in Chapter 4.

Suppose you need to compute the dot-product of two vectors, which requires you to form a sum of products. You can accumulate the sum in one of the 80387 registers, and form each product in another register. If ST holds the partial sum of products, you can perform one step of the vector dot-product by loading the next element of one vector into the accumulator stack, multiplying by the next element of the other vector, and then adding the result into the partial sum.

Figure 2.17 shows several pictures of the 80387 accumulator stack as this step of the vector dot-product operation proceeds. The first snapshot shows the accumulator stack with the partial sum 101.237 stored in ST, and the other registers empty (illustrated with shading). The physical register numbers are shown on the left, and the accumulator names are shown on the right. ST is in physical register 5 at the start of this example, so the TOP field is shown containing 101b.

The next element of the first vector (which has the value 1.21) is pushed onto the accumulator stack with a load instruction, leaving the stack with two elements, as illustrated in the next picture. The new value is loaded into physical register 4, which becomes the top-of-stack register, ST. The partial sum could now be addressed as ST(1), and it of course is still in physical register 5. The third picture shows the stack after multiplying ST by the next element of the second vector (which has the value 5.0). This changes the value in ST to 6.05, but does not push or pop the stack. The last picture shows the stack after an add and pop instruction (FADDP), which adds the new product into the partial sum register. This instruction adds ST (the new product) and ST(1) (the old partial sum), pops one element off the stack, and replaces ST with the result (107.287), which is the new partial sum. This leaves the stack as it was at the beginning of this example, with the partial sum in ST, so you are ready for the next iteration.

Sixteen-Bit Status and Control Registers

Three 16-bit registers (tag word, control word, and status word) control the operation of the floating-point instructions and provide status information.

Tag-Word Register

The 16-bit tag-word register, shown in Figure 2.18, contains eight 2-bit fields, one for each of the eight physical floating-point registers. These fields indicate whether the corresponding physical register holds a valid, zero, or special floating-point number, or is empty. The fields in the tag word correspond to the physical registers, rather than being relative to the stack top, to avoid the need to rotate the tag word as the accumulator stack is pushed and popped!

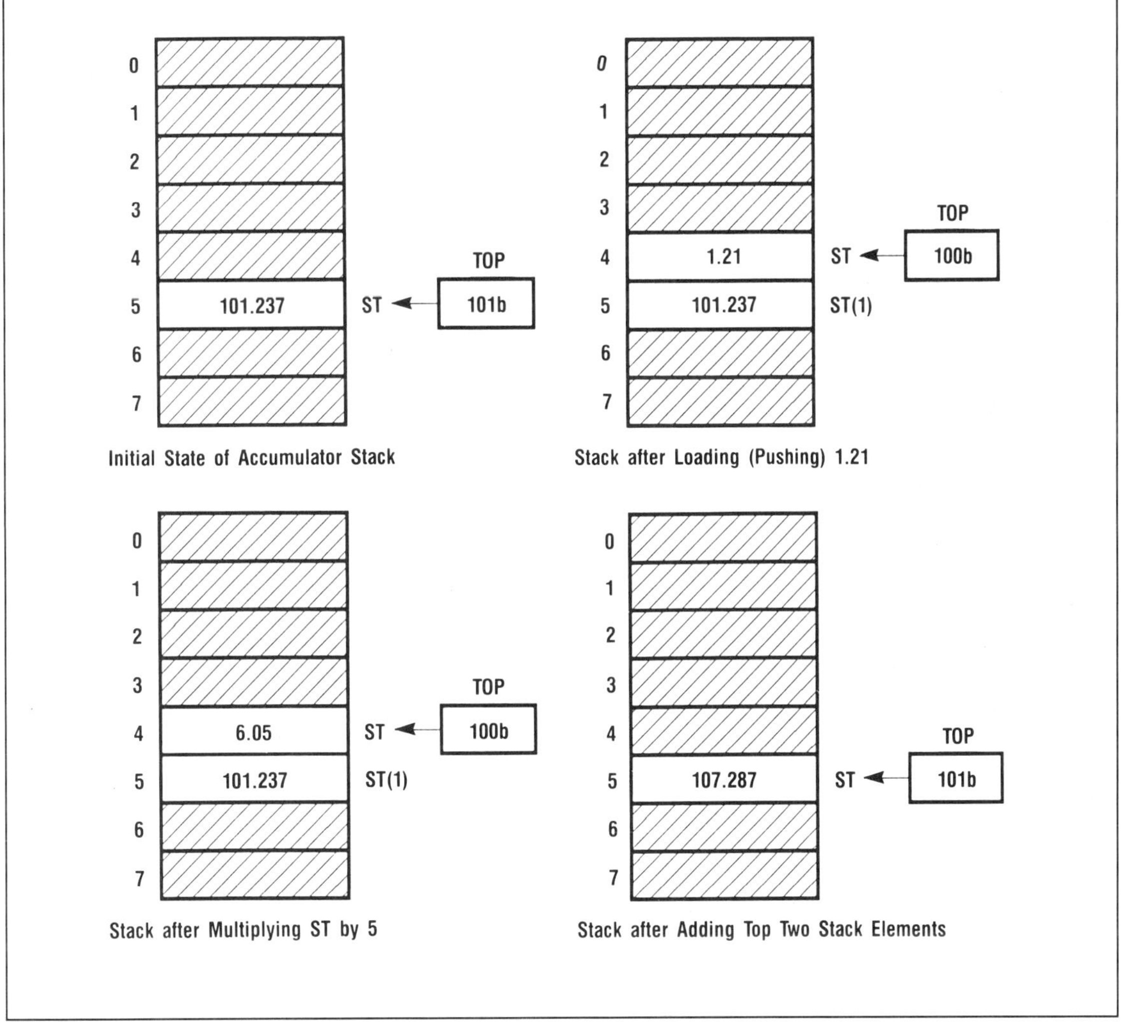

► **Figure 2.17:** 80387 accumulator stack operation

The tag fields are used to detect overflow or underflow of the accumulator stack. A stack overflow occurs if a push operation decrements TOP to point to a register that is not empty. A stack underflow occurs if an attempt is made to read or pop an empty register. Stack underflow or overflow will raise an invalid operation exception.

Control-Word Register

The control-word register can be set by the program to control the operation of the 80387. There are three fields within the control word, shown in Figure 2.19.

Each field in the control word is briefly described below.

- Bits 0...5 contain the exception masks for the conditions listed in Table 2.8. If an exception is detected by the 80387, the mask bit for that exception is tested to determine if the exception should be passed to a software error handler (mask = 0), or handled by a default error handler within the 80387 (mask = 1). An exception is said to be *masked* if its mask bit is 1.

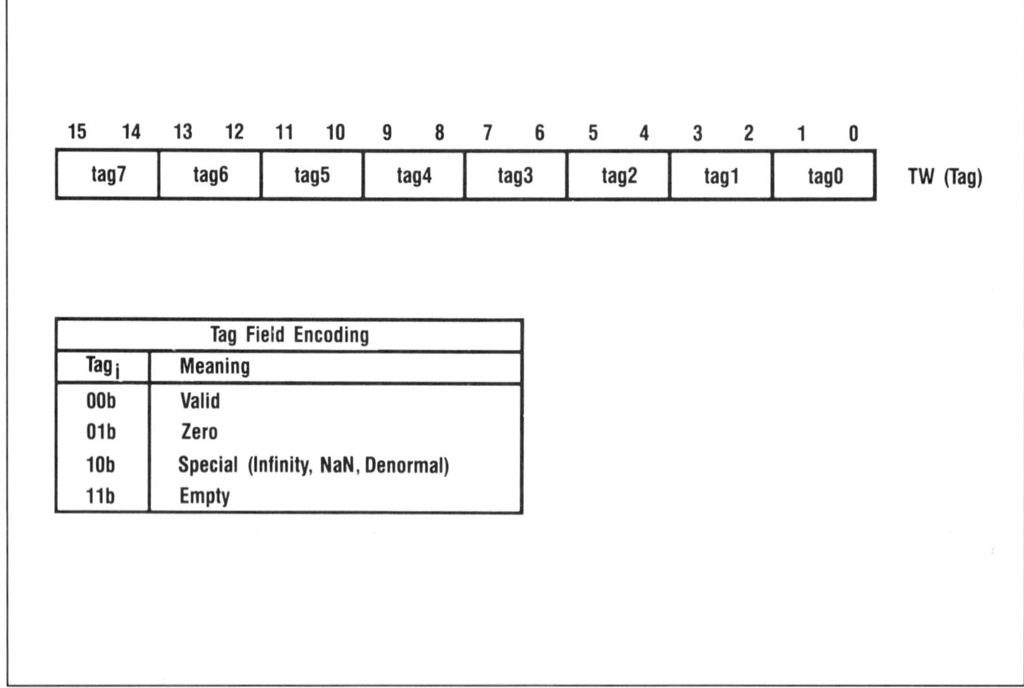

Tag Field Encoding	
Tag_i	Meaning
00b	Valid
01b	Zero
10b	Special (Infinity, NaN, Denormal)
11b	Empty

► **Figure 2.18:** Tag-word details

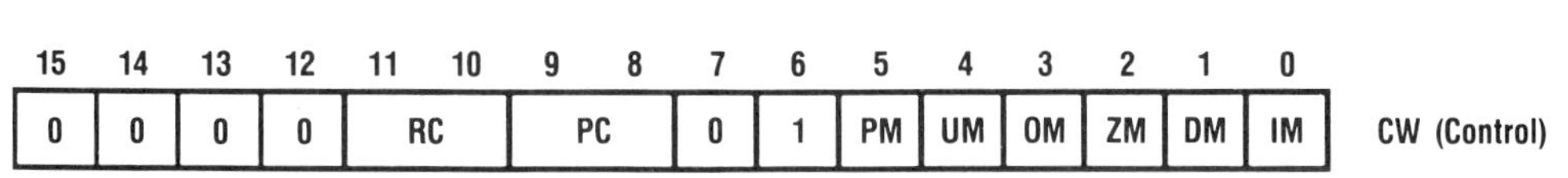

Precision Control	
PC	Precision of Significand
00b	24 bits (Short Real)
01b	(Reserved)
10b	53 bits (Long Real)
11b	64 bits (Temporary Real)

Rounding Control	
RC	Rounding Mode
00b	Round toward nearest or even
01b	Round toward −infinity
10b	Round toward +infinity
11b	Chop or truncate toward zero

► **Figure 2.19:** Control-word details

STATUS	MASK	CONDITION
IE	IM	Invalid Operation
DE	DM	Denormal
ZE	ZM	Zero Divide
OE	OM	Overflow
UE	UM	Underflow
PE	PM	Precision

► **Table 2.8:** Exception status and mask bits

- Bits 8...9 contain the *Precision Control* field, PC. Results of floating-point addition, subtraction, multiplication, division, and square root are rounded to one of the three precisions given in Figure 2.19 before being stored in the destination. All other operations use temporary real precision, or a precision specified in the instruction.
- Bits 10...11 contain the *Rounding Control* field, RC. The four rounding modes listed in Figure 2.19 are available to round results of floating-point operations.

The remaining bits in the control word are hard-wired to the values shown in Figure 2.19. When loading a value into these registers, these bits should have the values shown, or should be reloaded from a saved control-word image without change in order to support compatibility with other numeric coprocessors that may define additional control bits.

Rounding Whenever possible, the 80387 yields the correct result. It is possible, however, that during intermediate computations or during stores to a smaller data type a loss of precision may occur. When storing the internal temporary real format into a short integer, the possibility of precision loss is evident. When these situations arise, the 80387 will round the result so it will fit in the smaller operand.

There are four rounding modes on the 80387, specified in the RC field of the control-word register.

- Round to nearest
- Round down toward −infinity
- Round up toward +infinity
- Chop smaller in magnitude

The chop mode is useful when performing integer arithmetic, since it matches the way the integer divide instruction rounds the quotient.

Round to nearest is suitable to most applications. It is the default rounding mode, since the 80387 initializes the RC field to 00b when it is reset. If you are not experienced in numerical methods, this mode should be sufficient. It yields the most accurate results of the modes and never introduces bias into the computation.

The round to plus and minus infinity modes are provided for interval arithmetic. This is useful when you realize the answer is somewhat in error but would like to place bounds upon that error. By judicious use of the round to infinity modes, you can correctly establish the error bounds of the computation.

Infinities Prior members of the 86 family of numerics processors (8087 and 80287) could treat infinities in two modes, affine and projective, and used bit 12 of the control word to specify the mode. The 80387, per the IEEE standard discussed in Chapter 1, supports only the affine mode of infinity processing.

The 8087 and 80287 use 1 in bit 12 of the control-word register to specify use of affine mode, and 0 to indicate use of projective mode. These older coprocessors initialize this bit to 0 (projective mode setting) at reset, or after executing the FINIT instruction. This bit is also initialized to 0 on the 80387, so the control word is initialized to the same value on all coprocessors. Appendix B describes this and other differences between the 80387 and the 8087/80287 coprocessors in more detail.

Affine mode distinguishes between plus and minus infinity in computations. The sign indicates from which direction you reached infinity, which may be useful information in some cases. An algorithm, however, may yield plus or minus zero as the correct result. If you then perform 1/0 or 1/ −0, you get plus infinity or minus infinity, respectively. This seems like more information, but it may not be useful. In fact, in some cases it can be considered incorrect. Thus, careful interpretation of the sign of infinity is important.

Status-Word Register

The 80387 sets bits in the status word that can be tested by the program to check for special conditions. The status-word register is shown in Figure 2.20.

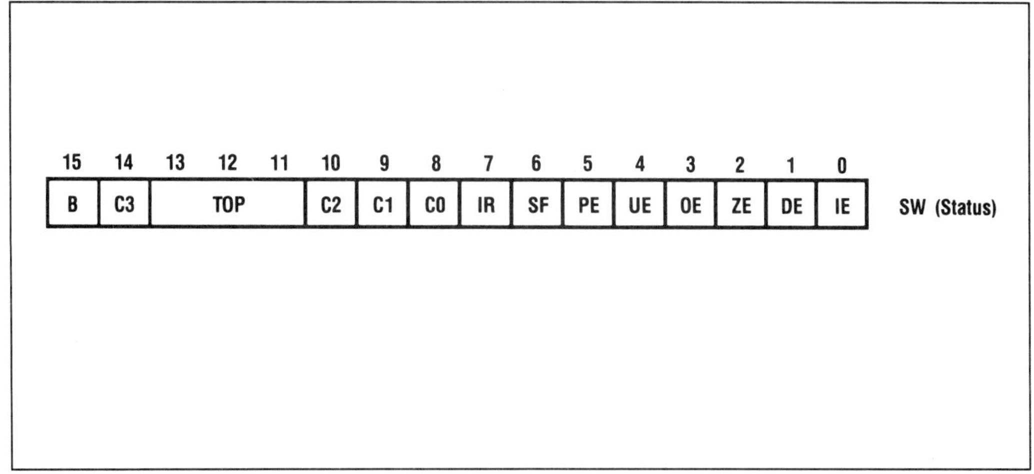

► **Figure 2.20:** Status-word details

Each field in the status word is briefly described below.

- Bits 0...5 are set if an exception is detected when executing a floating-point instruction. These bits are sticky. They are set by the 80387 whenever the condition is detected but must be explicitly reset by the program. Table 2.8 lists the correspondence between these bits and exceptions.
- Bit 6 (SF) is the *Stack Fault* flag. It is set if an invalid operation exception is due to overflow or underflow of the accumulator stack. Otherwise it is reset.
- Bits 8(C0), 9(C1), 10(C2), and 14 (C3) contain the floating-point condition code bits. A set of floating-point compare instructions are provided that set these bits to indicate the outcome of the comparison. These condition code bits are positioned so that they can be moved to the lower 8 bits of the 80386 EFLAGS register, so that the same set of conditional jumps can be used for floating-point conditions as for the conditions detected by the 80386. Chapter 4 contains an example that tests the floating-point condition codes.
- Bits 11...13 hold the TOP field, which indicates which physical register corresponds to the top of the accumulator stack.
- Bit 7 (IR) and bit 15 (B) are 1 if any unmasked exception is indicated by the exception bits in the lower 6 bits of the status word, as masked by the exception mask in the lower 6 bits of the control word. Otherwise IR and B are 0.

Error-Pointer Registers

The last set of 80387 registers shown in Figure 2.16 are four 32-bit registers that hold pointers to the last 80387 instruction executed, and its data. The first two registers, FIP and FCS, hold a pointer to the 80387 instruction that last executed along with the first two opcode bytes of that instruction (ignoring prefixes). FCS holds the selector and opcode, and FIP holds the offset. The second pair of registers, FOO and FOS, point to the memory operand of this last instruction. FOS holds the selector, and FOO holds the offset. If the last coprocessor instruction did not have a memory operand, the values in FOO and FOS are undefined. The FLDENV, FSTENV, FNSTENV, FRSTOR, FSAVE, and FNSAVE instructions, described in Chapter 3, are provided to load and store these error-pointer registers.

The opcode field is formed by combining the low-order 3 bits of the first (after prefixes) instruction byte with the second instruction byte, as illustrated in Figure 2.21. The two bytes selected come after any instruction prefixes, and so contain the opcode field and the first byte of the MODRM field. In Figure 2.21, the two instruction bytes are shown at the top as if they were a 16-bit number, with the low-order bits in the lower addressed byte. The first instruction byte is shown on the right at address m and contains bits I0 through I7. The second instruction byte is shown to the left at address m + 1 and contains bits I8 through I15. The low-order 3 bits of the first instruction byte (I0, I1, and I2) are placed into bits 8 through 10 of the opcode field. All 8 bits of the second instruction byte (I8 through I15) are placed into bits 0 through 7 of the opcode field. Since the high-order 5 bits of the first instruction byte (I3, I4, I5, I6, and I7) are the same for all floating-point instructions, they are not stored in the opcode field. The opcode format swaps the opcode bytes so that the discarded bits are in the high-order bit positions, rather than being in the middle of the opcode field. (Note that the early B1 version of the 386 did not store the opcode information.)

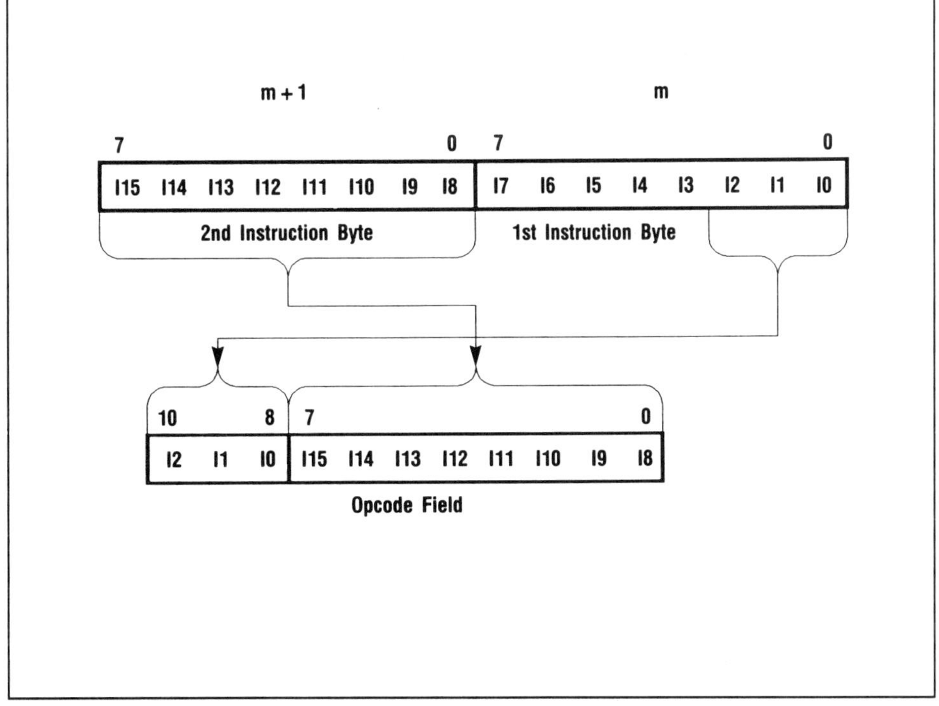

► **Figure 2.21:** Format of opcode field

The error pointers are useful for analyzing and reporting exceptions that occur during floating-point instructions. These pointers are necessary since the 80387 and 80386 can execute in parallel. Once a floating-point instruction is sent to the 80387, it can process it while the 80386 goes on to other instructions. If an error occurs in an 80387 instruction, the CS and EIP registers on the 80386 may be nowhere near the 80387 instruction that caused the exception. The error-pointer registers permit parallel processing by the 80386 and 80387, yet still provide necessary information to diagnose and recover from floating-point exceptions.

FLDENV, FSTENV, FNSTENV Operand Format

The FLDENV, FSTENV, and FNSTENV instructions described in Chapter 3 load and store the control-word, status-word, tag-word, and error-pointer registers from a 28-byte memory block shown in Figure 2.22. Bits shown as 0 in the figure are *reserved*. These reserved bits must be loaded as 0 and ignored when stored.

The FRSTOR, FSAVE, and FNSAVE instructions load and store all of the 80387 registers from a 108-byte memory block. The low 28 bytes

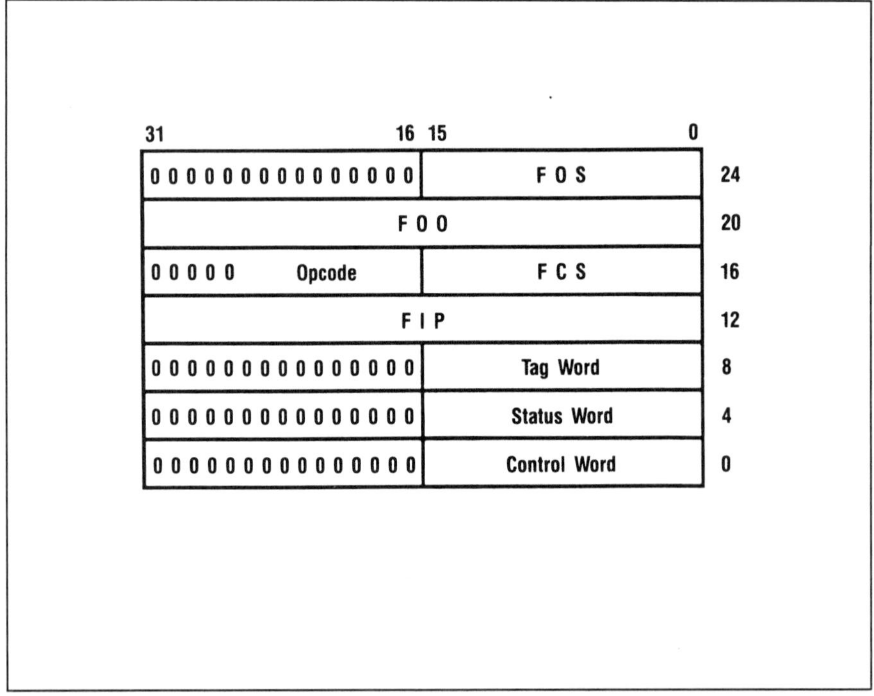

► **Figure 2.22:** FLDENV, FSTENV, FNSTENV operand format

of this block have the format shown in Figure 2.22. ST(0) is loaded or stored from offset 28, ST(1) from offset 38, and so on, with ST(7) loaded or stored from offset 98. The memory locations that correspond to accumulators tagged as empty are undefined after executing an FSAVE or FNSAVE, and are ignored by the FRSTOR instruction.

Instruction Set

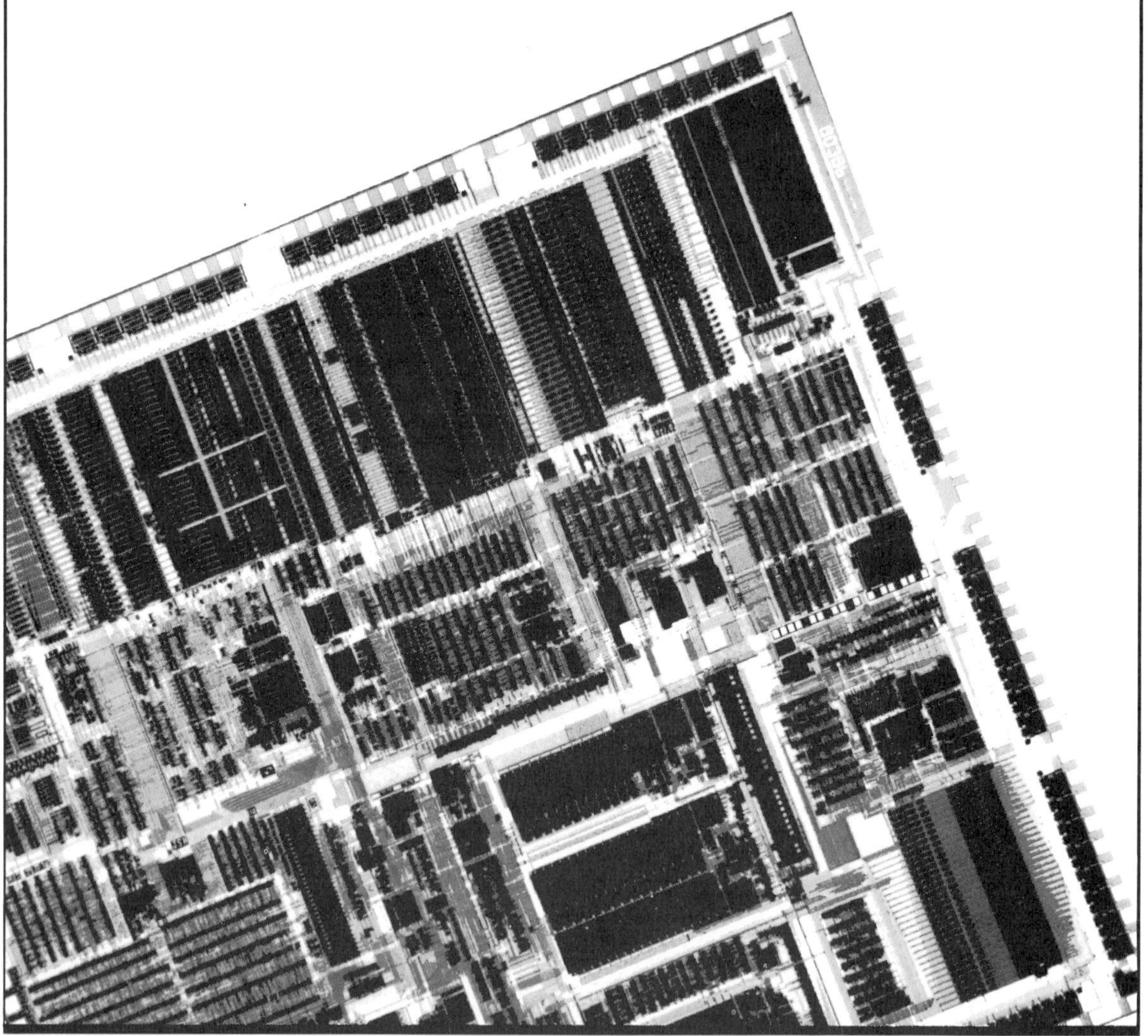

Chapter 3

Table of Contents

Introduction

Integer

Multiple Segment

Operating System

Floating point

▸ Introduction

Congratulations! You've made it through the preparatory material of Chapters 1 and 2, and now you are ready to understand exactly what the 80386 processor can do for you. So far you have learned of the data types, the internal machine state, and the method for addressing memory. Now you are ready to dive into the detailed description of every 386 instruction.

If you quickly leaf through this chapter, you will see that you have quite a bit of work to do. The 80386 and 80387 have very rich instruction sets. As we count them in this book, the 80386 has 152 instructions and the 80387 has 74. The 80386 instruction set has evolved from the early microcomputer days of the 8086 to the 80386: a multiprocessing, multitasking, virtual memory 32-bit processor. Thus, there are the familiar 8086 instructions as well as instructions that have been added in various generations to allow the machine to support some of the more advanced computer architecture features such as virtual memory.

This evolution leads us to the organization we use to present the instruction set. Rather than a simple alphabetic presentation, as many books present an instruction set, we have chosen an improved route that separates the instructions into categories of uses. We then present the instructions alphabetically within these categories. The categories we use are given in the following table.

Start Page	Category
119	Integer
269	Multiple Segment
290	Operating System
320	Floating Point

The 80386 applications programmer will want to read and reference the integer instruction set description. All arithmetic, logical, data movement, and simple control-flow instructions that an applications programmer requires are found in this section. This is by far the largest grouping of instructions.

The second section describes the instructions that are specifically intended for the programmer who is dealing with multiple segments in his or her programs. The applications programmer who is dealing with a single-segment or flat programming model (as was briefly presented in Chapter 2) need not go through the further complexities that this section presents.

The third section is intended solely for operating-system writers. These instructions were specifically added to the 80386 to ease the job of writing an operating system. Again, the applications programmer need not deal with the complexities of these instructions. In fact, most 80386 systems will not allow the applications programmer to use these instructions at all!

The fourth and final section contains the floating-point instructions of the 80387. As is the case throughout the book, we include the description of the 80387 as an integral part of the 80386 architecture. However, we separate the discussion of the floating-point instructions, as many programmers do not require the use of floating point.

Within these groupings, each instruction (or small group of highly related instructions) is given a complete page, or more as needed, to give a concise and complete description. This format, as well as the organization described above, is useful for reading and understanding the instructions of the machine. Moreover, this format provides an excellent reference manual for later use.

Alphabetical Index to Instructions

The following table summarizes the 80386 and 80387 instruction sets in alphabetic order. The page number and section of this chapter where each instruction is found is given, along with a brief description.

Instruction	Section	Page	Description
AAA	Integer	125	ASCII adjust after addition
AAD	Integer	127	ASCII adjust before division
AAM	Integer	128	ASCII adjust after multiplication
AAS	Integer	129	ASCII adjust after subtraction
ADC	Integer	131	Add with carry
ADD	Integer	133	Integer addition
AND	Integer	135	And
ARPL	Operating System	293	Adjust requested privilege level
BOUND	Integer	137	Check array index against bounds
BSF	Integer	138	Bit scan forward
BSR	Integer	140	Bit scan reverse
BT	Integer	142	Bit test
BTC	Integer	144	Bit test and complement

Instruction	Section	Page	Description
BTR	Integer	146	Bit test and reset
BTS	Integer	148	Bit test and set
CALL	Integer	150	Call procedure (intrasegment)
CALL	Multiple Segment	272	Call procedure (intersegment)
CBW/CWDE	Integer	152	Convert byte to word/ convert word to dword
CLC	Integer	153	Clear the carry flag
CLD	Integer	154	Clear the direction flag
CLI	Integer	155	Clear the interrupt flag
CLTS	Operating System	295	Clear the task-switched flag
CMC	Integer	156	Complement the carry flag
CMP	Integer	157	Compare
CMPS/CMPSB/ CMPSW/CMPSD	Integer	159	Compare string
CWD/CDQ	Integer	161	Convert word to dword/ convert dword to qword
DAA	Integer	163	Decimal adjust after addition
DAS	Integer	165	Decimal adjust after subtraction
DEC	Integer	167	Decrement
DIV	Integer	168	Unsigned divide
ENTER	Integer	170	Create stack frame
F2XM1	Floating Point	326	$2^x - 1$
FABS	Floating Point	327	Absolute value
FADD/FIADD/ FADDP	Floating Point	328	Addition
FBLD	Floating Point	330	BCD load
FBSTP	Floating Point	331	BCD store and pop
FCHS	Floating Point	332	Change sign
FCLEX/FNCLEX	Floating Point	333	Clear exceptions
FCOM/FCOMP/ FCOMPP	Floating Point	334	Compare
FCOS	Floating Point	336	Cosine

Instruction	Section	Page	Description
FDECSTP	Floating Point	337	Decrement stack pointer
FDIV/FIDIV/FDIVP	Floating Point	338	Division
FDIVR/FIDIVR/ FDIVRP	Floating Point	340	Division reverse
FFREE	Floating Point	342	Free register
FICOM/FICOMP	Floating Point	343	Integer compare
FILD	Floating Point	345	Integer load
FINCSTP	Floating Point	346	Increment stack pointer
FINIT/FNINIT	Floating Point	347	Initialize processor
FIST	Floating Point	348	Integer store
FISTP	Floating Point	349	Integer store and pop
FLD	Floating Point	350	Real load
FLD1	Floating Point	351	Load 1
FLDCW	Floating Point	353	Load control word
FLDENV	Floating Point	354	Load environment
FLDL2E	Floating Point	351	Load $\log_2 e$
FLDL2T	Floating Point	351	Load $\log_2 10$
FLDLG2	Floating Point	351	Load $\log_{10} 2$
FLDLN2	Floating Point	351	Load $\log_e 2$
FLDPI	Floating Point	351	Load π
FLDZ	Floating Point	351	Load zero
FMUL/FIMUL/ FMULP	Floating Point	355	Multiply
FNOP	Floating Point	357	No operation
FPATAN	Floating Point	358	Partial arctangent
FPREM	Floating Point	360	Partial remainder
FPREM1	Floating Point	362	Partial remainder — IEEE
FPTAN	Floating Point	364	Partial tangent
FRNDINT	Floating Point	365	Round to integer
FRSTOR	Floating Point	366	Restore state
FSAVE/FNSAVE	Floating Point	367	Save state

Instruction	Section	Page	Description
FSCALE	Floating Point	368	Power of two scaling
FSIN	Floating Point	370	Sine
FSINCOS	Floating Point	371	Sine and cosine
FSQRT	Floating Point	372	Square root
FST	Floating Point	373	Real store
FSTCW/FNSTCW	Floating Point	375	Store control word
FSTENV/FNSTENV	Floating Point	376	Store environment
FSTP	Floating Point	378	Real store and pop
FSTSW/FNSTSW	Floating Point	380	Store status word
FSTSW AX/ FNSTSW AX	Floating Point	381	Store status word into AX
FSUB/FISUB/FSUBP	Floating Point	382	Subtraction
FSUBR/FISUBR/ FSUBRP	Floating Point	384	Subtraction reverse
FTST	Floating Point	386	Test
FUCOM/FUCOMP/ FUCOMPP	Floating Point	388	Unordered compare
FXAM	Floating Point	390	Examine
FXCH	Floating Point	392	Exchange registers
FXTRACT	Floating Point	393	Extract exponent and significand
FYL2X	Floating Point	395	$y*\log_2 x$
FYL2XP1	Floating Point	397	$y*\log_2(x+1)$
HLT	Operating System	296	Halt
IDIV	Integer	172	Signed divide
IMUL	Integer	175	Signed multiplication
IN	Integer	178	Input from a port
INC	Integer	179	Increment
INS/INSB/ INSW/INSD	Integer	180	Input string
INT	Multiple Segment	274	Call to interrupt procedure
INTO	Multiple Segment	276	On overflow call interrupt procedure

Instruction	Section	Page	Description
IRET	Multiple Segment	278	Interrupt return
JB/JNAE/JC	Integer	182	Jump below
JBE/JNA	Integer	182	Jump below or equal
JCXZ/JECXZ	Integer	182	Jump CX/ECX zero
JE/JZ	Integer	182	Jump equal
JL/JNGE	Integer	182	Jump less
JLE/JNG	Integer	182	Jump less or equal
JMP	Integer	185	Jump (intrasegment)
JMP	Multiple Segment	280	Jump (intersegment)
JNB/JAE/JNC	Integer	182	Jump not below
JNBE/JA	Integer	182	Jump not below or equal
JNE/JNZ	Integer	182	Jump not equal
JNL/JGE	Integer	182	Jump not less
JNLE/JG	Integer	182	Jump not less or equal
JNO	Integer	182	Jump no overflow
JNP/JPO	Integer	182	Jump not parity
JNS	Integer	182	Jump not sign
JO	Integer	182	Jump overflow
JP/JPE	Integer	182	Jump parity
JS	Integer	182	Jump sign
LAHF	Integer	187	Load flags into AH register
LAR	Operating System	297	Load access rights
LDS	Multiple Segment	282	Load pointer to DS
LEA	Integer	188	Load effective address
LEAVE	Integer	189	Procedure exit
LES	Multiple Segment	282	Load pointer to ES
LFS	Multiple Segment	282	Load pointer to FS
LGDT	Operating System	300	Load global descriptor table
LGS	Multiple Segment	282	Load pointer to GS
LIDT	Operating System	301	Load interrupt descriptor table
LLDT	Operating System	302	Load local descriptor table

Instruction	Section	Page	Description
LMSW	Operating System	303	Load machine status word
LOCK	Integer	190	Bus lock
LODS/LODSB/ LODSW/LODSD	Integer	192	Load string
LOOP	Integer	194	Loop with ECX counter
LOOPNZ/LOOPNE	Integer	196	Loop with ECX and not zero / Loop with ECX and not equal
LOOPZ/LOOPE	Integer	198	Loop with ECX and zero / Loop with ECX and equal
LSL	Operating System	305	Load segment limit
LSS	Multiple Segment	282	Load pointer to SS
LTR	Operating System	308	Load task register
MOV	Integer	200	Move
MOV	Multiple Segment	284	Move to/from segment register
MOV	Operating System	309	Move to/from special register
MOVS/MOVSB/ MOVSW/MOVSD	Integer	201	Move string
MOVSX	Integer	203	Move and sign extend
MOVZX	Integer	205	Move and zero extend
MUL	Integer	207	Unsigned multiplication
NEG	Integer	209	Negate
NOP	Integer	210	No operation
NOT	Integer	211	Not
OR	Integer	212	Inclusive or
OUT	Integer	214	Write to port
OUTS/OUTSB/ OUTSW/OUTSD	Integer	215	Output string
POP	Integer	217	Pop off stack
POP	Multiple Segment	286	Pop off stack into segment register
POPA/POPAD	Integer	218	Pop all off stack
POPF/POPFD	Integer	220	Pop from stack into flags

Instruction	Section	Page	Description
PUSH	Integer	222	Push onto stack
PUSH	Multiple Segment	287	Push segment register onto the stack
PUSHA/PUSHAD	Integer	224	Push all onto stack
PUSHF/PUSHFD	Integer	226	Push flags onto stack
RCL	Integer	228	Rotate through carry left
RCR	Integer	230	Rotate through carry right
REP	Integer	232	Repeat
REPE/REPZ	Integer	233	Repeat while equal
REPNE/REPNZ	Integer	234	Repeat while not equal
RET	Integer	235	Return (intrasegment)
RET	Multiple Segment	288	Return (intersegment)
ROL	Integer	236	Rotate left
ROR	Integer	238	Rotate right
SAHF	Integer	240	Store AH register into flags
SAL/SHL	Integer	241	Shift arithmetic left
SAR	Integer	243	Shift arithmetic right
SBB	Integer	245	Subtract with borrow
SCAS/SCASB/ SCASW/SCASD	Integer	247	Scan string
SETB/SETNAE/ SETC	Integer	249	Set on below
SETBE/SETNA	Integer	249	Set on below or equal
SETE/SETZ	Integer	249	Set on equal
SETL/SETNGE	Integer	249	Set on less
SETLE/SETNG	Integer	249	Set on less or equal
SETNB/SETAE/ SETNC	Integer	249	Set on not below
SETNBE/SETA	Integer	249	Set on not below or equal
SETNE/SETNZ	Integer	249	Set on not equal
SETNL/SETGE	Integer	249	Set on not less
SETNLE/SETG	Integer	249	Set on not less or equal

Instruction	Section	Page	Description
SETNO	Integer	249	Set on no overflow
SETNP/SETPO	Integer	249	Set on not parity
SETNS	Integer	249	Set on not sign
SETO	Integer	249	Set on overflow
SETP/SETPE	Integer	249	Set on parity
SETS	Integer	249	Set on sign
SGDT	Operating System	311	Store global descriptor table
SHLD	Integer	251	Shift left double
SHR	Integer	253	Shift logical right
SHRD	Integer	255	Shift right double
SIDT	Operating System	312	Store interrupt descriptor table
SLDT	Operating System	313	Store local descriptor table
SMSW	Operating System	314	Store machine status word
STC	Integer	257	Set carry flag
STD	Integer	258	Set direction flag
STI	Integer	259	Set interrupt flag
STOS/STOSB/ STOSW/STOSD	Integer	260	Store string
STR	Operating System	315	Store task register
SUB	Integer	262	Subtract
TEST	Integer	264	Logical compare
VERR	Operating System	316	Verify segment for reading
VERW	Operating System	318	Verify segment for writing
WAIT	Floating Point	398	Wait for coprocessor
XCHG	Integer	265	Exchange
XLAT/XLATB	Integer	266	Table lookup translation
XOR	Integer	267	Exclusive or

Instruction Description Format

The lexicon of our instruction set description is given here. Anything can be described in several different ways. For instance, you can describe a hammer in terms of how it can be used. You can also describe it in terms of its properties, such as weight or shape, or you can describe what it looks like. Similarly, in the following instruction set description, each instruction is described in several ways.

We first give every assembly language syntax allowed with the instruction. We then give an English description of the instruction, which may be easier to understand than the formal definition in some cases. This is followed by a formal operational definition of the semantics of the instruction. Next, we show an example or two of how the instruction is used and what the effects of the instruction are. Finally, we give a list of exceptions (what may have gone wrong) with every instruction. Occasionally, an extra section of notes is included, where we list items that may be of particular interest to you. This section of notes may also include a reference to other pages of the book where this instruction is demonstrated or further explained.

Thus, by the various methods of description, we hope to give you a thorough description of every instruction.

Instruction Format

An example of an instruction format is given below.

ADD	op_1	,	op_2
	reg	,	reg
	reg	,	mem
	reg	,	imm
	mem	,	reg
	mem	,	imm

This indicates that the ADD instruction has five possible forms. It can have two register operands (reg, reg), a register and a memory (reg, mem) and so on. The shorthand op_1 and op_2 are used in the formal operational description that follows. Thus, in the operation section, we can simply refer to $op_1 = op_1 + op_2$ rather than specifically describing each possible form (i.e., reg = reg + reg, reg = reg + mem, and so on).

The list of all possible operand mnemonics and a brief description of each is given below.

reg — Any 8-, 16-, or 32-bit general registers as described in Chapter 2, Figure 2.1. The shorthand *reg* refers to a register of any size of these three. A particular register size will be referred to as reg8, reg16, or reg32. Some instructions use particular registers that are implicitly or explicitly specified, and other instructions allow several possible registers to be used with the register being specified.

mem Any of the memory addressing forms described in Chapter 2 can be used when *mem* is given in the instruction format. The memory forms themselves may reference any 8-, 16-, 32-, 48-, 64-, and 80-bit and 28- and 108-byte memory operand. These would be referred to as mem8, mem16, mem32, and so on in the instruction format description. The shorthand *mem* refers to mem8, mem16, or mem32. Any other memory size is called out explicitly.

imm Again, as described in Chapter 2, immediate constants are allowed in some instructions. An immediate of any length (8, 16, or 32 bits) is given the shorthand notation *imm*. An immediate of a particular length is called out specifically as imm8, imm16, or imm32.

sreg A segment register is referred to as *sreg*. A summary of these can be found in Chapter 2.

ST Many of the floating-point data types use the floating-point accumulator stack, which was described in Chapter 2. The top of the stack is called ST or ST(0), and elements beneath the stack top are ST(n). Refer to Chapter 2 for examples.

; The **;** (semicolon) is used as an assembler comment character. Thus

ADD EAX, EBX ; This is an add

is an assembly language statement with a comment. You will see the semicolon in the format section and the example section.

Note that reading across a line of one of the format statements (ADD reg, reg, for instance) requires the operands to be of the same length (unless the operand lengths are specifically called out). Thus, the format

ADD reg, reg

allows: reg8, reg8; reg16, reg16; or reg32, reg32, but not cases such as reg8, reg32; reg16, reg8; and so on. This same notion of equivalent operand lengths across a line in the format statement is also true for memory mnemonics. Thus,

ADD reg, mem

allows reg8, mem8; reg16, mem16; or reg32, mem32.

Also note that two-operand (binary) operations are normally of the form

$$op_1 = op_1 + op_2$$

where + is the appropriate operator for the instruction. Thus, op_1 is normally the destination of the operation. For example,

ADD reg, mem

causes reg to be assigned the value of reg + mem.

Instruction Description

An example of an instruction description follows.

> AAA will perform a BCD adjustment (unpacked) of the contents of the AL register following a byte addition. AAA normally follows a byte addition of the unpacked BCD contents of AL, but it can be used for other BCD conversions.
>
> If a decimal carry resulted from the addition, or the contents of the lower nibble of AL are greater than 9, then AL is incremented by 6, AH is incremented by 1, and the CF and AF bits are set. If no decimal carry occurred, then AH is unchanged, CF and AF are cleared to 0, and the lower 4 bits of AL are unchanged. If a decimal carry occurred or not, the upper 4 bits of AL are cleared.

This English description is from the AAA instruction. Where possible, an alternate algorithm from the one given in the operation section is given. Where appropriate, the purpose and use of the instruction is also given.

Instruction Operation

An example of the operation section of an instruction is given below.

```
AL = AL + (10 * AH);
AH = 0;
SF = B (7,AL)
ZF = AL == 0
PF = ~(B(7,AL) ^ B(6,AL) ^ . . . ^ B(0,AL));
AF = OF = CF = UNDEFINED;
```

This is an algorithmic description, from the AAD instruction. The order of statements is part of the semantics of the instruction. Thus, the statement

```
ZF = AL == 0;
```

refers to the value of AL after the first statement

```
AL = AL + (10 * AH)
```

has been executed. The operation section describes the complete effects of the instruction. If a register, flag, or operand is not included in the description, it is not affected by the instruction.

A description of the syntax used in the operation section (as well as in other portions of the instruction set description) is given below.

Instruction Examples

Examples are used to further clarify the operation of each instruction. All examples have been checked on a 386 system, to ensure accuracy. A representative instruction example is given below.

```
                                                                  OSZAPC
ADD EAX, EBX            Before:  EAX: 01234567  EBX: 76543210    XXXXXX
                        After :  EAX: 77777777  EBX: 76543210    000010

ADD mem32, 70000000h    Before:  Mem: 7FFFFFFF                   XXXXXX
                        After :  Mem: EFFFFFFF                   110010
```

This example, from the ADD instruction, is broken into two sections. On the left-hand side is the assembler language source for the instructions. This assembler syntax is valid on the 386 system we used. Yours may have slight differences from this, however. On the right-hand side is the state before and after the instruction execution. The register state is normally given in hex, even though it does not have an h suffix. The flag state shown on the far right is in binary. The shorthand column heading OSZAPC refers to the OF, SF, ZF, AF, PF, and CF bits. In examples, an X in either the register state or flag state indicates "don't care" or "unknown." In the example above, the state of the flags was unknown prior to the execution of the ADD instruction. Their state, however, cannot alter the execution of the ADD instruction. Thus, the flags are a "don't care" for this instruction.

U indicates unchanged. In the following example of the JO (jump on overflow) instruction, the flags (except for the overflow) are unknown or don't care prior to the execution of the JO, and the instruction does not modify them.

```
JO   near label1    ; label1 is 68h bytes forward in the program
                                        OSZAPC
          Before:  EIP : 00000300       1XXXXX
           After:  EIP : 00000368       UUUUUU
```

After this instruction, all of the flags remain unchanged, as indicated by the Us in the After picture of the flags.

Instruction Exceptions

Instructions have many possible exception conditions. In the instruction set description, a shorthand function call is used to summarize a potential exception condition. For example, any instruction that has a memory operand can generate one of several different exceptions due to the memory operand. Thus, a "call" to the Memory() function given below would check for the possible error conditions. Describing the error conditions in this shorthand way should eliminate repetitive exception descriptions that add little to the instruction description.

If an exception does in fact occur, the result is an exception of the level described below. Note that if no exceptions are given, the instruction cannot generate any exceptions. Exceptions are described in Chapter 6.

```
Memory(){
  /* All possible exceptions while accessing memory are
     embodied in the AccessVirtual() routine defined in Chapter 5.
     Please refer to Chapter 5 for further details.
  */
}
Stack(){
  /* All possible exceptions while accessing the stack are
     embodied in the AccessVirtual() routine defined in
     Chapter 5 with SReg equal to SS. Please refer to Chapter 5
     for further details.
  */
}
CodeReference(){
  /* The target of the control-transfer instruction is checked.
     A segment exception is reported in the control-transfer
     instruction if the first byte of the target is beyond
     the segment limit. Page exceptions are not reported until the
     instruction is fetched, as with segment exceptions in bytes
     beyond the first byte of the target instruction.
  */
if (EIP > CS.Limit)
  /* The SegmentException() routine is defined in Chapter 6.
     Please refer to Chapter 6 for further details.
  */
  SegmentException($GP,0);
}
AccessIO(){
  /* Defined in Chapter 5 with all possible exception
     conditions given. Please refer to Chapter 5 for further details.
  */
}
IOPLSensitive(){
  /* The SegmentException() routine is defined in Chapter 6.
     CPL and IOPL are discussed in detail in Chapter 5.
  */
  if (CPL > IOPL){
     SegmentException($GP,0)
  }
}
InvalidOpcode(){
  /* Defined in Chapter 6 */
}
```

Instruction Notes

The purpose of the instruction notes section is to point out particular items you should be aware of. For instance, any instruction new to the 386 or 387, or any instruction that operates differently than prior 86 family members, is specifically mentioned here. A peculiar side effect or unexpected result of an instruction is also pointed out here. A reference to an example or description located elsewhere in the book is often noted.

Instruction Description Syntax

This section gives a description of the syntax used to describe the instruction in the operation and exception sections. The syntax used is based on the C programming language. A summary of the C notation we use and the extensions we've made to it are given below. On several occasions, we may use syntax that is not strictly legal in C. This is done for further clarity or conciseness than would be allowed obeying strict C syntax.

Logical Operators

& Bitwise and

| Bitwise inclusive-or

^ Bitwise exclusive-or

<< Left shift

>> Right shift

~ One's complement (unary), not

Arithmetic Operators

+ Addition

− Subtraction

/ Division

% Modulus

++ Increment

−− Decrement

Relational Operators and Logical Connectives

> Greater than

< Less than

Relational Operators and Logical Connectives

>= Greater than or equal
<= Less than or equal
== Equality
!= Not equal
|| Or (logic connective)
&& And (logic connective)

Other

= Assignment
/* Begin comment
*/ End comment
{ Open block of statements
} Close block of statements
& Address of operand
[a] Operand at the address a
a is b If a is of type b, this is true
c in (s) If c is within the set specified by s, this is true

Constants

DENORMAL Floating-point denormal number
EMPTY Floating-point register empty
+INFINITY Floating-point positive infinity representation
−INFINITY Floating-point negative infinity representation
MSB Most significant bit
NaN Floating-point not a number
NORMAL Floating-point normal number
NUMOPS Number of operands specified
OPCODE The opcode of this instruction
QUIETNaN Floating-point quiet NaN
UNDEFINED Undefined result
UNSUPPORTED Unsupported floating-point representation

Register Mnemonics

EAX	32-bit EAX register
ECX	32-bit ECX register
EDX	32-bit EDX register
EBX	32-bit EBX register
ESP	32-bit ESP register
EBP	32-bit EBP register
ESI	32-bit ESI register
EDI	32-bit EDI register
AX	16-bit AX register
CX	16-bit CX register
DX	16-bit DX register
BX	16-bit BX register
SP	16-bit SP register
BP	16-bit BP register
SI	16-bit SI register
DI	16-bit DI register
AL	8-bit AL register
CL	8-bit CL register
DL	8-bit DL register
BL	8-bit BL register
AH	8-bit AH register
CH	8-bit CH register
DH	8-bit DH register
BH	8-bit BH register
CS	16-bit CS (code segment) register
DS	16-bit DS (data segment) register
SS	16-bit SS (stack segment) register
ES	16-bit ES (extra segment) register
FS	16-bit FS (extra segment) register
GS	16-bit GS (extra segment) register
EIP	32-bit instruction pointer

Register Mnemonics

CR0	32-bit control register 0
CR2	32-bit control register 2
CR3	32-bit control register 3
DR0	32-bit debug register 0
DR1	32-bit debug register 1
DR2	32-bit debug register 2
DR3	32-bit debug register 3
DR6	32-bit debug register 6
DR7	32-bit debug register 7
EFLAGS	32-bit flags register
MSW	Machine status word
LDTR	Local descriptor table register
IDTR	Interrupt descriptor table register
GDTR	Global descriptor table register
TR	Task register
TW	Floating-point tag word
SW	Floating-point status word
CW	Floating-point control word
ST	Floating-point stack top
ST(n)	nth register beneath floating-point stack top
TOP	Stack top pointer
FIP	Floating-point instruction pointer
FCS	Floating-point code segment
FOO	Floating-point operand offset
FOS	Floating-point operand segment

Flag Mnemonics

CF	Carry flag
PF	Parity flag
AF	Auxiliary carry flag
ZF	Zero flag

SF	Sign flag
TF	Trap enable flag
IF	Interrupt flag
DF	Direction flag
OF	Overflow flag
IOPL	I/O privilege level
NT	Nested task flag
RF	Debug fault enable
VM	Virtual 8086 mode
C0	Floating-point condition code 0
C1	Floating-point condition code 1
C2	Floating-point condition code 2
C3	Floating-point condition code 3

Other Flags/Bits/Pins

CPL	Current privilege level
DPL	Descriptor privilege level
LOCK	The LOCK bus pin
NMI	Nonmaskable interrupt pin
RPL	Requested privilege level
PE	Protection enable

Other Mnemonics

imm8	8-bit immediate
imm16	16-bit immediate
imm32	32-bit immediate
imm	8-, 16-, or 32-bit immediate
mem8	8-bit memory pointer
mem16	16-bit memory pointer
mem32	32-bit memory pointer
mem48	48-bit memory pointer
mem64	64-bit memory pointer
mem80	80-bit memory pointer

mem	8-, 16-, or 32-bit memory pointer
reg8	8-bit register
reg16	16-bit register
reg32	32-bit register
reg	8-, 16-, or 32-bit register
sreg	Segment register

General Variables

cnt	Variable used for bit counts
delta	Variable used in string descriptions
disp	Byte displacement
i	Loop variable
offset	Bit offset
quotient	Variable used for temporary quotient storage
tmp, temp	Miscellaneous variable

Type Casts

shortReal	Floating-point short real (32 bits)
longReal	Floating-point long real (64 bits)
tempReal	Floating-point temporary real (80 bits)
wordInt	80387 word integer (16 bits)
shortInt	80387 short integer (32 bits)
longInt	80387 long integer (64 bits)
int	Integer

Control Constructs

if (e) b1	If expression e is true, execute block b1
else b2	Else execute block b2
while (e) b3	While expression e is true, execute block b3
for(e1;e2;e3) b4	Execute e1; while e2 execute b4 and e3
switch (e1){case-block}	Multiway conditions statement
case c1:	True if constant c1 is matched
break:	Immediate exit of one program level

Most of these should be familiar or self-explanatory. A few, however, can use further explanation.

The *type casts* are much like the type casts of C. They allow conversion from one data type into another. For example

```
X = (shortInt) Y;
```

denotes that X is assigned the value of Y after the value of Y has been converted into the data type of short integer.

The *is* operator allows for the checking of data types. For example

```
if (op1 is mem){
    whatever...
}
```

executes "whatever..." if op_1 (the first operand) is a reference to memory.

The *in* operator allows for the notion of sets. For example

```
if (op1 in (mem32, mem64, mem80)) {
    Memory();
}
```

calls the Memory() exception routine if op_1 is in the set of items given: mem32, mem64, and mem80.

Functions

Several predefined procedures are used in the instruction set description. Below we define each of these.

```
/* Return bit "N" specified by bitN out of op */
B(bitN, op){
     return((op >> bitN) & 01b);
}

/* Return num bits at bit "N" out of op as specified by */
/* bitN and num                                         */
Bits(bitN, num, op){
     for(mask=0;i=0;i< num;i++){
          mask = (mask << 1) | 1 ;
     }
     return((op >> bitN) & mask);
}

/* Return the carryO of bitN from the most recent ALU */
/* operation. This assumes the existence of a special */
/* variable that contains the carry bits of the       */
/* most recent addition.                              */
CarryO(bitN){
     return((CarryChain >> bitN) & 01b);
}
```

```
/* Return the borrow0 of bitN from the most recent ALU*/
/* operation. This assumes the existence of a special */
/* variable that contains the borrow bits of the      */
/* most recent subtraction.                           */
Borrow0(bitN){
     return((BorrowChain >> bitN) & 01b);
}

/* The length in bits of op is returned.              */
/* Note sizeof is a C function that returns the size  */
/* of the given data type in terms of number of bytes.*/
Length(op){
     return(sizeof(op) * 8);
}

/* op of length OpLen is sign-extended to be of length*/
/* as specified by DesLen.                            */
SignEx(DesLen,OpLen,op){
     sign = B(OpLen-1,op);
     tmp = op;
     for(i=Oplen;i< DesLen;i++){
          tmp = (sign << i) | tmp;
     }
     return(tmp);
}
/* op1 is concatenated with op2, lenOfRes is the     */
/* final length, lenOfOp1 is the length of op1. The  */
/* lenOfRes minus lenOfOp1 gives the length of op2.  */
ConCat(lenOfRes, op2, lenOfOp1,op1){
     mask = 0;
     for(i=0;i<lenOfRes;i++){
          mask = (1 << i) | mask;
     }
     return(mask & ((op2 << lenOfOp1) | op1));
}

Push(op){
     len = Length(op) / 8;
     SS:[ESP-len] = op;
     ESP = ESP - len;
}

Pop(op){
     len = Length(op) / 8;
     tmp = SS:[ESP] ;
     ESP = ESP + len;
     return(tmp);
}

Port(op){
     /* The port routine is a simplified call to the      */
     /* AccessIO() routine defined in Chapter 5.          */
     /* AccessIO (port number, length-of-operation,       */
     /* address-of-data, write-or-readnot);               */
     /* Refer to Chapter 5 for further details.           */
```

```
        if (OPCODE in (OUT,OUTS)){
             AccessIO(op, Length(op)/8, &op2, 1 /* write */);
        } else { /* reading from port */
             AccessIO(op, Length(op)/8, &tmp, 0 /* read */);
             return (*tmp);
        }
   }
   /* Used by string instructions to determine which segment */
   /* to use for ESI string element reference.               */
   SegReg(op){
        if (op has Segment override){
             return(segment of op)
        } else {
             return(DS);
        }
   }

   /* The do this forever loop */
   StopExecution(){
        while(1);
   }
```

Now that you understand the syntax of our instruction set description language, you are ready to tackle the instruction-by-instruction description of the 80386.

▶ Integer

The Integer section gives the complete set of instructions used by the applications programmer. In this section you'll find all arithmetic, bit manipulation, data transfer, nonprivileged flag operation, high-level language, logical, and string instructions.

Each instruction includes one or two examples of how they are used. Chapter 4 gives more examples for the instructions in this section. Those examples are program segments consisting of several instructions to perform some useful function. Between the description and the examples given here, and the more extensive examples found in Chapter 4, you should be able to clearly understand the purpose and operation of these instructions.

The following tables summarize all the instructions in this section according to these subgroupings. Following the tables of instruction groups, the page-by-page description of each instruction begins.

Here are the integer arithmetic instructions that operate on signed and unsigned integers, ASCII data, and BCD data:

	Arithmetic
AAA	ASCII adjust after addition
AAD	ASCII adjust before division
AAM	ASCII adjust after multiplication
AAS	ASCII adjust after subtraction
ADC	Add with carry
ADD	Integer addition
CBW/CWDE	Convert byte to word/convert word to dword
CMP	Compare
CWD/CDQ	Convert word to dword/convert dword to qword
DAA	Decimal adjust after addition
DAS	Decimal adjust after subtraction
DEC	Decrement
DIV	Unsigned divide
IDIV	Signed divide
IMUL	Signed multiplication
INC	Increment
MUL	Unsigned multiplication
NEG	Negate
SBB	Subtract with borrow
SUB	Subtract

Here are the instructions that operate on bit data types:

	Bit
BSF	Bit scan forward
BSR	Bit scan reverse
BT	Bit test
BTC	Bit test and complement
BTR	Bit test and reset
BTS	Bit test and set

The following instructions allow conditional setting of a byte based on the flag state.

	Conditional Assignment
SETB/SETNAE/SETC	Set byte below
SETBE/SETNA	Set byte below or equal
SETE/SETZ	Set byte equal
SETL/SETNGE	Set byte less
SETLE/SETNG	Set byte less or equal
SETNB/SETAE/SETNC	Set byte not below
SETNBE/SETA	Set byte not below or equal
SETNE/SETNZ	Set byte not equal
SETNL/SETGE	Set byte not less
SETNLE/SETG	Set byte not less or equal
SETNO	Set byte no overflow
SETNP/SETPO	Set byte not parity
SETNS	Set byte not sign
SETO	Set byte overflow
SETP/SETPE	Set byte parity
SETS	Set byte sign

The following instructions allow conditional and unconditional transfer of control from the normal sequential instruction flow.

	Control Transfer
CALL	Call procedure
JB/JNAE/JC	Jump below
JBE/JNA	Jump below or equal
JCXZ/JECXZ	Jump CX zero/Jump ECX zero
JE/JZ	Jump equal
JL/JNGE	Jump less
JLE/JNG	Jump less or equal
JMP	Jump
JNB/JAE/JNC	Jump not below

Control Transfer

JNBE/JA	Jump not below or equal
JNE/JNZ	Jump not equal
JNL/JGE	Jump not less
JNLE/JG	Jump not less or equal
JNO	Jump no overflow
JNP/JPO	Jump not parity
JNS	Jump not sign
JO	Jump overflow
JP/JPE	Jump parity
JS	Jump sign
LOOP	Loop with ECX counter
LOOPNZ/LOOPNE	Loop with ECX and not zero/Loop with ECX and not equal
LOOPZ/LOOPE	Loop with ECX and zero/Loop with ECX and equal
RET	Return

The next set of instructions allow data to be moved to and from memory, the stack, input/output ports, and registers.

Data Transfer

IN	Input from a port
LEA	Load effective address
MOV	Move
MOVSX	Move and sign extend
MOVZX	Move and zero extend
OUT	Write to port
POP	Pop off stack
POPA/POPAD	Pop all off stack
PUSH	Push onto stack
PUSHA/PUSHAD	Push all onto stack
XCHG	Exchange

These next instructions allow individual flags to be altered and the flags as a group to be moved to and from the AH register and the stack.

	Flag Control
CLC	Clear the carry flag
CLD	Clear the direction flag
CLI	Clear the interrupt flag
CMC	Complement the carry flag
LAHF	Load flags into AH register
POPF/POPFD	Pop from stack into flags
PUSHF/PUSHFD	Push flags onto stack
SAHF	Store AH register into flags
STC	Set carry flag
STD	Set direction flag
STI	Set interrupt flag

The following instructions implement certain commonly performed high-level language operations.

	High-Level Language
BOUND	Check array index against bounds
ENTER	Create stack frame
LEAVE	Procedure exit

These instructions implement the standard logical operators.

	Logic
AND	And
NOT	Not
OR	Inclusive or
RCL	Rotate through carry left
RCR	Rotate through carry right
ROL	Rotate left
ROR	Rotate right
SAL/SHL	Shift arithmetic left/ Shift logical left

SAR	Shift arithmetic right
SHLD	Shift left double
SHR	Shift logical right
SHRD	Shift right double
TEST	Logical compare
XOR	Exclusive or

The next instructions perform operations on the string data types.

	String
CMPS/CMPSB/CMPSW/CMPSD	Compare string
INS/INSB/INSW/INSD	Input string
LODS/LODSB/LODSW/LODSD	Load string
MOVS/MOVSB/MOVSW/MOVSD	Move string
OUTS/OUTSB/OUTSW/OUTSD	Output string
REP	Repeat
REPE/REPZ	Repeat while equal/ Repeat while zero
REPNE/REPNZ	Repeat while not equal/ Repeat while not zero
SCAS/SCASB/SCASW/SCASD	Scan string
STOS/STOSB/STOSW/STOSD	Store string
XLAT/XLATB	Table lookup translation

Finally, the last instructions do not fit into any of the above categories.

	Other
LOCK	Bus lock
NOP	No operation

AAA

ASCII Adjust after Addition

Integer

Format:

AAA

Description:

AAA will perform a BCD adjustment (unpacked) of the contents of the AL register following a byte addition. AAA normally follows a byte addition of the unpacked BCD contents of AL, but it can be used for other BCD conversions.

If a decimal carry resulted from the addition, or the contents of the lower nibble of AL are greater than 9, then AL is incremented by 6, AH is incremented by 1, and the CF and AF bits are set. If no decimal carry occurred, then AH is unchanged, CF and AF are cleared to 0, and the lower 4 bits of AL are unchanged. If a decimal carry occurred or not, the upper 4 bits of AL are cleared.

Operation:

```
if ((AL & 0Fh) > 9) || (AF == 1) {
      AL = AL + 6;
      AH = AH + 1;
      AF = 1;
      CF = 1;
} else {
      AF = 0;
      CF = 0;
}
AL = AL & 0Fh;

OF = SF = ZF = PF = UNDEFINED;
```

Examples:

```
                                                              OSZAPC
ADD   AL,BL            Before:  AH:  05   AL:07   BL:  09   XXXXXX
                       After :  AH:  05   AL:10   BL:  09   000100
AAA                    Before:  AH:  05   AL:10   BL:  09   000100
                       After :  AH:  06   AL:06   BL:  09   XXX1X1

ADD   AL,BL            Before:  AH:  05   AL:07   BL:  02   XXXXXX
                       After :  AH:  05   AL:09   BL:  02   000010
AAA                    Before:  AH:  05   AL:09   BL:  02   000010
                       After :  AH:  05   AL:09   BL:  02   XXX0X0
```

Exceptions:

None.

AAD

ASCII Adjust before Division

Format:

AAD

Description:

AAD adjusts the numerator in AL before dividing two unpacked BCD numbers. The adjustment is done so the produced quotient of the divide will be a valid BCD result.

The AL register is set to the value: AL + (10 * AH). The AH register is zeroed. A subsequent divide operation will leave a valid BCD quotient in AL with the remainder in AH.

Operation:

```
AL = AL + (10 * AH);
AH = 0;
SF = B (7,AL)
ZF = AL == 0
PF = ~(B(7,AL) ^ B(6,AL) ^ ... ^ B(0,AL));
AF = OF = CF = UNDEFINED;
```

Example:

```
                                                   OSZAPC
AAD          Before:  AH: 05  AL:07  BL: 09       XXXXXX
             After :  AH: 00  AL:39  BL: 09       X00X1X
DIV BL       Before:  AH: 00  AL:39  BL: 09       X00X1X
             After :  AH: 03  AL:06  BL: 09       XXX1X1
```

Exceptions:

None.

AAM

ASCII Adjust after Multiplication

Format:

AAM

Description:

A MUL of two BCD digits may produce an invalid BCD result. AAM converts this result back into a pair of BCD digits, which are left in the AX register (AH and AL, respectively).

Thus, AAM normally follows a multiply operation of two BCD digits. The AH register receives the value of AL divided by 10. The new value of AL is the old value of AL modulus 10.

Operation:

```
AH = AL / 10;
AL = AL % 10;
SF = B(7,AL);
ZF = AL == 0;
PF = ~(B(7,AL) ^B(6,AL) ^... ^B(0,AL));
OF = AF  = CF  = UNDEFINED;
```

Example:

```
                                                    OSZAPC
MUL BL        Before:  AH:  00  AL:07  BL:  09  XXXXXX
              After :  AH:  00  AL:3F  BL:  09  0XXXX0
AAM           Before:  AH:  00  AL:3F  BL:  09  0XXXX0
              After :  AH:  06  AL:03  BL:  09  X00X1X
```

Exceptions:

None.

AAS

ASCII Adjust after Subtraction

Integer

Format:

AAS

Description:

AAS will perform a BCD adjustment (unpacked) of the contents of the AL register following a byte subtract operation. Thus, AAS should only be used following a byte subtract of the unpacked contents of AL.

If a decimal borrow resulted from the subtraction operation, then AL is decremented by 6, AH is decremented by 1, and the CF and AF bits are set. If no decimal carry occurred, then AH is unchanged, CF and AF are set to 0, and the lower 4 bits of AL are unchanged. If a decimal carry occurred or not, the upper 4 bits of AL are cleared.

Operation:

```
if ((AL & 0Fh) > 9) || (AF == 1) {
     AL = AL - 6;
     AH = AH - 1;
     AF = 1;
     CF = 1;
} else {
     AF = 0;
     CF = 0;
}
AL = AL & 0Fh;
OF = SF = ZF = PF = UNDEFINED;
```

Examples:

```
                                                                   OSZAPC
SUB   AL,BL              Before:  AH: 05   AL:07   BL: 09   XXXXXX
                         After :  AH: 05   AL:FE   BL: 09   010101
AAS                      Before:  AH: 05   AL:FE   BL: 09   010101
                         After :  AH: 04   AL:08   BL: 09   XXX1X1

SUB   AL,BL              Before:  AH: 05   AL:09   BL: 07   XXXXXX
                         After :  AH: 05   AL:02   BL: 07   000000
AAS                      Before:  AH: 05   AL:02   BL: 07   000000
                         After :  AH: 05   AL:02   BL: 07   XXX0X0
```

Exceptions:

None.

ADC

Add with Carry

Formats:

ADC	op_1	,	op_2
	reg	,	reg
	reg	,	mem
	reg	,	imm
	mem	,	reg
	mem	,	imm

Description:

An integer addition is performed on op_1, op_2, and c_i with the result placed into op_1. ADC is normally used as part of a multiple byte, word, or dword addition.

Operation:

```
op1  = op1  + op2  + CF;
OF = Carry0(MSB) ^ Carry0(MSB-1);
SF = B(MSB, op1);
ZF = op1 == 0;
AF = Carry0(3);
PF = ~(B(7,op1) ^ B(6,op1) ^ ... ^ B(0,op1));
CF = Carry0(MSB);
/*
      + is defined on a bitwise basis in the table below.
      ai and bi are the ith bits of op1 and op2. ci-1
      is the carry out of bit i-1 (which is the same as the
      carry into bit i). ri is the ith result bit and ci is
      the carry out of the ith bit. The bit variable i
      takes on values from 0 to MSB. ci for i-1 == -1
      is CF (value prior to ADC) for ADC.
      ai  bi  ci-1 | ri  ci
      ------------------------
      0   0   0    | 0   0
      0   0   1    | 1   0
      0   1   0    | 1   0
      0   1   1    | 0   1
      1   0   0    | 1   0
      1   0   1    | 0   1
      1   1   0    | 0   1
      1   1   1    | 1   1
*/
```

Examples:

```
                                                                          OSZAPC
ADC EAX, EBX           Before:  EAX: 01234567  EBX: 76543210  XXXXX1
                       After :  EAX: 77777778  EBX: 76543210  000010

ADC mem32, 70000000h Before:  Mem: 7FFFFFFF                    XXXXX0
                       After :  Mem: EFFFFFFF                    110010

ADC AL, AH             Before:  AL : F9        AH : 65        XXXXX1
                       After :  AL : 5F        AH : 65        000011
```

Exception:

```
Memory();
```

ADD

Integer Addition

Integer

Formats:

ADD	op_1	,	op_2
	reg	,	reg
	reg	,	mem
	reg	,	imm
	mem	,	reg
	mem	,	imm

Description:

An integer addition is performed on op_1 and op_2 with the result placed into op_1.

Operation:

```
op1  = op1 + op2;
OF   = Carry0(MSB) ^ Carry0(MSB-1);
SF   = B(MSB, op1);
ZF   = op1 == 0;
AF   = Carry0(3);
PF   = ~(B(7,op1) ^ B(6,op1) ^ ... ^ B(0,op1));
CF   = Carry0(MSB);
/*
        + is defined on a bitwise basis in the table below.
        ai and bi are the ith bits of op1 and op2. ci-1
        is the carry out of bit i-1 (which is the same as the
        carry into bit i). ri is the ith result bit and ci
        is the carry out of the ith bit. The bit variable i
        takes on values from 0 to MSB.  ci for i-1 == -1
        is 0 for ADD.
        ai  bi  ci-1 | ri  ci
        -------------+-------
        0   0   0    | 0   0
        0   0   1    | 1   0
        0   1   0    | 1   0
        0   1   1    | 0   1
        1   0   0    | 1   0
        1   0   1    | 0   1
        1   1   0    | 0   1
        1   1   1    | 1   1
*/
```

Examples:

```
                                                                      OSZAPC
ADD EAX, EBX            Before:  EAX: 01234567  EBX: 76543210  XXXXXX
                        After :  EAX: 77777777  EBX: 76543210  000010

ADD mem32, 70000000h Before:  Mem: 7FFFFFFF                    XXXXXX
                        After :  Mem: EFFFFFFF                    110010

ADD AL, AH              Before:  AL : F9        AH : 65        XXXXXX
                        After :  AL : 5E        AH : 65        000001
```

Exception:

```
Memory();
```

AND

And

Integer

Formats:

AND	op_1	,	op_2
	reg	,	reg
	reg	,	mem
	reg	,	imm
	mem	,	reg
	mem	,	imm

Description:

A logical AND is performed between op_1 and op_2. The result is stored in op_1.

Operation:

```
op1 = op1 & op2;
OF  = 0;
SF  = B(MSB, op1);
ZF  = op1 == 0;
AF  = UNDEFINED;
PF  = ~(B(7,op1) ^ B(6,op1) ^ ... ^ B(0,op1));
CF  = 0;
/*
      & is defined on a bitwise basis in the table below.
      ai and bi are the bits of op1 and op2.
      ri is the result bit.
      The bit variable i takes on values from 0 to MSB.
      ai bi | ri
      ------+---
      0  0  | 0
      0  1  | 0
      1  0  | 0
      1  1  | 1
*/
```

Examples:

```
                                                              OSZAPC
AND EAX, EBX        Before:  EAX: 01234567  EBX: 76543210  XXXXXX
                    After :  EAX: 00000000  EBX: 76543210  001X10

AND mem8, 70h       Before:  Mem: 7F                       XXXXXX
                    After :  Mem: 70                       000X00

AND AX, DI          Before:  AX : A5A5      DI : FFFF      XXXXXX
                    After :  AX : A5A5      DI : FFFF      010X10
```

Exception:

```
Memory();
```

BOUND

Check Array Index against Bounds

Formats:

BOUND	op_1	,	op_2
	reg16	,	mem32
	reg32	,	mem64

Description:

The signed array index given in op_1 (op_1 must be a register) is compared against the low and high bound data structure given in op_2. If the array index is not within the high and low bounds, an exception level 5 is raised.

The bound data structure is assumed to have two contiguous operands (either word or dword), where the first operand is the lower bound limit and the second is the upper bound limit.

Operation:

```
if ((op1 < op2) || (op1 > [&op2 + sizeof(op1)])) {
     Interrupt(5);
}
```

Example:

```
BOUND EAX, mem64     Before:  EAX      : 000092FD   mem: 00000000
                              [&mem+4]: 00000064
                     After :  Interrupt(5)
```

Exceptions:

```
Interrupt(5);
Memory();
```

BSF

Bit Scan Forward

Formats:

BSF	*op₁*	,	*op₂*
	reg16	,	reg16
	reg16	,	mem16
	reg32	,	reg32
	reg32	,	mem32

Description:

The word or dword specified by op_2 is scanned from right to left (bit 0 to bit 15 or 31) for the first 1 bit. The index of the first 1 bit when scanning right to left is stored into op_1.

If the entire word or dword is 0, the ZF bit is set and op_1 is undefined. If a 1 bit is found, the ZF bit is reset.

Operation:

```
if (op2 == 0){
      ZF = 1;
      op1 = UNDEFINED;
} else {             /* op2 is not all zeros: search */
      ZF = 0;
      temp = 0;
      while (B(temp, op2) == 0){
            temp = temp + 1;
      }
      op1 = temp;
}
OF = SF = AF = PF = CF = UNDEFINED;
```

Examples:

```
                                                                OSZAPC
BSF EAX, EBX          Before:  EAX: XXXXXXXX   EBX: 76543210   XXXXXX
                      After :  EAX: 00000004   EBX: 76543210   XX0XXX

BSF SI, mem16         Before:  SI : XXXX       mem: 0000       XXXXXX
                      After :  SI : XXXX       mem: 0000       XX1XXX
```

Exception:

```
Memory();
```

Note:

This instruction is new to the 80386.

BSR

Bit Scan Reverse

Formats:

BSR	op_1	,	op_2
	reg16	,	reg16
	reg16	,	mem16
	reg32	,	reg32
	reg32	,	mem32

Description:

The word or dword specified by op_2 is scanned from left to right (bit 31 or 15 to bit 0) for the first 1 bit. The index of the first 1 bit when scanning left to right is stored into op_1.

If the entire word or dword is 0, the ZF bit is set and op_1 is undefined. If a 1 bit is found, the ZF bit is reset.

Operation:

```
if (op2 == 0){
      ZF = 1;
      op1 = UNDEFINED;
} else {            /* op2 is not all zeros - do search */
      ZF = 0;
      temp = Length(op2) - 1;
      while (B(temp, op2) == 0){
            temp = temp - 1;
      }
      op1 = temp;
}
OF = SF = AF = PF = CF = UNDEFINED;
```

Examples:

```
                                                                OSZAPC
BSR BX, CX          Before:  BX : XXXX        CX : 0030         XXXXXX
                    After :  BX : 0005        CX : 0030         XX0XXX

BSR ESI, mem32      Before:  ESI: XXXXXXXX    mem: 000F0000     XXXXXX
                    After :  ESI: 00000013    mem: 000F0000     XX0XXX
```

Exception:

```
Memory();
```

Note:

This instruction is new to the 80386.

Bit Test

Formats:

BT	op_1	,	op_2
	reg16	,	reg16
	mem16	,	reg16
	reg16	,	imm
	mem16	,	imm
	reg32	,	reg32
	mem32	,	reg32
	reg32	,	imm
	mem32	,	imm

Description:

The bit of op_1 specified by op_2 is assigned to the carry flag.

op_2 is taken as a signed value. Thus, bit strings of $-32K$ to $32K-1$ and $-2G$ to $2G-1$ can be referenced.

If op_1 is a register, the bit assigned to CF is op_2 taken modulo the register size. If op_1 is a memory bit string, the word or dword of interest is found by adding op_2 (the bit index) divided by operand size (16 or 32) to the memory address of op_1. The bit within this word or dword is specified by op_2 modulo the operand size (16 or 32).

Operation:

```
offset = op2 % Length(op1);
disp   = op2 / Length(op1);
if (op1 in (reg16,reg32)){
     CF = B(offset, op1);
} else {          /* memory operand */
     CF = B(offset, [&op1 + disp]);
}
OF = SF = ZF = AF = PF = UNDEFINED;
```

Examples:

```
                                                                OSZAPC
BT BX, CX           Before: BX : 0A50       CX : 4218           XXXXXX
                    After : BX : 0A50       CX : 4218           XXXXX0

BT mem, EAX         Before: EAX                  : 004A6B48     XXXXXX
                            [&mem+04A6B48/20]: 54BBD231
                    After : EAX                  : 004A6B48     XXXXX0
                            [&mem+04A6B48/20]: 54BBD231
```


Exception:

```
Memory();
```

Notes:

This instruction is new to the 80386.

If op_1 is a memory operand, the processor may access the two or four bytes in memory beginning at

```
&mem + sizeof(op1)*disp
```

The programmer must thus be careful not to use BT near illegal portions of the address space. In particular, this instruction should not be used to reference memory-mapped I/O registers directly. In this case, we recommend that software use MOV instructions to load from or store to memory-mapped device registers, and use the register form of BT to manipulate the device-register image loaded into a processor register.

If op_2 is an immediate constant, only an 8-bit immediate field is provided in the instruction. This constant must be less than the operand size (32 or 16 bits), or the resulting bit offset is undefined. This permits specification of any bit offset in a register, and restricts immediate bit offsets in memory bit strings to be within the dword (or word) at the specified memory location. Larger immediate bit offsets in memory bit strings can be supported by an assembler by placing the low-order 5 bits (4 bits for 16-bit operand size) into the op_2 immediate field, and adjusting the memory byte displacement field by adding in the upper bits shifted to form a byte displacement.

BTC

Bit Test and Complement

Formats:

BTC	op_1	,	op_2
	reg16	,	reg16
	mem16	,	reg16
	reg16	,	imm
	mem16	,	imm
	reg32	,	reg32
	mem32	,	reg32
	reg32	,	imm
	mem32	,	imm

Description:

The bit of op_1 specified by op_2 is assigned to the carry flag. After CF has been set, this same bit of op_1 specified by op_2 is complemented.

op_2 is taken as a signed value. Thus, bit strings of $-32K$ to $32K-1$ and $-2G$ to $2G-1$ can be referenced.

If op_1 is a register, the bit assigned to CF and complemented is op_2 taken modulo the register size. If op_1 is a memory bit string, the word or dword of interest is found by adding op_2 (the bit index) divided by operand size (16 or 32) to the memory address of op_1. The bit within this word or dword is specified by op_2 modulo the operand size (16 or 32).

Operation:

```
offset = op2 % Length(op1);
disp   = op2 / Length(op1);
if (op1 in (reg16, reg32)){
     CF = B(offset, op1);
     B(offset, op1) = ~ B(offset, op1) ;
} else {        /* memory operand */
     CF = B(offset, [&op1 + disp]);
     B(offset, [&op1 + disp]) = ~ B(offset, [&op1 + disp]);
}
OF = SF = ZF = AF = PF = UNDEFINED;
```

Examples:

```
                                                                  OSZAPC
BTC EAX, EDX       Before: EAX: 0A50FF14   EDX: 00A4CCD4   XXXXXX
                   After : EAX: 0A40FF14   EDX: 00A4CCD4   XXXXX1

BTC mem, CX        Before: CX             : F4B8                XXXXXX
                           [&mem+F4B8/10]: D231
                   After : CX             : F4B8                XXXXX0
                           [&mem+F4B8/10]: D331
```


Exception:

```
Memory();
```

Notes:

This instruction is new to the 80386.

If op_1 is a memory operand, the processor may access the two or four bytes in memory beginning at

```
&mem + sizeof(op1)*disp
```

The programmer must thus be careful not to use BTC near illegal portions of the address space. In particular, this instruction should not be used to reference memory-mapped I/O registers directly. In this case, we recommend that software use MOV instructions to load from or store to memory-mapped device registers, and use the register form of BTC to manipulate the device-register image loaded into a processor register.

If op_2 is an immediate constant, only an 8-bit immediate field is provided in the instruction. This constant must be less than the operand size (32 or 16 bits), or the resulting bit offset is undefined. This permits specification of any bit offset in a register, and restricts immediate bit offsets in memory bit strings to be within the dword (or word) at the specified memory location. Larger immediate bit offsets in memory bit strings can be supported by an assembler by placing the low-order 5 bits (4 bits for 16-bit operand size) into the op_2 immediate field, and adjusting the memory byte displacement field by adding in the upper bits shifted to form a byte displacement.

BTR

Bit Test and Reset

Formats:

BTR	op_1	,	op_2
	reg16	,	reg16
	mem16	,	reg16
	reg16	,	imm
	mem16	,	imm
	reg32	,	reg32
	mem32	,	reg32
	reg32	,	imm
	mem32	,	imm

Description:

The bit of op_1 specified by op_2 is assigned to the carry flag. After CF has been set, this same bit of op_1 specified by op_2 is reset to 0.

op_2 is taken as a signed value. Thus, bit strings of $-32K$ to $32K-1$ and $-2G$ to $2G-1$ can be referenced.

If op_1 is a register, the bit assigned to CF and reset is op_2 taken modulo the register size. If op_1 is a memory bit string, the word or dword of interest is found by adding op_2 (the bit index) divided by operand size (16 or 32) to the memory address of op_1. The bit within this word or dword is specified by op_2 modulo the operand size (16 or 32).

Operation:

```
offset = op2 % Length(op1);
disp   = op2 / Length(op1);
if (op1 in (reg16,reg32)){
      CF = B(offset, op1);
      B(offset, op1) = 0;
} else {          /* memory operand */
      CF = B(offset, [&op1 + disp]);
      B(offset, [&op1 + disp]) = 0;
}
OF = SF = ZF = AF = PF = UNDEFINED;
```

Examples:

```
                                                          OSZAPC
BTR AX, 23h       Before: AX : 53FE                       XXXXXX
                  After : AX : 53F6                       XXXXX1

BTR mem, ESI      Before: ESI                : 532011D4   XXXXXX
                          [&mem+532011D4/20]: FFFFFFFF
                  After : ESI                : 532011D4   XXXXX1
                          [&mem+532011D4/20]: FFEFFFFF
```

Exception:

```
Memory();
```

Notes:

This instruction is new to the 80386. See example 4, page 412.

If op_1 is a memory operand, the processor may access the two or four bytes in memory beginning at

```
&mem + sizeof(op1)*disp
```

The programmer must thus be careful not to use BTR near illegal portions of the address space. In particular, this instruction should not be used to reference memory-mapped I/O registers directly. In this case, we recommend that software use MOV instructions to load from or store to memory-mapped device registers, and use the register form of BTR to manipulate the device-register image loaded into a processor register.

If op_2 is an immediate constant, only an 8-bit immediate field is provided in the instruction. This constant must be less than the operand size (32 or 16 bits), or the resulting bit offset is undefined. This permits specification of any bit offset in a register, and restricts immediate bit offsets in memory bit strings to be within the dword (or word) at the specified memory location. Larger immediate bit offsets in memory bit strings can be supported by an assembler by placing the low-order 5 bits (4 bits for 16-bit operand size) into the op_2 immediate field, and adjusting the memory byte displacement field by adding in the upper bits shifted to form a byte displacement.

BTS

Bit Test and Set

Formats:

BTS	op_1	,	op_2
	reg16	,	reg16
	mem16	,	reg16
	reg16	,	imm
	mem16	,	imm
	reg32	,	reg32
	mem32	,	reg32
	reg32	,	imm
	mem32	,	imm

Description:

The bit of op_1 specified by op_2 is assigned to the carry flag. After CF has been set, this same bit of op_1 specified by op_2 is set to 1.

op_2 is taken as a signed value. Thus, bit strings of $-32K$ to $32K-1$ and $-2G$ to $2G-1$ can be referenced.

If op_1 is a register, the bit assigned to CF and set is op_2 taken modulo the register size. If op_1 is a memory bit string, the word or dword of interest is found by adding op_2 (the bit index) divided by operand size (16 or 32) to the memory address of op_1. The bit within this word or dword is specified by op_2 modulo the operand size (16 or 32).

Operation:

```
offset = op2 % Length(op1);
disp   = op2 / Length(op1);
if (op1 in (reg16,reg32)){
      CF = B(offset, op1);
      B(offset, op1) = 1;
} else {        /* memory operand */
      CF = B(offset, [&op1 + disp]);
      B(offset, [&op1 + disp]) = 1;
}
OF = SF = ZF = AF = PF = UNDEFINED;
```

Examples:

```
                                                        OSZAPC
BTS EAX, 69h      Before: EAX : 0459B820                XXXXXX
                  After : EAX : 0459BA20                XXXXX0

BTS mem16, SI     Before: SI             : 3014         XXXXXX
                          [&mem+3014/10]: 0023
                  After : SI             : 3014         XXXXX0
                          [&mcm+3014/10]: 0033
```

Exception:

```
Memory();
```

Notes:

This instruction is new to the 80386. See example 4, page 412.

If op_1 is a memory operand, the processor may access the two or four bytes in memory beginning at

```
&mem + sizeof(op1)*disp
```

The programmer must thus be careful not to use BTS near illegal portions of the address space. In particular, this instruction should not be used to reference memory-mapped I/O registers directly. In this case, we recommend that software use MOV instructions to load from or store to memory-mapped device registers, and use the register form of BTS to manipulate the device-register image loaded into a processor register.

If op_2 is an immediate constant, only an 8-bit immediate field is provided in the instruction. This constant must be less than the operand size (32 or 16 bits), or the resulting bit offset is undefined. This permits specification of any bit offset in a register, and restricts immediate bit offsets in memory bit strings to be within the dword (or word) at the specified memory location. Larger immediate bit offsets in memory bit strings can be supported by an assembler by placing the low-order 5 bits (4 bits for 16-bit operand size) into the op_2 immediate field, and adjusting the memory byte displacement field by adding in the upper bits shifted to form a byte displacement.

CALL

Call Procedure

Formats:

CALL op_1
near_label
reg32
mem32

Description:

CALL causes instruction execution to continue at the given offset within the current code segment. Only calls within the same code segment are described here. Calls to different segments are described in the Multiple Segment section.

Intrasegment call offsets can be specified by a near label, a reg32, or a mem32, where the memory contents at mem32 give the offset.

Before control transfer occurs, the pointer to the next instruction to be executed is placed onto the stack. The pushed information can be used by the RET instruction to resume execution at this point in the program.

Note in the description that EIP is stored on the stack, and not EIP plus the length of the current call instruction. When the 80386 fetches an instruction, it increments the instruction pointer by the instruction length prior to execution. Thus, EIP can be stored directly.

Operation:

```
if (op1 is near_label) {
     Push(EIP);
     EIP   = near_label; /* † */
} else if (op1 is reg32) {
     Push(EIP);
     EIP   = reg32;
} else if (op1 is mem32) {
     Push(EIP);
     EIP   = mem32;
}
/*
     † The near label form is assembled into a simple 32b
     immediate offset.  This offset is relative to the current
     instruction pointer. Thus, a machine description of the EIP
     update would be:
          EIP = EIP + imm32
*/
```

Example:

```
CALL  near_label1  ; label1 is 32 bytes forward in the program
           Before:  EIP : 300    ESP : 200
           After :  EIP : 332    ESP : 1FC   SS:[ESP]: 300
```

Exceptions:

```
Memory();
Stack();
CodeReference() ;
```

Note:

See example 3a, page 409.

CBW / CWDE

Convert Byte to Word / Convert Word to Dword

Formats:

CBW

CWDE

Description:

The signed byte or word in AL or AX is sign-extended to fill the AX or EAX register. The value of bit 7 of AX or bit 15 of EAX is placed in every bit of AH or the upper 16 bits of EAX.

Thus, the value of the signed byte in AL or the signed word in AX becomes the signed word in AX or the signed dword in EAX.

Operation:

```
if (OPCODE == CWDE){
     EAX = SignEx(32, 16, AX);
} else {        /* CBW */
     AX = SignEx(16, 8, AL);
}
```

Examples:

```
CBW                Before:   AX: XX7F
                   After :   AX: 007F

CWDE               Before:  EAX: XXXXFDF3
                   After :  EAX: FFFFFDF3
```

Exceptions:

None.

Note:

CWDE differs from CWD in that CWD uses the DX and AX register pair rather than EAX.

CLC

Clear the Carry Flag

Format:

CLC

Description:

The carry flag is set to 0.

Operation:

```
CF = 0;
```

Example:

```
CLC            Before:  CF : 1
               After :  CF : 0
```

Exceptions:

None.

CLD

Clear the Direction Flag

Format:

CLD

Description:

The direction flag is set to 0. After the direction flag is set to 0, string instructions will increment their index registers (ESI and EDI).

Operation:

```
DF = 0;
```

Example:

```
CLD             Before:  DF : 1
                After :  DF : 0
```

Exceptions:

None.

Note:

See example 5, page 413.

CLI

Clear the Interrupt Flag

Format:

CLI

Description:

The interrupt enable flag is set to 0. The 80386 will ignore interrupts after the next instruction completes execution until the IF bit is set back to 1.

An exception is raised if the program does not have I/O privilege (see Chapter 5).

Operation:

```
IF = 0;
```

Example:

```
CLI             Before:  IF : 1
                After :  IF : 0
```

Exception:

```
IOPLSensitive();
```

Note:

See example 1, page 622.

CMC

Complement the Carry Flag

Format:

CMC

Description:

The carry flag is complemented.

Operation:

```
CF = ~CF;
```

Examples:

```
CMC            Before:  CF : 1
               After :  CF : 0

CMC            Before:  CF : 0
               After :  CF : 1
```

Exceptions:

None.

CMP

Compare

Integer

Formats:

CMP	op_1	,	op_2
	reg	,	reg
	reg	,	mem
	reg	,	imm
	mem	,	reg
	mem	,	imm

Description:

op_2 is subtracted from op_1 but the result is not stored anywhere. Only the flags are modified. CMP is often followed by a conditional jump or set byte instruction.

Operation:

```
temp = op1 - op2;
/* - is as defined under the SUB instruction below. */

OF  = Borrow0(MSB) ^ Borrow0(MSB-1);
SF  = B(MSB, temp);
ZF  = temp == 0;
AF  = Borrow0(3);
PF  = ~(B(7,temp) ^ B(6,temp) ^ ... ^ B(0,temp));
CF  = Borrow0(MSB);
```

Examples:

```
                                                                 OSZAPC
CMP EAX, EBX        Before:  EAX: 01234567  EBX:   01234568    XXXXXX
                    After :  EAX: 01234567  EBX:   01234568    010111
JZ  EQUAL           ; The jump is not taken

CMP AX, mem16       Before:  AX : 0000    mem16:   0000        XXXXXX
                    After :  AX : 0000    mem16:   0000        001010
JZ  EQUAL           ; The jump IS taken
```

Exception:

```
Memory();
```

Note:

See Chapter 4 examples, such as example 5, page 413.

CMPS / CMPSB / CMPSW / CMPSD

Compare String

Integer

Formats:

CMPSB
CMPSW
CMPSD

CMPS	mem_1	,	mem_2
	mem8	,	mem8
	mem16	,	mem16
	mem32	,	mem32

Description:

CMPS subtracts ES:[EDI] from [ESI]. The result of the subtraction is not stored, since only the flags are modified. The ESI and EDI registers are updated to point to the next element of the string. These registers are updated based upon the direction flag (DF) and the length of the operands (8, 16, or 32 bits) as indicated by mem_1 and mem_2 or by the OPCODE themselves (CMPSB, CMPSW, and CMPSD). If the DF flag is 0, the registers are updated by 1, 2, or 4. If the DF flag is 1, the registers are updated by -1, -2, or -4.

The CMPS operation may be preceded by REPE (REPZ) or REPNE (REPNZ). If preceded by REPE, the CMPS instruction is repeated while ECX is not 0 and the string elements are equal (ZF==1). If preceded by REPNE, the CMPS instruction is repeated while ECX is not 0 and the string elements are not equal (ZF==0). In this way, CMPS is useful to find first matches or mismatches in strings if they exist. Refer to REPE and REPNE for details of the prefixes.

The assembly language specification of mem_1 and mem_2 is used by the assembler to determine the length of the operation only. The strings are always taken from [ESI] and ES:[EDI]. CMPS may include a segment override prefix that affects the segment offset used for mem_1 ([ESI]). mem_2 always comes from ES:[EDI].

Operation:

```
if (OPCODE == CMPSB){
     delta = 1;
     temp = (byte)  DS:[ESI] - (byte)  ES:[EDI];
} else if (OPCODE == CMPSB){
     delta = 2;
     temp = (word)  DS:[ESI] - (word)  ES:[EDI];
} else if (OPCODE == CMPSB){
     delta = 4;
     temp = (dword) DS:[ESI] - (dword) ES:[EDI];
} else {               /* CMPS */
     /* Note that the default for SegReg(mem1) is DS */
     delta = Length(mem1);
     temp = SegReg(mem1):[ESI] - ES:[EDI]
}
/* - is as defined for the SUB instruction. */
OF  = Borrow0(MSB) ^ Borrow0(MSB-1);
SF  = B(MSB, temp);
ZF  = temp == 0;
AF  = Borrow0(3);
PF  = ~(B(7,temp) ^ B(6,temp) ^ ... ^ B(0,temp));
CF  = Borrow0(MSB);
if (DF == 1) {
     delta = - delta;
}
ESI = ESI + delta;
EDI = EDI + delta;
```

Examples:

```
                                                                  OSZAPC
CMPSB    Before: ESI        : 0008   EDI: 0016   [ESI]   : 67    XXXXXX
                 ES:[EDI]   :   65   DF : 0
         After : ESI        : 0009   EDI: 0017   [ESI-1]: 67     000010
                 ES:[EDI-1]:    65   DF : 0

REPE CMPS S1,S2   ; Note-S1 and S2 are 16-bit strings
                  ;  [ESI] points to S1, ES:[EDI] points to S2
     Before: ESI     : 0008     EDI    : 0016  [ESI]   : 0023   XXXXXX
             [ESI-2]: 7923    [ESI-4]: 7214  [ESI-6]: AA6D
             [EDI]   : 0023   [EDI-2]: 7923  [EDI-4]: 8215
             [EDI-6]: AA6D     ECX    : 4        DF : 1
     After : ESI     : 0002     EDI    : 0010  [ESI+6]: 0023    001010
             [ESI+4]: 7923    [ESI+2]: 7214  [ESI]   : AA6D
             [EDI+6]: 0023    [EDI+4]: 7923  [EDI+2]: 8215
             [EDI]   : AA6D     ECX    : 1        DF : 1
```

Exception:

```
Memory();
```

Note:

See example 5, page 413.

CWD / CDQ

Convert Word to Dword/ Convert Dword to Qword

Formats:

CWD

CWQ

Description:

The signed word in AX or double word in EAX is sign-extended to fill the DX or EDX register. The value of bit 15 or bit 31 of AX or EAX is placed in every bit of DX or EDX.

Thus, the valuc of the signed word in AX becomes the signed dword in DX:AX. Or, for 32-bit operands, the signed dword in EAX becomes the signed qword in EDX:EAX.

Operation:

```
if (OPCODE == CDQ){
     if (B(31, EAX) == 1){
          EDX = FFFFFFFFh;
     } else {
          EDX = 00000000h;
     }
} else {
     if (B(15, AX) == 1){
          DX = FFFFh;
     } else {
          DX = 0000h;
     }
}
```

Examples:

```
CWD                 Before:  AX: 7615   DX: XXXX
                    After :  AX: 7615   DX: 0000

CWD                 Before:  AX: F103   DX: XXXX
                    After :  AX: F103   DX: FFFF
```

Exceptions:

None.

Note:

CWD is different than CWDE in that CWDE uses the EAX register rather than the DX and AX register pair.

DAA

Decimal Adjust after Addition

Format:

DAA

Description:

DAA should only be used following an ADD instruction that operated on two packed BCD numbers (a packed byte) with the result left in AL.

DAA will take the AL register contents and convert this into a two-digit packed BCD number left in AL.

If the low nibble of AL is > 9 or AF was set, then add 6 to AL and set AF. Otherwise AF is reset. If the high nibble of AL is > 9F or the CF flag was set, then add 60h to AL and set CF. Otherwise CF is reset.

Operation:

```
if (((AL & 0Fh) > 9) || AF ) {
     AL = AL + 6;
     CF = CF | Carry0(7);
     AF = 1;
} else {
     AF = 0;
}
if ((AL > 9Fh) || CF) {
     AL = AL + 60h;
     CF = 1;
} else {
     CF = 0;
}
OF  = UNDEFINED;
SF  = B(7, AL);
ZF  = (AL == 0);
PF  = ~(B(7,AL) ^ B(6,AL) ^ ... ^ B(0,AL));
```

Examples:

```
                                                        OSZAPC
ADD   AL,BL        Before:  AL:77   BL:  13   XXXXXX
                   After :  AL:8A   BL:  13   110000
DAA                Before:  AL:8A   BL:  13   110000
                   After :  AL:90   BL:  13   X10110

ADD   AL,BL        Before:  AL:79   BL:  35   XXXXXX
                   After :  AL:AE   BL:  35   110000
DAA                Before:  AL:AE   BL:  35   110000
                   After :  AL:14   BL:  35   X00111
```

Exceptions:

None.

DAS

Decimal Adjust after Subtraction

Integer

Format:

DAS

Description:

DAS should only be used following a SUB instruction that operated on two packed BCD numbers (a packed byte) with the result left in AL.

DAS will take the AL register contents and convert this into a valid two-digit packed BCD number left in AL.

If thc low nibble of AL is > 9 or AF was set, then AL has 6 subtracted from it and the AF bit is set. Otherwise AF is reset. If the high nibble of AL is > 9Fh or the CF bit was set, then AL has 60h subtracted from it and CF is set. Otherwise CF is reset.

Operation:

```
if (((AL & 0Fh) > 9) || AF) {
     AL = AL - 6;
     CF = CF | Borrow0(7);
     AF = 1;
} else {
     AF = 0;
}
if ((AL > 9Fh) || CF) {
     AL = AL - 60h;
     CF = 1;
} else {
     CF = 0;
}
OF  = UNDEFINED;
SF  = B(7, AL);
ZF  = (AL == 0);
PF  = ~(B(7,AL) ^B(6,AL) ^... ^B(0,AL));
```

Examples:

```
                                                        OSZAPC
SUB   AL, BL            Before:  AL: 71   BL:  13       XXXXXX
                        After :  AL: 5E   BL:  13       000100
DAS                     Before:  AL: 5E   BL:  13       000100
                        After :  AL: 58   BL:  13       X00100
SUB   AL, BL            Before:  AL: 35   BL:  47       XXXXXX
                        After :  AL: EE   BL:  47       010111
DAS                     Before:  AL: EE   BL:  47       010111
                        After :  AL: 88   BL:  47       X10111
```

Exceptions:

None.

DEC

Decrement

Integer

Formats:

DEC *op_1*
mem
reg

Description:

op_1 has 1 subtracted from it, and the result is placed back into op_1.

Operation:

```
op1 = op1 - 1;
/* - is defined as it is for the SUB instruction. */

OF  = Carry0(MSB) ^ Carry0(MSB-1);
SF  = B(MSB, op1);
ZF  = op1 == 0;
AF  = Carry0(3);
PF  = ~(B(7,op1) ^ B(6,op1) ^ ... ^ B(0,op1));
CF  = CF;
```

Examples:

```
                                            OSZAPC
DEC EAX         Before:  EAX: 01234567      XXXXXX
                After :  EAX: 01234566      00001U

DEC mem16       Before:  Mem: 0000          XXXXXX
                After :  Mem: FFFF          01011U
```

Exception:

```
Memory();
```

Note:

The carry flag *is not* affected by the DEC instruction. The SUB instruction with an operand of 1 should be used if carry flag updates are desired.

DIV

Unsigned Divide

Formats:

DIV *op_1*
reg
mem

Description:

Unsigned division and remainder operations are performed upon the given operand (op_1) and an implicit register. The implicit register depends upon the length of op_1 (either 8 – AX, 16 – AX:DX, or 32 – EAX:EDX).

The quotient is placed into AL, AX, or EAX for 8-, 16- and 32-bit operands, respectively. The remainder is placed into AH, DX, or EDX for 8-, 16-, and 32-bit operands, respectively. Thus, the divisor is specified by op_1, and the dividend, quotient, and remainder always reside in implicit registers. The registers and operands used are summarized in the following table:

Length(op_1)	Dividend	Divisor	Quotient	Remainder
8	AX	op_1	AL	AH
16	DX:AX	op_1	AX	DX
32	EDX:EAX	op_1	EAX	EDX

Nonintegral quotients are truncated toward 0. Remainders are always less than the dividend.

If the quotient does not fit within the range of the quotient register (AL, AX or EAX), a divide by zero error occurs. A divide by zero error is 80386 interrupt 0. If a divide by zero error occurs, the quotient and remainder are undefined.

Operation:

```
if (op1 == 0) Interrupt(0);
if (Length(op1) == 8){
     if (( AX / op1) > FFh) Interrupt(0);
     temp= AX;
     AL  = temp / op1;
     AH  = temp % op1;
} else if (Length(op1) == 16){
     if (( ConCat(32,DX,16,AX) / op1) > FFFFh) Interrupt(0);
     temp= AX;
     AX  = ConCat(32,DX,16,temp) / op1;
     DX  = ConCat(32,DX,16,temp) % op1;
} else { /* Length(op1) == 32 */
     if (( ConCat(64,EDX,32,EAX) / op1) > FFFFFFFFh) Interrupt(0);
     temp= EAX;
     EAX = ConCat(64,EDX,32,temp) / op1;
     EDX = ConCat(64,EDX,32,temp) % op1;
}
OF = SF = ZF = AF = PF = CF = UNDEFINED
/*
     / is defined as unsigned division. Both AX or ConCat(DX,AX)
     or ConCat(EDX,EAX) and op1 are considered to be unsigned
     integer numbers.

     %, likewise, is defined as unsigned modulus or remainder.
*/
```

Examples:

```
                                                                 OSZAPC
DIV EBX          Before:  EDX: 76543210   EAX: 01234567   XXXXXX
                          EBX: 89014573
                 After :  EDX: 34DCEE8F   EAX: DD1A57C8   XXXXXX
                          EBX: 89014573

DIV mem8         Before:  AH: 78   AL: 21   mem: 5C        XXXXXX
                 After :  Interrupt(0) ;
                          AH: XX   AL: XX   mem: 5C        XXXXXX
```

Exceptions:

```
Memory();
Interrupt(0);
```

ENTER

Create Stack Frame

Formats:

ENTER *op₁* , *op₂*

imm16 , imm8

Description:

ENTER creates a stack frame. This is normally done by most high-level languages at every procedure call.

op_2 specifies the nesting depth of the routine. The nesting depth determines the number of stack frame pointers that are copied from the current stack frame into the new stack frame that is being built by this ENTER instruction. EBP is used to copy the frame pointers from the current stack frame into the new stack frame. EBP points to the new stack frame pointer at the end of the instruction.

op_1 specifies the number of bytes of local variables for which stack space is automatically allocated.

Operation:

```
level = op2 % 32;
Push(EBP);
frame = ESP;
if(level > 0) {
      while((--level)>0){
            EBP = EBP - 4;
            Push([EBP]);
      }
      Push(frame);
}
EBP = frame;
ESP = ESP - ConCat(32, 0000h, 16, op1);
```

Example:

```
ENTER 0Ch, 4
        Before: EBP          : 00000F38   SS:[EBP]     : 00000F4C
                SS:[EBP-4]   : 0000100B   SS:[EBP-8]   : 000010A4
                SS:[EBP-12]  : 00001102   ESP          : 00000F04
        After : SS:[ESP+28]  : 00000F38   SS:[ESP+24]  : 0000100B
                SS:[ESP+20]  : 000010A4   SS:[ESP+16]  : 00001102
                SS:[ESP+12]  : 00000F00   EBP          : 00000F00
                ESP          : 00000EE4
```

Exception:

```
Stack();
```

Note:

See example 3b, page 410.

IDIV

Signed Divide

Formats:

IDIV *op_1*
reg
mem

Description:

Signed division and remainder operations are performed upon the given operand (op_1) and one or more implicit registers. The implicit register depends upon the length of op_1 (either 8 – AX, 16 – AX:DX, or 32 – EAX:EDX).

The quotient is placed into AL, AX, or EAX for 8-, 16-, and 32-bit operands, respectively. The remainder is placed into AH, DX or EDX for 8-, 16-, and 32-bit operands, respectively. The registers and operands used are summarized by the following table:

Length(op_1)	Dividend	Divisor	Quotient	Remainder
8	AX	op_1	AL	AH
16	DX:AX	op_1	AX	DX
32	EDX:EAX	op_1	EAX	EDX

Nonintegral quotients are truncated toward 0. Remainders are always the same sign as the dividend and always have less magnitude than the divisor. The following table gives all sign combinations of the dividend and quotient for 4 divided by 3 and the resultant quotient and remainders.

Dividend	op_1 (Divisor)	Quotient	Remainder
+4	+3	+1	+1
+4	−3	−1	+1
−4	+3	−1	−1
−4	−3	+1	−1

The division always obeys the identity

dividend = quotient * divisor + remainder

If op_1 is 0 or the quotient does not fit within the range of the quotient register (AL, AX, or EAX) a divide by zero error occurs. A divide by zero error is 80386 interrupt 0. If a divide by zero error occurs, the quotient and remainder are undefined.

Operation:

```
if (op1 == 0) Interrupt(0);
if (Length(op1) == 8){
     if ( ((AX > 0) && (AX / op1) > 7Fh) ||
          ((AX < 0) && (AX / op1) < 80h) )
          Interrupt(0);
     temp= AX;
     AL  = temp / op1;
     AH  = temp % op1;
} else if (Length(op1) == 16){
     if ( ((ConCat(32,DX,16,AX) > 0) &&
           (ConCat(32,DX,16,AX) / op1) > 7FFFh) ||
          ((ConCat(32,DX,16,AX) < 0) &&
           (ConCat(32,DX,16,AX) / op1) < 8000h) )
          Interrupt(0);
     temp= AX;
     AX  = ConCat(32,DX,16,temp) / op1;
     DX  = ConCat(32,DX,16,temp) % op1;
} else { /* Length(op1) == 32 */
     if ( ((ConCat(64,EDX,32,EAX) > 0) &&
           (ConCat(64,EDX,32,EAX) / op1) > 7FFFFFFFh) ||
          ((ConCat(64,EDX,32,EAX) < 0) &&
           (ConCat(64,EDX,32,EAX) / op1) < 80000000h) )
          Interrupt(0);
     temp=EAX;
     EAX = ConCat(64,EDX,32,temp) / op1;
     EDX = ConCat(64,EDX,32,temp) % op1;
}
OF = SF = ZF = AF = PF = CF = UNDEFINED;
/*
  / is defined as signed division. Both AX or ConCat(DX,AX)
  or ConCat(EDX,EAX) and op1 are considered to be signed
  integer numbers.

  %, likewise, is defined as signed modulus or remainder.
*/
```

Examples:

```
                                                          OSZAPC
IDIV BX          Before:  DX: 3210   AX: 4567             XXXXXX
                          BX: 6773
                 After :  DX: 496E   AX: 7BE3             XXXXXX
                          BX: 6773

IDIV mem8        Before:  AH: D8   AL: D7   mem: AD       XXXXXX
                 After :  AH: BF   AL: 78   mem: AD       XXXXXX

IDIV BL          Before:  AH: 87   AL: B2   BL : 19       XXXXXX
                 After :  Interrupt(0);
                          AH: XX   AL: XX   BL : 19       XXXXXX
```

Exceptions:

```
Memory();
Interrupt(0);
```

Note:

See example 1 and discussion, page 406.

IMUL

Signed Multiplication

Formats:

IMUL	*op₁*				
	reg				
	mem				
IMUL	op_1	,	op_2		
	reg16	,	reg16		
	reg16	,	mem16		
	reg16	,	imm		
	reg32	,	reg32		
	reg32	,	mem32		
	reg32	,	imm		
IMUL	op_1	,	op_2	,	op_3
	reg16	,	reg16	,	imm
	reg16	,	mem16	,	imm
	reg32	,	reg32	,	imm
	reg32	,	mem32	,	imm

Description:

If the IMUL has only one operand, the second operand is implicitly taken from AL, AX, or EAX. The 16-, 32-, or 64-bit signed result is stored into AX, DX:AX, or EDX:EAX, respectively. If AH, DX, or EDX is only a sign extension of AL, AX, or EAX, respectively, CF and OF are set to 0. Otherwise they are set to 1.

The two-operand case has $op_1 * op_2$ stored into op_1. If the result of $op_1 * op_2$ is representable in the range of op_1, then CF and OF are set to 0. Otherwise they are set to 1.

The three-operand case has $op_2 * op_3$ stored into op_1. If the result of $op_2 * op_3$ is representable in the range of op_1, then CF and OF are set to 0. Otherwise they are set to 1.

Operation:

```
if (NUMOPS ==1){
     if (Length(op1 == 8){
          AX = AL * op1;
          if ((AH == 00h) || (AH == FFh)){
               CF = 0; OF = 0;
          } else {
               CF = 1; OF = 1;
          }
     } else if (Length(op1) == 16){
          DX = (AX * op1) >> 16;
          AX = (AX * op1) & 0FFFFh;
          if ((DX == 0000h) || (DX == FFFFh)){
               CF = 0; OF = 0;
          } else {
               CF = 1; OF = 1;
          }
     } else {      /* Length(op1) == 32 */
          EDX = (EAX * op1) >> 32;
          EAX = (EAX * op1) & 0FFFFFFFFh;
          if ((EDX == 00000000h) || (EDX == FFFFFFFFh)){
               CF = 0; OF = 0;
          } else {
               CF = 1; OF = 1;
          }
     }
} else if (NUMOPS == 2){
     doubleTemp = op1 * op2;
     op1 = op1 * op2;
     if (doubleTemp != op1){
          CF = 1; OF = 1;
     } else {
          CF = 0; OF = 0;
     }
} else {  /* NUMOPS == 3 */
     op1 = op2 * op3;
     doubleTemp = op2 * op3;
     if (doubleTemp != op1){
          CF = 1; OF = 1;
     } else {
          CF = 0; OF = 0;
     }
}
SF = ZF = AF = PF = UNDEFINED;
/* * is defined as signed multiplication. */
```

Examples:

```
                                                                      OSZAPC
IMUL BX            Before:  DX: XXXX  AX: 1862                        XXXXXX
                            BX: 8536
                   After :  DX: F44E  AX: 0EAC                        1XXXX1
                            BX: 8536

IMUL ECX, mem32    Before:  ECX: 00015792  mem32: 00052692            XXXXXX
                   After :  ECX: E99D9D44  mem32: 00052692            1XXXX1

IMUL CX, mem16, 8  Before:  CX: XXXX  mem16: 002A                     XXXXXX
                   After :  CX: 0150  mem16: 002A                     0XXXX0
```

Exception:

```
Memory();
```

Note:

See examples, page 3a and 3b, pages 409 and 410.

IN

Input from a Port

Formats:

IN	op_1	,	op_2
	AL	,	imm8
	AX	,	imm8
	EAX	,	imm8
	AL	,	DX
	AX	,	DX
	EAX	,	DX

Description:

IN transfers a data byte, word, or dword from the specified port into AL, AX, or EAX, respectively.

I/O ports are in the range 0 to 64K − 1. Instructions can access ports via two forms: an immediate byte and indirectly through the DX register.

The immediate-byte forms allow ports 0 to 255 to be accessed. The upper bits of the port address are always 0 in this case. The register form (DX) allows the full range of ports (0 to 64K − 1) to be accessed.

An exception occurs if the current task has insufficient privilege to perform I/O. See Chapter 5 for further details of privilege levels.

Operation:

```
op1 = port(op2);
```

Examples:

```
IN AL, 20h      Before:  AL: XX        port(20): 4A
                After :  AL: 4A        port(20): XX

IN EAX, DX      Before:  EAX: XXXXXXXX  DX: 4680
                         port(4680)       : FFA78201
                After :  EAX: FFA78201  DX: 4680
                         port(4680)       : XXXXXXXX
```

Exception:

```
AccessIO();
```

INC

Increment

Formats:

INC *op_1*
mem
reg

Description:

op_1 has 1 added to it and the result is placed back into op_1. All flags except CF are set according to the result.

Operation:

```
op1  = op1  + 1
/* + is as defined by the ADD instruction. */
OF  = Carry0(MSB) ^ Carry0(MSB-1);
SF  = B(MSB, op1 );
ZF  = op1  == 0;
AF  = Carry0(3);
PF  = ~(B(7,op1 ) ^ B(6,op1 ) ^ . . . ^ B(0,op1 ));
CF  = CF;
```

Examples:

```
                                               OSZAPC
INC AX           Before:  AX : 22D9            XXXXXX
                 After :  AX : 22DA            00000U

INC mem32        Before:  mem: 05621340        XXXXXX
                 After :  mem: 05621341        00001U
```

Exception:

```
Memory();
```

Note:

The carry flag *is not* affected by the INC instruction. The ADD instruction with an operand of 1 should be used if carry flag updates are desired.

INS / INSB / INSW / INSD

Input String

Formats:

INSB

INSW

INSD

INS	*mem_1*	,	*reg_2*
	mem8	,	DX
	mem16	,	DX
	mem32	,	DX

Description:

One, two, or four bytes of data (for 8-, 16-, and 32-bit operations) is transferred from the port specified by DX into ES:[EDI]. After the transfer is made, EDI is updated to point to the next string location. EDI is updated by 1, 2, or 4 if DF is 0. If DF is 1, EDI is updated by −1, −2, or −4.

The port to be used must be specified in the DX register. Immediate-port specifications are not allowed.

Note that the memory location is always specified by ES:[EDI]. No segment override is possible with INS. The mem_1 indication is used for operand length indication only.

INS can be preceded by the REP prefix. In this case ECX bytes, words, or dwords are transferred. The REP instruction describes this in more detail.

An exception is raised if the current task has insufficient privilege to perform I/O. See Chapter 5 for further details of privilege levels.

Operation:

```
if (OPCODE == INSB){
     ES:[EDI] = (byte) port(DX);
     delta = 1;
} else if (OPCODE == INSW) {
     ES:[EDI] = (word) port(DX);
     delta = 2;
```

```
} else if (OPCODE == INSD) {
     ES:[EDI] = (dword) port(DX);
     delta = 4;
} else {          /* INS */
     ES:[EDI] = (Length(mem1)) port(DX);
     delta = Length(mem1) / 8;
}
if (DF == 1) {
     delta = - delta ;
}
EDI = EDI + delta;
```


Examples:

```
INSD    Before: EDI      : 00000052  ES:[EDI]   : XXXXXXXX
                DX       :     004C  DF         : 0
                port(DX): FFFFD832
        After : EDI      : 00000056  ES:[EDI-4]: FFFFD832
                DX       :     004C  DF         : 0
                port(DX): FFFFD832

REP INS S1, DX; S1 is a 16-bit string
            Before: EDI         : 0374  ES:[EDI]   : XXXX
                    ES:[EDI-2]: XXXX  ES:[EDI-4]: XXXX
                    DX          : 4220  DF         : 1
                    port(DX,1): 6000  port(DX,2): 0455
                    port(DX,3): 6001  ECX        : 2
            After : DI          : 0370  ES:[EDI+4]: 6000
                    ES:[EDI+2]: 0455  ES:[EDI]   : XXXX
                    DX          : 4220  DF         : 1
                    port(DX,1): 6000  port(DX,2): 0455
                    port(DX,3): 6001  ECX        : 0
```

Exceptions:

```
Memory();
AccessIO();
```

Jcc

Conditional Jump Instructions

Formats:

Jcc near_label

Where the condition code is one of the following:

Mnemonics	Condition Codes	Description
JB/JNAE/JC	CF==1	Jump below/not above or equal/carry
JBE/JNA	CF==1 || ZF==1	Jump below or equal/not above
JCXZ	CX==0	Jump CX == 0
JE/JZ	ZF==1	Jump equal/zero
JECXZ	ECX==0	Jump ECX == 0
JL/JNGE	SF! =OF	Jump less/not greater or equal
JLE/JNG	SF! =OF || ZF==1	Jump less or equal/not greater
JNB/JAE/JNC	CF==0	Jump not below/above or equal/not carry
JNBE/JA	CF==0 && ZF==0	Jump not below or equal/above
JNE/JNZ	ZF==0	Jump not equal/not zero
JNL/JGE	SF==OF	Jump not less/greater or equal
JNLE/JG	ZF==0 && SF==OF	Jump not less or equal/greater
JNO	OF==0	Jump no overflow
JNP/JPO	PF==0	Jump not parity/parity odd

JNS	SF==0	Jump not sign
JO	OF==1	Jump overflow
JP/JPE	PF==1	Jump parity/parity even
JS	SF==1	Jump sign

Note that *less* and *greater* refer to signed integer comparisons, while *above* and *below* refer to unsigned integer comparisons.

Integer

Description:

The flags are tested for the conditions described above. If the flags meet the conditions stated above, the control transfer occurs to the specified label within the current code segment (the jump destination must be within the same segment). Otherwise, execution continues with the next sequential instruction.

The flags are assumed to have been set in some meaningful way by an instruction preceding it (not necessarily the instruction immediately prior to this one, however).

Multiple mnemonics are provided by the assembler allowing convenient interpretations of the flags. For instance, JA (jump above) and JNBE (jump not below or equal) are synonymous. The assembler conveniently allows both.

Operation:

```
if (ConditionCode) {
     EIP   = Offset(near_label); /* † */
}
/*
     † The near label is assembled into an immediate offset,
     which is relative to the current instruction pointer.
     Thus, a machine description of the EIP update would be:
          EIP = EIP + imm;
     The immediate offset can be 8 or 32 bits.
*/
```

Examples:

```
                                          OSZAPC
JO   near_label1    ; label1 is 68h bytes forward in the program
             Before:  EIP : 00000300      1XXXXX
             After :  EIP : 00000368      UUUUUU

JAE  near_label1    ; label1 is 537h bytes backward in the program
             Before:  EIP : 00000300      XXXXX1
             After :  EIP : 00000300      UUUUUU
       ; The next instruction would then be fetched, the EIP
       ; updated and the next instruction executed.
```

Exception:

```
CodeReference();
```

Notes:

See example 10, page 424.

JMP

Jump

Formats:

JMP *op1*
near_label
reg32
mem32

Description:

The jump instruction causes instruction execution to continue at the given offset within the current code segment.

Intrasegment jump offsets can be specified by a near label, a reg32, or a mem32. The near-label operand form specifies a direct jump to the given label. The reg32 and mem32 operand forms are indirect jumps, where the jump offset is taken from the specified register or memory location.

Note that no return information is stored for a JMP instruction as it is for a CALL instruction.

Operation:

```
if (op1 is near_label){
     EIP   = Offset(near_label); /* † */
} else if (op1 is reg32){
     EIP   = reg32;
} else if (op1 is mem32){
     EIP   = mem32;
}
/*
     † The near label is assembled into an immediate offset,
     which is relative to the current instruction pointer.
     Thus, a machine description of the EIP update would be:
          EIP = EIP + imm;
     The immediate offset can be 8 or 32 bits.
*/
```

Examples:

```
JMP   near_label1     ; label1 is 42h bytes forward in the program
              Before:  EIP : 300
              After :  EIP : 342

JMP CASETABLE[EAX*4]  ; CASETABLE is a jump table, EAX*4 gives an
                      ; index into this table that is jumped to.
              Before:  EIP : 5022AC
                       CASETABLE[EAX*4]: 60AA40
              After :  EIP : 60AA40
```

Exceptions:

```
Memory();
CodeReference();
```

Notes:

See also the multiple-segment form of the JMP instruction.

See example 2, page 407.

LAHF

Load Flags into AH Register

Format:

LAHF

Description:

The low byte of the flags word is transferred into AH. The flags in descending order from high bit to low bit are: sign, zero, value 0, auxiliary carry, value 0, parity, value 1, and carry. The following picture shows the low 8 flag bits of the EFLAGS register.

7	6	5	4	3	2	1	0
S F	Z F	0	A F	0	P F	1	C F

Operation:

```
AH = (EFLAGS & 0FFh);
```

Example:

```
                                            OSZAPC
LAHF         Before:  AH : XXXXXXXXb        X01110
             After :  AH : 01010110b        U01110
```

Exceptions:

None.

LEA

Load Effective Address

Formats:

LEA	op_1	,	op_2
	reg32	,	mem
	reg16	,	mem

Description:

The offset part of the address (not the value at that address) of op_2 is computed and placed into op_1. op_2 must be a memory specification. op_1 is always a register. If a 16-bit register is specified, the low-order 16 bits of the offset are stored into the specified register (this is not very useful!).

The memory address is formed per the guidelines in Chapter 2.

Operation:

```
op1 = &op2 ;
```

Examples:

```
LEA AX, [EBP+20h]        Before:   AX: XXXX       EBP: FFFA0246
                         After :   AX: 0266       EBP: FFFA0246

LEA ECX, [EAX*2+14Ch]    Before:  EAX: 0548901A   ECX: XXXXXXXX
                         After :  EAX: 0548901A   ECX: 0A912180
```

Exceptions:

None.

Notes:

LEA is useful for address arithmetic, such as computing the offset of a multidimensional array. It is also a versatile arithmetic instruction. It performs a general three-address register add:

$$r1 = r2 + r3 + \text{constant}$$

The address scaling (described in Chapter 2) can be used to compute small multipliers.

LEAVE

Procedure Exit

Format:

LEAVE

Description:

LEAVE removes the stack frame that was created by a corresponding ENTER instruction. The stack space is released by ESP being assigned the value of EBP (the frame pointer). The old frame pointer (seen on the top of the stack following the assignment of ESP to EBP) is popped into EBP to set up the frame pointer for the calling procedure.

Normally, a RET instruction is used to complete the control transfer back to the calling procedure. The RET follows the back-link and removes any parameters that were pushed onto the stack for the procedure that is now exiting.

Operation:

```
ESP   = EBP;
EBP   = Pop();
```

Example:

```
LEAVE        Before: EBP : 00000F00   SS:[EBP]    : 0000F38
                     ESP : 00000EB4
             After : EBP : 00000F38
                     ESP : 00000F04
```

Exception:

```
Stack();
```

Note:

See example 3a, page 409.

LOCK

Bus Lock

Format:

LOCK *instruction*

Description:

The LOCK# pin is asserted for the duration of the specified instruction to ensure that an indivisible read/modify/write operation takes place. When there are multiple processors on the bus, this signal is important to ensure indivisible access to the bus and any memory attached to the bus during sensitive operations. An example of such an operation is whenever a semaphore is being updated.

LOCK can only be used with the following instructions:

ADC, ADD, AND, BT	mem, reg/imm
BTS, BTR, BTC, OR	mem, reg/imm
SBB, SUB, XOR	mem, reg/imm
XCHG	reg, mem
XCHG	mem, reg
DEC, INC, NEG, NOT	mem

If a LOCK is specified with any instruction not in this list, an invalid opcode exception (described in Chapter 6) is raised.

Operation:

```
LOCK# = 0;
instruction;
LOCK# = 1;
```

Example:

```
;The LOCK# pin is asserted when BTS is executed.
LOCK BTS dword ptr [ESI],ECX
```

Exceptions:

```
InvalidOpcode();
```

Memory( ) exceptions may be generated by the instruction being locked.

Notes:

The list of lockable instructions on the 80386 is different from that of prior 86 family members. See Appendix A.

See example 4, page 412.

LODS / LODSB / LODSW / LODSD

Load String

Formats:

LODSB

LODSW

LODSD

LODS *mem₁*
mem8
mem16
mem32

Description:

One, two, or four bytes of data (for 8-, 16-, and 32-bit operations) is transferred from [ESI] into the AL, AX, or EAX register. After the transfer, ESI is updated to point to the next string location. ESI is updated by 1, 2, or 4 if DF is 0. If DF is 1, ESI is updated by −1, −2, or −4.

mem_1 specifies the length of the operand. The actual transfer is always done with the address specified in the ESI register. A segment override prefix can, however, be specified in mem_1, which is applied to [ESI].

Operation:

```
if (OPCODE == LODSB){
     AL = (byte) DS:[ESI];
     delta = 1;
} else if (OPCODE == LODSW){
     AX = (word) DS:[ESI];
     delta = 2;
} else if (OPCODE == LODSD){
     EAX = (dword) DS:[ESI];
     delta = 4;
} else {        /* LODS */
     /* Note that default of SegReg(mem1) == DS */
     if (Length(mem1) == 8){
          AL = SegReg(mem1):[ESI];
          delta = 1;
```

```
        } else if (Length(mem1) == 16){
            AX = SegReg(mem1):[ESI];
            delta = 2;
        } else if (Length(mem1) == 32){
            EAX = SegReg(mem1):[ESI];
            delta = 4;
        }
    }
    if (DF == 1) {
        delta = - delta ;
    }
    ESI = ESI + delta;
```


Example:

```
LODSB       Before: ESI   : 00000052  SS:[ESI]   : BF
                    AL    : XX        DF         : 0
            After : ESI   : 00000053  SS:[ESI-1]: BF
                    AL    : BF        DF         : 0
```

Exception:

```
Memory();
```

Note:

See examples 6a and 6b, pages 415 and 418.

LOOP

Loop with ECX Counter

Formats:

LOOP short_label

Description:

The ECX register is decremented without affecting flags. If the value in ECX after being decremented is not 0, control is transferred to the location specified by short label. If the ECX register is 0, the instruction following the LOOP instruction is next executed. A short label is within +127 bytes and −128 bytes of the LOOP instruction (the offset is −128 to 127 bytes from the current EIP).

Operation:

```
ECX = ECX - 1;      /* No flags are altered */
if (ECX != 0){
     EIP = short_label; /* † */
}
/*
     † The short label form is assembled into a simple
     8b immediate offset. This offset is relative to the
     current instruction pointer, which points to the next
     sequential instruction. Thus, a machine description
     of the EIP update would be:
          EIP = EIP + SignEx(32, 8, imm8)
*/
```

Example:

```
LOOP    near_label1     ; label1 is 4Eh bytes backward in the program
         Before:  EIP: 000DE300  ECX: 00000002
         After :  EIP: 000DE2B2  ECX: 00000001
LOOP    near_label1     ; label1 is 4Eh bytes backward in the program
         Before:  EIP: 000DE300  ECX: 00000001
         After :  EIP: 000DE300  ECX: 00000000 ; Execute next
                                              ; sequential instruction
```

Exception:

```
CodeReference();
```

Notes:

The LOOP instruction should be placed at the bottom of the loop, and the short label should be placed at the top.

See example 2, page 407.

LOOPNZ / LOOPNE

Loop with ECX and Not Zero / Loop with ECX and Not Equal

Formats:

LOOPNZ short_label

LOOPNE short_label

Description:

The ECX register is decremented without affecting flags. If the value in ECX after being decremented is not zero and the ZF bit is clear, control is transferred to the location specified by short label. If the ECX register is 0 or the ZF bit is set, the instruction following the LOOPNE or LOOPNZ instruction is next executed. A short label is within +127 bytes and −128 bytes of the LOOPNZ/LOOPNE instruction (the offset is −128 to 127 bytes from the current EIP).

Operation:

```
ECX = ECX - 1;     /* no flags are altered */
if ((ZF==0) && (ECX != 0)){
     EIP = short_label;   /* † */
}
/*
     † The short label form is assembled into a simple
     8b immediate offset. This offset is relative to the
     current instruction pointer, which points to the next
     sequential instruction. Thus, a machine description
     of the EIP update would be:
          EIP = EIP + SignEx(32, 8, imm8);
/*
```

Examples:

```
                                                          OSZAPC
LOOPNE   near_label2    ; label2 is 4Eh bytes backward in the program
          Before:  EIP: 000DE300  ECX: 00000008   XX1XXX
          After :  EIP: 000DE300  ECX: 00000007   UU1UUU
                   ; next sequential instruction is executed

LOOPNZ   near_label3    ; label3 is 3Ch bytes backward in the program
          Before:  EIP: 000C8300  ECX: 00000002   XX0XXX
          After :  EIP: 000C82C4  ECX: 00000001   UU0UUU
```

Exception:

```
CodeReference();
```

Notes:

LOOPNE and LOOPNZ are synonymous.

The LOOPNE/LOOPNZ instruction should be placed at the bottom of the loop, and the short label should be placed at thc top.

See example 11, page 428.

LOOPZ / LOOPE

Loop with ECX and Zero / Loop with ECX and Equal

Formats:

LOOPZ short_label

LOOPE short_label

Description:

The ECX register is decremented without affecting flags. If the value in ECX after being decremented is not zero and the ZF bit is set, control is transferred to the location specified by short label. If the ECX register is 0 or the ZF bit is clear, the instruction following the LOOPE or LOOPZ instruction is next executed. A short label is within +127 bytes and −128 bytes of the LOOPZ/LOOPE instruction (the offset is −128 to +127 bytes from the current EIP).

Operation:

```
ECX = ECX - 1;          /* no flags are altered */
if ((ZF==1) && (ECX != 0)){
     EIP = short_label; /* † */
}
/*
  †  The short label form is assembled into a simple
  8b immediate offset. This offset is relative to the
  current instruction pointer, which points to the next
  sequential instruction. Thus, a machine description
  of the EIP update would be:
      EIP = EIP + SignEx(32, 8, imm8);
/*
```

Examples:

```
                                                     OSZAPC
LOOPE   near label2     ; label1 is 4Eh bytes backward in the program
         Before:  EIP: 000DE300  ECX: 00000001    XX0XXX
         After :  EIP: 000DE300  ECX: 00000000    UU0UUU
                  ; The next sequential instruction is executed

LOOPZ   near label3     ; label3 is 3Ch bytes backward in the program
         Before:  EIP: 000C8300  ECX: 00000002    XX1XXX
         After :  EIP: 000C82C4  ECX: 00000001    UU1UUU
```

Exception:

```
CodeReference();
```

Notes:

LOOPE and LOOPZ are synonymous.

The LOOPE/LOOPZ instruction should be placed at the bottom of the loop, and the short label should be placed at the top.

MOV

Move

Formats:

MOV	op_1	,	op_2
	reg	,	reg
	reg	,	mem
	mem	,	reg
	reg	,	imm
	mem	,	imm

Description:

The contents of op_2 are copied into op_1. op_1 and op_2 can be a byte, word, or dword.

Operation:

```
op₁ = op₂;
```

Examples:

```
MOV AX, 0A80h        Before: AX : XXXX
                     After : AX : 0A80

MOV EAX, mem32       Before: EAX: XXXXXXXX mem: 0892ABDF
                     After : EAX: 0892ABDF mem: 0892ABDF

MOV mem8, AL         Before: AL : 4A       mem: XX
                     After : AL : 4A       mem: 4A
```

Exception:

```
Memory();
```

MOVS / MOVSB / MOVSW / MOVSD

Move String

Formats:

MOVSB

MOVSW

MOVSD

MOVS	*mem_1*	,	*mem_2*
	mem8	,	mem8
	mem16	,	mem16
	mem32	,	mem32

Description:

MOVS moves the byte, word, or dword specified by [ESI] into ES:[EDI]. The ESI and EDI registers are updated to point to the next element of the string. These registers are updated based upon the direction flag (DF) and the length of the operands (8, 16, or 32 bits) as indicated by mem_1 and mem_2 or the OPCODE itself (MOVSB, MOVSW, or MOVSD). If the DF bit is 0, the registers are updated by 1, 2, or 4. If the DF bit is 1, the registers are updated by -1, -2, or -4.

The MOVS operation may be preceded by the REP prefix. If preceded by REP, the MOVS instruction is repeated ECX times. Thus, a string of length ECX bytes, words, or dwords is moved from [ESI] to DS:[EDI].

The specification of mem_1 and mem_2 is used by the assembler to determine the length of the operation, and a possible segment override for mem_2. The strings are always taken from [ESI] and moved to ES:[EDI]. MOVS may include a segment override prefix, which affects the segment offset used for mem_2 ([ESI]). mem_1 always comes from ES:[EDI].

Operation:

```
if (OPCODE == MOVSB){
     delta = 1;
     ES:[EDI] = (byte) DS:[ESI];
} else if (OPCODE == MOVSW){
     delta = 2;
     ES:[EDI] = (word) DS:[ESI];
} else if (OPCODE == MOVSD){
     delta = 4;
     ES:[EDI] = (dword) DS:[ESI];
} else {                  /* MOVS */
     /* Note that the default for SegReg(mem2) is DS */
     delta = Length(mem1) ;
     ES:[EDI] = SegReg(mem2):[ESI];
}
if (DF == 1) {
     delta = - delta;
}
ESI = ESI + delta;
EDI = EDI + delta;
```

Examples:

```
MOVSD     Before: ESI      : 06533A40  EDI        : 07822CD4
                  [ESI]    : FFFFFFFF  ES:[EDI]   : XXXXXXXX
                  DF       : 0
          After : ESI      : 06533A44  EDI        : 07822CD8
                  [ESI-4]: FFFFFFFF    ES:[EDI-4]: FFFFFFFF
                  DF       : 0

REP MOVSD
         Before: ESI          : 00000008  EDI     : 00000010
                 ECX          : 00000002  [ESI]   : 01324567
                 ES:[EDI]     : XXXXXXXX  [ESI-4]: F421890A
                 ES:[EDI-4]: XXXXXXXX     DF      : 1
         After : ESI          : 00000000  EDI     : 00000008
                 ECX          : 00000000  [ESI+8]: 01324567
                 ES:[EDI+8]: 01324567     [ESI+4]: F421890A
                 ES:[EDI+4]: F421890A     DF      : 1
```

Exception:

```
Memory();
```

Note:

See example 1, page 618.

MOVSX

Move and Sign Extend

Formats:

MOVSX	*op₁*	,	*op₂*
	reg16	,	reg8
	reg16	,	mem8
	reg16	,	reg16
	reg16	,	mem16
	reg32	,	reg8
	reg32	,	mem8
	reg32	,	reg16
	reg32	,	mem16

Description:

The word or dword op_1 is updated with the sign-extended byte or word op_2. If op_1 and op_2 are both words, a normal move occurs.

Operation:

```
if (Length(op1) == 16){
     if (Length(op2) == 8){
          op1 = SignEx(16, 8, op2);
     } else {
          op1 = op2 ;    /* A normal move! */
     }
} else {                  /* Length(op1) == 32 */
     if (Length(op2) == 8){
          op1 = SignEx(32, 8, op2);
     } else {
          op1 = SignEx(32, 16, op2);
     }
}
```

Examples:

```
MOVSX AX, BH          Before:  AX: XXXX   BH: 9E
                      After :  AX: FF9E   BH: 9E

MOVSX EDX, mem16      Before:  EDX: XXXXXXXX  mem: 742D
                      After :  EDX: 0000742D  mem: 742D
```

Exception:

```
Memory();
```

Note:

This instruction is new to the 80386.

MOVZX

Move and Zero Extend

Formats:

MOVZX	op_1	,	op_2
	reg16	,	reg8
	reg16	,	mem8
	reg16	,	reg16
	reg16	,	mem16
	reg32	,	reg8
	reg32	,	mem8
	reg32	,	reg16
	reg32	,	mem16

Description:

The word or dword op_1 is updated with the zero-extended byte or word op_2. If op_1 and op_2 are both words, a normal move occurs!

Operation:

```
if (Length(op1) == 16){
     if (Length(op2) == 8){
          op1 = ConCat(16, 00h, 8, op2);
     } else {
          op1 = op2 ;    /* A normal move! */
     }
} else {                /* Length(op1) == 32 */
     if (Length(op2) == 8){
          op1 = ConCat(32, 000000h, 8, op2);
     } else {
          op1 = ConCat(32, 0000h, 16, op2);
     }
}
```

Examples:

```
MOVZX AX, BH           Before:  AX: XXXX  BH: 9E
                       After :  AX: 009E  BH: 9E

MOVZX EDX, mem16       Before:  EDX: XXXXXXXX  mem: 742D
                       After :  EDX: 0000742D  mem: 742D
```

Exception:

```
Memory();
```

Note:

This instruction is new to the 80386.

MUL

Unsigned Multiplication

Formats:

MUL *op₁*
reg
mem

Description:

The MUL instruction takes only one operand; the second is always implicit. op_1 is multiplied by the AL, AX, or EAX registers for 8-, 16-, or 32-bit operations, respectively. The 16-, 32-, or 64-bit unsigned result is stored into AX, DX:AX, or EDX:EAX, respectively. If AH, DX, or EDX is all 0s for 8-, 16-, or 32-bit operations, respectively, CF and OF are set to 0. Otherwise they are set to 1.

Operation:

```
if (Length(op1) == 8){
     AX = AL * op1;
     if (AH == 00h){
          CF = 0; OF = 0;
     } else {
          CF = 1; OF = 1;
     }
} else if (Length(op1) == 16){
     DX = (AX * op1) >> 16;
     AX = FFFFh & (AX * op1);
     if (DX == 0000h){
          CF = 0; OF = 0;
     } else {
          CF = 1; OF = 1;
     }
} else {      /* Length(op1) == 32 */
     EDX = (EAX * op1) >> 32;
     EAX = FFFFFFFFh & (EAX * op1);
     if (EDX == 00000000h){
          CF = 0; OF = 0;
     } else {
          CF = 1; OF = 1;
     }
}
SF = ZF = AF = PF = UNDEFINED;
/* * is defined as unsigned multiplication. */
```

Examples:

```
                                                                  OSZAPC
MUL BX      Before:  DX: XXXX  AX: 229A  BX : A431               XXXXXX
            After :  DX: 1631  AX: 477A  BX : A431               1XXXX1

MUL mem8    Before:  AH: XX    AL: 0A    mem: 12                 XXXXXX
            After :  AH: 00    AL: B4    mem: 12                 0XXXX0
```

Exception:

```
Memory();
```

NEG

Negate

Integer

Formats:

NEG *op₁*
mem
reg

Description:

NEG forms the two's complement of the given operand. op_1 is subtracted from 0, with the result placed into op_1.

The carry flag is set to 1 except when op_1 (the value of op_1 prior to the NEG instruction) was 0.

Operation:

```
CF  = op1 != 0;
op1 = 0 - op1;
/* - is defined as it is for the SUB instruction. */

OF  = Carry0(MSB) ^ Carry0(MSB-1);
SF  = B(MSB, op1);
ZF  = op1 == 0;
AF  = Carry0(3);
PF  = ~(B(7,op1) ^ B(6,op1) ^ ... ^ B(0,op1));
```

Examples:

```
                                             OSZAPC
NEG EAX        Before:  EAX: 01234567       XXXXXX
               After :  EAX: FEDCBA99       010111

NEG mem8       Before:  Mem: 00             XXXXXX
               After :  Mem: 00             001010
```

Exception:

```
Memory();
```

NOP

No Operation

Format:

NOP

Description:

NOP does nothing. The only effect this instruction has is altering the address of the next instruction to be executed.

Operation:

```
;
```

Example:

```
NOP      ; Nothing occurs
```

Exceptions:

None.

Notes:

NOP is useful for timing loops (it uses 3 clocks) and to align labels. Aligning labels to four-byte boundaries can speed execution, especially in code that is executed often, such as loops.

NOT

Not

Integer

Formats:

NOT *op_1*
reg
mem

Description:

A logical NOT or a one's complement is performed on op_1. The result is left in op_1. The flags are unaffected.

Operation:

```
op1 = ~op1;
/*
 ~ is defined on a bitwise basis in the table below.
 ai is the ith bit of op1. ri is the ith result bit.
 The bit variable i takes on values from 0 to MSB.
 ai | ri
 ---+---
 0  | 1
 1  | 0
*/
```

Examples:

```
NOT EAX          Before:  EAX: 01234567
                 After :  EAX: FEDCBA98

NOT mem8         Before:  mem: 72
                 After :  mem: 8D
```

Exception:

```
Memory();
```

OR

Inclusive Or

Formats:

OR	op_1	,	op_2
	reg	,	reg
	reg	,	mem
	reg	,	imm
	mem	,	reg
	mem	,	imm

Description:

A logical inclusive OR is performed between op_1 and op_2. The result is left in op_1.

Operation:

```
op1  = op1 | op2 ;
OF   = 0;
SF   = B(MSB, op1);
ZF   = op1 == 0;
AF   = UNDEFINED;
PF   = ~(B(7,op1) ^ B(6,op1) ^ ... ^ B(0,op1));
CF   = 0;
/*
  | is defined on a bitwise basis in the table below.
  ai,bi are the ith bits of op1 and op2, respectively.
  ri is the ith result bit.
  The bit variable i takes on values from 0 to MSB.
  ai  bi | ri
  -----------
  0   0  | 0
  0   1  | 1
  1   0  | 1
  1   1  | 1
/*
```

Examples:

```
                                                                    OSZAPC
OR EAX, EBX          Before:  EAX: 01234567  EBX: 76543210  XXXXXX
                     After :  EAX: 77777777  EBX: 76543210  000X10

OR mem16, 7878h      Before:  Mem: 1F90                      XXXXXX
                     After :  Mem: 7FF8                      000X00

OR AL, 0FFh          Before:  AL : A2                        XXXXXX
                     After :  AL : FF                        010X10
```


Exception:

```
Memory();
```

OUT

Write to Port

Formats:

OUT	op_1	,	op_2
	imm8	,	AL
	imm8	,	AX
	imm8	,	EAX
	DX	,	AL
	DX	,	AX
	DX	,	EAX

Description:

The OUT instruction transfers a data byte, word, or dword from AL, AX, or EAX to the specified port.

The port may be specified via an immediate byte allowing ports 0 to 255 to be accessed; the upper bits of the port address are always 0 in this case. The port may also be specified by placing the port number into the DX register. This allows the full range of ports (0 to 64K — 1) to be accessed.

Note that I/O port addresses 00F8 through 00FF have been reserved by Intel.

Operation:

```
port(op1) = op2 ;
```

Examples:

```
OUT 0C3h, AX     Before:  AX: 1C9B    port(00C3): XXXX
                 After :  AX: 1C9B    port(00C3): 1C9B

OUT DX, EAX      Before:  EAX: 96238887  DX: 4684
                          port(4684)       : XXXXXXXX
                 After :  EAX: 96238887  DX: 4684
                          port(4684)       : 96238887
```

Exception:

```
AccessIO();
```

OUTS / OUTSB / OUTSW / OUTSD

Output String

Formats:

OUTSB
OUTSW
OUTSD

OUTS	*reg_1*	,	*mem_2*
	DX	,	mem8
	DX	,	mem16
	DX	,	mem32

Description:

One, two, or four bytes of data (for 8-, 16-, and 32-bit operations), as indicated by mem_2 or by the OPCODE itself (OUTSB, OUTSW, or OUTSD), is transferred from memory at [ESI] to the port specified by DX. After the transfer is made, ESI is updated to point to the next string location. ESI is updated by 1, 2, or 4 if DF is 0. If DF is 1, ESI is updated by −1, −2 or −4.

The port to be used must be specified in the DX register. Immediate port specifications are not allowed.

mem_2 specifies the length of the operand. The actual transfer is always done with the address specified in the ESI register. A segment override can, however, be specified in mem_2 and applied to [ESI].

OUTS can be preceded by the REP prefix. In this case, ECX bytes, words, or dwords are transferred. The REP instruction describes this in more detail.

Operation:

```
if (OPCODE == OUTSB){
     port(DX) = (byte) DS:[ESI];
     delta = 1;
```

```
} else if (OPCODE == OUTSW){
     port(DX) = (word) DS:[ESI];
     delta = 2;
} else if (OPCODE == OUTSD){
     port(DX) = (dword) DS:[ESI];
     delta = 4;
} else {          /* OUTS */
     /* Note that default of SegReg(mem2) == DS */
     if (Length(mem2) == 8){
          port(DX) = (byte) SegReg(mem2):[ESI];
          delta = 1;
     } else if (Length(mem2) == 16){
          port(DX) = (word) SegReg(mem2):[ESI];
          delta = 2;
     } else if (Length(mem2) == 32){
          port(DX) = (dword) SegReg(mem2):[ESI];
          delta = 4;
     }
}
if (DF == 1) {
     delta = - delta ;
}
ESI = ESI + delta;
```

Examples:

```
OUTSW     Before: ESI       : 6240  [ESI]     : FFF6
                  DX        : 004C  DF        : 0
                  port(DX)  : XXXX
          After : ESI       : 6244  [ESI-4]   : FFF6
                  DX        : 004C  DF        : 0
                  port(DX)  : FFF6

REP OUTS DX, S1     ; S1 is a byte string
          Before: ESI : 00000040    [ESI]       : F2
                  [ESI+1]    : FF   [ESI+2]     : 00
                  DX         : 20   DF          : 0
                  port(DX)   : XX   CX          : 3
          After : ESI  : 00000043   [ESI-3]     : F2
                  [ESI-2]    : FF   [ESI-1]     : 00
                  DX         : 20   DF          : 0
                  port(DX,1) : F2   port(DX,2)  : FF
                  port(DX,3) : 00   CX          : 0
```

Exceptions:

```
Memory();
AccessIO();
```

POP

Pop off Stack

Formats:

POP *op₁*
mem16
reg16
mem32
reg32

Description:

POP moves a word or dword from the top of the stack into op_1. The top of stack is pointed to by SS:[ESP]. After the data transfer from the stack to op_1, the stack pointer is adjusted by adding 2 or 4 for 16- or 32-bit operand lengths, respectively.

Operation:

```
if (Length(op1) == 32){
      op1 = SS:[ESP];
      ESP = ESP + 4;
} else {
      op1 = SS:[ESP];
      ESP = ESP + 2;
}
```

Example:

```
POP AX      Before:  AX: XXXX  SS:[ESP]  : F340  ESP: F4320530
            After :  AX: F430  SS:[ESP-2]: F340  ESP: F4320532
```

Exceptions:

```
Memory();
Stack();
```

Note:

Be careful when popping 16-bit operands to avoid misaligning the stack, which causes performance degradations!

POPA / POPAD

Pop All off Stack

Formats:

POPA

POPAD

Description:

POPA/POPAD moves eight words or dwords from the top of the stack into the eight general-purpose registers. Thus, POPA/POPAD eliminates the need for eight consecutive POP instructions. The order of the registers popped is: DI, SI, BP, SP, BX, DX, CX, and AX for word (POPA); or EDI, ESI, EBP, ESP, EBX, EDX, ECX, and EAX for dword (POPAD).

Note that the value popped for ESP is discarded.

Operation:

```
if (OPCODE == POPAD){
      EDI = SS:[ESP+0];
      ESI = SS:[ESP+4];
      EBP = SS:[ESP+8];
      tmp = SS:[ESP+12];   /* Value for ESP is discarded */
      EBX = SS:[ESP+16];
      EDX = SS:[ESP+20];
      ECX = SS:[ESP+24];
      EAX = SS:[ESP+28];
      ESP = ESP + 32;
} else {
      DI  = SS:[ESP+0];
      SI  = SS:[ESP+2];
      BP  = SS:[ESP+4];
      tmp = SS:[ESP+6];   /* Value for SP is discarded */
      BX  = SS:[ESP+8];
      DX  = SS:[ESP+10];
      CX  = SS:[ESP+12];
      AX  = SS:[ESP+14];
      ESP = ESP + 16;
}
```

Example:

```
                                                                          OSZAPC
POPA     Before:  AX: XXXX   BX: XXXX   CX: XXXX   DX: XXXX    XXXXXX
                  SP: 7236   BP: XXXX   SI: XXXX   DI: XXXX
                  SS:[07236]: 42FF   SS:[07238]: AA2C
                  SS:[0723A]: B290   SS:[0723C]: 8861
                  SS:[0723E]: 0000   SS:[07240]: 0002
                  SS:[07242]: FFFF   SS:[07244]: 2133
         After :  AX: 2133   BX: FFFF   CX: 0002   DX: 0000    UUUUUU
                  SP: 7246   BP: B290   SI: AA2C   DI: 42FF
                  SS:[07236]: 42FF   SS:[07238]: AA2C
                  SS:[0723A]: B290   SS:[0723C]: 8861
                  SS:[0723E]: 0000   SS:[07240]: 0002
                  SS:[07242]: FFFF   SS:[07244]: 2133
```


Exception:

```
Stack();
```

POPF / POPFD

Pop from Stack into Flags

Formats:

POPF

POPFD

Description:

What is currently on the top of the stack is copied into the 32-bit flag register. After the transfer is complete, the stack pointer is incremented by 2 or 4 (16- or 32-bit operation) to point to the new top of stack.

The following figure shows the 32-bit flag word.

31	30	...	19	18	17	16	15	14	13	12	11	10	9	8	7	6	5	4	3	2	1	0
					V	R		N	IOP		O	D	I	T	S	Z		A		P		C
0	0	...	0	0	M	F	0	T	L		F	F	F	F	F	F	0	F	0	F	1	F

POPF only alters the low 16 bits of the flag word.

The I/O privilege level flag will only be altered if the current privilege level is 0. If you are not at level 0, the I/O privilege level flags will not be altered and no exception will result.

If the current privilege level is as privileged or more privileged than the current I/O privilege level, the interrupt enable flag will be altered. If not, the interrupt enable flag will be unchanged and no exception will result.

Operation:

```
RF = 0;
NT = ([ESP] & 00004000h) >> 14;
if (CPL == 00b){
     IOPL = ([ESP] & 00003000h) >> 12;
}
OF = ([ESP] & 00000800h) >> 11;
DF = ([ESP] & 00000400h) >> 10;
if (CPL <= IOPL){
     IF   = ([ESP] & 00000200h) >> 9;
}
```

```
TF = ([ESP] & 00000100h) >> 8;
SF = ([ESP] & 00000080h) >> 7;
ZF = ([ESP] & 00000040h) >> 6;
AF = ([ESP] & 00000010h) >> 4;
PF = ([ESP] & 00000004h) >> 2;
CF = ([ESP] & 00000001h) >> 0;
if (OPCODE == POPFD){
     ESP  = ESP + 4;
} else {
     ESP  = ESP + 2;
}
```


Example:

```
                                                                 II
                                                                 OO
                                                               VRNPPODITSZ A P C
                                                               MFTLLFFFFFF0F0F1F
POPFD ; The privilege level is 0
        Before:  ESP: 20143110 [ESP]: FFF601A5   0XXXXXXXXXXX0X0X1X
        After :  ESP: 20143114                   U0000000110000111
```

Exception:

```
Stack();
```

PUSH

Push onto Stack

Formats:

PUSH op_1
imm
mem
reg

Description:

op_1 is placed in the new top-of-stack position. The new top of stack is formed by decrementing the stack pointer ESP by 2 or 4 for 16- or 32-bit data, respectively. Immediate data is always considered to be 32 bits in size, although it may be encoded in the instruction as an 8-bit signed immediate, as was discussed in Chapter 2.

Operation:

```
if (Length(op1) == 32){
      SS:[ESP - 4] = op1;
      ESP = ESP - 4;
} else {       /* Length(op1) == 16 */
      SS:[ESP - 2] = op1;
      ESP = ESP - 2;
}
```

Examples:

```
PUSH 24h      Before:  ESP: FFFFF320   SS:[FFFFF31C]:  XXXXXXXX
              After :  ESP: FFFFF31C   SS:[FFFFF31C]:  00000024

PUSH AX       Before:  ESP: FFFFF31C   SS:[FFFFF31A]:      XXXX
                       AX : F799
              After :  ESP: FFFFF31A   SS:[FFFFF31A]:      F799
                       AX : F799
```

Exceptions:

```
Stack();
Memory();
```

Note:

Be careful when pushing 16-bit operands to avoid misaligning the stack, which causes performance degradations!

PUSHA / PUSHAD

Push All onto Stack

Formats:

PUSHA

PUSHAD

Description:

PUSHA/PUSHAD copies the eight word or dword registers onto the top of the stack. Thus, PUSHA/PUSHAD eliminates the need for eight consecutive PUSH instructions. The order of the registers pushed is: AX, CX, DX, BX, SP, BP, SI, and DI for word; or EAX, ECX, EDX, EBX, ESP, EBP, ESI, and EDI for dword.

Note that the value pushed for SP or ESP is the original value.

The order of the registers pushed by PUSHA is correct for a subsequent POPA.

Operation:

```
if (OPCODE == PUSHAD ){
      SS:[ESP-4]  = EAX;
      SS:[ESP-8]  = ECX;
      SS:[ESP-12] = EDX;
      SS:[ESP-16] = EBX;
      SS:[ESP-20] = ESP;     /* Note: original value of ESP */
      SS:[ESP-24] = EBP;
      SS:[ESP-28] = ESI;
      SS:[ESP-32] = EDI;
      ESP = ESP - 32;
} else {
      SS:[ESP-2]  = AX;
      SS:[ESP-4]  = CX;
      SS:[ESP-6]  = DX;
      SS:[ESP-8]  = BX;
      SS:[ESP-10] = SP;     /* Note: original value of SP */
      SS:[ESP-12] = BP;
      SS:[ESP-14] = SI;
      SS:[ESP-16] = DI;
      ESP = ESP - 16;
}
```

Example:

```
                                                             OSZAPC
PUSHA   Before:  AX: 0000  BX: 1111  CX: 2222  DX: 3333     XXXXXX
                 SP: 4444  BP: 5555  SI: 6666  DI: 7777
                 SS:[04442]: XXXX  SS:[04440]: XXXX
                 SS:[0443E]: XXXX  SS:[0443C]: XXXX
                 SS:[0443A]: XXXX  SS:[04438]: XXXX
                 SS:[04436]: XXXX  SS:[04434]: XXXX
        After :  AX: 0000  BX: 1111  CX: 2222  DX: 3333     UUUUUU
                 SP: 4434  BP: 5555  SI: 6666  DI: 7777
                 SS:[04442]: 0000  SS:[04440]: 1111
                 SS:[0443E]: 2222  SS:[0443C]: 3333
                 SS:[0443A]: 4444  SS:[04438]: 5555
                 SS:[04436]: 6666  SS:[04434]: 7777
```


Exception:

```
Stack();
```

PUSHF / PUSHFD

Push Flags onto Stack

Formats:

PUSHF

PUSHFD

Description:

The stack pointer is decremented by 2 or 4 (for a 16- or 32-bit flag word, respectively) to form the new top of stack. What is currently in the 16- or 32-bit flag register is copied into this new top of stack.

The following picture depicts the EFLAGS register.

31	30	...	19	18	17	16	15	14	13 12	11	10	9	8	7	6	5	4	3	2	1	0
0	0	...	0	0	VM	RF	0	NT	IOPL	OF	DF	IF	TF	SF	ZF	0	AF	0	PF	1	CF

Operation:

```
if (PUSHF){
    ESP = ESP - 2 ;
    SS: [ESP] =            (0    <<15)  |  (NT <<14)  |
          (IOPL <<12)  |  (OF <<11)  |  (DF <<10)  |  (IF << 9)  |
          (SF   << 7)  |  (ZF << 6)  |  (0   << 5)  |  (AF << 4)  |
          (0    << 3)  |  (PF << 2)  |  (1   << 1)  |  (CF << 0)  ;
} else {      /* PUSHFD */
    ESP = ESP - 4 ;
    SS: [ESP] = (0000h <<16)         |  (0   <<15)  |  (NT <<14)  |
          (IOPL <<12)  |  (OF <<11)  |  (DF <<10)  |  (IF << 9)  |
          (SF   << 7)  |  (ZF << 6)  |  (0   << 5)  |  (AF << 4)  |
          (0    << 3)  |  (PF << 2)  |  (1   << 1)  |  (CF << 0)  ;
}
```

Example:

```
                                                              II
                                                              OO
                                                            VRNPPODITSZ A P C
                                                            MFTLLFFFFFF0F0F1F
   PUSHFD
       Before:   [ESP-4]:  XXXXXXXX   ESP:  FFF42104  00100011011000011
       After :   [ESP]   :  000046C3   ESP:  FFF42100  00100011011000011
```

Exception:

```
   Stack();
```

Note:

See example 1, page 622.

RCL

Rotate through Carry Left

Formats:

RCL	op_1	,	op_2
	reg	,	imm8
	mem	,	imm8
	reg	,	CL
	mem	,	CL

Description:

The rotate count is specified in op_2. This count is masked to 5 bits (0–31). This 5-bit quantity is taken modulus the operand length plus 1 to form the rotate count.

The rotate is performed with op_1 and the carry flag as part of the rotated quantity. Thus, a 33-, 17-, or 9-bit quantity is being rotated for the dword, word, and byte quantities, respectively, by the adjusted rotate count.

The rotate instruction can be thought of as rotate-count left shifts, with the high-order bit being shifted into the carry and the carry filling in the least significant bit.

If the rotate count is 1, the overflow flag is set to 0 if the resulting carry flag (after this RCL instruction occurs) equals the high bit of the result. Otherwise it is set to 1. If the rotate count is not 1, the overflow flag is undefined.

Operation:

```
if (Length(op1) == 8){
     cnt = (op2 & 01Fh) % 9;
     if(cnt>0){
          temp = (op1 << cnt )          |
                 (CF  << (cnt - 1))     |
                 (op1 >> (9 - cnt));
           CF =  (op1  >> (8 - cnt)) & 01;
           op1 = temp;
     }
} else if (Length(op1) == 16){
     cnt = (op2 & 01Fh) % 17;
     if (cnt>0){
          temp = (op1 << cnt )          |
                 (CF  << (cnt - 1)      |
                 (op1 >> (17 - cnt));
           CF =  (op1 >> (16 - cnt)) & 01;
           op1 = temp;
     }
} else {        /* Length(op1) == 32 */
     cnt = op2 & 01Fh;
     if (cnt>0){
          temp = (op1 << cnt )          |
               (CF  << (cnt - 1))       |
               (op1 >> (33 - cnt));
           CF = (op1  >> (32 - cnt)) & 01;
           op1 = temp;
     }
}
if (op2 == 1){
     OF = B(MSB,op1) ^ CF;
} else {
     OF = UNDEFINED;
}
```

Examples:

				OSZAPC
RCL EAX,1	Before:	EAX: 01234567		XXXXX1
	After :	EAX: 02468ACF		0UUUU0
RCL mem8,CL	Before:	mem: 9B	CL: 11	XXXXX0
	After :	mem: 4D	CL: 11	XUUUU1

Exception:

```
Memory();
```

Notes:

Rotates with count equal to 0 do not alter the carry flag!

RCL of 32 or 33 bits (for dword) cannot be done, since only a count of 0 to 31 can be specified.

RCR

Rotate through Carry Right

Formats:

RCR	op_1	,	op_2
	reg	,	imm8
	mem	,	imm8
	reg	,	CL
	mem	,	CL

Description:

The rotate count is specified in op_2. This count is masked to 5 bits (0–31). This 5-bit quantity is taken modulus the operand length plus 1 to form the rotate count.

The rotate is performed with op_1 and the carry flag as part of the rotated quantity. Thus, a 33-, 17-, or 9-bit quantity is being rotated for the dword, word, and byte quantities, respectively, by the masked and modulus rotate count.

The rotate instruction can be thought of as rotate-count right shifts, with the low-order bit being shifted into the carry and the carry filling in the most significant bit.

If the rotate count is 1, the overflow flag is set to 0 if the two high-order bits of the result are equal. Otherwise it is set to 1. If the rotate count is not 1, the overflow flag is undefined.

Operation:

```
if (op2 == 1){
      OF = B(MSB, op1) ^ CF;
} else {
      OF = UNDEFINED;
}
if (Length(op1) == 8){
      cnt = (op2 & 01Fh) % 9;
      if(cnt>0){
            temp = (op1 >> cnt )       |
                   (CF << (8 - cnt     |
                   (op1 << (9 - cnt)) ;
             CF =  (op1 >> (cnt - 1)) & 01;
             op1 = temp;
      }
} else if (Length(op1) == 16){
      cnt = (op2 & 01Fh) % 17;
      if(cnt>0){
            temp = (op1 >> cnt )       |
                   (CF << (16 - cnt))  |
                   (op1 << (17 - cnt)) ;
             CF =  (op1 >> (cnt - 1)) & 01;
             op1 = temp;
      }
} else {         /* Length(op1) == 32 */
      cnt = op2 & 01Fh;
      if(cnt>0){
            temp = (op1 >> cnt )       |
                   (CF << (32 - cnt))  |
                   (op1 << (33 - cnt)) ;
             CF =  (op1 >> (cnt - 1)) & 01;
             op1 = temp;
      }
}
```

Examples:

			OSZAPC
RCR mem32,1	Before:	mem: 01234567	XXXXX0
	After :	mem: 0091A2B3	1UUUU1
RCR EDI,CL	Before:	EDI: A3214551 CL: 11	XXXXX0
	After :	EDI: 45515190 CL: 11	XUUUU1

Exception:

```
Memory();
```

Notes:

Rotates with count equal to 0 do not alter the carry flag!

RCR of 32 or 33 bits (for dword) cannot be done, since only a count of 0 to 31 can be specified.

REP

Repeat

Formats:

REP *String_Operation*
INS
MOVS
OUTS
STOS

Description:

REP is a prefix that causes the string operation following it to be repeated ECX times.

Operation:

```
while (ECX != 0) {
     ECX = ECX - 1;
     String_Operation;
}
OF, SF, ZF, AF, PF, CF  = As defined by String_Operation
```

Examples:

```
REP MOVSD
     Before: ESI        : 00000008  EDI     : 00000008
             ECX        : 00000002  [ESI]   : 01324567
             ES: [EDI]  : XXXXXXXX  [ESI-4]: F421890A
             ES: [EDI-4]: XXXXXXXX  DF      : 1
     After : ESI        : 00000000  EDI     : 00000010
             ECX        : 00000000  [ESI+8]: 01324567
             ES: [EDI+8]: 01324567  [ESI+4]: F421890A
             ES: [EDI+4]: F421890A  DF      : 1
```

Exceptions:

None as a result of REP, but String_Operation may cause an exception.

REPE / REPZ

Repeat While Equal / Repeat While Zero

Formats:

REPE/REPZ *String_Operation*
CMPS
SCAS

Description:

REPE is a prefix that causes the string operation following it to be repeated ECX times or until the ZF bit becomes 0. REPZ is synonymous with REPE.

Operation:

```
while (ECX != 0) {
     ECX = ECX - 1;
     String_Operation;
     if (ZF==0) break;
}
OF, SF, ZF, AF, PF, CF   = As defined by String_Operation
```

Examples:

```
REPE CMPSB
      Before: ESI : 00000008  EDI         : 16  ECX         : 04
              [ESI]      : 01  [ESI+1]     : 23  [ESI+2]     : 45
              [ESI+3]    : 67  ES: [EDI]   : 01  ES: [EDI+1]: 23
              ES: [EDI+2]: 44  ES: [EDI+3]: 67  DF          : 0
      After : ESI : 0000000B  EDI         : 19  ECX         : 01
              [ESI-3]    : 01  [ESI-2]     : 23  [ESI-1]     : 45
              [ESI]      : 67  ES: [EDI-3]: 01  ES: [EDI-2]: 23
              ES: [EDI-1]: 44  ES: [EDI]   : 67  DF          : 0
```

Exceptions:

None as a result of REPE/REPZ, but String_Operation may cause an exception.

Note:

See example 5, page 413.

REPNE / REPNZ

Repeat While Not Equal / Repeat While Not Zero

Formats:

REPNE/REPNZ *String_Operation*
CMPS
SCAS

Description:

REPNE is a prefix that causes the string operation following it to be repeated ECX times or until the ZF bit becomes 1. REPNZ is synonymous with REPNE.

Operation:

```
while (ECX != 0) {
      ECX = ECX - 1;
      String_Operation;
      if (ZF==1) break;
}
OF, SF, ZF, AF, PF, CF  = As defined by String_Operation
```

Examples:

```
REPNE CMPSB
    Before: ESI : 00000008  EDI         : 16  ECX         : 04
            [ESI]       : 01  [ESI+1]     : 23  [ESI+2]     : 45
            [ESI+3]     : 67  ES:[EDI]    : 01  ES:[EDI+1]: 23
            ES:[EDI+2]: 44  [EDI+3]     : 67  DF          : 0
    After : ESI : 00000009  EDI         : 17  ECX         : 03
            [ESI-1]     : 01  [ESI]       : 23  [ESI+1]     : 45
            [ESI+2]     : 67  ES:[EDI-1]: 01  ES:[EDI]    : 23
            ES:[EDI+1]: 44  ES:[EDI+2]: 67  DF          : 0
```

Exceptions:

None as a result of REPNE/REPNZ, but String_Operation may cause an exception.

Note:

See example 5, page 413.

RET

Return

Formats:

NEAR RET
RET imm16

Description:

RET causes instruction execution to resume at the instruction following a corresponding CALL instruction. The RET instruction uses the return address found upon the top of the stack to decide where to return. In other words, RET performs an indirect jump through the pointer at the top of the stack. On the top of the stack, the EIP value to be used is found.

An optional imm16 value can be specified. This value is added to the ESP value. This is useful when you want to remove several bytes of parameters from the stack.

Operation:

```
EIP    = Pop();
if (NUMOPS == 1) {
     ESP = ESP + imm16;
}
```

Examples:

```
RET       Before:  EIP: 804231AA   SS:[ESP]    : 032BBD4C
                   ESP: 04260988
          After :  EIP: 032BBD4C
                   ESP: 0426098C
```

Exceptions:

```
Stack();
CodeReference();
```

ROL

Rotate Left

Formats:

ROL	op_1	,	op_2
	reg	,	imm8
	mem	,	imm8
	reg	,	CL
	mem	,	CL

Description:

The rotate count is specified in op_2. This count is masked to 5 bits. Thus, rotates of 0 to 31 bits are performed.

The rotate is performed upon op_1 with the result being stored back into op_1.

The rotate instruction can be thought of as rotate-count left shifts, with the high-order bit being shifted into the least significant bit and the carry at each shift iteration. Thus, the final carry reflects the least significant bit of the result.

If the rotate count is 1, the overflow flag is set to 0 if the carry flag (after this ROL instruction occurs) equals the high bit of op_1 (the result). Otherwise it is set to 1. If the rotate count is not 1, the overflow flag is undefined.

Operation:

```
if (Length(op1) == 8){
      cnt = op2 % 8;
      if(cnt>0){
            op1 = (op1 << cnt ) |
                  (op1 >> (8 - cnt));
            CF = B(0, op1);
      }
} else if (Length(op1) == 16){
      cnt = op2 % 16;
      if(cnt>0){
            op1 = (op1 << cnt )    |
                  (op1 >> (16 - cnt));
            CF = B(0, op1);
      }
```

```
} else {        /* Length(op1) == 32) */
    cnt = op2 % 32;
    if(cnt>0){
        op1 = (op1 << cnt )      |
              (op1 >> (32 - cnt));
        CF = B(0, op1);
    }
}
if (op2 == 1){
    OF = (MSB,op1) ^ CF;
} else {
    OF = UNDEFINED;
}
```


Examples:

```
                                                  OSZAPC
ROL AL,1       Before:  AL: A6                    XXXXXX
               After :  AL: 4D                    1UUUU1

ROL BP,CL      Before:  BP: 6279   CL: 0A         XXXXXX
               After :  BP: E589   CL: 0A         XUUUU1
```

Exception:

```
Memory();
```

Note:

ROL with rotate count equal to 0 does not alter the carry or overflow flag!

ROR

Rotate Right

Formats:

ROR	op_1	,	op_2
	reg	,	imm8
	mem	,	imm8
	reg	,	CL
	mem	,	CL

Description:

The rotate count is specified in op_2. This count is masked to 5 bits. Thus, rotates of 0 to 31 bits are performed.

The rotate is performed upon op_1 with the result being stored back into op_1.

The rotate instruction can be thought of as rotate-count right shifts, with the low-order bit being shifted into the most significant bit and the carry at each shift iteration. Thus, the final carry reflects the most significant bit of the result.

If the rotate count is 1, the overflow flag is set to 0 if the top 2 bits of the result (op_1) are equal. Otherwise it is set to 1. If the rotate count is not 1, the overflow is undefined.

Operation:

```
if (Length(op1) == 8){
        cnt = op2 % 8;
        if(cnt>0){
                op1 = (op1 >> cnt )    |
                      (op1 << (8 - cnt));
                CF = B(7, op1);
        }
} else if (Length(op1) == 16){
        cnt = op2 % 16;
        if(cnt>0){
                op1 = (op1 >> cnt )     |
                      (op1 << (16 - cnt));
                CF = B(15, op1);
        }
} else {        /* Length(op1) == 32  */
        cnt = op2 % 32;
        if(cnt>0){
                op1 = (op1 >> cnt )      |
                     (op1 << (32 - cnt));
                CF = B(31, op1);
        }
```

```
} else {          /* Length(op1) == 32 */
     cnt = op2 % 32;
     if(cnt>0){
          op1 = (op1 >> cnt )      |
               (op1 << (32 - cnt));
          CF = B(31, op1);
     }
}
if (op2 == 1){
     OF = (MSB,op1) ^ (MSB-1,op1);
} else {
     OF = UNDEFINED;
}
```


Examples:

		OSZAPC
ROR mem16,1	Before: mem: E4A2	XXXXXX
	After : mem: 7251	1UUUU0
ROR EDI,7	Before: EDI: 07BDAF21	XXXXXX
	After : EDI: 420F7B5E	XUUUU0

Exception:

```
Memory();
```

Note:

Rotates with rotate count equal to 0 do not alter the carry or overflow flags!

SAHF

Store AH Register into Flags

Formats:

SAHF

Description:

AH is transferred into the low byte of the flags word. Bits 7, 6, 4, 2, and 0 of the AH register are loaded into the sign, zero, auxiliary carry, parity, and carry flags, respectively. The following figure depicts the low 8 bits of the EFLAGS register:

7	6	5	4	3	2	1	0
SF	ZF	0	AF	0	PF	1	CF

Operation:

```
SF = (AH & 80h) >> 7;
ZF = (AH & 40h) >> 6;
AF = (AH & 10h) >> 4;
PF = (AH & 04h) >> 2;
CF = (AH & 01h) >> 0;
```

Examples:

```
                                              OSZAPC
SAHF          Before:  AH : 10X1X0X0b         XXXXXX
              After :  AH : 10X1X0X0b         U10100
```

Exceptions:

None.

Note:

See example 7, page 421.

SAL / SHL

Shift Arithmetic Left / Shift Logical Left

Formats:

SAL/SHL	*op1*	,	*op2*
	reg	,	imm8
	mem	,	imm8
	reg	,	CL
	mem	,	CL

Description:

The shift count is specified in op_2. This count is masked to 5 bits. Thus, shifts of 0 to 31 bits are performed.

The shift is performed upon op_1 with the result being stored back into op_1. op_1 is shifted left shift-count times with the low-order bits being filled with 0s. The carry flag becomes the value of what is being shifted out of the most significant bit.

If the shift count is 1, the overflow flag is set to 0 if the carry flag (after this SAL/SHL instruction occurs) equals the high bit of op_1 (the result). Otherwise it is set to 1. If the shift count is not 1, the overflow flag is undefined.

Note that SAL and SHL are synonyms; arithmetic and logical left shifts are the same.

Operation:

```
cnt = op2 & 01Fh;
if(cnt < Length(op1)){
     if (cnt > 0){
          CF = B((Length(op1) - cnt), op1);
     }
     op1 = op1 << cnt;
} else {
     CF = 0;
     op1 = 0;
}
```

```
if (op2 == 1){
     OF = (MSB, op1 ) ^ CF;
} else {
     OF = UNDEFINED;
}
SF  = B(MSB, op1 );
ZF  = op1  == 0;
AF  = UNDEFINED;
PF  = ~(B(7, op1 ) ^ B(6, op1 ) ^ . . . ^ B(0, op1 ));
```

Examples:

```
                                                          OSZAPC
SAL BX,1         Before:  BX:  ADF3                       XXXXXX
                 After :  BX:  5BE6                       100X01

SHL mem32,CL     Before:  mem:  A6341209   CL:  09        XXXXXX
                 After :  mem:  68241200   CL:  09        X00X10
```

Exception:

```
Memory();
```

Note:

Shifts of zero do not alter the flags!

SAR

Shift Arithmetic Right

Formats:

SAR	op_1	,	op_2
	reg	,	imm8
	mem	,	imm8
	reg	,	CL
	mem	,	CL

Description:

The shift count is specified in op_2. This count is masked to 5 bits. Thus, shifts of 0 to 31 bits are performed.

The shift is performed upon op_1 with the result being stored back into op_1. op_1 is shifted right shift-count times, with the high-order bits being filled with the sign bit (most significant bit) of op_1. The carry flag becomes the value of what is being shifted out of the least significant bit.

If the shift count is 1, the overflow flag is set to 0. Otherwise it is unchanged.

Another way to look at this is that op_1 is being divided by 2, shift-count times. The divide in this case rounds to negative infinity, which is different than IDIV for negative numbers.

Operation:

```
cnt = op1 & 01Fh;
if (cnt > 0){
     CF = B(cnt, op1);
}
if (cnt < Length(op1){
     if(Length(op1) == 8){
          if(B(7,op1) == 1){
               op1 = (op1 >> cnt) | (FFh << (8-cnt));
          } else {
               op1 = (op1 >> cnt);
          }

     } else if(Length(op1) == 16){
          if(B(15,op1) == 1){
               op1 = (op1 >> cnt) | (FFFFh << (16-cnt));
```

```
                } else {
                        op1 = (op1 >> cnt);
                }
        } else {                /* Length(op1) == 32) */
                if (B(31,op1) == 1){
                        op1 = (op1 >> cnt) | (FFFFFFFFh << (32-cnt));
                } else {
                        op1 = (op1 >> cnt);
                }
        }
} else {
        if (B(Length(op1),op1) == 1){
                CF = 1;
                if (Length(op1) == 8){
                        op1 = FFh;
                } else {                /* must be 16 */
                        op1 = FFFFh;
                }
        } else {
                CF = 0;
                if (Length(op1) == 8){
                        op1 = 00h;
                } else {                /* must be 16 */
                        op1 = 0000h;
                }
        }
}
if (op2 == 1){
        OF = 0;
} else {
        OF = OF;
}
SF  = B(MSB,op1);
ZF  = op1 == 0;
AF  = UNDEFINED;
PF  = ~(B(7,op1) ^B(6,op1) ^... ^B(0,op1));
```

Examples:

```
                                                                OSZAPC
SAR mem8,1      Before:  mem: 84                                XXXXXX
                After :  mem: C2                                010X00

SAR EDI,CL      Before:  EDI: A6341209    CL: 13                XXXXXX
                After :  EDI: FFFFF4C6    CL: 13                X10X11
```

Exception:

```
Memory();
```

Notes:

Shifts of zero do not alter the flags!

SAR can be used to perform a fast divide by powers of two for unsigned integers. See example 1, page 406, for an example of this.

SBB

Subtract with Borrow

Formats:

SBB	op_1	,	op_2
	reg	,	reg
	reg	,	mem
	reg	,	imm
	mem	,	reg
	mem	,	imm

Description:

op_2 plus carry is subtracted from op_1, with the result being placed into op_1. The carry flag (borrow flag) indicates a borrow into the subtraction. This is equivalent to

```
op1 = op2 - (op2 + CF);
```

The SBB instruction is used as part of a multiple byte, word, or dword subtraction.

Operation:

```
op1 = op1 - (op2 + CF);
OF  = Borrow0(MSB) ^ Borrow0(MSB-1);
SF  = B(MSB, op1);
ZF  = op1 == 0;
AF  = Borrow0(3);
PF  = ~(B(7,op1) ^ B(6,op1) ^ ... ^ B(0,op1));
CF  = Borrow0(MSB);
/*
  - is defined on a bitwise basis in the table below.
  xi,yi are the ith bits of op1 and op2. bi-1 is
  the borrow out of the i-1 bit (this is the same as the
  borrow into the ith bit). ri is the ith result bit
  and bi is the borrow out of the ith bit.  The bit
  variable i takes on values from 0 to MSB. bi for
  i-1 == -1 is CF (the borrow flag) for SBB.
```

```
    xi yi bi-1 | ri bi
    ------------------
    0  0  0    | 0  0
    0  0  1    | 1  1
    0  1  0    | 1  1
    0  1  1    | 0  1
    1  0  0    | 1  0
    1  0  1    | 0  0
    1  1  0    | 0  0
    1  1  1    | 1  1
    Note that subtraction can also be defined in terms of
    addition. Comparing this to the addition table earlier:
        xi  =  ai
        yi  =  ~bi
        bi  =  ci
    Thus, the carry flag of the 80386 can also be considered
    the borrow flag.
*/
```

Examples:

				OSZAPC
SBB EAX, EBX	Before:	EAX: 0743CE21	EBX: 8D4BC956	XXXXX1
	After :	EAX: 79F804CA	EBX: 8D4BC956	010111
SBB mem8, 1Ah	Before:	mem: 72		XXXXX0
	After :	mem: 58		000100

Exception:

```
Memory();
```

► SCAS / SCASB / SCASW / SCASD

Scan String

Formats:

SCASB

SCASW

SCASD

SCAS *mem₁*
mem8
mem16
mem32

Description:

SCAS subtracts ES:[EDI] from AL, AX, or EAX for byte, word, or dword operations. The result of the subtraction is not stored, only the flags are modified. The EDI register is updated to point to the next element of the string, based upon the direction flag (DF) and the length of the operands (8, 16, or 32 bits) as indicated by mem_1 or by the OPCODE itself (SCASB, SCASW, or SCANSD). If the DF flag is 0, EDI is updated by 1, 2, or 4. If the DF flag is 1, EDI is updated by -1, -2, or -4.

The SCAS operation may be preceded by REPE (REPZ) or REPNE (REPNZ). If preceded by REPE, the SCAS instruction is repeated while ECX is not 0 and the string elements are equal to AL, AX, or EAX (ZF==1). If preceded by REPNE, the SCAS instruction is repeated while ECX is not 0 and the string element is not equal to AL, AX, or EAX (ZF==0). In this way, SCAS is useful to find the first mismatch (REPE) or match (REPNE) to AL, AX, or EAX in the string if they exist. Refer to REPE and REPNE for details of the prefixes.

The specification of mem_1, if it is present, is used by the assembler to determine the length of the operation only. The string is always taken from ES:[EDI]. No segment override is possible for SCAS.

Operation:

```
if ((Length(mem1) == 8) || (OPCODE == SCANSB)){
     delta = 1;
     temp = AL - (byte) ES:[EDI];
} else if ((Length(mem1) == 16) || (OPCODE == SCANSW)){
     delta = 2;
     temp = AX - (word) ES:[EDI];
} else { /*(Length(mem1) == 32) || (OPCODE == SCANSD)*/
     delta = 4;
     temp = EAX - (dword) ES:[EDI];
}
/* - is as defined for the SUB instruction. */
OF  = Borrow0(MSB) ^ Borrow0(MSB-1);
SF  = B(MSB, temp);
ZF  = temp == 0;
AF  = Borrow0(3);
PF  = ~(B(7,temp) ^ B(6,temp) ^ . . . ^ B(0,temp));
CF  = Borrow0(MSB);
if (DF == 1) {
     delta = - delta ;
}
EDI = EDI + delta;
```

Examples:

```
                                                                    OSZAPC
SCASW
      Before:  AX  : 0123  EDI : 0016  ES:[EDI]   : 3210          XXXXXX
               DF  : 0
      After :  AX  : 0123  EDI : 0018  ES:[EDI-2]: 3210           010001
               DF  : 0

REPNE SCAS S1   ; Note that S1 is a byte string
  Before: EDI        : 0008  AL          : 72  ES:[EDI]   : 23  XXXXXX
          ES:[EDI-1]: 23     ES:[EDI-2]: 72    ES:[EDI-3]: AA
          DF         : 0     ECX : 00000008
  After : EDI        : 0005  AL          : 72  ES:[EDI+3]: 23   001010
          ES:[EDI+2]: 23     ES:[EDI+1]: 72    ES:[EDI]   : AA
          DF         : 0     ECX : 00000005
```

Exception:

```
Memory();
```

Note:

See example 5, page 413.

SETcc

Byte Set on Condition Code

Formats:

SETcc *op₁*
reg8
mem8

Where the condition code is one of of the following:

Mnemonics	Condition Codes	Description
SETB/SETNAE/ SETC	CF==1	Set byte below/not above or equal/carry
SETBE/SETNA	CF==1 || ZF==1	Set byte below or equal/not above
SETE/SETZ	ZF==1	Set byte equal/zero
SETL/SETNGE	SF!=OF	Set byte less/not greater or equal
SETLE/SETNG	SF!=OF || ZF==1	Set byte less or equal/not greater
SETNB/SETAE/ SETNC	CF==0	Set byte not below/ above or equal/ not carry
SETNBE/SETA	CF==0 && ZF==0	Set byte not below or equal/above
SETNE/SETNZ	ZF==0	Set byte not equal/ not zero
SETNL/SETGE	SF==OF	Set byte not less/ greater or equal
SETNLE/SETG	ZF==0 && SF==OF	Set byte not less or equal/greater
SETNO	OF==0	Set byte no overflow

SETNP/SETPO	PF==0	Set byte not parity/ parity odd
SETNS	SF==0	Set byte not sign
SETO	OF==1	Set byte overflow
SETP/SETPE	PF==1	Set byte parity/ parity even
SETS	SF==1	Set byte sign

Note that *less* and *greater* refer to signed integer comparisons, while *above* and *below* refer to unsigned integer comparisons.

Description:

The flags are tested for the conditions described above. If the flags meet the conditions stated above, op_1 is set to 1. Otherwise op_1 is set to 0.

Note that the only size operand allowed by the SETcc instructions is a byte quantity.

Multiple mnemonics are provided by the assembler allowing convenient interpretations of the flags. For instance, SETA (set byte above) and SETNBE (set byte not below or equal) are synonymous. The assembler conveniently allows both.

Operation:

```
if (ConditionCode) {
     op1 = 1;
} else {
     op1 = 0;
}
```

Examples:

```
                                             OSZAPC
SETNO   mem8      Before: mem8: XX           1XXXXX
                  After : mem8: 00           1UUUUU

SETNBE AL         Before: AL  : XX           XX1XX0
                  After : AL  : 01           UU1UU0
```

Exceptions:

```
Code Reference();
Memory();
```

Note:

This instruction is new to the 80386.

SHLD

Shift Left Double

Formats:

SHLD	op_1	,	op_2	,	op_3
	reg16	,	reg16	,	imm8
	mem16	,	reg16	,	imm8
	reg16	,	reg16	,	CL
	mem16	,	reg16	,	CL
	reg32	,	reg32	,	imm8
	mem32	,	reg32	,	imm8
	reg32	,	reg32	,	CL
	mem32	,	reg32	,	CL

Description:

The shift count is specified in op_3. This count is masked to 5 bits. Thus, shifts of 0 to 31 bits can be performed.

The shift is performed upon op_1:op_2 with the result being stored back into op_1. op_1 is shifted left shift-count times, with the low-order bits being filled from the high-order bits of op_2. The carry flag becomes the value of what is being shifted out of the most significant bit of op_1.

If the shift count is 0, the instruction is equivalent to a NOP. If the shift count is 1, the overflow flag gets set to 1 if the most significant bit of the result does not match the carry flag. Otherwise it is cleared to 0. If a shift count greater than operand length is specified, the flags and result in op_1 are undefined.

Operation:

```
cnt = op3 & 01Fh;
if (cnt == 0) {
     /* nop */
} else if (cnt > Length(op1)){
     op1 = OF = SF = ZF = PF = CF = AF = UNDEFINED;
} else {
```

```
        CF   = B(Length(op1) - cnt,op1);
        op1  = (op1 << cnt) | (op2 >> (Length(op2) - cnt));
        OF   = B(MSB, op1) ^ CF);
        SF   = B(MSB,op1);
        ZF   = op1 == 0;
        PF   = (B(7,op1) ^ B(6,op1) ^ ... ^ B(0,op1));
        AF   = UNDEFINED;
}
```

Examples:

```
                                                             OSZAPC
SHLD mem16,AX,3  Before:  mem: 0084  AX: 00F3                XXXXXX
                 After :  mem: 0420  AX: 00F3                000X00

SHLD DI,SI,CL    Before:  DI : 1209  SI: 8552  CL: 0B        XXXXXX
                 After :  DI : 4C2A  SI: 8552  CL: 0B        000X00
```

Exception:

```
Memory();
```

Notes:

Shifts of zero do not alter the flags!
This instruction is new to the 80386.
See example 6b, page 418.

SHR

Shift Logical Right

Formats:

SHR	op_1	,	op_2
	reg	,	imm8
	mem	,	imm8
	reg	,	CL
	mem	,	CL

Description:

The shift count is specified in op_2. This count is masked to 5 bits. Thus, shifts of 0 to 31 bits are performed.

The shift is performed upon op_1 with the result being stored back into op_1. op_1 is shifted right shift-count times, with the high-order bits being filled with 0s. The carry flag becomes the value of what is being shifted out of the least significant bit.

If the shift count is 1 and the most significant 2 bits of the result are not equal, the overflow flag is set. Otherwise it is cleared to 0. If the shift count is not 1, the overflow flag is undefined.

Operation:

```
cnt = op2 & 01Fh;
if(cnt =< Length(op1)){
     if (cnt > 0){
          CF = B(cnt, op1);
     }
     op1 = op1 >> cnt;
} else {
     op1 = 0;
     CF = 0;
}
if (op2 == 1){
     OF = B(MSB, op1) ^ B(MSB-1, op1);
} else {
     OF = UNDEFINED;
}
```

```
SF  = B(MSB,op1);
ZF  = op1 == 0;
AF  = UNDEFINED;
PF  = ~(B(7,op1) ^ B(6,op1) ^ ... ^ B(0,op1));
```

Examples:

```
                                                            OSZAPC
SHR DX,1          Before:   DX:  84                         XXXXXX
                  After :   DX:  42                         000X10

SHR mem32,CL      Before:   mem:  F42BBD51   CL:  0C        XXXXXX
                  After :   mem:  000F42BB   CL:  0C        X00X11
```

Exception:

```
Memory();
```

Notes:

Shifts of zero do not alter the flags!
See example 6b, page 418.

SHRD

Shift Right Double

Integer

Formats:

SHRD	op_1	,	op_2	,	op_3
	reg16	,	reg16	,	imm8
	mem16	,	reg16	,	imm8
	reg16	,	reg16	,	CL
	mem16	,	reg16	,	CL
	reg32	,	reg32	,	imm8
	mem32	,	reg32	,	imm8
	reg32	,	reg32	,	CL
	mem32	,	reg32	,	CL

Description:

The shift count is specified in op_3. This count is masked to 5 bits. Thus, shifts of 0 to 31 bits are performed.

The shift is performed upon op_1:op_2 with the result being stored back into op_1. op_1 is shifted right shift-count times, with the high-order bits being filled from the low-order bits of op_2. The carry flag becomes the value of what is being shifted out of the least significant bit of op_1.

If the count is 0, the instruction is equivalent to a NOP. The overflow flag gets set to 1 if the 2 most significant bits of the result are not equal. Otherwise it is cleared to 0.

If a shift count greater than operand length is specified in op_3, the flags and result in op_1 are undefined.

Operation:

```
cnt = op3 & 01Fh;
if (cnt == 0) {
     /* nop */
} else if (cnt > Length(op1)){
     op1 = OF = SF = ZF = PF = CF = AF = UNDEFINED;
} else {
```

```
        CF  = B((cnt - 1),op1);
        op1 = (op1 >> cnt) | (op2 << (Length(op2) - cnt));
        OF  = B(MSB,op1) ^ B(MSB-1, op1);
        SF  = B(MSB,op1);
        ZF  = op1 == 0;
        PF  = ~(B(7,op1) ^ B(6,op1) ^ ... ^ B(0,op1));
        AF  = UNDEFINED;
}
```

Examples:

```
                                                          OSZAPC
SHRD mem16,BP,2     Before:  mem: 7AC0  BP: F43D          XXXXXX
                    After :  mem: 5EB0  BP: F43D          100X00
SHRD EAX,mem32,CL   Before:  EAX: 663B982F
                             mem: 9963120A  CL: 0A        XXXXXX
                    After :  EAX: 82998EE6
                             mem: 9963120A  CL: 0A        110X10
```

Exception:

```
Memory();
```

Notes:

Shifts of zero do not alter the flags!
This instruction is new to the 80386.
See example 6b, page 418.

STC

Set Carry Flag

Format:

STC

Description:

The carry flag is set to 1.

Operation:

```
CF = 1;
```

Example:

```
STC            Before:  CF : 0
               After :  CF : 1
```

Exceptions:

None.

STD

Set Direction Flag

Format:

STD

Description:

The direction flag is set to 1. After the direction flag is set to 1, string instructions will decrement their index registers (ESI and EDI).

Operation:

```
DF = 1;
```

Examples:

```
STD             Before:  DF : 0
                After :  DF : 1
```

Exceptions:

None.

STI

Set Interrupt Flag

Format:

STI

Description:

The interrupt enable flag is set to 1. The 80386 will respond to interrupts after the next instruction is executed.

If the current task does not have sufficient privilege to alter the interrupt flag, an undefined opcode fault is generated. Privilege levels are described in more detail in Chapter 5.

Operation:

```
IF = 1;
```

Examples:

```
STI             Before:  IF : 0
                After :  IF : 1
```

Exception:

```
IOPLSensitive();
```

STOS / STOSB / STOSW / STOSD

Store String

Formats:

STOSB

STOSW

STOSD

STOS *mem_1*
mem8
mem16
mem32

Description:

One, two, or four bytes of data (for 8-, 16-, and 32-bit operations) are transferred from the AL, AX, or EAX register into ES:[EDI]. After the transfer is made, EDI is updated to point to the next string location. EDI is updated based upon the direction flag (DF) and the length of the operand (8, 16, 32) as indicated by mem_1 or by the OPCODE itself (STOSB, STOSW, or STOSD). If DF is 0, EDI is updated by 1, 2, or 4. If DF is 1, EDI is updated by −1, −2, or −4.

mem_1 specifies the length of the operand. The actual transfer is always done with the address specified by ES:[EDI]. No segment override is possible.

The STOS instruction can be preceded by a REP prefix. This allows a string to be filled (initialized) with the contents of the AL, AX, or EAX register.

Operation:

```
if ((Length(mem1) == 8) || (OPCODE == STOSB)){
      delta = 1;
      ES:[EDI] = AL;
} else if ((Length(mem1) == 16) || (OPCODE == STOSW)){
      delta = 2;
      ES:[EDI] = AX;
} else { /*Length(mem1) == 32) || (OPCODE == STOSD))*/
      delta = 4;
      ES:[EDI] = EAX;
```

```
}
if (DF == 1) {
    delta = - delta;
}
EDI = EDI + delta;
```

Examples:

```
STOSW      Before: EDI  :  0052   ES:[EDI]   : XXXX
                   AX   :  FFFF   DF         : 0
           After : EDI  :  0054   ES:[EDI-2]: FFFF
                   AX   :  FFFF   DF         : 0
```

Exception:

```
Memory();
```

Note:

See example 1, page 619.

SUB

Subtract

Formats:

SUB	op_1	,	op_2
	reg	,	reg
	reg	,	mem
	reg	,	imm
	mem	,	reg
	mem	,	imm

Description:

op_2 is subtracted from op_1, with the result being placed into op_1.

Operation:

```
op1  = op1 - op2;
OF   = Borrow0(MSB) ^ Borrow0(MSB-1);
SF   = B(MSB, op1);
ZF   = op1 == 0;
AF   = Borrow0(3);
PF   = ~(B(7,op1) ^ B(6,op1) ^ ... ^ B(0,op1));
CF   = Borrow0(MSB);
/*
  - is defined on a bitwise basis in the table below.
  xi and yi are the ith bits of op1 and op2. bi-1 is
  the borrow out of the i-1 bit (this is the same as the
  borrow into the ith bit). ri is the ith result bit
  and bi is the borrow out of the ith bit.  The bit
  variable i takes on values from 0 to MSB. bi for
  i-1 == -1 is 0 for SUB.
  xi yi bi-1 | ri bi
  0  0  0    | 0  0
  0  0  1    | 1  1
  0  1  0    | 1  1
  0  1  1    | 0  1
  1  0  0    | 1  0
  1  0  1    | 0  0
  1  1  0    | 0  0
  1  1  1    | 1  1
```

```
  Note that subtraction can also be defined in terms of
  addition. Comparing this to the addition table earlier:
    xi  =   ai
    yi  =  ~bi
    bi  =   ci
  Thus, the carry flag of the 80386 can also be considered
  the borrow flag.
*/
```

Examples:

				OSZAPC
SUB EAX, EBX	Before:	EAX: 0743CE21	EBX: 8D4BC956	XXXXXX
	After :	EAX: 79F804CB	EBX: 8D4BC956	000101
SUB mem8, 3A	Before:	Mem: 72		XXXXXX
	After :	Mem: 38		000100

Exception:

```
Memory();
```

TEST

Logical Compare

Formats:

TEST	op_1	,	op_2
	reg	,	reg
	reg	,	mem
	reg	,	imm

Description:

A logical AND is performed between op_1 and op_2. The result is not stored. Only the flags are modified.

Operation:

```
temp = op1 & op2;
OF  = 0;
SF  = B(MSB, temp);
ZF  = temp == 0;
AF  = UNDEFINED;
PF  = ~(B(7,temp) ^ B(6,temp) ^ ... ^ B(0,temp));
CF  = 0;
/*
  & is defined on a bitwise basis in the table below.
  ai and bi are the bits of op1 and op2.
  ri is the ith result bit.
  The bit variable i takes on values from 0 to MSB.
  ai  bi | ri
  -----------
  0   0  | 0
  0   1  | 0
  1   0  | 0
  1   1  | 1
*/
```

Examples:

```
                                                                  OSZAPC
TEST EAX, EBX      Before:  EAX: 01234567  EBX: 76543210   XXXXXX
                   After :  EAX: 01234567  EBX: 76543210   001X10

TEST mem8, 75      Before:  Mem: 7F                        XXXXXX
                   After :  Mem: 7F                        000X00
```

Exception:

```
Memory();
```

XCHG

Exchange

Formats:

XCHG	op_1	,	op_2
	reg	,	reg
	mem	,	reg
	reg	,	mem

Description:

The contents of op_2 and op_1 are swapped. op_1 and op_2 can be a byte, word, or dword, but must always be the same length.

If one of op_1 or op_2 is a mem, the bus transfer is always performed as if a LOCK prefix is given (the LOCK# pin is asserted), even if LOCK was not specified. Thus, XCHG is useful for semaphore operations.

Operation:

```
temp = op1 ;
op1  = op2 ;
op2  = temp;
```

Examples:

```
XCHG AX, BX          Before:  AX: 0A8F   BX: 9042
                     After :  AX: 9042   BX: 0A8F

XCHG mem8, AL        Before:  AL: 4A   mem: 0F
                     After :  AL: 0F   mem: 4A
```

Exception:

```
Memory();
```

XLAT / XLATB

Table Lookup Translation

Formats:

XLATB

XLAT mem8

Description:

At the start of the instruction, AL is assumed to be the unsigned index into a table whose base is at [EBX]. XLAT replaces AL with the table entry at [EBX+AL]. AL is always taken as an unsigned value. The table is always based at [EBX] regardless of the mem8. mem8 does, however, allow a segment override to be specified rather than the default DS:[EBX].

Operation:

```
if (OPCODE == XLATB) {
     AL = DS: [EBX + ConCat(000000h,AL)];
} else {
     AL = SegReg(mem8): [EBX + ConCat(000000h,AL)];
}
```

Examples:

```
XLATB    Before: EBX      : F000   AL : 30
                 [EBX+AL]: 7D
         After : EBX      : F000   AL : 7D
```

Exception:

```
Memory();
```

Exclusive Or

Integer

Formats:

XOR	op_1	,	op_2
	reg	,	reg
	reg	,	mem
	reg	,	imm
	mem	,	reg
	mem	,	imm

Description:

A logical exclusive-OR is performed between op_1 and op_2. The result is stored into op_1.

Operation:

```
op1 = op1 ^ op2;
OF  = 0;
SF  = B(MSB, op1);
ZF  = op1 == 0;
AF  = UNDEFINED;
PF  = ~(B(7,op1) ^ B(6,op1) ^ ... ^ B(0,op1));
CF  = 0;
/*
  ^ is defined on a bitwise basis in the table below.
   ai and bi are the ith bits of op1 and op2, respectively.
   ri is the ith result bit. The bit variable i takes on
   values from 0 to MSB.
   ai  bi | ri
   -------+---
   0   0  | 0
   0   1  | 1
   1   0  | 1
   1   1  | 0
*/
```

Examples:

```
                                                                   OSZAPC
XOR EAX, EBX        Before:  EAX: 01234567  EBX: F0F0F0F0  XXXXXX
                    After :  EAX: F1D3B597  EBX: F0F0F0F0  010X00

XOR mem8, 70        Before:  Mem: 7F                       XXXXXX
                    After :  Mem: 0F                       000X10
```

Exception:

```
Memory();
```

▶ Multiple Segment

From the discussion of segmentation in Chapter 2, recall how the operating system can dictate a single-segment programming model (all segments are mapped into a single segment) or the operating system may allow a multiple-segmentation programming model. This choice is up to the programmer. This is true except that interrupt and exception handling always require the systems programmer to use the multiple-segment model. Interrupts and exceptions are described in detail in Chapter 6.

If you have chosen to use multiple segments, this section describes the particular instructions the 80386 includes to support this programming model. If you are not interested in this programming model, you can skip this section of instruction descriptions.

Chapters 5 and 7 describe the use of these instructions in more detail and give some examples of the use of these instructions. As you will see several times in the discussion of these instructions, you are referred to Chapter 5 for more details.

All the instructions in this section deal with the loading of selectors into segment registers. Both selectors and segment registers were described in Chapter 2, where loading a segment selector into a segment register makes the segment addressable. Data within the segment can be referenced with offsets from this segment register (see Chapter 2). The code segment is implicitly referenced on all instruction fetches, and the offset into this segment is given by the EIP register.

Function Definitions

At the beginning of this chapter, we defined several functions that allowed us to use a shorthand notation in instruction description and examples. Below is another routine with a similar purpose. We define it here, as it is used exclusively in this section of the instruction set description.

```
/* The IntExecTable routine returns either the        */
/* Segment or Offset of the interrupt service routine  */
/* that is being called. The actual semantics of       */
/* taking an interrupt are more complicated (gates,    */
/* task switches, and privilege level changes) than    */
/* shown here and are detailed in the interrupt routine*/
/* of Chapter 6. A call to this routine would be:      */
/* Interrupt(imm, 1)                                   */
/* where the second operand indicates that privilege   */
/* level checks need to be done and the first operand  */
/* is the immediate passed on the call to IntTable.    */
```

```
IntExecTable(type, imm){
    if (type==SEGMENT){
        return((word) IDTR.Base + 4);
    } else { /* OFFSET */
        return((dword) IDTR.Base + 0);
    }
}
```

Exception Routines

At the beginning of this chapter, we defined several exception routines allowing us to use a shorthand function call to summarize potential exception conditions. Below are several more exception routines that we did not define at the start of this chapter, since they are particular to the multiple-segment instructions.

```
CodeSegmentLoad(){
    /* All possible segment exceptions while loading a CS   */
    /* descriptor are embodied in the CSDescriptorLoad()    */
    /* routine defined in Chapter 5. Refer to Chapter 5 for */
    /* further details. */
}
SegmentLoad(){
    /* All possible segment exceptions while loading a   */
    /* descriptor are embodied in the DescriptorLoad()   */
    /* routine defined in Chapter 5. Refer to Chapter 5  */
    /* for further details. */
}
```

Instruction Set Summary

The following table summarizes the instructions that are found in this section of the instruction set description.

Multiple-Segment Instructions

CALL	Call procedure
INT	Call to interrupt procedure
INTO	On overflow call interrupt procedure
IRET	Interrupt return
JMP	Jump
LDS	Load pointer to DS
LES	Load pointer to ES
LFS	Load pointer to FS

LGS	Load pointer to GS
LSS	Load pointer to SS
MOV	Move to/from segment register
POP	Pop off stack into segment register
PUSH	Push onto stack
RET	Return

CALL

Call Procedure

Formats:

CALL *op₁*
far_label
mem48

Description:

CALL causes instruction execution to continue at a specified offset within a new code segment. The given pointer (a 48-bit pointer composed of a 16-bit segment selector and a 32-bit offset, as described in Chapter 2) points to a procedure in a different segment (intersegment call).

Before control transfer occurs, a 48-pointer to the next instruction to be executed is placed onto the stack. The pushed information can be used by a subsequent RET instruction.

Note in the description that the EIP value stored on the stack points to the instruction following the CALL. The 80386 fetches an instruction and then increments the instruction pointer prior to execution. Thus EIP can be stored directly, as it points "after" the CALL.

Note that when CS is pushed onto the stack, a full 32-bit word is pushed. This is done by the 80386 to keep the stack aligned (see Chapter 2). The upper 16 bits of this stack location are undefined. Stack alignment improves 80386 performance.

Operation:

```
/* far_label is assembled into a 48-bit pointer,
   composed of a 16-bit code segment selector, which is
   returned by the Segment routine below, and an
   instruction offset from the beginning of the segment,
   which is returned by the Offset routine below.
*/
if (op1 is far_label) { /* † */
    ESP   = ESP - 4 ;
    [ESP] = CS ;
    CS    = Segment(far_label);
    ESP   = ESP - 4 ;
    [ESP] = EIP ;
```

```
    EIP   = Offset(far_label);
} else if (op1 is mem48) { /* † */
    ESP   = ESP - 4 ;
    [ESP] = CS ;
    CS    = [&mem+4];
    ESP   = ESP - 4 ;
    [ESP] = EIP ;
    EIP   = [&mem];
}
/*
  † Since the far call instruction loads the CS
  register, which may cause privilege level transitions,
  gate traversal, and task switching, the exact effect
  may not be as described above. These more complicated
  forms are described in detail in Chapter 5.
*/
```

Example:

```
CALL  FAR label; label = 6320:0F03298A
        Before:  EIP     : 00000300   ESP  : 00000200   CS: 5028
        After :  EIP     : 0F03298A   ESP  : 00000198   CS: 6320
                 [ESP+4]: XXXX5028   [ESP]: 00000300
RET     Before:  EIP     : 0F03298A   ESP  : 00000198   CS: 6320
                 [ESP+4]: XXXX5028   [ESP]: 00000300
        After :  EIP     : 00000300   ESP  : 00000200   CS: 5028
```

Exceptions:

```
Memory();
Stack();
CodeSegmentLoad();
CodeReference();
```

Note:

For more details, see the description on page 533.
See also the intrasegment form of the CALL instruction (page 150).

INT

Call to Interrupt Procedure

Formats:

INT imm8

Description:

An INT instruction is basically a software call to an exception handler. The particular interrupt procedure to be used is specified by imm8. imm8 is the exception number.

The extended flags register, the code segment register, and the instruction pointer are pushed onto the stack. Control is transferred to the exception service routine (handler) for this particular exception number. At the end of the interrupt service processing, an IRET instruction is typically used to transfer control back to the interrupted execution location.

Note that when CS is pushed onto the stack, a full 32-bit word is pushed. This keeps the stack aligned (see Chapter 2). The upper 16 bits of this stack location are undefined. Stack alignment improves 80386 performance.

This instruction can be used as a "call" to the operating system.

Operation:

```
ESP    = ESP - 4;
[ESP]  = EFLAGS;
ESP    = ESP - 4;
[ESP]  = CS;        /* † */
ESP    = ESP - 4;
[ESP]  = EIP;
CS     = IntExecTable(SEGMENT,  imm8);
EIP    = IntExecTable(OFFSET,   imm8);
IF     = 0;
TF     = 0;
NT     = 0;
/*
  † Since the INT instruction loads the CS
  register, which may cause privilege level transitions,
  gate traversal, and task switching, the exact effect
  may not be as described above. These more complicated
  forms are described in detail in Chapters 5 and 6.
*/
```

Examples:

```
INT 5    Before: ESP    : FFFFF388  EIP    : 0000FA04
                 EFLAGS: 00004302  CS     :     F244
                 IntExecTable(SEGMENT, 5):     0400
                 IntExecTable(OFFSET , 5): 004AFDDC
         After : ESP    : FFFFF37C  EIP    : 004AFDDC
                 EFLAGS: 00000002  CS     :     0400
                [ESP+8]: 00004302 [ESP+4]: XXXXF244
                [ESP]  : 0000FA04
```

Exceptions:

```
Stack();
CodeSegmentLoad();
CodeReference();
```

Note:

The INT 3 instruction is a special single-byte form (the breakpoint instruction), which is useful for debugging. See Chapter 8 for details.

INTO

On Overflow Call Interrupt Procedure

Format:

INTO

Description:

An INTO instruction is basically a conditional software call to interrupt procedure 4. The call to exception handler 4 occurs if the overflow flag is set.

The extended flags register, the code segment register, and the instruction pointer are pushed onto the stack. Control is transferred to the interrupt service routine for the specified interrupt level. At the end of the interrupt service processing, an IRET instruction is typically used to transfer control back to the interrupting execution location.

Note that when CS is pushed onto the stack, a full 32-bit word is pushed. This keeps the stack aligned (see Chapter 2). The upper 16 bits of this stack location are undefined. Stack alignment improves 80386 performance.

Operation:

```
if (OF==0){      /* † */
     ESP    = ESP - 4;
     [ESP]  = EFLAGS;
     ESP    = ESP - 4;
     [ESP]  = CS;
     ESP    = ESP - 4;
     [ESP]  = EIP;
     CS     = IntExecTable(SEGMENT,  4);
     EIP    = IntExecTable(OFFSET,   4);
     IF     = 0;
     TF     = 0;
     NT     = 0;
}
/*
  † Since the INTO instruction loads the CS
  register, which may cause privilege level transitions,
  gate traversal, and task switching, the exact effect
  may not be as described above. These more complicated
  forms are described in detail in Chapters 5 and 6.
*/
```

Examples:

```
INTO    Before: ESP     : FFFFF388  EIP     : 0F822DDB    OSZAPC
                EFLAGS  : 00006FA7  CS      :     0008
                IntExecTable(SEGMENT, 4)    :     4A00
                IntExecTable(OFFSET , 4)    : 004AFDDC
        After : ESP     : FFFFF37C  EIP     : 004AFDDC    1UUUUU
                EFLAGS  : 00002CA7  CS      :     4A00
                [ESP+8] : 00006FA7  [ESP+4] : XXXX0008
                [ESP]   : 0F822DDB
```

Exceptions:

```
Stack();
CodeSegmentLoad();
CodeReference();
```

Interrupt Return

Format:

IRET

Description:

An IRET reverses the effect of an interrupt procedure entry. The EIP, CS, and EFLAGS registers are popped from the stack, and control resumes at the point the interrupt was taken. IRET is thus used at the end of an interrupt service routine to return control to the point of interrupt.

Note that when CS is popped off the stack, a full 32-bit word is popped. This is for stack alignment (see Chapter 2). The upper 16 bits of this stack location are discarded. Stack alignment improves 80386 performance.

Operation:

```
EIP    = [ESP];
ESP    = ESP + 4;
CS     = [ESP]; /* † */
ESP    = ESP + 4;
EFLAGS = [ESP];
ESP    = ESP + 4;
/*
  † Since the IRET instruction loads the CS
  register, which may cause privilege level transitions,
  gate traversal, and task switching, the exact effect
  may not be as described above. These more complicated
  forms are described in detail in Chapters 5 and 6.
*/
```

Examples:

```
IRET     Before: ESP      : FFFFF37C  EIP      : 004B0245
                 EFLAGS   : 00000002  CS       : 0400
                 [ESP+8]  : 00004302  [ESP+4]  : XXXXF244
                 [ESP]    : 0000FA04
         After : ESP      : FFFFF388  EIP      : 0000FA04
                 EFLAGS   : 00004302  CS       :     F244
```

Exceptions:

```
Stack();
CodeSegmentLoad();
CodeReference();
```

Note:

See example 1 on page 622. See also page 579.

JMP

Jump

Formats:

JMP *op₁*
far label
mem48

Description:

The jump instruction causes instruction execution to continue at the specified offset within another segment. The given pointer (a 48-bit pointer composed of a 16-bit selector and a 32-bit offset, as described in Chapter 2) points to a label in a different segment (intersegment jump).

This 48-bit far pointer can be specified directly (as a far label) or indirectly through memory (mem48).

Operation:

```
/* far_label is assembled into a 48-bit pointer
   composed of a 16-bit code segment selector, which is
   returned by the Segment routine below, and an
   instruction offset from the beginning of the segment,
   which is returned by the Offset routine below.
*/
if (op1 is far_label) {
     CS    = Segment(far_label);
     EIP   = Offset(far_label);
} else if (op1 is mem48) {  /* † */
     CS    = [&mem+4];
     EIP   = [&mem];
}
/*
  † Since the far jump instruction loads the CS
  register, which may cause privilege level transitions,
  gate traversal, and task switching, the exact effect
  may not be as described above. These more complicated
  forms are described in detail in Chapter 5.
*/
```

Example:

```
JMP  FAR label1     ; label1 = AC40:000000FB
             Before:  EIP : 00000300  CS: 2DF0
             After :  EIP : 000000FB  CS: AC40
```

Exceptions:

```
Memory();
CodeSegmentLoad();
CodeReference();
```

Note:

See the examples on pages 624 and 530.

Lsr

Load Pointer

Formats:

L*sr*	*reg*	,	*mem48*	
LDS	reg	,	mem48	; load pointer to DS
LES	reg	,	mem48	; load pointer to ES
LFS	reg	,	mem48	; load pointer to FS
LGS	reg	,	mem48	; load pointer to GS
LSS	reg	,	mem48	; load pointer to SS

Description:

An Lsr instruction loads a 48-bit full pointer into a segment register/ general register pair. The dword at mem48 is loaded into the register specified by reg. The word found at the location specified by mem48 plus 4 is loaded into the segment register given in the instruction mnemonic (one of DS, ES, FS, GS, or SS). Thus, mem48 specifies a complete 48-bit pointer, the first dword is the offset (which is loaded into the specified register), and the last word is the segment descriptor (which is loaded into the specified segment register).

Loading a segment register with a selector makes a segment addressable as described in Chapter 2. Lower-level details of segment register loads are given in Chapter 5.

CS cannot be loaded by an Lsr instruction (LCS). CS can only be loaded by far control-flow transfer instructions (CALL far label, IRET, JMP far label, INT).

Operation:

```
reg    = (dword) [&mem48];
sr     = (word)  [&mem48+4];
```

Example:

```
LGS EAX, mem48       Before:    EAX    :   XXXXXXXX   GS:  XXXX
                                mem48:     8034:0F4BC319
                     After :    EAX    :   0F4BC319   GS:  8034
                                mem48:     8034:0F4BC319
```

Exceptions:

```
Memory();
SegmentLoad();
```

Notes:

LSS, LFS, and LGS are new to the 80386 instruction set. Use

LSS ESP,mem48

to point to a new stack. Since both SS and ESP are assigned by this instruction, any potential problems that may arise if they are updated by separate instructions are eliminated.

See example 1, page 621.

MOV

Move to/from Segment Register

Formats:

MOV	op_1	,	op_2
	sreg	,	reg16
	sreg	,	mem16
	reg16	,	sreg
	mem16	,	sreg

Description:

The contents of op_2 are copied into op_1.

If op_1 is a segment register, a new segment is made addressable by loading its selector into sreg. In order to access data in a segment, a selector identifying the segment must be loaded into one of the segment registers.

If op_1 is SS, interrupts are disabled until the next instruction execution is complete.

A thorough treatment of segmentation and the loading of segment registers is given in Chapter 5.

Operation:

```
op₁ = op₂;
```

Examples:

```
MOV AX, GS          Before:  AX: XXXX    GS: F433
                    After :  AX: F433    GS: F433

MOV AX,Segment1     ; This causes the selector of Segment1 to be
                    ;  loaded into AX.
MOV GS,AX           ; The selector is then moved into GS.
ADD GS:sum,DX       ; The data at location 'sum' within the GS
                    ;  segment (Segment1) is now addressable and
                    ;  used in this ADD instruction.
```

Exceptions:

```
SegmentLoad();
Memory();
```

Notes:

op_1 cannot be CS.
See page 517.

POP

Pop off Stack into Segment Register

Formats:

POP op_1
DS
ES
SS
FS
GS

Description:

POP moves the word (selector) from the stack into the specified segment register (DS, ES, SS, FS, or GS). Loading the segment register makes the segment referred to by the selector on the top of the stack addressable. The top of the stack is pointed to by SS:[ESP]. After the data transfer from the stack to op_1, the stack pointer is automatically updated by adding 4 to it.

As noted above, the segment register load may entail a complete segment descriptor load. The semantics of a segment register load are described in Chapter 5.

POP SS inhibits interrupts until the next instruction completes execution.

It is illegal to specify CS in a POP instruction.

Operation:

```
op1 = SS: [ESP];
ESP = ESP + 4;
```

Example:

```
POP ES      Before: ES: XXXX  SS: [ESP]  : F340  ESP: F4320530
            After : ES: F430  SS: [ESP-4]: F340  ESP: F4320534
```

Exceptions:

```
SegmentLoad();
Stack();
```

PUSH

Push onto Stack

Formats:

PUSH *op_1*
DS
ES
CS
SS
FS
GS

Description:

op_1 is placed in the new top of stack. The new top of stack is formed by decrementing the stack pointer (ESP) by 4.

Operation:

```
SS: [ESP-2] = op1;
ESP = ESP - 4;
```

Example:

```
PUSH SS      Before:  SS: 8042  ESP: 0424  [SS:420]: XXXX
             After :  SS: 8042  ESP: 0420  [SS:420]: 8042
```

Exception:

```
Stack();
```

RET

Return

Formats:

RET

RET imm16

Description:

RET causes instruction execution to resume at the instruction following a corresponding CALL instruction. The RET instruction uses the return pointer (a 48-bit pointer composed of CS and EIP, as described in Chapter 2) found on the top of the stack. The far pointer is popped into the EIP register and CS register. Another way to consider the RET instruction is as an indirect far jump through the memory pointer at SS:[ESP] with the appropriate stack updates.

An optional imm16 value can be specified with the RET instruction. This value is added to ESP to remove several bytes of parameters from the stack.

Note that when CS is popped off the stack, a full 32-bit word is popped. This is for stack alignment (see Chapter 2). The upper 16 bits of this stack location are discarded. Stack alignment improves 80386 performance.

Operation:

```
EIP = [ESP];
ESP = ESP + 4;
CS  = [ESP];   /* † */
ESP = ESP + 4;
if (NUMOPS == 1){
     ESP = ESP + imm16;
}
/*
  † Since the RET instruction loads the CS register,
  which may cause privilege level transitions, gate
  traversal, or task switching, the exact effect may not
  be as described above. These more complicated forms
  are described in detail in Chapter 5.
*/
```

Example:

```
FAR RET
          Before:  EIP     : 0F03429A   ESP  : 00000198    CS: 6320
                   [ESP+4]: XXXX5028   [ESP]: 00000300
          After :  EIP     : 00000300   ESP  : 00000200    CS: 5028
```

Exceptions:

```
Stack();
CodeSegmentLoad();
CodeReference();
```

Note:

See the detailed description on page 539.

▸ Operating System

As has been mentioned several times in this book, the 80386 supports several advanced operating-system features in hardware. To take advantage of this hardware, the instructions needed to implement multitasking, multiuser, and virtual-memory operating systems are provided to the operating-system writer.

This section describes the instructions that are explicitly provided for the operating-system writer. If you are an applications programmer, you can skip this section of instructions without any loss of completeness. In fact, most operating systems will not allow the applications programmer to use these instructions!

As was the case in the multiple-segment instructions of the last section, Chapter 5 explains why this set of instructions is provided. Thus, we recommend you read Chapter 5 before reading this section. After you read Chapter 5, the operating-system instructions should be clear and easy to understand. We include a complete instruction description here, however.

All instructions can be executed at all privilege levels unless noted otherwise by the Level0( ) exception.

Function Definitions

At the beginning of this chapter, we defined several functions that allowed us to use a shorthand notation in instruction descriptions and examples. Below is another routine with a similar purpose. We define it here because it is used exclusively in this section of the instruction set description.

```
/* The FetchDescriptor() routine is defined in detail in */
/* Chapter 5. The attributes structure is also defined   */
/* in Chapter 5. */
Descr(num, op){
    FetchDescriptor(op, &dword1, &dword2, &attributes);
    if (num==1) return(dword1);
    else        return(dword2);
}
```

Exception Routines

At the beginning of this chapter, we defined several exception routines allowing us to use a shorthand function call to summarize potential exception conditions. Below are several more exception routines that we did not define at the start of this chapter, since they are particular to the operating-system instructions.

```
SegmentLoad(){
    /* All possible segment exceptions while loading a        */
    /* descriptor are embodied in the DescriptorLoad() routine */
    /* defined in Chapter 5. Refer to Chapter 5 for further    */
    /* details.*/
}
Level0(){
    /* CPL is defined in Chapter 5.*/
    /* The SegmentException() routine is defined in Chapter 6. */
    if (CPL != 0){
        SegmentException($GP,0);
    }
}
8086Mode(){
    /* 8086Mode() signals an InvalidOpcode() exception if the */
    /* 80386 is executing in real or virtual-8086 mode, as    */
    /* described in Chapter 9. The processor is in real mode  */
    /* if the PE bit in CR0 is 0. The processor is in         */
    /* virtual-8086 mode if PE is 1 and the VM bit in the     */
    /* EFLAGS register is 1.

    if ( (CR0 & 1b == 0) /* real mode */
        || ( ((CR0 & 1b) == 1) &&
             ( EFLAGS.VM == 1) ) /* virtual-8086 mode */   )
       InvalidOpcode();
}
```

Instruction Set Summary

The following table summarizes the instructions that are found in this section of the instruction set descriptions.

	Operating-System Instructions
ARPL	Adjust requested privilege level
CLTS	Clear the task-switched flag
HLT	Halt
LAR	Load access rights
LGDT	Load global descriptor table
LIDT	Load interrupt descriptor table
LLDT	Load local descriptor table
LMSW	Load machine status word
LSL	Load segment limit
LTR	Load task register
MOV	Move to/from special register

SGDT	Store global descriptor table
SIDT	Store interrupt descriptor table
SLDT	Store local descriptor table
SMSW	Store machine status word
STR	Store task register
VERR	Verify segment for reading
VERW	Verify segment for writing

ARPL

Adjust Requested Privilege Level

Formats:

ARPL	op_1	,	op_2
	reg16	,	reg16
	mem16	,	reg16

Description:

ARPL checks the RPL (requested privilege level) of op_1 against the RPL of op_2. The RPL is specified in the 2 least significant bits of op_1 and op_2. If RPL of op_1 is less than RPL of op_2, the zero flag is set to 1 and the 2 least significant bits of op_1 are set equal to the 2 least significant bits of op_2. Either op_1 or op_2 can be the null selector.

ARPL is not used in application programs; it is normally only used in operating-system code. Usually, op_2 is the code segment selector of the caller. op_1 is a selector for a segment that the caller desires the subroutine to access. This comparison is used to ensure that the caller does not request more privilege than the caller is allowed.

Operating System

Operation:

```
if ((op1 & 03h) < (op2 & 03h)){
    ZF = 1;
    op1 = (op1 & FFFCh) | (op2 & 03h);
} else {
    ZF = 0;
}
```

Examples:

```
                                                          OSZAPC
ARPL  mem16, AX   Before:  mem16: 6DD3  AX: 456A          XXXXXX
                  After :  mem16: 6DD3  AX: 456A          UU0UUU

ARPL   CX  , AX   Before:  CX   : FF44  AX: 62F1          XXXXXX
                  After :  CX   : FF45  AX: 62F1          UU1UUU
```

Exceptions:

```
Memory();
8086Mode();
```

CLTS

Clear the Task-Switched Flag

Formats:

CLTS

Description:

The task-switched flag in the machine status word (MSW or CR0) is set to 0. Every time a task switch occurs, this flag is automatically set to 1 (refer to Chapter 5 for details on task switching). The TS flag is used to minimize the overhead of context switching when an 80387 is present in the system. If a task switch has occurred (TS == 1) and the new task attempts to use the 80387, a fault will occur. The corresponding fault routine must then save the context of the 80387 and execute a CLTS instruction. The new task can then use the 80387 without destroying any of the data of the prior task.

Thus, only tasks that use the 80387 will incur the overhead of saving the prior state of the 80387.

CLTS appears only in operating-system code. It can only be executed at privilege level 0.

Operation:

```
TS = 0;
```

Example:

```
CLTS                Before:  TS : 1
                    After :  TS : 0
```

Exception:

```
Level0();
```

HLT

Halt

Format:

HLT

Description:

HLT causes the 80386 to stop execution. Following a halt, execution can only be resumed by the receipt of an enabled interrupt (note that NMI is always enabled) or by a reset of the computer. Interrupts, and how they can be enabled, are discussed in detail in Chapter 6.

Example:

```
HLT      ; Execution stops
```

Exception:

```
Level0();
```

LAR

Load Access Rights

Formats:

LAR	op_1	,	op_2
	reg16	,	reg16
	reg16	,	mem16
	reg32	,	reg32
	reg32	,	mem32

Description:

LAR loads the first operand with the segment attributes field (access rights) from the descriptor for the segment specified by the selector in the second operand.

The segment attributes field is simply the high-order four bytes of the descriptor ANDed with 00FxFF00h, where x indicates that bits 16 through 19 are undefined in the value loaded by LAR.

The descriptor specified by the selector op_1 must be within the descriptor table limits, have a valid Type field, and be accessible at both CPL and RPL of the selector in op_2 compared to DPL. If so, ZF is set to 1 and op_1 is loaded with the segment attributes field. Otherwise, ZF is cleared to 0 and op_1 is not modified.

Any memory segment descriptor (indicated by a 1 in the DType field) can have any value in its Type field and be valid for use with LAR. The valid types for system segments and gates (DType = 0) are given in the following table:

Descriptor Type	Valid?
0 Undefined	Invalid
1 Available286TSS	Valid
2 LDT	Valid
3 Busy286TSS	Valid
4 286CallGate	Valid

5 TaskGate	Valid
6 286InterruptGate	Invalid
7 286TrapGate	Invalid
8 Undefined	Invalid
9 Available386TSS	Valid
A Undefined	Invalid
B Busy386TSS	Valid
C 386CallGate	Valid
D Undefined	Invalid
E 386InterruptGate	Invalid
F 386TrapGate	Invalid

Operation:

```
if ( (op2 & 0FFFCh) == 0 /* Null selector */ )
    goto ClearZF;

/* Routine FetchDescriptor is defined in Chapter 5. */
/* Returns 0 if descriptor is beyond table limit.   */
if (FetchDescriptor(op2, &dword1, &dword2, &Attributes) == 0)
    goto ClearZF;

/* Otherwise descriptor within table limits */
if (Attributes.DType == 1 /* memory segment */)
    switch (Attributes.Type){
      case 0: case 1: /* Read-only */
      case 2: case 3: /* Read/write */
      case 4: case 5: /* Read-only, expand-down */
      case 6: case 7: /* Read/write, expand-down */
      case 8: case 9: /* Execute-only */
      case 10: case 11: /* Execute/read */
         /* Do privilege check only for nonconforming segments */
         if ( (Attributes.DPL<CPL) ||
              (Attributes.DPL<op2.RPL))
            goto ClearZF;
         break;
         /* DPL is ignored for a conforming segment. */
      case 12: case 13: /* Execute-only, conforming */
      case 14: case 15: /* Execute/read, conforming */
         break;
    } /* end switch */

else /* DType ==0, system segment or gate */
    switch (Attributes.Type) {
        Case 1: /* Available 286 TSS   */
        Case 2: /* LDT                 */
        Case 3: /* Busy      286 TSS   */
        Case 4: /* 286 Call gate       */
        Case 5: /* Task gate           */
```

```
        Case 9: /* Available 386 TSS    */
        Case 11:/* Busy      386 TSS    */
        Case 12:/* 386 Call gate        */
           /* Type is valid, check DPL */
           if ( Attributes.DPL<CPL || Attributes.DPL<op2.RPL )
              goto ClearZF;
           break;

    Default: /* other types are invalid */
                goto ClearZF;

    } /*end switch */

/* Fall out to here only if all checks pass.  */
/* Set ZF to 1, load Attributes into op1.     */
    ZF = 1;
    op1 = Attributes & 0FxFF00h;
    return;

/* Jump to ClearZF if something goes wrong. */
/* Clear ZF to 0 and do not change op1.     */
ClearZF:
    ZF = 0;
    return;
```

Examples:

```
                                                          OSZAPC
LAR   EAX, mem32   ; Assume the descriptor is visible
            Before:  Descr(0, mem32): 1F0FACFE   XXXXXX
                     EAX: XXXXXXXX
            After :  Descr(0, mem32): 1F0FACFE   XX1XXX
                     EAX: 000XAC00

LAR   EAX, mem32   ; Assume the descriptor is not visible
            Before:  Descr(0, mem32): 1F0FACFE   XXXXXX
                     EAX: XXXXXXXX
            After :  Descr(0, mem32): 1F0FACFE   XX0XXX
                     EAX: UUUUUUUU
```

Exceptions:

```
Memory();
8086Mode();
```

LGDT

Load Global Descriptor Table

Format:

LGDT op_1
mem48

Description:

LGDT loads the global descriptor table register from the 48-bit pseudo-descriptor (mem48) given in the instruction. The pseudo-descriptor has two components: the limit and the base. The 16-bit limit is stored at the low word, and the 32-bit base is stored at the high dword.

LGDT appears only in operating-system code; it should never be found in applications code.

Operation:

```
GDTR.Limit = mem48;          /* 16-bit GDT limit */
GDTR.Base  = [&mem48+2];     /* 32-bit GDT Base  */
```

Example:

```
LGDT mem48     Before:  mem48      : 4132   [&mem48+2]: AC405B10
                        GDTR.Limit: XXXX   GDTR.Base : XXXXXXXX
               After :  mem48      : 4132   [&mem48+2]: AC405B10
                        GDTR.Limit: 4132   GDTR.Base : AC405B10
```

Exceptions:

```
Memory();
Level0();
```

Note:

See page 623.

LIDT

Load Interrupt Descriptor Table

Format:

LIDT *op₁*
mem48

Description:

LIDT loads the interrupt descriptor table register from the 48-bit pseudo-descriptor (mem48) given in the instruction. The pseudo-descriptor has two components: the limit and the base. The limit is in the lower 16 bits, and the base is in the high-order 32 bits. LIDT loads the interrupt descriptor table register from the address (mem48) given in the instruction. The interrupt descriptor table register has two components: the 16-bit limit is stored at the low word, and the 32-bit base is stored at the high dword.

LIDT appears only in operating-system code; it should never be found in applications code.

Operation:

```
IDTR.Limit = mem48;       /* 16-bit IDT limit */
IDTR.Base  = [&mem48+2];  /* 32-bit IDT limit */
```

Example:

```
LIDT mem48   Before: mem48      :AAC3  [&mem48+2]: 0BF4103D
                    IDTR.Limit:XXXX  IDTR.Base  : XXXXXXXX
             After : mem48      :AAC3  [&mem48+2]: 0BF4103D
                    IDTR.Limit:AAC3  IDTR.Base  : 0BF4103D
```

Exceptions:

```
Memory();
Level0();
```

Note:

See pages 619 and 620.

LLDT

Load Local Descriptor Table

Formats:

LLDT *op₁*
reg16
mem16
reg32
mem32

Description:

LLDT loads the local descriptor table register with the selector in op_1, addressing a new LDT segment.

The given selector must point to a global descriptor table (GDT) entry that is of descriptor type Local Descriptor Table (LDT). If this is the case, the LDT register is loaded. Chapter 5 describes these checks in detail.

op_1 may be a null selector, which will cause the LDT to be marked invalid. Loading a selector naming an LDT segment will raise a segment load exception if LDTR contains a null selector.

LLDT appears only in operating-system code; it should never be found in applications code.

Operation:

```
LDTR = op1;
```

Example:

```
LLDT AX        Before:  AX : 001C     LDTR : XXXX
               After :  AX : 001C     LDTR : 001C
```

Exceptions:

```
SegmentLoad();
Memory();
Level0();
8086Mode();
```

Note:

See page 526.

LMSW

Load Machine Status Word

Formats:

LMSW *op₁*
reg16
mem16
reg32
mem32

Description:

LMSW loads the MSW register from op_1. MSW (the low 16 bits of CR0) is described in Chapter 2.

LMSW can be used to enter protected mode by setting the PE bit of MSW to 1. If this is done, the LMSW instruction must be immediately followed by an intrasegment jump instruction.

Also note that for strict 80286 compatibility, the ET bit of MSW is not altered by the LMSW instruction.

Note that the PE bit of MSW is sticky to the LMSW instruction. This means that after the PE bit of MSW has been set to 1 (protected mode has been entered), the PE bit cannot be cleared (set to 0) by an LMSW instruction. See Chapter 5 for further details of protected mode and Chapter 9 for further details of real mode.

LMSW appears only in operating-system code; it should never be found in applications code.

Operation:

```
MSW = (op1 & FFEFh) | (MSW & 0011h);
    /* CR0 = (CR0 & FFFF0011h) | (0000FFEFh & op1); */
```

Examples:

```
LMSW AX      Before: AX: 0007      MSW: 0010
             After : AX: 0007      MSW: 0017

LMSW AX      Before: AX: 0010      MSW: 0007
             After : AX: 0010      MSW: 0001
```

Exceptions:

```
Memory();
Level0();
```

Note:

The LMSW instruction is provided for strict compatibility with the 80286. When programming the 80386, MOV CR0 should be used rather than LMSW.

LSL

Load Segment Limit

Formats:

LSL	op_1	,	op_2
	reg16	,	reg16
	reg16	,	mem16
	reg32	,	reg32
	reg32	,	mem32

Description:

LSL loads the first operand with the limit field (segment limit) from the descriptor for the segment specified by the selector in the second operand.

The resultant limit placed into op_1 is the byte limit. Thus, if the specified descriptor had a page granular limit (G=1, the G bit of the descriptor, is described in Chapter 5), the limit is shifted left 12 bits and filled with 12 low-order bits of 1s.

The descriptor specified by the selector in op_2 must be within the descriptor table, a valid type for LSL (see the table below), and visible at the CPL (current privilege level) and the RPL (requested privilege level) compared against the DPL (descriptor privilege level). If this is the case, the zero flag is set and op_1 is modified. If not, the zero flag is cleared and op_1 is not modified.

Any memory segment descriptor (indicated by a 1 in the DType field) can have any value in its Type field and be valid for use with LSL. The valid types for system segments and gates (DType = 0) are given in the following table.

Descriptor Type	Valid?
0 Undefined	Invalid
1 Available286TSS	Valid
2 LDT	Valid
3 Busy286TSS	Valid
4 286CallGate	Invalid

5 TaskGate	Invalid
6 286InterruptGate	Invalid
7 286TrapGate	Invalid
8 Undefined	Invalid
9 Available386TSS	Valid
A Undefined	Invalid
B Busy386TSS	Valid
C 386CallGate	Invalid
D Undefined	Invalid
E 386InterruptGate	Invalid
F 386TrapGate	Invalid

Operation:

```
if ( (op2 & 0FFFCh) == 0 /* Null selector */ )
     goto ClearZF;

/* Routine FetchDescriptor is defined in Chapter 5.*/
/* Returns 0 if descriptor is beyond table limit.  */
if (FetchDescriptor(op2, &dword1, &dword2, &Attributes) == 0)
     goto ClearZF;

/* Otherwise descriptor within table limits */
if (Attributes.DType == 1 /* memory segment */)
    switch (Attributes.Type){
      case 0: case 1: /* Read-only */
      case 2: case 3: /* Read/write */
      case 4: case 5: /* Read-only, expand-down */
      case 6: case 7: /* Read/Write, expand-down */
      case 8: case 9: /* Execute-only */
      case 10: case 11: /* Execute/read */
         /* Do privilege check only for nonconforming segments */
         if ( (Attributes.DPL<CPL) ||
              (Attributes.DPL<op2.RPL) )
            goto ClearZF;
         break;

      /* DPL is ignored for a conforming segment.   */
      case 12: case 13: /* Execute-only, conforming */
      case 14: case 15: /* Execute/read, conforming */
      break;
   } /* end switch */

else /* DType ==0, system segment or gate */
    switch (Attributes.Type) {
        Case 1: /* Available 286 TSS  */
        Case 2: /* LDT                */
        Case 3: /* Busy      286 TSS  */
```

```
        Case 9: /* Available 386 TSS  */
        Case 11:/* Busy      386 TSS  */
              break;
        Default: /* other types are invalid */
              goto ClearZF;

       } /* end switch */

/* Fall out to here only if all checks pass.  */
/* Set ZF to 1, load segment limit into op1    */
    ZF = 1;
    if (B(23, dword1) == 0){ /* A byte granular segment */
         op1 =    (dword2 & 000F0000h) |
                  (dword1 & 0000FFFFh) ;
    } else {                /* A page granular segment */
         op1 = (((dword2 & 000F0000h) |
                  (dword1 & 0000FFFFh) ) << 12) | FFFh ;
    }
    return;

/* Jump to ClearZF if something goes wrong.   */
/* Clear ZF to 0 and do not change op1.       */
ClearZF:
    ZF = 0;
    return;
```

Example:

```
                                                      OSZAPC
LSL  EAX, mem32  ; Assume the descriptor is visible
           Before:  Descr(0, mem32): 1F0FACFE    XXXXXX
                    Descr(1, mem32): 008F8100
                    EAX: XXXXXXXX
           After :  Descr(0, mem32): 1F0FACFE    UU1UUU
                    Descr(1, mem32): 008F8100
                    EAX: FACFEFFF
```

Exceptions:

```
Memory();
8086Mode();
```

Operating System

LTR

Load Task Register

Formats:

LTR *op₁*
reg16
mem16
reg32
mem32

Description:

LTR loads the task register with the selector in op_1, making a TSS segment addressable. The TSS (task state segment) loaded is marked busy.

The given selector must point to a global descriptor table (GDT) entry that is of descriptor type TSS. If this is the case, the task register is loaded. Chapter 5 describes the checks in detail.

LTR appears only in operating-system code; it should never be found in applications code.

Operation:

```
TR = op1;
```

Example:

```
LTR  mem32   Before:  mem32 :  XXXX0014  TR : XXXX
             After :  mem32 :  UUUU0014  TR : 0014
```

Exceptions:

```
SegmentLoad();
Memory();
8086Mode();
Level0();
```

Note:

See pages 527 and 721.

MOV

Move to/from Special Register

Formats:

MOV	op_1	,	op_2
	reg32	,	CR0
	reg32	,	CR2
	reg32	,	CR3
	CR0	,	reg32
	CR2	,	reg32
	CR3	,	reg32
	reg32	,	DR0
	reg32	,	DR1
	reg32	,	DR2
	reg32	,	DR3
	reg32	,	DR6
	reg32	,	DR7
	DR0	,	reg32
	DR1	,	reg32
	DR2	,	reg32
	DR3	,	reg32
	DR6	,	reg32
	DR7	,	reg32

Description:

The contents of op_2 are copied into op_1.

The control registers and the exact effects of loading them are described in Chapter 5. The debug registers and the exact effects of loading them are described in Chapter 8.

Note that only 32-bit register operands can be used with the MOV special register instruction.

The special register move can only be used when operating at privilege level 0.

Operation:

```
op₁ = op₂; /* † */
/*
   † Since the loading of these special registers may
   have side effects, this description is not complete in
   all cases.
*/
```

Example:

```
MOV CR0, EAX          Before: EAX: 80000003 CR0: XXXXXXXX
                      After : EAX: 80000003 CR0: 80000003
```

Exception:

```
Level0();
```

Note:

See page 620.

SGDT

Store Global Descriptor Table

Format:

SGDT *op_1*
mem48

Description:

The global descriptor table register contents are stored into the pseudo-descriptor at the six-byte location specified by op_1. The 16-bit limit is stored at the low word, and the 32-bit base is stored at the high dword.

SGDT appears only in operating-system code; it should never be found in applications code.

Operation:

```
mem48        = GDTR.Limit;
[&mem48+2]   = GDTR.Base;
```

Example:

```
SGDT  mem48   Before:  GDTR.Limit : 0032   GDTR.Base   : 0BD542FF
                       mem48      : XXXX   [&mem48+2]  : XXXXXXXX
              After :  GDTR.Limit : 0032   GDTR.Base   : 0BD542FF
                       mem48      : 0032   [&mem48+2]  : 0BD542FF
```

Exception:

```
Memory();
```

SIDT

Store Interrupt Descriptor Table

Format:

SIDT *op₁*

mem48

Description:

The interrupt descriptor table register contents are stored into the pseudo-descriptor at the six-byte location specified by op_1. The 16-bit limit is stored at the low word, and the 32-bit base is stored at the high dword.

SIDT appears only in operating-system code; it should never be found in applications code.

Operation:

```
mem48        = IDTR.Limit;
[&mem48+2]   = IDTR.Base;
```

Example:

```
SIDT  mem48   Before:  IDTR.Limit : 0032   IDTR.Base   : 0BD542FF
                       mem48      : XXXX   [&mem48+2]  : XXXXXXXX
              After :  IDTR.Limit : 0032   IDTR.Base   : 0BD542FF
                       mem48      : 0032   [&mem48+2]  : 0BD542FF
```

Exception:

```
Memory();
```

SLDT

Store Local Descriptor Table

Formats:

SLDT *op₁*

reg16
mem16
reg32
mem32

Description:

The local descriptor table register contents are stored into op_1. This register contains a selector that points to the current LDT.

SLDT appears only in operating-system code; it should never be found in applications code.

Operation:

```
op1 = LDTR;
```

Example:

```
SLDT mem16   Before:  LDTR : 5569   [&mem16] : XXXX
             After :  LDTR : 5569   [&mem16] : 5569
```

Exceptions:

```
Memory();
8086Mode();
```

SMSW

Store Machine Status Word

Formats:

SMSW *op_1*
reg16
mem16
reg32
mem32

Description:

SMSW places the contents of the MSW register into op_1. MSW (which corresponds to the low 16 bits of CR0) is described in Chapter 2.

Operation:

```
op1 = MSW;
```

Example:

```
SMSW AX       Before: AX: XXXX        MSW: FF10
              After : AX: FF10        MSW: FF10
```

Exception:

```
Memory();
```

Note:

The SMSW instruction is provided for strict compatibility with the 80286. When programming the 80386, MOV CR0 should be used rather than SMSW.

STR

Store Task Register

Formats:

STR *op_1*
reg16
mem16

Description:

The task register contents are stored into op_1.

STR appears only in operating-system code; it should never be found in applications code.

Operation:

```
op1 = TR;
```

Example:

```
STR mem16    Before: TR: FFD5      mem: XXXX
             After : TR: FFD5      mem: FFD5
```

Exceptions:

```
Memory();
8086Mode();
```

Note:

See example 2, page 627.

VERR

Verify Segment for Reading

Formats:

VERR *op₁*

reg16
mem16
reg32
mem32

Description:

The VERR instruction determines if the segment identified by the selector in op_1 is suitable for reading.

The selector must be a valid descriptor (within the LDT or GDT), a memory segment descriptor, and readable and visible at the current privilege level. If the segment identified by the selector in op_1 meets these requirements, the zero flag is set to 1. Otherwise the zero flag is cleared to 0.

The verification steps that are executed, with the results left in the zero flag, are identical to those done if the referenced descriptor were loaded and a read performed to that segment.

Operation:

```
if ( (op2 & 0FFFCh) == 0 /* Null selector */ )
    goto ClearZF;

/* Routine FetchDescriptor() is defined in Ch. 5. */
/* Returns 0 if descriptor is beyond table limit. */
if (FetchDescriptor(op2, &dword1, &dword2, &Attributes) == 0)
    goto ClearZF;

/* Otherwise descriptor within table limits */
if (Attributes.DType == 1 /* memory segment */)
    switch (Attributes.Type){
      case 0: case 1: /* Read-only */
      case 2: case 3: /* Read/write */
      case 4: case 5: /* Read-only, expand-down */
      case 6: case 7: /* Read/write, expand-down */
      case 10: case 11: /* Execute/read */
```

```
        /* Do privilege check only for nonconforming */
        /* segments.*/
        if ( (Attributes.DPL<CPL) ||
             (Attributes.DPL<op2.RPL) )
           goto ClearZF;
        break;
        /* DPL is ignored for a conforming segment. */
        case 14: case 15: /* Execute/read, conforming */
        break;
        Default: /* other types are invalid */
             goto ClearZF;
      } /* end switch */

else /* DType ==0, system segment or gate */
    goto ClearZF;    /* all system segments are invalid */

/* Fall out to here only if all checks pass. */
/* Set ZF to 1 */
    ZF = 1;
    return;

/* Jump to ClearZF if something goes wrong. */
/* Clear ZF to 0 */
ClearZF:
    ZF = 0;
    return;
```

Example:

```
VERR  mem16   ; Assume the segment is readable      OSZAPC
                  Before:                           XXXXXX
                  After :                           XX1XXX
```

Exceptions:

```
Memory();
8086Mode();
```

VERW

Verify Segment for Writing

Formats:

VERW op_1
reg16
mem16
reg32
mem32

Description:

The VERW instruction determines if the segment identified by the selector in op_1 is suitable for writing.

The selector must be a valid descriptor (within the LDT or GDT), a memory segment descriptor, and writable and visible at the current privilege level. If the segment identified by the selector in op_1 meets these requirements, the zero flag is set to 1. Otherwise the zero flag is cleared to 0.

The verification steps that are executed, with the results left in the zero flag, are identical to those done if the referenced descriptor were loaded and a write performed to that segment.

Operation:

```
if ( (op2 & 0FFFCh) == 0 /* Null selector */ )
    goto ClearZF;

/* Routine FetchDescriptor() is defined in Ch. 5.     */
/* Returns 0 if descriptor is beyond table limit.     */
if (FetchDescriptor(op2, &dword1, &dword2, &Attributes) == 0)
    goto ClearZF;

/* Otherwise descriptor within table limits */
if (Attributes.DType == 1 /* memory segment */)
    switch (Attributes.Type){
      case 2: case 3: /* Read/write */
      case 6: case 7: /* Read/write, expand-down */
         /* Do privilege check only for nonconforming */
         /* segments */
         if ( (Attributes.DPL<CPL) ||
              (Attributes.DPL<op2.RPL) )
           goto ClearZF;
      break;
```

```
        Default: /* other types are invalid  */
             goto ClearZF;
      } /* end switch */
 else /* DType ==0, system segment or gate */
    goto ClearZF;    /* all system segments are invalid */

/* Fall out to here only if all checks pass. */
/* Set ZF to 1 */
    ZF = 1;
    return;

/* Jump to ClearZF if something goes wrong. */
/* Clear ZF to 0 */
ClearZF:
    ZF = 0;
    return;
```

Example:

```
VERW  mem16   ; Assume the segment is writable     OSZAPC
                  Before:                           XXXXXX
                  After :                           XX1XXX
```

Exceptions:

```
Memory();
8086Mode();
```

▸ Floating Point

This section of instructions gives the complete set of the floating-point instructions available in an 80386/80387 system. All the arithmetic, data transfer, comparison, transcendental, constant, and control instructions supported by the 80387 are described herein.

Each instruction includes one or two examples of how they are used. In the second half of Chapter 4 are more examples of the use of the instructions in this section. These examples are program segments consisting of several instructions to perform some useful functions. Between the description and the examples given here, and the more extensive examples found in Chapter 4, you should be able to clearly understand the purpose and operation of these instructions.

Since some of the syntax for floating-point instructions is significantly different from that used so far to describe the instructions of the 80386, let's take a few paragraphs to review the syntax used throughout this section.

Instruction Mnemonics

The assembler mnemonics for the floating-point instructions follow a standard notation.

F	All floating-point instructions begin with F (e.g., FADD, FLD, etc.). No other 86 family instructions begin with F.
FI	All instructions that operate upon integer data types begin with FI (e.g., FIADD, FILD, etc.).
FB	All instructions that operate with BCD data types begin with FB (e.g., FBLD, FBST, etc.).
FxxP	All instructions that cause the stack to be popped once end in P (e.g., FSTP, FADDP, etc.).
FxxPP	All instructions that cause the stack to be popped twice end in PP (e.g., FCOMPP, FUCOMPP, etc.).
FNxx	All instructions except those beginning with FN check for unmasked numeric exceptions prior to execution. The FNxx instructions do not check for numeric exceptions (e.g., FNINIT, FNSAVE, etc.).

Stack

As we mentioned in Chapter 2, the 80387 uses an accumulator stack and almost all operations must have the stack top as one operand. The stack top is referred to as *ST*. The other accumulators are referenced relative to ST using the notation ST(n). This indicates the nth stack element beneath the current top of stack. Thus, ST(3) indicates the third accumulator beneath the top of stack.

Since many floating-point operations push or pop elements on or off the stack, it is often helpful to indicate what happens to the stack top in certain operations. For this, we use the notation TOP in examples. Thus, TOP = 3 indicates that the current top-of-stack register is the third physical floating-point register.

Example

Below is an example of a floating-point instruction. This is the compare and pop instruction. The stack top ST is numerically compared against ST(3), the third element below the stack top, in this case. After the comparison is complete, the top of stack is popped, as is seen by TOP changing from 4 to 5.

```
FCOMP ST(3)   Before: ST    : 2.4560 * 10^6
                      ST(3) : 9.4102 * 10^4
                      TOP   : 4   C3: X C2: X C0: X
              After : ST(2) : 9.4102 * 10^4
                      TOP   : 5   C3: 0 C2: 0 C0: 0
```

Note that pushes cause the stack-top pointer to decrement (place a new item on the stack), and pops cause the stack-top pointer to increment (remove an item from the stack) as is the case in this example. This was described in Chapter 2, and you can see a visual representation of it in Figure 2.24.

Function Definitions

At the beginning of this chapter, we defined several functions that allowed us to use a shorthand notation in instruction descriptions and examples. Below are additional routines with similar purpose. We define them here, as they are exclusively used in this section of the instruction set description.

```
/* Pop the floating-point accumulator stack.      */
/* Causes stack-top pointer TOP to be incremented. */
FPop(){
     TOP = TOP + 1;
     if (TOP > 7) {
          TOP = 0;
     }
}
```

```
/* Push the floating-point stack. Causes stack to */
/* be decremented.                                */
FPush(){
      TOP = TOP - 1;
      if (TOP < 0) {
            TOP = 7;
      }
}

/* Note that the FIP (Floating-point Instruction Pointer), FCS */
/* (Floating-point Code Segment), FOO (Floating-point Operand  */
/* Offset), and FOS (Floating-point Operand Segment) are loaded*/
/* beginning at [memp+12].                                     */
/* Note that the FIP and FCS are just copies of the EIP        */
/* and CS value at the most recent floating-point instruction. */
/* FOO and FOS are simply the offset and segment of the ''mem''*/
/* of the most recent floating-point instruction (if one       */
/* existed).                                                   */
LdErrorPointer(memp){
      FIP  = [memp + 12];
      FCS  = [memp + 16];
      FOO  = [memp + 20];
      FOS  = [memp + 24];
}

StErrorPointer(memp){
      [memp + 12] =  FIP;
      [memp + 16] =  FCS;
      [memp + 20] =  FOO;
      [memp + 24] =  FOS;
}

/* The following routines perform the arithmetic           */
/* function given by their name.                           */
abs(op);     /* return the absolute value of op            */
arctan(op); /* return the arctan of op (op is in radians) */
cos(op);     /* return the cos of op (op is in radians)    */
log2(op);    /* return the log base 2 of op                */
sin(op);     /* return the sin of op (op is in radians)    */
sqrt(op);    /* return the square root of op               */
tan(op);     /* return the tan of op (op is in radians)    */
```

Exception Routines

At the beginning of this chapter, we defined several exception routines allowing us to use a shorthand function call to summarize potential exception conditions. Below is another exception routine that we did not define at the start of this chapter, since it is particular to the floating-point instructions.

```
Float(Src){
        if(exception Src not masked){
            Interrupt(16);
        }
      /* case Src of:
        IS: Invalid operation caused by stack
            overflow or underflow
```

```
        I : Invalid operation for any reason
        D : Denormal operand
        Z : Zero divide
        O : Overflow
        U : Underflow
        P : Precision
    */
}
```

Instruction Summary

The following tables give a summary of all the instructions in this section according to subgroupings. Following the tables of instruction groups, the page-by-page description of each instruction begins.

Data Transfer

FBLD	BCD load
FBSTP	BCD store and pop
FILD	Integer load
FIST	Integer store
FISTP	Integer store and pop
FLD	Real load
FST	Real store
FSTP	Real store and pop
FXCH	Exchange registers

Arithmetic

FABS	Absolute value
FADD/FIADD/FADDP	Addition
FCHS	Change sign
FDIV/FIDIV/FDIVP	Division
FDIVR/FIDIVR/FDIVRP	Division reverse
FMUL/FIMUL/FMULP	Multiply
FPREM	Partial remainder
FPREM1	Partial remainder—IEEE
FRNDINT	Round to integer
FSCALE	Power of two scaling
FSUB/FISUB/FSUBP	Subtraction

FSUBR/FISUBR/FSUBRP	Subtraction reverse
FSQRT	Square root
FXTRACT	Extract exponent and significand
	Comparison
FCOM/FCOMP/FCOMPP	Compare
FICOM/FICOMP	Integer compare
FTST	Test
FUCOM/FUCOMP/FUCOMPP	Unordered compare
FXAM	Examine
	Transcendental
F2XM1	$2^x - 1$
FCOS	Cosine
FPATAN	Partial arctangent
FPTAN	Partial tangent
FSIN	Sine
FSINCOS	Sine and cosine
FYL2X	$y*\log_2 x$
FYL2XP1	$y*\log_2(x+1)$

Note: FCOS, FPTAN, FSIN, and FSINCOS expect their operands and deliver their results in radians.

	Constant
FLD1	Load 1
FLDL2E	Load $\log_2 e$
FLDL2T	Load $\log_2 10$
FLDLG2	Load $\log_{10} 2$
FLDLN2	Load $\log_e 2$
FLDPI	Load π
FLDZ	Load zero
	Control
FCLEX/FNCLEX	Clear exceptions
FDECSTP	Decrement stack pointer

FFREE	Free register
FINCSTP	Increment stack pointer
FINIT/FNINIT	Initialize processor
FLDCW	Load control word
FLDENV	Load environment
FNOP	No operation
FRSTOR	Restore state
FSAVE/FNSAVE	Save state
FSTCW/FNSTCW	Store control word
FSTENV/FNSTENV	Store environment
FSTSW/FNSTSW	Store status word
FSTSW AX/FNSTSW AX	Store status word into AX
WAIT	Wait for coprocessor

F2XM1

$2^X - 1$

Format:

F2XM1

Description:

The item in the top of stack is ST in the computation of $2^{ST} - 1$. The result of this computation replaces the initial ST.

Note that the input operand range is bounded by -0.5 and 0.5. If the operand is out of this range, the results are undefined.

Operation:

```
if (-0.5 <= ST <= 0.5){
    ST = 2^ST - 1;
} else {
    UNDEFINED;
}
```

Example:

```
F2XM1   Before: ST: 3.49921 * 10^-2
        After : ST: 2.45512 * 10^-2
```

Exception:

```
Float(IS,I,D,U,P);
```

Note:

The 80287 input range allowed is 0.0 to 0.5, where the 80387 allows input operands in the range -0.5 to $+0.5$.

FABS

Absolute Value

Format:

FABS

Description:

The top stack element is changed to its absolute value. The top stack element is always positive following FABS.

Operation:

```
if (ST < 0 ){
    ST = - ST;
}
```

Example:

```
FABS   Before: ST: -7.324 * 10^-402
       After : ST:  7.234 * 10^-402
```

Exception:

```
Float(IS);
```

FADD / FIADD / FADDP

Addition

Formats:

```
FADD                        ; Real addition ST(1), ST
FADD    op1                 ; Real addition
        ST(n)
        mem32               ;      short real
        mem64               ;      long real
FIADD   op1                 ; Integer addition
        mem16               ;      word integer
        mem32               ;      short integer
FADDP   op1    ,  op2       ; Real addition and pop
        ST     ,  ST(n)
        ST(n)  ,  ST
FADD    op1    ,  op2       ; Real addition
        ST     ,  ST(n)
        ST(n)  ,  ST
```

Description:

The explicitly or implicitly specified floating-point operands are added (ST(1)+ST, ST+op_1, or op_1+op_2 when 0, 1, and 2 operands are specified, respectively), with the result being stored into the destination. The destination is the stack top in all cases except the two-operand form, where the destination can be ST(n).

If op_1 is a memory operand (word or short integer, short or long real), it is automatically converted to temporary real (the internal format) before any operations are performed with it.

An FADDP or FADD without any operands causes the stack to be popped. Thus, FADD with no operands is synonymous with FADDP ST(1),ST.

Operation:

```
if(NUMOPS == 0){
    ST(1) = ST(1) + ST;
    FPop();                /* pop the stack, result in ST */
```

```
} else if (NUMOPS == 1){
    ST = ST + (tempReal) op1;
} else {                    /* NUMOPS == 2 */
    op1 = op1 + op2;
    if (OPCODE == FADDP){
        FPop();             /* pop the stack */
    }
}
```

Example:

```
FADD mem32  Before: ST: 4.51200 * 10^5  mem: 3.664 * 10^3
            After : ST: 4.54864 * 10^5  mem: 3.664 * 10^3
```

Exceptions:

```
Memory();
Float(IS,I,D,U,O,P);
```

Note:

The following table summarizes the add operation (all varieties) with infinities.

Original Operands		Results (op_1)	
op_1	op_2	Sign	Value
$+\infty$	$+\infty$	$+$	∞
$-\infty$	$-\infty$	$-$	∞
$-\infty$	$+\infty$	Invalid operation	
$+\infty$	$-\infty$	Invalid operation	
$\pm z$	$\pm\infty$	Sign of ∞	∞
$\pm\infty$	$\pm z$	Sign of ∞	∞

where $0 \leq z < \infty$.

FBLD

BCD Load

Format:

FBLD mem80

Description:

The ten-byte packed BCD memory operand pointed to by mem80 is converted to a temporary real value and pushed onto the top of the stack. The conversion is always exact. The BCD digits of mem80 are assumed to be in the range 0h to 9h.

Operation:

```
FPush();
ST = (tempReal) mem80;
```

Example:

```
FBLD mem80  Before: mem80: -000000000000005698  TOP: 4
            After : mem80: -000000000000005698  TOP: 3
                    ST   : -5.698 * 10^3
```

Exceptions:

```
Float(IS);
Memory();
```

Note:

An attempt to load invalid BCD digits puts an undefined temporary real value into ST.

FBSTP

BCD Store and Pop

Format:

FBSTP mem80

Description:

The stack top is converted to an 18-digit BCD number, which is stored into the ten-byte location pointed to by mem80. The stack is then popped. The ST is rounded to an integer using the rounding mode specified by RC. Thus, a FRNDINT is not needed prior to FBSTP.

Operation:

```
tmp = (BCD) ST;
FPop();
mem80 = tmp;
```

Example:

```
                                                  ; Round Down
FBLD mem80  Before: ST   : 8.99033 * 10^3  TOP: 7  RC: RD
                    mem80: XXXXXXXXXXXXXXXXXX
            After : ST   : 8.99033 * 10^3  TOP: 0  RC: RD
                    mem80: 000000000000008990
```

Exceptions:

```
Float(IS,I);
Memory();
if (ST is QUIETNaN){
    Float(I);
}
```

Notes:

ST for FBSTP can be a denormal, where it could not be in the 80287.

This instruction is very slow and may cause an interrupt latency problem.

If ST is a quiet NaN, an invalid operation exception will be generated. Operations with quiet NaNs do not normally generate exceptions.

FCHS

Change Sign

Format:

FCHS

Description:

The sign of the top stack element is complemented. If the stack top was +0.0, it is changed to −0.0 by FCHS.

Operation:

```
ST = - ST;
```

Example:

```
FCHS  Before: ST:   6.221 * 10^37
      After : ST:  -6.221 * 10^37
```

Exception:

```
Float(IS);
```

FCLEX / FNCLEX

Clear Exceptions

Formats:

FCLEX
FNCLEX

Description:

FCLEX/FNCLEX causes the 80387 to clear all exceptions and the busy bit of the status-word register.

FCLEX checks for unmasked numeric exceptions; FNCLEX does not.

Operation:

```
SW = SW & 7F00h;
```

Example:

```
FCLEX  Before: SW: F450
       After : SW: 7400
```

Exceptions:

None.

FCOM / FCOMP/ FCOMPP

Compare

Formats:

FCOM	op_1	; compare
	mem32	
	mem64	
	ST(i)	
FCOMP	op_1	; compare and pop
	mem32	
	mem64	
	ST(i)	
FCOMPP		; compare and pop two

Description:

The given operand is numerically compared with the top of stack. The condition codes are set according to the following table. If the opcode was FCOMPP, the operand compared against the top of stack is ST(1).

	C3	C2	C0
ST > op_1	0	0	0
ST < op_1	0	0	1
ST == op_1	1	0	0
Unordered	1	1	1

If the operand was FCOMP, the stack is popped once after comparison. If the operand was FCOMPP, the stack is popped twice after comparison.

Unordered comparison occurs if either of the two operands were NaNs.

The sign of zero is ignored in comparisons.

Operation:

```
if (OPCODE == FCOMPP){
   op1 = ST(1);
```

```
}
if ((ST is NaN) || (op1 is NaN)){
    C3 = 1; C2 = 1; C0 = 1;
} else if (ST > op1){
    C3 = 0; C2 = 0; C0 = 0;
} else if (ST < op1){
    C3 = 0; C2 = 0; C0 = 1;
} else if (ST == op1){
    C3 = 1; C2 = 0; C0 = 0;
}
if (OPCODE == FCOMP){
    FPop();
} else if (OPCODE == FCOMPP){
    FPop();
    FPop();
}
```

Example:

```
FCOMP ST(3)   Before: ST   : 2.4560 * 10^6
                      ST(3): 9.4102 * 10^4
                      TOP : 4   C3: X C2: X C0: X
              After : TOP : 5   C3: 0 C2: 0 C0: 0
```

Exceptions:

```
Float(IS,I,D);
if ((ST is QUIETNaN) || (op1 is QUIETNaN)){
    Float(I);
}
```

Notes:

FCOM generates an invalid operation exception if either operand was a quiet NaN. Normally, operations with quiet NaNs do not cause operation exceptions.

An example of jumping on the condition code flags of the 80387 is given in example 7, page 421.

FCOS

Cosine

Format:

FCOS

Description:

The cosine of ST is computed. After the computation is complete, the stack top is set to the cosine of ST and 1.0 is pushed onto the stack. Thus

$$ST(1) / ST = \cos(ST')$$

where ST′ is the stack top prior to the cosine instruction, ST is always 1.0, and ST(1) is the cosine of ST′.

The input operand to FCOS must be in the range of 0 to $\pi * 2^{62}$. If the source operand is within this range, C2 is set to 0. Otherwise C2 is set to 1, ST is left intact, and the stack-top pointer is also unchanged (TOP).

Operation:

```
if (ST < π * 2⁶²) {
    ST = cos(ST);
    FPush();
    ST = 1.0;
    C2 = 0;
} else {
    /* Note: no change to ST */
    C2 = 1;
}
```

Example:

```
FCOS  Before: ST   : 4.51200 * 10⁵     TOP: 4  C2: X
      After : ST   : 1.00000 * 10⁰     TOP: 3  C2: 0
              ST(1): 4.53137 * 10⁻¹
```

Exception:

```
Float(IS,I,D,U,P);
```

Note:

This instruction is new to the 80387.

FDECSTP

Decrement Stack Pointer

Format:

FDECSTP

Description:

One is subtracted from the stack-top pointer TOP in the status word. The tag word or the stack top itself is not updated. If an FDECSTP is executed when the TOP is 0, ST becomes 7. Pushing a new element onto the stack causes the stack pointer to be decremented, as does FDECSTP.

Operation:

```
TOP = TOP - 1;
if (TOP < 0){
    TOP = 7;
}
```

Example:

```
FDECSTP  Before: TOP: 4
         After : TOP: 3
```

Exceptions:

None.

Notes:

This instruction allows direct control of the stack pointer. This can be useful if a "virtual" accumulator stack that is larger than the eight hardware accumulators provided on the 80387 is needed. The "virtual" stack registers would reside in memory, and software would manage the virtual stack when stack invalid operation exceptions were detected. FDECSTP, FINCSTP, and FFREE are provided to support a virtual accumulator stack.

FDIV / FIDIV / FDIVP

Division

Formats:

FDIV				; Real divide and pop ST(1), ST
FDIV	*op₁*			; Real divide
	ST(n)			
	mem32			; short real
	mem64			; long real
FIDIV	*op₁*			; Integer divide
	mem16			; word integer
	mem32			; short integer
FDIVP	*op₁*	,	*op₂*	; Real divide and pop
	ST	,	ST(n)	
	ST(n)	,	ST	
FDIV	*op₁*	,	*op₂*	; Real divide
	ST	,	ST(n)	
	ST(n)	,	ST	

Description:

The explicitly or implicitly specified floating-point operands are divided (ST(1)/ST, ST/op_1, or op_1/op_2 when 0, 1, and 2 operands are specified, respectively), with the result being stored into the destination. The destination is the stack top in all cases except the two-operand form, where the destination can be ST(n).

If op_1 is a memory operand (word or short integer, short or long real), it is automatically converted to temporary real (the internal format) before any operations are performed with it.

An FDIV without any operands causes the stack to be popped. Thus, FDIV with no operands is synonymous with FDIVP ST(1),ST.

Operation:

```
if(NUMOPS == 0){
    ST(1) = ST(1) / ST;
    FPop();               /* pop the stack, result in ST */
```

```
} else if (NUMOPS == 1){
    ST = ST / (tempReal) op1;
} else {                    /* NUMOPS == 2 */
    op1 = op1 / op2;
    if (OPCODE = FDIVP){
        FPop();             /* pop the stack */
    }
}
```

Examples:

```
FDIV ST, ST(3)   Before: ST    : 2.240 * 10^-2
                         ST(3): 3.664 * 10^3
                 After : ST    : 6.113 * 10^-6
                         ST(3): 3.664 * 10^3
```

Exceptions:

```
Memory();
Float(IS,I,Z,U,P,D,O);
```

Notes:

The following table summarizes the divide operation (all varieties) with infinities.

Operands		Results (op_1)	
op_1	op_2	Sign	Value
$\pm\infty$	$\pm\infty$	Invalid operation	
$\pm\infty$	$\pm z$	Exclusive-or of operand signs	∞
$\pm z$	$\pm\infty$	Exclusive-or of operand signs	0
$\pm\infty$	± 0	Exclusive-or of operand signs	∞
$\pm z$	± 0	Exclusive-or of operand signs	∞

where $0 \leq z < \infty$

See example 11, page 428.

FDIVR / FIDIVR / FDIVRP

Division Reverse

Formats:

FDIVR				; Real divide reverse, ST(1)/ST
FDIVR	*op₁*			; Real divide reverse
	ST(n)			
	mem32			; short real
	mem64			; long real
FIDIVR	*op₁*			; Integer divide reverse
	mem16			; word integer
	mem32			; short integer
FDIVRP	*op₁*	,	*op₂*	; Real divide reverse and pop
	ST	,	ST(n)	
	ST(n)	,	ST	
FDIVR	*op₁*	,	*op₂*	; Real divide reverse
	ST	,	ST(n)	
	ST(n)	,	ST	

Description:

The explicitly or implicitly specified floating-point operands are divided (ST/ST(1), op_1/ST, or op_2/op_1 when 0, 1, and 2 operands are specified, respectively), with the result being stored into the destination. The destination is the stack top in all cases except the two-operand form, where the destination can be ST(n).

These operations are equivalent to FDIV/FIDIV/FDIVP except numerator and divisor are reversed (op_2/op_1 for FDIVR, rather than op_1/op_2 for FDIV, for instance).

If op_1 is a memory operand (word or short integer, short or long real), it is automatically converted to temporary real (the internal format) before any operations are performed with it.

An FDIVR without any operands causes the stack to be popped. Thus, FDIVR with no operands is synonymous with FDIVRP ST(1),ST.

Operation:

```
if(NUMOPS == 0){
    ST(1) = ST / ST(1);
    FPop();                 /* pop the stack, result in ST */
} else if (NUMOPS == 1){
    ST = (tempReal) op1 / ST;
} else {                    /* NUMOPS == 2 */
    op1 =  op2 / op1;
    if (OPCODE = FDIVRP){
        FPop();             /* pop the stack */
    }
}
```

Example:

```
FDIVR ST, ST(3)  Before: ST   : 2.240 * 10^-2
                         ST(3): 3.664 * 10^3
                 After : ST   : 1.636 * 10^5
                         ST(3): 3.664 * 10^3
```

Exceptions:

```
Memory();
Float(IS,I,Z,U,P,D,O);
```

Notes:

The following table summarizes the divide reverse operation (all varieties) with infinities.

Operands		Results (op_1)	
op_1	op_2	Sign	Value
$\pm\infty$	$\pm\infty$	Invalid operation	
$\pm\infty$	$\pm z$	Exclusive-or of operand signs	0
$\pm z$	$\pm\infty$	Exclusive-or of operand signs	∞
± 0	$\pm\infty$	Exclusive-or of operand signs	∞
± 0	$\pm z$	Exclusive-or of operand signs	∞

where $0 \leqslant z < \infty$

FFREE

Free Register

Format:

FFREE ST(n)

Description:

The tag-word bits associated with the specified register are set to 11b. This indicates that the specified stack element is changed to empty. Neither the floating-point stack nor the floating-point stack pointer is modified.

Operation:

```
tmp = ((TOP + n) % 8); /* physical register number */
TW = TW | (11b << (tmp * 2));
```

Example:

```
FFREE  ST(3)  Before: TOP: 3  TW: 0FC0
              After : TOP: 3  TW: 3FC0
```

Exceptions:

None.

Notes:

The tag word describes the physical stack registers, and FFREE gives an accumulator stack reference that is relative to the stack top.

FICOM / FICOMP

Integer Compare

Formats:

FICOM	*op₁*	;	Integer compare
	mem16	;	word integer
	mem32	;	short integer
FICOMP	*op₁*	;	Integer compare and pop
	mem16	;	word integer
	mem32	;	short integer

Description:

The given operand is converted from word or short integer into temporary real and numerically compared against the top of the stack. The condition codes are set according to the following table.

	C3	C2	C0
ST > op_1	0	0	0
ST < op_1	0	0	1
ST = = op_1	1	0	0
Unordered	1	1	1

If the operand was FICOMP, the stack is popped.

Unordered comparison occurs if the stack top was a NaN. The sign of zero is ignored in comparisons.

Operation:

```
tmp = (tempReal) op1;
if (ST is NaN){
    C3 = 1; C2 = 1; C0 = 1;
} else if (ST > tmp){
    C3 = 0; C2 = 0; C0 = 0;
} else if (ST < tmp){
    C3 = 0; C2 = 0; C0 = 1;
} else if (ST == tmp){
    C3 = 1; C2 = 0; C0 = 0;
}
if (OPCODE == FICOMP){
    FPop();
}
```

Example:

```
FICOMP mem16  Before: mem16: 94320   ST   : 6.0059 * 10^3
                      TOP : 4  C3: X C2: X C0: X
              After : mem16: 94320
                      TOP : 5  C3: 0 C2: 0 C0: 1
```

Exceptions:

```
Float(IS,I,D);
if (ST is QUIETNaN){
    Float(I);
}
```

Note:

An example of jumping on the condition codes of the 80387 is given in example 7, page 421.

FILD

Integer Load

Formats:

```
FILD   op1
       mem16   ; word integer
       mem32   ; short integer
       mem64   ; long integer
```

Description:

The memory word, short, or long integer given by op_1 is read from memory and converted into temporary real format. The stack is pushed, and the temporary real is placed in the new top of stack.

Operation:

```
FPush();
ST = (tempReal) op1;
```

Example:

```
FILD mem32  Before: mem32: F234D9A1          TOP: 6
            After : mem32: F234D9A1          TOP: 5
                    ST   : -2.31417439*10^8
```

Exceptions:

```
Float(IS);
Memory();
```

FINCSTP

Increment Stack Pointer

Format:

FINCSTP

Description:

One is added to the stack pointer in the status word. The tag word (TW) and the contents of the floating-point stack are not updated. If an FINCSTP is executed when the stack-top pointer (TOP) is 7, ST becomes 0. Popping an element off the stack causes the stack pointer to be incremented.

Operation:

```
TOP = (TOP + 1) % 8;
```

Example:

```
FINCSTP  Before: TOP: 7
         After : TOP: 0
```

Exceptions:

None.

Notes:

This instruction allows direct control of the stack pointer. This can be useful if a "virtual" accumulator stack that is larger than the eight hardware accumulators provided on the 80387 is needed. The "virtual" stack registers would reside in memory, and software would manage the virtual stack when stack invalid operation exceptions were detected. FDECSTP, FINCSTP, and FFREE are provided to support a virtual accumulator stack.

FINIT / FNINIT

Initialize Processor

Formats:

FINIT
FNINIT

Description:

FINIT/FNINIT sets all the control-word, status-word, and tag-word registers to their default values. After this instruction is executed, the machine rounding control is set to round to nearest, all exceptions are masked, precision is set to 64 bits, the status word (SW) is cleared except for the four condition code bits that are undefined, and all floating-point stack registers (TW) are set to empty.

FINIT checks for unmasked numeric exceptions; FNINIT does not.

Operation:

```
CW = 037Fh;   /* Round to nearest, mask all exceptions */
              /* 64-bit precision */
SW = SW & 4700h;
TW = FFFFh ;
```

Example:

```
FINIT  Before: CW: 1D7E  SW: D401  TW: 3FFC
       After : CW: 037F  SW: 4400  TW: FFFF
```

Exceptions:

None.

FIST

Integer Store

Formats:

FIST op_1
mem16 ; word integer
mem32 ; short integer

Description:

The stack top is rounded to an integer whose length matches that of op_1: word or short integer. The rounding is as specified by the round control (RC) bits of the control word (CW). The integer is then stored into op_1. Negative zero is converted to two's complement positive zero before storing.

Operation:

```
if (op1 is mem16){
    op1 = (wordInt) ST;
} else {    /* mem32 */
    op1 = (shortInt) ST;
}
```

Example:

```
                                                         ; Round Up
FIST mem16  Before: ST    : 8.90133*10^1   TOP: 5   RC: RU
            After : ST    : 8.90133*10^1   TOP: 5   RC: RU
                    mem16: 005A
```

Exceptions:

```
Float(IS,I,P);
Memory();
if (ST is QUIETNaN){
    Float(I);
}
```

Notes:

FIST cannot store a long integer.

If ST is a quiet NaN, an invalid operation exception is generated. Operating with a quiet NaN does not normally cause an operation exception.

FISTP

Integer Store and Pop

Formats:

FISTP *op₁*

FISTP	op_1	
	mem16	; word integer
	mem32	; short integer
	mem64	; long integer

Description:

The stack top is rounded to an integer whose length matches that of op_1: word, short, or long integer. The rounding is as specified by RC. The integer is then stored into op_1. Negative zero is converted to two's complement positive zero. The stack is popped.

Operation:

```
if (op1 is mem16){
    op1 = (wordInt)  ST;
} else if (op1 is mem32){
    op1 = (shortInt) ST;
} else {   /*  mem64   */
    op1 = (longInt)  ST;
}
FPop();
```

Floating Point

Examples:

```
                                                 ; Round Nearest
FISTP mem64  Before: ST    : -4.32990*10^3       TOP: 5  RC: RN
             After : mem64: FFFFFFFFFFFFEF16     TOP: 6  RC: RN
```

Exceptions:

```
Float(IS,I,P);
Memory();
```

Note:

FISTP can store a long integer, where FIST cannot.

FLD

Real Load

Formats:

FLD *op₁*
mem32 ; short real
mem64 ; long real
mem80 ; temp real
ST(i)

Description:

The stack is pushed. The short, long, or temporary real or stack operand specified by op_1 is stored into the new top of stack. If op_1 is a short or long real, the operand is converted to a temporary real before being stored into the new top of stack.

Operation:

```
FPush();
ST = (tempReal) op1 ;
```

Example:

```
FLD  mem32   ; mem32 is a short real
             Before: mem32: 3.2611 * 10^2   TOP: 2
             After : mem32: 3.2611 * 10^2   TOP: 1
                     ST   : 3.2611 * 10^2
```

Exceptions:

```
Memory();
if (op1 in (mem32,mem64)){
    Float(I,D);
}
Float(IS);
```

Note:

The 80287 will flag Float(D) exceptions in all formats including extended, where the 80387 will only flag Float(D) for short and long reals.

FLDcon

Load Constant

Formats:

FLD1	; load 1.0
FLDL2E	; load $\log_2 e$
FLDL2T	; load $\log_2 10$
FLDLG2	; load $\log_{10} 2$
FLDLN2	; load $\log_e 2$
FLDPI	; load π
FLDZ	; load 0.0

Description:

The stack is pushed. The constant value that is specified by the instruction itself is loaded into the new top of stack.

Operation:

```
FPush();
switch (OPCODE) {
  case FLD1   : ST = +1.0  ; break;
  case FLDL2E : ST = log₂e ; break;
  case FLDL2T : ST = log₂10; break;
  case FLDLG2 : ST = log₁₀2; break;
  case FLDLN2 : ST = logₑ2 ; break;
  case FLDPI  : ST = π     ; break;
  case FLDZ   : ST = +0.0  ; break;
}
```

Examples:

```
FLD1    Before: TOP: 6
        After : TOP: 5   ST: 1.0 * 10⁰

FLDPI   Before: TOP: 0
        After : TOP: 7   ST: 3.1416 * 10⁰
```

Floating Point

Exception:

```
Float(IS);
```

Note:

See example 9, page 423.

FLDCW

Load Control Word

Format:

FLDCW mem16

Description:

FLDCW loads the control word with the value found in mem16. An exception will be flagged if any of the exception flags in SW are unmasked by the new CW.

Operation:

```
CW = mem16;
```

Example:

```
FLDCW mem16   Before: CW: XXXX  mem16: 1F4F
              After : CW: 1F4F  mem16: 1F4F
```

Exception:

```
Float(I,IS,D,Z,O,U,P,S)
```

FLDENV

Load Environment

Format:

FLDENV mem

Description:

FLDENV loads the machine environment from the given memory area. The environment consists of the control-word, status-word, and tag-word registers, and the error-pointer registers of the most recent floating-point instruction executed. The detailed format of the error-pointer registers was given in Chapter 2. The error-pointer registers contain information on the most recent opcode and the data referenced.

Operation:

```
CW = mem;
SW = [&mem+4];
TW = [&mem+8];
LdErrorPoint(&mem);
```

Example:

```
FLDENV mem
      Before: CW : XXXX   SW : XXXX        TW : XXXX   FIP: XXXXXXXX
              FCS: XXXX   FDP: XXXXXXXX   FDS: XXXX
              [&mem+0 ]: XXXX137F   [mem+4 ]: XXXX0400
              [&mem+8 ]: XXXXA0FE   [mem+12]: 0000FFD0
              [&mem+16]: XXXX0241   [mem+20]: 005F3DD0
              [&mem+24]: XXXX3015
      After : CW : 137F   SW : 0400        TW : A0FE   FIP: 0000FFD0
              FCS: 0241   FOO: 005F3DD0   FOS: 3015
              [&mem+0 ]: XXXX137F   [mem+4 ]: XXXX0400
              [&mem+8 ]: XXXXA0FE   [mem+12]: 0000FFD0
              [&mem+16]: XXXX0241   [mem+20]: 005F3DD0
              [&mem+24]: XXXX3015
```

Exceptions:

```
Float(I,IS,D,Z,O,U,P,S)
```

FMUL / FIMUL / FMULP

Multiply

Formats:

FMUL				; Real multiply, ST(1), ST
FMUL	*op₁*			; Real multiply
	ST(n)			
	mem32			; short real
	mem64			; long real
FIMUL	*op₁*			; Integer multiply
	mem16			; word integer
	mem32			; short integer
FMULP	*op₁*	,	*op₂*	; Real multiply and pop
	ST	,	ST(n)	
	ST(n)	,	ST	
FMUL	*op₁*	,	*op₂*	; Real multiply
	ST	,	ST(n)	
	ST(n)	,	ST	

Description:

The explicitly or implicitly specified floating-point operands are multiplied (ST(1)*ST, ST*op_1, or op_1*op_2 when 0, 1, and 2 operands are specified, respectively), with the result being stored into the destination. The destination is the stack top in all cases except the two-operand form, where the destination can be ST(n).

If op_1 is a memory operand (word or short integer, short or long real), it is automatically converted to temporary real (the internal format) before any operations are performed with it.

An FMUL without any operands causes the stack to be popped. Thus, FMUL with no operands is synonymous with FMULP ST(1),ST.

Floating Point

Operation:

```
if(NUMOPS == 0){
    ST(1) = ST(1) * ST;
    FPop();              /* pop the stack, result in ST */
```

```
} else if (NUMOPS == 1){
    ST = ST * (tempReal) op1;
} else {                    /* NUMOPS == 2 */
    op1 = op1 * op2;
    if (OPCODE == FMULP){
        FPop();             /* pop the stack */
    }
}
```

Examples:

```
FMULP ST, ST(3)   Before: ST   : 8.410 * 10^-12   TOP: 4
                          ST(3): 9.934 * 10^9
                  After : ST   : 8.354 * 10^-2    TOP: 3
                          ST(2): 9.934 * 10^9
```

Exceptions:

```
Memory();
Float(IS,I,O,P,D,U);
```

Notes:

The following table summarizes the multiply operation (all varieties) with infinities.

Operands		Results (op_1)	
op_1	op_2	Sign	Value
$\pm\infty$	$\pm\infty$	Exclusive-or of operand signs	∞
$\pm\infty$	$\pm x$	Exclusive-or of operand signs	∞
± 0	$\pm\infty$	Invalid operation	
$\pm\infty$	± 0	Invalid operation	

where $0 < x < \infty$.

See example 10, page 424.

FNOP

No Operation

Format:

FNOP

Description:

FNOP stores the stack top to the stack top, which is effectively a NOP.

Operation:

```
ST = ST;
```

Example:

```
FNOP
```

Exceptions:

None.

FPATAN

Partial Arctangent

Format:

FPATAN

Description:

The arctangent of ST(1)/ST is computed. After the computation is complete, the stack is popped once and the result is placed in the new top of stack.

The 80387 places no limits on the operand range allowed by the FPATAN instruction. The results, however, are in the range given by the following table.

Sign(ST(1))	Sign(ST)	|ST(1)| < |ST|	Result
+	+	Yes	ATAN(ST(1)/ST)
+	+	No	$\pi/2$ − ATAN(ST(1)/ST)
+	−	Yes	π − ATAN(ST(1)/−ST)
+	−	No	$\pi/2$ − ATAN(−ST(1)/ST)
−	+	Yes	− ATAN(ST(1)/ST)
−	+	No	$-\pi/2$ + ATAN(ST(1)/−ST)
−	−	Yes	$-\pi$ + ATAN(—ST(1)/−ST)
−	−	No	$-\pi/2$ − ATAN(−ST(1)/−ST)

Operation:

```
ST(1) = arctan(ST(1) / ST);
FPop();    /* result in ST after FPop */
```

Example:

```
FPATAN  Before: ST   : 4.51200 * 10^5     TOP: 4
                ST(1): 3.664   * 10^3
        After : ST   : 8.12039 * 10^-3    TOP: 5
```

Exception:

```
Float(IS,I,D,U,P);
```

Notes:

The 80287 operand range allowed is

$$0 \leqslant |ST(1)| < |ST(0)| < +\infty$$

where the 80387 operand range is not restricted.

FPREM

Partial Remainder

Format:

FPREM

Description:

FPREM computes the partial remainder of ST/ST(1). The remainder produced is exact (no precision error is possible). The remainder is computed by a series of successive scaled subtractions. When the operands differ greatly in magnitude, this series of subtractions can take a very long time. To prevent severely degrading interrupt latency, the instruction only partially computes the remainder, and a software loop is required to complete the reduction. Thus the mnemonic: partial remainder.

The instruction reduces a magnitude difference up to 2^{64} in one execution. If the reduction is complete, condition code 2 is set to 0 and condition code bits 0, 3, and 1 reflect the least significant 3 bits of the quotient. If the reduction was incomplete, condition code 2 is set to 1.

The result obeys the relation

$$REM = ST - ST(1) * quotient;$$

where the remainder always has the sign of the original ST.

FPREM was important on the 80287, since most of the periodic transcendental functions had their range restricted from 0 to $\pi/4$. FPREM would then reduce the argument to the proper range. Since all such bounds on the arguments have been removed on the 80387 (hurray!), this instruction is not as important to the 80387 as it was to the 80287.

Operation:

```
if (|ST| < |ST(1)| * 2^64){
    C2 = 0;
    quotient = ST / ST(1);
    ST = ST % ST(1);
    /* / and mod result in the sign of ST being */
    /* the same as the original ST.             */
```

```
        if ((quotient % 8) >= 4 ) C0 = 1;
        if ((quotient % 4) >= 2 ) C3 = 1;
        if ((quotient % 2) == 1 ) C1 = 1;
    } else {
        if (ST > 0) {
            ST = ST - ST(1) * (2^64 -1);
        } else { ST = ST + ST(1) * (2^64 -1); }
        C2 = 1;
    }
```

Example:

```
                                                 CCCC
                                                 3210
FPREM  Before: ST    : -4.317 * 10^2             XXXX
               ST(1):   6.283 * 10^0
       After : ST    : -4.443 * 10^0             0000
               ST(1):   6.283 * 10^0
```

Exceptions:

```
Float(IS,I,U,D);
```

Notes:

The condition codes (C0, C3, C1) are reliably set on the 80387, where they were not on the 80287.

See also FPREM1.

If ST(1) was initially ∞, ST is unchanged and the quotient (condition codes) is set to 0.

See example 8, page 422.

FPREM1

Partial Remainder — IEEE

Format:

FPREM1

Description:

FPREM1 computes the partial remainder of ST/ST(1). The remainder produced is exact (no precision error is possible). The remainder is computed by a series of successive scaled subtractions. When the operands differ greatly in magnitude, this series of subtractions can take a very long time. To prevent severely degrading interrupt latency, the instruction only partially computes the remainder, and a software loop is required to complete the reduction. Thus the mnemonic: partial remainder.

The instruction reduces a magnitude difference up to 2^{64} in one execution. If the reduction is complete, condition code 2 is set to 0 and condition code bits 0, 3, and 1 reflect the least significant 3 bits of the quotient. If the reduction was incomplete, condition code 2 is set to 1.

The result obeys the relation

$$REM = ST - ST(1) * quotient;$$

where the quotient is the integer nearest to the exact value of ST/ST(1). Whenever

$$|Q - ST/ST(1)| = 1/2$$

Q is even. Rounding mode and precision control do not affect the results except when ST(1) exactly divides into ST. In this case, the result is plus zero for rounding control of nearest, up, or chop and minus zero for down.

FPREM was important on the 80287, since most of the periodic transcendental functions had their range restricted from 0 to $\pi/4$. FPREM would then reduce the argument to the proper range. Since all such bounds on the arguments have been removed on the 80387 (hurray!), FPREM is not as important to the 80387 as it was to the 80287.

Operation:

```
if (|ST| < |ST(1)| * 2^64){
    C2 = 0;
    quotient = ST / ST(1);
    ST = ST % ST(1);
    /* / and % result in ST being in the range */
    /* -abs(ST(1)/2) to abs(ST(1)/2)           */
    if ((quotient % 8) >= 4 ) C0 = 1;
    if ((quotient % 4) >= 2 ) C3 = 1;
    if ((quoticnt % 2) == 1 ) C1 = 1;
} else {
    if (ST > 0) {
        ST = ST - ST(1) * (2^64-1);
    } else { ST = ST + ST(1) * (2^64-1); }
    C2 = 1;
}
```

Example:

```
                                             CCCC
                                             3210
FPREM1  Before: ST   :  -4.317 * 10^2        XXXX
                ST(1):   6.283 * 10^0
        After : ST   :   1.827 * 10^0        0010
                ST(1):   6.283 * 10^0
```

Exceptions:

```
Float(IS,I,U,D);
```

Notes:

FPREM1 is new to the 87 family. FPREM1 is for the purpose of IEEE compatibility. The example of FPREM and FPREM1 emphasizes the differences of the two instructions.

Note the difference with FPREM. The remainder for FPREM1 is always in the range −abs(ST(1)/2) to abs(ST(1)/2), where FPREM placed the remainder in the range 0 to abs(ST(1)) and −abs(ST(1)) to 0 for positive and negative dividends ST, respectively. This may lead to a difference of 1 between the condition code settings of FPREM and FPREM1.

If ST(1) was initially ∞, ST is unchanged and the quotient (condition codes) is set to 0.

FPTAN

Partial Tangent

Format:

FPTAN

Description:

The tangent of ST is computed. After the computation is complete, the stack top is set to the tangent of ST and 1.0 is pushed onto the stack. Thus

$$ST(1)/ST = \tan(ST')$$

where ST′ is the stack top prior to the tangent instruction, ST is always 1.0, and ST(1) is the tangent of ST′.

The input operand to FPTAN must be in the range of 0 to $\pi * 2^{62}$. If the source operand is within this range, C2 is cleared to 0. Otherwise, C2 is set to 1 and ST is unchanged as well as the stack-top pointer (TOP).

Operation:

```
if (ST < π * 2^62) {
    ST = tan(ST);
    FPush();
    ST = 1.0;
    C2 = 0;
} else {
    /* Note that ST and TOP are unaltered */
    C2 = 1;
}
```

Example:

```
FPTAN  Before: ST   : 9.47103 * 10^22   TOP: 4   C2: X
       After : ST   : 1.00000 * 10^0    TOP: 3   C2: 0
               ST(1): 1.51273 * 10^0
```

Exception:

```
Float(IS,I,D,U,P);
```

FRNDINT

Round to Integer

Format:

FRNDINT

Description:

The top-of-stack element is rounded to an integer. The rounding obeys the setting of the RC (round control) field in the control word. The four rounding modes are chop (11), minus infinity (01), plus infinity (10), and nearest (00).

Operation:

```
ST = (int) ST ;
```

Examples:

```
                                       ; Round to nearest
FRNDINT  Before:  ST: -4.317 * 10^0   RC: 00
         After :  ST: -4.000 * 10^0   RC: 00
                                       ; Round to -infinity
FRNDINT  Before:  ST: -4.317 * 10^0   RC: 01
         After :  ST: -5.000 * 10^0   RC: 01
```

Exceptions:

```
Float(IS,I,D,P);
```

FRSTOR

Restore State

Format:

FRSTOR mem

Description:

FRSTOR reloads the complete state of the 80387 from the 108-byte location given by mem. Included in this is the 80387 environment and the eight 80b floating-point stack registers.

The format of the load memory is identical with that of the FSAVE instruction.

Any exception is possible if the combination of the status word and control word are in an exception combination.

Operation:

```
CW = mem;
SW = [&mem+4];
TW = [&mem+8];
LdErrorPoint(&mem);
for(i=0;i<8;i++){
     STi = [&mem+28+i*10] ;
}
```

Example:

```
FRSTOR mem    ; mem is a 108-byte data location.
```

Exceptions:

```
Float(I,IS,D,Z,O,U,P,S)
Memory();
```

FSAVE / FNSAVE

Save State

Formats:

FSAVE mem
FNSAVE mem

Description:

FSAVE/FNSAVE stores the complete state of the 80387 into the memory location mem. The environment consists of the control-word, status-word, and tag-word registers; the error-pointer registers; and the complete floating-point stack (eight 80b registers). The detailed format of the error pointers and save area was given in Chapter 2. The error pointers contain information on the most recent instruction executed and any data address used.

After storing the 80387 state, FSAVE initializes the 80387, in the same way the FINIT instruction does.

FSAVE checks for unmasked numeric exceptions, FNSAVE does not.

Operation:

```
mem = CW;
[&mem+4] = SW;
[&mem+8] = TW;
StErrorPointer(&mem);
for(i=0;i<8;i++){
    [&mem+28+i*10] = STi;
}
FINIT;
```

Example:

```
FSAVE mem    ; mem is a 108-byte data location.
```

Exception:

```
Memory();
```

FSCALE

Power of Two Scaling

Format:

FSCALE

Description:

The top of stack is scaled by the power of two given in ST(1). The value in ST(1) is treated as an integer and is added to the exponent of ST. This is useful as a quick way of multiplying by powers of two.

FSCALE uses the nearest integer smaller in magnitude than ST(1) (that is, ST(1) is chopped).

Operation:

```
ST = ST * 2^ST(1)
```

Examples:

```
FSCALE  Before: ST   : -1.0111b * 2^6
                ST(1): -1.0110b * 2^4
        After : ST   : -1.0111b * 2^-16
                ST(1): -1.0110b * 2^4
```

Exception:

```
Float(IS,I,D,O,U,P);
```

Notes:

FSCALE on the 80387 has no restriction on the range of ST(1) as the 80287 did. Operands in the range

$$0 < |ST(1)| < 1$$

are treated as zero, where operands in this range on the 80287 gave an undefined result. Operands that cause overflow or underflow signal exceptions.

The following table summarizes the FSCALE operations with infinities.

Original Operands		Results (ST)	
ST	ST(1)	Sign	Value
$\pm\infty$	$-\infty$	Invalid operation	
$\pm\infty$	$+\infty$	Sign of ST	∞
$\pm\infty$	$\pm z$	Sign of ST	∞
± 0	$\pm\infty$	Sign of ST	0
$\pm x$	$+\infty$	Overflow	
$\pm x$	$-\infty$	Underflow	

where $0 < x < \infty$ and $0 \leq z < \infty$

FSIN

Sine

Format:

FSIN

Description:

The sine of ST is computed. After the computation is complete, the stack top is set to the sine of ST and 1.0 is pushed onto the stack. Thus

$$ST(1) / ST = \sin(ST')$$

where ST′ is the stack top prior to the sine instruction, ST is always 1.0, and ST(1) is the sine of ST′.

The input operand to the FSIN must be in the range of 0 to $\pi * 2^{62}$. If the source operand is within this range, C2 is set to 0. Otherwise, C2 is set to 1, and ST, as well as the stack-top pointer (TOP), is unchanged.

Operation:

```
if (ST < π * 2^62) {
    ST = sin(ST);
    FPush();
    ST = 1.0;
    C2 = 0;
} else {
    /* Note that ST and TOP are unaltered */
    C2 = 1;
}
```

Example:

```
FSIN  Before: ST   :   8.41229 * 10^3    TOP: 4   C2: X
      After : ST   :   1.00000 * 10^0    TOP: 3   C2: 0
              ST(1):  -7.80288 * 10^-1
```

Exception:

```
Float(IS,I,D,U,P);
```

Note:

This instruction is new to the 80387.

FSINCOS

Sine and Cosine

Format:

FSINCOS

Description:

The sine and cosine of ST are computed. After the computation is complete, the stack top is set to the sine of ST. The cosine is then pushed onto the stack. Thus, at the end of execution, ST(1) = sin(ST′) and ST = cos(ST′), where ST′ is the stack top prior to the FSINCOS instruction.

The input operand to the FSINCOS instruction must be in the range of 0 to $\pi*2^{62}$. If the source operand is within this range, C2 is set to 0. Otherwise, C2 is set to 1, and ST, as well as the stack-top pointer (TOP), is unchanged. The sine result of FSINCOS may be less precise than the FSIN and FCOS instructions.

Operation:

```
if (ST < π * 2^62) {
    tmp = cos(ST);
    ST = sin(ST);
    FPush();
    ST = tmp;
    C2 = 0;
} else {
    /* Note that ST and TOP are unaltered */
    C2 = 1;
}
```

Example:

```
FSINCOS  Before: ST    :  2.97421 * 10^6    TOP: 4   C2: X
         After : ST    :  9.86024 * 10^-1   TOP: 3   C2: 0
                 ST(1):  1.66602 * 10^-1
```

Exception:

```
Float(IS,I,D,U,P);
```

Note:

This instruction is new to the 80387.

FSQRT

Square Root

Format:

FSQRT

Description:

The top of stack is replaced with the square root of the top of the stack. Note that

FSQRT(−0) = −0

FSQRT(+∞) = +∞

and FSQRT(−∞) is an invalid operation.

Operation:

```
ST = sqrt(ST);
```

Example:

```
FSQRT  Before: ST : 8.410 * 10⁴
       After : ST : 2.900 * 10²
```

Exception:

```
Float(IS,I,U,P,D);
```

Note:

See example 11, page 428.

FST

Real Store

Formats:

FST *op_1*

mem32 ; short real

mem64 ; long real

ST(i)

Description:

The top of stack is stored into op_1. If op_1 is a short or long real, the top of stack is first converted to the type according to RC (round control). If the top of stack is a NaN or an infinity, the stack-top exponent and significand are chopped rather than rounded to fit the destination sizes.

Operation:

```
if (op1 is mem32){
    op1 = (shortReal) ST;
} else if (op1 is mem64){
    op1 = (longReal) ST;
} else {
    op1 = ST;
}
```

Example:

```
FST  mem64  ; mem64 is a long real
            Before: ST   : 2.9921 * 10^-9   TOP: 2
                    mem64: X.XXXX * 10^X
            After : ST   : 2.9921 * 10^-9   TOP: 2
                    mem64: 2.9921 * 10^-9
```

Exceptions:

```
Memory();
Float(IS,I,O,U,P);
```

Notes:

The D exception is not flagged during FST, to maintain compatibility with the 80287.

FST cannot store a temporary real operand to memory, where FSTP can.

FSTCW / FNSTCW

Store Control Word

Formats:

FSTCW mem16

FNSTCW mem16

Description:

FSTCW/FNSTCW stores the control word into mem16. FSTCW checks for unmasked numeric exceptions; FNSTCW does not.

Operation:

```
mem16 = CW;
```

Example:

```
FSTCW mem16  Before: CW: 1F4D  mem16: XXXX
             After : CW: 1F4D  mem16: 1F4D
```

Exceptions:

None.

FSTENV / FNSTENV

Store Environment

Formats:

FSTENV mem

FNSTENV mem

Description:

FSTENV/FNSTENV stores the machine environment into the given memory location. The environment consists of the control-word, status-word, and tag-word registers, and the error pointers of the most recent floating-point instruction executed. The detailed format of the error pointers was given in Chapter 2. The error pointers contain information on the most recent instruction executed and any data address used in that instruction.

FSTENV checks for unmasked numeric exceptions; FNSTENV does not.

Operation:

```
mem = CW;
[&mem+4] = SW;
[&mem+8] = TW;
StErrorPointer(&mem);
```

Example:

```
FSTENV mem
          Before: CW : 137F   SW : 0400      TW : A0FE   FIP: 0000FFD0
                  FCS: 0241   FOS: 005F3DD0  FOS: 3015
                  [&mem+0 ]: XXXXXXXX   [mem+4 ]: XXXXXXXX
                  [&mem+8 ]: XXXXXXXX   [mem+12]: XXXXXXXX
                  [&mem+16]: XXXXXXXX   [mem+20]: XXXXXXXX
                  [&mem+24]: XXXXXXXX
          After : CW : 137F   SW : 0400      TW : A0FE   FIP: 0000FFD0
                  FCS: 0241   FOS: 005F3DD0  FOS: 3015
                  [&mem+0 ]: XXXX137F   [mem+4 ]: XXXX0400
                  [&mem+8 ]: XXXXA0FE   [mem+12]: 0000FFD0
                  [&mem+16]: XXXX0241   [mem+20]: 005F3DD0
                  [&mem+24]: XXXX3015
```

Exception:

```
Memory();
```

FSTP

Real Store and Pop

Formats:

FST *op_1*
mem32 ; short real
mem64 ; long real
mem80 ; temp real
ST(i)

Description:

The top of stack is stored into op_1. If op_1 is a short or long real, the top of stack is first converted to this type as specified by RC. If the top of stack is a NaN or an infinity, the stack-top exponent and significand are chopped rather than rounded to fit the destination sizes.

FSTP can store a temporary real number to memory, where FST cannot.

Operation:

```
if (op1 is mem32){
    op1 = (shortReal) ST;
} else if (op1 is mem64){
    op1 = (longReal) ST;
} else {
    op1 = ST;
}
FPop();
```

Example:

```
FSTP  mem64  ; mem32 is a short real
            Before: ST    : 8.9901 * 10^-102    TOP: 7
                    mem64: X.XXXX * 10^X
            After : ST    : 8.9901 * 10^-102    TOP: 0
                    mem64: 8.9901 * 10^-102
```

Exceptions:

```
Memory();
Float(IS,I,O,U,P);
```

Notes:

The D exception is not flagged during FSTP, to maintain compatibility with the 80287.

See example 10, page 424.

FSTSW / FNSTSW

Store Status Word

Formats:

FSTSW mem16
FNSTSW mem16

Description:

FSTSW/FNSTSW stores the current status word into mem16. FSTSW checks for unmasked numeric exceptions; FNSTSW does not.

Operation:

```
mem16 = SW;
```

Example:

```
FSTSW mem16  Before: SW: FF81  mem16: XXXX
             After : SW: FF81  mem16: FF81
```

Exception:

```
Memory();
```

FSTSW AX / FNSTSW AX

Store Status Word into AX

Formats:

FSTSW AX
FNSTSW AX

Description:

FSTSW/FNSTSW stores the current status word into the 80386 AX register. This instruction is useful for control-flow changes based upon the condition flag settings of the 80387.

FSTSW checks for unmasked numeric exceptions; FNSTSW does not.

Operation:

```
AX = SW;
```

Example:

```
FSTSW AX   Before: SW: 0900  AX: XXXX
           After : SW: 0900  AX: 0900
```

Exceptions:

None.

Note:

See example 7, page 421.

FSUB / FISUB / FSUBP

Subtraction

Formats:

```
FSUB                          ; Real subtraction, ST(1) - ST
FSUB    op1                   ; Real subtraction
        ST(n)
        mem32                 ;     short real
        mem64                 ;     long real
FISUB   op1                   ; Integer subtraction
        mem16                 ;     word integer
        mem32                 ;     short integer
FSUBP   op1    ,  op2         ; Real subtraction and pop
        ST     ,  ST(n)
        ST(n)  ,  ST
FSUB    op1    ,  op2         ; Real subtraction
        ST     ,  ST(n)
        ST(n)  ,  ST
```

Description:

The explicitly or implicitly specified floating-point operands are subtracted (ST(1) − ST, ST − op_1, or $op_1 - op_2$ when 0, 1, and 2 operands are specified, respectively), with the result being stored into the destination. The destination is the stack top in all cases except the two-operand form, where the destination can be ST(n).

If op_1 is a memory operand (word or short integer, short or long real), it is automatically converted to temporary real (the internal format) before any operations are performed with it.

An FSUB without any operands causes the stack to be popped. Thus, FSUB with no operands is synonymous with FSUBP ST(1),ST.

Operation:

```
if(NUMOPS == 0){
    ST(1) = ST(1) - ST;
    FPop();              /* pop the stack, result in ST */
```

```
} else if (NUMOPS == 1){
    ST = ST - (tempReal) op1;
} else {                    /* NUMOPS == 2 */
    op1 = op1 - op2;
    if (OPCODE == FSUBP){
        FPop();             /* pop the stack */
    }
}
```

Example:

```
FSUB ST, ST(3)    ; ST = ST - ST(3);
                   Before: ST    : 8.410 * 10^12   TOP: 7
                           ST(3): 9.934 * 10^11
                   After : ST    : 7.419 * 10^12   TOP: 7
                           ST(3): 9.934 * 10^11
```

Exceptions:

```
Memory();
Float(IS,I,O,P,D,U);
```

Notes:

The following table summarizes the subtract operation (all varieties) with infinities.

Original Operands		Results (op_1)	
op_1	op_2	Sign	Value
$+\infty$	$-\infty$	$+$	∞
$-\infty$	$+\infty$	$-$	∞
$+\infty$	$+\infty$	Invalid operation	
$-\infty$	$-\infty$	Invalid operation	
$\pm\infty$	$\pm z$	Sign of ∞	∞
$\pm z$	$\pm\infty$	Sign of z	∞

where $0 \leq z < \infty$

Floating Point

FSUBR / FISUBR / FSUBRP

Subtraction Reverse

Formats:

FSUBR				; Real subtraction reverse, ST − ST(1)
FSUBR	*op₁*			; Real subtraction reverse
	ST(n)			
	mem32			; short real
	mem64			; long real
FISUBR	*op₁*			; Integer subtraction
	mem16			; word integer
	mem32			; short integer
FSUBRP	*op₁*	,	*op₂*	; Real subtraction reverse and pop
	ST	,	ST(n)	
	ST(n)	,	ST	
FSUBR	*op₁*	,	*op₂*	; Real subtraction reverse
	ST	,	ST(n)	
	ST(n)	,	ST	

Description:

The explicitly or implicitly specified floating-point operands are subtracted (ST − ST(1), $op_1 - ST$, or $op_2 - op_1$ when 0, 1, and 2 operands are specified, respectively), with the result being stored into the destination. The destination is the stack top in all cases except the two-operand form, where the destination can be ST(n).

If op_1 is a memory operand (word or short integer, short or long real), it is automatically converted to temporary real (the internal format) before any operations are performed with it.

An FSUBR without any operands causes the stack to be popped. Thus, FSUBR with no operands is synonymous with FSUBRP ST(1),ST.

Operation:

```
if(NUMOPS == 0){
    ST(1) = ST - ST(1);
    FPop();                /* pop the stack, result in ST */
```

```
} else if (NUMOPS == 1){
    ST = (tempReal) op1 - ST;
} else {                      /* NUMOPS == 2 */
    op1 = op2 - op1;
    if (OPCODE == FSUBRP){
        FPop();               /* pop the stack */
    }
}
```

Example:

```
FSUBR mem     ; ST = mem - ST
           Before: mem:    9934
                   ST :    8.410    * 10^4
           After : mem:    9934
                   ST : -7.74166 * 10^4
```

Exceptions:

```
Memory();
Float(IS,I,O,P,D,U);
```

Notes:

The following table summarizes the subtract reverse operation (all varieties) with infinities.

Original Operands		Results (op_1)	
op_1	op_2	Sign	Value
$+\infty$	$-\infty$	$-$	∞
$-\infty$	$+\infty$	$+$	∞
$+\infty$	$+\infty$	Invalid operation	
$-\infty$	$-\infty$	Invalid operation	
$\pm\infty$	$\pm z$	Sign of z	∞
$\pm z$	$\pm\infty$	Sign of ∞	∞

where $0 \leq z < \infty$

FTST

Test

Format:

FTST

Description:

The stack top is numerically compared against 0. The condition code bits in the status word are set according to the following table.

	C3	C2	C0
ST > 0.0	0	0	0
ST < 0.0	0	0	1
ST == 0.0	1	0	0
Unordered	1	1	1

Unordered comparison occurs if ST is a NaN. The sign of zero is ignored in comparisons.

Operation:

```
if (ST is NaN){
    C3 = 1; C2 = 1; C0 = 1;
} else if (ST > 0.0){
    C3 = 0; C2 = 0; C0 = 0;
} else if (ST < 0.0){
    C3 = 0; C2 = 0; C0 = 1;
} else if (ST == 0.0){
    C3 = 1; C2 = 0; C0 = 0;
}
```

Example:

```
FTST  Before: ST: 2.4560 * 10^6    TOP: 4
              C3: X C2: X C0: X
      After : ST: 2.4560 * 10^6    TOP: 4
              C3: 0 C2: 0 C0: 0
```

Exceptions:

```
Float(IS,I,D);
if (ST is QUIETNaN) {
    Float(I);
}
```

FUCOM / FUCOMP / FUCOMPP

Unordered Compare

Formats:

```
FUCOM     op1      ; Unordered compare
          mem32    ;    short real
          mem64    ;    long real
          ST(i)
FUCOMP    op1      ; Unordered compare and pop
          mem32    ;    short real
          mem64    ;    long real
          ST(i)
FUCOMPP            ; Unordered compare and pop two
```

Description:

The given operand is numerically compared with the top of stack. The condition codes are set according to the following table. If the opcode was FUCOMPP, the operand compared against the top of stack is ST(1).

	C3	C2	C0
ST > op₁	0	0	0
ST < op₁	0	0	1
ST = = op₁	1	0	0
Unordered	1	1	1

If the operand was FUCOMP, the stack is popped once. If the operand was FUCOMPP, the stack is popped twice.

Unordered comparison occurs if either of the two operands are NaNs. The sign of zero is ignored in comparisons.

Operation:

```
if (OPCODE == FUCOMPP){
   op1 = ST(1);
}
if ((ST is NaN) || (op1 is NaN)){
    C3 = 1; C2 = 1; C0 = 1;
} else if (ST > op1){
    C3 = 0; C2 = 0; C0 = 0;
} else if (ST < op1){
    C3 = 0; C2 = 0; C0 = 1;
} else if (ST == op1){
    C3 = 1; C2 = 0; C0 = 0;
}
if (OPCODE == FUCOMP){
    FPop();
} else if (OPCODE == FUCOMPP){
    FPop();
    FPop();
}
```

Example:

```
FUCOMPP  Before: ST    : 6.1224 * 10^-4
                 ST(1): 5.3210 * 10^-11
                 TOP   : 4  C3: X C2: X C0: X
         After : TOP   : 6  C3: 0 C2: 0 C0: 0
```

Exception:

```
Float(IS,I,D);
```

Notes:

FUCOM (and all variant pop forms) are identical to FCOM (and its variants), except that FUCOM does not cause an exception on either operand being a quiet NaN, where FCOM does.

FXAM

Examine

Format:

FXAM

Description:

The stack top is examined. The condition codes of the status word are modified according to the following table.

C3	C2	C1	C0	ST Value
0	0	0	0	+ Unsupported
0	0	0	1	+ NaN
0	0	1	0	− Unsupported
0	0	1	1	− NaN
0	1	0	0	+ Normal
0	1	0	1	+ ∞
0	1	1	0	− Normal
0	1	1	1	− ∞
1	0	0	0	+ 0
1	0	0	1	+ Empty
1	0	1	0	− 0
1	0	1	1	− Empty
1	1	0	0	+ Denormal
1	1	0	1	+ Empty
1	1	1	0	− Denormal
1	1	1	1	− Empty

The *Unsupported* entry in the table refers to any of the following: pseudo-NaN, pseudo-infinity, unnormal, or pseudo-zero, as described in Chapter 1.

Operation:

```
if (ST < 0.0){
    C1 = 1;
}
if      (ST is UNSUPPORTED){ C3 = 0 ; C2 = 0 ; C0 = 0 ; }
else if (ST is NaN        ){ C3 = 0 ; C2 = 0 ; C0 = 1 ; }
else if (ST is NORMAL     ){ C3 = 0 ; C2 = 1 ; C0 = 0 ; }
else if (ST is INFINITY   ){ C3 = 0 ; C2 = 1 ; C0 = 1 ; }
else if (ST == 0.0        ){ C3 = 1 ; C2 = 0 ; C0 = 0 ; }
else if (ST is DENORMAL   ){ C3 = 1 ; C2 = 1 ; C0 = 0 ; }
else if (ST is EMPTY      ){ C3 = 1 ; C2 = 0 ; C0 = 1 ; }
```

Example:

```
FXAM  Before: ST : 3.21950 * 10^-131   TOP: 2
              C3 : X  C2: X  C1: X  C0: X
      After : ST : 3.21950 * 10^-131   TOP: 2
              C3 : 0  C2: 1  C1: 0  C0: 0
```

Exceptions:

None.

Note:

See the floating-point section of Chapter 1 for further details of these data types.

FXCH

Exchange Registers

Format:

FXCH
FXCH *op₁*
ST(n)

Description:

The contents of op_1 are exchanged with the contents of the top of stack. Since many 80387 instructions operate only on the stack top (for example: FSQRT, FSIN, FPATAN), FXCH provides a convenient way to use these instructions on other stack elements.

Operation:

```
if (NUMOPS == 1){
    tmp = ST;
    ST = ST(n);
    ST(n) = tmp;
} else {
    tmp = ST;
    ST = ST(1);
    ST(1) = tmp;
}
```

Example:

```
FXCH ST(3)   Before: ST   :  9.99321 * 10^-92    TOP: 3
                     ST(3): -7.22964 * 10^75
             After : ST   : -7.22964 * 10^75     TOP: 3
                     ST(3):  9.99321 * 10^-92
```

Exception:

```
Float(IS);
```

Note:

See example 11, page 428.

FXTRACT

Extract Exponent and Significand

Format:

FXTRACT

Description:

The exponent (unbiased) of the original stack top is placed in the stack top as a real number. The significand and sign are pushed onto the stack (the new top of stack). Thus, the original stack top is decomposed into a true exponent (ST(1)) — unbiased — and a significand (ST) portion. The significand has an exponent of zero.

Operation:

```
tmp = ST;
if(tmp == 0){
    ST = -INFINITY;
} else {
    /* Note that the bias (16383) is subtracted out */
    ST  = (tempReal) ((tmp >> 64) & 7FFFh) - 16383;
}
FPush();
                                /* 64 bits */
ST  = (tempReal) (tmp & FFFFFFFFFFFFFFFFh/2^63);
if (tmp < 0.0){
    ST = -ST;
}
```

Example:

```
FXTRACT  Before:   ST:     1.1001101b * 2^39  TOP = 3
         After :   ST:     1.1001101b * 2^0   TOP = 2
                ST(1):     1.00111b   * 2^5
```

Exception:

```
Float(IS,I,Z,D);
```

Notes:

If the operand was 0, ST(1) (exponent) is set to $-\infty$ and ST (significand) is set to 0 with the same sign as the original stack top. This differs from the setting by the 80287. If the operand was ∞, the ST(1) exponent is $+\infty$ and ST (significand) is ∞ with the sign of the original stack top.

FYL2X

$y^*\log_2 x$

Format:

FYL2X

Description:

The top two stack elements are used in the computation of the function

$ST(1) * \log_2 ST$

The stack is popped, and the new stack top is replaced with the result of this computation.

The ST must be in the range of 0 to $+\infty$. The ST(1) operand can be $-\infty$ to $+\infty$. If the operands are not in this range, the instruction will produce an undefined result and no exception will be detected.

FYL2X works well to calculate the log to any base other than two because a multiplication is always required. You can see this in the following equation, which computes $\log_n x$:

$$\log_n x = (1/\log_2 n) * \log_2 x$$

Operation:

```
if ((0 <= ST < +INFINITY) &&
    ( -INFINITY < ST(1) < +INFINITY)){
    tmp = ST(1) * log2(ST);
    FPop();
    ST = tmp;
} else {
    UNDEFINED;
}
```

Example:

```
FYL2X  Before: ST   :  9.87311 * 10^9
               ST(1): -2.79022 * 10^-3
       After : ST   : -9.26377 * 10^-2
```

Exception:

```
Float(IS,I,D,U,P);
```

Note:

See example 9, page 423.

FYL2XP1

$y^*\log_2(x+1)$

Format:

FYL2XP1

Description:

The top two stack elements are used in the computation of the function

$$ST(1) * \log_2(ST+1.0)$$

The stack is popped, and the new stack top is replaced with the result of this computation.

The ST must be in the range of

$$-(1-\sqrt{2}/2) \quad \text{to} \quad +(1-\sqrt{2}/2)$$

ST(1) operand can be $-\infty$ to $+\infty$. If the operands are not in this range, the instruction will produce an undefined result and no exception will be detected.

Operation:

```
if ((-(1-sqrt(2)/2) < ST    < (1-sqrt(2)/2)) &&
    ( -INFINITY      < ST(1) < +INFINITY    )){
    tmp = ST(1) * log2(ST + 1.0);
    FPop();
    ST = tmp;
} else {
    UNDEFINED;
}
```

Example:

```
FYL2XP1  Before: ST   :  1.17230 * 10^0
                 ST(1):  2.99013 * 10^13
         After : ST   : -7.58600 * 10^13
```

Exception:

```
Float(IS,I,D,U,P);
```

Floating Point

WAIT

Wait for Coprocessor

Format:

WAIT

Description:

WAIT causes suspension of 80386 operation until the numerics coprocessor becomes not busy.

This instruction is useful in that it allows the main processor and its numerics coprocessor to become synchronized.

Operation:

```
while (80387 is busy)
{
}
```

Example:

```
WAIT     ; Nothing occurs
```

Exceptions:

None.

Notes:

This instruction is needed only after floating-point stores to memory (e.g., FST(P), FIST(P), and FBSTP), before the stored data is used by an 80386 instruction. This ensures that the data is stored by the 80387 before it is accessed by the 80386. No WAIT is required after a floating-point store if another 80387 instruction is executed before the 80386 accesses the stored data. The 8086/8087 and 80286/80287 required use of the WAIT instruction in more cases.

Instruction Set Examples

Chapter

THIS CHAPTER PRESENTS A SET OF EXAMPLES to further explain the instructions described in Chapter 3 as well as the material of Chapters 1 and 2. We only cover the integer and floating-point examples in this chapter. Examples for the multiple-segment and operating-system instructions are in Chapter 7.

It may seem rather surprising, but in eleven examples—six integer and five floating-point—we will show at least one example of every class or group of instructions provided in the integer and floating-point portions of the 80386. The classes of integer instructions are arithmetic, bit, control transfer, data transfer, flag control, high-level language, logic, and string. The classes of floating-point instructions are data transfer, arithmetic, comparison, transcendental, constant, and control.

► Syntax

In Chapter 2, the assembly language syntax used to address registers and memory was presented. Chapter 3 developed this syntax further, presenting multiple-operand forms of instructions as well as all possible assembly language instructions allowed by an 80386 and 80387 assembler. In this chapter, we present complete instruction sequences that implement some common or demonstrative subroutines. Thus, we need to extend the assembly language syntax we have developed so far with other assembler directives and formats.

The assembler syntax given here may not be exactly the same as the syntax on the machine you are using. Since we have assembled and tested all examples given here, they are valid on the assembler we are using. You may find slight differences with your assembler.

Types

All variables and memory references have a *type* associated with them. The type of a variable or reference identifies the number of bytes that are being referenced. Type information allows the assembler to generate the correct instruction. Sometimes the type information can be inferred from the instruction or other operands, and in other cases the programmer must explicitly give the type. For example

```
INC [ESI]
```

is ambiguous, as the pointer [ESI] does not specify if this is a byte, word, or dword. This is called an *anonymous pointer.* Any of the following would be valid:

```
INC byte  ptr [ESI]
INC word  ptr [ESI]
INC dword ptr [ESI]
```

The following case is also ambiguous

```
MOV [EBX], 5
```

because the immediate does not imply type. The following is a valid form:

```
MOV word ptr [EBX], 5
```

Two-operand forms need to have a type specified by only one of the operands, however. For example

```
MOV [EBX], EAX
MOV [EBX], AX
MOV [EBX], AL
```

are all valid, as the type of the first operand is implied by the second. Valid types are listed in Table 4.1.

Note that ptr, short for pointer, is misleading. For example, *byte ptr* gives the type of the memory operand (for example, [EBX]). It in no way denotes that [EBX] is a memory pointer. You can see this in the two-operand forms, where the memory operand is anonymous in MOV [EBX], EAX.

TYPE	DESCRIPTION
byte	1 byte
word	2 bytes
dword	4 bytes
pword	6 bytes
qword	8 bytes
tword	10 bytes
short	label within segment, within +127 and −128 bytes
near	label within segment (short or long)
far	label in different segment

► **Table 4.1:** Valid types

Data Allocation

To reserve storage, you can use db, dw, or dd to reserve bytes, words, or dwords of storage. The general form allows you to specify a variable (a symbolic name to reference it by), a size, and an initial value for the storage.

```
fred db 1       ; define 1 byte of storage named fred with
                ;  initial value of 1
joe  dw 10,8,7  ; define 3 words of storage named joe with
                ;  initial values of 10,8,7
     dd ?       ; define 1 dword of storage with no name and
                ;  no initial value
```

There are two special forms of data allocation. The first form allows a character string to initialize consecutive bytes in a db. The second form allows the special DUP construct to initialize multiple units of storage. The DUP statement can be nested, as it is in the last example here.

```
string1 db 'Hello World'
stack   dd 50 dup (0)      ; 50 dwords, all initialized to 0
funny   dw  2 dup (3, 2 dup (?), 4) ; initialize 8 words to
                                    ; 3, ?, ?, 4, 3, ?, ?, 4
```

Offset

The offset operator returns the offset of a variable or label from the base of the segment that it is defined in. Here's an example.

```
string1     db 'Hello World'
string1_end db 0
string2     db 'Goodbye World'
string2_end db 0
< ... >
MOV ESI, offset string1
MOV EAX, offset string1 - offset string2
```

This code segment moves the offset of string1 from the base of the segment in which it is defined into the ESI register. The second example shows that you can use the offset operator in arithmetic computations to form an immediate constant.

Labels

Labels are a symbolic reference to a location in a code sequence. Labels provide a convenient means to jump to certain locations.

```
label1:  MOV EAX, 1
         .
         .
         .
         LOOPNZ label1
```

PROC/ENDP

The PROC directive is an alternative means of defining a label as well as a means to define a sequence of instructions that are interpreted as a subroutine. The sequence of instructions that represent this subroutine is terminated with the ENDP directive. The subroutine is normally referenced in a CALL instruction.

```
JunkProc PROC
    .
    .
    .
JunkProc ENDP
    .
    .
    .
  call JunkProc
```

EQU

The EQU assembler directive allows you to equate a symbol to some other expression. You can use the expression to provide a different mnemonic to specify a constant, label, address, or register. For instance

```
reg1 EQU EAX
reg2 EQU EBX
```

allows you to use reg1 and reg2 rather than the normal register names. Other examples follow:

```
Length EQU 100
My_word EQU word ptr [ESI + EBP]
```

In this chapter, you will see the EQU directive being used to mnemonically reference stack-relative temporary or local variables, as shown below.

```
Error EQU SS: byte ptr [EBP-1]
```

This defines a byte Error, which is located in the stack segment addressed by SS at the offset given by the contents of the EBP register minus 1.

► Integer Examples

In this section, we will give examples of the integer instructions.

Signed Divide

In the description of the SAR (shift arithmetic right) instruction in Chapter 3, we noted that SAR is equivalent to a signed divide by a power of two, except that the rounding of the quotient is toward minus infinity rather than toward 0, as is the case for the IDIV instruction. For example, dividing −17 by 4 yields a quotient of −4 using the IDIV instruction. If, however, a SAR of 2 were used to divide −17 by 4, the resultant quotient would be −5. This difference is displayed below.

```
IDIV ECX     Before: EDX: FFFFFFFF  EAX: FFFFFFEF
                     ECX: 00000004
             After : EDX: FFFFFFFF  EAX: FFFFFFFC
                     ECX: 00000004

SAR EAX,CL   Before: EAX: FFFFFFEF  ECX: 00000002
             After : EAX: FFFFFFFB  ECX: 00000002
```

Since IDIV is a rather slow instruction, you could write more efficient code if you could avoid the use of IDIV for power-of-two divisors. It is important, however, that all integer divides operate the same! The code in Listing 4.1 detects the condition when incorrect rounding will occur (a negative non-power-of-two dividend). It also adjusts the dividend so correct rounding occurs when the shift is actually done, if needed.

```
; Use SAR for power-of-two divisions. Need to be careful with
; quotient rounding, though, which is checked by the following
; routines. The first example is quicker when no adjustment is
; required. The second is faster when adjustment is needed.
;   N:   the power of two to be divided by
;   EAX: dividend
;
; SAR divide routine 1:
  OR  EAX,EAX
  LEA EAX,[EAX+2^N - 1]
  JL  Adj
  SUB EAX,2^N - 1
Adj:
  SAR EAX,N
;
; SAR divide routine 2:
;
  OR  EAX,EAX
  JGE NoAdj
  ADD EAX,2^N - 1
NoAdj:
  SAR EAX,N
```

► **Listing 4.1:** Example 1—Signed divide

The normal IDIV instruction for a register source takes 43 clocks. The routines in Listing 4.1 compute the quotient in 12 or 15 clocks if the dividend was positive, and in 17 or 10 clocks if the dividend was negative. Thus, the SAR routines are significantly faster than IDIV or power-of-two division, and they round correctly.

Note that we do not show the SAR divide as a subroutine. Because of the clocks needed to perform a call and return, a subroutine would negate almost all the savings of the fast power-of-two SAR divide. Thus, to get the desired performance improvement, the SAR routines need to be executed as in line code. To save on typing and to have a nice concise form of this, you may be able to use assembler equates (EQU) or macros (if your assembler supports them).

Sort

A common operation performed on a sequence of numbers is sorting the list. The function in Listing 4.2 will sort the list of numbers pointed

```
; Sort: Sort the list of numbers pointed to by ESI. The length of
; the list is given in ECX. Length is one less than the actual count
; since you start counting from 0 (e.g., [0:ECX]). The smallest number
; of the list is stored at ESI, and the largest number is stored
; at [ESI+ECX*4]. The sort algorithm used is a simple bubble sort.
; The list is assumed to be a list of dword numbers.
;    ESI: pointer to the start of number string
;    ECX: count of the number of elements of the list.
SORT PROC
OutLoop:
  MOV EDX,0
  InnerLoop:
    CMP  EDX,ECX
    JGE  Bottom
    MOV  EAX, [ESI+EDX*4+4]
    CMP  [ESI+EDX*4], EAX
    JGE  NoSwap
    ; [ESI+EDX*4] > [ESI+EDX*4+4] thus they need to be swapped
    XCHG [ESI+EDX*4+4], EAX
    MOV  [ESI+EDX*4], EAX
  NoSwap
    INC EDX
    JMP InnerLoop
  Bottom:
    LOOP OutLoop
Done:
  RET
SORT ENDP
```

► **Listing 4.2:** Example 2—Sort

to by ESI upon the call. The length of the list is given in ECX. The algorithm used to sort the list is a bubble sort.

A *bubble sort* has two nested loops (execution time is $O(n^2)$). The inner loop compares each entry with the one immediately above it in the list. If an entry is larger than the one above it, the two entries are switched. Thus, the larger datum "bubbles" to the top of the list. This inner loop is repeated the number of data element times. Each succeeding inner loop need only operate on data array items from 0 up to the value of the outer loop counter minus 1. The outer loop counter counts down from the initial length of the list. After the first execution of the inner loop, the largest datum will be at the highest entry in the data array. After the second iteration, the largest entry is at the highest address, the second largest entry is at the second highest address, and so on for each subsequent iteration.

Thus, the second inner loop iteration need not compare the second highest address item to the highest address, since the highest address is guaranteed to be the largest entry. Similarly, on the third iteration the two highest address data elements need not be compared, and so on.

Factorial

The example in Listing 4.3 gives a routine that receives its parameter in the EAX register, then computes the factorial of this number and returns the result in the EAX register. The mathematical equation describing a factorial is

$$n! = n*(n-1)*(n-2)*\ldots*(1)$$

The routine given uses a recursive procedure call. The initial procedure (Fact) performs some initial checks and calls the recursive procedure _Fact. _Fact checks if the argument given is 0. If the argument is not 0, _Fact is recursively called with the argument minus 1. If the argument is 0, then the result register (EAX minus partial factorial results computed so far) is set to 1 and the procedure returns to the caller. On each return to caller, the factorial partial product computed so far is multiplied by the value of the argument given to _Fact at this recursive call. Thus, _Fact is called $n+1$ recursive times, with the $n+1^{st}$ call receiving 0 as its argument. On the return, the multiplications are performed (1*1, 1*2, 2*3, 6*4,...).

In this example, _Fact is termed a dummy procedure of Fact. _Fact is never seen by the caller of Fact. Fact eases the writing of the code for the recursive procedure, _Fact. A dummy procedure such as _Fact is common in recursive programming.

The factorial is a powerful mathematical function. In fact, it turns out that 13! is the largest factorial that can be computed whose result is representable in the range of a 32-bit signed integer. Thus, it is important to have careful error checking for overflow, as this routine does.

Note the PUSH and POP of EBX and ECX at the beginning and end of the subroutine in Listing 4.3. This guarantees that the register state of the caller is unaltered by the callee. In general, there are two choices.

1. Always have the caller save the registers it needs kept intact.
2. Have the callee save any registers it uses.

Each of these may save more registers than needed, since the caller may save registers the callee doesn't use or the callee may save registers the caller doesn't care about. You may also want to keep other machine state

```
; Fact: Recursively compute the factorial of the value given in
; the EAX register. The result of the factorial computation is
; returned in the EAX register. If an error is encountered
; while computing the factorial of the given number, -1 is
; returned in the EAX register.
;    EAX: number to compute the factorial of. After the
;         execution, EAX holds the result.
; Dummy recursive procedure of Fact: _Fact
Error EQU SS: byte ptr [EBP-1]
_Fact PROC
 CMP ECX,0
 JZ  done
 PUSH ECX
 DEC ECX
 CALL _Fact
 POP ECX
 IMUL EAX,ECX
 SETO BL
 OR Error, BL
 RET
done:
 MOV EAX,1
 RET
_Fact ENDP

; The actual procedure to compute factorial. Perform a
; check and call the recursive procedure _Fact.
FACT PROC
 ENTER 4,0
 PUSH EBX
 PUSH ECX        ; Save EBX and ECX, as they are used in this routine
                 ; and we do not want to alter register
                 ; state of caller.
 MOV Error,0
 MOV ECX, EAX
 CMP ECX,0
 JB Fail
 CALL _Fact
;Finished with factorial computation
 CMP Error,1
 JNZ Done
Fail:
 MOV EAX,-1
Done:
 POP ECX
 POP EBX
 LEAVE
 RET
FACT ENDP
```

► **Listing 4.3:** Example 3a—Recursive factorial

intact, such as the flag state. The rest of the examples in this chapter do not deal with register state and the saving of it. You do need to consider this, however.

It is often the case in recursive routines such as _Fact that recursion is not needed. You can convert some recursive procedures to simple iteration, as you can see in the example in Listing 4.4.

The iterative factorial turns out to be significantly faster than the recursive factorial procedure. The actual speed increase depends on the data value for which the factorial is being computed. On a couple of test cases, we had a speed increase of almost 50 percent. Some sophisticated

```
; Fact: Iteratively compute the factorial of the value given in
; the EAX register. The result of the factorial computation is
; returned in the EAX register. If an error is encountered
; while computing the factorial of the given number, -1 is
; returned in the EAX register.
;    EAX: number to compute the factorial of
;
Error EQU SS: byte ptr [EBP-1]
FACT PROC
  ENTER 4,0
  MOV Error,0
  MOV ECX,EAX
  CMP ECX,0
  JB  Fail
  MOV EAX,1
  JE  Done
top:
  IMUL EAX, ECX
  SETO BL
  OR    Error, BL
  LOOP top
Done:
; Finished with factorial computation
  CMP Error,1
  JZ  Fail
  LEAVE
  RET
Fail:
  MOV EAX,-1
  LEAVE
  RET
FACT ENDP
```

► **Listing 4.4:** Example 3b—Iterative factorial

high-level language compilers will analyze recursive procedure calls and determine if they can be replaced with iteration.

Semaphore

A common problem of multitasking systems is the allocation of system resources between tasks. For instance, if two processes are requesting a disk, tape, or file, you want to be sure that both do not attempt to use it at the same time. The result of not guaranteeing mutual exclusion between system resources can be disastrous. One solution to this problem is semaphores. *Semaphores* are special flags that are accessed and/or changed in an indivisible operation.

Imagine the use of a memory byte that is a semaphore flag. A processor will read this byte when it needs to use a system resource, determine if the resource is free, and then mark the flag as being busy. This is wonderful as long as the read/modify/write of the flag is indivisible. If this were not the case, two processors could read the same flag, and each could determine the semaphore flag was free and conclude it could use the system resource—disaster! Thus, when the semaphore flag is read, no other processor in the system can be allowed to access memory until the read/modify/write cycle is complete. The 80386 supports this via the LOCK instruction prefix, described in Chapter 3. An instruction with a LOCK prefix locks the memory for the duration of the instruction to guarantee that the read/modify/write cycle is indivisible. No other processor in the system can access memory until this instruction is complete. Thus the indivisible nature is met. The LOCK prefix is demonstrated in the routines in Listing 4.5. These routines give examples of *Get* (have this process become the owner) and *Free* (allow other process to become the owner) operations.

The following piece of code shows use of the basic operators GetSem and FreeSem.

```
MOV ESI, offset SemWord
MOV ECX, SemBitWeNeed
CALL GetSem

< critical code requiring exclusive >
< use of semaphored resource        >

MOV ESI, offset SemWord
MOV ECX, SemBitWeNeed
CALL FreeSem
```

The above code works correctly. Unfortunately, it does not work efficiently. If the semaphore is not free when Get is entered, it loops

```
; GetSem (get Semaphore): the semaphore bit is 0 when
; the semaphore is busy, thus loop until CF is set
; when BTR is encountered.
;     Semaphore=0    Busy
;     Semaphore=1    Free
;
;     ECX: bit location in semaphore
;     ESI: address (in DS) of semaphore
GetSem PROC
LoopGet:
  LOCK BTR dword ptr [ESI],ECX
  JNC LoopGet
  RET
GetSem ENDP
; FreeSem: mark semaphore free. If it was already free
; (freeing a free semaphore) an error code of -1 is
; returned in the EAX register.
FreeSem PROC
  LOCK BTS dword ptr [ESI],ECX
  JNC Done
  MOV EAX,-1     ; error: freeing a free semaphore
  Done: RET
FreeSem ENDP
```

► **Listing 4.5:** Example 4—Semaphore

without end until the semaphore is free. This is termed *busy waiting.*

Now a busy loop such as this is expensive, since it does no useful work but ties up CPU and memory resources while waiting. You can often redefine the semaphore operators (which we won't do here) to place a process waiting for a free semaphore into a waiting queue and then call the scheduler to execute a different process while waiting for the semaphore.

String Search

A common procedure is to search for a substring within a string. Functions such as this are often performed by command interpreters, text editors, and database management systems. Searching for a substring is such a common function that it has become one of a standard set of benchmarks called the EDN benchmarks. Most computer manufacturers use this set of benchmarks to compare their processors against the competitors. The routine given in Listing 4.6 is the EDN string-search benchmark coded for the 80386.

```
; EDN Benchmark E: String Search.
; Find a substring within a string and return the starting
; position in the EAX register. EAX is -1 if the substring
; was not found in the string.
;
; Parameters:
;    ESI = PTR (in DS) to Substring to search for.
;    EDI = PTR (in ES) to String to search for substring.
;    ECX = Length of string.
;    EDX = Length of substring.
;
Srch_Len EQU SS: dword ptr [EBP-4]    ; StringLen-SubStrLen

BENCHE PROC
  PUSH  EBP          ; Fast enter 0 code...
  MOV   EBP, ESP
  SUB   ESP, 4       ; Local Frame Size
  CLD

; Need to scan for first byte only for StrLen-SubStrlen+1 (assume > 0)
  LODSB               ; AL = first byte of SubStr
  MOV   EBX, ESI      ; EBX points to 2nd byte of SubStr. for CMPS
  DEC   EDX           ; Length of remainder of substring.
  SUB   ECX, EDX      ; Length for SCAS
  MOV   Srch_Len, ECX ; Save for final offset computation.

; Scan for first byte of target string.
Scan_Loop:
  JECXZ SHORT NotFnd ; Test for completion of subsequent iterations
  REPNE SCASB
  JNE   SHORT NotFnd ; Failed to match first Character

; First Byte matched. If SubStrLen was 1, we're done,
; otherwise do a CMPS on rest of SubStr.
  CMP   EDX, 0
  JE    SHORT Match

; Save current Scan Ptr (points to next char for SCAS if CMPS fails)
  PUSH  ECX
  PUSH  EDI

; Load ESI with addr. of 2nd byte of SubStr (stored in EBX).
  MOV   ESI, EBX      ; Addr. of source for CMPS
  MOV   ECX, EDX      ; Length for CMPS
  REPE  CMPSB         ; See if SubStr matches
  POP   ECX
  POP   EDI           ; Restore pointers/count for SCAS
  JNE   Scan_Loop     ; Continue with SCAS (if any left)
; Fall through if SubStr matched. ECX points to 2nd byte of substr,
; Srch_Len holds original search length-1, so SRCH_LEN-ECX is offset.
Match:
  MOV   EAX, Srch_Len
  SUB   EAX, ECX
```

► **Listing 4.6:** Example 5—String search

```
    JMP    Epilogue
  ; If no match, set EAX to -1 and return.
  NotFnd:
    MOV    EAX, -1

  Epilogue:
    LEAVE
    RET

  BENCHE ENDP
```

► **Listing 4.6:** Example 5—String search (continued)

The algorithm used in the string search first uses a SCAS instruction to search for the first byte of the substring to be found in the string. The REPNE SCASB instruction is quite efficient in this case, as it compares up to the first matching byte or until the string is exhausted. When the first byte of the substring is found, the entire string is compared against the potential matching substring by a REPE CMPSB instruction. The CMPSB instruction is also quite efficient in this case, as it compares up to the first mismatch or until the substring is exhausted. If this turns out not to be a matching substring (even though the first byte matched), the string is searched again for the first matching first byte of the substring. This process continues until a match is found or the string being searched is exhausted. One special case of the routine is when the substring being searched for is only one byte in length. When this is the case, the CMPS portion of the routine is not needed. If a matching substring is found, the offset to the start of the string is returned in the EAX register. If no matching substring is found, a −1 is returned in the EAX register.

This procedure serves as a good example of the string instructions using the LODS, SCAS, and CMPS string instructions. Whenever you are programming using strings of byte, word, or dword data, you will find the string instructions (LODS, CMPS, SCAS, STOS, MOVS) to be useful and efficient.

Also notice the "fast" enter code:

```
PUSH EBP          ; Fast enter 0 code...
MOV  EBP, ESP
SUB  ESP, 4       ; Local Frame Size
```

The ENTER instruction, when used for level 0 operation, uses 10 clocks to execute. The above code, which specifically performs a level 0 entry, requires only 6 clocks to execute. The speed increase is possible because ENTER is a general-purpose instruction. The 80386 must first perform checks to determine level 0 operation. You the programmer can "skip" these checks as is done here when only level 0 operation is needed.

Also notice the use of SHORT directives in Listing 4.6. Most assemblers use a single pass over the source code to generate instructions that implement the program you have specified. But forward references, such as the

```
JNE     SHORT NotFnd
```

instruction, are jumps to a label (NotFnd) that has not been encountered yet. So the assembler cannot determine if the label is in fact short (+127 to −128 bytes from the JNE). Thus, the single-pass assembler will insert a full 32-bit displacement jump rather than attempt to use a short jump. The specification of a SHORT directive, as is done here, allows the programmer to override the assembler and force it to generate code for a short label jump.

Bit Block Transfer

Graphics operations, as well as others, often deal with data that is a simple sequence of bits. One of the most common operations to perform on bit data is the transfer of a string (or block) of bits from one location to another. The routine in Listing 4.7 performs a bit transfer from a

```
; BitBlt: move arbitrarily located source bit string pointed
; to by ESI into the aligned destination pointed to by
; EDI. The amount to be moved needs to be an exact multiple
; of 32 bits.
;  ESI: offset of the source string, assumed visible by DS.
;  EDI: offset of the destination string, assumed visible by ES.
;  EBX: dword count of bits to be moved (thus, bits to be moved
;       is a multiple of 32).
;  ECX: offset from 0 within the source string.
BitBlt PROC
  MOV  EDX, dword ptr [ESI]
  ADD  ESI, 4
  CLD
BitLoop:
  LODS                ; new high-order part
  SHRD EDX, EAX, CL   ; EDX gets aligned dword
  XCHG EAX,EDX        ; swap high and low order
  STOS                ; write out next result portion
  DEC  EBX
  JA   BitLoop
  RET
BitBlt ENDP
```

► **Listing 4.7:** Example 6a—Simple bit block transfer

source string pointed to by ESI into a destination string pointed to by EDI. This routine requires the destination to be aligned on a dword boundary, and the length of the bit string to be moved is exactly a multiple of 32 bits. This simplifies the example to illustrate the heart of the BitBlt operation. The source string can be at any arbitrary bit offset within the source string. The bit string is processed from the low-order address to higher order. The shift right double works best to process the string in this manner.

The routine in Listing 4.7 shows one use for and a particular benefit of the 80386's double-wide shift instruction. In the example, the loop can process 32 bits upon each iteration. If a double-wide shift were not present in the 80386, the best that could be done would be 16 bits per iteration using a 32-bit shift rather than the double shift. Thus, the double-wide shift allows the performance of bit block transfers to be doubled.

This example demonstrates how bit block transfers are performed as well as how the double-wide right shift of the 80386 can be used to facilitate the transfer. Unfortunately, this simple procedure is not very useful, since bit strings are not normally only multiples of 32 bits in length, and the destination strings are not always aligned on a dword boundary. The procedure in Listing 4.8 gives a general and far more useful bit block transfer routine. This routine allows bit strings of any length to be transferred. The source and destination strings can be aligned on any arbitrary bit offset. Unfortunately, this more general procedure is significantly more complicated!

The procedure is really composed of three parts: prelude, main, and postlude. The prelude aligns the destination onto a dword boundary. This was also a requirement of the first simple bit block transfer procedure. The destination alignment requires transferring the first bits from source to destination while keeping intact any destination string bits before the starting offset of the destination string. The prelude, as well as the postlude, follows slightly different algorithms depending on whether the source offset or the destination offset is greater. This is required since if the destination offset is greater than the source offset, the prelude consumes all bits of the first dword of the source string.

After the prelude, the main loop is entered. The main loop first computes the shift-count, which is the difference of the offset between the source and destination strings. The main loop is similar to the routine given in Listing 4.7. The two requirements of the simple bit block transfer routine are the same as the conditions on the main loop here. The prelude and postlude accounts for aligning the destination on a dword boundary, as well as accounting for nonmultiples of 32 bits to be transferred. Each iteration of the loop processes 32 bits of data from the source string to the destination string.

```
; General BitBlt: Move any length bit string from any bit location in
; the source string into any bit location of the destination string.
;  EAX: (BitCount) the number of bits to be moved.
;  ESI: dword address of the source string.
;  EDI: dword address of the destination string.
;  ECX: (SrcOff) bit offset into the dword of the source string
;          specified by ESI.
;  EDX: (DestOff) bit offset into the dword of the destination string
;          specified by EDI.
BitCount  EQU SS: dword ptr [EBP-4]
SrcOff    EQU SS: dword ptr [EBP-8]
DestOff   EQU SS: dword ptr [EBP-12]
SrcOffFlg EQU SS: dword ptr [EBP-16]

BitBlt PROC
  ENTER 16,0            ; 16 bytes of local temporaries
  CLD

;****
;** PRELUDE:  Start-up portion of BitBlt
;****
  MOV BitCount,EAX      ; Save parameters passed in registers into
  MOV SrcOff,ECX        ;  local stack temporaries
  MOV DestOff,EDX       ;
  MOV EDX,dword ptr [ESI]     ; load of high- and low-order source
  MOV EAX,dword ptr [ESI+4]   ; string bits
; Determine first dword of destination.
  SHRD EDX, EAX, CL     ; At this point EDX contains the first 32 bits
                        ;  of the source string.
  MOV EAX,dword ptr [EDI]     ; Now grab residual bits from destination
  MOV ECX,DestOff       ;  that are not to be affected by this bit
  ROR EAX, CL           ;  string, move and include them into the
  SHLD EDX,EAX,CL       ;  dword of the destination.
  MOV EBX,32            ; This code checks the case where the entire
  SUB EBX,DestOff       ;  string is within a single (the first
  SUB EBX,BitCount      ;  and only) dword. If it is within the
  JBE DestMoreThan1     ;  first destination dword, jump to the end
  MOV ECX,32            ;  for cleanup, which will include any high-
  SUB ECX,EBX           ;  order residual bits.
  MOV EBX,ECX
  JMP CommonEnd
DestMoreThan1:
  MOV dword ptr [EDI],EDX ; store first dword result
  ADD EDI,4
  JZ Done               ; Exact fit into first dword of destination.

; Compute correct shift count
  SUB ECX,SrcOff        ; If SrcOff > DestOff then CL=SrcOff-DestOff
  JL SrcLrgStr          ; Else             CL = 32 - (DestOff-SrcOff)
  MOV BL, 32
  SUB BL, CL
  MOV CL, BL
  JMP BeginBitBlt
```

► **Listing 4.8:** Example 6b—Bit block transfer

```
SrcLrgStr:
  MOV ECX,SrcOff
  SUB ECX,DestOff
  ADD ESI,4              ; Since DestOff <= SrcOff all of first Src
                         ;  dword has been consumed.
  MOV SrcOffFlg,1        ; Simple flag denoting the SrcOff > DestOff

;****
;** MAIN: Body of BitLoop
;****
;
; Body of BitBlt. At this point Dest is aligned to a 32-bit
; boundary. CL holds the shift amount, ESI points to source
; and EDI to destination at the correct point to begin the
; main bit string transfer.
BeginBitBlt:
  MOV EBX,BitCount
  ADD EBX,DestOff
  SUB EBX,32             ; EBX holds the # of bits still to be moved
  MOV EDX,dword ptr [ESI]
  ADD ESI,4
; Loop portion of BitBlt. 32 bits are moved from the source into
; the destination bit strings on each iteration of the loop. The
; loop stops when less than 32 bits remain to be moved.
BitLoop:
  SUB EBX,32
  JLE FixEnd
  LODSD
  SHRD EDX,EAX,CL
  XCHG EDX,EAX           ; EAX: aligned part for Dest string, EDX is
                         ;  residual portion of source string for next
                         ;  shift loop iteration.
  STOSD                  ; Store EAX into Dest string.
  JMP BitLoop

;****
;** POSTLUDE: Tail end portion of BitBlt
;****
FixEnd:
  JZ Done                ; If no bits in tail portion, we are done!
  CMP SrcOffFlg,1
  JZ SrcLrgEnd
  LODSD
  SHRD EDX,EAX,CL
  JMP CommonEnd
SrcLrgEnd:
  SHR EDX,CL
CommonEnd:               ; At this point EDX contains final residual
                         ; source string bits aligned to the
                         ; destination.
  MOV EAX,dword ptr [EDI]
  MOV CL,BL
  ROR EDX,CL
```

► **Listing 4.8:** Example 6b—Bit block transfer (continued)

```
 ROR EAX,CL
 MOV BL,32
 SUB BL,CL
 MOV CL,BL
 SHRD EDX,EAX,CL     ; Perform final shift putting the destination
                     ;  bits after the end of the bit string along
                     ;  with final source string bits into EDX
 XCHG EAX,EDX
 STOSD               ; Store the final dword into destination.
Done:
 LEAVE
 RET
BitBlt ENDP
```

► **Listing 4.8:** Example 6b—Bit block transfer (continued)

The postlude handles the transfer of the final bits into the destination string, while maintaining any bits after the final destination bit string intact. A special case that needs to be considered (checked for in the prelude) is when the entire destination bit string fits within a single dword. The number of bits transferred to the destination string by the postlude is given by:

```
(BitCount - DestOffset) % 32
```

Even though the general bit block transfer routine in Listing 4.8 is significantly more complicated than the short example given in Listing 4.7, decomposing the routine into the three sections (prelude, main, and postlude) and analyzing each of these separately can lead to a clear understanding of its function.

As is often the case, this procedure uses local storage on the stack. This allows recursion and in general provides a convenient way to manage local temporary variables, since storage is only required as it is used. As mentioned in Chapter 2, the EBP register is often used as a frame pointer onto the stack, and ESP provides a dynamic top-of-stack pointer. Thus, local temporary variables are often addressed via the EBP register, as you have seen in this procedure:

```
BitCount  EQU SS: dword ptr [EBP-4]
```

Thus, you can use a mnemonic BitCount that equates to a stack-based temporary value referenced indirectly via the EBP register.

The model of using EBP as a stack frame pointer is supported by the ENTER and LEAVE instructions, which are also demonstrated in this example. The ENTER 16,0 instruction here creates a level 0 stack frame with room for 16 bytes of local variables. A level 0 stack frame indicates that no display is built in the new stack frame. A display is often used when nested procedures and variable scoping within the nested procedures (as seen in some high-level languages such as Pascal) are supported. The complement of ENTER is a LEAVE instruction that destroys the stack frame just before returning to the caller.

► Floating-Point Examples

In this section, we will give several examples of the floating-point instructions.

Floating-Point Flags

The floating-point condition codes were discussed in Chapter 2. These four condition codes are part of the status-word register of the 80387. In Chapter 3, when we discussed the floating-point instructions of the 80387, we also gave several instructions that modify these condition codes as part of their operation. For example, the

```
FCOM op1
```

instruction numerically compares the given operand (op_1) to the top of the stack and sets the condition codes as given in the following table.

	C3	C2	C0
ST > op_1	0	0	0
ST < op_2	0	0	1
ST = op_1	1	0	0
Unordered	1	1	1

Now let's discuss how you can use these condition codes to alter the flow of execution. A special instruction of the 80386 and 80387 pair is the FSTSW AX instruction. This instruction copies the status word of the 80387 into the AX register of the 80386. If the FSTSW AX instruction is followed by a SAHF instruction (store the AH register into the flags), the conditional jumps of the 80386 can be used to jump on the condition flags of the

80387. If FSTSW AX is followed by SAHF, the diagram in Figure 4.1 depicts the upper part of the status word and the associated flag bits of the 80386.

The code sequence in Listing 4.9 shows a jump table based on the settings of the 80387 condition codes after a FCOM instruction. The first accumulator beneath the stack top is compared against the stack top with the appropriate jump taken as a result of the comparison.

A similar sequence can be used for the FTST, FICOM, FUCOM, and all pop variants of these instructions.

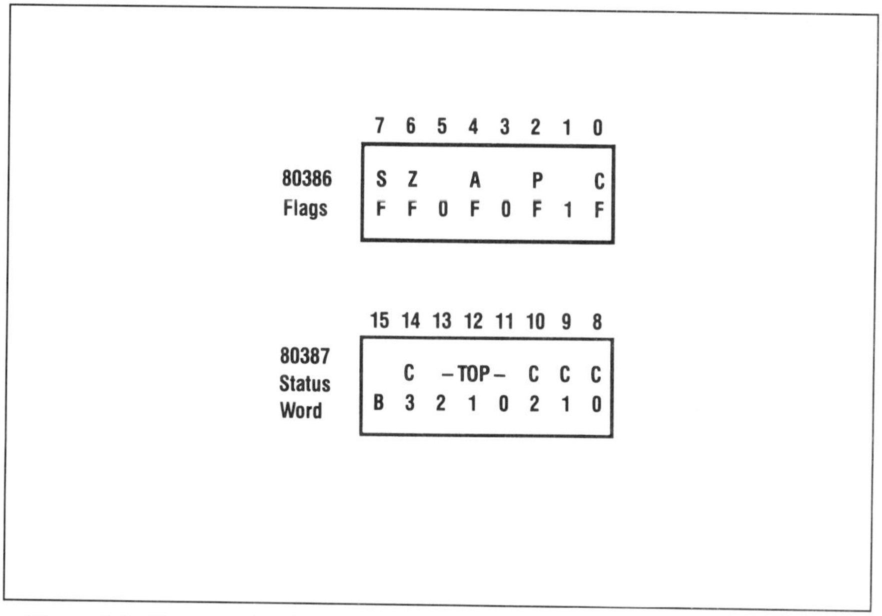

80386 Flags	7	6	5	4	3	2	1	0
	SF	ZF	0	AF	0	PF	1	CF

80387 Status Word	15	14	13	12	11	10	9	8
	B	C3	2	1	0	C2	C1	C0
			–TOP–					

► **Figure 4.1:** Flags transfer from 80386 to 80387

```
; Comparison and jump table
FCOM ST(1)    ; perform comparison
FSTSW AX      ; move status word to AX register of 80386
SAHF          ; move condition codes into flags register
JP Error      ; ST or ST(1) is a NaN - Error condition
JE STeqST1    ; ST == ST(1)
JB STltST1    ; ST <  ST(1)
JA STgtST1    ; ST >  ST(1)
```

► **Listing 4.9:** Example 7—Floating-point flags

Partial Remainder

In the presentation of the partial remainder instructions in Chapter 3 (FPREM, FPREM1), we pointed out that because these instructions may have very long execution times, they stop partway through the reduction. This allows interrupts to be taken at these boundaries. The routine in Listing 4.10 presents a short instruction loop that will check for the completion of the reduction and iterate if needed.

In this example, notice the use of the flag transfer instruction sequence as was demonstrated by an earlier example.

```
; Complete partial reminder
RemLoop:
   FPREM
   FSTSW AX
   SAHF
   JP RemLoop          ; If C2==1 reduction was incomplete,
                       ; try again.
```

► **Listing 4.10:** Example 8—Partial remainder

Exponential Computations

Recall from Chapter 3 that the F2XM1 instruction computes

$$ST = 2^{ST} - 1$$

Notice that there is not an F10XM1 instruction. The three examples in Listing 4.11 implement algorithms to compute three other exponential computations using F2XM1 as a basis. The conversion equations are given below.

$$10^X = 2^{x * \log_2 10}$$
$$e^X = 2^{x * \log_2 e}$$
$$Y^X = 2^{x * \log_2 Y}$$

Note in the last example how convenient the FYL2X instruction is for this case. Remember that FYL2X implements the function

```
ST = ST(1) * log₂ST    ; pop ;
```

```
; Exponential computations for other than 2^x-1

; 10^X    ; ST = X
  FLDL2T
  FMULP ST,ST(1)    ; ST = X * log2 10
  F2XM1             ; ST = 2^(X * log2 10) - 1
  FLD1
  FADDP ST,ST(1)    ; ST = 2^(X * log2 10) = 10^X

; e^X     ; ST = X
  FLDL2E
  FMULP ST,ST(1)    ; ST = X * log2 e
  F2XM1             ; ST = 2^(X * log2 e) - 1
  FLD1
  FADDP ST,ST(1)    ; ST = 2^(X * log2 e) = e^X

; Y**X     ; ST = Y, ST(1) = X
  FYL2X    ; ST = X * log2 Y
  F2XM1    ; ST = Y^X - 1
  FLD1
  FADDP ST,ST(1)    ; ST = Y^X
```

► **Listing 4.11:** Example 9—Exponential computations

Matrix Multiplication

Mathematical data is commonly stored in matrices. One of the common functions performed on matrices is to multiply two matrices together to form a third matrix. Matrix multiplication takes two matrices, X and Y, where X is of dimension $i*k$ and Y is of dimension $k*j$. The result matrix, Z, is of dimension $i*j$. The k dimension of the X and Y matrices must be the same. The elements of the Z matrix obey the relation

$$Z_{ij} = \sum_{n=1}^{k} (X_{in} * Y_{nj})$$

for all result elements of the Z matrix.

The routine in Listing 4.12 performs matrix multiplication. The locations of two input matrices are passed in the ESI and EDI registers,

```
; This routine performs a matrix multiplication of two matrices
; X and Y to produce a resultant matrix Z. Matrix X is of
; dimension i*k, matrix Y is of dimension k*j, and the result
; matrix Z is of dimension i*j. Note that the matrices are
; assumed to be stored in row-major form.
;    ESI: offset of X in the DS segment
;    EDI: offset of Y in the DS segment
;    EAX: Di, i dimension
;    ECX: Dk, k dimension
;    EBX: Dj, j dimension
;    EDX: offset of Z in the DS segment
;
; The Loops used are:
; for (iCnt = 0; iCnt < Di; iCnt ++){
;    for (jCnt = 0; jCnt < Dj; jCnt ++){
;       for (ECX = Dk; ECX >= 0; ECX--){
;          load element from X
;          load element from Y
;          multiply; add to partial sum
;       }
;       store into Z
;    }
; }
Di   EQU SS: dword ptr [EBP-4]
Dk   EQU SS: dword ptr [EBP-8]
Dj   EQU SS: dword ptr [EBP-12]
Zoff EQU SS: dword ptr [EBP-16]
iCnt EQU SS: dword ptr [EBP-20]
jCnt EQU SS: dword ptr [EBP-24]

MatMult PROC
  ENTER 24,0      ; No display copied, 24 bytes of local parameters
  MOV Di   ,EAX   ; Save contents of registers before using
  MOV Dk   ,ECX   ;  "
  MOV Dj   ,EBX   ;  "
  MOV Zoff,EDX    ;  "
  CMP EAX,0       ; Make sure no dimensions are zero
  JZ  Done        ;  "
  CMP ECX,0       ;  "
  JZ  Done        ;  "
  CMP EBX,0       ;  "
  JZ  Done        ;  "
  MOV iCnt,0      ;  i Loop variable
  MOV EDX,0       ;  z element pointer
  Loop_i:
    mov jCnt,0  ;  j Loop variable
    Loop_j:
      MOV  EAX,iCnt
      IMUL EAX,Dk
      MOV  EBX,jCnt
      FLDZ        ;  zero  Z sum
```

► **Listing 4.12:** Example 10—Matrix multiplication

```
        MOV ECX, Xk
        Loop_k:
        DEC    ECX
        FLD    qword ptr [ESI + EAX*8]   ; fetch X array element
        INC    EAX
        FLD    qword ptr [EDI + EBX*8]   ; fetch Y array element
        ADD    EBX, Dj
        FMULP  ST(1), ST
        FADDP  ST(1), ST
        CMP    ECX,0
        JA     Loop_k
      MOV  EAX,Zoff
      FSTP qword ptr [EAX+EDX*8]         ; Store into z array
      INC  EDX                           ; Next z element
      INC  jCnt
      MOV  EAX,Dj
      CMP  EAX,jCnt
      JA  Loop_j
    INC iCnt
    MOV EAX,Di
    CMP EAX,iCnt
    JA  Loop_i
Done:
 LEAVE
 RET
MatMult ENDP
```

► **Listing 4.12:** Example 10—Matrix multiplication (continued)

respectively. The location where the results are to be stored is passed in the EDX register. All three are in the segment addressed by the DS register. All three matrices are stored in row-major format.

Row-major format dictates how a two-dimensional array gets mapped into a one-dimensional memory (remember the discussion of memory organization in Chapter 1). If you have an array A with elements A_{ij}, does $A_{0,1}$ or $A_{1,0}$ follow $A_{0,0}$? In a row-major form, sequential elements of a row are stored in sequential memory locations, with sequential column elements stored a stride apart in memory. Note that in row-major format

$A_{0,0}$, $A_{0,1}$, $A_{0,2}$,...$A_{0,n}$ (row 0)

are stored sequentially, followed by

$A_{1,0}$, $A_{1,1}$, $A_{1,2}$,...$A_{1,n}$ (row 1)

and so on.

The i and k dimensions of the X matrix are passed in the EAX and ECX registers, and the k and j dimensions of the Y matrix are passed in the ECX and EBX registers. The k dimension of the X and Y matrices must be the same to allow matrix multiplication to occur.

Note that this routine can multiply matrices of any size and does not know the size of the matrices to be multiplied prior to being called. Matrix multiplications that operate on fixed-size matrices can be coded more efficiently than this general one. Every element of the X and Y matrices is loaded k times. A fixed-size matrix-multiply routine could limit the loading of one of the matrix elements (the X matrix elements, for example) to once, and use the element repetitively from the accumulator stack, rather than loading it k times.

The procedure uses a triply nested loop. The outermost loop repeats i times, the second loop repeats j times, and the innermost loop repeats k times. The inner loop is the one computing the Z_{ij} elements. The second loop runs down the rows of X, and thus fills the rows of Z while traversing each column of Y. The outer loop is repeated for each row of X and Z. Thus, the Z matrix is filled sequentially in memory, since it is in row-major format.

Statistics

A common operation is computing statistics on a set of numbers. For instance, an instructor, when reporting the grades for a class, may give the mean and standard deviation of test scores. The mean statistic gives the average of the class scores. The equation for mean is given by

$$\mu = \frac{\sum_{i=0}^{n-1} x_i}{n}$$

where Σ is the summation operator computing the sum of all x_i from i equals 0 to $n-1$. In the remainder of the discussion, we will use the shorthand notation for the summation operator: Σx.

The standard deviation gives a measure of the average dispersion about the mean. The following equation gives the standard deviation:

$$s = \sqrt{\frac{\Sigma(x - \mu)^2}{n - 1}}$$

If you wanted to compute the standard deviation of a set of numbers, this equation would require you to first compute the mean of the numbers, and then to make a second pass over the list of numbers to compute the standard deviation. A better equation to use in a statistics procedure would require only a single pass over the set of data. Fortunately, the standard deviation equation can be proven equivalent (we will not repeat the proof here) to the following equation:

$$s = \sqrt{\frac{\sum x^2 - \frac{(\Sigma x)^2}{n}}{n - 1}}$$

The function in Listing 4.13 uses this second equation in computing the standard deviation. The main loop of the following function computes Σx and Σx^2. At the conclusion of the loop, the standard deviation and mean are computed with the results left in ST and ST(1), respectively.

The later portion of the procedure makes extensive use of the floating-point accumulator stack. In fact, it may be a bit difficult to follow exactly what is occurring on the stack at each instruction through the sequence. Table 4.2 gives a horizontal stack trace, which may help you to understand the exact operation on the stack at each point. The stack trace given on the right shows the contents of the floating-point accumulator stack after the operation given on the left of the same line is complete. For conciseness, the following identity is used in the table:

$$a = \sum x^2 - \frac{(\Sigma x)^2}{n}$$

```
; Stat: the following procedure computes the standard deviation
; and the mean of a list of numbers. The list of numbers is a
; list of long real numbers in memory pointed to by ESI. The
; length of the list is given by ECX. The standard deviation is
; computed and returned in the stack top. The mean is computed and
; returned in ST(1).
; The standard deviation is given by the following equation:
;     s=sqrt((sum(x²) - sum(x)²/n)/(n-1))
; The mean is given by the equation: u=sum(x)/n
;   ECX: number of long reals
;   ESI: pointer (in DS) to list of long reals
Count EQU SS: dword ptr [EBP-4]
STAT PROC
 ENTER 4,0
 MOV Count,ECX     ; save the count for later use
 FLDZ              ; zero sum(x)
 FLDZ              ; zero sum(x²)
; The following loop computes sum(x), which is left in ST(1),
; and sum(x²), which is left in ST.
LoopTop:
 FLD   qword ptr [ESI+ECX*8]
 FADD  ST(2),ST   ; add to sum(x)
 FMUL  ST,ST(0)   ; create x²
 FADDP ST(1),ST   ; add to sum(x²)
 LOOPNZ LoopTop

; At this point ST=sum(x²) and ST(1)=sum(x)
 FLD   ST(1)
 FMUL  ST,ST(1)   ; compute sum(x)²
 FILD  Count      ; After: ST=n
 FDIV  ST(1),ST   ; After: ST(1)=sum(x)²/n
 FXCH  ST,ST(1)
 FSUBP ST(2),ST   ; After: ST(1)=sum(x²)-sum(x)²/n
 FLD1
 FSUBR ST,ST(1)   ; After: ST=n-1
 FDIVP ST(2),ST   ; After: ST(1)=(sum(x²)-sum(x)²/n)/(n-1)
 FDIVP ST(2),ST   ; After: ST(1)=u=sum(x)/n
 FSQRT            ; After: ST=s
; ST=s, ST(1)=u
 LEAVE
 RET
STAT ENDP
```

► **Listing 4.13:** Example 11—Statistics

INSTRUCTION		STACK AFTER EXECUTION				
		ST	ST(1)	ST(2)	ST(3)	ST(4)
		Σx^2	Σx			
FLD	ST(1)	Σx	Σx^2	Σx		
FMUL	ST,ST(0)	$(\Sigma x)^2$	Σx^2	Σx		
FILD	Count	n	$(\Sigma x)^2$	Σx^2	Σx	
FDIV	ST(1),ST	n	$(\Sigma x)^2/n$	Σx^2	Σx	
FXCH	ST,ST(1)	$(\Sigma x)^2/n$	n	Σx^2	Σx	
FSUBP	ST(2),ST	n	a	Σx		
FLD1		1	n	a	Σx	
FSUBR	ST,ST(1)	n − 1	n	a	Σx	
FDIVP	ST(2),ST	n	s^2	Σx		
FDIVP	ST(2),ST	s^2	μ			
FSQRT		s	μ			

► **Table 4.2:** Horizontal stack trace

Memory Management, Protection, and Tasks

Chapter 5

THIS CHAPTER AND CHAPTER 6 DESCRIBE THE 80386 features that support operating systems. These chapters are less tutorial than the previous chapters, which described the 80386 facilities available to the applications programmer. In this chapter, we assume you are familiar with the basic concepts incorporated in a multitasking operating system that supports virtual memory. We provide a brief introduction to review the relevant concepts and to acquaint you with our terminology. This chapter is aimed primarily at developers of operating-system software. However, applications programmers may find the first half of this chapter helpful in understanding the concepts behind 80386 memory management, protection, and task support. Applications programmers who use the multiple-segment model discussed in Chapter 2 may find this information especially helpful.

Operating systems, even for single-user personal computers, must be able to work on several things at once in order to make the most of the computer's hardware facilities as well as the user's time. A computer with a 386 has enough computing power to do several things in the background, and it will even allow you to run your word processor or a game program while you wait for the background programs to complete. Alternatively, while using the word processor you may need to call up the spreadsheet program to cook up some numbers for your report. You can freeze the word processor in a background window while you run the spreadsheet. Once you have fudged the numbers to your satisfaction, you can transfer the data from the spreadsheet to the word processor, and continue editing your report. You can switch back and forth from spreadsheet to word processor as needed.

Each program constitutes a separate *task,* whether it is a spreadsheet recalculation or download operation from a mainframe database running unattended in the background, or a word processor or game program requiring continuous interaction. Each task is the "sequential thread of execution" of a single program. Within a task, the program executes sequentially. However, the tasks themselves share processor time in a fashion that makes the different tasks appear to simultaneously execute asynchronously to each other. One task may suspend execution to wait for a disk access to complete, permitting another task to use the processor. Later an interrupt will arrive to signal completion of the disk access. The task then executing is suspended so the interrupt can be processed, which may indicate that another task is to resume execution. Or you may control the task switching, as when you switch from one window to another to suspend one application and resume another.

The operating system uses the facilities described in this chapter and Chapter 6 to allocate and protect the computer's resources: main memory space, execution time, and peripheral devices. The operating system allocates these resources to the tasks in the system so that all tasks run efficiently to completion. The resource allocation and protection policies of the operating system are enforced by the 80386 hardware memory-management and protection mechanisms. The operating system uses the 80386 memory-management and protection mechanisms to ensure that each task is protected from every other task. For example, the operating system typically uses the memory-management mechanisms to ensure that the memory areas allocated to the different tasks do not overlap (unless they purposely share memory), and it uses the protection mechanisms to ensure that none of the tasks can access memory allocated to the operating system.

Most of the facilities described in this chapter and Chapter 6 are used to allocate and protect resources. These facilities can be divided into three groups, which mirror the three categories of resources defined above: main memory space, processor time, and peripheral devices. Memory-management facilities support the allocation and protection of memory space. These memory-management facilities, along with the interrupt and exception mechanism described in Chapter 6, support the allocation of processor time. An I/O management facility supports the allocation and protection of peripheral devices. The memory-management and I/O-management facilities are the topics of the remainder of this chapter.

Exceptions are an important operating-system facility, but they will not be described in detail until Chapter 6. Certain key aspects of exceptions are covered in this chapter to allow the remaining operating-system facilities to be presented. An exception is like an invisible CALL instruction that is executed any time an unusual or invalid operation occurs. The target of the invisible CALL is a predefined operating-system procedure written to handle the occurrence of the exception. This procedure may either terminate the program raising the exception, or fix the cause of the exception and return to resume the program at the point where the exception occurred. Exceptions are used to report unusual or invalid events to operating-system software. As you shall see, exceptions are the enforcement mechanism that allows the operating system to keep control of resources. If a program attempts to use or obtain resources it does not own, an exception occurs to report the attempt to the operating system.

► Memory-Management Facilities

There are two key parts to any complete memory-management system: protection and address translation. Protection is provided to prevent a task from accessing memory belonging to another task or the operating system. Address translation gives the operating system flexibility in allocating memory to tasks, and it is also a key protection mechanism.

Address Translation

As defined in Chapter 1, the physical memory in a computer is a linear array of bytes, each byte having a unique address known as its *physical address*. Chapter 2 defined the addresses used by programs to access memory. These addresses had two parts to address the two-dimensional segmented memory used by the 80386. This two-part address is not used directly to access physical memory. Instead, program addresses are translated, or mapped, into physical memory addresses by an address translation mechanism. This translation mechanism supports the concept of a *virtual address,* which is a two-part address generated by a program. The term *virtual address* is used since these addresses do not correspond directly to physical memory locations, but only indirectly through the virtual-to-physical address mapping function.

Note that every address generated by a program is a two-part virtual address, whether in the inner sanctum of the operating system or in the most mundane application program. No matter what kind of program is running, the memory-management mechanism operates to translate virtual addresses into physical memory addresses.

The virtual-to-physical address translation also provides for memory protection, since you can arrange that certain physical addresses are not mapped from any virtual address. In addition to this basic protection, the address translation function is extended so that virtual addresses can be identified as invalid. Rather than generating a physical address when presented with an invalid virtual address, the translation mechanism reports an exception so that operating-system software can take appropriate action.

Segmentation and Paging

To minimize the amount of information needed to specify the address translation function, large seqential blocks of memory are mapped as single units. This permits the mapping to be specified once for an entire block of memory rather than requiring a separate specification for each byte. Segmentation and paging are two widely used address translation techniques. They differ in how virtual memory is organized into blocks for mapping, how the translation information is specified, and how the programmer views their operation.

Both segmentation and paging use memory-resident tables to specify their respective translation functions. These tables are stored in memory accessible only by the operating system, to prevent modification by application programs. This is important, since changing the contents of the translation tables changes the translation function, which in turn has the effect of changing the virtual address space. Typically, the operating system will maintain a different set of translation tables for each task. This allows each task to use addresses that span the entire virtual address space. The effect is that each task has a different virtual address space, and the tasks are isolated from each other.

The 80386 uses both segmentation and paging in a two-stage virtual-to-physical address translation mechanism, illustrated in Figure 5.1. The first stage uses segmentation to translate a two-part address in the virtual address space into an address in an intermediate address space, called the *linear address space.* The second stage uses paging to translate this linear address to a physical address. Segmentation is always enabled, but paging can be enabled or disabled as required. If paging is disabled, the linear addresses produced by the segmentation translation stage are used directly as physical addresses, as if the page translation function was the identity map. This is illustrated as a bypass path around the paging function in Figure 5.1. So if paging is disabled, the physical address is the linear address. Otherwise, it is translated with the page table.

The linear address space has the same structure as the physical address space. Both are one-dimensional address spaces, in contrast to the two-dimensional virtual address space. The virtual address space contains up to 16K segments, each of which can be up to 4G in size, making the virtual address space 64 terabytes (2^{46}) in size. Both the linear and physical address spaces are 4G (2^{32}) bytes in size. In fact, if paging is turned off, the linear address space *is* the physical address space!

The two translation mechanisms, segmentation and paging, are distinct mechanisms, each providing a separate stage of the overall address translation function. Although both mechanisms make use of translation tables stored in main memory, they use separate table structures. In fact, the segment tables are stored in the linear address space, whereas the page tables are stored in the physical address space. One consequence of this is that the segment translation tables can be relocated by the paging mechanism without the knowledge or cooperation of the segmentation mechanism! The segment translation mechanism translates virtual addresses into linear addresses, and accesses its tables at linear addresses, but is not aware that the paging mechanism translates these linear addresses into physical addresses.

Similarly, the paging mechanism knows nothing about the virtual address space that is used by programs to generate addresses. Paging

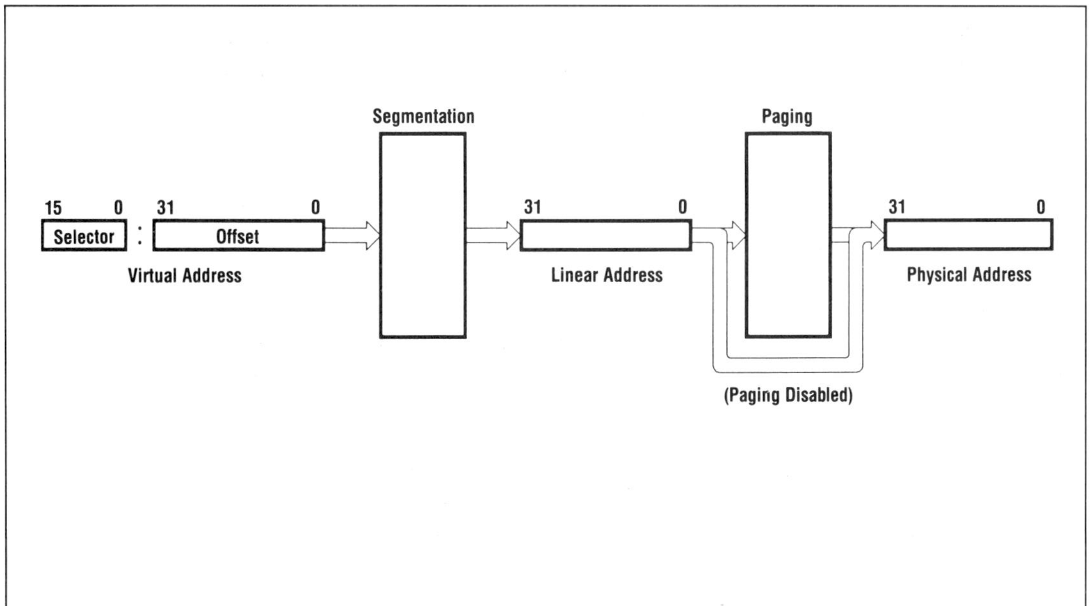

► **Figure 5.1:** Virtual-to-physical address translation function

simply translates linear addresses to physical addresses, and accesses its translation tables in physical memory, unaware that the virtual address space exists, or even that a segment translation mechanism exists.

The next section contains a brief digression on virtual memory, including a brief discussion of the relative merits of segmentation and paging. After that, we introduce some basic protection concepts before returning to describe segmentation and paging individually.

Virtual Memory

Virtual memory is a technique used to provide the illusion of a memory space that is much larger than the physical main memory available in a computer system. This illusion allows programs to be written without regard to the exact size of physical memory. One benefit is that a program can easily run on a wide range of configurations with radically different physical memory sizes. Another benefit is that you can write a program that uses a virtual memory size that is much larger than the physical memory on any configuration.

The virtual memory illusion is supported by the memory translation mechanism, in conjunction with a large amount of fast hard-disk storage. At any time, the virtual address space is mapped such that a small part is in main memory, with the rest stored on the disk. Since only the part of the virtual memory that is stored in main memory is available to the processor, this technique relies on locality of reference within a program to ensure that only a small amount of the total virtual memory needs to be in main memory at any instant during the execution of a program. As the program executes, the neighborhood of memory references changes, necessitating that some parts of the virtual memory be brought in from the disk to main memory, while other parts of the virtual memory can be moved from main memory out to disk storage.

For example, a large application program might provide a large menu of functions. As you select one function from the menu, you would execute several subroutines specific to that function, but would not reference the subroutines that implement the remaining functions. In a virtual memory system, the execution of the selected menu function would be supported by bringing the code and data for the selected function into main memory (if not already there). Code and data for the inactive functions could be moved out to (or remain on) the disk. As long as the physical memory was large enough to hold the code and data for any single function, the total size of the physical memory could be much smaller than the total size of the application.

The address translation mechanism supports virtual memory in two ways. First, it is used to mark only the parts of the virtual memory actually in main memory as valid, and it is set up to translate virtual addresses corresponding to the resident parts of the virtual memory to their respective physical memory addresses. If a program references a virtual address corresponding to a part of the virtual memory that is not resident, the reference will cause an exception due to invalid mapping information. The operating system can handle this exception by reading the missing part into main memory from the disk, and updating the address translation tables as needed. After the cause of the exception has been removed, the program can be resumed by returning from the exception handler. This will reexecute the instruction that raised the exception, and the instruction should now complete successfully.

The address translation mechanism also supports virtual memory by collecting usage statistics on the parts of the virtual memory that are resident in main memory. These usage statistics help the operating system decide what can be moved back to the disk when main memory space is tight.

On the 80386, paging is the best choice for supporting virtual memory. As described in later sections, paging uses fixed-size blocks and segmentation uses variable-size blocks to manage memory. The fixed-size blocks used by paging turn out to be better suited for managing physical memory, whether it is in main memory or on the disk. This superiority in handling the physical side of the virtual memory illusion makes paging the technique of choice for supporting virtual memory.

On the other hand, the variable-size blocks used by segmentation make it better suited for handling the logical partitioning of a complex system. Units of memory can be defined as appropriate to their logical meaning without regard for artificial constraints imposed by fixed-size pages. Each segment can be handled as a single unit, simplifying the protection and sharing of segments.

Protection

There are two broad classes of protection supported by the 80386. One is the ability to completely separate tasks by giving each task a different virtual address space. This is done by giving each task a different virtual-to-physical address translation map. The other protection mechanisms operate within a task to protect operating-system memory segments and special processor registers from access by application programs.

Protection between Tasks

An important aspect of protection is the ability to protect application tasks from each other. On the 80386, this is accomplished by putting each task in a different virtual address space, by giving each task a different virtual-to-physical address translation map. The address translation function in each task is defined so that the virtual addresses in one task map to one part of the physical memory, while the virtual addresses in another task map to different areas in the physical memory. Since one task cannot generate any virtual address that maps to a part of physical memory used by the other task, the tasks are isolated from each other.

Each task is given a different address translation function simply by having a separate set of mapping tables for each task. On the 80386, each task has its own segment tables and page tables. When the processor switches to execute a new task, a key part of this task switch is switching to the translation tables for the new task.

The operating system could be stored in a separate task, in order to isolate it from all of the applications. However, the protection mechanism described in the next section, which operates within a task, is better suited to protecting the operating system from applications. This mechanism allows the operating system to be shared by all tasks, and accessed from within each task, while still protecting the operating system from the applications. The operating system is shared by all tasks by arranging to have a part of the virtual-to-physical address map the same in all tasks, and storing the operating system within this common part of the virtual address space. This part of the virtual address space that is common to all tasks is called the *global address space.*

The part of the virtual address space that is unique to a single task—that is, the part that is not shared with any other task—is called the *local address space.* The local address space contains the code and data private to the task that needs to be isolated from the other tasks in the system.

One consequence of having a different local address space in each task is that a reference to the same virtual address in two different tasks will translate to different physical addresses. This allows the operating system to give each task memory at common virtual addresses, yet ensure task isolation. On the other hand, a reference to the same virtual address in the global address space will translate to the same physical address in all tasks. This supports sharing of common code and data, such as the operating system. The global and local address spaces will be discussed in more detail, with examples, in the sections of this chapter that describe the segmentation and paging mechanisms in detail.

The initialization example in Chapter 7 demonstrates how the global and local address spaces can be defined as suggested here. In that example, the operating system is in the global address space and is shared by all tasks. The application code and data for each task is stored in the local address space.

Protection within a Task

Within a task, four execution privilege levels are defined to restrict access to the segments in the task according to the sensitivity of the data contained in the segment and the degree to which different parts of the program in the task can be trusted. The most sensitive data is assigned to the most privileged level, where it can be accessed only by the most trusted part of the task. Less sensitive data is assigned to lesser privileged levels, where it can be accessed by the less trusted parts of the task.

The levels are numbered from 0 to 3, with 0 the most privileged and 3 the least privileged. The numeric assignment of the levels from 0 to 3 makes sense, as long as you remember that a level with a higher number has a lower privilege! To avoid this ambiguity, we will not use the terms *greater than* or *less than* when comparing privilege levels. Instead, we will use the terms *inner* to mean more privileged, with lower numeric level, and *outer* to mean less privileged, with higher numeric level. Level 0 is known as the innermost privilege level, and level 3 is the outermost level. This four-level hierarchy is illustrated in Figure 5.2 as a set of concentric circles.

Each memory segment is associated with a privilege level. This privilege level limits access to the segment to programs with sufficient privilege. Recall from Chapter 2 that the processor fetches and executes instructions from the segment addressed by the CS register. The *Current Privilege Level,* or CPL, is simply the privilege level of this currently active code segment, and it defines the level of privilege of the program currently executing. The CPL determines which segments can be accessed by the program.

Whenever the program attempts to access a segment, the current privilege level is compared to the privilege level of the segment to determine if the access is permitted. A program executing at a given CPL is permitted access to a data segment in the same level, or in an outer level. An attempt to reference a segment at an inner level is illegal, and raises an exception to report the violation to the operating system.

Each privilege level has its own program stack (Chapter 2), to avoid protection problems associated with a shared stack. As a program switches execution from one privilege level to another, the stack segment is changed to the stack for the new level. The method used to switch from one level to another is described later in this chapter, in the section on control-transfer methods.

Typical usage of privilege levels is to put the kernel of the operating system in level 0, the rest of the operating system at level 1, and applications at level 3. This leaves level 2 free for use by intermediate software

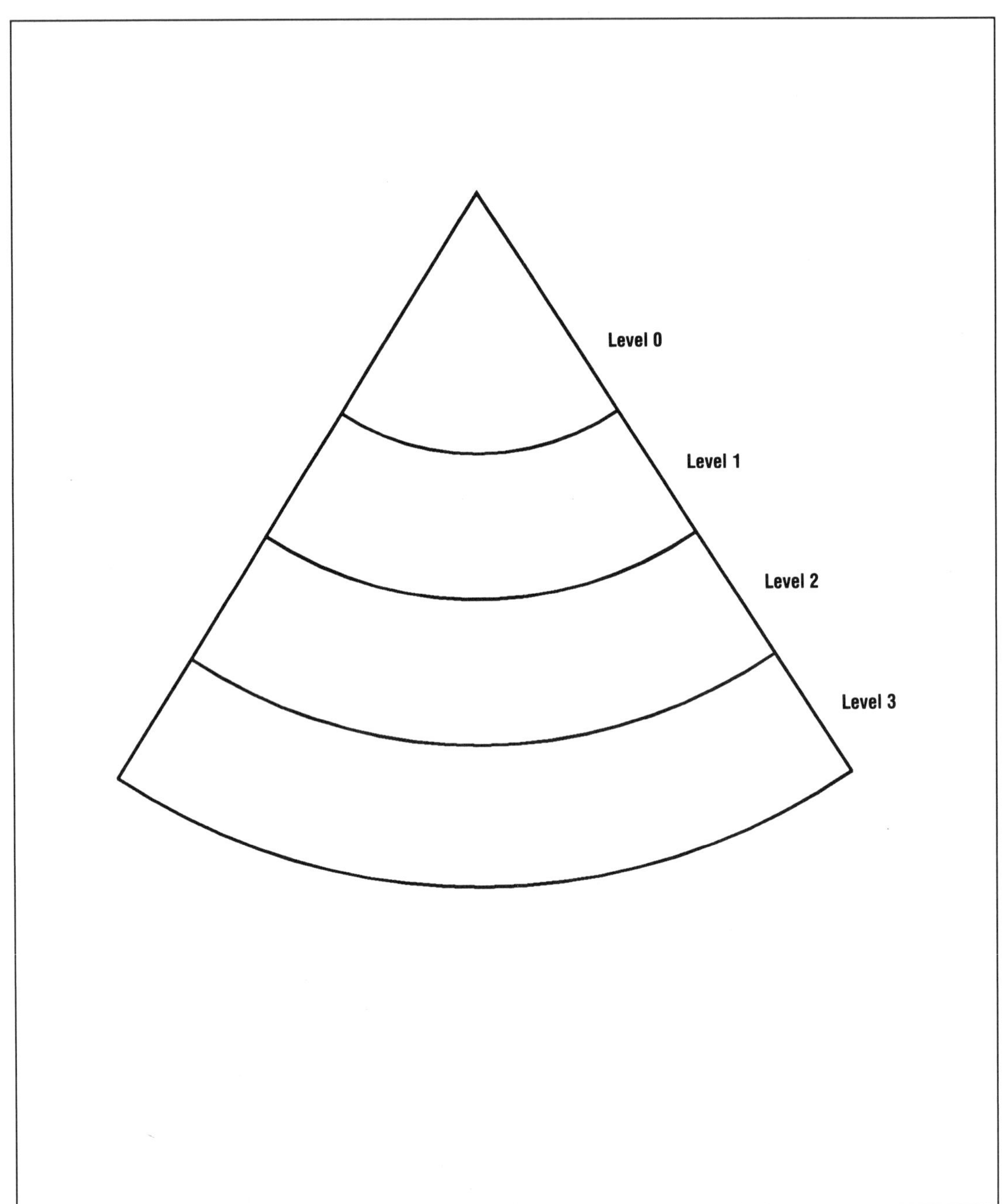

► **Figure 5.2:** Four levels of privilege

levels. Given this allocation of privilege levels, the operating-system (OS) kernel at level 0 has access to every segment in the task. The rest of the operating system in level 1 has access to all segments except those at level 0. The application at level 3 can only access its own segments, which are also at level 3. This allocation protects the OS kernel from the rest of the operating system, and prevents the application program from accessing any operating-system segments.

Figures 5.3, 5.4, and 5.5 illustrate the four privilege levels, the assignment of segments to privilege levels, and the access rules for segments based on the current execution privilege level, CPL. The OS kernel at level 0 is stored in a level 0 code segment named $Code_k$ and a level 0 data segment named $Data_k$. The rest of the operating system at level 1 is stored in the segments $Code_{os}$ and $Data_{os}$, and the application is stored at level 3 in $Code_{ap}$ and $Data_{ap}$. These examples do not use level 2. When the application code in the segment $Code_{ap}$ is executing, CPL is 3, and only the application segments $Code_{ap}$ and $Data_{ap}$ are accessible, as shown in Figure 5.3.

Figure 5.4 illustrates how the operating system executes with CPL = 1, and can access its own segments as well as the application segments.

Figure 5.5 illustrates how the OS kernel can access all six segments in this small system as it executes at CPL = 0.

Combined Protection Levels

The two previous sections detailed the two aspects of protection provided on the 80386: protection between tasks, and protection within a task. This section describes how these two aspects work together to protect applications from each other, to allow all applications to share the operating system, yet to protect the operating system from all of the applications.

Each application is put into a separate task, with the code and data specific to that application stored in segments at level 3 that are local to the task. The operating system is stored in level 1 segments that are global to all tasks. The kernel is stored in global level 0 segments.

This mapping of applications and operating system is illustrated in Figure 5.6, where the concentric circles illustrate protection levels, and the radial lines through the level 3 ring indicate task boundaries. This arrangement has the operating system and kernel shared by all tasks, since they are mapped in the global address space, signified by the absence of radial lines through levels 0 and 1. Yet the operating system is protected from each application, since the applications are at level 3, and the operating system is at levels 0 and 1. Although all of the applications are at level 3, they are stored in different virtual address spaces in different tasks to provide protection between applications.

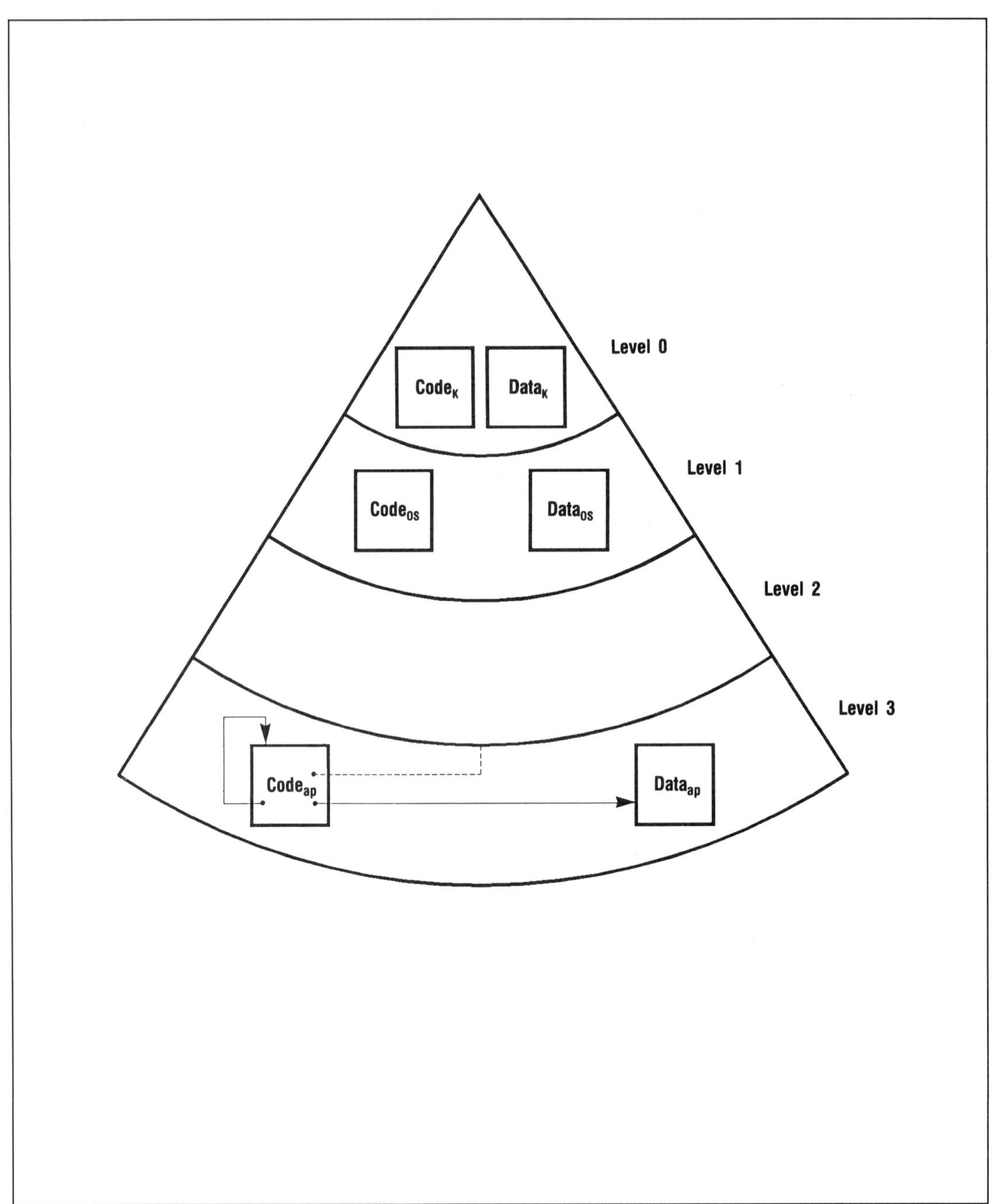

► **Figure 5.3:** Segments accessible at privilege level 3

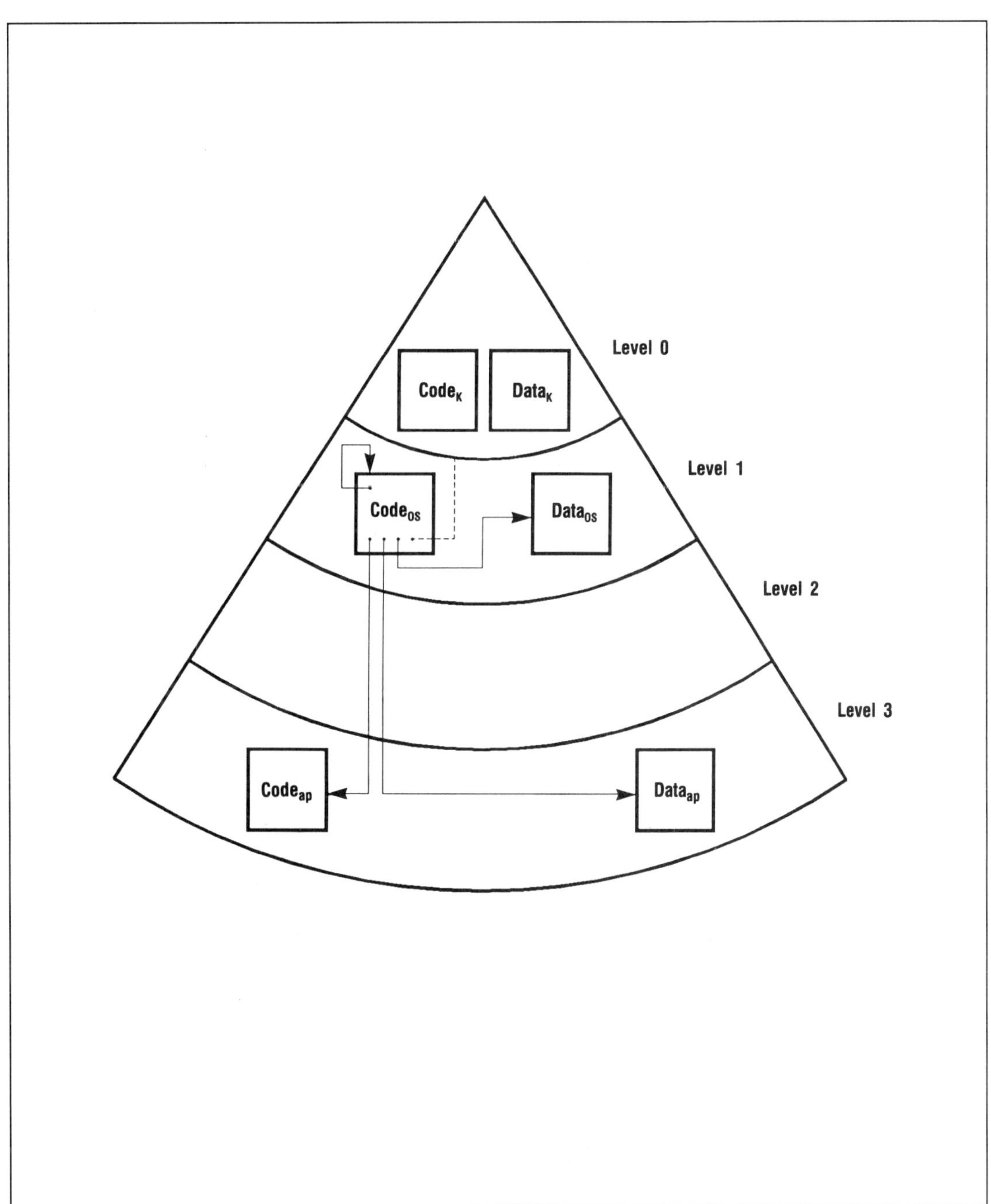

► **Figure 5.4:** Segments accessible at privilege level 1

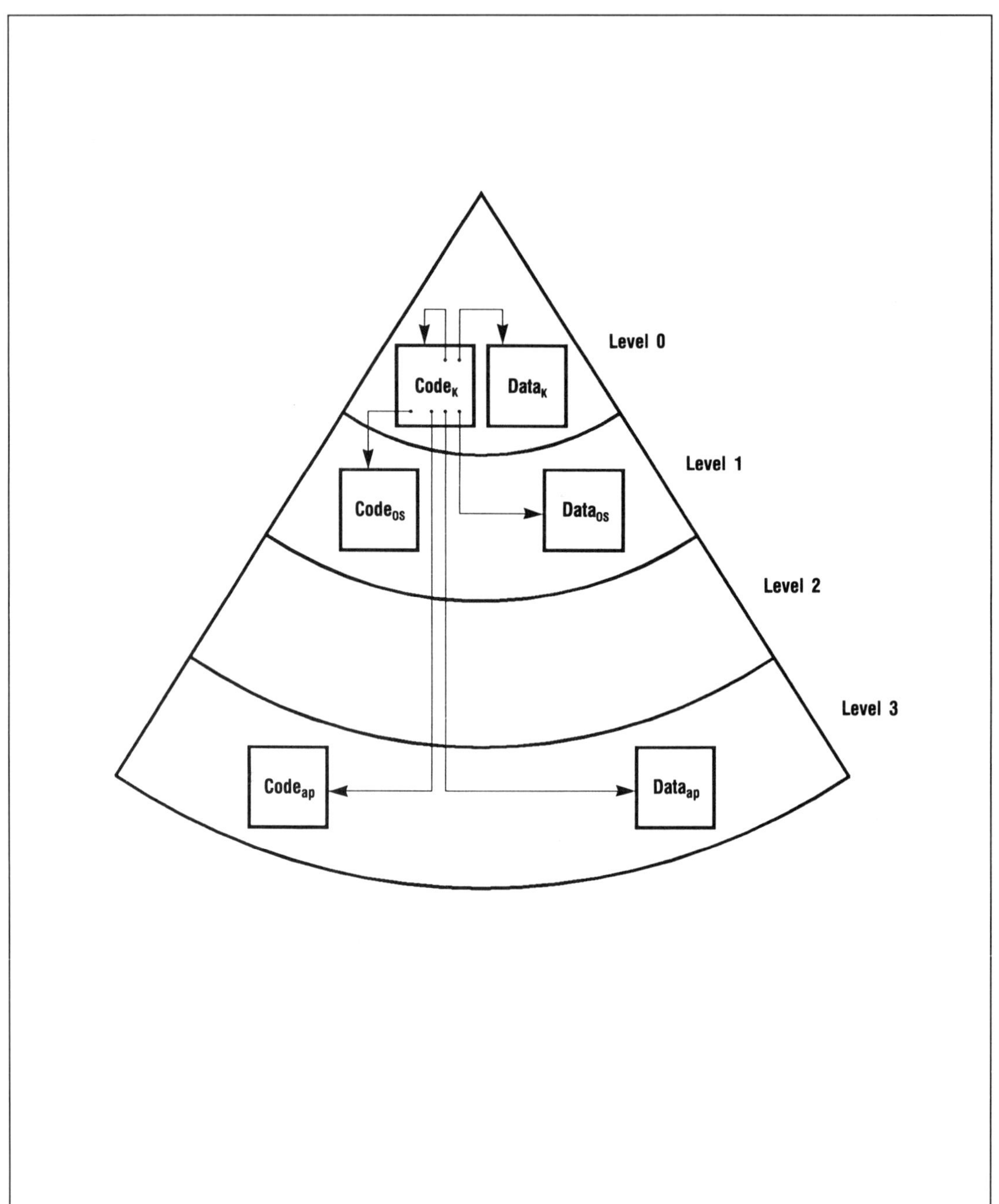

► **Figure 5.5:** Segments accessible at privilege level 0

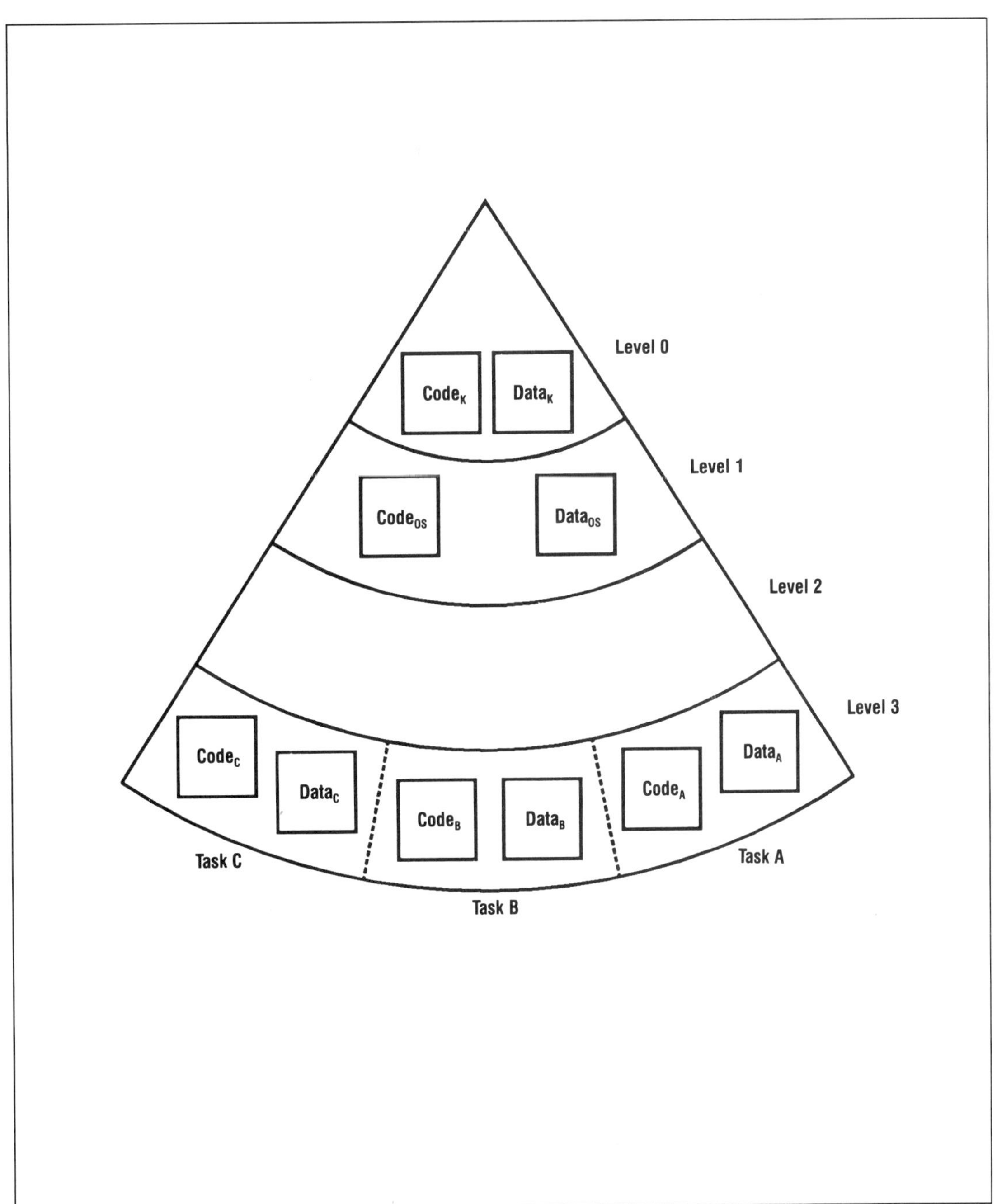

► **Figure 5.6:** Protection between and within tasks

► Segmentation

Segmentation organizes virtual memory as a collection of variable-size units, called *segments.* The 80386 segmentation model uses a two-part virtual address: a segment part and an offset part. Chapter 2 introduced these two-part virtual addresses, described the segment registers provided to hold the segment parts of addresses, and detailed the address modes available to generate the offset parts of addresses. This chapter describes the segment part of the virtual address in detail by describing how segments are defined and how virtual addresses are translated to linear addresses. Chapter 3 described the instructions available for loading selectors into segment registers to make segments addressable. This chapter describes in detail the process used to make a segment addressable when a segment register is loaded.

Segments form the basis of the virtual-to-linear address translation mechanism. Each segment is defined by three parameters, two of which relate virtual addresses given by offsets within the segment to linear addresses:

1. The *base address* of the segment specifies the starting address of the segment in the linear address space. The base address is the linear address corresponding to the virtual address at offset 0 within the segment.
2. The segment *limit,* which is the largest offset that can be used with the segment in a virtual address. This defines the size of the segment.
3. *Attributes* of the segment, which indicate segment characteristics such as whether the segment can be read from, written to, or executed as a program; the privilege level of the segment; and so on.

The segment limit defines the size of the segment in the virtual address space. The base address and limit define the range of linear addresses mapped by the segment. Virtual addresses within the segment at offsets ranging from 0 to *limit* correspond to linear addresses ranging from *base* to *base* + *limit.* A virtual address in the segment with an offset larger than the segment limit makes no sense, and if used, will cause an exception. An exception also occurs if an access is not permitted by the segment's attributes. For example, the 80386 detects an exception if you attempt to write into a read-only segment.

Figure 5.7 illustrates how segments are relocated from the virtual address space to the linear address space. The virtual address space is shown on the left. There are three segments defined—A, B, and C—

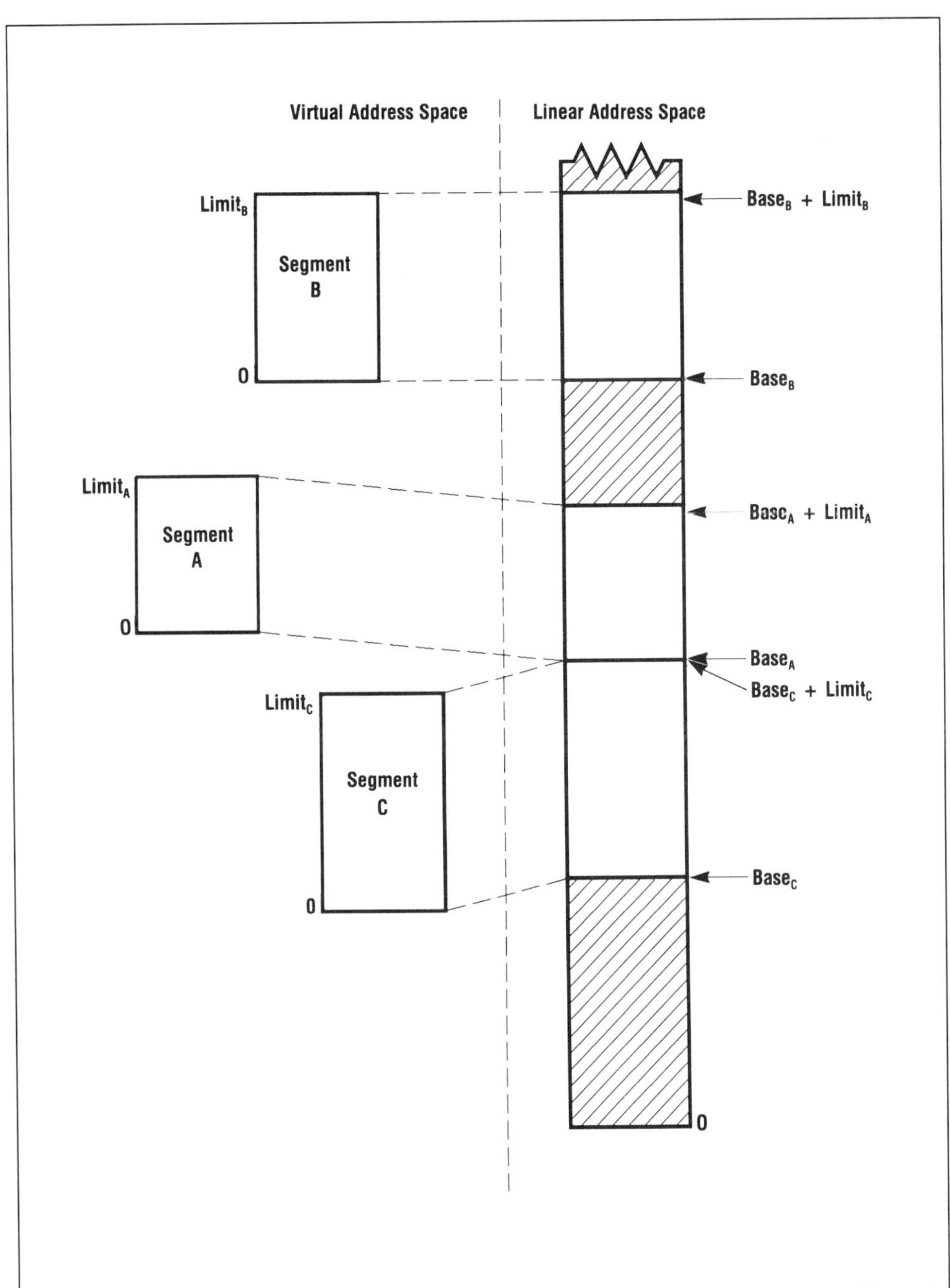

► **Figure 5.7:** Virtual-to-linear address translation

with sizes given by $Limit_A$, $Limit_B$, and $Limit_C$. The virtual-to-linear translation is defined by the segment base addresses $Base_A$, $Base_B$, and $Base_C$. This translation is shown symbolically by dotted lines connecting segments A, B, and C in the virtual space to the corresponding regions of the linear space defined by $Base_A$ to $Base_A + Limit_A$ for segment A, $Base_B$ to $Base_B + Limit_B$ for segment B, and $Base_C$ to $Base_C + Limit_C$ for segment C. Note that segment A is stored just above segment C. This means that $Base_A = Base_C + Limit_C + 1$. There is a gap between the end of segment A and the beginning of segment B.

Because each memory reference checks to ensure that the offset part of an address is within the segment limits, a very large offset in segment C (an offset larger than $Limit_C$) does not address memory in segment A, but instead will raise an exception to report the segment limit violation to the operating system. This limit check permits the operating system to allocate segment A to privilege level 3 and segment C to an inner privilege level, and ensure that a level 3 program cannot use an "illegal" offset within segment A to access memory in segment C, even though the segments are close together in the linear address space.

The base address, limit, and protection attributes for a segment are stored in a *segment descriptor,* which is referenced during the virtual-to-linear address translation process. Segment descriptors are stored in memory in *descriptor tables,* which are simply arrays of segment descriptors. The segment selector introduced in Chapter 2 identifies a segment by specifying the location of the descriptor for the segment. Descriptor tables, selectors, and descriptors are described in more detail in the following sections.

Segment Descriptor Tables

The *Global Descriptor Table* (GDT) and the *Local Descriptor Table* (LDT) are special segments that contain the segment descriptor tables. Descriptor tables are stored in special segments that are maintained by the operating system and referenced by the memory-management hardware in the processor. These segments should be stored in protected memory accessible only by operating-system software to prevent application software from modifying the address translation information.

The virtual address space is divided into two equal halves: one half is mapped by the GDT, the other half by the LDT. The total virtual address space consists of 2^{14} segments. Half of this space, or 2^{13} segments, is the global virtual address space mapped by the GDT. The other half is the local virtual address space mapped by the LDT. A segment descriptor is located by indicating a descriptor table (GDT or LDT), along with a descriptor number within the indicated table.

When a task switch occurs, the LDT is changed to the LDT for the new task, but the GDT is unchanged. Consequently, the half of the virtual address space mapped by the GDT is common to all tasks in the system, but the half mapped by the LDT is changed at a task switch. Segments shared by all tasks in the system are mapped by the GDT. Such segments would include the segments containing the operating system, and the LDT segments for all of the tasks in the system. The LDT segment can be thought of as data belonging to the operating system.

The LDT contains descriptors for the segments private to a single task. Several tasks can share a common LDT. In this case the same set of segments are available to all of these tasks, since they have the same LDT, and all tasks share a single GDT. Two tasks can also have a descriptor for a shared segment in both of their LDTs, in order to share a segment without having to put its descriptor in the GDT for all tasks to share. In this case, the shared segment must be treated specially by the operating system, since it has two descriptors in two different LDTs that must be updated together.

Figure 5.8 illustrates how the segments in a task can be split between the GDT and LDT. There are eight segments that hold two application programs (A and B) plus the operating system and kernel. There are two tasks in the system, one for each application program, and each task has its own LDT. Application A runs in Task A, which has LDT_A mapping the segments $Code_A$ and $Data_A$, which contain the code and data for application A. Similarly, application B runs in Task B, with $Code_B$ and $Data_B$ mapped by LDT_B. The two segments that hold the operating system, $Code_{OS}$ and $Data_{OS}$, and the kernel segments $Code_K$ and $Data_K$ are mapped by the GDT so they can be shared by both tasks. The LDT segments LDT_A and LDT_B are also mapped by the GDT.

The set of segments accessible when Task A is executing include $Code_A$ and $Data_A$ mapped by LDT_A, plus the operating-system segments $Code_{OS}$, $Data_{OS}$, $Code_K$, and $Data_K$, mapped by the GDT. When Task B is executing, the set of addressable segments changes to $Code_B$ and $Data_B$ mapped by LDT_B, plus the operating-system and kernel segments mapped by the GDT.

This example illustrates how the virtual address space can be structured to isolate application tasks from each other by use of separate LDTs per task. When Task A is executing, the segments for Task B are not part of the virtual address space, so there is no way for Task A to access memory in Task B. Similarly, when Task B is executing, the segments for Task A cannot be addressed. This use of LDTs isolates application tasks from each other, meeting one of the key protection requirements outlined earlier in this chapter.

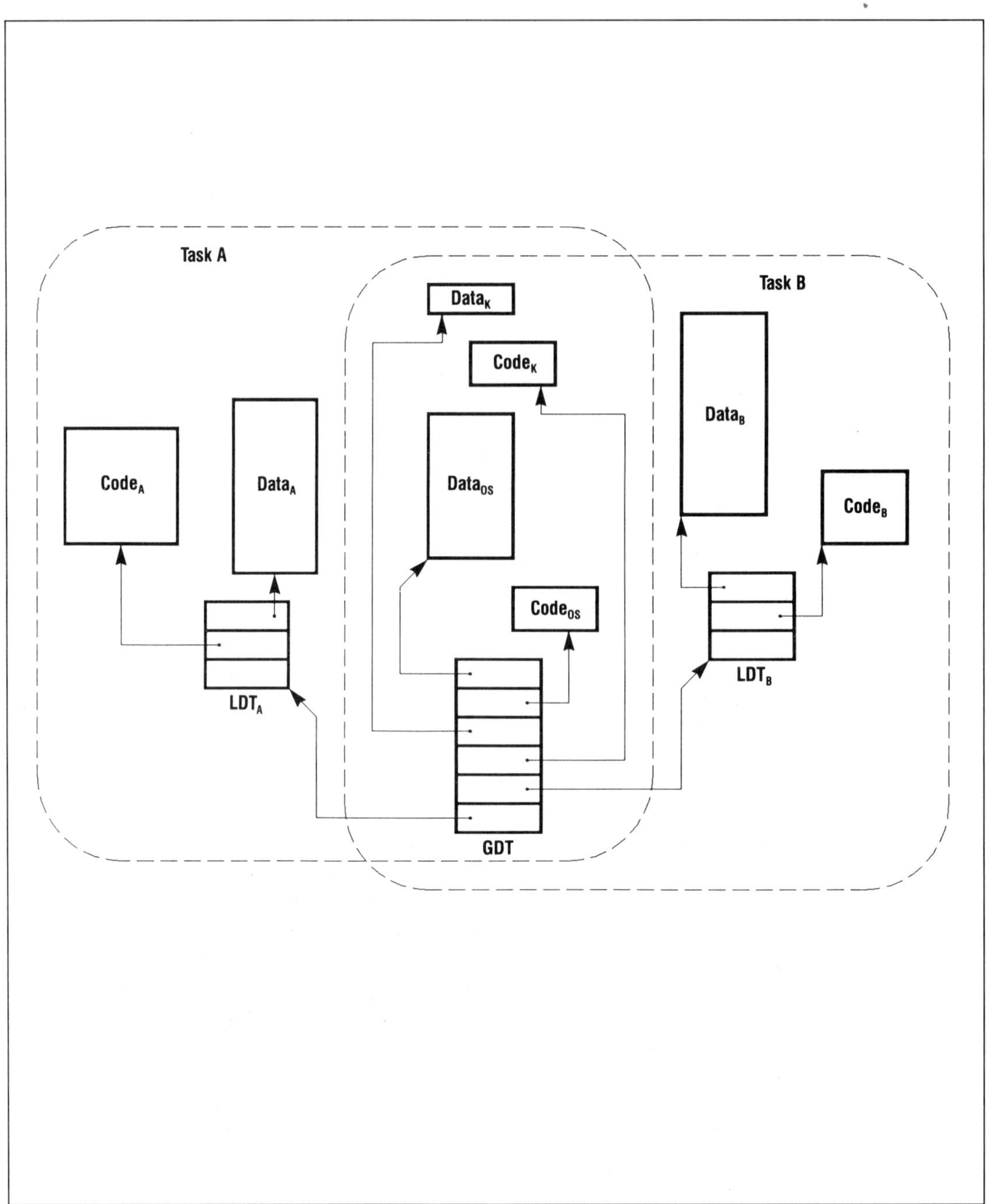

► **Figure 5.8:** Global and local address spaces

Segment Selectors

The segment selector was introduced in Chapter 2 as the segment part of a two-part virtual address. A segment selector identifies a segment, and can be thought of as the name of the segment. As shown in Figure 5.9, a segment selector is 16 bits in size, and contains three subfields. The RPL (requested privilege level) field is in the low-order 2 bits. It provides a key part of the segment protection model, and is described in more detail below. The TI bit in bit 2 identifies the descriptor table containing the descriptor of the segment. TI = 0 indicates that the descriptor for the segment is in the GDT. TI = 1 indicates that the descriptor is in the LDT. The index field is in the high-order 13 bits of the selector, and it gives the index of the descriptor for the segment within the GDT or LDT.

As you can see, a selector names a segment by locating the descriptor for the segment. The TI bit identifies the descriptor table containing the descriptor, and the index field identifies the descriptor within the indicated table. The descriptor holds all of the information needed to access a segment, such as the segment base address, size, and attributes. Segment selectors can be thought of as placeholders for descriptors, or as indirectly specifying the descriptor.

For example, the following selector identifies segment 3 within the GDT, with RPL = 0. The index field is 11b, or 3, and the TI bit is 0, indicating the GDT.

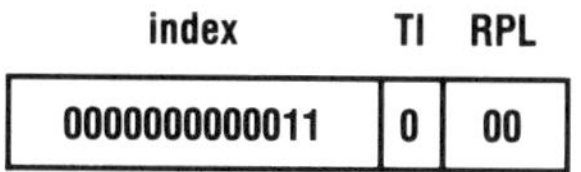

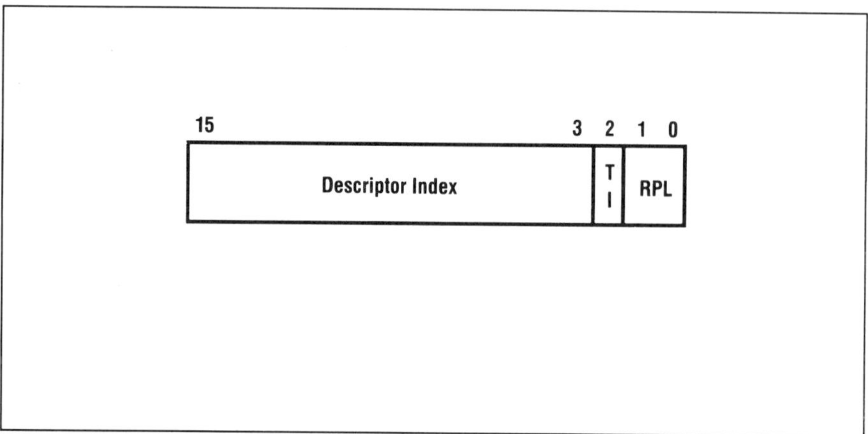

► **Figure 5.9:** Selector format

The following selector identifies segment 8191 within the LDT, with RPL = 3. The index field is 1111111111111b, or 8191, and the TI bit is 1, indicating the LDT. Note that this is the largest index that can be given.

index	TI	RPL
1111111111111	1	11

Null Selector

The following selector is a special value called the *null selector.* It has TI = 0 and index = 0, but it can have any value in the RPL field. As noted in the detailed descriptions given in the section on Memory Data Access Details later in this chapter, any memory reference that uses a segment register containing the null selector will raise an exception. The null selector is a useful value that can be used when a placeholder selector is needed, but when no segment makes sense. Note that a selector that has TI = 1 and index = 0 is not a null selector, but instead identifies the segment described by the first descriptor in the LDT.

index	TI	RPL
0000000000000	0	RPL

Because the null selector has TI = 0 and index = 0, it occupies the first descriptor slot in the GDT. When the operating system builds descriptor tables, it must build in a "dummy" descriptor in the first GDT descriptor slot to account for the null selector. This descriptor is never referenced by the processor.

RPL Field Usage

Whenever the program attempts to access a segment, the current privilege level (CPL) is compared to the privilege level of the segment to determine if the access is permitted. The RPL field of the selector modifies this privilege level test by checking as if the program was executing at a privilege level given by the outermost of CPL and RPL.

RPL allows the operating system to "weaken" its CPL when operating with selectors passed in as parameters by outer-level routines. The operating system simply sets the RPL of all selector parameters to the CPL of the program that passed the selector. This is efficiently done by using the ARPL instruction described in Chapter 3. Then, when the operating system uses the selector to access a segment, the privilege level checks will be done using the CPL of the calling program (stored in RPL) rather than the CPL of the operating system. This ensures that the operating system does not access a segment on behalf of a calling program unless that program itself has access to the segment.

CPL is stored in the RPL field of the CS register. Whenever a code segment selector is loaded into the CS register, the processor automatically stores CPL into the RPL field of CS. A program can examine CPL by storing the CS selector into a general register or memory.

Segment Descriptors

Previous sections have introduced the descriptor tables that contain descriptors, and the segment selectors that identify segments by locating their descriptors. Now it is time to describe the descriptors themselves. Before we give the exact format of a segment descriptor, we will abstractly describe the key fields of a descriptor. (If you are impatient, you can look ahead to Figure 5.10 to see the detailed format of a segment descriptor). Each segment descriptor is eight bytes in size, and contains three fields: a segment base address, a segment limit, and segment attributes.

Base and Limit

The base address is 32 bits, in order to allow a segment to start at any byte address in the 32-bit linear address space. The limit is also 32 bits, but is specified with only 20 bits in the descriptor. Segment limits can be byte granular or 4K byte granular, as defined by one of the 12 attribute bits. Therefore, the 20-bit limit permits specification of segment sizes from one byte to one megabyte in one-byte increments, or sizes from 4K bytes to 4G bytes in 4K byte increments. Use of 4K granularity permits specification of large segment limits, but leaves 12 bits available for segment attributes, described below.

For example, a segment with

Base = 012345678

Limit = 0

Granularity = 0 (byte granular)

describes a segment that is one byte long, at linear address 12345678. Within this segment the only valid offset is 0, to access the single byte in the segment, and all other offsets will generate exceptions.

When a 4K granular limit is specified, the full limit is computed from the 20-bit limit stored in the descriptor using the following formula:

```
Segment Limit = Descriptor Limit * 4K + 4095
              = Descriptor Limit << 12 + 0FFFh
```

In other words, the 20 bits in the descriptor limit field give the upper 20 bits of the segment limit, with the bottom 12 bits set to 0FFFh. The bottom 12 bits of the segment limit are set to 0FFFh so that a descriptor limit of 0 specifies a 4K segment. More importantly, the largest descriptor limit, $2^{20}-1$ (0FFFFFh), specifies a segment that is 4G in size.

For example, a segment with

Base = 12345000h

Limit = 0

Granularity = 1 (4K granular)

describes a segment that starts at linear address 12345000h, and is 4K long. Offsets from 0 to 0FFFh are valid in this segment, and translate to linear addresses from 12345000h to 12345FFFh.

Another good example is a segment with

Base = 0

Limit = 0FFFFFh

Granularity = 1 (4K granular)

which describes a segment that encompasses all 4G of the linear space. The limit is 0FFFFFh 4K chunks, so the largest offset that can be specified is 0FFFFFh * 1000h + 0FFFh, or 0FFFFFFFFh. If you count the Fs in that offset correctly, you will see that this results in a segment that is exactly 4G in size. Since the base address is 0, this large segment is mapped directly on top of the entire 4G linear address space.

Segments can be extended in size by increasing the segment limit (which may require moving segments within the linear address space to make room for the larger segment!). This works well for data segments that can grow "up" in memory, but is no help for the segment containing a stack. Recall from Chapter 2 that the program stack is stored in the segment addressed by the SS segment register, the ESP register holds the offset of the top of the stack, and the stack grows toward lower offsets within this segment as elements are pushed. Because the program stack grows "down," it is usually allocated so that it starts at the top of the segment (at the segment limit), and grows down toward offset 0 in the segment. Expand-down segments are provided to support expansion of stacks in the natural direction for stacks: down!

An expand-down segment has the role of the limit reversed. In a normal segment, the limit field divides the 4G range of possible offsets into two subranges: from 0 to the limit are the legal offsets, and from limit + 1 to 4G − 1 are the illegal offsets. In an expand-down segment, the legal vs. illegal interpretation is reversed. The offsets from 0 to the limit are illegal offsets (which will signal exceptions), and offsets from limit + 1 to 4G − 1 are the legal offsets.

The expansion direction for the segment is another segment attribute that is stored in the segment descriptor. This attribute is referenced to determine how to use the limit field to check for limit violations.

Segment Attributes

The segment privilege level is stored in the attribute field in every type of segment descriptor, and so is named the *Descriptor Privilege Level,* or DPL. This field is 2 bits in size in order to hold a privilege level that is a number from 0 to 3.

The *Present* (P) bit is a second attribute bit common to all descriptor types. If set, it indicates that the descriptor is valid for use in translating virtual addresses to linear addresses. If it is clear, it indicates that the descriptor is not valid for address translation, and any attempt to use the descriptor should report an exception.

Another attribute bit common to all descriptors is the *DType* bit, which distinguishes two kinds of descriptors. If the DType bit is 1, the descriptor is for a memory segment. If it is 0, the descriptor is for a system segment or a gate. The LDT is one system segment that has already been introduced. Gates will be described later in this chapter.

The following sections describe the encoding of descriptors for memory segments, system segments, and gates. Although the format of memory segments and system segments is similar, they have different attributes, and so are discussed in separate sections. The format of gate descriptors is quite different from memory or system segment descriptors.

Memory Segment Descriptor Format

Memory segments hold all of the code and data that can be accessed directly by a program. Figure 5.10 illustrates the format of a memory segment descriptor. The eight-byte descriptor is shown with the lowest addressed byte (assumed to be at address *m*) on the right, with the relative byte addresses shown along the top. The attributes stored in the bytes at offsets 5 and 6 are shown in a magnified view that includes bit offsets as well as byte offsets. The DType bit is bit 4 of the byte at offset 5. It is 1 for memory segments (labeled as DT1 in Figure 5.10) and 0 for system segments and gates.

The base address is split into two pieces: bits 23...0 are stored in three bytes beginning at offset 2, and bits 31...24 are stored in the byte at offset 7. The limit field is also split into two parts: bits 15...0 are stored in the two bytes at offset 0, and bits 19...16 are stored in the low-order 4 bits of the byte at offset 6. Segment attributes are stored in the two bytes at offset 5 and 6, and are discussed separately in the following list.

G The G bit is the limit *Granularity* attribute discussed above. G = 0 indicates a byte granular limit. G = 1 indicates a 4K granular limit. Note that the G bit only affects the granularity of the segment limit. The segment base is always byte granular.

D The D bit should always be 1 for 80386 software. As discussed in Chapter 9, 80286 software should have this bit set to 0. This bit gives a *Default* for segments that are executable or expand-down, or that are addressed by the SS register, as follows:

1. Executable segments use the D bit to set the default size for addresses and operands referenced by the instructions in the segment. D = 1 indicates that the

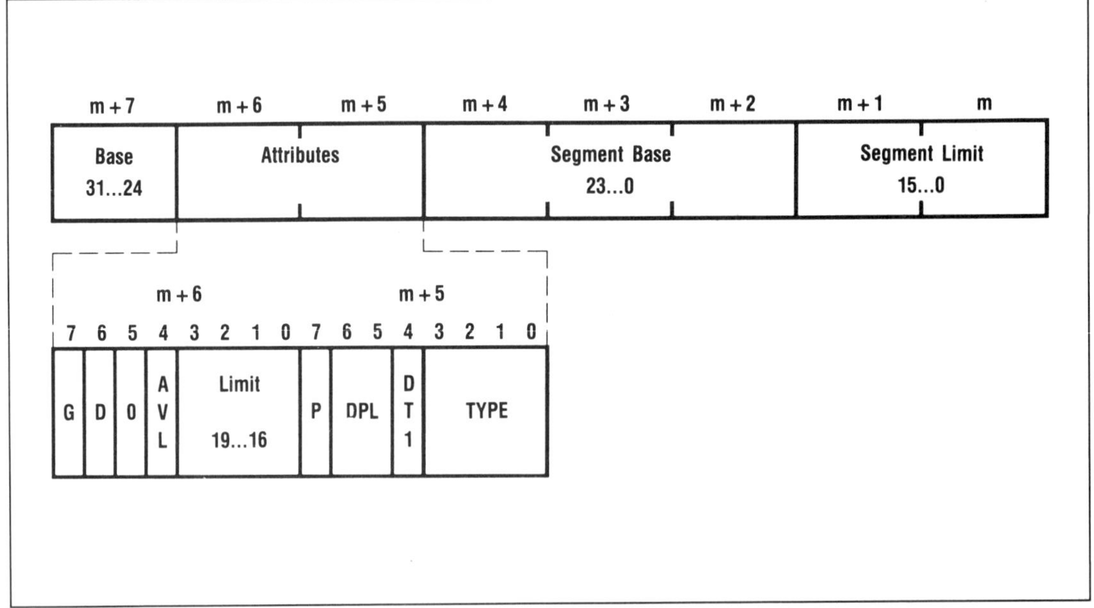

► **Figure 5.10:** Memory segment descriptor format

default is 32-bit addresses and 32-bit or 8-bit operands, the normal setting for 80386 programs. D = 0 indicates the default is 16-bit addresses and 16-bit or 8-bit operands, for compatibility with the 286. An instruction prefix can be used to get a size other than the default.

2. Expand-down segments use the D bit to determine the upper bound of the segment. D = 1 indicates a 4G upper limit for the segment. D = 0 indicates a 64K upper limit for compatibility with the 286.
3. Segments addressed by the SS register use the D bit to determine whether to use the 32-bit ESP register (if D = 1) for implicit stack references such as the PUSH and POP instructions, or to use the 16-bit SP register (D = 0) for 286 compatibility.

AVL The *Available-to-Software* bit is available for software use. The 80386 does not interpret this bit, and Intel promises that all future processors compatible with the 80386 will not define a use for this bit.

P The *Present* bit is discussed above. P = 1 indicates that the descriptor is valid for address translation. P = 0 indicates that the descriptor is not valid, and use of the descriptor will cause an exception.

DPL The *Descriptor Privilege Level* defines the privilege level associated with the segment.

DT The *DType* bit distinguishes memory segments (DType = 1) from the system segments and gates (DType = 0). This field is labeled DT1 in Figure 5.10.

Type The 4-bit Type field defines the *type* of the memory descriptor. The codes are given in Table 5.1. The read, write, and execute attributes in Table 5.1 need no further explanation. The expand-down limit attribute was discussed above, and the conforming attribute for code segments will be discussed in a later section. A descriptor is marked as "accessed" by the 80386 when the corresponding selector is loaded into a segment register. The "accessed" attribute can be examined by operating-system software to see if a descriptor has been accessed by the processor since the last time software cleared the bit to 0.

System Segments and Gates

System segments are special segments used by the 80386 segmentation mechanism. Gates do not describe segments, but instead contain pointers. System segments and gates are described in detail later in this chapter. The definition of their descriptor format is included here as reference information.

Figure 5.11 illustrates the format for system segment descriptors. The base and limit fields are the same as for memory segment descriptors, as are the limit granularity (G) bit, the present (P) bit, the DPL field, the DType bit, and even the Available-to-Software (AVL) field. The Type field is present, but is encoded differently. Only the default (D) bit is missing, and is ignored (labeled as X in Figure 5.11). The DType bit is 0 (labeled as DT0), identifying this as a system segment or gate descriptor.

TYPE	DEFINES
0	Read-only
1	Read-only, accessed
2	Read/write
3	Read/write, accessed
4	Read-only, expand-down limit
5	Read-only, expand-down limit, accessed
6	Read/write, expand-down limit
7	Read/write, expand-down limit, accessed
8	Execute-only
9	Execute-only, accessed
A	Execute/read
B	Execute/read, accessed
C	Execute-only, conforming
D	Execute-only, conforming, accessed
E	Execute/read, conforming
F	Execute/read, conforming, accessed

► **Table 5.1:** Memory segment descriptor types

As with memory segment descriptors, the byte at offset 5 contains a 4-bit Type field, which determines whether the descriptor is for a system segment or a gate. The Type field codes for both system segments and gates are given in Table 5.2. The LDT system segment type has already been introduced. The busy and available 386 TSS system segment types, the 386 call gate type, and the task gate type will be described later in this chapter. The 386 trap and interrupt gate types will be described in Chapter 6. The 286 TSS types and the 286 gate types are the 16-bit counterparts of the 386 types and will be discussed in Chapter 9.

Figure 5.12 illustrates the format for gate descriptors. Gates contain a 48-bit full pointer, plus 16 bits of attributes. The 48-bit pointer has the same information as the full pointer data type introduced in Chapter 2, but is stored with the offset split into two pieces. The selector part of the pointer is stored in bytes at offset 2 and 3. The 32-bit offset is stored in two different pieces. The low-order 16 bits of the offset are stored at offset 0, and the high-order 16 bits are stored at offset 6.

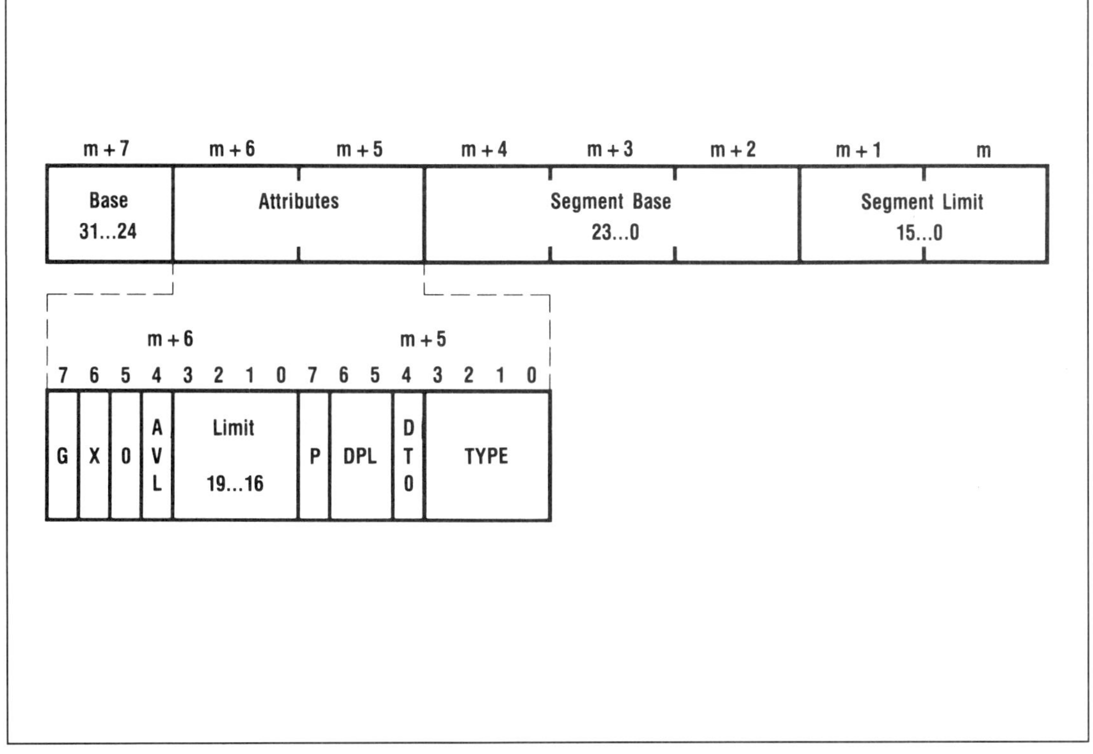

► **Figure 5.11:** System segment descriptor format

TYPE	DEFINES
0	Undefined
1	Available 286 TSS
2	LDT
3	Busy 286 TSS
4	286 Call Gate
5	Task Gate
6	286 Interrupt Gate
7	286 Trap Gate
8	Undefined
9	Available 386 TSS
A	Undefined
B	Busy 386 TSS
C	386 Call Gate
D	Undefined
E	386 Interrupt Gate
F	386 Trap Gate

► **Table 5.2:** Type field encoding for system segments and gates

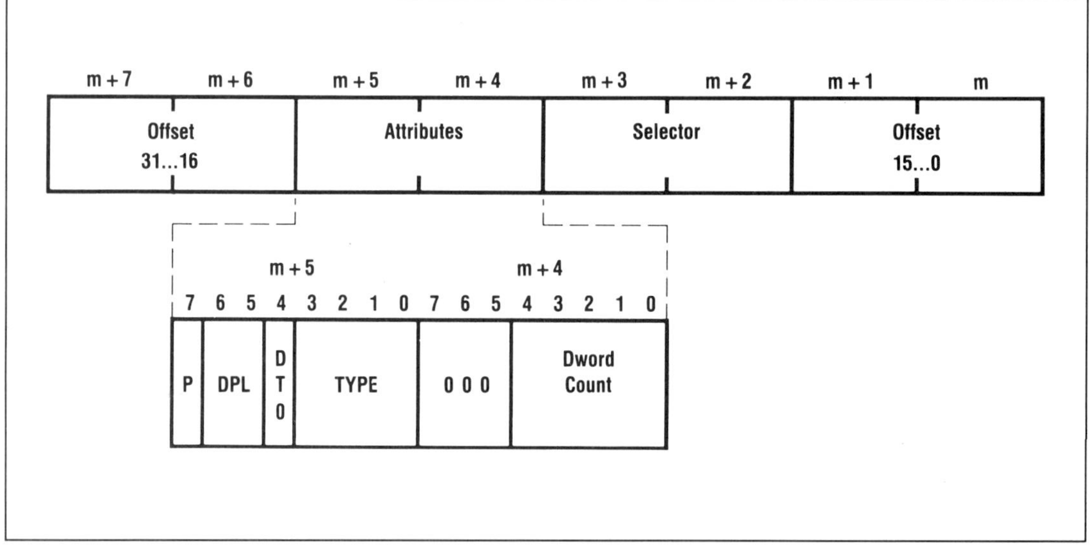

► **Figure 5.12:** Gate descriptor format

In a gate descriptor, the attributes are stored in the bytes at offset 4 and 5, as follows:

P	This is the *Present* bit. P = 1 indicates that the gate is valid. P = 0 indicates that it is not valid, and use of the gate should cause an exception.
DPL	This is the *Descriptor Privilege Level,* which defines the privilege level associated with the gate.
DT	This is the *DType* bit, which distinguishes memory segments (DType = 1) from systems segments and gates (DType = 0).
Type	This 4-bit field defines the *type* of the gate, given in Table 5.2 above.
Dword Count	This field gives the number of dwords (4 bytes) of parameters to copy from one stack to another if use of the gate results in a level transition and a stack change. As described later, this allows procedure parameters to be passed on the program stack, as described in Chapter 2, even if a level transition and stack change occur.

Descriptor Shadow Registers

To avoid referencing the descriptor table to read and decode a segment descriptor for every memory reference, each segment register has associated with it a set of descriptor shadow registers. These registers hold the descriptor information for the segment identified by the selector in the segment register. The segment register is visible to the programmer, either as one of the six segment registers defined in Chapter 2, or as one of the registers described later in this chapter. The associated registers that hold the descriptor are not visible to the programmer, and so are called *shadow registers.* Figure 5.13 shows the six segment registers with their shadow registers. The segment registers are drawn with solid lines, to indicate that they are visible to the programmer. The shadow registers are drawn with dashed lines to indicate they are not visible.

The shadow registers hold the base, limit, and attributes for the segment addressed by the corresponding segment register. They are loaded with the descriptor information whenever the corresponding segment register is loaded with a selector. This allows the descriptor to be loaded only once for many references to the segment. Since the shadow registers are stored on-chip on the 80386, they can be accessed rapidly by the segmentation hardware. High-performance execution is achieved, since most instructions reference data in segments whose selectors have already been loaded into segment registers.

The instructions in the Multiple Segment section of Chapter 3 each load a new selector into a segment register. Each of these instructions will also load the corresponding descriptor information into the shadow registers. Chapter 3 described these instructions as viewed by the programmer; that is, as instructions that load selectors into segment registers. Later sections of this chapter expand on this definition to detail how the corresponding descriptors are checked by these instructions, and, if all checks pass, how they are loaded into the shadow registers. If any of the checks fail, an exception is raised and none of the selector or shadow registers are modified.

Because the shadow registers contain a copy of the descriptor information, the operating system must take care to ensure that changes to the descriptor table are reflected in the shadow registers. Otherwise, a segment might have its base address or limit changed in the descriptor table

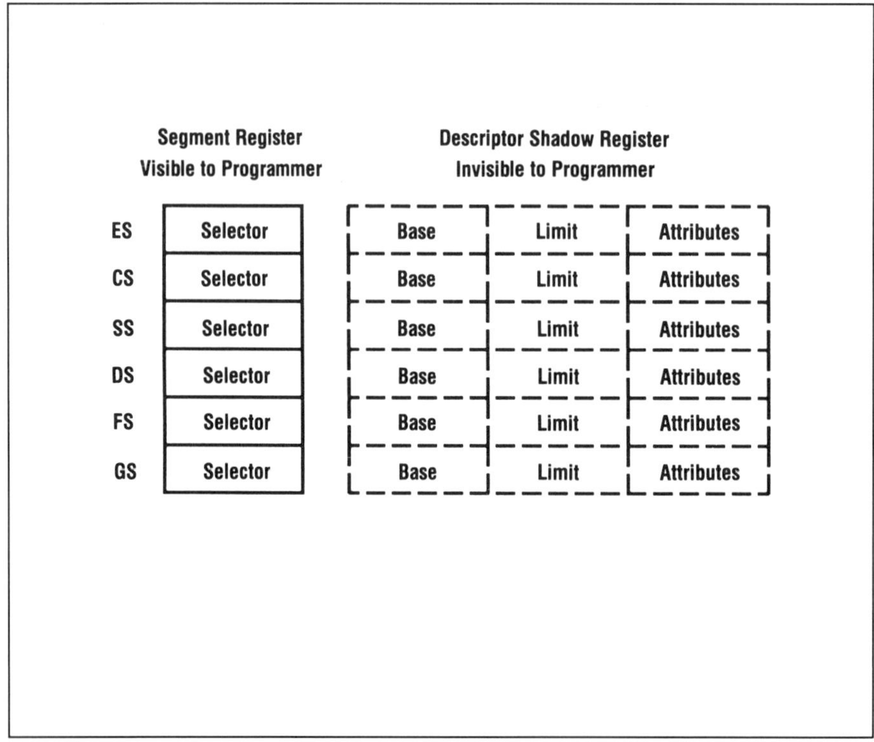

► **Figure 5.13:** Descriptor shadow registers

but not in the shadow registers. The easiest way to handle this is to reload all six segment registers after changing any descriptors in the descriptor table. This will reload the shadow registers with the latest information from the descriptor table.

► Paging

Paging is the second part of the 80386 memory-management mechanism. It operates underneath segmentation to complete the virtual-to-physical address translation process. Segmentation translates virtual addresses to linear addresses. Paging translates the linear addresses put out by segmentation to physical addresses.

The paging mechanism is enabled by the PG bit in CR0. If PG = 1, paging is enabled and linear addresses are translated to physical addresses using the mechanism described in this section. If PG = 0, paging is disabled and the linear addresses generated by the segmentation mechanism are used directly as physical addresses.

Unlike segmentation, which operates with variable-size chunks of memory, paging operates with fixed-size chunks of memory called *pages*. Paging divides both the linear and physical address spaces into pages. Any page in the linear address space can map to any page in the physical address space. Figure 5.14 illustrates how paging divides both the linear and physical address spaces into pages and provides an arbitrary mapping between the spaces. The linear address space is illustrated on the left as a sequence of fixed blocks representing pages. The physical address space is shown on the right, also as a sequence of pages. The arrows in the figure connect a page in the linear space to the corresponding page in the physical space. Note the arbitrary correspondence of pages in the linear space to pages in the physical space.

The 80386 uses a 4K byte page size. Every page is 4K bytes in size, and is aligned to a 4K boundary. This means that the paging mechanism divides the 2^{32} byte (4G) linear address space into 2^{20} pages each 2^{12} bytes (4K) in size. Paging operates by relocating pages from the linear address space into the physical address space. Since an entire 4K page is mapped as a unit and pages are aligned at 4K boundaries, the lower 12 bits of the linear address are passed through the paging mechanism directly as the lower 12 bits of the physical address. The relocation function performed by paging can be thought of as a function that translates the upper 20 bits of a linear address to the upper 20 bits of the corresponding physical address.

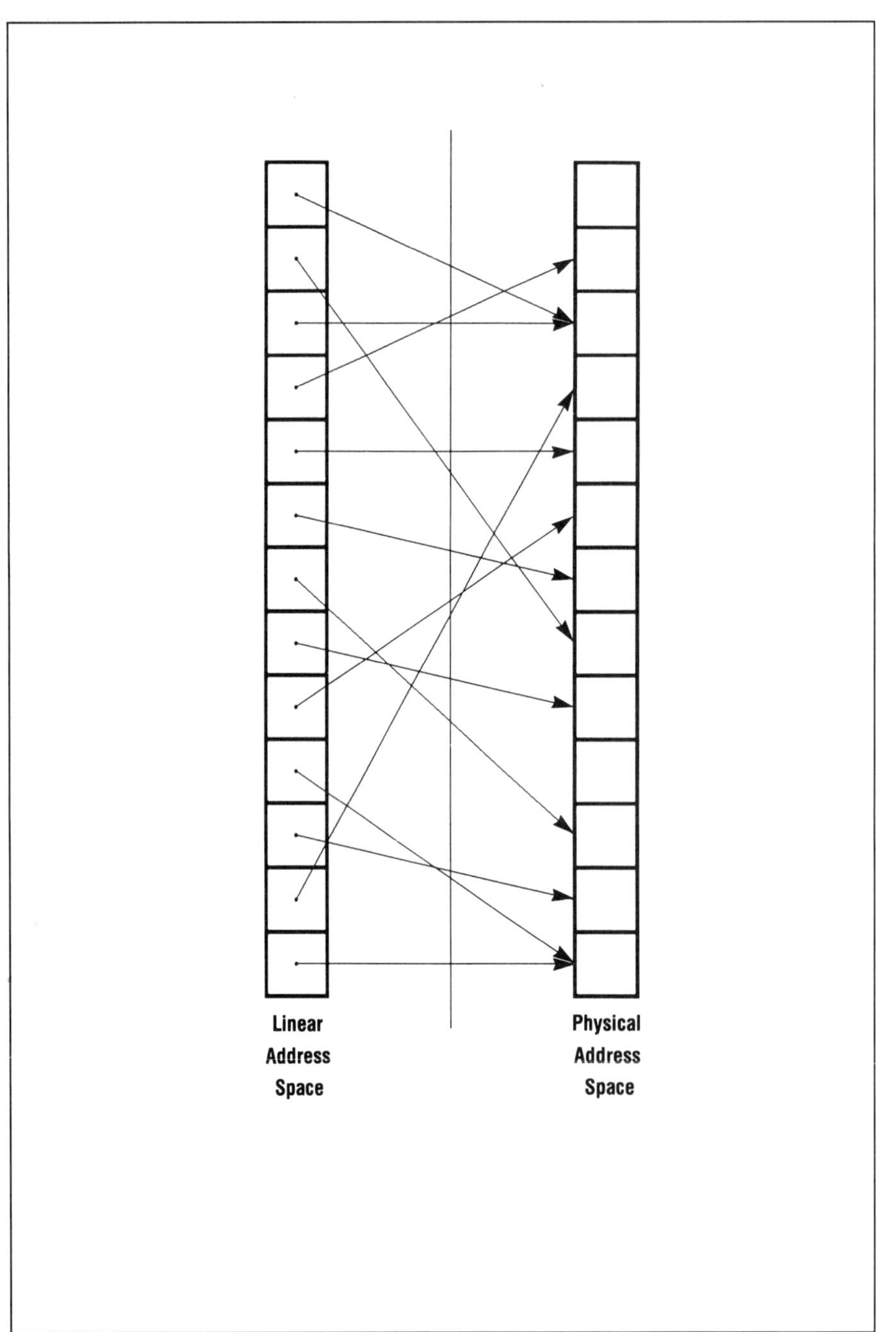

► **Figure 5.14:** Paging translates linear addresses to physical addresses

The linear-to-physical address translation function is extended to permit a linear address to be marked as invalid rather than producing a physical address. A page can be marked invalid either because it is simply a linear address not supported by the operating system, or because it corresponds to a page in a virtual memory system that is stored on disk rather than in physical memory. In the first case, the program generating the invalid address must be terminated. In the second case, the invalid address is really a request to the virtual memory manager of the operating system to move the page from the disk into physical memory so it can be accessed by the program. Because invalid pages are usually associated with a virtual memory system, they are known as not-present pages, and are identified by an attribute in the page table called the *present* attribute.

Page Table Structure

The paging translation function is described by a memory-resident table called the *page table,* which is stored in the physical address space. The page table can be thought of as a simple array of 2^{20} physical addresses. The linear-to-physical mapping function is simply an array lookup. The upper 20 bits of the linear address form the index into this array, which selects the correponding physical address of the page. The lower 12 bits of the linear address give an offset into this page, which is added to the base address to obtain the final physical address. Since the page base addresses are aligned at 4K boundaries, the lower 12 bits of the page base address are 0. This means that the 12-bit offset is not really added, but is simply concatenated with the upper 20 bits of the page base address. That is, the base address provides the upper 20 bits of the physical address and the offset provides the lower 12 bits.

Each page table entry is 32 bits in size. Since only 20 bits of the 32-bit entry are needed to store the physical address, 12 bits are left over for page attributes, such as whether the page is present. If the page table entry indexed by the linear address is marked present, the entry is valid and the physical address is obtained from another field in the entry. If the entry is tagged as not present, a page exception is raised to report the invalid address to operating-system software.

Two-Level Page Table Structure

The page table contains 2^{20} entries, each of which is four bytes wide. If stored as one table, it would occupy 4 megabytes of contiguous physical memory! Rather than dedicate this amount of memory to the page table, the table is stored as a two-level table. Furthermore, the linear-to-physical address translation of the upper 20 address bits is done in two steps, with each step using 10 bits.

The first level of the table is called the *page directory.* It is stored in a single 4K byte page and has 2^{10} (1K) four-byte entries that point to second-level tables. The high-order 10 linear address bits (bits 31...22) are used to index this first-level table to select one of the 2^{10} second-level tables.

The second-level tables are called *page tables* and are also exactly one page in size and contain 1K four-byte entries. Each four-byte entry contains the physical base address of a page. The second-level page tables are indexed by the middle 10 linear address bits (bits 21...12) to obtain the page table entry containing the physical base address of a page. The upper 20 bits of this physical address are combined with the low-order 12 bits (the page offset) from the linear address to form the final physical address that is the output of the page translation process.

Figure 5.15 illustrates this two-level table lookup process. Register

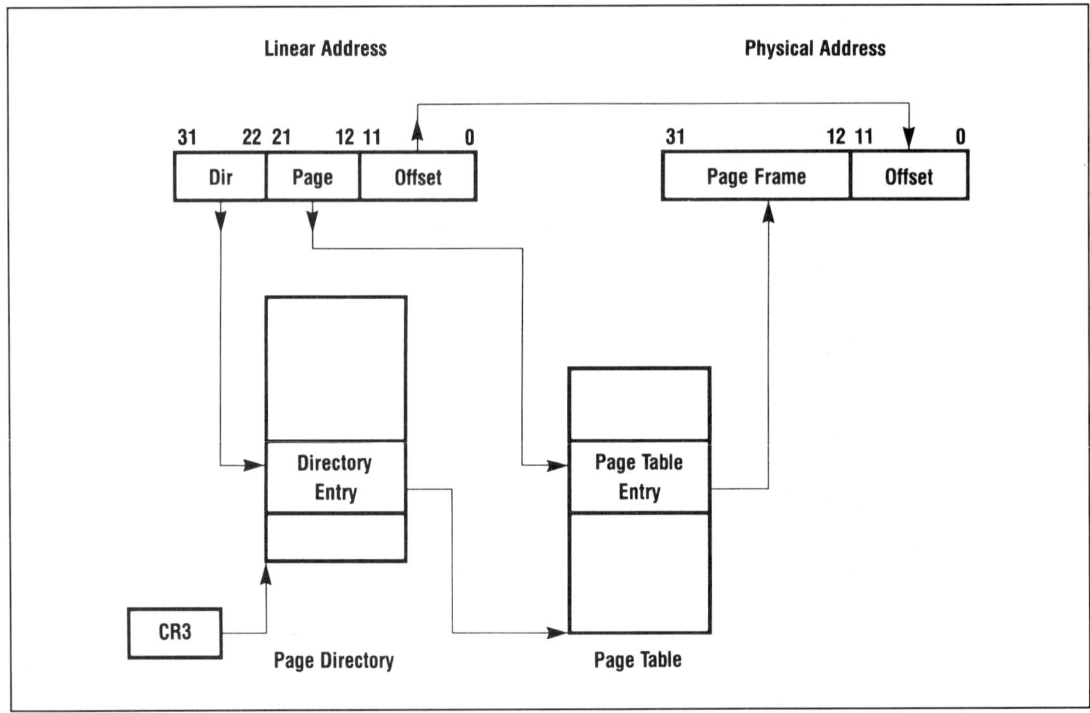

► **Figure 5.15:** Two-level page table structure

CR3, described in a later section, roots the page table structure by pointing to the directory page. The upper 10 bits of a linear address are used to index this directory to obtain a pointer to the appropriate second-level page table. The middle 10 bits of the linear address are used to index this second-level table to obtain the upper 20 bits of the resulting physical address. The low-order 12 bits of the linear address pass through the paging mechanism unchanged, and are concatenated to the upper 20 physical address bits obtained from the page table to form the full physical address.

Not-Present Page Tables

By using a two-level table structure, we have not solved the problem of needing 4 megabytes of memory to store the page table. In fact, we have made the storage problem slightly worse, since we need an extra page for the directory! However, the two-level structure allows the page table to be scattered in pages throughout memory rather than being stored in one contiguous 4-megabyte chunk. Furthermore, second-level tables need not be allocated for nonexistent or unused parts of the linear address space. The directory page must always be present in physical memory, but the second-level tables can be allocated only as needed. This allows the size of the page table structure to correspond to the size of the linear address space actually used.

Every entry in the directory has a *present* attribute that is analogous to the present attribute in page table entries. The present attribute in a directory entry indicates if the corresponding second-level table is available for use in page translation. If the directory entry indicates that the second-level table is present, the second level of table lookup proceeds as described above by accessing the second-level table. If the present bit indicates that the second-level table is not present, a page exception is raised to report the use of an invalid linear address to operating-system software. The present attribute in directory entries allows the operating system to allocate only as many second-level tables as are needed to cover the linear address range that is actually used.

The present attribute in directory entries can also be used to store second-level page tables in virtual memory. This means that only a subset of the second-level tables need be in physical memory at any time, with the rest stored on disk. Directory entries for tables in physical memory would be marked *present* to indicate they are valid for page translation. Directory entries for tables on disk would be marked *not present* to indicate they are invalid for address translation. A page exception due to a not-present second-level page table would signal the operating system to bring in the missing table from disk. Storing the page tables in virtual memory minimizes the amount of physical memory required to store the paging translation tables.

Global vs. Local Page Tables

Unlike the segment table structure, there is no provision for splitting the page table into a global table and a local table. However, by arranging for each task to share a part of the linear-to-physical address mapping function, a global part of the linear address space can be defined. This part of the linear address space is mapped the same in every task in the system because the same linear-to-physical mapping information is used in each task. Pages in this part of the linear address space are called *global pages,* since they are mapped to the same physical addresses in all tasks. The remaining part of the linear address space is local to each task. The table structure is set up so that a different address mapping function is used for the local part of the linear address space. Pages within this local part of the linear address space are called *local pages.*

The two-level page table structure supports the efficient sharing of parts of the linear address space by sharing second-level page tables as well as the global pages themselves. Figure 5.16 illustrates this technique. The figure shows the page table structure for two tasks, A and B. DIR_A is the directory page for task A, and DIR_B for task B. The first entry (at offset 0) of each directory points to a global page table, which maps up to 2^{10} (1K) global pages. The second entry (at offset 4) of each directory points to a local page table unique to each task, each of which maps up to 2^{10} local pages.

This simple example has the lowest 4 megabytes of the linear address space global to both tasks, and has the next 4 megabytes local to each task. Additional page tables can be allocated to the global area as required, providing expansion of the global part of the linear address space in 4-megabyte chunks. Also note that the shared page tables are pointed to by the same directory entries in both page directories. This is important, since it ensures that the same linear address range in both tasks will map to this global area. In this example, the first 4 megabytes of the linear address space (addresses 0 to 3FFFFFh) are in the global linear address space.

Sharing second-level tables that map the global part of the linear address space has several benefits. First, only one set of second-level page tables needs to be allocated to map the global pages. These page tables are then shared by all tasks rather than requiring a duplicate copy in each task. A second advantage is that if the status of a shared page changes, there is only one page table entry that needs to be updated to

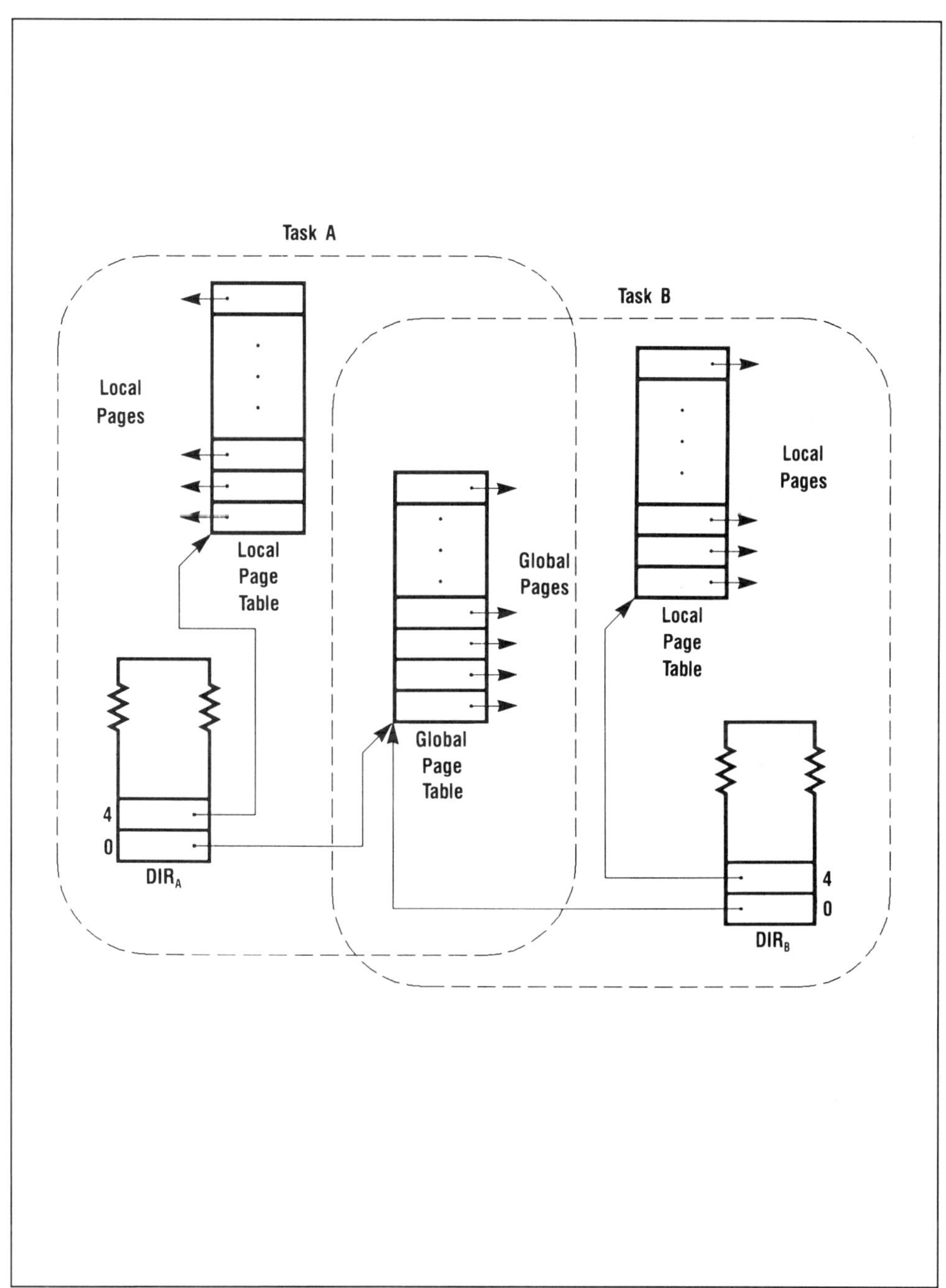

► **Figure 5.16:** Global and local page tables

reflect the change in status. If a global page is swapped to or from disk in a virtual memory system, only one page table entry needs to change.

As with segmentation, such things as the operating-system code and data and the segment descriptor tables would normally be stored in global pages. Code and data unique to a task would be stored in the local pages. The segment and page tables should be set up so that the segments mapped by the GDT are stored in global pages, and segments mapped by the LDT are stored in pages local to a task.

Page Table Entry Format

The entries at both the directory and page table levels use the format shown in Figure 5.17. Bits 31...12 contain the upper 20 bits of a physical address to locate a page "frame" in the physical address space. The lower 12 bits contain page attributes. The present attribute has been discussed already. The remaining attributes are briefly described here, and are discussed in detail in the following sections. Bit positions indicated as 0 are reserved by Intel for use in future processors and must be set to 0 to ensure upward compatibility.

P — Bit 0 is the *Present* bit introduced above, which indicates whether the entry is valid for address translation (P = 1) or not (P = 0). An exception is raised if an invalid entry is encountered in either the directory or the page table during the page translation process. If P = 0, the remaining bits in the entry are available for software use, as illustrated in Figure 5.18. The 80386 does not interpret any other bits for entries that have P = 0.

R/W — Bit 1 is the R/W (*Read/Write*) bit. If it is 1, the page can be read, written, or executed. If it is 0, the page can be read or executed, but not written. As discussed below, the R/W bit is ignored if the procesor is executing at one of the supervisor privilege levels (0, 1, or 2). The R/W bit in a directory entry applies to all pages mapped by that entry.

U/S — Bit 2 is the U/S (*User/Supervisor*) bit. If it is 1, the page is accessible to programs executing at any privilege level including the user level (level 3). If it is 0, the page is accessible only to programs executing at one of the supervisor privilege levels (0, 1, or 2). The U/S bit in a directory entry applies to all pages mapped by that entry.

A — Bit 5 is the A or *Accessed* bit. The A bit in a page table entry is set to 1 by the processor before any access to the page mapped by the entry. The A bit in a directory entry is set to 1 by the processor before any access to any of the pages mapped by the entry. The A bit is never cleared by the processor, but can be cleared periodically by operating-system software to obtain page usage statistics.

D — Bit 6 is the D or *Dirty* bit. The D bit in the second-level page table entry is set to 1 by the processor before any write access to the page mapped by the entry. The processor does not modify the D bit of entries in the page directory.

AVL — The AVL field is available for use by software. It is not modified by the processor, and it is not reserved for use by future processors.

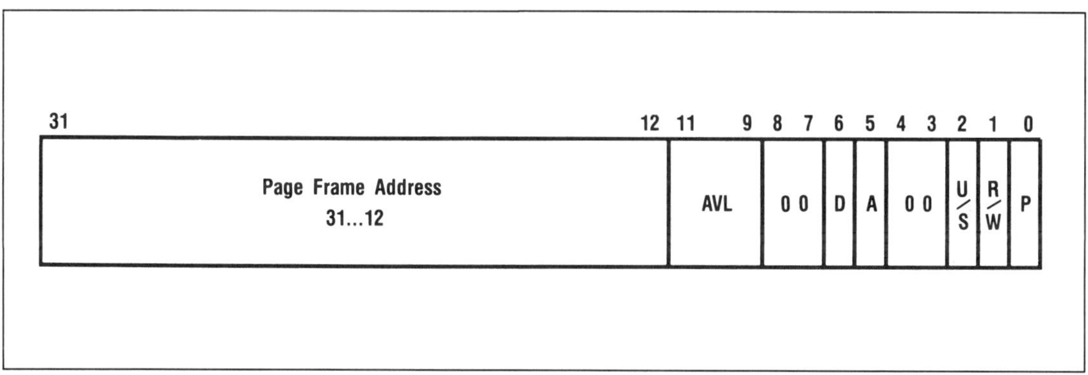

► **Figure 5.17:** Page directory/table entry format

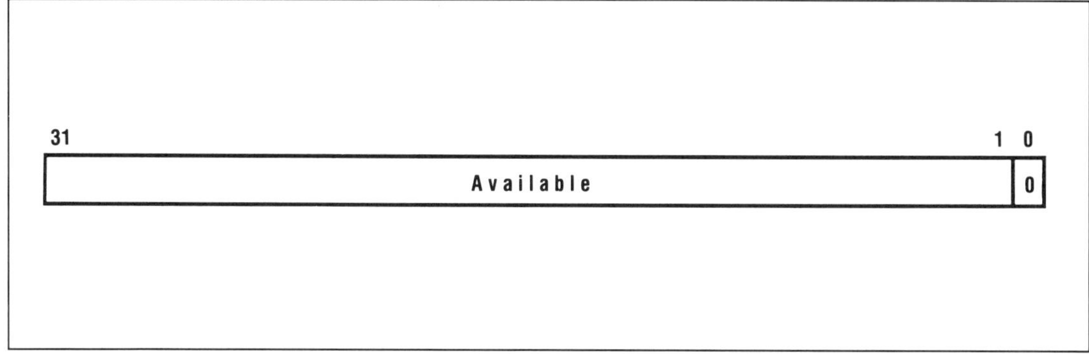

► **Figure 5.18:** Not-present page directory/table entry format

The following example illustrates in detail how a linear address is translated to a physical address by traversing the two levels of the page table. Suppose you want to translate the linear address 11111678h to a physical address, and CR3 contains the value 8000h. The 32-bit linear address 11111678h is first split into three fields:

31 22	21 12	11 0
0001000100	0100010001	011001111000

Bits 31...22 are used to index the directory page. Bits 21...12 index the second-level page table pointed to by the selected directory entry. Bits 11...0 give the byte offset into the page pointed to by the selected page table entry.

The four-byte directory entry is addressed by extracting the directory index, bits 31...22 of the linear address, and then shifting left by 2 (multiply by 4) to get the byte offset into the directory page: 0001000100b = 44h shifted left 2 is 0100010000b = 110h. This byte offset is added to the physical base address of the directory page contained in CR3—in this case, the value 8000h. So the directory entry is read from physical address 8110h.

The page table is addressed by the upper 20 bits of this directory entry. If the directory entry at address 8110h contained the value 00023021h, the page table base is 00023000h, and the P bit and A bits are 1, indicating the second-level page table is present, and the directory entry has been accessed before. The address of the page table entry is addressed by using bits 21...12 of the linear address as an index into the page table at address 00023000h. The table index is 100010001b or 111h. This is shifted left 2 to form a byte offset 444h into the page table. The page table entry is then read from physical address 00023444h. If it contains the value 12345021h, the page frame address is 12345000h, and the page is present and accessed.

The physical address corresponding to the original linear address is formed by adding the lower 12 bits of the linear address to the page frame address from the page table entry:

```
page frame address  12345000h
page offset        +     678h  =  011001111000b
                   ----------
physical address    12345678h
```

In this example, the linear address 11111678h was translated to the physical address 12345678h by traversing the two levels of the page table. Register CR3 pointed to the page directory at physical address

8000h. The directory entry was read from address 8110h, and it pointed to a page table at physical address 23000h. The page table entry was read from address 23444h, and it pointed to the page frame at physical address 12345000h. The final physical address was formed by adding the page offset from the linear address to this page frame address, yielding 12345678h as the final physical address.

Virtual Memory

The P bit provides the critical attribute for supporting virtual memory with paging. Pages in the linear address space that are present in physical memory will be marked present (P = 1), with the corresponding physical address available in the entry. Pages that are not present in physical memory will of course be marked not present (P = 0). If a program accesses a not-present page, a page exception occurs so that the operating system can bring the missing page in from the disk, store the corresponding physical address in the entry, and then mark it present before resuming the program that raised the exception.

The A and D bits assist the efficient implementation of virtual memory. By periodically examining and clearing all of the A bits, the operating system can determine which pages have not been referenced recently. These pages might be good candidates to move out to disk storage. If the D bit is set to 0 when a page is read in from disk, and it is still 0 when the page is to be moved out to disk, the page need not be written. If the D bit is 1, the page must be written, since at least one write has occurred to the page since the last time it was moved in from the disk.

Another important consideration for virtual memory systems is not visible in the page table structure. All instructions are restartable after a paging exception. Once the cause of the exception is fixed, for example, by reading in a not-present page from disk and marking it *present,* the instruction raising the exception can be resumed simply by returning from the interrupt handler for the page exception. The mechanisms used to report and return from exceptions are covered in Chapter 6. The causes of page exceptions, and the information made available to the page exception handler, are covered later in this chapter.

Page-Level Protection

The R/W and U/S bits provide a subset of the protection attributes supported by segmentation. These page-level protection attributes are summarized in Table 5.3. Only two privilege levels are recognized by paging.

Privilege levels 0, 1, and 2 are grouped together as a supervisor privilege level. Privilege level 3 is known as the user privilege level. Pages at the user level can be marked as read/execute-only or as read/write/execute. Supervisor level pages are always read/write/execute to the supervisor, but no user access is allowed. As with segmentation, a program executing at the outer user level can only access user-level pages, but a program executing at any supervisor level (0, 1, 2) can access user-level pages as well as supervisor-level pages. Unlike segmentation, a program executing at the inner supervisor level has read/write/execute access to any page, even to those marked read/execute-only at the user level. This allows a page to be restricted to read/execute-only access at the user level, but allows read/write/execute access by the supervisor.

Just as paging operates after segmentation in the overall 80386 address translation mechanism, page-level protection operates after the protection provided by segmentation. First, all of the segment-level protection checks are tested. If these pass, the page-level protection checks are tested. For example, a byte of memory is accessible to a program executing at privilege level 3 only if it is in a segment accessible to level 3, and in a page marked as a user-level page. It is writable only if both segmentation and paging permit writing. If the segment is typed as a read/write segment, but the page is marked read/execute-only, no write access is permitted. If the segment is typed read/execute-only, no write access is permitted regardless of the page protection assigned.

The protection attributes for a page are computed as the combination of the attributes at the directory and page level. The U/S and R/W bits from a page table entry apply to the single page mapped by that entry. The U/S and R/W bits from a directory entry apply to all 1K pages mapped by that entry. Table 5.4 defines the combined page protection

U/S	R/W	USER-PERMITTED ACCESS	SUPERVISOR-PERMITTED ACCESS
0	0	None	Read/write/execute
0	1	None	Read/write/execute
1	0	Read/execute	Read/write/execute
1	1	Read/write/execute	Read/write/execute

► **Table 5.3:** Page-level protection attributes

attributes from the attributes at both levels of the page tables. The combined attributes are formed by performing the AND operation on the attributes from the two levels, and so are the more restrictive of the two levels. For example, suppose the directory entry has U/S = 1 and R/W = 1 indicating a user read/write/execute page, but the page table entry had U/S = 1 and R/W = 0 indicating a user read/execute-only page. In this case, the combined protection attribute would be U/S = 1 and R/W = 0, indicating a user read/execute-only page.

Software Issues in Modifying Page Table Entries

This section provides some guidelines for operating-system software to follow when modifying page table entries. The use of a paging translation cache requires all systems to adhere to certain guidelines. Multiprocessor systems where one processor can change the page table entries of another concurrently executing processor must adhere to additional guidelines.

DIRECTORY U/S	PAGE U/S	COMBINED U/S
0	0	0
0	1	0
1	0	0
1	1	1
DIRECTORY R/W	**PAGE R/W**	**COMBINED R/W**
0	0	0
0	1	0
1	0	0
1	1	1

► **Table 5.4:** Combined page protection attributes

Coherency of the Paging Translation Cache

To increase speed by avoiding accesses to the memory-resident page tables for every memory reference, the most recently used linear-to-physical address translations are stored in a page translation cache within the processor. This cache is consulted before the memory-based page tables are referenced. Only if the necessary translation is not in the cache are the two levels of the page table traversed. The page translation cache is the paging counterpart of the shadow descriptor registers, described earlier in this chapter, which are used to speed up segment translations. Another term for the paging translation cache used in other computers is *Translation Lookaside Buffer*, or TLB.

Coherence between the data in the paging translation cache and the data in the page table is not maintained by the 80386 processor, but must be guaranteed by operating-system software. That is, the processor does not recognize when page tables are modified by software, for example, to change the base address of a page, or to mark a page not present. In a reasonable system, the page tables can be modified only by the operating system, which can straightforwardly ensure coherence by flushing the cache after any software modification of the page tables. The cache is flushed simply by loading the processor control register CR3, described in a later section of this chapter. This can be accomplished with the following code sequence, which reloads CR3 with its current value:

```
MOV  EAX, CR3 ; Move CR3 value to EAX
MOV  CR3, EAX ; And move it back to flush the cache
```

One important special case of modifying a page table entry does not require the page translation cache to be flushed. That is when any part of a not-present entry is changed, even if the P bit is changed from 0 to 1 to mark the entry as valid for page translation. Since invalid entries are never cached, there is no need to flush the cache when an invalid entry is changed. This means that you do not need to flush the cache after reading in a page from disk to make it present.

Multiple-Processor Considerations

In a system with multiple processors, special care must be taken if a program executing on one processor modifies a page table that may be accessed simultaneously by a second processor. The 80386 processor supports this configuration by using indivisible read/modify/write cycles whenever it updates a page table entry to set the D or A bits. Software updates to the page table will work properly provided the LOCK prefix (see Chapter 3) is used to ensure use of indivisible read/modify/write cycles on instructions that modify the page table. Before changing a page table entry that may be used by another procesor, software should use a locked AND instruction to clear the P bit to 0 in an indivisible operation. Then the entry can be changed as required, and made available by later setting the P bit to 1.

At some point in the modification of a page table entry, all processors in the system that may have the entry cached must be notified (usually with an interrupt) to flush their page translation caches to remove any old copies of the entry. Until these old copies are flushed, these processors can continue to access the old page, and may also set the D bit in the entry being modified. If this may cause the modification of the entry to fail, the paging caches should be flushed after the entry is marked not present, but before the entry is otherwise modified.

Processor-Control Registers and System Segments

This section describes the registers and memory segments that control the operation of the segmentation and paging mechanisms. The registers contain the base addresses of the segment and page translation tables, and bits that control the operation of the processor. The registers are accessible only to programs at privilege level 0, the innermost level. If a program at an outer privilege level attempts to write into these registers, an exception is raised so the operating-system kernel can take appropriate action.

Figure 5.19 illustrates the control registers of the 80386. There are four 32-bit control registers, named CR0, CR1, CR2, and CR3. There are two 48-bit registers named GDTR and IDTR, and two 16-bit selector registers named LDTR and TR. The figure also illustrates the descriptor shadow registers associated with LDTR and TR, which are drawn in dashed lines to indicate that they are not visible to the programmer.

Processor-Control Registers

CR0, CR1, CR2, and CR3 are the four 32-bit control registers. CR1 is reserved for future processors, and is undefined for the 80386. Use of an instruction that encodes CR1 as the register will result in an invalid opcode exception, as described in Chapter 6. CR0 contains bits that enable and disable paging and protection, and bits that control the operation of the floating-point coprocessor. CR2 and CR3 are used by the paging mechanism. Bits 30 through 5 of CR0, and bits 11 through 0 of CR3 are reserved and must be loaded with 0s.

The processor-control registers can be loaded and stored only by programs executing at privilege level 0, by using special forms of the MOV instruction described in Chapter 3.

CR0 Coprocessor Control Bits

Four CR0 bits named ET, TS, EM, and MP control the operation of the 80387 floating-point coprocessor. The ET bit selects the protocol to use when communicating with the coprocessor. The TS, MP, and EM bits determine if floating-point or WAIT instructions should raise a *Device Not Available* (DNA) exception, which is described in Chapter 6. The coprocessor exception handler example in Chapter 7 illustrates how the DNA exception can be used to save and restore the floating-point registers only for tasks that use floating-point arithmetic. This expedites task switches between tasks that do not use floating-point.

ET The *Extension Type* bit controls the protocol used to send floating-point instructions to the coprocessor. ET = 1 indicates

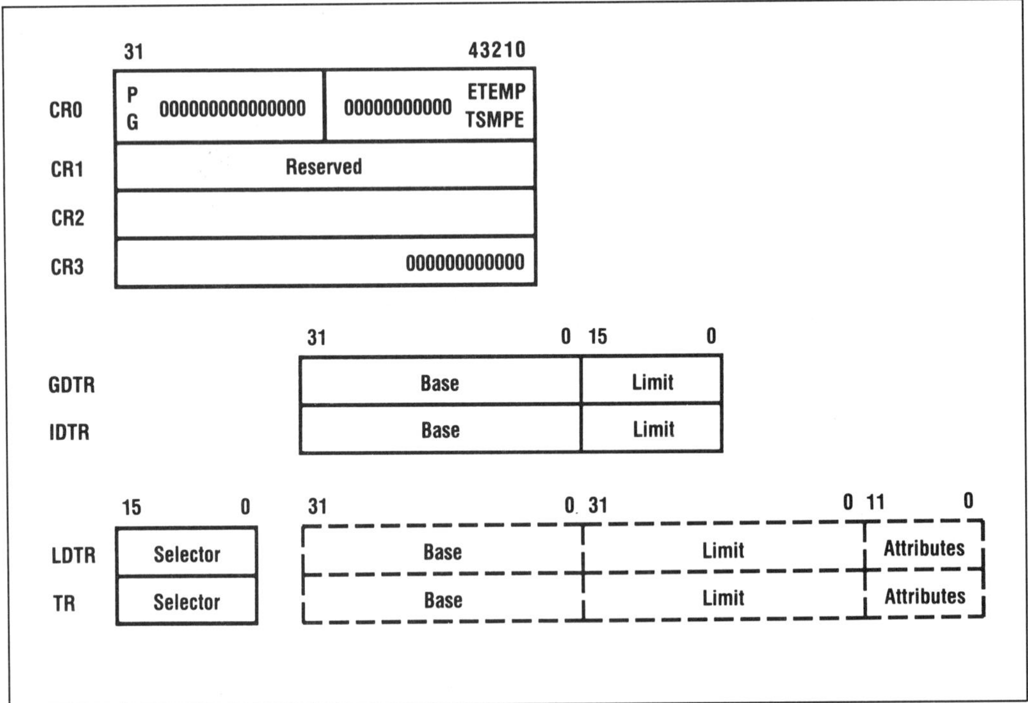

► **Figure 5.19:** Processor-control registers

the presence of an 80387 coprocessor, indicating that the high-performance 32-bit coprocessor protocol is to be used. ET = 0 indicates the use of 16-bit protocol to communicate to an 80287 coprocessor. This field is ignored if the EM bit is 1.

TS The *Task-Switched* bit is used to speed task switches by allowing the coprocessor registers to be swapped only when necessary. The processor sets TS to 1 whenever a task switch occurs. A floating-point instruction will raise a DNA exception if TS = 1. The WAIT instruction will raise a DNA exception if TS = 1 and MP = 1.

MP The *Math Present* bit controls whether WAIT instructions will raise a DNA exception if TS = 1. If MP = 1, a WAIT executed with TS = 1 will raise an exception. If MP = 0, the WAIT instruction will ignore the TS bit.

EM The *Emulate* bit controls whether floating-point instructions will raise a DNA exception (EM = 1), or will be sent to the coprocessor (EM = 0). Note that the WAIT instruction ignores the setting of the EM bit.

Table 5.5 summarizes the use of the EM, TS, and MP bits to raise DNA exceptions. WAIT instructions use the MP bit to qualify the TS bit and are not affected by the EM bit. Floating-point instructions ignore the MP bit, but are affected by the EM bit.

CR0 BIT			INSTRUCTION TYPE	
EM	TS	MP	FLOATING-POINT	WAIT
0	0	0	Execute	Execute
0	0	1	Execute	Execute
0	1	0	DNA Exception	Execute
0	1	1	DNA Exception	DNA Exception
1	0	0	DNA Exception	Execute
1	0	1	DNA Exception	Execute
1	1	0	DNA Exception	Execute
1	1	1	DNA Exception	DNA Exception

► **Table 5.5:** EM, TS, and MP bit summary

The ET bit is initialized when the processor is reset to indicate the type of numeric coprocessor in the system. If a 387 coprocessor is present, the ET bit is set to 1. Otherwise, if a 287 is present or if no coprocessor is present, ET is cleared to 0. Refer to the Intel data sheets for the 80386, 80387, and 80287 for more information about hardware reset.

CR0 Protection Control Bits

The PE bit (bit 0) and the PG bit (bit 31) control the operation of the segmentation and paging mechanisms. PE controls the segmentation mechanism. If PE = 1, the processor operates with the segmentation mechanism enabled and operating as described in this chapter. When PE = 1, the processor is said to be executing in protected mode. If PE = 0, the segmentation mechanism is turned off, and the processor operates in real mode as an 8086, as described in Chapter 9. PG controls the paging mechanism. If PG = 1, paging is enabled and operates as described in this chapter. If PG = 0, paging is disabled and the linear addresses produced by the segmentation mechanism are passed through as physical addresses.

Table 5.6 summarizes the processor modes that can be selected using the PE and PG bits. Note that only three of the four possible combinations are legal. Loading CR0 with a value that has PG = 1 and PE = 0 will raise a general protection exception.

Care must be taken when the PG and PE bits are changed. The PG bit should be changed only when executing a program that has its code

PG	PE	EXECUTION MODE
0	0	Real mode (see Chapter 9)
0	1	Protected mode, paging disabled
1	0	Illegal combination, do not use
1	1	Protected mode, paging enabled

► **Table 5.6:** Processor modes selected by PG and PE bits

and at least some of its data in pages that have the same address in both the linear and physical address spaces, as illustrated in Chapter 7. This code provides a bridge between the paged and nonpaged worlds that has the same address whether paging is on or not. Also, the paging cache must be flushed before setting PG to 1.

The program must execute a jump instruction immediately after changing the value of the PE bit in order to flush the execution pipeline of any instructions that may have been fetched in the wrong mode. Before setting the PE bit, the program must initialize the system segments and control registers. The processor is initialized with PE = 0 and PG = 0 (real mode) to permit bootstrap code to initialize the registers and data structures needed to support segmentation and paging before these mechanisms are enabled. Refer to Chapter 7 for an example of how to initialize the processor, and to Chapter 9 for more information about real mode.

CR2 and CR3

CR2 and CR3 are used by the paging mechanism. CR3 contains the physical address of the page containing the first level of the page table, the directory. Because the directory is page-aligned, only the top 20 bits of this register are significant. The bottom 12 bits are reserved for use in future processors. They must be 0 when loading a new value into CR3, and must be ignored when storing CR3.

Loading CR3 using the *MOV CR3, reg* instruction described in Chapter 3 has the side effect of invalidating the paging cache. CR3 can be loaded even if the PG bit in CR0 is off. This permits initialization of the paging mechanism. CR3 is also changed by task switches, but if the new task has the same CR3 value as the old task, the processor need not flush the paging cache. This permits faster execution when tasks share page tables.

CR2 is used to report error information when a page exception is raised. The processor stores the linear address that caused the exception into CR2 when reporting a page exception. The page exception handler in the operating system can examine the contents of CR2 to determine which page in the linear address space caused the exception.

Segmentation Table Base Registers

GDTR, IDTR, LDTR, and TR are the base registers for the segments that contain tables important to the segmentation system. GDTR, IDTR, and LDTR address segments that contain descriptor tables, and TR addresses a special *Task State Segment* (TSS), described in the next section, which contains important information about the task that is currently executing.

The GDTR points to the GDT. The 48-bit GDTR defines the base and limit of the GDT directly with a 32-bit linear address, and a 16-bit limit. The GDTR provides the "root" for the segment table structure. Descriptors for the LDT and for the TSS current task are stored in the GDT, so these system segments can be identified with selectors, just like all other segments. Since the GDT cannot be defined by a descriptor within itself, the GDTR provides a pseudo-descriptor for this special system segment to root the segment table structure in the linear address space.

The IDTR contains a 48-bit pseudo-descriptor for the *Interrupt Descriptor Table* (IDT). The IDT is rooted directly in the linear address space with a pseudo-descriptor, rather than with a descriptor in the GDT, in order to avoid a level of indirection when accessing interrupt descriptors. The IDT, and descriptor types unique to the IDT, are described in detail in Chapter 6.

The memory format of a 48-bit pseudo-descriptor is shown in Figure 5.20. The high-order 32 bits contain the base address of the segment within the linear address space. The low-order 16 bits contain the limit field, which is a byte granular limit providing a table size from one byte to 64K bytes. Since descriptors are eight bytes in size, the operating system should ensure that the limit field for a table containing N descriptors is set to the value 8*N – 1.

The LDTR register contains the selector for the LDT of the current task. This selector must identify a segment of type LDT mapped by the

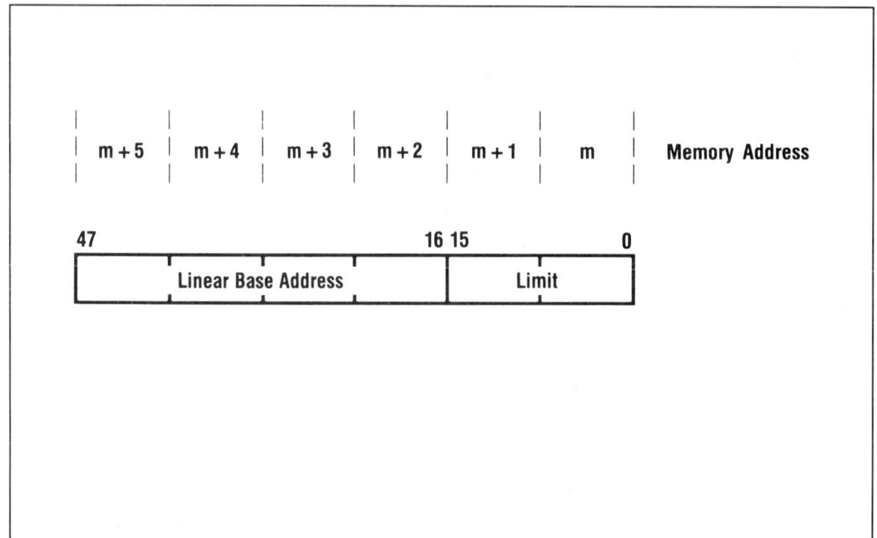

► **Figure 5.20:** Pseudo-descriptor format

GDT. That is, the TI bit in this selector must be 0 to indicate that the associated descriptor is stored in the GDT, and the type field in this descriptor must indicate a segment of type LDT.

It is possible to load LDTR with a null selector to indicate that the current task has no LDT. In this case, an exception is raised if an address is generated with a selector that has the TI bit set to 1, indicating that it is stored in the LDT. If LDTR is loaded with a null selector, all addresses must use selectors for segments mapped through the GDT.

The TR register contains the selector for the task state segment (TSS) of the current task. The TSS is described in the next section. This selector must identify a segment mapped by the GDT, with TI cleared to 0. This selector cannot be null, and must identify a segment of type TSS. The TSS addressed by the TR register contains important information about the task currently executing on the processor.

Note that all of these system segments are defined as contiguous regions of the linear address space, just like all other segments. Because they are in the linear address space, these system tables can be relocated by the paging mechanism. Furthermore, in a virtual memory system with many tasks, the LDT and TSS segments for inactive tasks can be paged out to disk, to be brought back on demand. Since the IDT and GDT are referenced by every task, these system segments should always be resident in physical memory.

None of these system segments can be referenced directly by a program, not even by the operating-system kernel at level 0. The special descriptor types used for the LDT and TSS segments will cause faults if an attempt is made to load a selector naming one of them into one of the six segment registers. The GDT and IDT segments don't even have selectors or segment descriptors! To permit the operating-system kernel to inspect or modify the contents of these segments, read-only or read/write segments must be defined with the same base address and limits, but with attributes suitable for loading into one of DS, ES, FS, or GS for program access. These extra segments are known as *aliases,* since they provide a different name for the same area of the linear address space.

Task State Segment Format

The task state segment, or TSS, is a special segment that contains important information about a task. The TSS for the active task is addressed by the TR register. The TSS for an inactive task contains a "frozen" view of the task. The TSS supports task suspension and resumption by holding a complete image of the register state of the task. When a task is suspended, the current processor register values are written into fields in the TSS. When a task is resumed, the registers are loaded from the values saved in the TSS to reestablish the state of the task, and thus to permit execution to continue as if the task was never suspended. The layout of a TSS is shown in Figure 5.21, and contains five different types of information:

- Link field
- Inner-level stack pointers
- Address mapping base registers
- Register save area
- Miscellaneous fields

The 80386 processor defines the format of the first 104 bytes of the TSS. The operating system can store additional information about the task above this hardware-defined area. As described above, an alias memory segment must be defined for the TSS to permit the operating system to read or write fields in the TSS.

Since the TSS is stored in the linear address space, it can be relocated by the paging mechanism, and can even be paged out to disk in a virtual memory system. The only special requirement on paging a TSS is that a page exception cannot occur in the middle of a task switch. A page exception can be handled properly on the first reference to a paged-out TSS, so a few simple strategies suffice to satisfy this restriction. One strategy, of course, is to never page out a TSS, or otherwise mark it not present. Another strategy is to ensure that if a TSS is swapped, either the entire TSS is present, or the entire TSS is not present, by ensuring that no TSS crosses a page boundary. This can easily be done by aligning each TSS at a 128-byte boundary in the linear address space, since only the first 104 bytes of a TSS are referenced by the processor during a task-switch operation. If the base of the TSS is aligned on a 128-byte boundary, the first 104 bytes cannot cross a page (4K) boundary.

Link Field

The link field is at offset 0 in the TSS, and it is a 32-bit field with a selector in the low-order 16 bits, with the upper 16 bits undefined. It is used together with the NT bit in the EFLAGS register to link the TSSs for tasks suspended by CALL instructions or interrupts. Tasks can be suspended by executing a CALL instruction that references a task, as described in the Task-Switch Details section later in this chapter. Or, a task can be suspended if an interrupt is received that specifies handling with a task switch, as described in Chapter 6. If the current task was activated by a CALL instruction or interrupt, the link field in its TSS

31	0	
I/O Permission Bitmap Offset	000000000000000 | T	64h
0000000000000000	LDT	60h
0000000000000000	GS	5Ch
0000000000000000	FS	58h
0000000000000000	DS	54h
0000000000000000	SS	50h
0000000000000000	CS	4Ch
0000000000000000	ES	48h
EDI		44h
ESI		40h
EBP		3Ch
ESP		38h
EBX		34h
EDX		30h
ECX		2Ch
EAX		28h
EFLAGS		24h
EIP		20h
CR3		1Ch
0000000000000000	SS2	18h
ESP2		14h
0000000000000000	SS1	10h
ESP1		0Ch
0000000000000000	SS0	8
ESP0		4
0000000000000000	LINK	0

► **Figure 5.21:** Task state segment format

contains the selector for the TSS of the suspended task, and the NT bit is set to 1 to indicate that the link field is valid. An IRET instruction executed with the NT bit in the EFLAGS register set to 1 will follow this back-link field to resume execution of the previous task on the link, as described in Chapter 6.

Figure 5.22 illustrates a chain of tasks linked by the back-link chain. The TSS for the current task (described by TSS_C) is addressed by the TR register. The TSSs for the suspended tasks (TSS_B and TSS_A) are linked via the link field, as shown in the figure. As described in a later section, the NT bit in the EFLAGS register would be 1 when task C is executing, indicating it is a nested task. Also, the NT bit of the EFLAGS register image in TSS_B would be 1, indicating that task B was nested inside another task. The NT bit in TSS_A would be 0, indicating that task A is not nested within another task. Note that having NT = 0 indicates the end of the link chain in task A, and the link field of TSS_A is not referenced.

The chain of linked TSSs illustrated in Figure 5.22 would be built by a series of nested task switches caused by CALL instructions or interrupts. A CALL or interrupt received when task A was executing specifies a task-switch to task B. This causes task A to be suspended, task B to be activated, and the link field in task B to point to TSS_A. During the execution of task B, another CALL or interrupt specifies a task-switch to

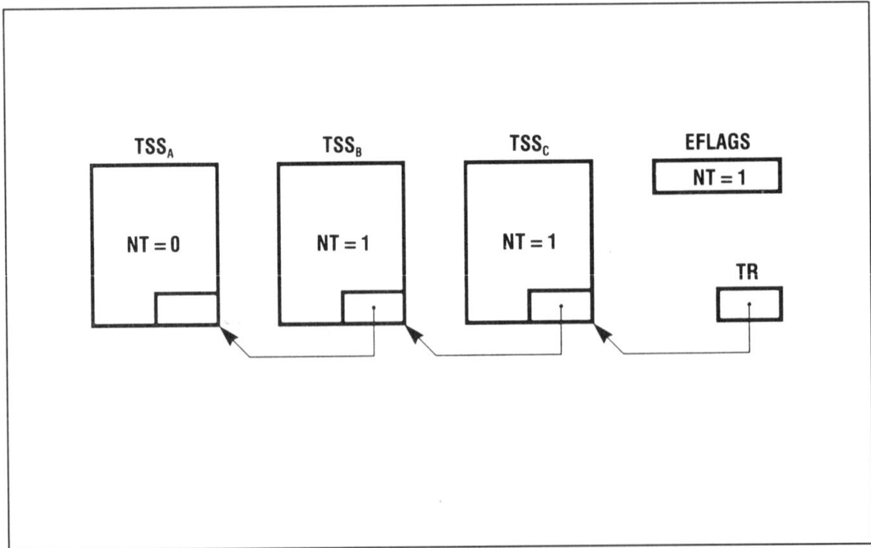

► **Figure 5.22:** Chain of linked TSSs

task C, causing task B to be suspended, task C to be activated, and the link field in TSS_C to point to TSS_B. This results in the TSS link chain shown in the figure.

Inner-Level Stack Pointers

Previous sections have described how each privilege level has a separate stack to avoid protection problems with a shared stack. When a level change to an inner level occurs, the stack for that inner level is initialized by loading the appropriate stack pointer from this area of the TSS. The stack pointer from the outer level is pushed onto this inner stack so that the outer-level stack can be restored upon return. Privilege level changes and associated stack switches are described in the Control-Transfer Methods section later in this chapter.

The stack pointers are simply full 48-bit pointers to the tops of the stacks for levels 0, 1, and 2. They are stored at offsets 4, 12, and 20, respectively, within the TSS. When a transition to an inner level occurs, the appropriate pointer is loaded into the SS and ESP registers to switch to the inner stack. There is no stack pointer for level 3, the outermost level, since it is not possible to enter level 3 during a transition to an inner level! If a task is suspended at level 3, the pointer to its stack will be held in the SS and ESP register images, which are saved in another part of the TSS.

The 80386 processor reads the inner stack pointers from this area, but never writes into this area. This means that inner-level transitions always initialize the inner stack to the same point, always starting with a "fresh" stack on each inner transition. This is correct, since it is not possible for inner-level transitions to be recursive. Once an inner-level transition occurs, the only way to get back to an outer level is through a matching outer-level return, which pops the inner-level stack back to its initial configuration.

Address Mapping Base Registers

When a task switch into a task occurs, the LDTR and CR3 registers are loaded from fields in the TSS of the new task. The LDTR register is loaded with a selector at offset 60h in the TSS, and CR3 is loaded with the dword at offset 1Ch.

Loading CR3 with a new value changes the page table to that of the new task, which changes the linear-to-physical translation function. Similarly, loading the LDTR register changes the LDT to that of the new task, changing the virtual-to-linear mapping function of the half of the virtual address space mapped by the LDT. As described above, this ability to change the address translation function between tasks is the part of the protection mechanism that serves to isolate tasks from each other.

Note that the 80386 processor reads these fields in the TSS to load the appropriate registers during a task switch into the task, but the processor never writes these fields even when a task switch out of the task occurs. Because of this, if a program changes either LDTR or CR3, the new value must also be stored in the TSS for the currently executing task.

Register Save Area

The register save area of the TSS is a save area for the general registers, processor-control registers, and segment registers. When the task described by this TSS is the currently executing task, these fields are undefined. When a task switch out of a task occurs, the current values of these registers are stored in this area, so that when a task switch into the task occurs later, the register values can be restored from this area to resume execution.

The register save area occupies offsets 20h through 5Fh, as shown in Figure 5.21. The segment registers are saved in 32-bit fields that have the upper 16 bits undefined, and the selector is saved in the lower 16 bits.

Miscellaneous Fields

The offset within the TSS of the I/O permission bitmap is stored in the word at offset 66h. As described in a later section, the I/O permission bitmap is stored in the TSS, and it defines the I/O addresses that can be accessed by this task. The I/O permission bitmap itself is another field in the TSS.

The word at offset 64h is intended to supply special attributes for the task. In the 80386, only one attribute is defined, a *Debug Trap* (T) attribute, which is stored in the low-order bit of this word. The remaining bits must be 0 for compatibility with future processors. If a task switch occurs into a task that has the debug trap bit set to 1, a debug trap is taken after the task switch is complete, but before the first instruction of the new task is executed. This debug trap bit allows software to efficiently share the debug registers between tasks as required, without burdening the standard task switch with this function. Debug traps and the debug registers are described in Chapter 8.

► Instructions Sensitive to Privilege Level

Certain 80386 instructions execute differently depending on the privilege level of the program that executes them. *Privileged* instructions can only be executed at privilege level 0, and will raise an exception if executed at other privilege levels. *I/O-sensitive* instructions can only be executed at the same or an inner privilege level relative to the IOPL field in the EFLAGS register (Chapter 2), or if they access an address in the I/O space marked accessible to the current task by the I/O permission bitmap, a special data structure stored in the TSS. Finally, the instructions that modify the EFLAGS register will not change the values of certain fields unless executing at privilege level 0, or other fields unless executing at the same or an inner privilege level relative to IOPL.

Privileged Instructions

The instructions that access key protection-model registers are privileged instructions. These instructions restrict access to these registers only to programs that execute at privilege level 0. These registers must be protected from unauthorized access to ensure the integrity of the protection model. Table 5.7 lists the privileged instructions on the 80386. Note that the instructions that *load* the GDTR, IDTR, LDTR, TR, and MSW (low 16 bits of CR0) are privileged, but the instructions that *store* these registers are not privileged. This means that any program can store these registers, but only level 0 programs can change them. In contrast, the instructions that store the control registers and the debug registers (Chapter 8) are privileged, along with the instructions that load these registers.

MNEMONIC	FUNCTION
CLTS	Clear TS bit in CR0
HLT	Halt
LGDT	Load GDTR
LIDT	Load IDTR
LLDT	Load LDTR
LMSW	Load MSW (low 16 bits of CR0)
LTR	Load TR
MOV CRn, reg	Load Control Register *n*
MOV reg, CRn	Store Control Register *n*
MOV DRn, reg	Load Debug Register *n*
MOV reg, DRn	Store Debug Register *n*

► **Table 5.7:** Privileged instructions

I/O Space Protection

Two mechanisms control access to the I/O address space and I/O-related instructions:

1. The IOPL field in the EFLAGS register.
2. The I/O permission bitmap in the TSS.

The IOPL field in the EFLAGS register defines the outermost privilege level that can execute all I/O-related instructions and access all addresses in the I/O space. The I/O permission bitmap contained in the TSS defines which addresses in the I/O space can be accessed by programs executing at any privilege level.

Programs executing at the I/O privilege level (IOPL) or an inner level can execute all of the instructions listed in Table 5.8. The CLI and STI instructions will raise an exception if they are executed at an outer level. The IN, INS, OUT, and OUTS instructions will raise an exception at outer levels only if the I/O address is marked inaccessible in the I/O permission bitmap. That is, if one of these I/O instructions is executed at an outer level relative to IOPL, an appeal is made to the I/O permission bitmap before an exception is generated. If access to the specific I/O addresses referenced by the instruction is granted by the bitmap, the instruction operates normally. Otherwise an exception is raised.

MNEMONIC	FUNCTION
CLI	Clear IF bit in EFLAGS
STI	Set IF bit in EFLAGS
IN	Read data from I/O address
INS	Read string from I/O address
OUT	Write data to I/O address
OUTS	Write string to I/O address

► **Table 5.8:** I/O-sensitive instructions

Since each task has its own TSS and EFLAGS register, each task can have a different IOPL and can define a different I/O permission bitmap. For example, a task executing a game program may have a bitmap that allows access to a joystick. A task executing a communications application might have a bitmap that allows access to networking hardware.

I/O Permission Bitmap

The I/O permission bitmap defines which addresses in the 64K byte I/O space can be accessed by programs executing at any privilege level. A 64K bit string is stored in the current TSS. Each bit in the bit string corresponds to a single byte-wide I/O address. Bit 0 corresponds to I/O address 0, bit 1 to address 1, and so on. A 0 in the bitmap indicates that the corresponding I/O address is accessible to programs at any privilege level. A 1 in the bitmap indicates that the I/O address is only accessible to programs at IOPL or an inner level. An exception will be raised if a program attempts to access an I/O address corresponding to a 1 in the bitmap while executing at an outer level relative to IOPL.

Since the I/O address space is byte-addressable and up to four bytes can be accessed in one instruction, multiple-byte transfers must check the bits for all I/O addresses referenced. If all the referenced bits are 0, the I/O will be allowed. If any of the permission bits are 1, the I/O operation will raise an exception.

This multiple-bit check must work for any possible length and alignment combination. This requires that two bytes be read from the bitmap in the worst case. To access the bitmap as quickly as possible, the 80386 always reads two bytes whether needed or not. To avoid problems at the highest I/O address mapped by the bitmap, there must always be a byte containing all 1s after the last bitmap byte that contains valid mapping information but before the TSS limit. This provides a filler byte that allows the processor to read two bytes from the bitmap, even at the top of the I/O address space.

The I/O permission bitmap can be stored anywhere within the first 64K bytes of the TSS, and can be any length that is a multiple of 8 bits. The word at offset 66h in the current TSS defines the starting offset of the I/O permission bitmap, which must be less than 56K. Thus, the bitmap can start anywhere in the first 56K of the TSS. The end of the bitmap is either this offset plus 8K or the TSS limit, whichever is smaller. A full 8K bitmap can be defined by making the TSS limit larger than the starting offset plus 8K. Or, the TSS limit can be made closer to the starting offset to dedicate less storage to the bitmap. Bits beyond the TSS limit are taken as 1s to raise exceptions if the corresponding I/O addresses are accessed at levels outside IOPL. The bitmap can be made empty by having the TSS limit less than or equal to the starting offset of the bitmap.

For example, setting the TSS limit to

BitMapOffset + 32

provides a bitmap for the first 256 I/O addresses, and will raise an exception if an I/O address greater than 255 is used. This eliminates the commitment of 8K of memory when it's not required, while allowing the fully general case if desired.

I/O Address Space References The detailed description of references to the I/O address space is given in our C-like notation in the routine AccessIO( ) in Listing 5.1. This description makes use of the Access-Linear( ) routine defined later in this chapter (Listing 5.4) to read data from the TSS. Also, the TR.Base register is referenced to obtain the linear address of the base of the current TSS. The SegmentException( ) routine is called to report a segment exception if necessary. Refer to the detailed descriptions of memory references and exceptions given later in this chapter.

The AccessIO( ) routine first compares CPL against IOPL, since if CPL is at the same or an inner level relative to IOPL, all I/O addresses are accessible and the bitmap is not checked. Otherwise, the bitmap is checked.

The offset of the start of the bitmap is read from the word at offset 66h in the current TSS. The location of the needed bits within the bitmap is computed by obtaining the byte and bit offset from the I/O address to be checked. The byte offset is the I/O address shifted right by 3. The bit offset within this byte is the I/O address modulo 8. Two bytes are read at the indicated byte offset within the bitmap to ensure that the necessary bits are read for all possible I/O address alignments and lengths. If these bytes are beyond the segment limit, an exception is raised. This supports the definition of a bitmap less than the full 8K byte size.

The length mask is formed based on the size of the I/O reference. It can be from 1 to 4 bits long for one- to four-byte I/O references. This length mask is shifted left by the bit offset to align the low-order mask bit with the bitmap bit corresponding to the lowest I/O address. The AND operates on the length mask with the bytes read from the bitmap to clear the irrelevant bits. If the result is 0, the I/O access is allowed. If the result is nonzero, one or more of the I/O addresses spanned by the reference are not accessible, and a segment exception is raised.

If the I/O access is allowed, it is carried out by a call to the routine AccessPhysicalIO( ). This routine abstracts the operation of accessing

```
AccessIO(IOAddress, Length, RW, Data)
   int IOAddress, /* I/O Address to check for accessibility */
       Length,    /* number of bytes to check */
       RW,        /* 0 if read, 1 if write    */
       *Data;     /* pointer to data to read or write */
{
   shortint ptr2, ptrbits;
   int      BitOffset, ByteOffset, Mask, Result;

/* If CPL <= IOPL, all I/O addresses are accessible. */
/* If CPL >  IOPL, check the I/O permission bitmap.  */
if (CPL > IOPL)   {
   /* Read offset of bitmap from offset 66h in TSS */
   AccessLinear(TR.Base + 66h, 2, 0 /* PL 0 */, 0 /* Read */, &ptr2);

   /* compute bit and byte offset within bitmap */
   ByteOffset = IOAddress >> 3;
   BitOffset  = IOAddress & 0111b;

   /* Mask is formed by shifting a field of 1, 2, or 4 bits */
   /* left by the BitOffset within the map.                 */
   Mask       = (01111b >> (4-Length)) << BitOffset;

   /* Read two bytes containing 1 to 4 bits we need for test */
   /* Test TSS limit to see if indicated bits are beyond the */
   /* end of the bitmap.                                     */
   if (TR.Limit < ptr2 + ByteOffset + 1)
      SegmentException($GP, 0);
   AccessLinear(TR.Base+ptr2+ByteOffset,
                2, 0 /* PL 0 */, 0 /* Read */, &ptrbits);

   /* If Mask anded with permission bits is not zero, */
   /* access is denied so generate an exception.      */
   /* Otherwise access is OK so return to caller.     */
   Result = ptrbits & Mask;
   if (Result != 0)
      SegmentException($GP, 0);
   } /* end CPL>IOPL */

   /* Fall through to here only if I/O access is allowed. */
   AccessPhysicalIO(IOAddress, Length, RW, &Data);
}
```

► **Listing 5.1:** AccessIO( ) subroutine

physical I/O addresses. It is not described in this book, since the operation in the memory system is external to the 80386 processor. The routine takes the same parameters as the AccessIO( ) routine.

The bitmap shown in Figure 5.23 is used in the following examples to illustrate the operation of the I/O permission bitmap. The bitmap is stored within the TSS for the current task beginning at the offset given in the word at offset 66h in the TSS. In this example, the offset is *m*. The I/O addresses mapped by each dword are shown on the right, along with the address of the dword relative to the start of the bitmap at offset *m*. The bit offsets within bytes are tabulated at the top, as are the byte offsets within dwords. This bitmap contains 17 bytes plus one filler byte at the highest address. The 17 significant bytes map I/O addresses from 0 to 135.

This bitmap permits access to I/O addresses 2...9, 12...13, 15, 20...24, 27, 33...34, 40...41, 48, 50, 52...53, 58...60, 62...63, and

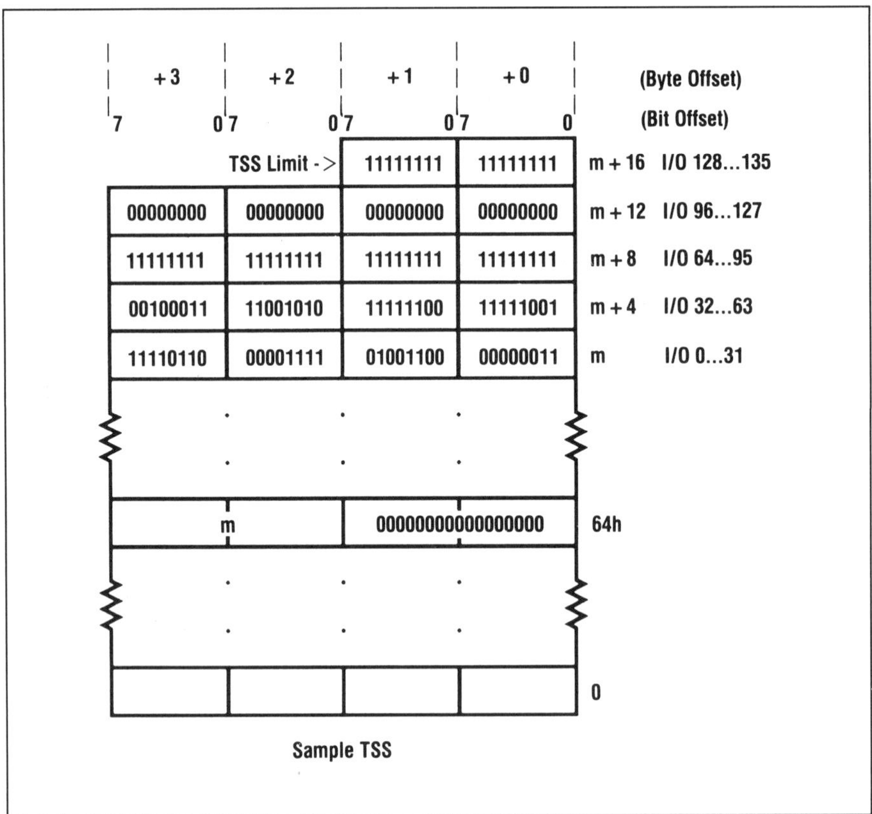

► **Figure 5.23:** Sample I/O permission bitmap

96...127. The other I/O addresses are accessible only to programs executing at a level that is the same or inner relative to IOPL. Note that the last byte before the TSS limit is a filler byte that must be all 1s.

For example, suppose a program executing at an outer level relative to IOPL has the sample bitmap in Figure 5.23, and tries to access a dword at I/O address 7. This means that the bits for I/O addresses 7, 8, 9, and 10 must be checked. Using the algorithm above, we form a mask that has four 1 bits shifted by 7 modulo 8, or 7. The AND operates on this mask with the two bytes read from the bitmap at offset 7/8, or 0. Since I/O address 10 is not accessible, indicated by a 1 in bit position 10 in the map, the result is not zero and so an exception is generated. This process is illustrated algorithmically below:

```
Offset = Byte 0, bit 7
Mask   = (1111b >> (4-Length))<< 7
       = (1111b >> 0) << 7
       = 1111b << 7 = 78h

       BitString 0100110000000011 (See map)
   AND Mask      0000011110000000
       Result    0000010000000000 (Not equal to zero)

Exception!
```

This example illustrates a case where the bits to check span two bytes in the bitmap. The bit for I/O address 7 is in the byte at offset 0 from the start of the bitmap, and the bits for addresses 8, 9, and 10 are in the next sequential byte.

For another example, suppose a program executing at an outer level relative to IOPL has the sample bitmap in Figure 5.23, and tries to access a word at I/O address 33. This means that the bits for I/O addresses 33 and 34 must be checked. Using the algorithm above, we form a mask that has two 1 bits shifted by 33 modulo 8, or 1. The AND operates on this mask with the two bytes read from the bitmap at offset 33/8, or 4. In this example, both bits are 0, and so the access is permitted.

```
Offset = Byte 4, bit 1
Mask   = (1111b >> (4-Length))<< 1
       = (1111b >> 2) << 1
       = 11b << 1 = 110b

       BitString 1111110011111001 (See map)
   AND Mask      0000000000000110
       Result    0000000000000000 (Zero)

I/O allowed!
```

Instructions That Change EFLAGS

Certain fields in the EFLAGS register are handled differently, depending on the privilege level of the program that tries to access or modify them. As mentioned in Chapter 2, the IF, IOPL, and VM bits are handled differently from the other fields in EFLAGS. The IRET, CLI, STI, and POPF instructions (Chapter 3) are available to change these fields in EFLAGS.

The IOPL and VM bits can only be modified by programs executing at privilege level 0. The IF bit can only be modified by programs executing at the same or an inner level relative to IOPL. A program at an outer privilege level that executes a POPF or IRET that attempts to modify one of these fields does not generate an exception. Instead, these fields are simply not modified, with no special notification given. Table 5.9 summarizes the handling of these special flags.

In addition to this special handling of these fields, the POPF instruction does not modify the VM bit, and the PUSHF instruction always pushes a 0 in the VM bit position. This is necessary to prevent programs from testing the VM bit to determine if they are in virtual 8086 mode or real mode. These modes are described in Chapter 9.

EXECUTION		EFLAGS FIELD	
PRIVILEGE	VM	IOPL	IF
CPL = 0	Modified*	Modified	Modified
0 < CPL ≤ IOPL	Unchanged	Unchanged	Modified
IOPL < CPL	Unchanged	Unchanged	Unchanged

* VM is not modified by the POPF instruction.

► **Table 5.9:** Special handling of EFLAGS fields

► Control-Transfer Methods

This section describes the methods used by intersegment jumps, calls, and returns to transfer control between programs in different code segments. We present two views of these control transfers. The first view is discussed in this section. The different methods for transferring control include a direct transfer to an offset in another code segment, a transfer through a gate to an entry point in another code segment, or a transfer through a task gate to another task. In this view, we introduce the concepts needed to understand all of the different ways to transfer control outside of the current code segment. The second view, given in later sections, considers the JMP, CALL, and RET instructions that can be used to transfer control by one or more of these methods. Chapter 6 describes how interrupts and IRET instructions use the same methods to transfer to and return from interrupts.

The "methods" view of task switches, the transfer of control from onc task to another, is deferred to a later section, which also includes the detailed description. Task switches are the most complex part of the 80386 segmentation model, but are not needed by every 80386 system. By deferring the description of task switches, we hope to provide a clearer view of the other control-transfer methods that must be used in every 80386 system.

Chapter 3 included a description of the JMP, CALL, and RET instructions in which the transfer to another code segment was described as changing the CS and EIP registers to point to an instruction in a different code segment. This is the effect seen by the applications programmer, who sees the program execute the control-transfer instruction and then start executing in a different code segment. More activity is visible to the systems programmer. The CS descriptor shadow registers are loaded with the descriptor for the new code segment after many protection checks are applied to the CS selector and the associated descriptor. The transfer may even go to a code segment at a different privilege level within the same task, or to a code segment in a different task.

Same Level, Same Task

The simplest intersegment transfer uses a JMP, CALL, or RET instruction to transfer to a code segment at the same privilege level in the same task. This transfer is specified by having the new CS selector identify a present executable memory segment with DPL = CPL, or a present conforming executable segment (described below) with

DPL $\leqslant$ CPL. This kind of control transfer is similar to loading a data segment register with a selector for a data segment, and can be thought of as the method used to load the CS register. Several tests are applied to the new CS selector, and if these pass, the associated descriptor is read from the descriptor table and more tests are applied to the descriptor. If these tests also pass, the descriptor is loaded into the CS shadow registers, the new selector is loaded into CS, and a new offset is loaded into EIP to successfully complete the control transfer.

Conforming executable segments are a special type of memory segment provided to support sharing of subroutines by programs at more than one privilege level without requiring changes in privilege. For example, a numerics library might be shared by programs executing at different levels by putting the library subroutines in a conforming segment. Then a program at any level could call a routine in the library using an intersegment call, and the routine would execute with the privilege level of the caller.

A control transfer to a conforming segment will execute the conforming segment at the privilege level of the caller rather than the DPL of the conforming segment. Instead, the DPL of a conforming segment is used to specify the innermost privilege level that can transfer to the conforming segment. This interpretation of DPL is the opposite of the normal interpretation of DPL. Normally, DPL is used to specify the outermost privilege level permitted to access a segment. Conforming segments use DPL to specify the innermost privilege level permitted to transfer to the segment. This means that a level 3 program can transfer to any conforming segment, but level 0 routines can only transfer to conforming segments that have DPL = 0.

Different Level, Same Task

The ability to transfer between segments at the same privilege level is important, but is not sufficient, since there are four privilege levels on the 80386, not just one! The CALL instruction permits transfer to an inner level through use of a call gate. The RET instruction permits transfer to a segment at an outer level to return from an inner-level CALL. The JMP instruction cannot transfer to a different level.

Inward calls and outward returns are supported to allow applications to directly call operating-system subroutines in inner levels to obtain necessary services such as memory allocation or file accesses. Outward calls and inward returns are not supported, since it is unlikely that the operating system will call an application-level program to obtain a service. In the few cases where the operating system must transfer to an outer level other than returning from a call, the pointer to the appropriate segment and offset at the outer level can be pushed onto the stack and the RET instruction executed. This technique is useful for transferring to a program just after it is loaded so it can begin to execute, as illustrated in the initialization example in Chapter 7.

Transfers to inner levels must be carefully controlled to ensure the integrity of the protection mechanism. Outer levels are permitted to transfer to inner levels only through entry points defined by the operating system. The operating system must control both the segment and the offset of the entry points. Otherwise, if only the segment part is controlled, an application may transfer to any offset in the segment. For example, it could specify an offset that is just past the code that checks the parameters passed to the inner level. Worse yet, the outer level might specify an offset that lies in the middle of an instruction!

Call Gates

Call gates provide the mechanism needed to control access to inner-level routines. Call gates are special descriptor types that contain pointers to entry points. The gate descriptor contains a full 48-bit pointer to the entry point, including both the segment part and the offset part. A CALL through a call gate is like an indirect CALL through the gate. To use the gate, the outer-level routine specifies a selector for the gate as the selector to be "loaded" into CS. When the CALL instruction checks the new CS descriptor and discovers a call gate instead of an executable memory segment, the pointer is retrieved from the gate and used as the pointer for the control transfer. The offset from the gate is used instead of the offset given in the instruction to control the entry point of the inner-level segment. The selector from the gate is used to read another descriptor, which must be an executable segment that is the actual target of the call. Gates to gates are not permitted!

Figure 5.24 illustrates how the call gate indirectly specifies the target of a call. Note that the offset from the instruction is discarded and the offset from the gate is used instead. The selector in the gate is used to access another descriptor, which must be for an executable segment.

The DPL field in the gate descriptor controls access to the gate using the same privilege rules as for data access. Only procedures that execute at the same level or an inner level relative to the gate DPL can use the gate. The RPL field of the selector for the gate is also checked to ensure it is at the same level or an inner level relative to the gate DPL. Thus, the gate is placed at the outermost level for which access to it will be permitted.

A different set of privilege-level checks is applied to the descriptor of the executable segment pointed to by the selector in the gate. The RPL field of the selector in the gate is ignored. Only the DPL field of the executable segment is used in these privilege-level checks. If DPL = CPL, or if the segment is conforming with DPL ≤ CPL, the gate transfers are within the same level. JMP and CALL instructions can use call gates to transfer to a segment at the same level. If DPL is less than CPL, a transfer to an inner level is performed. Only CALL instructions can use call gates to transfer to inner levels. DPL>CPL is not permitted, to prevent calls to outer levels. RET instructions cannot use call gates, regardless of privilege levels.

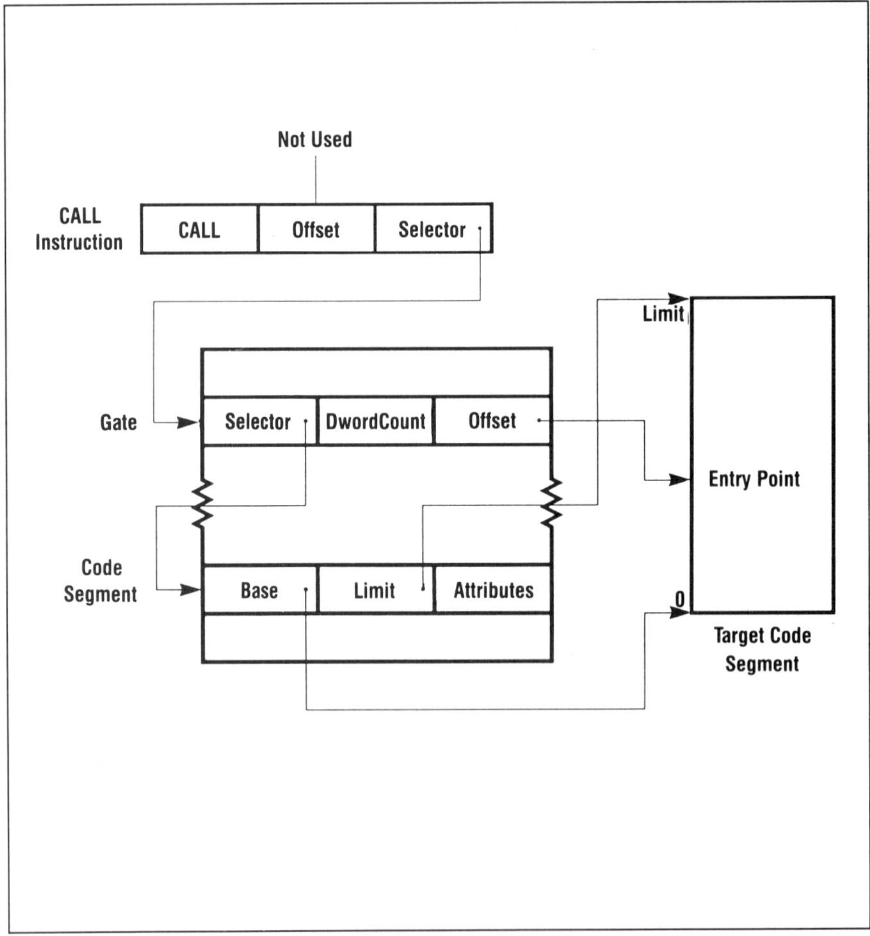

► **Figure 5.24:** Transfer through a call gate

Figure 5.25 illustrates the permissible relationships for a CALL instruction between CPL, the level of the gate, and the level of the executable segment pointed to by the gate. A program executing at level 2

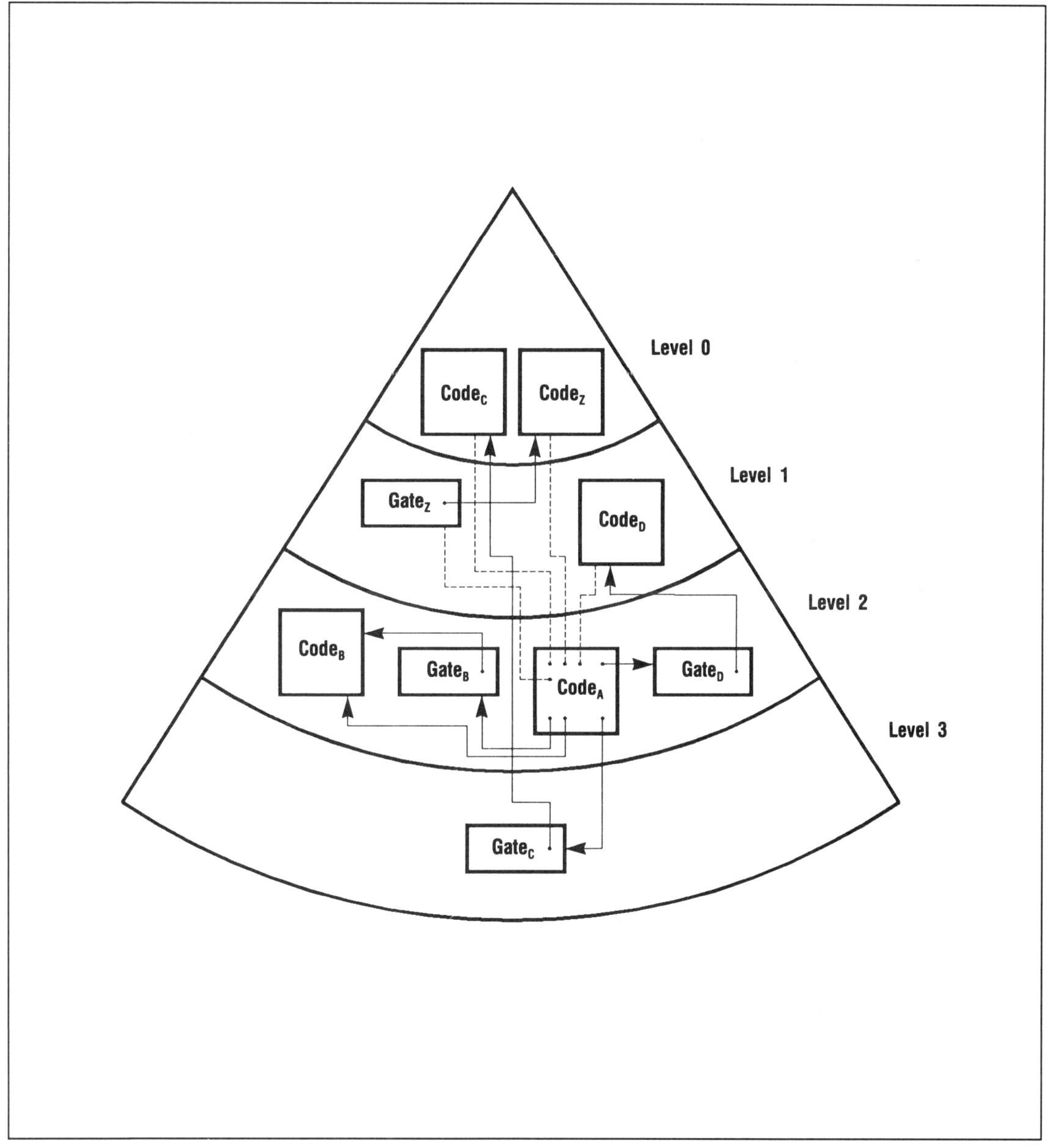

► **Figure 5.25:** Privilege levels and gates

in the segment $Code_A$ can access the gates at levels 2 and 3. These gates must point to executable segments at level 2 or inner levels (0 or 1). The permissible relationships are illustrated with solid arrows. The illegal relationships are illustrated with dotted lines.

$Gate_B$ at level 2 points to an executable segment at level 2 ($Code_B$), so use of $Gate_B$ from level 2 results in no change in privilege level. In fact, $Code_B$ is accessible directly without the gate, as shown in the figure. $Gate_C$ at level 3 points to a level 0 segment $Code_C$, so use of $Gate_C$ from level 2 results in a privilege-level transition. $Code_C$ is not accessible directly, but only indirectly through $Gate_C$. Similarly, $Gate_D$ at level 2 points to a level 1 code segment $Code_D$, which is not directly accessible from level 2. Use of $Gate_D$ from level 2 also results in a privilege-level transition. $Gate_Z$ at level 1 is not accessible from level 2, nor is the segment $Code_Z$ accessible at level 0.

Stack Switch A CALL through a call gate to an inner level not only switches the privilege level and transfers control to a new code segment, but it also switches to the stack segment for the inner level. The stack remains unchanged if the CALL is to the same level, even if the CALL is through a gate. Recall that the TSS contains pointers to stacks for levels 0, 1, and 2. During an interlevel CALL, the SS and ESP registers are initialized with the appropriate pointer from the TSS. This sets up an empty stack at the new level, since the ESP pointer in the TSS is typically set to point to the upper limit of the new stack segment. However, the stack does not stay empty for long!

When the SS register is loaded with the selector for the inner-level stack segment, the same privilege checks are applied as if a MOV SS, selector instruction was executed at the inner privilege level. This means that the segment must be a read/write segment, and must have RPL = DPL = CPL at the inner level.

After initializing the stack with the pointer from the TSS, the old SS and ESP register values are pushed onto the inner-level stack to permit the matching outer return to restore the stack of the outer level. After this, 0 to 31 dwords (124 bytes) can be copied from the outer-level stack to the inner-level stack. This copies parameters that were pushed onto the outer stack before the call, but that need to be on the new stack to be easily accessed by the inner-level procedure. The number of dwords to copy is given in the DwordCount field of the call gate descriptor.

Figure 5.26 illustrates the stack-switch operation that occurs as part of a gated CALL to an inner level. The outer-level stack is shown on the right as containing four dword parameters (P1, P2, P3, and P4) pushed before the CALL instruction. The inner-level stack is shown on the left after successful completion of the CALL. The SS and ESP values for the outer stack are pushed onto the inner stack first. Then, the four dword parameters are copied from the outer stack to the inner stack, assuming the gate has four in its DwordCount field. Finally, the return address is pushed as the CS and EIP values for the outer-level program. After the CALL instruction, SS addresses the stack segment for the inner level, and ESP points within this segment to the EIP value pushed by the CALL.

Although gates are most useful to transfer to an inner level, a gate can specify a code segment that is at the current privilege level, or is conforming. In this degenerate usage of call gates, no privilege-level switch is performed, and no stack switch occurs. Both CALL and JMP instructions can use gates to transfer to a segment at the same privilege level. This use of a gate is similar to an indirect CALL or JMP instruction.

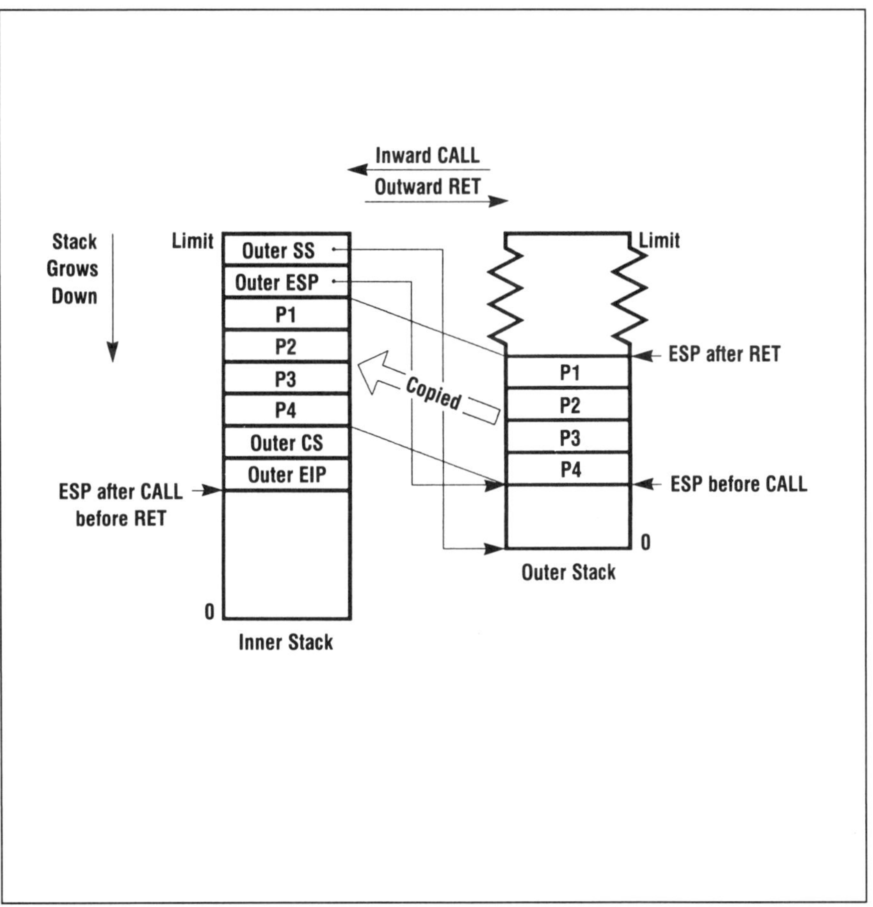

► **Figure 5.26:** Switching to inner-level stack

Transparency An important property of gates is that they are transparent to the calling program. That is, the calling program uses the standard intersegment CALL instruction to transfer to a different segment and cannot tell whether the selector given in the call identifies the memory segment, or identifies a gate that indirectly specifies the new segment and substitutes a new offset. Because the operating system controls the contents of the descriptor tables, it can use gates to intercept transfers to routines placed at different privilege levels.

Using gates to directly call operating-system procedures fits very well into the multiple-segment programming model, and is a major benefit of the use of that model. However, since the single-segment programming model does not use intersegment calls, the benefit of tranparency is not evident. In the single-segment model, a call to an operating-system procedure is typically an intrasegment call to a utility library routine that contains an intersegment call that can go through a gate.

Outward Returns

CALLs through call gates transfer control from outer-level routines to inner-level routines. This section describes how the RET instruction can be used to return from the inner level to the outer level. The intersegment RET instruction pops the return pointer from the stack, and can also adjust ESP to remove parameters pushed on the stack before the corresponding call. The selector part of the return pointer identifies the segment to return to. The RPL field of this selector identifies the privilege level to return to. Note that the RPL field of this selector is used, and not the DPL field of the corresponding descriptor. This is necessary because the return may be to a conforming segment that may execute at a level other than that given in its DPL field.

If the RPL field of the selector specifies an outer level relative to CPL, an outward return occurs. The pointer to the outer-level stack is popped off the inner-level stack, and loaded into SS and ESP to restore the outer stack after CPL is adjusted to the outer level. ESP is then adjusted to remove parameters pushed on the outer stack before the matching call. Before resuming execution at the outer level, the data-segment registers DS, ES, FS, and GS are checked to ensure that the segments they address are accessible at the outer level. If a segment register addresses a segment that is not accessible at the outer level, it is loaded with a null selector to avoid a protection hole upon return.

Note that the parameter bytes are popped off both the inner-level and outer-level stacks by the outward return. This makes sense, since there are two copies of the parameters! The parameters copied to the inner-level stack must be popped off in order to access the stack pointer to the outer-level stack. The parameters must be popped off the outer-level stack to adjust the stack used after the return completes.

Figure 5.26, used to illustrate the stack-switch operation in an interlevel call, also illustrates the stack switch that occurs during the matching outward return. Just before the RET instruction executes, the inner stack contains the return address, the four dword parameters copied during the inner-level call, and the SS:ESP pointer to the outer-level stack. The outer-level stack has the four dword parameters pushed before the inner-level call executed. A RET instruction with a parameter count of 16 will undo the effects of the interlevel call. The CS:EIP return address is popped from the inner stack, and the inner ESP adjusted by 16 to remove the parameter bytes. This leaves ESP pointing to the SS:ESP pointer to the outer-level stack. The RPL field of the return CS selector indicates an outer level, so these SS and ESP values are popped from the stack, CPL is changed to the outer level, and then the outer ESP is adjusted by 16 to remove the original parameters. After the return, the inner-level stack is discarded, SS addresses the outer-level stack, and ESP points just above the four parameters, as shown.

► Segmentation Details

The next several sections describe the operation of the segmentation mechanism in detail with our C-like notation. In these sections and in the corresponding sections in Chapter 6, we will present a collection of subroutines that precisely describe the memory-management model of the 80386. These subroutines are presented in an order that provides a good progression of concepts, but does not always define terms before using them as a C compiler would require! These subroutines are dependent upon and build upon each other. For example, most of the subroutines call other subroutines to handle memory references. The subroutines that describe task switches reference several levels of subroutines to describe these complex operations. We believe that the subroutine approach is best for presenting this material because it lets you digest a concept embodied in a subroutine, and then use it as a higher-level abstraction to build more complex operations. The collection of subroutines provides a complete description of the exact 80386 actions when referencing memory, loading segment registers, and executing intersegment control transfers.

A key part of the following description is the exceptions that are raised to report protection violations to the operating system. Although most of the details of exceptions are covered in Chapter 6, this chapter details the conditions that cause exceptions, and what information is reported with an exception. We give a brief overview of how exceptions are described in this chapter before we dive into the detailed descriptions.

The descriptions are divided into three major parts:

1. Access to data in memory data segments
2. Intersegment control transfers
3. Task switches

The first section expands our C-like notation to include structure definitions and pointer dereferencing operators, and then includes a definition of the structure types and global variables used throughout the rest of this chapter. It also includes a description of the paging mechanism, which is a key part of referencing memory.

The detailed descriptions in these sections provide a formal specification of the operation of the memory-management model on the 80386 that supplements the descriptive material presented earlier in this chapter. The detailed descriptions provide a concise, exact specification of the 80386 memory-management mechanism, whereas the descriptive material presented earlier in the chapter is more verbose and glosses over some of the less important details. If you're reading this material for the first time, you may want to read Chapters 6 and 7 to get a better idea of the entire set of operating system facilities available in the 80386 before returning to these detailed descriptions. Other readers may find these descriptions most useful as reference material.

Exceptions Summary

In the following detailed instruction descriptions, several different types of segment exceptions can occur if a program attempts an operation that violates the segmentation protection model. If paging is enabled, page exceptions can also occur even during operations primarily involving the segmentation mechanism. Chapter 6 describes how exceptions interrupt the program sequence. The detailed instruction descriptions in this chapter describe the conditions that cause segment and page exceptions, and the information made available to software when these exceptions are reported.

Segment Exceptions

The segment exceptions referenced in this chapter and their names as used in the detailed descriptions are as follows:

Task Switch $TS

Not Present	$NP
Stack Segment	$SS
General Protection	$GP

A segment exception reports an error code that can be used by exception handler software to discover and fix the cause of the exception, or to provide diagnostic information when terminating the offending program. The format of the error code is shown in Figure 5.27. The error code is a 16-bit value formed from the selector value that caused the exception, or 0 if no selector is involved. Operations that load a selector into a segment register take the upper 14 bits directly from the selector: bit 2 is the TI bit, and bits 15...3 are the index field. Other operations, for example a data access, use a zero-error code, since no selector is directly involved in the operation. The RPL field from the selector is discarded, and replaced with two bits that indicate the operation that caused the exception. Bit 0 is the EXT bit and is set to 1 if the exception occurred when processing another exception, or an external interrupt. Bit 1 is the IDT bit and is set if the exception occurred reading an entry from the IDT, which occurs only during interrupt or exception processing, described in Chapter 6. The detailed descriptions in this chapter specify exactly how the error code is formed for each possible exception.

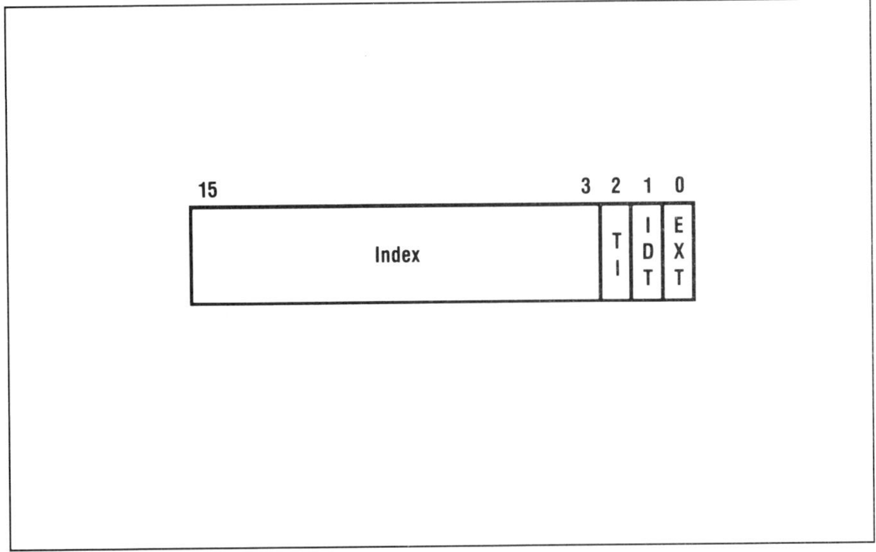

► **Figure 5.27:** Segment-exception error-code format

In the detailed descriptions below, exceptions are indicated by calls to the subroutine SegmentException( ), defined in Chapter 6, which takes two parameters:

1. The vector number to use when reporting the exception. These are indicated mnemonically with the predefined names $TS, $NP, $SS, and $GP. The correspondence of vector numbers to exceptions is covered in Chapter 6.
2. The selector to use in the error code reported with the exception.

Page Exceptions

Page exceptions are also raised by the operations described in this chapter. Whereas segment exceptions have several types, there is only one type of page exception. When a page exception occurs, the processor loads CR2 with the linear address causing the exception. Page exceptions also report an error code, to help operating-system software diagnose the exception.

The error code for a paging exception has only 3 significant bits, as shown in Figure 5.28. Bit 0 is the P bit, which indicates whether the exception was due to a not-present page (P = 0) or to a page protection violation (P = 1). Bits 1 and 2 indicate the type of access that caused the exception. Bit 1 is the W bit, which is 1 if the access was a write, and is 0 for reads. Bit 2 is the U bit and is 1 if the access came from a program executing at privilege level 3 (user level), and is 0 for programs at levels 0, 1, and 2.

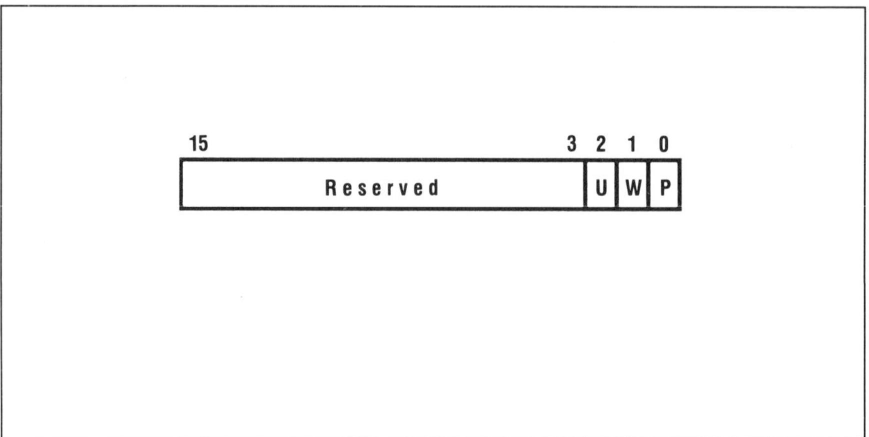

► **Figure 5.28:** Page-exception error-code format

In the detailed descriptions below, page exceptions are indicated by calls to the subroutine PageException( ), defined in Chapter 6, which takes four parameters:

1. The linear address causing the exception.
2. The privilege level of the attempted access. This is used to form the U bit of the error code.
3. The W bit of the error code (1 if a write, 0 if a read).
4. The P bit of the error code (1 if a protection exception, 0 if a not-present exception).

Aborting Execution of Instruction Descriptions

Unlike the other subroutines used in the detailed descriptions, the PageException( ) and SegmentException( ) routines do not return to their caller. Instead, they abort the "execution" of the instruction description, terminating all subroutines backward along the chain of nested procedure calls. This allows us to more concisely describe the normal cases yet still precisely describe exception handling.

Memory Data Access Details

As described in Chapter 2, both the segment part and the offset part of a virtual address must be specified in order to access data in memory. The segment part is given as a segment register that has been loaded with a selector for the segment containing the desired data. The offset is a simple byte offset within this segment, and can be generated from the sum of a base register, a scaled index register, and a constant displacement. This means that accessing data in memory is a two-step process. First, a segment register must be loaded with a selector for the segment containing the data. Then, the data can be referenced by specifying the segment register along with the components of the offset (base register, index register, displacement).

The description of a memory access is split into three parts. The first part introduces the types and global variables, such as those used to describe registers. The second part describes a memory reference using a segment register that is assumed to be already loaded. Finally, we describe the process of loading a segment register in detail to conclude this section on memory data access. We describe memory references first, since the operation of loading a segment register itself requires several memory references.

Notation, Struct Definitions, and Global Variables

Before diving into the descriptions, we need to extend the C notation introduced in Chapter 3 with two new key constructs. We use the *struct* construct to build structures or records as composites of several basic data types such as *int* (for integer), *char* (for characters), or other structs. The struct operator lets us define our own data types for complex structures such as segment descriptors and selectors. We also use the pointer dereference operator (*) to reference data in memory whose address is obtained from a pointer variable. If *ptr* is a pointer to an integer, the construct *ptr can be used to name the integer pointed to by ptr. In variable definitions, the * operator is used to define a pointer, as in the following example. The code declares I and J as integers and PTR as a pointer to an integer, then assigns PTR the address of J, and assigns the value in I to J by dereferencing PTR to access J.

```
int I, J, *PTR; /* I, J are integers, PTR points to an
integer. */
PTR = &J;        /* PTR now points to J. */
*PTR = I;        /* Same effect as J = I; */
```

The detailed descriptions of data accesses and segment register loads rely on the struct definitions and global variables defined in Listing 5.2. The struct definitions make use of two built-in types that are not standard C constructs. The *Bit* type is assumed to define a struct field as a given number of bits. Within a struct definition, the bit fields are assigned from the low-order bit position to the high-order bit position. The *filler* type is defined to reserve bits of space in the structure, to reflect bits that are not used.

The structure of a selector is defined by the struct definition SelectorType, which details the allocation of bits to the RPL field, the TI bit, and the index field. This definition matches the graphical presentation of the selector format given in Figure 5.9. The structure of the segment attributes is described by the struct definition SegAttributes. It describes the layout of the second dword (at offset 4) of a descriptor. It includes all of the possible attribute fields, the combination of the fields for gates and segment descriptors illustrated in Figures 5.10, 5.11, and 5.12. The DType and Type fields determine which of the remaining attribute fields are valid.

The structure of a segment register and associated shadow registers is described by the struct definition SegmentRegister. It contains four subfields to reflect the structure illustrated in Figure 5.13: a selector defined to have the struct type SelectorType, an attributes field defined to have the struct type SegAttributes, and two 32-bit integers to describe the base

```
struct SelectorType{
   Bit(2)  RPL;
   Bit(1)  TI;     /* 0 if GDT, 1 if LDT */
   Bit(13) Index; /* Index into GDT or LDT of descriptor */
}

/* The following structure maps the second dword of descriptors.   */
/* The DType and Type fields control which other fields are valid. */
struct SegAttributes{
   Bit(5) DwordCount; /* Parameter count for call gates only */
   filler(3);
   Bit(4) Type;
   Bit(1) DType; /* 0 if System Segment or Gate, 1 if Memory Segment */
   Bit(2) DPL;
   Bit(1) P;      /* Present Bit */
   filler(6);
   Bit(1) D;      /* Default size (16 vs. 32), see Chapter 9 */
   Bit(1) G;      /* Limit Granularity.  0=byte, 1=4K byte granular */
}

struct SegmentRegister {
   SelectorType Selector;     /* visible selector register  */
   SegAttributes Attributes; /* invisible shadow registers */
   int  Base,
        Limit;
}

SegmentRegister CS, SS, DS, ES, FS, GS, /* Segment registers */
                TR, LDTR,          /* System Segment registers */
                IDTR, GDTR; /* use only base and limit fields */

int CR0, CR2, CR3;      /* 32-bit processor-control registers */
int CPL;                /* Current Privilege Level           */

/* 32-bit general registers */
int EAX, EBX, ECX, EDX, ESP, EBP, ESI, EDI;

/* Processor-control registers */
struct EflagsType {
   Bit(1) CF;
   filler(1);
   Bit(1) PF;
   filler(1);
   Bit(1) AF;
   filler(1);
   Bit(1) ZF, SF, TF, IF, DF, OF;
   Bit(2) IOPL;
   Bit(1) NT;
   filler(1);
   Bit(1) RF, VM;
   filler(14);
}

EflagsType EFLAGS;
int        EIP;
```

► **Listing 5.2:** Struct definitions and global variables

and limit. The segment limit is stored as a full 32-bit byte-granular limit. Segment-register loads will translate 4K byte-granular limits to byte limits before storing into the limit register.

Given the above predefined types, the six segment registers CS, SS, DS, ES, FS, and GS are defined as having the struct type SegmentRegister. The system registers LDTR, TR, IDTR, and GDTR are also defined as having the struct type SegmentRegister. IDTR and GDTR do not use the selector or attributes fields. CPL is defined as a 32-bit integer. The control registers CR0, CR2, and CR3 are defined as 32-bit integers, as are the general registers EAX, EBX, ECX, EDX, ESP, EBP, ESI, and EDI.

The structure of the EFLAGS register is given by the struct definition EflagsType, which matches the graphic definition given in Figure 2.2. The EFLAGS register is, of course, of this type. The EIP register is defined as a 32-bit integer.

Data References

Assuming a selector has been loaded into a segment register and the corresponding descriptor into the shadow registers, data within the segment addressed by the register can be referenced. Every data reference makes several protection checks, given in detail in the routine AccessVirtual( ) in Listing 5.3. Most protection checks are done when the segment register is loaded. The number of checks made at each memory reference is minimized to ensure high performance, since there are typically many more memory references than segment register loads.

The operation section of many detailed instruction descriptions in Chapter 3 contained references to instruction operands stored in memory. These memory references are all "calls" to the routine AccessVirtual( ), even though none of the notations used in Chapter 3 make any mention of this routine. The AccessVirtual( ) routine contains the detailed description of the memory reference, which is abstracted in Chapter 3.

Within the AccessVirtual( ) routine, first the segment register is checked to see if it contains a null selector by testing the Attributes.P bit in the shadow descriptor registers. The offset is checked to ensure it is within the segment limit. Two different limit tests are required: one for normal (expand-up) segments, and a second for expand-down segments. The type of reference is checked against the segment attributes to prevent a write into a read-only segment, or a read or write to an execute-only segment. If any check fails, an exception is reported and no memory reference is made. If all checks pass, the memory reference is allowed by segmentation and is passed down to the paging mechanism by calling the AccessLinear( ) routine, passing the linear address of the

```
/* Access data in a segment addressed by a Segment Register SReg */
AccessVirtual(SReg, Offset, Length, RW, IntNumber, Data)
   SegmentRegister SReg;
   int Offset, Length, /* offset in segment, and length of data  */
       RW,          /* 0 if read, 1 if write                     */
       IntNumber,   /* $SS for SS access, $GP for other registers */
       *Data;       /* Pointer to Data to read or write          */
{
   if  (SReg.Attributes.P == 0) /* Invalid Segment register (Null) */
        SegmentException(IntNumber, 0);

   switch (SReg.Attributes.Type   /* Ignore Accessed attribute */)  {
      case 0: case 1: /* Read-only */
      case 10: case 11: /* Execute/Read */
      case 14: case 15: /* Execute/Read, Conforming */
         /* Test for writing a read-only segment, */
         /* then fall through to limit test.      */
         if (RW == 1)
            SegmentException(IntNumber, 0);
      case 2: case 3: /* Read/Write */
         /* Test for normal (expand-up) segment limit */
         if ( (Offset+Length-1) > SReg.Limit )
            SegmentException(IntNumber, 0);
         break;

      case 4: case 5: /* Read-only,  Expand-Down */
         /* Test for writing a read-only segment, */
         /* then fall through to limit test.      */
         if (RW == 1)
            SegmentException(IntNumber, 0);
      case 6: case 7: /* Read/Write, Expand-Down */
         /* Test for expand-down segment limit */
         if ( (Offset <= SReg.Limit) || ((Offset+Length-1)>=4G) )
            SegmentException(IntNumber, 0);
         break;

      case 8: case 9: /* Execute-only */
      case 12: case 13: /* Execute-only, Conforming */
         /* Can't read or write an execute-only segment */
         SegmentException(IntNumber, 0);
         break;
   } /* end switch */

    AccessLinear(SReg.Base+Offset, Length, CPL, RW, Data);
} /* end AccessVirtual */
```

► **Listing 5.3:** AccessVirtual( ) subroutine

data obtained by adding the segment base to the indicated offset of the data. If all of the paging access checks pass, the instruction can complete normally. Note that for these data references generated directly by the program, CPL is used as the privilege level of the access.

Paging The operation of the paging mechanism is encapsulated into two subroutines: AccessLinear( ) and TranslateLinear( ). AccessLinear( ), shown in Listing 5.4, calls TranslateLinear( ) to translate the linear addresses to physical addresses, and then calls the routine AccessPhysical( ) described below to actually reference physical memory. AccessLinear( ) also handles the case where a reference is split across two pages. For example, referencing the dword at address 0FFFh would cross two pages: the first byte of the dword is in page 0, at address 0FFFh. The last three bytes of the dword are stored in page 1, at address 1000h through 1003h. In cases such as these, AccessLinear( ) splits the reference into two references on the two different pages.

The heart of the paging mechanism is encapsulated in the routine TranslateLinear( ), shown in Listing 5.5. It first checks the PG bit in CR0 to see if paging is enabled. If paging is disabled, it simply returns the input linear address as the output physical address. If paging is enabled, it reads both levels of the page table to translate a linear address to a physical address. It tests both the directory and page table entries, and detects an exception if the entry at either level is marked *not present,* or if a page protection violation is detected. This description is written to always read both levels of the page table for all memory references. As described earlier in this chapter, the real 80386 has a paging cache to ensure that the memory-resident page tables need be read only infrequently.

Access to Physical Memory The subroutine AccessPhysical( ) abstracts the operation of accessing physical memory in our instruction descriptions. We don't include a detailed description of this routine, since this operation occurs in the memory system external to the 80386 processor. This routine takes four parameters:

1. The physical address to access.
2. The length of the data to reference.
3. Whether to read or write.
4. A pointer to the data to access.

```
/* The following routines AccessLinear and TranslateLinear          */
/* encapsulate the page translation mechanism.                       */
/* TranslateLinear performs linear-to-physical address translation. */
/* AccessLinear uses this function to support read and write access */
/* to the Linear Address space.                                      */

AccessLinear(LAddress, Length, PL, RW, Data)
    int LAddress, Length, /* Linear address and length of data */
        PL,               /* Privilcgc lcvel of access */
        RW,               /* 0 if read, 1 if write */
        *Data;            /* Pointer to Data to read or write */
{
    int PAddress,
        LAddress2, PAddress2,
        Len1,
        Len2;

/* Check for split references */
if ( ((LAddress % 4096) + Length) > 4096)
   {/* Access split into two pieces, on two different pages. */
    /* First piece of data is at address LAddress,          */
    /* and extends to the end of the page.                  */
    Len1 = 4096 - (LAddress % 4096);
    PAddress = TranslateLinear(LAddress, PL, RW);

    /* Second piece of data is on next page (LAddress+Len1), */
    /* of length Length-Len1 */
    LAddress2 = LAddress + Len1;
    Len2 = Length-Len1;
    PAddress2 = TranslateLinear(Laddress2, PL, RW);

    /* Both pieces are accessible (an exception will abort   */
    /* in TranslateLinear), so access physical memory.       */
    AccessPhysical(PAddress,  Len1, RW, Data);
    AccessPhysical(Paddress2, Len2, RW, Data+Len1);

   } /* end Split-page access */

else { /* access lies entirely within one page */
   PAddress = TranslateLinear(Laddress, PL, RW);
   AccessPhysical(PAddress, Length, RW, Data);
   } /* end single page access */

} /* end AccessLinear */
```

► **Listing 5.4:** AccessLinear( ) subroutine

```
TranslateLinear(LAddress, PL, RW)
   int LAddress,
       PL,        /* Privilege Level of access */
       RW;        /* 0 if read, 1 if write     */

{  /* The PTE structure defines the format of page table entries at */
   /* both levels of the page table.                                */
   struct PTE     {bit(1)  P;  /* 1 if valid for translation */
                   bit(1) RW;  /* 1 if writable              */
                   bit(1) SU;  /* 1 if accessible to PL 3    */
                   filler(2);
                   bit(1)  A;  /* Accessed bit               */
                   bit(1)  D;  /* Dirty bit                  */
                   filler(5);
          Bit(20) PageFrame;} /* Physical Address 31..12    */

   PTE DEntry,    /* Directory  (1st level) entry */
       PEntry;    /* Page Table (2nd level) entry */
   int PAddress;

/* Test PG bit in CR0 to see if paging is enabled. If not, simply */
/* return the linear address as the physical address.             */
if ((CR0 & 80000000h) == 0)
   return(LAddress);

/* If PG=1, read Directory Entry using top 10 bits of Laddress as */
/* an index into the Page Directory Table pointed to by CR3.      */
/* Note that page attributes are not checked until both levels of */
/* the page table have been read in.                              */
PAddress =  (CR3    & 0FFFFF000h) + ( (LAddress>>20) & 0FFCh);
AccessPhysical(PAddress, 4, 0 /* Read */, &DEntry);
if (DEntry.P == 0) /* Not Present */
    PageException(LAddress, PL, RW, DEntry.P);

/* update A bit for present entries */
DEntry.A = 1;
AccessPhysical(PAddress, 4, 1 /* Write */, &DEntry);

/* Read Page Table Entry using middle 10 bits of LAddress as an */
/* index into the Page table pointed to by the Directory Entry  */
PAddress =  (DEntry & 0FFFFF000h) + ( (LAddress>>10) & 0FFCh);
AccessPhysical(Paddress, 4, 0 /* Read */, &PEntry);
if ( (PEntry.P == 0) /* Not Present */
     || ( (PL == 3) &&
              ( /* Check for page protection violations */
                (DEntry.U == 0)
             || (PEntry.U == 0)
             || ( (DEntry.RW == 0) && (RW == 1) )
             || ( (PEntry.RW == 0) && (RW == 1) )
              )
        )
   )
    PageException(LAddress, PL, RW, PEntry.P);
```

► **Listing 5.5:** TranslateLinear( ) subroutine

```
    /* If translation is valid, update D and A bits */
    PEntry.A = 1;
    if (RW == 1) /* Write */
       PEntry.D = 1;
    AccessPhysical(Paddress, 4, 1 /* Write */, &PEntry);

    Return( (PEntry & 0FFFFF000h) /* bits 31..12 from Page Table */
          + (LAddress & 0FFFh)    /* bits 11..0 from linear address */);

} /* end TranslateLinear */
```

► **Listing 5.5:** TranslateLinear( ) subroutine (continued)

Loading a Segment Register

Before data in a memory segment can be accessed by a program, the segment must be made addressable by loading the selector for the segment into one of the segment registers (for example, by a MOV). This section describes in detail how a segment register is loaded, including how the segment descriptor is loaded into the associated shadow descriptor registers.

Only the DS, ES, FS, GS, and SS registers can be loaded with the simple load instructions described here. CS is loaded only by intersegment control transfers, which are described later in this chapter. Note that data within the current code segment can be referenced by giving CS as the segment register and specifying the offset of the desired data in this segment. Because segments loaded into CS must either be execute-only or execute/read, only read access is supplied to the current code segment.

The detailed description of a segment register load is given in the routine SRegLoad( ), shown in Listing 5.6. It takes three parameters:

1. SReg, the segment register to be loaded.
2. Selector, the selector to load.
3. GPorTS, which selects whether certain exceptions will be reported as $GP exceptions or as $TS exceptions. Segment loads in the instructions MOV, POP, and Lsr use $GP. Segment loads in task switches (the subroutine TaskSwitch( ) described later) use $TS.

The SRegLoad( ) routine only loads the descriptor shadow registers if all protection checks pass. It is the responsibility of the caller to load the

```
/* SRegLoad loads SS, DS, ES, FS, or GS shadow registers with a */
/* descriptor.                                                   */
SRegLoad(SReg, Selector, GPorTS)
   SegmentRegister SReg;
   SelectorType    Selector;
   int GPorTS; /* 13 or 10 to select GP or TS exceptions for all but */
               /* Not Present Exceptions.                              */
{
   SegAttributes Attributes;
   SelectorType GSelector;
   int Base, Limit, GOffset;

/* One set of tests for SS, another for DS, ES, FS, GS */
if (SReg == SS) {
   if ( ((Selector & 0FFFCh) == 0 /* Null */)
        || (Selector.RPL != CPL) )
      SegmentException(GPorTS, 0);

   /* If Selector tests pass, read Descriptor and test it */
   ReadDescriptor(Selector,&Attributes,&Base,&Limit,&GSelector,&GOffset);
   if ( (Attributes.DPL != CPL)
      || (Attributes.DType == 0) /* System segment or Gate */ )
      SegmentException(GPorTS, 0);
   switch (Attributes.Type   /* Ignore Accessed attribute */ ){
      case 2: case 3: /* Read/Write */
      case 6: case 7: /* Read/Write, Expand-down */
         /* Type is OK, check Present bit */
         if (Attributes.P == 0)
            SegmentException(12, Selector);
         break;

      case 0: case 1: /* Read-only */
      case 4: case 5: /* Read-only, Expand-down */
      case 8: case 9: /* Execute-only */
      case 10: case 11: /* Execute/read */
      case 12: case 13: /* Execute-only, Conforming */
      case 14: case 15: /* Execute/read, Conforming */
         /* Type is no good, report segment violation */
         SegmentException(GPorTS, 0);
      } /* end switch */
   } /* end SS tests

 else {/* DS, ES, FS, or GS load */

    if ( (Selector & 0FFFCH) == 0 /* Null */)
       {/* Mark descriptor invalid (not present) and return */
        SReg.Attributes.P = 0;
        Return;
       }
```

► **Listing 5.6:** SRegLoad( ) subroutine

```
    /* If Selector is not Null, load Descriptor and test it */
    ReadDescriptor(Selector,&Attributes,&Base,&Limit,&GSelector,&GOffset);
    if (Attributes.DType == 0) /* System segment or Gate */
       SegmentException(GPorTS, 0);
    switch (Attributes.Type   /* Ignore Accessed attribute */ ){
       case 0: case 1: /* Read-only */
       case 2: case 3: /* Read/Write */
       case 4: case 5: /* Read-only, Expand-down */
       case 6: case 7: /* Read/Write, Expand-down */
       case 10: case 11: /* Execute/read */
          /* Type is OK, check DPL against RPL and CPL */
          if ( (Attributes.DPL<CPL) || (Attributes.DPL<Selector.RPL) )
             SegmentException(GPorTS, Selector);

          /* DPL is ignored when loading a conforming segment as */
          /* a data segment.                                     */
       case 14: case 15: /* Execute/read, Conforming */

          /* Check Present bit last. */
          if (Attributes.P == 0)
             SegmentException(11, Selector);
          break;

       case 8: case 9: /* Execute-only */
       case 12: case 13: /* Execute-only, Conforming */
          /* Type is no good, report segment violation */
          SegmentException(GPorTS, 0);
       } /* end switch */

    } /* end DS, ES, FS, GS */

 /* Fall out to here only if all checks pass.                 */
 /* Set Accessed bit in descriptor.                           */
 /* Load descriptor into shadow registers.                    */

 SetAccessed(Selector);

 SReg.Attributes = Attributes;
 SReg.Base       = Base;
 SReg.Limit      = Limit;

 } /* end SRegLoad */
```

► **Listing 5.6:** SRegLoad( ) subroutine (continued)

visible part of the segment register, the selector part. Two different sets of protection checks are used: one for selectors loaded into DS, ES, FS, and GS, and a stricter set of tests for selectors loaded into the SS (stack segment) register.

When a selector is loaded into a segment register, first the selector is checked for validity. If these checks fail, an exception is raised and the segment register is not modified. A null selector is valid for loading into the DS, ES, FS, and GS registers, but not SS. If a null selector is loaded, no descriptor is loaded and the P bit is set to 0 in the segment attributes field in the shadow descriptor register to indicate an invalid descriptor. Then any subsequent memory reference that uses the segment register will raise an exception.

If the selector is valid and not null, the corresponding descriptor is retrieved from the memory-resident segment descriptor table, and another set of checks is applied. If these checks fail, an exception is raised and the segment register is not modified. If the descriptor checks pass, the descriptor is stored into the corresponding shadow registers. Then, when the segment register is specified in an address, the descriptor is available on-chip in special registers for efficient processing.

A segment-register load can have one of three outcomes. First, an exception can be raised if there is a problem with either the selector or the descriptor. Second, a null selector can be loaded into DS, ES, FS, or GS (but not SS). Third, the segment register can be successfully loaded with the selector, and the descriptor can be successfully stored in the shadow registers. If an exception is raised, neither the segment register nor the shadow registers are modified.

Selector Tests Recall that selectors have three fields: 1 bit specifies the table (LDT or GDT) containing the associated descriptor, 13 bits specify the index in this table for the descriptor, and 2 bits specify RPL, which can be used to "weaken" the current privilege level (CPL).

The selector is first checked to see if it is null. Null selectors can be loaded into the DS, ES, FS, and GS registers. No exceptions are raised when one of these registers is loaded with a null, but any subsequent memory references that use the register will cause an exception. Attempting to load the SS register with a null selector will raise an exception at the load rather than waiting for the first stack reference after the load.

Selectors loaded into the SS register are checked to ensure RPL is equal to CPL. The other segment registers do not require this RPL check.

Descriptor Checks If the selector is valid, and is not null, the index field is used to read the descriptor from the indicated descriptor table. The ReadDescriptor( ) routine in Listing 5.7 describes the descriptor read in

```
/* Routine to read a descriptor from a descriptor table.          */
/* Returns attributes field, plus unscrambled base, limit,        */
/* and Gate selector and offset fields.                           */
/* Caller must examine attributes field to determine whether      */
/* to use base and limit (memory or system segments), or          */
/* Gate selector and offset fields.                               */
ReadDescriptor(Selector, Attributes, Base, Limit, GSelector, GOffset)

   SelectorType  Selector;     /* Selector to load           */
   SegAttributes *Attributes;  /* return attributes here     */
   int           *Base,        /* return segment base here   */
                 *Limit;       /* return segment limit here  */
   SelectorType  *GSelector;   /* return gate selector here  */
   int           *GOffset;     /* return gate offset here    */
{
int DTBase, Dword1, Dword2;

if (Selector.TI == 1 /* LDT */) {
   if (LDTR.Attributes.P == 0 /* Null LDT */)
        || (((Selector.Index * 8) + 7) > LDTR.Limit)
      )
      SegmentException($GP, Selector);
   DTBase = LDTR.Base;
   }
else /* GDT */ {
   if ( ((Selector.Index * 8) + 7) > GDTR.Limit)
      SegmentException($GP, Selector);
   DTBase = GDTR.Base;
   }

/* Table limits are OK, read descriptor entries in Linear Space.    */
/* Read descriptor table using privilege level 0 regardless of CPL. */
AccessLinear(DTBase+Selector.Index*8,     4, 0 /* PL */, 0 /* Read */,
             &Dword1);
AccessLinear(DTBase+Selector.Index*8 + 4, 4, 0 /* PL */, 0 /* Read */,
             &Dword2);

/* unscramble base and limit fields. */
*Limit = (Dword1 & 0FFFFh) | (Dword2 & 0F0000h);
*Base  = (Dword1>>16) | ((Dword2 & 0FFh)<<16) | (Dword2 & 0FF000000h);
*Attributes = Dword2;
if (*Attributes.G == 1)
   *Limit = (*Limit << 12) | 0FFFh;  /* 4K granular limit */

/* unscramble Gate selector and offset */
*GSelector = Dword1 >> 16;
*GOffset   = (Dword1 & 0FFFFh) | (Dword2 & 0FFFF0000h);

} /* end ReadDescriptor */
```

► **Listing 5.7:** ReadDescriptor( ) routine

detail. This descriptor read itself can raise an exception for any of the following reasons:

1. If the LDT was indicated, and the LDTR register contains a null selector, a $GP exception is raised, with the new selector as the error code.
2. If the index field specifies a descriptor that is partially or wholly outside the descriptor table limit, a $GP exception is raised, with the new selector as the error code.
3. If part or all of the descriptor is stored in a page that is not present, a page exception is raised.

The first two checks are made by the ReadDescriptor( ) routine. Note that unlike the SRegLoad( ) routine, ReadDescriptor( ) has no parameter for choosing a $GP exception or a $TS exception. Only $GP exceptions are reported when reading descriptors, even during task switches.

Page exceptions are possible when reading descriptors, since descriptor tables are stored in the linear address space just like all other segments. This means that a call to the AccessLinear( ) routine is required to read the descriptor, which may result in a page exception. Note that when ReadDescriptor( ) calls the AccessLinear( ) routine to read the descriptor, it uses 0 as the privilege level of the read. This means that all descriptor table reads are performed at privilege level 0, regardless of the privilege level (CPL) of the current program. This permits the descriptor tables to be stored in pages not accessible to level 3 programs, but still permit level 3 programs to load segment registers.

The FetchDescriptor( ) routine in Listing 5.8 is similar to the ReadDescriptor( ) routine. FetchDescriptor( ) is used in Chapter 3 in the detailed description of instructions that test segment attributes. Instead of reporting an exception if the descriptor is outside the segment limits, FetchDescriptor( ) returns the value 0 to indicate that the descriptor cannot be read. Otherwise, the value 1 is returned, along with the two dwords containing the descriptor, as well as the second dword formatted as a struct of type SegAttributes.

After returning to the SRegLoad( ) subroutine but before the descriptor is loaded, many checks are made to ensure that the segment is valid for use at the current privilege level and in the manner implied by the segment register loaded. These checks are done once when the segment register is loaded, rather than every time a memory reference uses the segment. As with the selector tests, the checks applied depend on the segment register loaded: the DS, ES, FS, and GS segment registers have one set of checks, and SS has a separate set of stricter tests.

```
/* Routine to read a descriptor from a descriptor table.        */
/* Returns both dwords of the descriptor, plus the second dword */
/* as a SegAttributes struc type. Returns 0 if there are any    */
/* problems reading the descriptor, otherwise returns 1.        */
/* No segment exceptions can occur, but page exceptions can     */
/* occur (see AccessLinear routine).                            */
FetchDescriptor(Selector, Dword1, Dword2, Attributes)

SelectorType  Selector;     /* Selects desired descriptor      */
int   *Dword1, *Dword2;     /* return both dwords of descriptor */
SegAttributes *Attributes; /* return attributes here          */
{

int DTBase;

if (Selector.TI == 1 /* LDT */) {
   if (LDTR.Attributes.P == 0 /* Null LDT */)
       || (((Selector.Index * 8) + 7) > LDTR.Limit)
      )
      return(0);
   DTBase = LDTR.Base;
   }
else /* GDT */ {
   if ( ((Selector.Index * 8) + 7) > GDTR.Limit)
      return(0);
   DTBase = GDTR.Base;
   }

/* Table limits are OK, read descriptor entries in Linear Space.    */
/* Read descriptor table using privilege level 0 regardless of CPL. */
AccessLinear(DTBase+Selector.Index*8,     4, 0 /* PL */, 0 /* Read */,
             &Dword1);
AccessLinear(DTBase+Selector.Index*8 + 4, 4, 0 /* PL */, 0 /* Read */,
             &Dword2);

*Attributes = Dword2;
return(1);

} /* end FetchDescriptor */
```

► **Listing 5.8:** FetchDescriptor( ) subroutine

A privilege-level test is done for all descriptors loaded. The SS register requires that the descriptor privilege level (DPL) be equal to CPL. Since RPL was checked earlier to ensure it was equal to CPL, for loads into SS we require DPL = RPL = CPL. The other segment registers require that both CPL and RPL specify an inner level relative to DPL. This is specified as:

DPL ⩾ CPL && DPL ⩾ RPL

Since we report an exception if this condition is not met, the SRegLoad( ) routine negates this test to see if an exception occurs, resulting in the test

DPL < CPL | | DPL < RPL

A segment with execute/read access can be loaded into the DS, ES, FS, or GS register, but not SS. Conforming segments omit the privilege-level test. Conforming segments with execute/read access can be read from any privilege level.

The Type field in the descriptor is checked to ensure it is appropriate. Loads into SS require that the segment be typed as a read/write segment, since presumably the stack will be written to at least once! Loads into the other segment registers only require that the segment be readable.

If any of the above tests fail, either a $GP exception or a $TS exception is reported, as determined by the third parameter to SRegLoad( ). If all of these tests pass, the present attribute bit is tested. If the segment is not present (P == 0), a $SS exception is reported for loads into the SS register, and a $NP exception is reported for loads into other registers.

If all of the protection tests pass, the accessed attribute in the Type field is set by calling the routine SetAccessed( ) shown in Listing 5.9. Then, the shadow registers are loaded with the descriptor information read earlier. The segment-register load is successful!

Loading LDTR with the LLDT Instruction

The routine LLDT( ) in Listing 5.10 contains the detailed description of the LLDT instruction. It takes one parameter, the selector for the new LDT segment. The LLDT instruction is a privileged instruction, and so can only be executed at level 0. First, the selector is tested to ensure that it identifies a segment with a descriptor in the GDT. It is possible to load a null selector into the LDTR. If this is done, any subsequent segment-register loads with selectors identifying segments in the LDT will cause segment exceptions. Otherwise, the descriptor for the new LDT segment is read and tested. It must be a system segment or gate, with type LDT, and it must be present. If all of these checks pass, the descriptor is loaded into the LDTR shadow registers, and the selector is loaded into the visible LDTR selector register.

Loading TR with the LTR Instruction

The routine LTR( ) in Listing 5.11 contains the detailed description of the LTR instruction. It takes one parameter, the selector for the new TSS segment. The LTR instruction is a privileged instruction, and so can only be executed at level 0. Next, the selector is tested to ensure that it identifies a segment with a descriptor in the GDT, and is not null. If

```
/* Routine to set the Accessed bit in segment descriptors. */
SetAccessed(Selector)
   SelectorType Selector; /* selector for descriptor to change */

{int DTBase, Dword2;

 /* simply read the second Dword of a descriptor,               */
 /* set the low order bit of the Type field to 1, then write the */
 /* modified Dword back. No type checking is done in this routine.*/
 /* The caller is responsible for type checking.                 */

 /* Determine linear address of base of descriptor table containing */
 /* the descriptor to modify. */
if (Selector.TI == 1 /* LDT */) {
   if (LDTR.Attributes.P == 0 /* Null LDT */)
       || (((Selector.Index * 8) + 7) > LDTR.Limit)
      )
      SegmentException($GP, Selector);
   DTBase = LDTR.Base;
   }
else /* GDT */ {
   if ( ((Selector.Index * 8) + 7) > GDTR.Limit)
      SegmentException($GP, Selector);
   DTBase = GDTR.Base;
   }

AccessLinear(DTBase+Selector.Index*8 + 4, 4, 0 /* PL */, 0 /* Read */,
             &Dword2);
Dword2 = Dword2 | 100h; /* set low bit of type field */
AccessLinear(DTBase+Selector.Index*8 + 4, 4, 0 /* PL */, 1 /* Write */,
             &Dword2);
}
```

► **Listing 5.9:** SetAccessed( ) subroutine

```
/* Detailed description of the LLDT instruction */
LLDT(Selector)
   SelectorType    Selector;
{
   SegAttributes Attributes;
   SelectorType GSelector;
   int Base, Limit, GOffset;

/* Must be at level 0 to execute the LLDT instruction */
if (CPL != 0)
   SegmentException($GP, 0);

/* Selector tests */
if (Selector.TI == 1 /* descriptor in LDT */)
   SegmentException($GP, 0);

if ( (Selector & 0FFFCh) == 0 /* Null */)
   /* Can load a Null selector into LDTR to indicate no LDT */
   {LDTR.Selector = Selector;
    LDTR.Attributes.P = 0;
    return;
   }

/* If Selector tests pass, read Descriptor and test it. */
/* Must be a system segment or gate, of type LDT.       */
ReadDescriptor(Selector,&Attributes,&Base,&Limit,&GSelector,&GOffset);
if ( (Attributes.DType == 1) /* Memory segment */
      || (Attributes.Type != 2 /* LDT */) )
   SegmentException($GP, 0);

if (Attributes.P == 0)
   Segment Exception($NP, 0);

/* Load descriptor into shadow registers, */
/* selector into visible part of LDTR.    */
LDTR.Attributes = Attributes;
LDTR.Base       = Base;
LDTR.Limit      = Limit;
LDTR.Selector   = Selector;
} /* end LLDT */
```

► **Listing 5.10:** Detailed description of LLDT instruction

```
/* Detailed description of the LTR instruction */
LTR(Selector)
   SelectorType    Selector;
{
   SegAttributes Attributes;
   SelectorType GSelector;
   int Base, Limit, GOffset;

/* Must be at level 0 to execute the LTR instruction */
if (CPL != 0)
   SegmentException($GP, 0);

/* Selector tests */
if ( (Selector.TI == 1 /* descriptor in LDT */)
  || ((Selector & 0FFFCh) == 0 /* Null */) )
   SegmentException($GP, 0);

/* If Selector tests pass, read Descriptor and test it.          */
/* Must be a system segment or gate, and of type Available 286 TSS */
/* or Available 386 TSS.                                          */
ReadDescriptor(Selector,&Attributes,&Base,&Limit,&GSelector,&GOffset);
if ( (Attributes.DType == 1) /* Memory segment */
   || (  (Attributes.Type != 1 /* Available 286 TSS */)
       &&(Attributes.Type != 9 /* Available 386 TSS */) ) )
   SegmentException($GP, 0);

if (Attributes.P == 0)
   Segment Exception($NP, 0);

/* Mark TSS as busy by changing type field in descriptor */
AccessLinear(GDT.Base+Selector.Index*8 + 4, 4, 0 /* PL */, 0 /* Read */,
             &Dword2);
Dword2 = Dword2 | 200h; /* set bit 1 of type field */
AccessLinear(GDT.Base+Selector.Index*8 + 4, 4, 0 /* PL */, 1 /* Write */,
             &Dword2);

/* Load descriptor into shadow registers, */
/* selector into visible part of TR.      */
TR.Attributes = Attributes;
TR.Base       = Base;
TR.Limit      = Limit;
TR.Selector   = Selector;
} /* end LTR */
```

► **Listing 5.11:** Detailed description of LTR instruction

so, the descriptor for the new TSS is read and tested. It must be a system segment or gate, with type available 286 TSS or available 386 TSS, and it must be present. If all of these checks pass, the descriptor is loaded into the TR shadow registers, and the selector is loaded into the visible TR selector register after the descriptor type is modified to busy 286 TSS or busy 386 TSS.

Control-Transfer Details

This section describes each of the intersegment control-transfer instructions with programs in our C-like notation. This description presents an orthogonal view to the description of intersegment control-transfer methods presented earlier in this chapter. These descriptions make use of some of the routines given in the detailed description of paging and segment-register loads given in previous sections.

The subroutine CSDescriptorLoad( ), shown in Listing 5.12, is used by all of the control-transfer instructions to check a descriptor to be loaded into the CS shadow registers. CSDescriptorLoad( ) only loads the CS shadow registers. The calling routine is responsible for loading the selector part of the CS register.

The CSDescriptorLoad( ) subroutine checks the Type field and DPL of the descriptor against CPL and the RPL field of the selector to determine if the descriptor is valid. The checks are for a direct transfer to a present executable memory segment, with the privilege-level test dependent on whether a normal or conforming segment is given. This test is appropriate for JMP and CALL instructions directly to executable segments, and for RET instructions that do not change privilege levels. The more complex transfers will change privilege levels or tasks before calling this routine, so these tests are still appropriate.

CSDescriptorLoad( ) includes a test of the RPL of the CS selector. Since transfers through gates ignore the RPL field of the selector read from the gate, the descriptions of these transfers will set this RPL field to 0 before calling CSDescriptorLoad( ).

The JMP Instruction

The routine JMP( ) shown in Listing 5.13 contains the detailed description of the JMP instruction. It takes two parameters, the selector and the offset of the target of the jump. If the selector is not null, the associated descriptor is read with the routine ReadDescriptor( ) shown in Listing 5.7. The descriptor checks are split into two parts, based on the DType bit.

```
/* Common Subroutine to load a descriptor into CS shadow registers,  */
/* provided it defines an executable memory segment with DPL=CPL     */
/* and DPL>=RPL, or a conforming segment with DPL<=CPL. Only the     */
/* CS shadow registers are loaded (base, limit, attributes).         */
/* CS selector must be loaded by the caller.                         */
CSDescriptorLoad(Selector, Attributes, Base, Limit, GPorTS)
   SelectorType Selector;
   SegAttributes Attributes;
   int     Base, Limit,
                GPorTS; /* $GP or $TS exception for exceptions */
                        /* other than not-present.             */
{
/* Tests vary depending on Type of memory segment */
switch (Attributes.Type   /* Ignore Accessed attribute */ ){
   case 8: case 9: /* Execute-only */
   case 10: case 11: /* Execute/read */
      /* Non-conforming segment, check DPL against CPL and RPL */
      if ((Attributes.DPL != CPL) || (Attributes.DPL < Selector.RPL))
         SegmentException(GPorTS, Selector);
      break;

   case 12: case 13: /* Execute-only, Conforming */
   case 14: case 15: /* Execute/read, Conforming */
      /* Conforming segment, check DPL against CPL */
      if (Attributes.DPL > CPL)
         SegmentException(GPorTS, Selector);
      break;

   case 0: case 1: /* Read-only */
   case 2: case 3: /* Read/Write */
   case 4: case 5: /* Read-only, Expand-down */
   case 6: case 7: /* Read/Write, Expand-down */
      /* Type is no good, report segment violation */
      SegmentException(GPorTS, 0);
   } /* end switch */

/* Check Present bit last. */
if (Attributes.P == 0)
   SegmentException($NP, Selector);

/* Get to here only if all checks pass. Set Accessed bit, */
/* load descriptor into shadow registers, and return.     */

SetAccessed(Selector);

CS.Attributes = Attributes;
CS.Base       = Base;
CS.Limit      = Limit;

} /* end CSDescriptorLoad */
```

► **Listing 5.12:** CSDescriptorLoad( ) subroutine

```
/* Detailed description of JMP instruction. */
JMP(Selector, Offset)
   SelectorType Selector;
   int Offset;
{
   SegAttributes Attributes;
   SelectorType GSelector;
   int Base, Limit, GOffset;

/* Selector tests for JMP */
if ( (Selector & 0FFFCh) == 0) /* Null */
   SegmentException($GP, 0);

/* Read and test descriptor */
ReadDescriptor(Selector,&Attributes,&Base,&Limit,&GSelector,&GOffset);
if (Attributes.DType == 1) /* Memory Segment */ {
   /* Call common routine to complete CS Descriptor load. */
   CSDescriptorLoad(Selector, Attributes, Base, Limit, $GP);
   /* Verify target is within segment limit */
   if (Offset > CS.Limit)
      SegmentException($GP, 0);

   /* Get to here only if all protection checks pass.      */
   /* Complete instruction with "visible" register loads. */
   CS.Selector     = Selector;
   CS.Selector.RPL = CPL;
   EIP             = Offset;
   } /* end Memory Segment */

else /* System segment or Gate */ {
   /* check DPL against CPL and RPL */
   if ( (Attributes.DPL < CPL) || (Attributes.DPL < Selector.RPL) )
      SegmentException($GP, Selector);

   switch (Attributes.Type){
   case 1: /* Available 286 TSS */
      if (Attributes.P == 0)
         SegmentException($NP, Selector);
      TaskSwitch286(Selector, Attributes, Base, Limit, 0 /* NoLink */);
      /* See Chapter 9. */
      break;

   case 5: /* Task Gate */
      if (Attributes.P == 0)
         SegmentException($NP, Selector);
      TaskGate(GSelector, 0 /* NoLink */);
      break;

   case 9: /* Available 386 TSS */
      if (Attributes.P == 0)
         SegmentException($NP, Selector);
      TaskSwitch(Selector, Attributes, Base, Limit, 0 /* NoLink */);
      break;
```

► **Listing 5.13:** Detailed description of JMP instruction

```
    case 4: /* 286 Call Gate */
       if (Attributes.P == 0)
          SegmentException($NP, Selector);
       JumpGate286(GSelector, GOffset, $GP); /* See Chapter 9. */
       break;

    case 12: /* 386 Call Gate */
       if (Attributes.P == 0)
          SegmentException($NP, Selector);
       JumpGate(GSelector, GOffset, $GP);
       break;

    Default: /* Other Types raise $GP exceptions */
       SegmentException($GP, Selector);
    } /* end switch */
 } /* end System segment or Gate */

 } /* end JMP */
```

► **Listing 5.13:** Detailed description of JMP instruction (continued)

If DType = 1, a memory segment is indicated, and the routine CSDescriptorLoad( ) in Listing 5.12 is called to complete the descriptor checks. It returns if the descriptor was loaded successfully. If the new offset is within the CS limit, the instruction completes by loading the CS selector register, setting RPL of this CS selector to CPL, and loading EIP with the offset from the instruction.

If DType = 0, a system segment or gate is indicated. First, the DPL field is tested to ensure it is at the same level or an outer level relative to both CPL and RPL. Then the Type field is tested, with different actions for each of the valid types provided that the P bit is set to 1, indicating that the descriptor entry is valid.

If the descriptor Type field indicates an available 286 TSS, available 386 TSS, or task gate, a task switch occurs without linking or unlinking a task from the suspended task chain. The detailed descriptions of task switches are given in three other routines. Both TaskGate( ) and TaskSwitch( ) are described later in this chapter. We do not include a detailed description of the TaskSwitch286( ) subroutine, which performs a task switch through a 286 TSS. Chapter 9 discusses how a task switch through a 286 TSS differs from the 80386 task switch described in the TaskSwitch( ) routine.

Jump through Call Gate A descriptor type of 286 call gate or 386 call gate specifies a jump through a call gate. The routine JumpGate( ) shown in Listing 5.14 describes a jump through an 80386 call gate. It takes three parameters:

1. The selector from the gate.
2. The offset from the gate.
3. GPorTS, which indicates if a $GP or $TS exception is to be signaled for certain exceptions. GPorTS permits this routine to also be used by the detailed description of task switches.

First, the selector is tested to ensure it is not null. Then, the descriptor is read from the descriptor table. If its DType field indicates it is a memory segment, it is passed to the common routine CSDescriptorLoad( )

```
JumpGate(Selector, Offset, GPorTS)
   SelectorType Selector;
   int Offset,
   int GPorTS; /* 13 or 10 to select GP or TS exceptions for all but */
               /* Not Present Exceptions.                             */
{
   SegAttributes Attributes;
   SelectorType GSelector;
   int Base, Limit, GOffset;

/* Selector tests for JMP */
if ( (Selector & 0FFFCh) == 0) /* Null */
   SegmentException(GPorTS, 0);

/* Read and test descriptor */
ReadDescriptor(Selector,&Attributes,&Base,&Limit,&GSelector,&GOffset);

if (Attributes.DType == 0) /* Can't be System segment or gate */
   SegmentException(GPorTS, Selector);

/* Call common routine to complete CS descriptor load */
Selector.RPL = 0; /* ignore RPL in selector read from gate. */
CSDescriptorLoad(Selector, Attributes, Base, Limit, GPorTS);
/* Verify target is within segment limit */
if (Offset > CS.Limit)
   SegmentException(GPorTS, 0);

/* Visible part of JMP instruction follows! */
CS.Selector     = Selector;
CS.Selector.RPL = CPL;
EIP             = Offset;
} /* end JumpGate */
```

► **Listing 5.14:** JumpGate( ) subroutine

shown in Listing 5.12. Since the RPL field in the selector from the gate is ignored, the RPL field of the selector is set to 0 to nullify the RPL test in that routine. If CSDescriptorLoad( ) succeeds in loading the descriptor, it returns. If the new offset is within the CS limit, the instruction completes by loading the CS selector register, setting RPL of this CS selector to CPL, and loading EIP with the offset from the gate.

We do not include a detailed description of the JumpGate286( ) routine, which performs a jump through a 286 call gate. Chapter 9 discusses how a jump through a 286 call gate differs from a jump through a 386 call gate described in the JumpGate( ) routine.

The CALL Instruction

The routine CALL( ) in Listing 5.15 contains the detailed description of the CALL instruction. It is similar in structure to the JMP( ) routine

```
/* Detailed Description of Inter-Segment CALL instruction.      */
CALL(Selector, Offset)
   SelectorType Selector;
   int Offset;
{
   SegAttributes Attributes;
   SelectorType  GSelector;
   int  Base, Limit, GOffset;

/* Selector tests for CALL */
if ( (Selector & 0FFFCh) == 0) /* Null */
   SegmentException($GP, 0);

/* Read and test descriptor */
ReadDescriptor(Selector,&Attributes,&Base,&Limit,&GSelector,&GOffset);
if (Attributes.DType == 1) /* Memory Segment */ {
   /* Call common routine to complete CS Descriptor load */
   CSDescriptorLoad(Selector, Attributes, Base, Limit, $GP);
   /* Verify target is within segment limit */
   if (Offset > CS.Limit)
      SegmentException($GP, 0);

   /* Get to here only if all protection checks pass.              */
   /* Push return pointer onto stack, then load CS selector and EIP */
   ESP = ESP-4;
   /* push 4 bytes, with CS selector in low 2 */
   AccessVirtual(SS, ESP, 4, 1 /* Write */, $SS, &CS.Selector);
   ESP = ESP-4;
   AccessVirtual(SS, ESP, 4, 1 /* Write */, $SS, &EIP);

   CS.Selector     = Selector;
   CS.Selector.RPL = CPL;
   EIP             = Offset;
   } /* end Memory Segment */
```

► **Listing 5.15:** Detailed description of CALL instruction

```
else /* System segment or Gate */ {
   /* check DPL against CPL and RPL */
   if ( (Attributes.DPL < CPL) || (Attributes.DPL < Selector.RPL) )
      SegmentException($GP, Selector);

   switch (Attributes.Type){
   case 1: /* Available 286 TSS */
      if (Attributes.P == 0)
         SegmentException($NP, Selector);
      TaskSwitch286(Selector, Attributes, Base, Limit, 1 /* Link */);
      /* See Chapter 9. */
      break;

   case 5: /* Task Gate */
      if (Attributes.P == 0)
         SegmentException($NP, Selector);
      TaskGate(GSelector, 1 /* Link */);
      break;

   case 9: /* Available 386 TSS */
      if (Attributes.P == 0)
         SegmentException($NP, Selector);
      TaskSwitch(Selector, Attributes, Base, Limit, 1 /* Link */);
      break;

   case 4: /* 286 Call Gate */
      if (Attributes.P == 0)
         SegmentException($NP, Selector);
      CallGate286(GSelector, GOffset, Attributes.DwordCount);
         /* See Chapter 9. */
      break;

   case 12: /* 386 Call Gate */
      if (Attributes.P == 0)
         SegmentException($NP, Selector);
      CallGate(GSelector, GOffset, Attributes.DwordCount);
      break;

   Default: /* Other Types raise $GP exceptions */
      SegmentException($GP, Selector);
   } /* end switch */
} /* end System segment or Gate */

} /* end CALL */
```

► **Listing 5.15:** Detailed description of CALL instruction (continued)

described above. It takes two parameters: the selector and the offset of the target of the call. If the selector is not null, the associated descriptor is read and tested based on the setting of the DType bit.

If DType = 1, a memory segment is indicated, and the routine CSDescriptorLoad( ) shown in Listing 5.12 is called to complete the descriptor checks. If it returns, the descriptor was loaded successfully. If the new offset is within the CS limit, the instruction completes by performing the "visible" part of the instruction. The old CS selector is pushed, then EIP is pushed to provide the return address. Finally, the CS selector register is loaded, its RPL is set to CPL, and EIP is loaded with the offset from the instruction.

If DType = 0, a system segment or gate is indicated. First, the DPL field is tested to ensure it is at the same level or an outer level relative to both CPL and RPL. Then the Type field is tested, with different actions for each of the valid type fields provided that the P bit is set to 1, indicating that the descriptor entry is valid.

If the descriptor Type field indicates an available 286 TSS, available 386 TSS, or task gate, a task switch occurs, which links the current task to the new task on the suspended task chain. The detailed descriptions of task switches are given later in this chapter.

We do not include a detailed description of the TaskSwitch286( ) subroutine, which performs a task switch through a 286 TSS. Chapter 9 discusses how a task switch through a 286 TSS differs from the 80386 task switch described in the TaskSwitch( ) routine.

Call through Call Gate A descriptor type of 286 call gate or 386 call gate specifies a call through a call gate. The routine CallGate( ) shown in Listing 5.16 describes a call through a 386 call gate. It takes three parameters:

1. The selector from the gate.
2. The offset from the gate.
3. The dword count from the gate, which gives the number of dwords to copy if a stack switch is required.

First, the selector is tested to ensure it is not null. Then the descriptor is read from the descriptor table, and its DType field checked to ensure it is a memory segment and not a system segment or gate. Next, the descriptor attributes are checked to see if a privilege-level change is required. If the descriptor indicates a present nonconforming executable segment with DPL at an inner level relative to CPL, a privilege-level switch is indicated.

```
CallGate(Selector, Offset, DwordCount)
   SelectorType Selector;
   int Offset,
       DwordCount; /* number of parameter dwords to copy */
                   /* for inter-level Calls.             */
{
   SegAttributes Attributes;
   SelectorType GSelector;
   int Base, Limit, GOffset;

/* Selector tests for CALL */
if ( (Selector & 0FFFCh) == 0) /* Null */
   SegmentException($GP, 0);

/* Read and test descriptor */
ReadDescriptor(Selector,&Attributes,&Base,&Limit,&GSelector,&GOffset);

if (Attributes.DType == 0) /* Can't be System segment or gate */
   SegmentException($GP, Selector);

/* CALL to inner level non-conforming executable present segment */
/* is OK, but requires switch to inner stack and inner CPL. */
if ( (Attributes.Type>=8) && (Attributes.Type<=11)
     && (Attributes.DPL < CPL) && (Attributes.P == 1) )
            InnerStack(Attributes.DPL, DwordCount, Selector);

/* Call common routine to finish CS descriptor load */
Selector.RPL = 0; /* ignore RPL in selector read from gate. */
CSDescriptorLoad(Selector, Attributes, Base, Limit, $GP);
/* Verify target is within segment limit */
if (Offset > CS.Limit)
   SegmentException($GP, 0);

/* Get to here only if all protection checks pass.            */
/* Push return pointer onto stack, then load CS selector and EIP */
ESP = ESP-4;
/* push 4 bytes, with CS selector in low 2 */
AccessVirtual(SS, ESP, 4, 1 /* Write */, $SS, &CS.Selector);
ESP = ESP-4;
AccessVirtual(SS, ESP, 4, 1 /* Write */, $SS, &EIP);

CS.Selector     = Selector;
CS.Selector.RPL = CPL;
EIP             = Offset;
} /* end CallGate */
```

► **Listing 5.16:** CallGate( ) subroutine

We do not include a detailed description of the CallGate286( ) routine, which performs a call through a 286 call gate. Chapter 9 discusses how a call through a 286 call gate differs from a call through a 386 call gate described in the CallGate( ) routine.

Privilege-Level and Stack-Switch Details The privilege-level change and the associated stack switch is described in the routine InnerStack( ) shown in Listing 5.17. It takes three parameters:

1. NewCPL gives the new privilege level.
2. The DwordCount field from the gate gives the number of dwords of parameters to copy.
3. The NewCSSelector gives the CS selector from the gate, which is only needed to pass as an error code for exceptions.

First, the inner-level stack is initialized by reading the stack pointer for this level from the TSS. Before loading SS with the selector and descriptor for the inner stack, the old SS selector and descriptor registers and the outer CPL are saved for the stack copy operation. Then CPL is changed to the inner level, and SS is loaded by calling the routine SRegLoad( ). CPL must be changed before the call to SRegLoad( ), so that the protection checks in that routine work properly.

The pointer to the outer-level stack is saved on the inner stack by pushing the old SS and ESP values. Then the dword parameters are copied from the outer stack to the inner stack. The copy operation is illustrated as running in the same order as the original pushes onto the outer stack, but the order is not significant. What is significant is that the reads from the outer stack are done with CPL set to the outer CPL, and the writes to the inner stack are done with CPL set to the inner CPL. This is necessary to ensure that the paging protection checks will operate properly, and it avoids a protection hole that might occur if the outer stack were read using the inner privilege level. At the end of the parameter copy loop, ESP is set to point to the last parameter pushed, and the routine InnerStack( ) returns with the privilege-level transition complete.

Completing the Call Gate Once the privilege level and stack have been changed, if necessary, the routine CSDescriptorLoad( ) shown in Listing 5.12 is called to complete the descriptor checks. The RPL field of the selector from the gate is ignored by setting it to 0 before calling CSDescriptorLoad( ). If it returns, the descriptor was loaded successfully. If the new offset is within the CS limit, the instruction completes by performing the "visible" part of the instruction. The old CS selector is pushed, then EIP is pushed to provide the return address. Finally, the CS selector register is loaded, its RPL is set to CPL, and EIP is loaded with the offset from the gate.

```
/* Routine to switch stacks for inter-level transitions. */
InnerStack(NewCPL, DwordCount, NewCSSelector)
   int NewCPL,     /* Switch to stack for this privilege level       */
       DwordCount;/* Count of parameter dwords to copy to new stack */
   SelectorType NewCSSelector; /* need CS selector for error code.   */
{
   SelectorType NewSSSelector;
   SegmentRegister OldSS;
   int TSSOffset, NewESP, tempESP, OldCPL, Dword1;

/* Read new SS and ESP from TSS. */
TSSOffset = NewCPL*8 + 4;
if ( (TSSOffset + 7) > TR.Limit)
   SegmentException($TS, NewCSSelector);
AccessLinear(TR.Base+TSSOffset,   0 /* PL 0 */, 0 /* Read */, &NewESP);
AccessLinear(TR.Base+TSSOffset+4, 0 /* PL 0 */, 0 /* Read */,
                                                    &NewSSSelector);

/* Save old SS and CPL to use during parameter copy loop. */
OldSS = SS;
OldCPL = CPL;

/* Load SS with selector for new stack after changing to new CPL */
/* and loading descriptor into shadow registers.                 */
CPL = NewCPL;
SRegLoad(SS, NewSSSelector, $TS);
/* return if SS load was successful. */
SS.Selector = NewSSSelector;

/* Push old SS and ESP.      */
NewESP = NewESP - 4;
AccessVirtual(SS, NewESP, 4, 1 /* Write */, $SS, &OldSS.Selector);
NewESP = NewESP - 4;
AccessVirtual(SS, NewESP, 4, 1 /* Write */, $SS, &ESP);

/* Copy parameters. Writing to new stack uses new CPL.          */
/* Reading from old stack uses old CPL.                         */
/* Order of parameter copying is irrelevant, but is illustrated */
/* as the same order as originally pushed on the outer stack by */
/* pointing tempESP at the opposite end of the parameter block  */
/* from ESP.  With this order, we exit the loop with NewESP     */
/* pointing to the top of the new stack.                        */
tempESP = ESP + DwordCount*4;
for (i=1; i<=DwordCount; i++){
   CPL = OldCPL;
   tempESP = tempESP - 4;
   AccessVirtual(OldSS, tempESP, 4, 0 /* Read */,  $SS, &Dword1);
   CPL = NewCPL;
   NewESP = NewESP - 4;
   AccessVirtual(SS,     NewESP, 4, 1 /* Write */, $SS, &Dword1);
   } /* end parameter copy loop */

ESP = NewESP; /* exit loop with NewESP pointing to new stack top */
} /* end InnerStack */
```

► **Listing 5.17:** InnerStack( ) subroutine

The RET Instruction

The routine RET( ) shown in Listing 5.18 contains the detailed description of the RET instruction. It takes one parameter, which is the number of bytes of parameters to remove from the stack after popping

```
/* Detailed description of inter-segment RET */
RET(ParmCount)
   int ParmCount; /* number of parameter bytes to remove */
                  /* from stack.                          */
{
   SelectorType Selector, GSelector;
   SegAttributes Attributes;
   int Base, Limit, Offset, GOffset;

/* Pop return address from stack */
AccessVirtual(SS, ESP, 4, 0 /* Read */, $SS, &Offset);
ESP = ESP + 4;
AccessVirtual(SS, ESP, 4, 0 /* Read */, $SS, &Selector);
ESP = ESP + 4;
/* Remove parameter bytes from the stack */
ESP = ESP + ParmCount;

/* Selector tests for RET */
if ( ((Selector & 0FFFCh) == 0) || (Selector.RPL < CPL))
   SegmentException($GP, 0);
if (Selector.RPL > CPL) {
   /* Inter-level RET is required if Selector.RPL > CPL.      */
   /* Call subroutine to restore (outer level) stack from     */
   /* SS:ESP stack pointer now at top of (inner level) stack. */
   OuterStack(Selector.RPL, ParmCount);
   }

/* Read and test CS descriptor */
ReadDescriptor(Selector,&Attributes,&Base,&Limit,&GSelector,&GOffset);
if (Attributes.DType == 0) /* Can't be System segment or gate */
   SegmentException($GP, Selector);

/* Call common routine to complete CS descriptor load. */
CSDescriptorLoad(Selector, Attributes, Base, Limit, $GP);
/* Verify target is within segment limit */
if (Offset > CS.Limit)
   SegmentException($GP, 0);

/* Get to here if all protection tests pass.  Complete visible */
/* part of instruction by loading CS selector and EIP.         */
CS.Selector = Selector;
EIP = Offset;

} /* end RET */
```

► **Listing 5.18:** Detailed description of RET instruction

off the return address. There are two forms of the intersegment RET instruction. One form includes a 16-bit immediate field containing this parameter byte count. The other form has no immediate field, so its parameter byte count is taken as 0.

First, the return pointer is popped off the stack, and ESP is adjusted by adding the parameter byte count. Then, the CS selector popped from the stack is tested. Its RPL field defines the privilege level to return to. An exception is raised if the selector is null, or if its RPL field specifies an inner level relative to CPL. If its RPL field indicates an outer level relative to CPL, a return to an outer level is indicated.

Privilege Level and Stack Switch The routine OuterStack( ) shown in Listing 5.19 is called to switch stacks and privilege levels. OuterStack( ) takes two parameters:

1. NewCPL gives the new privilege level.
2. ParmCount gives the parameter byte count to pop from the outer-level stack after switching stacks.

First, the outer-level stack pointer is popped from the inner-level stack. Then CPL is changed to the outer level, and the SS register is loaded by calling the routine SRegLoad( ). CPL is changed before calling SRegLoad( ) so that the privilege-level checks in that routine work properly. Then, ESP is loaded with the value popped from the inner stack after adding the parameter byte count to remove parameters from the outer stack. Finally, the segments addressed by the DS, ES, FS, and GS registers are tested to be sure they are accessible at the outer level. Each register that is not accessible is loaded with a null selector, and the P bit in the shadow register is cleared to prevent access through that register until a new selector is loaded.

Completing the RET Instruction Once the privilege level and stack have been changed, if necessary, the routine CSDescriptorLoad( ) shown in Listing 5.12 is called to complete the descriptor checks. Since CPL was assigned from the RPL field of the selector, the RPL test in CSDescriptorLoad( ) is guaranteed to pass. If the routine returns, the descriptor was loaded successfully. If the new offset is within the CS limit, the instruction completes by performing the "visible" part of the instruction, loading CS and EIP with the selector and offset popped from the stack.

Task Switches

CALL and JMP instructions can also transfer control to a different task, as can interrupts and the IRET instruction described in Chapter 6.

```
/* Subroutine to switch to outer level stack.          */
OuterStack(NewCPL, ParmCount)
   int NewCPL,     /* CPL of outer level we're returning to  */
       ParmCount;  /* number of parameter bytes to remove    */
                   /* from stack.                            */
{
   SelectorType NewSSSelector;
   int          NewESP;

   /* Pop outer SS and ESP from (inner level) stack. */
   AccessVirtual(SS, ESP, 4, 0 /* Read */, $SS, &NewESP);
   ESP = ESP + 4;
   AccessVirtual(SS, ESP, 4, 0 /* Read */, $SS, &NewSSSelector);
   ESP = ESP + 4;

   /* Load SS with selector for outer-level stack after changing CPL */
   CPL = NewCPL;
   SRegLoad(SS, NewSSSelector, $GP);
   /* return if SS load was successful. */
   SS.Selector = NewSSSelector;

   /* Load ESP with outer ESP adjusted by removing parameter bytes. */
   ESP = NewESP + ParmCount;

   /* Verify that segments addressed by DS, ES, FS, and GS              */
   /* are accessible at the new privilege level.  A segment             */
   /* is accessible if it is conforming regardless of DPL,              */
   /* otherwise if DPL ≥ the new CPL. If not, load Null                 */
   /* to avoid a protection hole. No need to check RPL,                 */
   /* since the register could not be loaded at the inner               */
   /* level if RPL > new CPL > old CPL.                                 */
   if ( (DS.Attributes.Type < 12) && (DS.Attributes.DPL < CPL) )
      {DS.Selector = 0; DS.Attributes.P = 0;}
   if ( (ES.Attributes.Type < 12) && (ES.Attributes.DPL < CPL) )
      {ES.Selector = 0; ES.Attributes.P = 0;}
   if ( (FS.Attributes.Type < 12) && (FS.Attributes.DPL < CPL) )
      {FS.Selector = 0; FS.Attributes.P = 0;}
   if ( (GS.Attributes.Type < 12) && (GS.Attributes.DPL < CPL) )
      {GS.Selector = 0; GS.Attributes.P = 0;}
   } /* end OuterStack */
```

► **Listing 5.19:** OuterStack( ) subroutine

The 80386 processor can perform a complete task switch as part of executing these instructions. The TSS system segment type described earlier supports this task switching by encapsulating the state of a task. The TSS contains a register save area, a field to link tasks, and pointers to the segmentation and paging tables. This permits the 80386 to save and load the processor registers, link suspended tasks, and change the virtual-to-physical address mapping to implement a full task switch.

The ability to switch tasks in a single instruction does not add any capability to the 80386 over what is available from the rest of the instruction set. The task-switch operations described here can be implemented in software using a sequence of simpler instructions. The hardware-supported task-switch operation is more efficient than software solutions if there is a close match between the task model of the 80386 and that of the operating system. If there is a large difference between the task models, a software task-switching mechanism may be a better choice.

If the selector for the target of an interrupt, or a JMP, CALL, or IRET instruction identifies a TSS or a task gate, a task switch occurs to the indicated TSS, or the TSS pointed to by the task gate. Task gates are similar to call gates in that they indirectly specify the target of the control transfer. Only the selector part of the pointer in the task gate is used, which must identify a TSS.

Privilege checks are applied to task switches to ensure the TSS or task gate is accessible. Task switches use the same privilege checks as call gates and data segment loads. The TSS or task gate must have its DPL at the same or an outer level relative to both CPL and RPL. The DPL of the TSS pointed to by a task gate is not checked.

The type of the TSS descriptor must be appropriate to the kind of transfer. A TSS can be either busy or available, as indicated in the Type field of its descriptor. A task is busy if it is the current task, or if it is linked to the current task along the list of suspended tasks with the link field of each TSS. Otherwise a task is available. A CALL, JMP, or interrupt must be to an available TSS. An IRET transfers to the previous task on the list of suspended tasks, which must be a busy task.

As described earlier in this chapter, the link field in the TSS is used to build a list of suspended tasks. The current task is suspended and added to the front of the suspended task list if a call or interrupt to another task occurs. A task is removed from the suspended list when the matching IRET is executed. This IRET follows the back link to resume the most recently suspended task.

Task switches cannot be recursive. A CALL or interrupt must be to an available TSS, and these operations leave the old TSS busy, preventing recursive tasks. An interrupt source that can generate nested interrupts cannot be handled with a task switch. After receipt of an interrupt handled by a task switch, the interrupt task must complete and execute a JMP or IRET instruction to mark the interrupt task available, before the next interrupt from the same source can be accepted.

The NT bit in the EFLAGS register is used to indicate when there is a suspended task linked to the current TSS. This bit is referenced by the IRET instruction to determine if a task switch is required to return, or if the return is to a program in the current task. If NT = 1, IRET will follow the link field to resume the most recently suspended task. If NT = 0, the IRET pops a return address off the stack to return to a program in the current task.

A program at any privilege level can alter the value in the NT bit. If a program sets the NT bit to 1 and then executes an IRET, a task switch to the TSS pointed to by the link field of the current TSS will occur. If the link field has not been set by a corresponding call or interrupt, unpredictable results may occur. Therefore, the operating system should take care to initialize the link field of every TSS before a jump to that TSS occurs. This way, a malicious or erroneous program can set the NT bit and execute an IRET, and the operating system can stay in control.

Task Gate Details

The routine TaskGate( ) shown in Listing 5.20 contains the detailed description of transfers through task gates. It takes two parameters:

1. The selector from the task gate descriptor.
2. A linkage indication, which controls how the list of suspended tasks is handled.

The selector must not be null, and must indicate a descriptor in the GDT. If so, the descriptor is read and tested. The descriptor must specify a system segment or gate descriptor by having a 0 in the DType field. Next, the Type field is tested according to the setting of the linkage parameter. If the Type field is appropriate, and the P bit is 1, the appropriate TaskSwitch( ) routine is called to complete the task switch.

We do not include a detailed description of the TaskSwitch286( ) subroutine, which performs a task switch through a 286 TSS. Chapter 9 discusses how a task switch through a 286 TSS differs from the 80386 task switch described in the TaskSwitch( ) routine.

Task-Switch Details

The routine TaskSwitch( ) shown in Listing 5.21 contains the detailed description of a task switch through a 386 TSS. Before calling this routine, the detailed instruction descriptions must verify that the current program has sufficient privilege to switch to the new task, and that the

```
TaskGate(Selector, Linkage)
   SelectorType Selector;    /* Selector from task gate descriptor   */
   int          Linkage;     /* 0=NoLink, 1=Link, -1=UnLink on chain */
                             /* of nested tasks.                     */
{
   SegAttributes Attributes;
   SelectorType  GSelector;
   int  Base, Limit, GOffet;

/* Selector must identify a TSS, stored in GDT */
if (   ((Selector & 0FFFCh) == 0 /* Null */)
     || (Selector.TI == 1 /* in LDT */)    )
   SegmentException($GP, Selector);

ReadDescriptor(Selector,&Attributes,&Base,&Limit,&GSelector,&GOffset);
if (Attributes.DType == 1) /* Memory Segment */
   SegmentException($GP, Selector);

switch (Attributes.Type) {
case 1: /* Available 286 TSS */
   if (Linkage == -1 /* UnLink */)
      SegmentException($GP, Selector);
   if (Attributes.P == 0)
      SegmentException($NP, Selector);
   TaskSwitch286(Selector, Attributes, Base, Limit, Linkage);
   break;

case 3: /* Busy 286 TSS */
   if (Linkage != -1 /* Unlink */)
      SegmentException($GP, Selector);
   if (Attributes.P == 0)
      SegmentException($NP, Selector);
   TaskSwitch286(Selector, Attributes, Base, Limit, Linkage);
   break;

case 9: /* Available 386 TSS */
   if (Linkage == -1 /* UnLink */)
      SegmentException($GP, Selector);
   if (Attributes.P == 0)
      SegmentException($NP, Selector);
   TaskSwitch(Selector, Attributes, Base, Limit, Linkage);
   break;

case 11: /* Busy 386 TSS */
   if (Linkage != -1 /* Unlink */)
      SegmentException($GP, Selector);
   if (Attributes.P == 0)
      SegmentException($NP, Selector);
   TaskSwitch(Selector, Attributes, Base, Limit, Linkage);
   break;

Default: /* Other system segment or gate types are illegal */
   SegmentException($GP, Selector);
} /* end switch */
} /* end TaskGate */
```

► **Listing 5.20:** TaskGate( ) subroutine

```
TaskSwitch(Selector, Attributes, Base, Limit, Linkage)
   SelectorType Selector;
   SegAttributes Attributes;
   int    Base, Limit,
              Linkage;      /* 0=NoLink, 1=Link, -1=UnLink on chain */
                            /* of nested tasks.                     */
{
if (Limit < 103)
   SegmentException($TS, Selector);

/* Save current machine state in old task's TSS */
AccessTSSState(1 /* Write */);

/* Point TR and Shadow registers to new TSS */
TR.Base       = Base;
TR.Limit      = Limit;
TR.Attributes = Attributes;
OldTSS        = TR.Selector; /* Save old task's TSS selector for link*/
TR.Selector   = Selector;

 /* Load machine state from new task's TSS */
AccessTSSState(0 /* Read */);

/* Handle differences in Linkage */
if (Linkage == 1 /* Link */) {
   /* Save old TSS selector in new TSS, set NT bit.  Leave old */
   /* TSS descriptor marked as busy. */
   AccessLinear(TR.Base, 2, 0 /* Level 0 */, 1 /* Write */, &OldTS);
   EFLAGS.NT = 1;
   SetTSSBusy(Selector, 1);    /* Mark new TSS descriptor busy    */
   } /* end Link */
else if (Linkage == -1 /* UnLink */) {
   SetTSSBusy(OldTSS, 0);     /* Mark old TSS descriptor not busy */
   } /* end UnLink */
else if (Linkage == 0 /* NoLink */) {
   SetTSSBusy(OldTSS, 0);     /* Mark old TSS descriptor not busy */
   SetTSSBusy(Selector, 1);   /* Mark new TSS descriptor busy     */
   } /* end NoLink */

CR0.TS = 1; /* Set Task Switched bit */
CPL = CS.Selector.RPL; /* Get CPL from RPL field of CS selector */

/* Visible state now restored.  Load descriptors into shadow */
/* registers for LDTR and segment registers.                 */
/* Mark all descriptors invalid for fault handling.          */
LDTR.Attributes.Present = 0;
CS.Attributes.Present = 0;
SS.Attributes.Present = 0;
DS.Attributes.Present = 0;
ES.Attributes.Present = 0;
FS.Attributes.Present = 0;
GS.Attributes.Present = 0;
```

► **Listing 5.21:** TaskSwitch( ) subroutine

new task has a valid TSS descriptor. Any exceptions detected there will be taken in the current task, not the new task. The remaining steps of a task switch are described in TaskSwitch( ):

1. Call the routine AccessTSSState( ), shown in Listing 5.22, to store the current values of the general registers, segment registers, EIP, and EFLAGS into the current TSS. The EIP value

```
/* Must load LDTR first */
if (LDTR.Selector.TI == 1 /* in LDT */)
   SegmentException($TS, LDTR.Selector);
if ((LDTR.Selector & 0FFFCh) = 0 /* Null */) {
   /* OK if LDTR is null. */
   LDTR.Attributes.P = 0;
   }

else {/* Read and test descriptor if selector is not null */
   ReadDescriptor(LDTR.Selector,&Attributes,&Base,&Limit,
                  &GSelector,&GOffset);
   if ( (Attributes.DType == 1)
        || (Attributes.Type != 2 /* LDT */)
        || (Attributes.Present == 0) )
      SegmentException($TS, LDTR.Selector);
   /* Load LDTR shadow registers if all checks pass */
   SetAccessed(LDTR.Selector);
   LDTR.Attributes = Attributes;
   LDTR.Base       = Base;
   LDTR.Limit      = Limit;
   } /* end LDTR.Selector not Null */

/* Load remaining shadow registers */
/* CS load is same as a jump through a call gate */
JumpGate(CS.Selector, EIP, $TS);

SRegLoad(SS, SS.Selector, $TS);
SRegLoad(DS, DS.Selector, $TS);
SregLoad(ES, ES.Selector, $TS);
SRegLoad(FS, FS.Selector, $TS);
SregLoad(GS, GS.Selector, $TS);

/* Clear local enable bits in DR7. See Chapter 8 */
DR7.L0 = 0;
DR7.L1 = 0;
DR7.L2 = 0;
DR7.L3 = 0;
DR7.L0 = 0;

} /* end TaskSwitch */
```

► **Listing 5.21:** TaskSwitch( ) subroutine (continued)

```
/* Save or restore machine state from TSS. */
AccessTSSState(RW)
   int     RW; /* 0 if Read, 1 if Write */
{
if (TR.Limit < 103)
   SegmentException($TS, TR.Selector);

AccessLinear(TR.Base+ 20h, 4, 0 /* Level 0 */, RW, &EIP);
AccessLinear(TR.Base+ 24h, 4, 0 /* Level 0 */, RW, &EFLAGS);
AccessLinear(TR.Base+ 28h, 4, 0 /* Level 0 */, RW, &EAX);
AccessLinear(TR.Base+ 2Ch, 4, 0 /* Level 0 */, RW, &ECX);
AccessLinear(TR.Base+ 30h, 4, 0 /* Level 0 */, RW, &EDX);
AccessLinear(TR.Base+ 34h, 4, 0 /* Level 0 */, RW, &EBX);
AccessLinear(TR.Base+ 38h, 4, 0 /* Level 0 */, RW, &ESP);
AccessLinear(TR.Base+ 3Ch, 4, 0 /* Level 0 */, RW, &EBP);
AccessLinear(TR.Base+ 40h, 4, 0 /* Level 0 */, RW, &ESI);
AccessLinear(TR.Base+ 44h, 4, 0 /* Level 0 */, RW, &EDI);
AccessLinear(TR.Base+ 48h, 2, 0 /* Level 0 */, RW, &ES.Selector);
AccessLinear(TR.Base+ 4Ch, 2, 0 /* Level 0 */, RW, &CS.Selector);
AccessLinear(TR.Base+ 50h, 2, 0 /* Level 0 */, RW, &SS.Selector);
AccessLinear(TR.Base+ 54h, 2, 0 /* Level 0 */, RW, &DS.Selector);
AccessLinear(TR.Base+ 58h, 2, 0 /* Level 0 */, RW, &FS.Selector);
AccessLinear(TR.Base+ 5Ch, 2, 0 /* Level 0 */, RW, &GS.Selector);

/* CR3 and LDTR.Selector are only accessed if reading. */
if (RW == 0 /* Read */) {
   AccessLinear(TR.Base+ 60h, 2, 0 /* Level 0 */, RW, &LDTR.Selector);
   AccessLinear(TR.Base+ 1Ch, 4, 0 /* Level 0 */, RW, &NewCR3);
   if (NewCR3 != CR3) {
      /* Avoid flush of TLB if new CR3 is same as old CR3 */
      FlushTLB;
      CR3 = NewCR3;
      } /* end CR3 load */
   } /* end Read special cases */

} /* end AccessTSSState */
```

► **Listing 5.22:** AccessTSSState( ) subroutine

saved points to the instruction after the one that caused the task switch. This freezes the state of the current task so it can be resumed later.

2. Load TR (the task register) with the selector for the TSS of the new task, and load the descriptor into the shadow registers. From this point on, any exceptions that occur are taken in the new task.
3. Call AccessTSSState( ) to load the general registers, segment registers, EFLAGS, and EIP from the new TSS. To properly handle exceptions that occur while loading segment registers for the new task, all of the selector registers are loaded before any of the descriptors are loaded. All of the descriptor shadow registers are marked *not present* at this point, since no descriptors are loaded yet.
4. AccessTSSState( ) will also load LDTR and CR3 from the new TSS. This changes the virtual-to-physical address mapping to that of the new task. Note that neither of these registers was written into the old TSS during the state-saving in step 1. Since CR3 is changed in the middle of accessing the new TSS, the page mapping must ensure that TSSs are mapped the same way in all tasks.
5. Call the routine SetTSSBusy( ), shown in Listing 5.23, to update the Type fields in the descriptors for both the old and new TSS to be busy or available, based on the linkage type requested. If the linkage parameter indicates that we are to link to the suspended task chain, the NT bit in the EFLAGS register (just loaded from the new TSS) is set to 1 and the selector for the old TSS is stored into the link field of the new TSS.
6. Set the TS bit in CR0. This will cause the next coprocessor instruction to trap so that the coprocessor registers can be saved to the old task, and reloaded from the new task. Coprocessor state save/restore is illustrated in Chapter 7. The CPL of the new task is taken from the RPL field of the CS selector in the new TSS. A task switch can occur from any level in one task (provided the new TSS or a task gate to the new TSS is accessible) to any level in the other task.
7. Load the descriptors corresponding to the selectors loaded previously. If an exception occurs loading a descriptor, the exception may be raised before all of the descriptors are loaded. In this case, these segment registers will contain the selectors, but the P bit will be 0 to prevent access. Exception handlers need to take care to handle this case properly.

8. The local enable bits in debug register DR7 are set to 0 to clear any breakpoints, or exact mode, local to the old task. The debug registers are described in Chapter 8.

Segment Register Loads during Task Switches As noted above, the segment register values are loaded from the new TSS in two stages. This two-stage process is necessary because an exception raised during the loading of one segment register will abort the task switch, leaving the rest of the segment registers with undefined values.

The first stage in step 3 loads the selector registers with the values read from the TSS without checking these selectors or the associated descriptors. To avoid problems with stale values, the P bit is cleared to 0 in all of the shadow registers to ensure the segment registers cannot be used to address memory until either the task switch completes successfully, or a new selector is successfully loaded.

The second stage in step 6 loads the descriptors for each segment register and performs protection checks on the selectors and descriptors. Exceptions at this point will abort the task switch, leaving one or more segment registers with the selector part containing an untested selector read from the TSS, but with P = 0 to prevent any access. These untested selectors act like null selectors for subsequent accesses, but may have values other than null.

```
/* Routine to change the type in a TSS descriptor. */
SetTSSBusy(Selector, Busy)
   SelectorType Selector; /* Selector for TSS descriptor.      */
   int          Busy;     /* 0 to set Available, 1 to set Busy. */
{
   int dword1;

/* Caller has verified selector is not null and is in the GDT.  */
/* Simply read descriptor and modify bit 2 of the Type field.   */
AccessLinear(GDT.Base+Selector.Index*8 + 4, 4, 0 /* PL 0 */,
             0 /* Read */, &dword1);
dword1 = dword1 & 0FFFFFDFFh;   /* Clear bit 2 of type field, */
dword1 = dword1 | (Busy << 9); /* and set to value in Busy.  */
AccessLinear(GDT.Base+Selector.Index*8 + 4, 4, 0 /* PL 0 */,
             1 /* Write */, &dword1);
} /* end SetTSSBusy */
```

► **Listing 5.23:** SetTSSBusy( ) subroutine

Most 80386 systems will simply abort a task if the TSS contains a bad selector value. Only systems that may mark segments *not present* will need to recover from segment exceptions during a task switch.

Two methods can be used to resume or complete the task-switch operation. The simplest is to handle these exceptions with task gates, as described in Chapter 6. Then, after the cause of the exception is fixed, the IRET will perform a task switch back to the aborted task to restart the task switch. These interrupt handlers should verify all of the segment register values in the faulting task to ensure that the task switch can complete successfully.

The second method is to handle the exceptions with trap gates (Chapter 6), but have the interrupt routine push all of the segment register values on the stack at entry, and pop them off just before the IRET. When the bad selector is popped off before the interrupt return, it will load successfully, assuming the cause of the exception was fixed. Other selectors may cause exceptions when they are popped if they were not processed before the exception aborted the task switch. The only constraint here is that the operating system must be able to tolerate recursive exceptions just before the IRET from these exceptions.

Interrupts and Exceptions

Chapter 6

INTERRUPTS AND EXCEPTIONS ARE SPECIAL control-transfer methods that operate outside of the normal programmed instruction stream. Rather than transfer control from one procedure to another by executing a CALL instruction, interrupts and exceptions transfer control without executing an instruction, as if a CALL instruction were inserted between two instructions. Control is transferred to an interrupt or exception *handler* procedure, which can return to the interrupted program by executing an IRET instruction (described in Chapter 3). The process of transferring control to the handler is termed *handling* the interrupt or exception.

Interrupts are caused by external events and have no relation to the instruction executing when an interrupt is received. Typically, an interrupt is used to indicate that an I/O device such as a disk drive or a keyboard has finished with the last operation, or has data for the processor. These external events are unrelated to the instruction executing at the time the interrupt is received. The interrupt causes a control transfer to an interrupt handler in the operating system that starts the next operation for the I/O device, reads data, checks status, and so on. When the interrupt handler is finished, it resumes the interrupted program at the point of interrupt by executing an IRET instruction.

Exceptions are unusual or invalid conditions detected during the execution of an instruction, and are directly associated with that instruction. For example, the segment and page exceptions outlined in Chapter 5 are detected during execution of an instruction and prevent the successful completion of this instruction. The "software interrupt" instructions INT *n* and INTO are classified as exceptions rather than interrupts, since the execution of these instructions will cause an exception. Other examples of exceptions are the debugging facilities described in Chapter 8.

Interrupts and exceptions are normally handled between instructions. The repeated string instructions (Chapter 3) are defined to update the pointer and count registers and handle interrupts after each repeat step to provide good interrupt response while ensuring that the instruction will eventually complete. Repeated string instructions also permit an exception to be reported without losing the results of the steps completed already. If an exception occurs on step 1902 of a repeated string move with a count of 2000, the exception is reported with the pointer and count registers having the values held after the 1901st iteration, the last step to complete successfully. After the cause of the exception is fixed, the instruction can be resumed to complete the unfinished 99 steps.

Each interrupt and exception has an 8-bit number associated with it called a *vector number.* Exceptions have preassigned vector numbers in the range of 0 to 31. For example, the divide error exception has vector number 0, and the page exception has vector number 14. You can assign interrupts to any vector number in the range 0 to 255, but they should be restricted to the range 32 to 255 to avoid conflicts with the preassigned exception vector numbers. The vector number selects the handler for a given interrupt or exception from the interrupt descriptor table, described later in this chapter.

Interrupts and exceptions can normally occur between any two instructions. However, mechanisms described in this chapter can be used to mask interrupts and certain exceptions so that they are ignored until they are later unmasked. Only the exceptions that support program debugging described in Chapter 8 can be masked. The other exceptions, including the segment and page exceptions described in Chapter 5, cannot be masked and so can occur at any time.

► Interrupts

As defined above, interrupts are caused by asynchronous external events. Special processor pins are used by external hardware to signal interrupts to the 80386 processor. Two classes of interrupts, each corresponding to a pin, are supported by the 80386: INTR and NMI.

INTR Interrupts

INTR interrupts are maskable interrupts and can have any vector number. When external hardware signals an INTR interrupt, it supplies the 8-bit interrupt vector number. The Intel 8259A Programmable Interrupt Controller is designed to work with the 80386 to multiplex up to 64 interrupt lines onto the single INTR pin provided on the 80386. A single 8259A can support up to eight interrupts. Up to nine 8259A Interrupt Controllers can be used to support up to 64 interrupt lines, each of which can be assigned a different vector number. In addition to supplying the vector number to the 80386, the 8259As can be used to assign and arbitrate priorities of interrupts. This is an important function, since the 80386 recognizes only one priority for INTR interrupts.

INTR interrupts can be masked by the IF bit in the EFLAGS register. If IF = 1, INTR interrupts can occur between any two instructions. If IF = 0, INTR interrupts are masked. If an INTR interrupt is signaled when IF = 0, it is held pending until either IF is set to 1 or the external hardware removes the INTR request. IF can be used to mask interrupts during critical regions of code that must be guaranteed to execute in sequence with no interruptions.

NMI

The *Nonmaskable Interrupt* (NMI) is not masked by the IF bit, and uses a preassigned vector number of 2 rather than receiving its vector number from external hardware. An NMI is typically used to signal serious system conditions such as bus time-outs, power-fail detection, and so on. NMI interrupts are masked only during the execution of the NMI handler. Unlike INTR interrupts, which are masked by the IF bit, there is no NMI mask visible to software. Upon receipt of an NMI, the 80386 internally masks further NMIs until an IRET instruction is executed, which is normally used to return from the NMI handler.

► Exceptions

Exceptions are unusual or invalid conditions associated with the execution of a particular instruction. The 80386 recognizes several different classes of exceptions, and assigns a different vector number to each class. Each exception is further classified as a fault, trap, or abort, depending on when it is reported, and whether the program causing the exception can be resumed.

A *fault* is an exception that is reported before the instruction that causes the exception. The CS and EIP values saved when transferring control to the handler for the fault will point to the instruction causing the fault. Faults are fully restartable on the 80386. This means that once the cause of the exception has been fixed, the faulting program can be resumed by executing an IRET instruction to return to the instruction causing the fault.

Faults are detected either before an instruction begins to execute or during the execution of an instruction. If detected in the middle of an instruction, the faulting instruction is canceled by restoring any source operands of the instruction to the values held before the instruction began to execute. This way, when the faulting program is resumed, the faulting instruction will be reexecuted with exactly the same input conditions to guarantee the proper results are obtained.

A *trap* is an exception that is reported after the instruction causing the exception. The CS and EIP values saved when transferring control to the handler for the trap point to the instruction dynamically after the instruction causing the trap. Because CS and EIP point to the next instruction, the instruction causing the trap cannot generally be identified. Before a trap is reported, the instruction causing the trap completes normally, which may result in changes to registers or memory.

An *abort* is an exception that is reported under severe conditions such as hardware failures or illegal or inconsistent values in system tables. The instruction causing the abort may not be identifiable. The program executing when an abort is reported cannot be resumed. Upon receipt of an abort, the handler may need to restart the operating system after rebuilding system tables.

The segment and page exceptions introduced in Chapter 5 are examples of faults. If one of these exceptions is detected during execution of an instruction, the instruction is canceled as described above and the exception is reported with CS and EIP pointing to the faulting instruction. The single-step and data breakpoint exceptions described in Chapter 8 are good examples of traps. If these exceptions are detected during the execution of an instruction, the instruction completes normally and reports the trap with CS and EIP pointing to the next instruction.

The misnamed *software interrupt instructions* INT *n* and INTO described in Chapter 3 are really programmed trap instructions rather than interrupts. They will generate a trap as part of their execution, which results in a control transfer to the trap handler with CS and EIP pointing to the following instruction.

Instruction Restart

All instructions are restartable after a fault. Operating-system software need not participate in the restart process, as the processor will report a fault with the machine in a state that permits clean restart of the faulting instruction after correcting the condition causing the fault. The CS and EIP values saved at a fault will point to the instruction that faulted. After the operating system has corrected the cause of the fault, the faulting instruction can be restarted simply by executing an IRET instruction to return from the fault handler.

Exception Types

This section lists the exception types by vector number, with a brief description included with each type. Each exception is classified as a fault, trap, or abort. Some of the exceptions provide additional information in the form of an error code passed to the exception handler.

Most exceptions are fairly simple and are adequately described in this brief format. Chapter 5 has more detail on segment and page exceptions, and Chapter 8 has more detail on debug exceptions. Coprocessor error exceptions are discussed in a special section later in this chapter.

Exception 0—Divide Error

The divide error is a fault that occurs if a DIV or IDIV instruction is executed with a divisor of 0, or if the quotient is too big to fit in the result operand. At entry to the divide error handler, the saved CS and EIP values point to the faulting instruction. No error code is provided with the divide error.

Exception 1—Debug Exceptions

The debug exceptions described in Chapter 8 use vector number 1. Some debug exceptions are faults, others are traps. Register DR6, described in Chapter 8, can be referenced by the debug exception handler to determine the condition(s) causing the debug exception and whether these exceptions are faults or traps. More than one debug exception can be detected in an instruction, resulting in several bits being set in DR6. Debug faults, but not debug traps, are masked if the RF bit in the EFLAGS register is set to 1. No error codes are provided to the debug exception.

Exception 3—Single-Byte INT 3

A special one-byte form of the INT *n* instruction is provided for INT 3. This can be used by debuggers to support code breakpoints, as described in Chapter 8. This INT 3 instruction is a programmed trap, not an interrupt. At entry to the exception handler, the saved CS and EIP values point to the instruction immediately following the INT 3, one byte past the INT 3 instruction. No error code is provided with the INT 3 trap.

Exception 4—Overflow

The overflow trap is reported through vector 4. The INTO instruction provides a conditional trap through vector 4. INTO will trap if the OF bit in the EFLAGS register is 1. If OF = 0, no trap is taken and execution continues with the instruction following INTO. At entry to the overflow exception handler, the saved CS and EIP values point to the instruction following the INTO. No error code is provided with the overflow trap.

Exception 5—Bounds Check

The bounds check fault occurs if a BOUND instruction finds that the tested value is outside the specified range. At entry to the bounds check handler, the saved CS and EIP values point to the faulting BOUND instruction. No error code is provided with the bounds check fault.

Exception 6—Invalid Opcode

The invalid opcode fault occurs if CS and EIP point to a bit pattern that is not recognized as an instruction by the 80386. This may happen if the opcode field specifies a code that is not a valid 80386 instruction, or if a register operand is specified for an instruction that requires a memory operand, or if the LOCK prefix is used on an instruction that cannot be locked. At entry to the invalid opcode fault handler, the saved CS and EIP values point to the first byte of the invalid instruction. No error code is provided with the invalid opcode fault.

Exception 7—Device Not Available

The device not available fault supports the 80387 numerics coprocessor. You can use it to substitute a software emulator in systems that do not include the 80387 coprocessor hardware. You can also use it to delay context switching of the 80387 (hardware or emulated) register state after a task switch until another task uses a floating-point instruction. The CS and EIP values saved at entry to the device not available fault point to the faulting instruction. No error code is provided with this fault.

The device not available fault is caused by the following conditions:

1. A floating-point instruction is executed, and either the EM bit or the TS bit in control register CR0 is a 1.
2. A WAIT instruction is executed, and both the TS and MP bits in CR0 are 1.

Refer to Chapter 5 for a discussion of the EM, TS, and MP bits in CR0.

Exception 8—Double Fault

If a segment or page exception is detected while reporting another exception, the processor will attempt to report a double fault rather than the second exception. Double faults are classified as aborts. That is, the CS and EIP values saved at entry to the double fault handler may not point to the instruction causing the double fault, and instruction restart is not supported for double faults. An error code of 0 is provided for double faults.

Double faults usually indicate serious problems in systems tables such as the segment descriptor tables, page tables, or the interrupt descriptor table. The double fault exception can be useful when debugging an operating system that may not yet handle system tables properly. In a production system, the double fault handler will probably have to restart the operating system after rebuilding the system tables.

It is possible to get a page fault while attempting to report a segment fault. In this case, a page fault is reported rather than a double fault. However, a segment fault detected when reporting a segment or page fault will cause a double fault, and a page fault when reporting a page fault will also cause a double fault.

If a segment or page exception is detected in the process of reporting a double fault exception, the processor will stop executing instructions and will enter the shutdown mode. The shutdown mode is similar to the state of the processor after executing a HLT instruction: no instructions are fetched, and no processor activity occurs. The processor will remain in this idle state until an NMI is received or the processor is reset. INTR interrupts are masked while in the shutdown state.

Exception 9—Coprocessor Segment Overrun

The coprocessor segment overrun is an abort that occurs if a floating-point instruction operand exceeds the segment limit. No error code is provided for this exception.

For example, if a floating-point instruction has an eight-byte operand stored at offset 0FFFFFFFCh in a segment that is 0FFFFFFFDh in size, this exception will be reported.

The coprocessor segment overrun is an abort, since the instruction causing the exception cannot be restarted. The 80387 coprocessor must be reinitialized with the FNINIT instruction before returning from the coprocessor segment overrun handler. The CS and EIP values saved at entry to the exception handler will point to the aborted instruction to assist in diagnosing the problem. This exception only affects the program executing when the condition is detected.

Exception 10—Invalid TSS

The invalid TSS fault occurs if a segment exception other than the not-present exception is detected when loading a selector from the TSS. It provides an error code containing the selector of the segment causing the exception. The format of this error code and the conditions that cause invalid TSS faults are detailed in Chapter 5, where the exception is referenced with the symbol $TS.

Since this exception is a fault, the CS and EIP values saved at entry to the exception handler will point to the instruction causing the fault, or to the first instruction of a task if the fault occurs as part of a task switch.

Exception 11—Segment Not Present

The segment not-present fault occurs when the processor finds the P bit 0 when accessing an otherwise valid descriptor that is not to be loaded into the SS register. If the SS descriptor has P = 0, a stack segment exception is reported instead of a segment not-present fault. The segment not-present fault provides an error code containing the selector for the segment causing the exception. The format of this error code and the conditions that cause segment not-present faults are detailed in Chapter 5, where the exception is referenced with the symbol $NP.

Since this exception is a fault, the CS and EIP values saved at entry to the exception handler will point to the instruction causing the fault, or to the first instruction of a task if the fault occurs as part of a task switch.

Exception 12—Stack Segment

The stack segment fault occurs when the processor detects certain problems with the segment addressed by the SS segment register. It provides an error code whose value depends upon the detected condition.

The format of the error code and the conditions that cause stack segment faults are detailed in Chapter 5, where the exception is referenced with the symbol $SS. The conditions that can cause this exception can be summarized in the following three categories.

1. A limit violation in the segment addressed by the SS register will cause a stack segment fault with an error code of 0.
2. A limit violation in the inner stack during an interlevel call or interrupt will cause a stack segment fault with an error code that contains the selector for the inner stack.
3. If a descriptor to be loaded into the SS register has its present bit 0, a stack segment fault is reported with an error code that contains the selector for the not-present segment.

The last two conditions result in faults with nonzero error codes. The stack segment fault handler can examine the descriptor for the segment identified by the selector in the error code to distinguish between the two conditions. If the present bit is 1 in this descriptor, the limit violation in the inner stack is indicated. Otherwise, a not-present stack segment exception is indicated.

The stack segment exception is a fault, so the CS and EIP values saved at entry to the exception handler will point to the instruction that caused the exception, or to the first instruction of the new task if the exception is detected as part of a task-switch operation. This exception is restartable.

Faults with a 0 error code can be used to indicate when to expand the stack segment in systems that support expandable stack segments.

Exception 13—General Protection

A segment exception that is not one of the previous categories is reported as a general protection fault. It provides an error code whose value depends upon the detected condition. The format of the error code and the conditions that cause general protection faults are detailed in Chapter 5, where the exception is referenced with the symbol $GP.

Since this exception is a fault, the CS and EIP values saved at entry to the exception handler will point to the instruction causing the fault, or to the first instruction of a task if the fault occurs as part of a task switch.

The conditions that can cause this exception can be grouped into two classes, based on the possible responses by the general protection exception handler.

1. The exception can indicate a violation of the protection model by an application program executing a privileged instruction or I/O reference. Systems that support virtual 8086 programs (Chapter 9) or virtual I/O references will need to emulate these instructions and restart the interrupted program after the faulting instruction. These exceptions are all reported with an error code of 0.
2. The exception can indicate a violation of the protection model that should result in termination of the faulting program. These cases may have an error code of 0, or they may include a selector value in the error code.

These two cases can be distinguished by examining the instruction causing the fault along with the error code. Because the general protection exception is a fault, the CS and EIP saved at entry to the fault handler will point to this faulting instruction. If the error code is 0 and the instruction is one for which emulation is supported, the handler will emulate it and return to the following instruction. If the instruction is not one for which emulation is supported, the faulting program may need to be terminated.

Exception 14—Page Exceptions

A page fault occurs if paging is enabled (PG = 1 in register CR0) and an instruction makes a memory reference to a linear address in a not-present page or to a page with attributes that are not appropriate to the type of access. The processor loads register CR2 with the linear address causing the fault, and also provides an error code that indicates the type of memory access that caused the page fault. The format of the error code and the conditions that cause page faults are detailed in Chapter 5.

Page exceptions are faults, so the CS and EIP values saved at entry to the page fault handler point to the faulting instruction. More importantly, page exceptions are restartable so that once the cause of the page fault has been fixed, the faulting instruction can be restarted simply by executing an IRET instruction to return from the page fault handler.

Exception 16—Coprocessor Error

A coprocessor error fault is reported with a vector number 16. It indicates that an unmasked numeric error such as overflow or underflow has occurred. It is reported as a fault on the next floating-point instruction or WAIT after the floating-point instruction that caused the problem. No error code is provided. A more detailed description of the coprocessor error exception is given later in this chapter.

Exception Summary

Table 6.1 summarizes the exception conditions discussed in this section. The exceptions are ordered by their associated vector number. The

VECTOR NUMBER	EXCEPTION TYPE	EXCEPTION CLASS	ERROR CODE	SIGNALING INSTRUCTION
0	Divide Error	Fault	NO	DIV, IDIV
1	Debug Exceptions	Fault/Trap	NO	Any instruction
3	Single-byte INT 3	Trap	NO	INT 3
4	Overflow	Trap	NO	INTO
5	Bounds Check	Fault	NO	BOUND
6	Invalid Opcode	Fault	NO	An invalid instruction encoding or operand
7	Device Not Available	Fault	NO	Floating-point instruction or WAIT
8	Double Fault	Abort	YES	Any instruction
9	Coprocessor Segment Overrun	Abort	NO	Floating-point instruction that references memory
10	Invalid TSS	Fault	YES	JMP, CALL, IRET, interrupt
11	Segment Not Present	Fault	YES	Any instruction that loads a segment register
12	Stack Segment	Fault	YES	Any instruction that loads SS or references memory in the segment addressed by the SS register
13	General Protection	Fault	YES	Any privileged instruction, or any instruction that references memory
14	Page Exception	Fault	YES	Any instruction that references memory
16	Coprocessor Error	Fault	NO	Floating-point instruction or WAIT
0–255	Software Interrupt	Trap	NO	INT *n*

► **Table 6.1:** Exception summary

table lists the instructions that can cause the given exception, categorizes each exception as a fault, trap, or abort, and indicates if an error code is provided with the exception.

► Priority of Interrupts and Exceptions

This section details how interrupts are ordered for processing if more than one interrupt or exception is detected during the execution of an instruction. Table 6.2 lists the interrupts and exceptions recognized by the 80386 in order from highest priority to lowest priority. If more than one interrupt or exception is detected, the one with the highest priority is reported. Lower priority exceptions are discarded, and lower priority interrupts are held pending. An exception discarded when reporting a higher priority exception will probably be detected again when the instruction is reexecuted after the cause of the higher priority exception is fixed.

For example, if both an NMI and INTR are signaled, the NMI is taken since it has higher priority, and the INTR interrupt is held pending. A more complex example is if a debug trap and a page fault are detected in the same instruction. In this case, the page fault is reported and the debug trap is discarded. After the page fault is fixed and the instruction is restarted, the debug trap will occur again and will be reported, assuming no higher priority exception occurs.

INTERRUPT/EXCEPTION TYPE	PRIORITY
Debug Faults	Highest
Non-debug Faults	
Trap Instructions INT *n*, INTO	
Debug Traps	
NMI Interrupt	
INTR Interrupt	Lowest

► **Table 6.2:** Simultaneous interrupt/exception priority

Note that these cases of multiple exceptions and interrupts detected in a single instruction are quite different from the double fault exception. The cases described here determine which exception to report if more than one occurs during the execution of an instruction. Only one of these simultaneous exceptions or interrupts will be reported. If a segment or page exception occurs while reporting the highest priority exception or interrupt, the selected exception or interrupt is discarded and a double fault is reported. Double faults do not arise from the presence of multiple fault conditions occurring in a single instruction. Instead, a double fault occurs if a segment or page exception occurs when transferring control to the exception handler.

► Masking Interrupts and Exceptions

Certain conditions and processor flag settings will cause interrupts and debug exceptions to be ignored, or masked. In these cases, the interrupts are held pending and the debug exceptions are discarded.

1. INTR interrupts are masked if the IF bit in the EFLAGS register is 0.
2. An STI instruction executed with IF = 0 will mask INTR interrupts until after the next instruction.
3. Debug faults (but not traps) are masked if the RF bit in the EFLAGS register is 1.
4. After reporting an NMI, further NMIs are masked until an IRET instruction is executed.
5. A MOV or POP instruction with the SS register as the destination will mask interrupts and debug exceptions until after the next instruction.

The first three cases were mentioned earlier in this chapter. The last condition supports an indivisible load of a new stack pointer into the SS and ESP registers with a pair of instructions. If a MOV or POP into SS is followed by a MOV or POP into ESP, no interrupts or debug exceptions will be reported between the two instructions, allowing the full stack pointer to be updated safely. As long as no segment or page exceptions occur on the load of ESP in the second instruction, the two instructions will be executed without interruption. The LSS instruction described in Chapter 3 is a new instruction on the 80386 that loads both SS and a general register (usually ESP) from a 48-bit pointer in memory. If possible, the LSS instruction should be used to load a new stack pointer rather than the old method using two instructions, since it loads both SS and ESP in a single instruction.

► Interrupt/Exception Transfer Methods

Two views of the interrupt and exception control transfers are presented in this chapter. The result of these transfers is to begin execution of the handler selected by the vector number for the interrupt or exception. The first view, given in this section, is a high-level view of the methods used for these transfers. The second view, given in later sections, is a detailed description of the mechanism presented in our C-like notation. The methods and mechanism are similar to those used for intersegment CALLs through call and task gates presented in Chapter 5. You should thoroughly understand that material before reading the next several sections of this chapter.

Interrupts and exceptions use the interrupt descriptor table (IDT), which is pointed to by the IDTR register, as described in Chapter 5. The vector number is used to index the IDT to obtain an eight-byte gate descriptor. Figure 6.1 illustrates the format of a gate descriptor. Gates

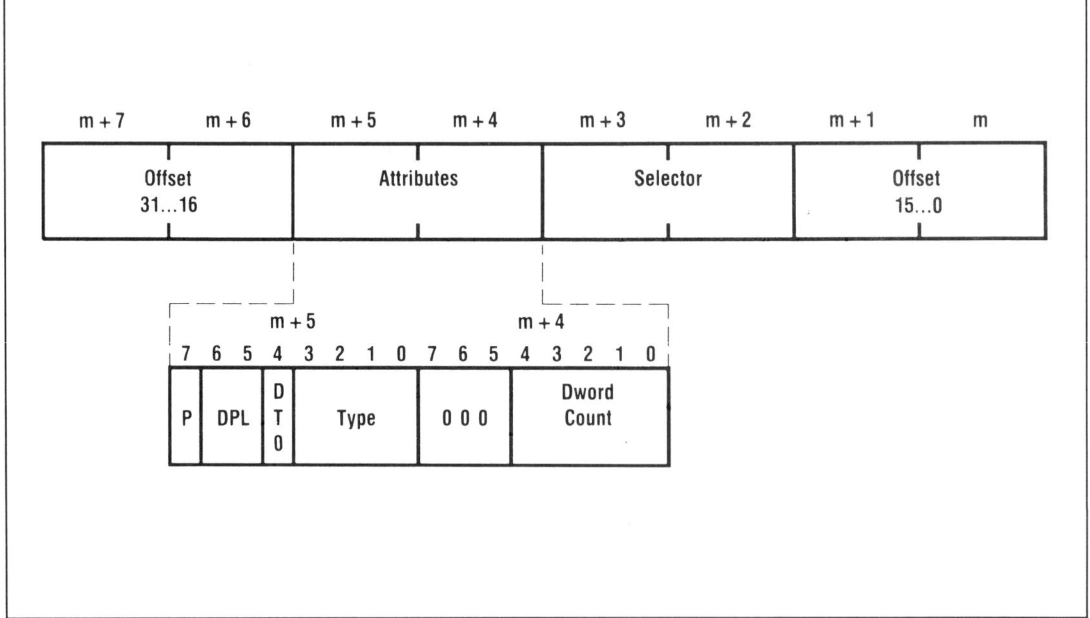

► **Figure 6.1:** Gate descriptor format

contain a 48-bit full pointer, plus 16 bits of attributes. The 48-bit pointer has the same information as the full pointer data type introduced in Chapter 2, but it is stored with the offset split into two pieces. The selector part of the pointer is stored in bytes at offset 2 and 3. The 32-bit offset is stored in two different pieces. The low-order 16 bits of the offset are stored at offset 0, and the high-order 16 bits are stored at offset 6.

In a gate descriptor, the attributes are stored in the bytes at offset 4 and 5, as follows:

P — P is the *Present* bit. P = 1 indicates that the gate is valid. P = 0 indicates that it is not valid, and use of the gate should cause an exception.

DPL — DPL is the *Descriptor Privilege Level,* which defines the privilege level associated with the gate. The Gate DPL is checked only for the INT *n* and INTO programmed trap instructions to prevent an application program from executing an INT *n* to any vector number, such as the vector number assigned for disk interrupts. The Gate DPL is ignored for all other exceptions and interrupts.

DT — DT is the *DType* bit, which distinguishes memory segments (DType = 1) from system segments and gates (DType = 0). It is 0 to indicate a gate.

Type — The 4-bit *Type* field defines the type of the gate, given in Table 6.3.

Descriptors in the IDT must have one of the following types:

- Task gate
- 286 Interrupt gate
- 286 Trap gate
- 386 Interrupt gate
- 386 Trap gate

DwordCount — The DwordCount field is not used in task, interrupt, or trap gates.

The 286 interrupt and trap gates are discussed in Chapter 9. This chapter describes transfers through task gates and 80386 interrupt and trap gates. Transfers through task gates transfer to a handler located in a different task. Transfers through interrupt and trap gates transfer to a handler located in the current task. As we shall see, the interrupt and trap gate names do not directly correspond to their uses, which is fortunate since there is no fault or abort gate type! Interrupts, faults, traps, and aborts can be handled by any of the three kinds of gates: task, interrupt, or trap.

Transfers through task gates perform a complete task switch to begin executing a handler in a different task. This task switch is identical to the method used when executing a CALL through a task gate. Interrupt and trap gates perform a much simpler transfer to a handler procedure located in the current task. This transfer is similar, but not identical, to the method used when executing a CALL through a call gate.

TYPE	DEFINES
0	Undefined
1	Available 286 TSS
2	LDT
3	Busy 286 TSS
4	286 Call Gate
5	Task Gate
6	286 Interrupt Gate
7	286 Trap Gate
8	Undefined
9	Available 386 TSS
A	Undefined
B	Busy 386 TSS
C	386 Call Gate
D	Undefined
E	386 Interrupt Gate
F	386 Trap Gate

► **Table 6.3:** System segment and gate descriptor types

Interrupt and Trap Gates

If the IDT descriptor indexed by the vector number is a gate of type 386 interrupt gate or 386 trap gate, a transfer to a handler procedure in the current task is indicated. Like a CALL through a call gate, the 48-bit pointer to the handler procedure is obtained from the interrupt or trap gate. Figure 6.2 illustrates how an interrupt or trap gate in the IDT specifies the interrupt handler procedure. The selector from the gate is used to access a descriptor in the GDT or LDT, which must specify an executable memory segment. The offset in the gate descriptor specifies the offset of the entry point of the handler procedure within this segment.

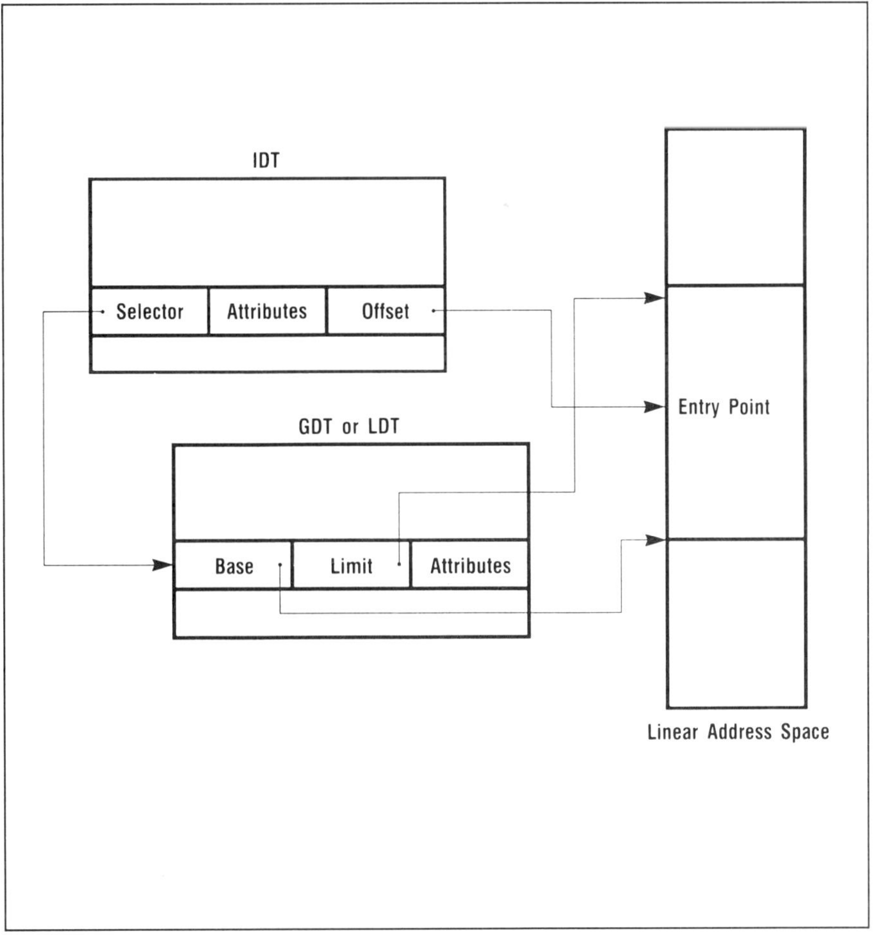

► **Figure 6.2:** Transfer through an interrupt or trap gate

The gate DPL is checked only for the INT *n* and INTO programmed trap instructions to prevent an application program from executing an INT *n* to any vector number, such as the vector number assigned for disk interrupts. The gate DPL is ignored for all other exceptions and interrupts.

The selector from the gate must specify a present, executable memory segment. The Type and DPL fields of the descriptor for this segment determine if the interrupt or exception is to a procedure at the current privilege level, or if a transfer to a new privilege level is required. Interrupts and exceptions can transfer to a procedure at the same privilege level, or to an inner privilege level. The matching IRET instruction can transfer to the same privilege level or to an outer privilege level. This matches the inward call, outward return rules for CALL and RET instructions.

If the selector from the gate identifies a conforming segment with DPL at the same or an inner level relative to CPL, or a nonconforming segment with DPL = CPL, then a transfer to a procedure at the current privilege level is indicated. A nonconforming segment with DPL at an inner level relative to CPL indicates a transfer to the inner level given by DPL of this segment. As with a CALL through a call gate, the stack segment is switched to the stack for this inner level as part of this privilege-level switch. The initial SS and ESP values for the new stack are obtained from fields in the current TSS, as described in Chapter 5. The old SS and ESP values are pushed onto the new stack so the matching IRET can restore the outer-level stack pointer. Unlike a CALL through a call gate, no parameters are copied from the old stack to the new stack for transfers through interrupt or trap gates. The DwordCount field of interrupt and trap gates is ignored.

Once the privilege level and stack have been switched, if needed, the rest of the interrupt or exception processing can proceed. The EFLAGS register is pushed onto the stack so it can be restored by the matching IRET instruction. Then the NT and TF bits in the EFLAGS register are set to 0. TF = 0 indicates that the handler is entered with single-stepping disabled (see Chapter 8). NT = 0 indicates that an IRET should return within the same task rather than to a nested task. If the transfer is through an interrupt gate, the IF bit in EFLAGS is also set to 0 so the handler will be entered with INTR interrupts masked. If the transfer is through a trap gate, the IF bit is unchanged.

Next, the return pointer is pushed onto the stack by pushing the current value of CS and EIP. CS is then loaded with the selector from the gate, after setting its RPL field to CPL. EIP is loaded with the offset from the gate to complete the transfer to the handler procedure.

The last part of exception processing is to push an error code onto the stack, if required. Error codes are provided only for certain exceptions, as described earlier and summarized in Table 6.1. The error code is a 16-bit value whose format is described in Chapter 5. To keep the stack aligned, the error code is pushed as a 32-bit value that has its upper 16 bits undefined.

Interrupt and trap gates are identical except for the setting of the IF bit in the EFLAGS register after transfer through the gate. Interrupt gates set IF to 0 to mask INTR interrupts at entry to the handler, but trap gates leave IF unchanged. As their name implies, interrupt gates are best for handling INTR interrupts, since they will mask interrupts before entering the interrupt handler. Trap gates are best for handling exceptions (including software traps), since they will not change the state of the IF bit.

Figure 6.3 illustrates the stack switch operation that occurs during an

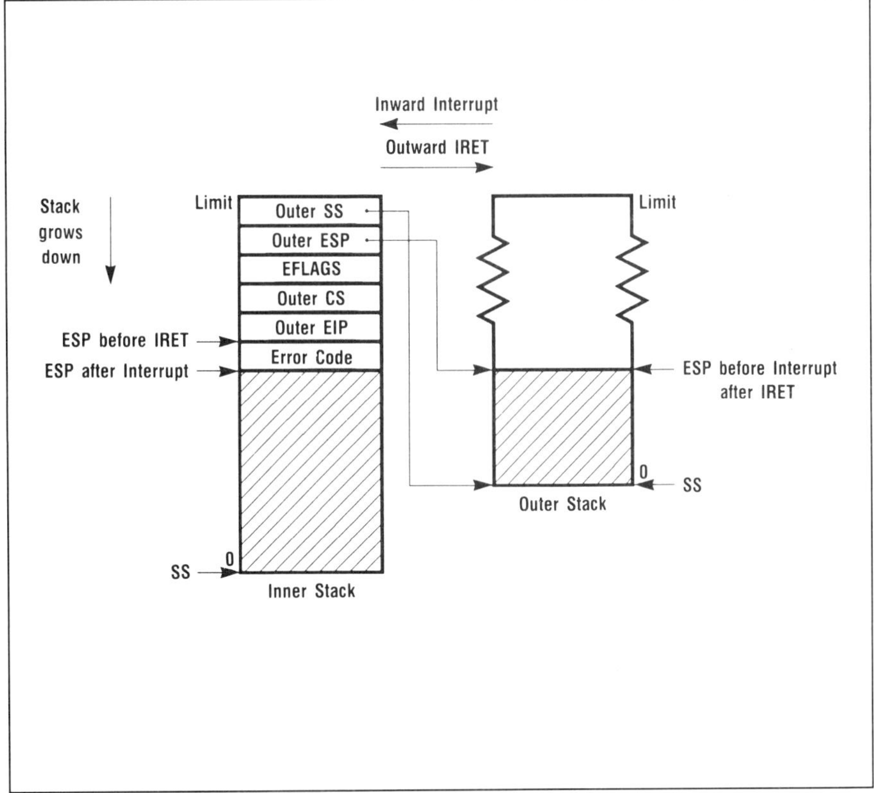

► **Figure 6.3:** Interrupt or trap gate to inner level

inter-level transfer through an interrupt or trap gate for an exception that provides an error code. The outer-level stack addressed by the SS and ESP registers is shown to the right. The new stack for the inner level is shown on the left, at entry to the handler. The first item pushed (at the highest address) is a pointer to the outer-level stack given by the old SS and ESP values. Next, the old EFLAGS value is pushed. Then the return address is pushed as the outer level CS and EIP values. The error code is pushed last. At entry to the handler, SS addresses the stack segment for the inner level and ESP gives the offset of the error code, which is at the top of this stack.

IRET with NT = 0

The IRET instruction is used to return from the interrupt or exception handler. A handler entered with an interrupt or trap gate will have NT = 0 in the EFLAGS register when the IRET instruction is executed, which indicates that IRET can find the return information on top of the current stack. IRET with NT = 0 can return to a procedure at the same privilege level, or to an outer level.

IRET pops the EIP and CS return pointer from the top of the stack, then pops the EFLAGS value. The RPL field of the popped CS selector identifies the privilege level to return to. As with the RET instruction described in Chapter 5, the RPL of the return CS selector is used rather than DPL of the segment identified by that selector, in order to permit return to a conforming segment that may execute at a level other than that given in its DPL field.

If the return selector RPL is the same as CPL, no privilege-level change is required. If RPL specifies an outer level, a privilege-level change is needed. In this case, the ESP and SS values needed to restore the outer stack are popped from the inner stack to complete the IRET.

IRET expects to find the return pointer and saved EFLAGS value on top of the stack, so handlers for exceptions that provide error codes must remove the error code from the stack before executing the IRET instruction.

Figure 6.3, used to illustrate the inner-level transfer through an interrupt or trap gate, also serves to illustrate the stack before and after an inter-level IRET is executed. The outer-level stack is shown on the right. The current stack is the inner-level stack shown on the left. Before executing the IRET instruction, the handler procedure must pop the error code from the stack so that ESP points to the EIP part of the return address pointer pushed by the transfer through the corresponding interrupt or trap gate. The return pointer's EIP and CS are popped from the stack to resume the interrupted program, and the EFLAGS register is restored by popping the saved EFLAGS value from the stack. The RPL field of the popped CS selector is examined to determine if an outer-level return is required. In this example, RPL specifies an outer level relative to CPL, so the outer-level stack is restored by popping the saved ESP and SS values into the corresponding registers. The interrupted program is resumed with the SS, ESP, EFLAGS, CS, and EIP values saved when the corresponding interrupt or exception was reported. The figure illustrates that SS and ESP address the outer stack after the IRET instruction completes.

Transfers through Task Gates

If the IDT descriptor indexed by the vector number is a gate of type task gate, a transfer to a handler procedure in a different task is indicated. Like a CALL through a task gate, the gate contains a 16-bit selector of the TSS segment describing the handler task. This selector must identify a segment of type available 286 TSS or available 386 TSS. A transfer through a 286 TSS is discussed in Chapter 9. A transfer to an interrupt or exception handler through a task gate to an available 386 TSS is identical to a CALL through a task gate to an available 386 TSS, as described in Chapter 5. The only difference is that exceptions providing error codes will push the error code onto the stack of the new task after the task switch is complete. To keep the stack aligned, the 16-bit error code is pushed as a 32-bit value with the upper 16 bits undefined.

The transfer through a task gate will enter the interrupt or exception handler with NT = 1 in the EFLAGS register to indicate that the matching IRET instruction must return to a nested task. The IRET instruction will reference the link field in the current TSS to obtain the selector of the TSS for the task to return to. Refer to Chapter 5 for more details about task switches and the nested task chain defined by the link field in the TSS.

Task vs. Interrupt/Trap Gates

The 80386 allows an interrupt or exception to be handled by a *procedure* within the current task by use of an interrupt or trap gate, or to be handled by a separate *task* by use of a task gate. Handler procedures within the current task are simpler and result in faster transfers to the handler, but the handler procedure is responsible for saving and restoring the processor registers. Handler tasks take longer to get to the handler, but include the overhead of saving and restoring registers as part of the task switch. Use of a handler procedure provides direct access to the state of the task executing when an interrupt or exception is signaled, but requires that every task contain a handler procedure. Use of a separate task provides better isolation of the handler, but may complicate access to the state of the task signaling the interrupt or exception.

Invalid TSS exceptions must be handled by a task gate to ensure a valid task context for the handler. Other exceptions are generally best handled in the context of the task in which they are detected and do not need to mask interrupts, and so should use trap gates. The exception handler pointed to by the trap gate is a procedure shared by all tasks, and so it should be located in the global address space. If a different handler is required for each task, the global exception handler can keep a table of these handlers and call the appropriate one for the task causing the exception.

Interrupts are usually unrelated to the task executing when the interrupt is received, and they may benefit from the task isolation provided by use of a task gate. Interrupts that require fast response may be better handled by an interrupt gate. Systems that do not use the built-in 386 task-switching mechanism will also use interrupt gates. Since an interrupt can occur at any time, interrupt handlers accessed through interrupt gates must be located in the global address space so they are addressable in all tasks. Chapter 7 contains a long example that illustrates the use of interrupt gates and how the handler is placed in the global address space.

Use of a task gate provides an automatic dispatch of the handler task when an interrupt or exception is received. This task dispatch is performed directly by the 80386 hardware and bypasses the software task dispatcher contained in the operating system. This provides a faster task switch to the handler, but may require the handler to call the software dispatcher to notify it of the task switch.

► Interrupt/Exception Details

The following sections present the second view of interrupt and exception control-transfer methods: the detailed description of interrupt and exception handling presented in our C-like notation. These descriptions reference subroutines, global variables, and global types defined in Chapter 5.

Interrupt Description

The routine Interrupt( ) in Listing 6.1 contains the detailed description

```
/* Process an Interrupt or Exception. */
Interrupt(VecNumber, CheckDPL)

int VecNumber, /* Vector Number */
    CheckDPL;  /* 0 = ignore DPL of gate in IDT,           */
               /* 1 = check DPL of IDT gate against CPL */
{  SegAttributes Attributes;
   SelectorType Selector;
   int Dword1, Dword2, Offset, Base, Limit;

/* Read IDT entry for indicated vector number,    */
/* switch on the type of the descriptor obtained. */
if (VecNumber*8+7 > IDTR.Limit)
   SegmentException($GP, VecNumber*8+2);
AccessLinear(IDTR.Base+VecNumber*8,   4, 0 /* PL 0 */, 0 /* Read *
             &Dword1);
AccessLinear(IDTR.Base+VecNumber*8+4, 4, 0 /* PL 0 */, 0 /* Read *,
             &Dword2);

Attributes = Dword2; /* Gate attributes are in high-order dword. */
/* Unscramble Gate selector and offset. */
Selector = Dword1 >> 16;
Offset   = (Dword1 & 0FFFFh) | (Dword2 * 0FFFF0000h);

/* Test descriptor DType and Type fields. */
if (
     (Attributes.DType == 0) /* Memory Segment */
  || /* Check DPL of gate if CheckDPL parameter is 1. */
     ( (CheckDPL == 1) && (Attributes.DPL < CPL) )
  ||   (Attributes.Type < 5) /* Type must be 5, 6, 7, 14, or 15. */
  || ( (Attributes.Type > 7) && (Attributes.Type < 14) )
   )
   SegmentException($GP, VecNumber*8+2);

/* General Protection violations checked before Not Present. */
if (Attributes.P == 0 /* Not Present IDT entry */)
   SegmentException($NP, VecNumber*8+2);

switch (Attributes.Type) {
 5: /* TaskGate */
    TaskGate(Selector, 1 /* Link */); /* See Chapter 5 */
    break;
 6: /* IntGate286 */
    IntTrapGate286(Selector, Offset, 1 /* Clear IF */);
    break;
 7: /* TrapGate286 */
    IntTrapGate286(Selector, Offset, 0 /* IF Unchanged */);
    break;
```

► **Listing 6.1:** Detailed description of interrupt handling

```
14: /* IntGate386 */
    IntTrapGate(Selector, Offset, 1 /* Clear IF */);
    break;
15: /* TrapGate386 */
    IntTrapGate(Selector, Offset, 0 /* IF Unchanged */);
    break;

} /* end switch */
} /* end Interrupt */
```

► **Listing 6.1:** Detailed description of interrupt handling (continued)

of interrupt and exception handling. It takes two parameters:

1. The vector number associated with the interrupt or exception.
2. A flag to indicate whether to check the DPL of the gate in the IDT.

The vector number is used to index the IDT to obtain a gate descriptor. The DType field must be 0, indicating a system segment or gate descriptor. The Type field must be 5, 6, 7, 14, or 15, indicating a task gate, 286 interrupt gate, 286 trap gate, 386 interrupt gate, or 386 trap gate. If the CheckDPL parameter is 1, the IDT gate DPL is checked to ensure it is at the same or an outer level relative to CPL. If any of these tests fail, a $GP (general protection) segment exception is reported. The P bit must be 1, indicating a valid descriptor. Otherwise, a $NP (not-present) segment exception is reported. The $GP and $NP exceptions provide an error code containing the vector number in the selector index field, with bit 1 of the error code set to 1 to indicate the error code refers to the IDT.

The Type field in the gate determines how the interrupt is handled. A task gate indicates handling with a task switch to the task described by the TSS identified by the selector in the gate. The description of this task switch is contained in the TaskGate( ) routine in Chapter 5. A 286 interrupt or trap gate indicates handling within the current task using a 16-bit transfer compatible with 286 interrupt handling. Transfers through these gates are discussed in Chapter 9.

Interrupt and Trap Gates

A 386 interrupt or trap gate indicates handling within the current task with a control transfer that is similar to a CALL through a call gate. The routine IntTrapGate( ) in Listing 6.2 contains the detailed description of this control transfer. It takes three parameters:

1. A selector for the code segment containing the handler procedure.

```
IntTrapGate(Selector, Offset, ClearIF)
/* Similar to CallGate routine in Chapter 5. */
   SelectorType Selector;
   int Offset,
       ClearIF; /* if 1, clear IF before entering handler. */
                /* if 0, leave IF unchanged.               */
{
   SegAttributes Attributes;
   SelectorType GSelector;
   int Base, Limit, GOffset;

/* Selector test */
if ( (Selector & 0FFFCh) == 0) /* Null */
   SegmentException($GP, 0);

/* Read and test descriptor */
ReadDescriptor(Selector,&Attributes,&Base,&Limit,&GSelector,&GOffset);

if (Attributes.DType == 0) /* Can't be System segment or gate */
   SegmentException($GP, Selector);

/* Interrupt to inner level nonconforming executable present        */
/* segment is OK, but requires switch to inner stack and inner CPL. */
if ( (Attributes.Type>=8) && (Attributes.Type<=11)
     && (Attributes.DPL < CPL) && (Attributes.P == 1) )
          InnerStack(Attributes.DPL, 0, Selector);

/* Call common routine to finish CS descriptor load. */
Selector.RPL = 0; /* Ignore RPL in selector read from gate. */
CSDescriptorLoad(Selector, Attributes, Base, Limit, $GP);

/* Verify target is within segment limit. */
if (Offset > CS.Limit)
   SegmentException($GP, 0);

/* Get to here only if all protection checks pass.  */
/* Push EFLAGS and return pointer,                  */
/* then modify EFLAGS and load CS selector and EIP. */
ESP = ESP-4;
AccessVirtual(SS, ESP, 4, 1 /* Write */, $SS, &EFLAGS);
ESP = ESP-4;
/* Push 4 bytes, with CS selector in low-order 2 bytes. */
AccessVirtual(SS, ESP, 4, 1 /* Write */, $SS, &CS.Selector);
ESP = ESP-4;
AccessVirtual(SS, ESP, 4, 1 /* Write */, $SS, &EIP);

EFLAGS.TF = 0; /* Turn off single stepping (Chapter 8). */
EFLAGS.NT = 0; /* Interrupt not handled by nested task. */
if (ClearIF == 1)
   EFLAGS.IF = 0;

CS.Selector     = Selector;
CS.Selector.RPL = CPL;
EIP             = Offset;
} /* end IntTrapGate */
```

► **Listing 6.2:** IntTrapGate( ) subroutine

2. The offset of the handler procedure in this segment.
3. A flag to indicate whether to set IF to 0, or leave it unchanged before transfer to the handler.

First, the selector is tested to ensure it is not null. Then the descriptor is read from the descriptor table with a call to the routine ReadDescriptor( ) defined in Chapter 5. The DType field must be 1, indicating a memory segment. If the descriptor indicates a present nonconforming executable segment with DPL at an inner level relative to CPL, a privilege-level change is indicated. This privilege-level transition includes a change to a different stack and is handled by a call to the routine InnerStack( ) defined in Chapter 5.

Once the privilege level and stack have been changed, if necessary, the routine CSDescriptorLoad( ) defined in Chapter 5 is called to complete the descriptor checks. The RPL of the selector from the gate is ignored by setting it to 0 before calling CSDescriptorLoad( ). It returns if the descriptor was loaded successfully. If the new offset is within the CS limit, the "visible" part of interrupt handling is performed by pushing EFLAGS, CS, and EIP, clearing certain EFLAGS fields, and loading CS and EIP with the selector and offset from the gate.

IRET Instruction

The routine IRET( ) shown in Listing 6.3 contains the detailed description of the IRET instruction, which enlarges upon the description of IRET given in Chapter 3. First, the NT bit in the EFLAGS register is tested to see if a return to a nested task is indicated (NT = 1), or if the return is within the current task (NT = 0). If NT = 1, a return to a nested task is performed by reading the selector for the TSS of the nested task from the link field at offset 0 in the current TSS, and calling the routine TaskGate( ) to perform the task switch.

If NT = 0, a return within the current task is indicated, and the return information (EIP, CS, and EFLAGS) is popped off the stack. The RPL field of the popped CS selector determines the privilege level to return to. If it indicates an outer level relative to CPL, a return to an outer level is indicated. This privilege-level transition includes a change of the stack segment and is handled with a call to the routine OuterStack( ) defined in Chapter 5. Then the CS descriptor is read, tested, and loaded into the shadow registers by calls to two routines defined in Chapter 5: ReadDescriptor( ) and CSDescriptorLoad( ). Finally, if the return offset is within the CS limit, the "visible" part of the IRET instruction is executed by loading EFLAGS, CS, and EIP with the values popped from the stack earlier.

```
/* Detailed description of the IRET instruction. */
IRET()
{
   SelectorType Selector, GSelector;
   SegAttributes Attributes;
   int Base, Limit, Offset, GOffset;

/* Test NT bit to see if we do a Task return. */
if (EFLAGS.NT == 1)
   {/* Return through Task identified in Link field of current TSS. */
    AccessLinear(TR.Base, 2, 0 /* PL 0 */, 0 /* Read */, &Selector);
    TaskGate(Selector, -1 /* Unlink */); /* see Chapter 5. */
   }

else {
   /* Otherwise pop interrupt return information from the stack. */
   AccessVirtual(SS, ESP, 4, 0 /* Read */, $SS, &Offset);
   ESP = ESP + 4;
   AccessVirtual(SS, ESP, 4, 0 /* Read */, $SS, &Selector);
   ESP = ESP + 4;
   AccessVirtual(SS, ESP, 4, 0 /* Read */, $SS, &NewEFLAGS);
   ESP = ESP + 4;

   /* Selector tests for IRET */
   if ( ((Selector & 0FFFCh) == 0) || (Selector.RPL < CPL))
      SegmentException($GP, 0);
   if (Selector.RPL > CPL) {
      /* Inter-level IRET is required if Selector.RPL > CPL.     */
      /* Call subroutine to restore (outer level) stack from     */
      /* SS:ESP stack pointer now at top of (inner level) stack. */
      OuterStack(Selector.RPL, 0);
      }

   /* Read and test CS descriptor */
   ReadDescriptor(Selector,&Attributes,&Base,&Limit,&GSelector,&GOffset);
   if (Attributes.DType == 0) /* Can't be System segment or gate */
      SegmentException($GP, Selector);

   /* Call common routine to complete CS descriptor load. */
   CSDescriptorLoad(Selector, Attributes, Base, Limit, $GP);

   /* Verify target is within segment limit. */
   if (Offset > CS.Limit)
      SegmentException($GP, 0);

   /* Get to here if all protection tests pass.  Complete visible  */
   /* part of instruction by loading EFLAGS, CS selector, and EIP. */
   EFLAGS = NewEFLAGS;
   CS.Selector = Selector;
   EIP = Offset;
   } /* end NT=0 */
} /* end IRET */
```

► **Listing 6.3:** Detailed description of IRET

Exception Reporting

These sections provide detailed descriptions of the SegmentException( ) and PageException( ) routines used in Chapter 5 to report segment and page exceptions. Before diving into these descriptions, a few more global variables and a basic instruction fetch-execute loop shown in Listing 6.4 need to be introduced. The global variable EXT is used to form the error code for segment exceptions. It is normally 0, and is set to 1 when processing an external interrupt or an exception other than the INT *n* or INTO software trap instructions. OldEIP saves the offset of the current instruction within the current code segment addressed by the CS register. If a fault occurs, OldEIP is moved back into EIP so the exception is reported with the saved EIP (saved on the stack or in the TSS for a nested task) pointing to the instruction causing the fault.

The loop headed by the label DispatchInstruction is a basic fetch-execute loop. Before each instruction, EXT is cleared to 0, and EIP is copied to OldEIP. Then, the FetchInstruction( ) routine (not given in this book) is called to fetch the instruction pointed to by EIP. This routine will also increment EIP to point to the next sequential instruction. After the instruction is fetched, it is executed by a call to the routine Execute( ), which is a placeholder for any of the routines given in this chapter or Chapter 5 that contain the detailed descriptions of instructions (for example, the IRET( ) routine). This "execute" routine will return if the instruction executed successfully (without faulting), and then the loop is traversed again.

```
/* EXT and OldEIP are global variables that are assigned whenever */
/* a new instruction is fetched and executed. This fragment       */
/* specifies the handling of EXT, EIP, and OldEIP at an           */
/* Instruction Boundary.                                          */

int EXT,     /* 1 if processing external interrupt or exception, */
             /* used to form error code for segment exceptions.  */
    OldEIP;  /* Save EIP of current instruction here to support  */
             /* exception handling.                              */

/* Actions when fetching and executing an instruction.            */
/* Exception handling routines jump here to abort an instruction  */
/* and resume with first instruction of the exception handler.    */
DispatchInstruction:
   EXT = 0;
   OldEIP = EIP;             /* Save pointer to current instruction. */
   FetchInstruction();       /* Increments EIP to next instruction.  */
   Execute();       /* "Calls" proper routine to execute instruction. */
   goto DispatchInstruction; /* Fetch-Execute loop.                  */
```

► **Listing 6.4:** Global variables and fetch-execute loop

As noted in Chapter 5, the routines PageException( ) and Segment-Exception( ) do not return to their caller, but instead abort the "execution" of an instruction description. This abort is handled by a jump to the label DispatchInstruction, hardly a standard C construct, but one that should be familiar to most programmers. This jump will "unwind" the procedure-call stack to terminate any nested procedures before resuming at the DispatchInstruction label.

The detection and reporting of double faults are not included in these detailed descriptions to avoid complicating the descriptions. Double faults were discussed earlier in this chapter.

SegmentException( ) Routine

Segment exceptions are reported with the routine Segment-Exception( ), shown in Listing 6.5, which takes two parameters:

1. The vector number used to report the exception.
2. The selector used to form the error code provided with the exception.

```
SegmentException(VecNumber, ErrorCode)
/* Raise a Segmentation exception. */

   int VecNumber,   /* Exception Number */
       ErrorCode;   /* Top 15 bits of error code */
{
/* Compute error code before processing the interrupt, to permit  */
/* EXT to be set to 1 here without affecting this exception code. */
ErrorCode = (ErrorCode & 0FFFEh) | EXT;
EXT = 1; /* EXT=1 for subsequent exceptions. */

/* Back up EIP so it points to faulting instruction.             */
/* Recall that EIP is incremented after fetching every instruction. */
/* EIP of the current (faulting) instruction is saved in OldEIP.    */
EIP = OldEIP;

/* Signal exception with vector number given in VecNumber. */
Interrupt(VecNumber, 0 /* Don't check DPL of IDT gate */);

/* Push error code onto stack after processing interrupt. */
ESP = ESP-4;
AccessVirtual(SS, ESP, 4, 1 /* Write */, $SS, &ErrorCode);

/* Abort processing of faulting instruction,           */
/* continue with first instruction of exception handler. */
GOTO DispatchInstruction;
} /* end SegmentException                               */
```

► **Listing 6.5:** SegmentException( ) subroutine

The error code for the exception is formed by concatenating the upper 15 bits passed as the second parameter with the EXT bit. The error code format for segment exceptions is described in Chapter 5. Then, EIP is backed up to point to the faulting instruction by copying OldEIP (saved in the fetch-execute loop) to EIP. After the exception is processed as described by the routine Interrupt( ), the error code is pushed onto the stack. Finally, the faulting instruction is aborted by jumping to the DispatchInstruction label, where the fetch-execute loop will resume with the first instruction of the exception handler.

PageException( ) Routine

The routine PageException( ) shown in Listing 6.6 is similar to SegmentException( ) except for two things: how the error code is formed, and the vector number passed to the Interrupt( ) routine. The format of

```
PageException(LAddress, U, W, Present) {
   int LAddress,
       U,        /* 1 if user access, 0 if supervisor    */
       W,        /* 1 if write access, 0 if read         */
       Present;  /* 1 if entry present, 0 if not present */

{int ErrorCode;

/* Set up error information.  Store Linear Address into CR2, and  */
/* prepare error code based on attempted access plus present bit. */
CR2 = LAddress;
if (U==3)
     ErrorCode = 4 + 2*W + Present;
else ErrorCode =     2*W + Present;
EXT = 1;  /* EXT=1 for subsequent exceptions. */

/* Back up EIP so it points to faulting instruction.                */
/* Recall that EIP is incremented after fetching every instruction. */
/* EIP of the current (faulting) instruction is saved in OldEIP.    */
EIP = OldEIP;

/* Signal exception with vector number 14. */
Interrupt(14, 0 /* Don't check DPL of IDT gate */);

/* Push error code onto stack after processing interrupt. */
ESP = ESP-4;
AccessVirtual(SS, ESP, 4, 1 /* Write */, $SS, &ErrorCode);

/* Abort instruction processing,                        */
/* continue with first instruction of exception handler. */
GOTO DispatchInstruction;
} /* end PageException */
```

► **Listing 6.6:** PageException( ) subroutine

the error code for page exceptions is described in Chapter 5. PageException( ) takes four parameters:

1. The linear address causing the exception.
2. The privilege level of the attempted access, used to form the U bit of the error code.
3. The W bit of the error code (1 if a write, 0 if a read).
4. The P bit of the error code (1 if a protection exception, 0 if a not-present exception).

► Coprocessor Error Exceptions

The following sections describe the exceptions detected by the 80387 numerics coprocessor. Chapter 2 described the 80387 status-word and control-word registers, which contain fields important to the handling of these exceptions. Chapter 3 listed the exceptions that can be raised for each instruction.

Coprocessor error exceptions are grouped into the six categories listed in Table 6.4. Each category is discussed in detail below. This table gives the code used for the exception in the instruction descriptions in Chapter 3, the name of the corresponding status bit in the status-word register, and the corresponding mask bit in the control-word register.

CODE	STATUS	MASK	CONDITION
I,IS	IE	IM	Invalid operation (numeric, stack)
D	DE	DM	Denormal
Z	ZE	ZM	Zero divide
O	OE	OM	Overflow
U	UE	UM	Underflow
P	PE	PM	Precision (IEEE inexact)

► **Table 6.4:** Coprocessor error exception summary

Masked vs. Unmasked Exceptions

The mask bit in the control-word register determines the action taken if an exceptional condition is detected. If the mask bit is 1, the exception is *masked,* and it is handled within the 80387 by returning a reasonable result value and continuing without reporting the exception. If the mask bit is 0, the exception is *unmasked* and is reported using vector number 16.

Note that the status bit is set for a masked exception even though a coprocessor error exception is not reported. This permits software to determine if a masked exception occurs during a sequence of numeric calculations by clearing the status bits, setting the mask bits, performing the computations, and then examining the status bits for the masked exceptions to determine if any exception occurred during the intervening computations.

If an unmasked exception occurs, it is reported as a fault on the next floating-point or WAIT instruction to be executed. This means that the CS and EIP values saved at entry to the coprocessor error handler point to the next floating-point instruction, *not* to the floating-point instruction causing the exception. The 80387 error-pointer registers can be read using the FSTENV or FSAVE instructions to obtain a pointer (in FCS and FIP) to the instruction causing the coprocessor error exception, the opcode of that instruction, and its memory operand (in FOS and FOO), if any.

Unmasked exceptions are further classified as pre-execution or post-execution exceptions. A *pre-execution* exception is reported before a result is stored, so it leaves the source operands unchanged. A *post-execution* exception is reported after a value is stored, which may change one or more of the source operands. A pre-execution exception is analogous to a fault, except that the saved CS and EIP values do not point to the instruction causing the exception. Similarly, a post-execution exception is analogous to a trap.

The I, IS, D, and Z exceptions are always pre-execution exceptions. The P exception is always a post-execution exception. The U and O exceptions are pre-execution exceptions for store instructions (FST(P), FIST(P), and FBST(P)) to memory. Otherwise, U and O are post-execution exceptions, including stores to the accumulator stack.

The coprocessor error handler may simply report the error to the screen or a debugger and terminate the program causing the exception. If the coprocessor error handler wishes instead to resume the program causing the exception, it must complete the floating-point instruction causing the exception either by interpreting the instruction (for pre-execution exceptions) or adjusting the result (for post-execution exceptions) before returning. The exception handler can read the status-word register to determine which unmasked exception occurred, and can read and decode the instruction by using the instruction-pointer registers FCS and FIP. Before returning from the coprocessor error handler, the unmasked status-word exception status bits must be cleared by executing an FCLEX, FLDENV, or FRSTOR instruction.

The masked exception response provided by the 80387 is best in most cases. We recommend that all exceptions except invalid operation be masked. An invalid operation exception occurs only when a reasonable result cannot be provided that would permit the computation to continue, such as adding $+\infty$ and $-\infty$, or dividing 0 by 0.

Coprocessor Error Categories

The six categories of coprocessor error exceptions are described in the following sections. These descriptions divide the floating-point instructions into two classes: computational and noncomputational. The computational instructions are those in the data transfer, arithmetic, comparison, and transcendental instruction subgroupings defined in Chapter 3, except that the following instructions are in the noncomputational class:

1. FLD with a register or temporary real memory source operand.
2. FST(P) with a register or temporary real memory destination operand.
3. FXCH, FABS, FCHS, and FXAM.

Invalid Operation Exceptions

There are two categories of invalid operation exceptions: those that are due to numerics errors, and those due to overflow/underflow of the 80387 accumulator stack. The SF bit in the status-word register distinguishes invalid operation exceptions due to stack underflow/overflow (SF = 1) from those due to numerics exceptions (SF = 0). The invalid operation exception is a pre-execution exception, so unmasked exceptions are reported before a result is stored.

Invalid Numeric Operation (SF = 0) An invalid operation exception is triggered for any of the cases listed in Table 6.5. If the invalid operation exception is masked, the indefinite quiet NaN value is returned (except FIST(P) stores the integer indefinite, and FBSTP stores the BCD indefinite). For operations that return two results, both are returned as indefinite quiet NaNs. Special cases are marked with footnotes.

If the invalid operation exception is unmasked, a coprocessor error exception is raised and no result is stored. The source operands are available to the exception handler.

Accumulator Stack Underflow/Overflow (SF = 1) An invalid operation exception is also triggered if an instruction attempts to read an accumulator tagged as empty (underflow), or to push a result onto the accumulator stack when the new stack top is not tagged as empty (overflow). Note that the destination register of FST(P) or FXCH is not considered as a push on the stack, so these instructions can write to a non-empty register. The C1 condition code bit in the status-word register indicates whether an underflow (C1 = 0) or overflow (C1 = 1) occurred.

INVALID OPERATION CONDITIONS

Operand of a computational instruction is in an unsupported format

Operand of a computational instruction is a signaling NaN

Operand of FCOM or FTST is a signaling or quiet NaN[1]

Operand of FUCOM is a signaling NaN[1]

Operands of FADD are infinities with opposite signs

Operands of FSUB are infinities with the same sign

Operands of FMUL are zero and infinity

Operands of FDIV are both infinity or both zero

Divisor is zero or dividend is infinity for FPREM or FPREM1[2]

Operand of FCOS, FPTAN, FSIN, or FSINCOS is infinity

Operand of FSQRT or FYL2X is less than 0

Operand of FYL2XP1 is less than −1

Operand of FIST or FBSTP is a NaN or infinity, or will not fit in destination

[1] If the invalid operation exception is masked, condition codes are set to "unordered": C3, C2, C0 all set to 1.

[2] If the invalid operation exception is masked, C2 is set to 1.

► **Table 6.5:** Invalid numeric operation summary

Denormal Exception

The denormal exception is reported if a source operand of a computational instruction is a denormal. If this exception is masked, the DE bit in the status-word register is set and the instruction proceeds using the denormal number. If masked, use of a denormal short or long real memory operand results in a conversion to a normal temporary real. Due to its expanded range, a normalized temporary real can hold a denormal short or long real.

If the exception is unmasked, the DE bit in the status-word register is set, a coprocessor exception is raised, and no result is stored, since the denormal exception is a pre-execution exception.

Since denormals have fewer significant bits than normal numbers, you may have to avoid denormals in certain algorithms. However, in most cases this exception should be masked so that the computation proceeds using the denormal operand.

Zero Divide Exception

The zero divide exception is reported if an FDIV or FYL2X instruction attempts to divide a finite operand by 0, or if the FXTRACT instruction has its operand 0. If the exception is masked, the result for FDIV or FYL2X is infinity with a sign that is the exclusive-or of the signs of the input operands. The masked result for FXTRACT is $-\infty$. In all cases, the ZE bit in the status word is set. If the exception is not masked, the ZE bit is set, a coprocessor exception is raised, and no result is stored, since the zero divide exception is a pre-execution exception.

Overflow Exception

The overflow exception is reported if the true result is too large to fit into the destination format. If this exception is masked, the OE bit in the status-word register is set, and the result that is stored depends on the rounding mode selected by the RC field in the control-word registers, as given in Table 6.6.

If the exception is unmasked, the OE bit is set and a coprocessor exception is reported. If an overflow occurs in an FST instruction with a memory destination, no result is stored. This allows the exception handler to take appropriate action with the source data still available in the accumulator stack.

A result is stored before reporting the coprocessor error exception if the destination is the accumulator stack. The value stored is the true result divided by $2^{24,576}$ after rounding the significand. Note that $24,576 = 3 * 2^{13}$. This extends the exponent range by "rebiasing" the exponent.

Underflow Exception

The underflow exception is reported if the true result is too small to fit into the destination format. If this exception is masked, the true result is denormalized and stored into the destination operand. If the exception is masked, the UE bit in the status-word register is set only if the denormalization results in a loss of precision, in which case the precision exception is also raised. This masked response supports gradual underflow through the use of denormals.

If the underflow exception is unmasked, the UE bit is set whether or not a loss of precision occurs, and a coprocessor exception is reported. If an underflow occurs in an FST instruction with a memory destination, no result is stored. This allows the exception handler to take appropriate action with the source data still available in the accumulator stack.

A result is stored before reporting the coprocessor error exception if the destination is the accumulator stack. The value stored is the true result multiplied by $2^{24,576}$ after rounding the significand. Note that $24,576 = 3 * 2^{13}$. This extends the exponent range by "rebiasing" the exponent.

Precision (IEEE Inexact) Exception

The precision exception is reported if the result cannot be represented exactly in the destination format, or if an underflow results in a loss of

ROUNDING MODE	RESULT SIGN	MASKED RESULT
To nearest	+	$+\infty$
	–	$-\infty$
Toward $-\infty$	+	Largest finite positive number
	–	$-\infty$
Toward $+\infty$	+	$+\infty$
	–	Largest finite negative number
Toward 0	+	Largest finite positive number
	–	Largest finite negative number

► **Table 6.6:** Masked overflow results

accuracy. Note that the C1 condition code bit in the status-word register indicates the direction of the last rounding in computational instructions. C1 = 0 indicates that the last operation rounded down, so the result delivered is smaller than the true result. C1 = 1 indicates that the last operation rounded up, so the result delivered is larger than the true result. If the exception is masked, the PE bit is set in the status-word register, and the rounded result is stored into the destination. If the exception is unmasked, the PE bit is set, the rounded result is stored into the destination, and a coprocessor error exception is raised.

The precision exception provides notice when a computation is inexact. This is important in few cases, such as when operating with money. This exception should be masked in most applications.

Precedence of Coprocessor Error Exceptions

If more than one exception condition is detected in an instruction, only one is reported. Which exception is reported is determined by the exception precedence listed in Table 6.7. Note that a precision exception can be reported with an underflow or overflow exception.

EXCEPTION	PRECEDENCE
Invalid operation	Highest
• Stack underflow	
• Stack overflow	
• Unsupported format	
• Signaling NaN	
• Other	
Zero divide	
Denormal	
Overflow/underflow	
Precision	Lowest

► **Table 6.7:** Coprocessor error exception precedence

Operating System Examples

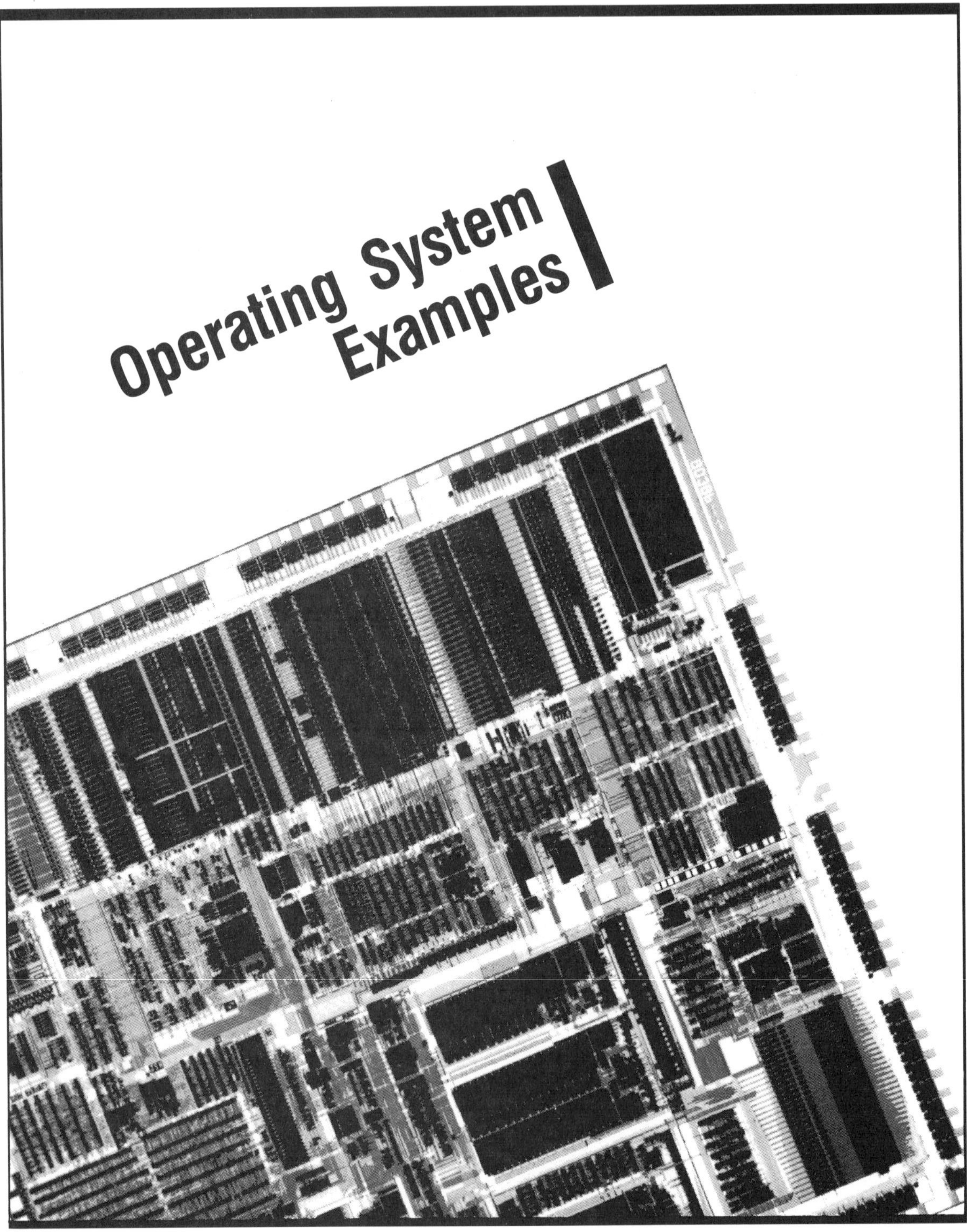

Chapter 

CHAPTER 4 PRESENTED A SET OF EXAMPLES demonstrating the features and instructions of the 80386 available to the applications programmer. These features were presented in Chapters 1 and 2, and part of Chapter 3. Chapters 5 and 6, and part of Chapter 3, presented features and instructions of the 80386 intended for the operating-system programmer. This chapter will present examples on the use of these operating-system features.

► Syntax

As in Chapter 4, we need to present a bit more syntax of the assembly language. Most of the new constructs relate to the definition of segments.

SEGMENT/ENDS

SEGMENT and ENDS are assembler directives that define the beginning and end of a segment. Directives such as these do not generate any code; rather, they tell the assembler how to generate code.

USE32/USE16

USE is an assembler directive that indicates whether the contents of this segment are 32-bit or 16-bit code or data. A USE32 segment will cause the assembler to generate code assuming the descriptor for this segment has the D bit equal to 1. Note that the programmer could have made an error (the assembler does not check) and not set the D bit for this descriptor. In this case, the program would fail, since the code or data in this segment is of incorrect size.

ORG

ORG is an assembler directive that defines an offset within a segment.

ASSUME

ASSUME is the final directive presented here. ASSUME is only meaningful for code segments. It indicates what to assume the segment register contents are within this segment. Without this directive, the assembler will issue messages warning that the addressed segment may not be currently addressable. This directive does not generate any code to load the indicated segment register with the specified segment.

Syntax Example

Below is a brief example demonstrating all the above directives.

```
Test_Code_Seg SEGMENT USE32
ASSUME DS:My_Segment
        MOV AX, My_Segment_Sel
        MOV DS, AX
        ; Code
        ORG 0FF0h
        ; More Code
Test_Code_Seg ENDS
```

A segment name Test_Code_Seg is defined by the SEGMENT and ENDS directives. It is a 32-bit segment as indicated by the USE32 directive. The segment is assembled assuming that DS addresses the segment named My_Segment. The first two lines of code in the segment satisfy this assumption. Finally, part of the code is given an origin in the segment of 0FF0h.

► Initialization Example

The first example is an initialization example that takes the machine from its reset state to a 32-bit flat machine, with paging enabled to run multiple tasks.

Overview of Example 1

Before beginning a detailed description of the code, it is helpful to first present a picture of what we want the final machine state to be. After this is presented, the details of how the machine gets into this state should be easier to understand.

This initialization example provides a simple core of an operating system. A real operating system is composed of thousands, if not millions, of lines of code (and we certainly aren't going to explain a million-line example here). Many, many things are missing, but enough of the basics remain to demonstrate most of the operating-system and multiple-segment instruction semantics.

Assumptions

We make a few assumptions about the underlying hardware.

1. The operating-system code resides in a ROM (read-only memory) in highest physical memory. The ROM is assumed to be at least 64K bytes in size (begins at FFFF0000h and ends at FFFFFFFFh).
2. RAM (random access memory) begins at address 0, and the machine has at least 48K bytes of memory. Our example does not try to figure out exactly how much memory the hardware provides (a necessary thing for a complete operating system to do). It simply assumes at least 48K bytes are present.

Other than these assumptions, the example is complete and self-contained.

Multitasking and Protection

At the conclusion of the example, the necessary operating-system tables will have been developed and a single user task will be invoked. We've taken care, however, to allow multiple tasks to be executing on this machine at one time. Two protection levels are used in the example: 0 for the operating system and 3 for the application program. The operating system, however, is typically shared by all tasks within the system. Each task has its own private code and data regions, which are stored in the local address space and so are not visible to other tasks within the system. The operating system is shared by all tasks and is therefore stored in the global address space. Figure 7.1 demonstrates this. The concentric circles represent the protection levels (we make use of only 0 and 3), and the radial lines distinguish between tasks within the system.

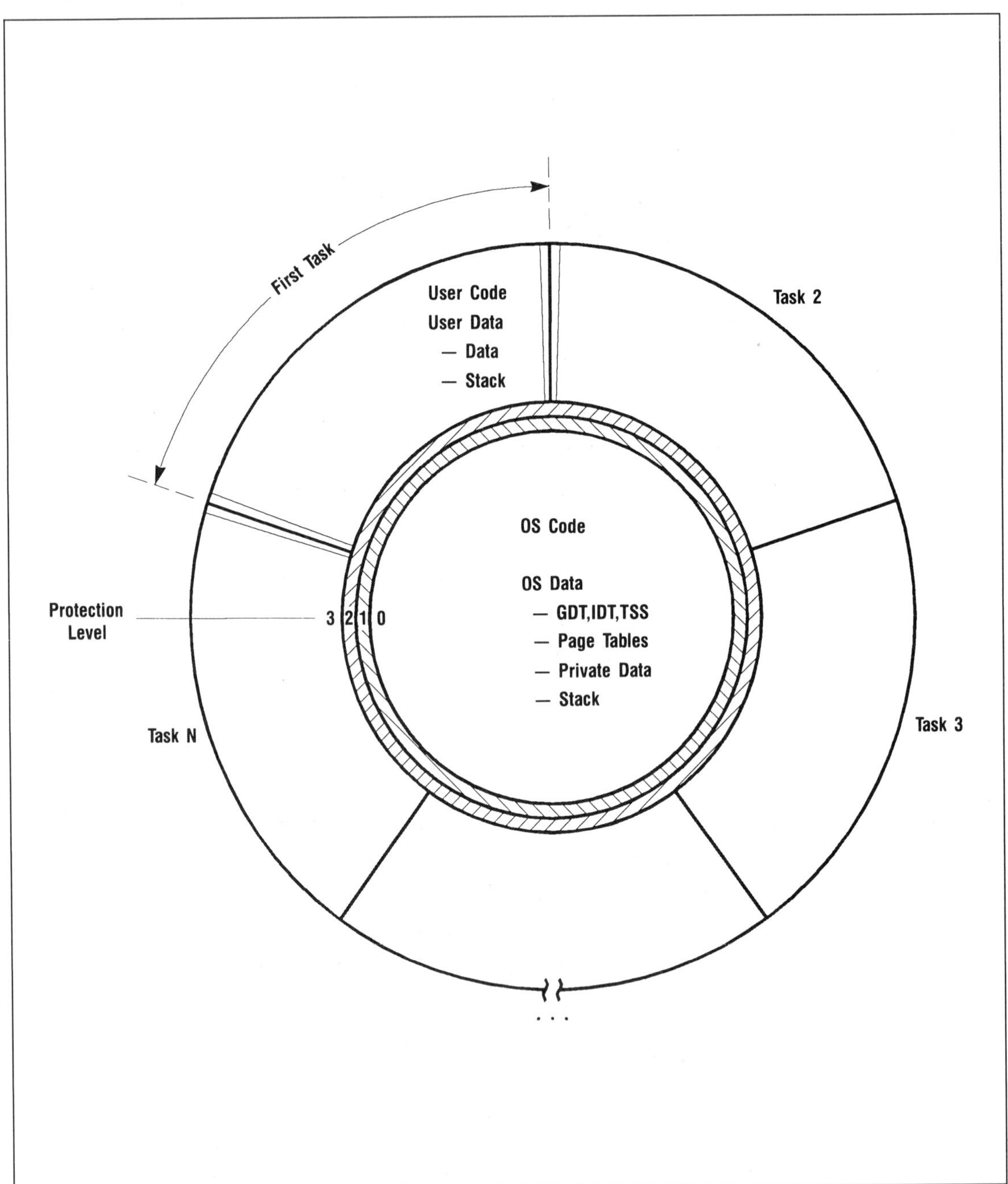

► **Figure 7.1:** Multiple-task system

Each radial slice of the pie indicates a task boundary. Except for the global address regions of each task's virtual address space, an address in task 1 is unrelated to an equal-value address in task 2.

Virtual Address Space

Figure 7.2 depicts the virtual address space of each task. The virtual address space is composed of the global address space mapped by the GDT and the local address space mapped by the LDT. The global address space contains five segments.

1. The GDT itself, which contains descriptors that define the other four segments in this global address space.
2. The TSS of the first task. When many tasks are executing, a TSS would be defined for each.
3. The operating-system data segment.
4. The operating-system code segment.
5. The LDT of the first task, which maps the segments in the local address space. When many tasks are executing, a LDT would be defined for each.

The local address space contains two segments.

1. The user code segment.
2. The user data segment containing data and stack.

Applications see a single-segment model containing a single data segment and a single code segment, as discussed in Chapter 5.

Linear Address Space

The linear address space is shown in Figure 7.3. There are four segments in the linear address space, which are described below.

1. Operating-system data (OS Data), a 16M segment beginning at linear address 0 and continuing to 00FFFFFFh. This segment contains the system segment tables (GDT, IDT, TSS), the page tables (directory and second-level tables), local data for the operating system, and the stack for the operating system.
2. User code, a 1M segment beginning at 01000000h and continuing to 010FFFFFh. The choice of 1M in size is arbitrary. When the task is actually loaded, the code segment size will be known exactly and the segment limit can be adjusted appropriately.

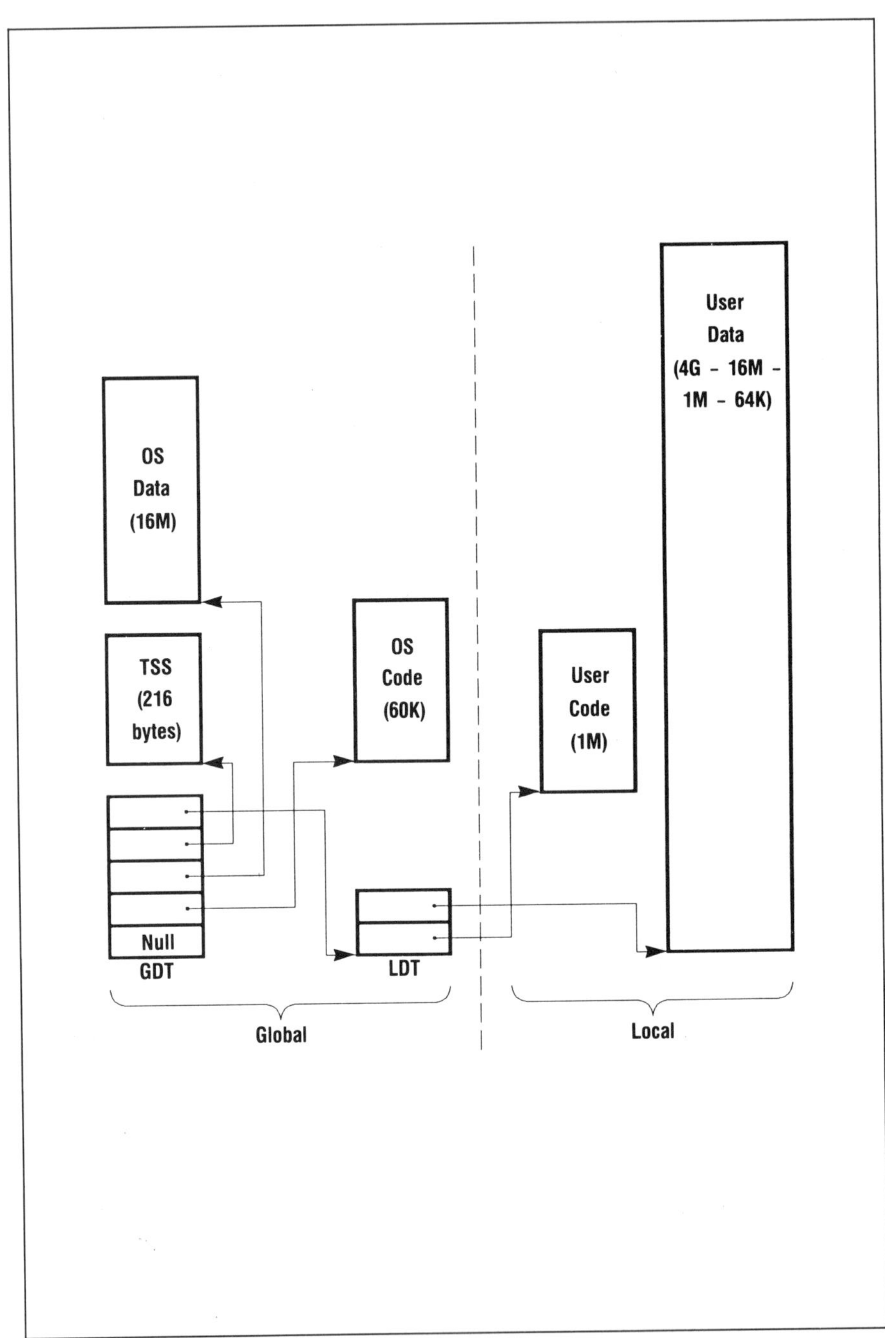

► **Figure 7.2:** Virtual address space

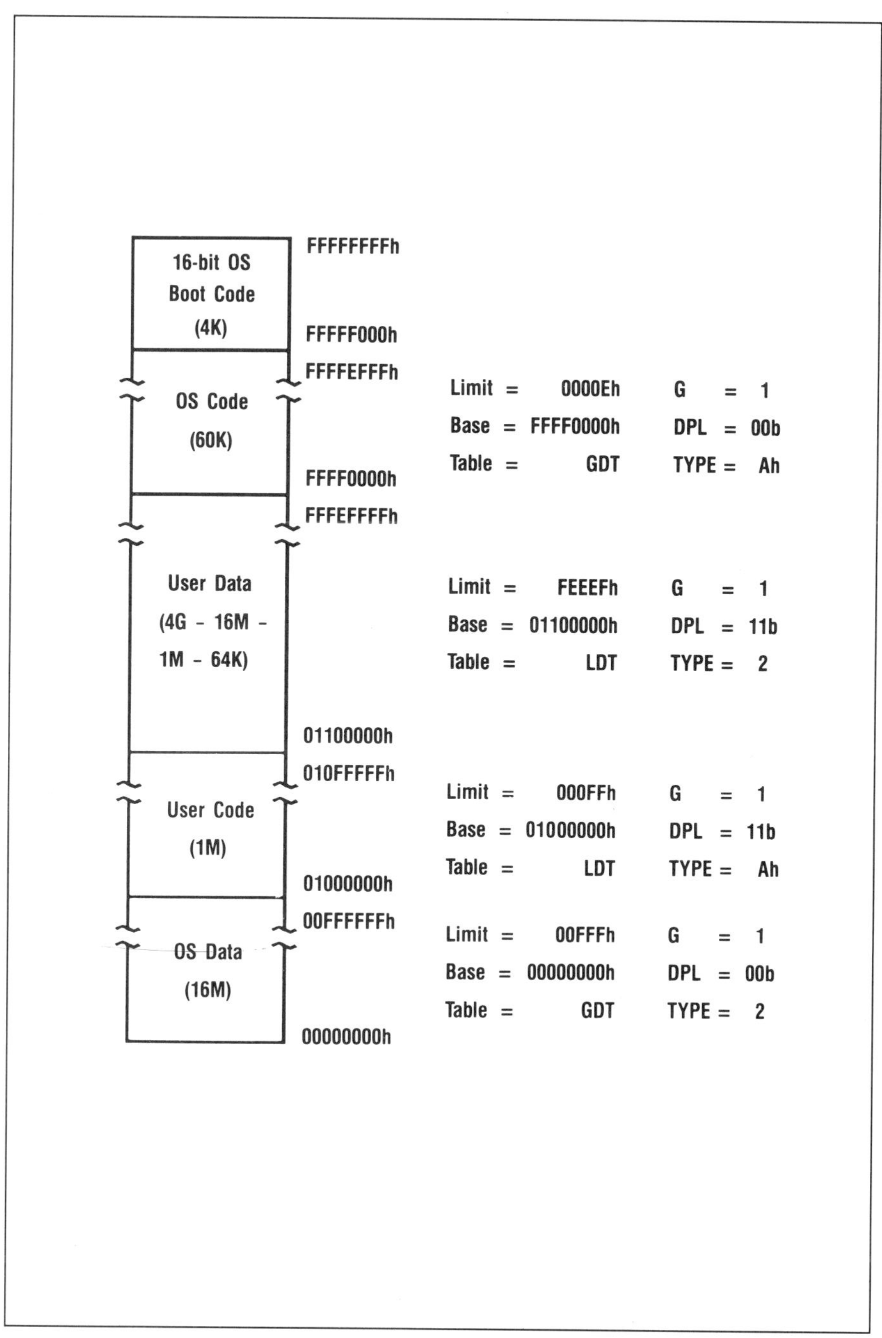

► **Figure 7.3:** Linear address space of each task

3. User data. All memory not required by the operating system or by the user's code is given to the user's program in one enormous data segment. The segment begins at linear address 01100000h and continues to FFFEFFFh. Thus, the size of this segment is

   4G – 16M – 1M – 64K

   (quite a large data array indeed!). In this segment, the stack starts at the top and grows down, and the data starts at the bottom and grows up.
4. Operating-system code (OS Code). This segment begins at linear address FFFF0000h and ends at FFFFEFFFh (the top of a task's virtual memory space). The example assumes that all code within the operating system fits within a 64K ROM (not likely for a real operating system, but fine for this example).
5. The boot code segment begins at linear address FFFFF000h and continues to FFFFFFFFh. Thus, the upper 4K of the boot ROM are dedicated to the 16-bit start-up code. Note that this segment is not addressable in the example after protection has been enabled.

The choice of where these segments reside in the linear address space is completely arbitrary except for the boot code, which must begin at physical address FFFFFFF0h. The mapping for both the operating-system code and data are chosen so their linear and physical addresses are the same. We'll give a thorough explanation of this in the detailed discussion of the initialization code below. The linear address location of the application code and data segment is somewhat arbitrary.

Page Mapping

The linear address space—the address space after translation by the segmentation mechanism—is mapped by the page tables, as shown in Figure 7.4. The figure shows the linear address space divided into 4M regions. This is the amount of memory that is mapped by a page table (1K page entries with 4K bytes per page). Five tables with pointers from the page directory are set up. A sixth directory entry points back to the page directory itself. A directory entry pointing to the directory is a simple means of mapping the page tables back into the linear address space to allow access to them, as explained in detail below. The six-page directory entries and page tables that are set up are:

1. Common operating-system data. GDT, IDT, and TSS tables in particular.

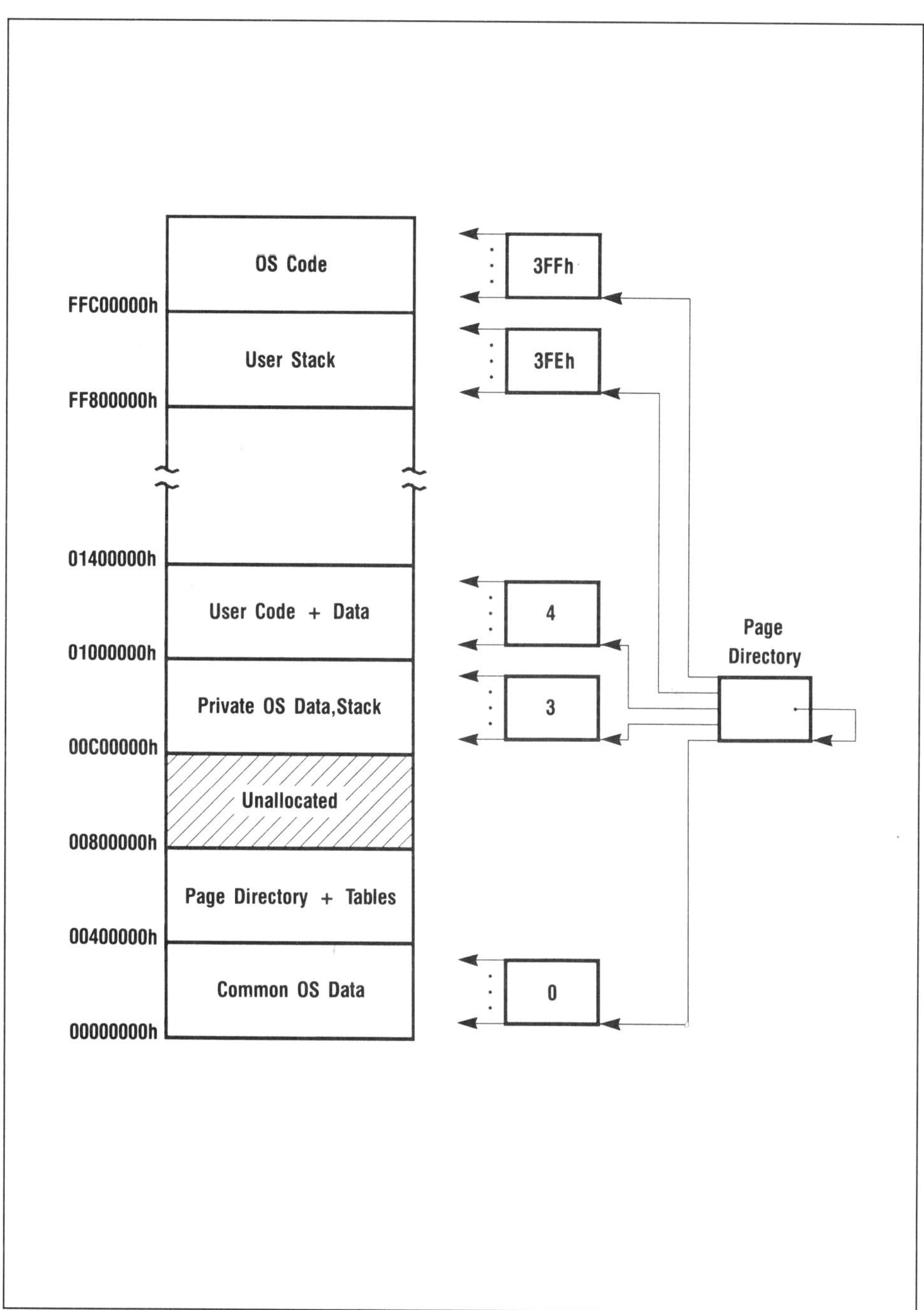

► **Figure 7.4:** Page tables map linear address space

2. Page directory and page tables.
3. Private operating-system data. Miscellaneous operating-system data and the operating-system stack.
4. User code and data.
5. User stack.
6. Operating-system code.

Physical Address

The physical address space is given in Figure 7.5. A total of 28 pages (each page is 4K) have been allocated. The lower 12 pages are defined in the RAM area beginning at address 0, continuing up to the page starting at address 0B000h. Sixteen pages are allocated in high memory, beginning at address 0FFFF0000h. These pages match exactly the 64K ROM area in high memory, which we discussed earlier in this chapter.

Now that we've discussed both linear and physical address spaces, it is very interesting to compare them and make several observations.

1. The operating-system code region is at the high 64K bytes in both. As the machine is being initialized, this is helpful, as we will see in the detailed code below. The code could have been at different addresses in the different address spaces, but this would have made the example more difficult to understand as well as write! This is particularly true when protection and, later, paging are enabled.
2. The GDT, IDT, TSS, and LDT tables are located at the same address in both. If this were not the case, these tables would have to be re-created or moved, and descriptors reloaded after protection was enabled and again after paging was enabled. To avoid this complication, we have kept them at the same address. Thus, we only need to load and build them once.
3. The physical addresses for the remainder of the pages do not match the linear addresses. This is done to minimize the amount of physical memory required to map the linear address space. This is one of the major benefits of paging: a linear address space that is larger than physical memory is allowed. We have, however, kept the physical pages in approximately the same order as they appear in the linear address space. Except for points 1 and 2 above, the location of the pages in physical memory is arbitrary. In fact, these pages could be moved later, as the paging mechanism replaces certain inactive pages with other

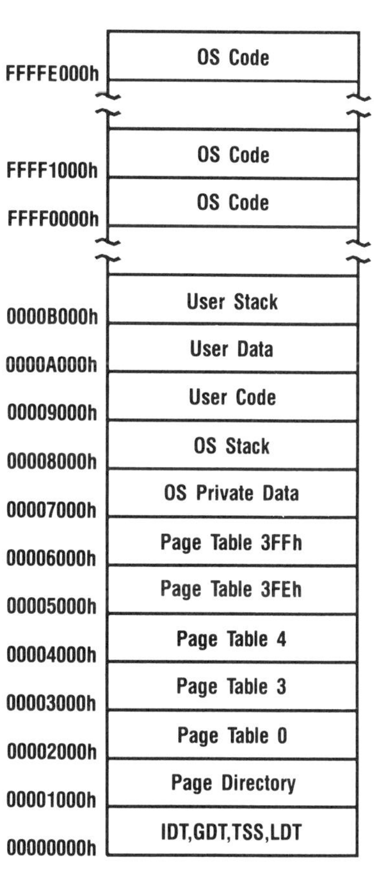

► **Figure 7.5:** Physical address space

active pages. Not only can we swap portions of the linear address space by paging, we can even page the page tables (this may be necessary to minimize the amount of physical memory dedicated to the operating system, since the page tables can get quite large). To page the page tables, some care has to be taken in updating the invalid page table entries and distinguishing them from simple page entries. The page directory needs to remain in the same location and must always be present. Changing the location of the page directory requires the page directory base register (CR3) to be updated.

Task Switch

We do not go through the details of building and switching to a new task (such as the second task in the system), but it is helpful to point out what is needed to accomplish this.

1. An LDT needs to be built for the new task. It would be identical to the one in the example except for the different code space sizes possible. A GDT entry would have to be created for this LDT.
2. A TSS would have to be built. It is similar to the one built in the example, except that the LDT is the one described above. A GDT entry would have to be created for this TSS.
3. A page directory needs to be built. The page tables that map the global address space are identical to the first task, and these page directory entries are shared by both (and all future) tasks. The directory entries for the local page tables (user code and data and stack) are, of course, different.
4. Page tables for the local address space for the new task need to be built. They are the same as the page tables for the first task, except that they map to different physical pages.
5. To switch to the new task requires the loading of TR, LDTR, and CR0. The actual task switch can be accomplished by the techniques described in Chapter 5.

Details of Initialization Example

With the overview of the desired final machine state given above, we are now ready to dig into the details of the example. The example in Listing 7.1 (beginning on page 614) can actually be considered many short examples that are executed in the proper sequence to form a complete initialization sequence.

Equates

The first section of the example simply defines some mnemonics for later use. All seven selectors (five in the GDT and two in the LDT) are defined. The physical addresses of all pages are also defined. Since the linear addresses and physical addresses for these tables do not all match, we define the physical address mnemonics here. Note that these physical addresses do match Figure 7.5, which shows the physical address space.

Segment Definitions

The four segments of the example are defined next (OS_Data_Seg, User_Code_Seg, User_Data_Seg and OS_Code_Seg). These segment definitions exactly match the picture of virtual and linear address spaces given in Figures 7.2 and 7.3, respectively. The segment definitions given here enable us to use symbolic references to the segments throughout the remainder of the example. Declaring the segments in this way does not initialize these memory segments.

Also note that the OS_Code segment does not cover the upper 4K of memory. The upper 4K of operating-system code is contained within a separate segment (BootRom16). This segment is a 16-bit segment, whereas OS_Code_Seg is a 32-bit segment. Since the 80386 begins in a 16-bit mode of operation, we need at least a small region of code to take us from 16-bit mode into the 32-bit mode of operation. After protected mode is entered, this 16-bit segment is not addressable. The example minimizes the amount of time spent in this backward-compatible 16-bit mode of operation. The goal of minimizing 16-bit code matches the theme of the book—focus on the 32-bit 80386.

Code Sequence 1—Cold Start

At reset, the 80386 begins operation in what is termed *real mode.* This mode is defined in detail in Chapter 9. For our purposes, real mode is simply a 16-bit machine where the maximum size of a segment is 64K bytes. In real mode, the selector is shifted left by 4 and added to the offset within the segment to form the physical address (see Figure 9.2). Thus, the maximum physical address is 0FFFFFh or a total address space of 1M byte. The machine state at reset is given in Table 9.3. Reference is made to the initial machine state in the following sections.

At reset, the CS register is initialized to F000h and IP is initialized to FFF0h. Thus, the first instruction fetch after reset would be done to address FFFF0h. In addition, the 80386 keeps the address bits A31 to A20 asserted such that the first instruction fetch is done to address FFFFFFF0h. So the 16-bit code segment is located at address

FFFF0000h to match the initial CS value, and the ORG of the cold start code (JMP Start16, on page 624) is to offset 0FFF0h. Address bits A31 to A20 remain asserted until the first intersegment control transfer. It is common practice for machines to begin execution at the highest memory location, as the 80386 does. This allows a boot ROM to be placed in high memory.

Code Sequence 2—Miscellaneous

This sequence begins at the *Start16* label (see page 622). The first instruction clears the IF (interrupt enable) bit, masking all maskable interrupts. Clearing IF is not really needed, since the 80386 reset sequence clears IF also, but it is shown here for emphasis. The IDT (interrupt descriptor table) is also set to have a limit of 0. This causes any nonmaskable interrupts to generate a shutdown (discussed in Chapter 6). Since the LIDT instruction requires a memory operand, we need to first initialize the DS register to point at the OS_Data_Seg. Since the DS register is initialized to 0 and OS_Data_Seg is at address 0, this was not needed. But since in most cases (except a few like this one) loading a segment register is needed prior to addressing a segment, we do so here.

Code Sequence 3—Build GDT, LGDT

The third section of code builds the GDT (global descriptor table) and loads the GDT pseudo-descriptor into the processor.

The first step is to fill the GDT with the appropriate information. In the example, we have five GDT entries (Null, OS Code, OS Data, LDT, and TSS). Table 7.1 summarizes the contents of these five descriptors. The code shows the appropriate decomposition of this information into the descriptor format (given in Figure 5.10). Table 7.2 summarizes the descriptor types used here.

The last step is to build a pseudo-descriptor in memory. The low word is the limit of the GDT. The limit is eight times the number of GDT entries minus 1, the largest valid offset within the GDT. The upper dword of the pseudo-descriptor is the linear address of the GDT. This pseudo-descriptor is then loaded into the processor with the LGDT instruction.

Code Sequence 4—Enter Protected Mode

The next step is to set the PE (protection enable) bit of the machine status word. After the PE bit is set, it is important to immediately perform a jump. This causes the on-chip prefetch and decode queues to be flushed (set to empty). This is necessary because any prefetched and predecoded information pertains to real mode, which is no longer valid.

The machine is now in 16-bit protected mode. For our purposes, this mode is similar to what we have discussed so far in the book, except that all data and offsets are 16 bits. This mode is discussed in more detail in Chapter 9.

After protected mode has been entered, a far JMP is executed. The JMP references the Start32 location within the OS Code segment. Since

NAME	TABLE	LIMIT	BASE	TYPE	DT	DPL	P	D	G
Null	GDT	00000	00000000	0	0	0	0	0	0
OS Code	GDT	0000E	FFFF0000	A	1	0	1	1	1
OS Data	GDT	FFFFF	00000000	2	1	0	1	1	1
User Code	LDT	000FF	01000000	A	1	3	1	1	1
User Data	LDT	FEEEF	01100000	2	1	3	1	1	1
TSS1	GDT	000D7	000000B0	9	0	0	1	0*	0
LDT1	GDT	0000F	00000188	2	0	0	1	0*	0

* *Note:* The D bit for a system segment has no meaning.

► **Table 7.1:** Summary of descriptor contents

TYPE	DT	DESCRIPTION
2	1	Memory Segment—Read/Write
A	1	Memory Segment—Execute/Read
9	0	System Segment—Available 386 TSS
2	0	System Segment—LDT

► **Table 7.2:** Descriptor types

the GDT entry for the OS Code segment defines a 32-bit code segment (as indicated by the D bit of the descriptor), the machine will be executing as a 32-bit machine when the JMP is completed. At this point, the machine is (finally) in the state assumed by Chapters 1 through 6.

Code Sequence 5—Load Segment Descriptors

This sequence begins at the label Start32 on page 617. Since the machine is now in protected mode, it is necessary to reload the segment registers to make the data segments addressable. Note the difference between the load of the DS register performed here and the one done in Code Sequence 2, when the machine was still in real mode. In the load of the DS register in real mode, the selector value loaded into DS is simply shifted left by 4 and added to the offset to form the final physical address. Now that we have enabled protected mode, loading a selector into DS causes the descriptor given in the GDT to be loaded (as discussed in Chapter 5). The selector is also loaded into ES for use by string instructions. SS will be loaded with this selector later.

Code Sequence 6—Build LDT, LLDT

The local address space of the task is mapped by the LDT (local descriptor table). The LDT contains two entries, one for the user code segment and one for the user data segment, as seen in Figure 7.2. When the GDT was built, an LDT entry was included that defined an LDT of two entries. The LDT segment is defined as a piece of the OS_Data segment. The initialization example uses alias locations in the OS_Data segment to access the LDT, while the 80386 uses the actual LDT segment. The first part of this example fills this LDT with the appropriate information for these two segments (user code and data). The code shows the appropriate decomposition of the descriptor information into the descriptor format. Table 7.1 summarizes the descriptor information for the two segments mapped by the LDT. After the LDT is built, the selector for the LDT is loaded into the LDTR.

Much of the protected model initialization (GDT, IDT, TSS) can be done either before or after entering protected mode. Since our goal was to minimize the amount of 16-bit code written, all of these except for the GDT are done after entering protected mode. Since loading of the LDTR can only be done in protected mode, we did not have a choice where to perform it.

Code Sequence 7—Build IDT

A very important part of initialization is building the IDT (interrupt descriptor table). In our example, after user mode (level 3) execution begins, the only way for the task to access the operating-system services is via the exception processing mechanism. Gates, as discussed in Chapter 5, allow levels of lesser privilege to access levels of greater privilege, but we have defined no gates in our example.

The IDT entries themselves are interrupt gates. Since in our flat machine model the entire operating system is visible to the current task, we need not use a task gate for the IDT entries. The format for gate descriptors is given in Figure 5.12. The basic contents of our interrupt gate descriptor are summarized in the following table. If an exception or interrupt is taken from level 3, a privilege-level change to level 0 will occur. As discussed in Chapter 5, each protection level (0–3) has a separate stack. Thus, as part of the transition from level 3 to 0, the stack is switched to the level 0 stack.

Field	**Value**
Offset	offset Default_Hand
Selector	OS_Code_Sel
DwordCount	0, copy no parameters
Type	E, 386 Interrupt Gate
DPL	0

Aliases in the OS_Data segment are used to access the IDT. Initially, all 17 interrupt gates are filled with the same information. These 17 interrupt levels are those predefined by the 80386, and we don't define any additional ones at this point. After the 17 descriptors have been set to the default, we explicitly replace this information for interrupts that have specific handlers provided for them by the operating system. In this way, many interrupts that the operating system has no interest in distinguishing between go to the same default handler. The exception handlers given at the start of the OS_Code_Seg are obviously trivial, and are for the purpose of demonstrating the declaration of an exception handler. A more elaborate example of an exception handler (a coprocessor device not available—exception 7) is the subject of the second example in this chapter.

Code Sequence 8—Build Page Directory

Now that the segmentation model is built, we are ready to begin setting up the paging mechanism of the 80386. As discussed in Chapter 5, the paging mechanism has two levels of memory-resident translation tables: the page directory and page tables (see Figure 5.15 for details of the two-level paging mechanism). This code sequence discusses building the page directory, and the following section discusses building the individual page tables. The format for the page table entries is given in Figure 5.17.

Each entry (of the 1024 possible) in the page directory points to a page table. Since each page table has 1024 entries, each pointing to a 4096-byte page, each page directory entry is mapping up to 4M of memory. If the page directory entry is marked not present, the corresponding 4M of the linear address space is not present (unmapped). The first step of this code sequence marks all tables not present (bit 0 of each entry is the P or present bit, which is set to 0). Each page directory entry that is to map a valid section of the linear address space is then updated with the pertinent information. This information is:

1. Present bit (= 1)
2. User/supervisor privilege level
3. Read/write
4. Physical address of the page table this entry points to

All entries are marked supervisor read-only except the user code and data and user stack directories, which are marked user-writable. The page table address inserted into each of these is the physical address of the page table.

The second page table entry is particularly interesting. This directory entry points to the directory itself. This may seem a bit confusing at first, but this is a convenient means to map the page directory and page tables into the linear address space. Figure 7.6 demonstrates this. Page directory entry 0000000001b points to the page directory.

A linear address of 00C00010h

31 ... 22	21 ... 12	11 ... 0
0000000011	0000000000	000000010000

is a normal access through page directory entry 3, through page table 0 to address 10h within this page, as is seen in the first part of Figure 7.6.

The second example shows that linear address 00403000h

31 ... 22	21 ... 12	11 ... 0
0000000001	0000000011	000000000000

will access the first entry (dword) in page table 3, as seen in the second part of Figure 7.6.

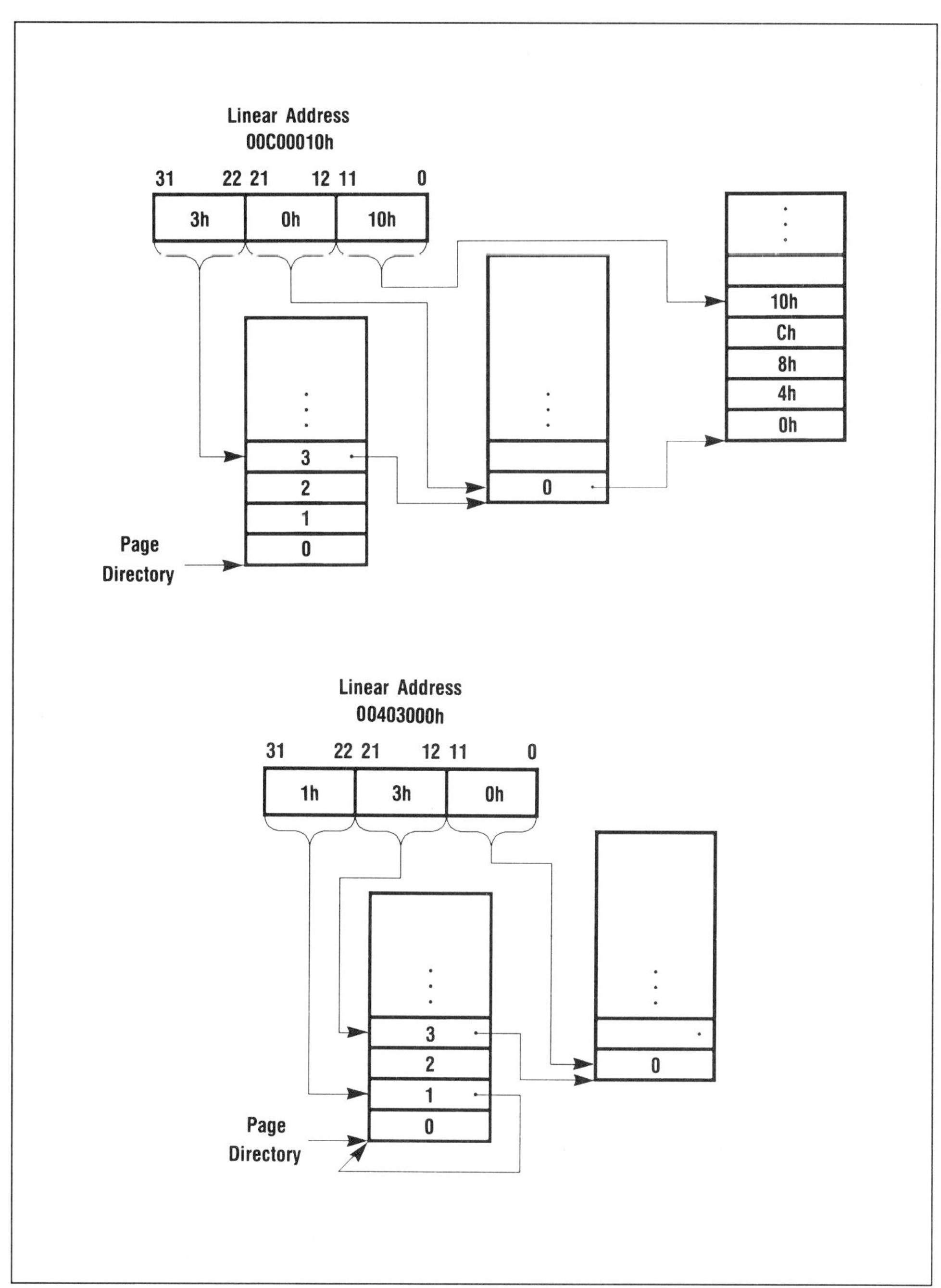

► **Figure 7.6:** Page directory pointing to self

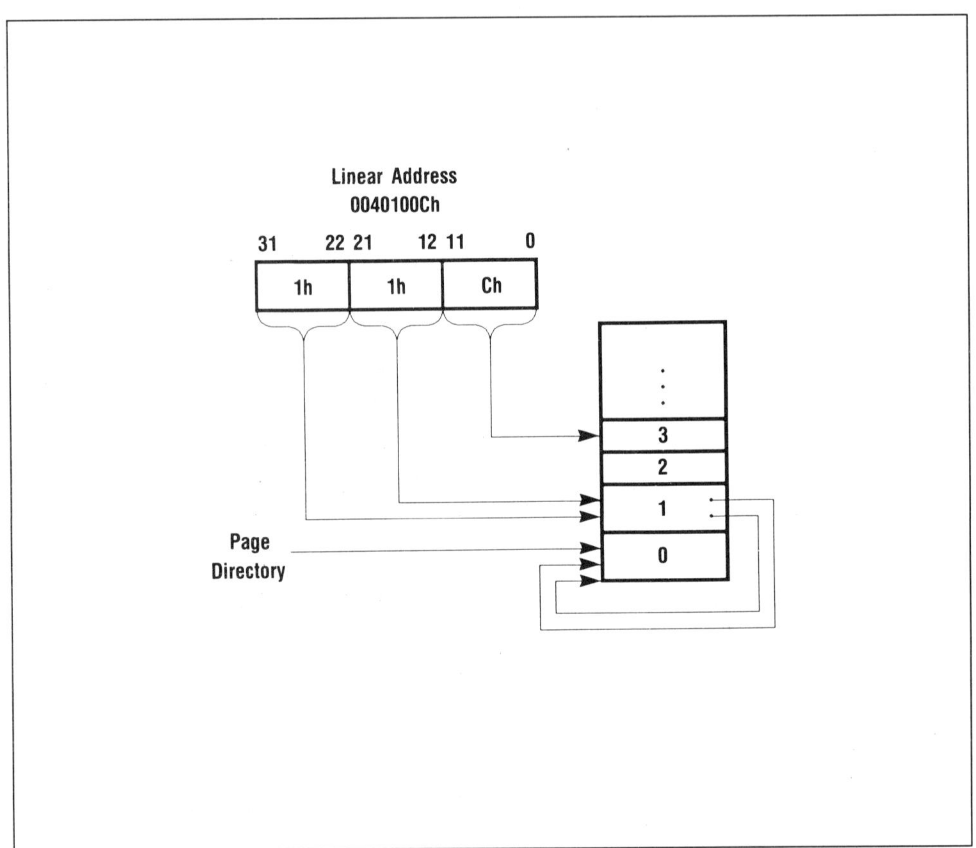

► **Figure 7.6:** Page directory pointing to self (continued)

The third example shows how linear address 0040100Ch

31 … 22	21 … 12	11 … 0
0000000001	0000000001	000000001100

will access the fourth entry (dword) in the page directory, as seen in the third part of Figure 7.6.

Code Sequence 9—Build Page Tables

After the page directory is built, tables need to be built for each valid directory entry. As was the case for building the directory, the first thing to do is fill the entire table with not-present entries and then selectively insert valid entries into the tables. As discussed above, making the linear address space identical to the physical is an important consideration in building the page table. At this point, we need to keep the following addresses the same in the linear and physical address spaces:

1. The operating-system code executing out of ROM, 16 pages starting at physical address FFFF0000h, FFFF1000h...FFFFF000h, are given identical locations in the linear and physical address spaces. Otherwise, a *magic jump* will be executed when paging is enabled. *Magic* means that the next instruction will be fetched from the linear address that maps to a different physical address than the one prior to enabling paging.
2. The GDT, IDT, and TSS are stored in the page beginning at physical address 00000000h, which is also given the same linear address. Otherwise, we need to reload these registers and rebuild the associated tables after paging is enabled.

Refer to Figure 7.5 (the physical address space) and compare the page table entries that are filled to the allocated pages in the figure. Table 7.3 summarizes the pages allocated and the access allowed to them.

DIRECTORY ENTRY	TABLE ENTRY	USER	WRITE	COMMENT
0	0	No	No	IDT, GDT, TSS
1	0	No	No	Page Table 0
1	1	No	No	Page Directory
1	3	No	No	Page Table 3
1	4	No	No	Page Table 4
1	3FEh	No	No	Page Table 3FE
1	3FFh	No	No	Page Table 3FF
3	0	No	No	OS Private Data
3	3FFh	No	No	OS Stack
4	0	Yes	No	User Code
4	100h	Yes	Yes	User Data
3FEh	3FFh	Yes	Yes	User Stack
3FFh	3F0-3FFh	No	No	OS Code

► **Table 7.3:** Allocated pages

Code Sequence 10—Enable Paging

The page directory and tables are ready. All that is needed to enable paging is to set the PG bit of CR0. After paging is enabled, it is important to perform a jump that will flush both the prefetch queue and the instruction decode queue. As was the case when protection was being enabled above, the information in these queues was prefetched and decoded when paging was disabled and is no longer valid.

Code Sequence 11—Load Operating-System Stack Pointer

This code segment simply loads the operating-system stack pointer. As discussed in Chapter 5, each protection level (0–3) has a different stack. Since our example only uses levels 0 and 3, only two stacks are required. Note the use of the LSS instruction. LSS avoids any of the difficulties that may arise when SS and ESP are loaded separately. In this case, interrupts are disabled and no possible exceptions can occur, so using LSS would not be needed. Nevertheless, it is good practice to always use LSS rather than two separate instructions.

Code Sequence 12—Build TSS

During privilege-level changes or task switches, the TSS will be referenced to retrieve or store information for later use. For example, the first exception (maybe a page fault, for instance) will require a privilege-level transition from 3 (the user level) to 0 (the operating-system level). As part of this change, stacks will be changed. The 80386 expects to find the level 0 stack selector and offset at the appropriate locations in the TSS. The only information we need to put in the TSS is

1. Level 0 stack offset
2. Level 0 stack selector
3. Page directory base (CR3)
4. LDT
5. Offset of I/O Bit Map
6. Debug Trap bit (set to 0)

The I/O Bit Map offset is set to 8000h, which is beyond the TSS limit, to specify an empty map.

The TR (task register) is then loaded to make the TSS visible to the processor.

Also note that the TSS has room allocated for floating-point state. The uppermost byte of the TSS is set to 0 to indicate this task has not yet used the coprocessor.

Load User Task

Almost all aspects of initialization are now complete, and we are ready to load the user's task. The example assumes the existence of a procedure *loader,* which takes the selectors for the code segment and data segment for the task. The loader routine will then read the code and data for the task from disk (for instance) into memory. Since the task may be quite large, the first page of code and data are loaded into memory while the rest of the task is kept in virtual storage on the swapping disk until the appropriate page faults force them to be read into memory. The loader routine returns the offset of the start of the task (the first instruction to be executed in the task) in the EAX register.

When the local descriptors were built (Code Sequence 6), we arbitrarily made the user code area 1M in size and gave the rest of memory (most of the 4G of linear address space) to the user data area. The loader would readjust the User_Code_Seg limit and User_Data_Seg base appropriately, as the task was loaded.

Prepare for User Task Invocation

As discussed in Chapter 5, calls to outer levels are not allowed. Instead, returns are done to outer levels. Thus, we put an image on the stack composed of

- Stack selector
- Stack offset
- Flags
- Code selector
- Code offset (returned by loader)

for the user task. When a subsequent IRET is done, it will *return* to the user program at level 3 to begin execution of the first user task of the system.

Note that interrupts are enabled by setting the IF bit in the flags image on the stack. As part of the IRET, interrupts will be enabled, not prematurely as would be the case if a STI would be executed while still in the operating-system code.

Invoke User Task

Finally, we reach the magic IRET. The first user-level task is invoked, and our example is complete. The IRET will retrieve the information just pushed onto the stack and change machine state appropriately. In this case, the protection level, stack, CS:EIP, and flags are changed.

```
; ****************************************************************
; * Take the machine from its reset state to completely
; * initialized as a flat machine and invoke the first
; * user task. Major portions of this program are building the
; * appropriate segmentation tables and building the paging
; * tables.
; *
; * The example is composed of 15 steps:
; * 1)  Boot Address cold start
; * 2)  Misc: Disable interrupts, load DS, null IDTR
; * 3)  Build GDT, LGDT
; * 4)  Enter protected mode/32b code
; * 5)  Load segment registers
; * 6)  Build LDT, LLDT
; * 7)  Build IDT, LIDT
; * 8)  Build page directory
; * 9)  Build page tables
; * 10) Enable paging
; * 11) Load OS stack
; * 12) Build TSS, LTR
; * 13) Load user task
; * 14) Prepare for user task invocation
; * 15) Invoke user task!
; ****************************************************************

                  NAME    Initial
; Miscellaneous Constants
IDT_Entries       EQU     17
GDT_Entries       EQU     5          ; Null, OS Data, LDT
                                     ; OS Code, TSS
LDT_Entries       EQU     2          ; User Code, User Data

Page_Size         EQU     4096
Page_Entries      EQU     1024
Not_Present       EQU     0
PE                EQU     1
PG                EQU     80000000h
Int_Flag          EQU     0200h

; GDT Selectors
Null              EQU     0h
OS_Code_Sel       EQU     8h         ; 1,GDT,RPL=00
OS_Data_Sel       EQU     10h        ; 2,GDT,RPL=00
LDT1_Sel          EQU     18h        ; 3,GDT,RPL=00
TSS1_Sel          EQU     20h        ; 4,GDT,RPL=00

; LDT Selectors
User_Code_Sel     EQU     7h         ; 0,LDT,RPL=11
User_Data_Sel     EQU     0Fh        ; 1,LDT,RPL=11
```

► **Listing 7.1:** Initialization code

```
; Physical Address Constants. Use these to initialize
; the page tables.
P_OS_GData      EQU     00000h
P_Page_Dir      EQU     01000h
P_Page_Tab0     EQU     02000h
P_Page_Tab3     EQU     03000h
P_Page_Tab4     EQU     04000h
P_Page_Tab3FE   EQU     05000h
P_Page_Tab3FF   EQU     06000h
P_OS_PData      EQU     07000h
P_OS_Stack      EQU     08000h
P_User_Code     EQU     09000h
P_User_Data     EQU     0A000h
P_User_Stack    EQU     0B000h

TSS_Size        EQU       104  ; Minimum TSS size
FP_Save         EQU       112  ; Save area is 108+4 (extra
                               ; word for flag that FP used)

; *********************
; *********************
; ** OS Data Segment
; *********************
; *********************
; Contains the segmentation and paging tables.
; Locate this segment at linear address 0.
OS_Data_Seg     SEGMENT  RW USE32  ; Locate AT 00000000h

; IDT_Table at Offset 0, GDT immediately above it,
; TSS immediately above GDT, LDT immediately
; above TSS.
IDT_Table       db IDT_Entries*8 DUP (?)
GDT_Table       db GDT_Entries*8 DUP (?)
TSS1_Table      db (TSS_Size+FP_Save) DUP (?)
LDT1_Table      db LDT_Entries*8 DUP (?)

pdescr          db 6 dup(?)  ;Build Pseudo-descriptor for IDTR, GDTR here.

; *****
; ** Page Directory and Page tables area in the physical address space,
; ** used to initialize the page tables before enabling paging.
; *****
                ORG 00001000h              ;  Physical Address
Page_Dir        dd Page_Entries DUP(?)
Page_Tab0       dd Page_Entries DUP(?)     ; OS Common Data(IDT, GDT, TSS)
Page_Tab3       dd Page_Entries DUP(?)     ; OS Private (stack)
Page_Tab4       dd Page_Entries DUP(?)     ; User Code and Data
Page_Tab3FE     dd Page_Entries DUP(?)     ; User Stack
Page_Tab3FF     dd Page_Entries DUP(?)     ; OS Code
```

► **Listing 7.1:** Initialization code (continued)

```
; *****
; ** Page Directory and Page tables area in the linear address space.
; ** 4M linear space for full directory and tables.
; *****
                ORG 00400000h
L_Page_Tab0     dd Page_Entries DUP (?)    ; OS Common Data(IDT, GDT, TSS)
L_Page_Dir      dd Page_Entries DUP (?)    ; Page Directory
                ORG 00403000h
L_Page_Tab3     dd Page_Entries DUP (?)    ; OS Private (stack)
L_Page_Tab4     dd Page_Entries DUP (?)    ; User Code and Data
                ORG 007FE000h
L_Page_Tab3FE   dd Page_Entries DUP (?)    ; User Stack
L_Page_Tab3FF   dd Page_Entries DUP (?)    ; OS Code

; *****
; * OS data. 4M linear space. Not used in example.
; *****
ORG     0800000h

; *****
; ** OS data. 4M linear space for data and stack private to OS.
; *****
ORG     0C00000h         ; Linear Address
Unshared_OS_Data        dd      ?
; Unshared OS Data Area, Temps, etc.
temp    db      10 dup (?)
fptss   dw      ?

; *****
; ** OS Stack.
; *****
ORG             0FFFFFCh        ; Top of OS stack
Top_OS_Stack    dd      ?
OS_Data_Seg     ENDS

; ***********************
; ***********************
; ** User Code Segment
; ***********************
; ***********************
; Locate this segment at linear address  1000000h.
User_Code_Seg  SEGMENT ER USE32 ; Locate AT 1000000h.
  ; Start of User's code segment in linear address space.
  ; Define a 1 Megabyte region.
User_Code_Seg  ENDS

; ***********************
; ***********************
; ** User Data Segment
; ***********************
; ***********************
; Locate this segment at linear address 1100000h.
User_Data_Seg  SEGMENT RW USE32 ; Locate AT 1100000h
```

► **Listing 7.1:** Initialization code (continued)

```
  ; Start of User's code segment in linear address space.
  ; The rest of memory (enormous) is defined for user data.
  ORG 0FEEEFFFCh
  Top_User_Stack   dd ?
User_Data_Seg  ENDS

; ****************************
; ****************************
; ** 32-bit OS Code Segment
; ****************************
; ****************************
; 32-bit OS code.
; Locate this segment at linear address 0FFFF0000h.
OS_Code_Seg SEGMENT ER   USE32 ; Locate AT 0FFFF0000h
        Extrn   loader:NEAR

Default_Hand:
        ; < Default Handler Code >
        IRET
DNA_Hand:
        ; < DNA Handler Code: Example 2 >
        IRET
Page_Fault_Hand:
        ; < Page Fault Handler Code >
        IRET
Debug_Hand:
        ; < Debug Handler Code >
        IRET
Start32:

    ; *****
    ; ** [5] Make OS_Data segment addressable by loading
    ; ** it into DS and ES segment registers.
    ; *****
        MOV AX, OS_Data_Sel
        MOV DS, AX
        MOV ES, AX
        ASSUME DS:OS_Data_Seg

    ; *****
    ; ** [6] Build LDT, LLDT
    ; *****
        MOV EAX, offset LDT1_Table
        ; entry 0 --> User Code Descriptor
        ; Base=00100000h, Limit=000FFh,G=1,D=1,Type=A,DPL=3
        MOV word ptr [EAX],000FFh       ; Limit[15..0]
        MOV word ptr [EAX+2],0000h      ; Base[15..0]
        MOV byte ptr [EAX+4],000h       ; Base[23..16]
        MOV byte ptr [EAX+5],0FAh       ; Type = data
                                        ; descriptor,DPL=11
        MOV byte ptr [EAX+6],0C0h       ; G,D,Limit[19..16]
        MOV byte ptr [EAX+7],01h        ; Base[31..24]
        ADD EAX,8
```

► **Listing 7.1:** Initialization code (continued)

```
    ; entry 1 --> User Data Descriptor
    ; Base=00110000h, Limit=FEEEFh,G=1,D=1,Type=A,DPL=3
    MOV word ptr [EAX],0EEEFh       ; Limit[15..0]
    MOV word ptr [EAX+2],0000h      ; Base[15..0]
    MOV byte ptr [EAX+4],010h       ; Base[23..16]
    MOV byte ptr [EAX+5],0F2h       ; Type = data
                                    ; descriptor, DPL=11
    MOV byte ptr [EAX+6],0CFh       ; G,D,Limit[19..16]
    MOV byte ptr [EAX+7],01h        ; Base[31..24]

    MOV AX, LDT1_Sel
    LLDT AX

; *****
; ** [7] Build IDT
; *****
    ; Fill in first 16 entries in IDT. First fill with the
    ; Default Handler, then come back and update.
    MOV EAX, offset IDT_Table
    MOV EBX, offset Default_Hand
    MOV word ptr [EAX], BX           ; Offset[15..0]
    MOV word ptr [EAX+2], OS_Code_Sel
    MOV byte ptr [EAX+4], 00h        ; WordCnt=0
    MOV byte ptr [EAX+5], 8Eh        ; Type=E, DPL=00
    SHR EBX, 16
    MOV word ptr [EAX+6], BX         ; Offset[31..16]
    ; Now that one is built, copy into rest.
    MOV ESI, offset IDT_Table
    MOV EDI, (offset IDT_Table + 8)
    MOV ECX, (IDT_Entries-1)*2
    REP MOVSD
    ; Now come back and fill nondefault pointers.
    ; entry 1: Debugger
    MOV EAX, (offset IDT_Table + (1 * 8))
    MOV EBX, offset Debug_Hand
    MOV word ptr [EAX], BX           ; Offset[15..0]
    SHR EBX, 16
    MOV word ptr [EAX+6], BX         ; Offset[31..16]

    ; entry 7: Device Not Available
    MOV EAX, (offset IDT_Table + ( 7 * 8))
    MOV EBX, offset DNA_Hand
    MOV word ptr [EAX], BX           ; Offset[15..0]
    SHR EBX, 16
    MOV word ptr [EAX+6], BX         ; Offset[31..16]

    ; entry 14: Page fault handler
    MOV EAX, (offset IDT_Table + (14 * 8))
    MOV EBX, offset Page_Fault_Hand
    MOV word ptr [EAX], BX           ; Offset[15..0]
    SHR EBX, 16
    MOV word ptr [EAX+6], BX         ; Offset[31..16]
```

► **Listing 7.1:** Initialization code (continued)

```
    ; load IDTR
    MOV word ptr pdescr, (IDT_Entries * 8 - 1)
    MOV dword ptr pdescr[2], offset IDT_Table
    LIDT pword ptr pdescr

; *****
; ** [8] Build Page Directory
; *****
    MOV EAX,Not_Present
    MOV ECX, Page_Entries
    CLD
    MOV EDI, offset Page_Dir
    REP STOSD             ; mark entire directory not present

    ; Entry 0: OS Shared Data Table. No user-level access.
    ; Locate at 0 so linear=physical and the loaded GDT, IDT,
    ; and TSS , are still valid after paging is enabled.
    MOV Page_Dir[   0], P_Page_Tab0 OR 001h
    ; Entry 1: Pointer to Directory. No user-level access.
    ; This maps the PageDir and PageTables into the linear
    ; address space.
    MOV Page_Dir[   4], P_Page_Dir OR 001h

    ; Entry 3: OS Private Data Table. No user-level access.
    MOV Page_Dir[  12], P_Page_Tab3 OR 001h

    ; Entry 4: User code and Data. User read/write access.
    MOV Page_Dir[  16], P_Page_Tab4 OR 007h

    ; Entry 3FEh: User Stack, put at highest area of user
    ; data space.  User read/write access.
    MOV Page_Dir[4088], P_Page_Tab3FE OR 007h

    ; Entry 3FFh: OS Shared Code Table. No user-level access.
    ; It is very important this entry is at high memory to map
    ; to the same address as is currently being executed.
    MOV Page_Dir[4092], P_Page_Tab3FF OR 001h

; *****
; ** [9] Build Tables: Directory has been built, now we must
; ** build each page table.
; *****
    ; Page Table 0: OS common data
    ; First thing is to clear entire table.
    MOV EAX, Not_Present
    MOV ECX, Page_Entries
    CLD
    MOV EDI, offset Page_Tab0
    REP STOSD
    ; Now allocate page for IDT, GDT, TSS, ...
    MOV Page_Tab0[   0h], P_OS_GData OR 001h
```

► **Listing 7.1:** Initialization code (continued)

```
    ; Page Table 3: OS private data
    ; First thing is to clear entire table.
    MOV EAX, Not_Present
    MOV ECX, Page_Entries
    CLD
    MOV EDI, offset Page_Tab3
    REP STOSD
    ; Allocate pages for private data and OS stack.
    MOV Page_Tab3[0000h], (P_OS_PData OR 001h)
    MOV Page_Tab3[0FFCh], (P_OS_Stack OR 001h)

    ; Page Table 4: User code, data and stack
    ; First thing is to clear entire table.
    MOV EAX, Not_Present
    MOV ECX, Page_Entries
    CLD
    MOV EDI, offset Page_Tab4
    REP STOSD
    ; Allocate pages for user code and data.
    MOV Page_Tab4[0000], (P_User_Code OR 005h)
    MOV Page_Tab4[1024], (P_User_Data OR 007h)

    ; Page Table 3FE: User Stack
    ; First thing is to clear entire table.
    MOV EAX, Not_Present
    MOV ECX, Page_Entries
    CLD
    MOV EDI, offset Page_Tab3FE
    REP STOSD
    ; Allocate page for user stack: highest linear address.
    MOV Page_Tab3FE[4092], (P_User_Stack OR 007h)

    ; Page Table 3FFh: OS code. All pages are readable to
    ; user, the upper 64K of memory is mapped such that
    ; physical and linear addresses match.
    MOV EAX, 0FFFFF005h        ; highest PTE,
    MOV ECX, Page_Size
    LoopTop:
        SUB ECX, 4
        MOV Page_Tab3FF[ECX], EAX
        SUB EAX, 1000h
        CMP ECX, 4032
        JNZ LoopTop
; *****
; ** [10] Enable Paging
; *****
    MOV EAX, P_Page_Dir
    MOV CR3, EAX
    MOV EAX, CR0
    OR  EAX, PG
    MOV CR0, EAX
    JMP pflush
  pflush:
```

► **Listing 7.1:** Initialization code (continued)

```
; *****
; ** [11] Load the OS Stack pointer
; *****
    MOV dword ptr temp[0],offset Top_OS_stack
    MOV word  ptr temp[4],OS_Data_Sel
    LSS ESP,pword ptr temp

; *****
; ** [12] Build TSS. Only load up the parts referenced
; ** by OS. All other parts are written over on first
; ** transition to inner-level or unneeded. Also load
; ** the task register.
; *****
    ; Level 0 stack offset
    MOV dword ptr TSS1_Table[ 4 ], offset Top_OS_stack
    ; Level 0 stack selector
    MOV dword ptr TSS1_Table[ 8 ],OS_Data_Sel
    ; CR3
    MOV EAX, CR3
    MOV dword ptr TSS1_Table[1Ch],EAX
    ; LDT
    MOV dword ptr TSS1_Table[60h],0
    ; I/O Bit Map Offset
    MOV word ptr TSS1_Table[66h], 8000h
    ; Debug Trap Bit
    MOV word ptr TSS1_Table[64h], 0
    MOV AX, TSS1_Sel
    LTR AX

    ; Initialize floating-point status bytes needed by example 2.
    ; These are discussed in detail in that example.
    MOV byte ptr TSS1_Table[TSS_Size + FP_Save - 1], 0
    MOV fptss, 0

; *****
; ** [13] Load User Task
; *****
    MOV EAX, User_Code_Sel  ; Selector for user code
    MOV ECX, User_Data_Sel  ; Selector for user data
    ; The loader will fetch the first user task from disk
    ; and load it into the locations as specified by the
    ; selectors passed to it. The loader routine returns
    ; the offset of the start of the user task in the EAX
    ; register.
    CALL loader

    ; *****
    ; ** [14] Prepare for user task invocation. Push user's
    ; ** SS:ESP, push the flags, push the CS:EIP, and IRET
    ; ** will invoke the user code.
    ; *****
        MOV  ECX, User_Data_Sel ; Stack for user routine,
                                ; as data selector.
```

► **Listing 7.1:** Initialization code (continued)

```
        PUSH ECX
                                  ; Stack pointer for user.
        MOV  ECX, offset Top_User_Stack
        PUSH ECX

        PUSHF
                                  ; Set IF on the stack.
        OR SS: dword ptr [ESP],Int_Flag

        MOV ECX, User_Code_Sel    ; Code Segment of user routine.
        PUSH ECX
        PUSH EAX                  ; Offset to start in user task.

    ; *****
    ; ** [15] Invoke user task
    ; *****

        ; The magic IRET, switch to user routine as indicated
        ; on the stack.
        IRET

OS_Code_Seg ENDS

; 16-bit Bootstrap code.
; Segment origin is at 0FFFF0000h, to match addressing through CS just
; after reset. ORG to offset 0F000h to assemble boot code in top 4K
; of memory.
BootRom16  SEGMENT EO   USE16; Locate AT 0FFFF0000h
        ORG 0F000h              ; 16-bit OS code is in upper 4K of memory.
Start16:
    ; *****
    ; ** [2] Misc: CLI, DS, null IDT
    ; *****
        CLI                     ; disable interrupts
        MOV AX, 0               ; initial Data segment in real mode.
        MOV DS, AX
        ASSUME DS:OS_Data_Seg   ; tell assembler DS addresses OS data.

       ;  Set up empty IDT, will cause shutdown on any interrupts.
        MOV  word ptr  pdescr[0],0
                                ; set up for zero limit IDT,Base
        MOV  dword ptr pdescr[2],0
        LIDT pword ptr pdescr

    ; *****
    ; ** [3] Set up GDT
    ; *****
        MOV EAX, offset GDT_Table
        ; entry 0 --> Null
        MOV dword ptr [EAX],0
        MOV dword ptr [EAX+4],0
        ADD EAX,8
```

► **Listing 7.1:** Initialization code (continued)

```
; entry 1 --> OS Code Descriptor
; Base=FFFF0000h, Limit=0000Eh,G=1,D=1,Type=A,DPL=0
MOV word ptr [EAX],0000Eh       ; Limit[15..0]
MOV word ptr [EAX+2],0000h      ; Base[15..0]
MOV byte ptr [EAX+4],0FFh       ; Base[23..16]
MOV byte ptr [EAX+5],09Ah       ; Type = code
                                ; descriptor, DPL=0
MOV byte ptr [EAX+6],0C0h       ; G,D,Limit[19..16]
MOV byte ptr [EAX+7],0FFh       ; Basc[31..24]
ADD EAX,8

; entry 2 --> OS Data Descriptor
; Base=00000000h, Limit=0FFFFFh,G=1,D=1,Type=9,DPL=0
; Map entire data space into OS Address Space --> this provides
; access to memory to load a user task, for instance.
MOV word ptr [EAX],0FFFFh       ; Limit[15..0]
MOV word ptr [EAX+2],0000h      ; Base[15..0]
MOV byte ptr [EAX+4],00h        ; Base[23..16]
MOV byte ptr [EAX+5],092h       ; Type = data
                                  ; descriptor, DPL=0
MOV byte ptr [EAX+6],0CFh       ; G,D,Limit[19..16]
MOV byte ptr [EAX+7],00h        ; Base[31..24]
ADD EAX,8

; entry 3 --> LDT
; Base=(offset LDT1_Table), Limit=(LDT_Entries * 8),
; G=0, Type=LDT, DPL=00
MOV word ptr [EAX], (LDT_Entries * 8 - 1) ; Limit[15..0]
MOV EBX, offset LDT1_Table
MOV word ptr [EAX+2], BX                  ; Base[15..0]
SHR EBX, 16
MOV byte ptr [EAX+4], BL                  ; Base[23..16]
MOV byte ptr [EAX+5],082h                 ; Type=LDT
MOV byte ptr [EAX+6],000h                 ; Limit[19..16]
MOV byte ptr [EAX+7], BH                  ; Base[31..24]
ADD EAX,8

; entry 4 --> TSS for this task
; Base=(offset TSS1_Table), Limit=(TSS_Size + FP_Save),
; G=0, Type=Available 386 TSS, DPL=00
MOV word ptr [EAX], (TSS_Size + FP_Save - 1) ; Limit[15..0]
MOV EBX, offset TSS1_Table
MOV word ptr [EAX+2], BX                     ; Base[15..0]
SHR EBX, 16
MOV byte ptr [EAX+4], BL                     ; Base[23..16]
MOV byte ptr [EAX+5],089h                    ; Type=Available 386 TSS
MOV byte ptr [EAX+6],000h                    ; Limit[19..16]
MOV byte ptr [EAX+7], BH                     ; Base[31..24]

; Set up GDT pseudo-descriptor (limit and base), and load it into GDTR.
MOV  word ptr  pdescr[0],(GDT_Entries*8 - 1)
MOV  dword ptr pdescr[2],offset GDT_Table
LGDT pword ptr pdescr
```

► **Listing 7.1:** Initialization code (continued)

```
        ; *****
        ; ** [4] Enter Protected Mode
        ; *****
            SMSW AX
            OR   AX,PE
            LMSW AX                    ; Set protection enable bit
            JMP  Flush
          Flush:
            JMP far ptr Start32        ; Jump through GDT to 32-bit
                                       ; OS code.
        ; *****
        ; ** [1] Cold Start Code!
        ; *****
            ORG 0FFF0h
            JMP Start16
BootRom16 ENDS

END
```

► **Listing 7.1:** Initialization code (continued)

► Coprocessor Exception Handler

The second example is a coprocessor *Device Not Available* (DNA) exception handler. This example is an extension of the first. The exception handler is given in Listing 7.2 (beginning on page 627).

Overview of Example 2

This example will demonstrate the details of a fault handler and specifically the coprocessor device not available handler. A device not available exception (vector number 7) can be generated for any of the following reasons (these were discussed in Chapter 6).

1. A floating-point instruction is executed and the EM bit in control register CR0 is a 1. EM indicates that a math coprocessor is to be emulated.
2. A floating-point instruction is executed and the TS bit in control register CR0 is a 1. TS indicates the fast task-switch mode discussed below.
3. A WAIT instruction is executed and both the TS and MP bits in CR0 are 1.

In our example, we deal with the fast task-switch mode. If the system is to emulate the coprocessor (discussed in Chapter 1), a simple call to the routine DNA_Emulate is done. It is the responsibility of this routine to emulate the operation of the coprocessor.

The fast task-switch mode is an optimization that allows the state of the coprocessor to be saved only when it is accessed by a task. If most tasks in the system do not use the coprocessor, this can be a large benefit, since unloading and reloading the coprocessor state is quite time-consuming.

When a DNA exception occurs, the coprocessor device not available handler would be called. This handler is written to be inserted directly into the first example of this chapter, the initialization example. In fact, you could insert the DNA handler exactly at the location in the first example seen as:

```
<DNA Handler Code - Example 2>
```

Several items in example 1 are exclusively for the purpose of this example. For example, the TSS has enough space allocated in it to allow the floating-point state to be stored into it.

On an exception, if a task had been using the coprocessor, the coprocessor state is stored into the TSS of the task using it (if there was one). The current task's coprocessor state (if it already made use of it) is then loaded into the coprocessor. The operating system keeps a variable containing the selector for the TSS of the last task using the coprocessor. This is updated as part of loading the coprocessor with its new state. Throughout this example, interrupt latency is a concern, and will be further discussed below.

Details of Exception Handler

Before anything else is done, interrupts are enabled. Since loading and storing coprocessor state can take a while, we will disable interrupts only when absolutely needed. Interrupts need to be enabled, since all the handlers from example 1 are interrupt gates that disable interrupts as they are taken.

Code Sequence 1—Emulation

If the exception was caused by the EM bit being set in CR0, the emulator is called. An emulator is not part of the example. After emulation, simply return.

Code Sequence 2—Current Task Base

The *fptss* variable contains the selector for the TSS of the task whose state is currently in the coprocessor. The coprocessor state is stored in the upper part of the TSS. Thus, we need to determine the selector and the base of the current task's TSS. This is done rather nicely by working backward, beginning at the TR. The TR gives the selector for the current TSS, accessing the GDT and unscrambling the base from the descriptor. The selector is kept in SI and the base in ECX for future use.

Code Sequence 3—Save Old State

The initialization sequence clears the fptss variable to 0. This is done to indicate that no task has yet used the coprocessor. If this is the case, the current coprocessor state need not be stored anywhere, and the coprocessor will be initialized with the FNINIT instruction below. If fptss was not zero, the coprocessor state is stored into the TSS of the old task at the appropriate location. As above, this location is determined by following the fptss selector to determine the base of the TSS. Another optimization is if the last task to use the coprocessor is the current task. If this is the case, do nothing and return.

Code Sequence 4—Load New State

While the new state is being loaded into the coprocessor, it is necessary to disable interrupts, since the machine is not in a valid state. Consider the case when the coprocessor state has been stored into the prior task's TSS and the state for the new task is loaded into the coprocessor, but fptss has not yet been updated. In this case, the coprocessor state and fptss are inconsistent. If an interrupt were taken at this point, a subsequent invocation of this fault handler (prior to return to this invocation) could corrupt the old task's coprocessor state.

It is unfortunate that interrupts are disabled during the loading of a new coprocessor state: interrupt latency suffers, since the FRSTOR instruction is very long. You can avoid the disabling of interrupts throughout this instruction, but you'd need two semaphores, and the exception handler becomes much trickier to write. Rather than complicate this example handler to the point of being unintelligible, this exercise is left to the interested and able reader.

The highest byte in the coprocessor state portion of the TSS is a byte indicating that the coprocessor state has been saved in this TSS. The part of the operating system that initiates tasks takes care to zero this byte (we did so in our initialization example). If this byte is 0, the coprocessor state need not be restored from the current task, as the current task has never used the coprocessor and the coprocessor is simply reset by the FNINIT instruction. If this byte is 1, this task has state to be loaded into the coprocessor. Finally, the fptss variable is updated, and the highest byte of the TSS coprocessor state is set to 1 to indicate the new status of the coprocessor and this task's use of it.

```
; *******************************************************************
; * Example 2 - Device Not Available Handler.
; *
; * Several items are assumed (Example 1 meets these assumptions):
; * 1. fptss is a selector of the TSS of the most recent task
; *    that used the coprocessor (the state from this task is still
; *    in the coprocessor). If none, it is 0.
; * 2. The TSS has a floating-point save area immediately above
; *    the minimal TSS.
; * 3. The floating-point save area of the TSS is 108 (normal save
; *    area) plus 4 bytes. The highest addressed byte is a flag,
; *    indicating if the task has coprocessor state (0 indicates
; *    no state).
; *******************************************************************

DNA_Hand:
        STI
     ; *****
     ; * [1] Determine if fault is caused by Emulation
     ; *****
        ; Remember CR0 layout:      3
        ;                           1 ... 4 3 2 1 0
        ;                           P     E T E M P
        ;                           G     T S M P E
        MOV  EAX, CR0
        BT   EAX, 2
        JNC  DNA_Task_Ex
        CALL DNA_Emulate
        IRET

    ; *****
    ; * [2] Determine current task TSS base
    ; *****
    DNA_Task_Ex:
        XOR  ESI,ESI
        STR  SI            ; ESI holds TSS selector of current task
        MOV  ECX, [ESI + offset GDT_Table + 0]
        MOV  EDX, [ESI + offset GDT_Table + 4]
        SHRD ECX,EDX,16
        AND  ECX,000FFFFFFh
        AND  EDX,0FF000000h
        OR   ECX,EDX        ; ECX now holds base of current task
```

► **Listing 7.2:** Device not available exception handler

```
; *****
; * [3] Fault is caused by task switch. If state of old task needs
; * to be saved, do so.
; *****
    XOR EDI,EDI
    MOV DI, fptss
    CMP DI,0
    JE  DNA_Restor     ; No prior task used Coprocessor.
    CMP DI,SI          ; If the last user is the current task
                       ; we don't need to save and restore.
    JNE  DNA_Save
    IRET
 DNA_Save:
    ; determine base of TSS of last task
    MOV  EAX,[EDI + offset GDT_Table + 0]
    MOV  EDX,[EDI + offset GDT_Table + 4]
    SHRD EAX,EDX,16
    AND  EAX,000FFFFFFh
    AND  EDX,0FF000000h
    OR   EAX,EDX      ; EAX now holds base of prior task TSS

    FNSAVE [EAX + TSS_Size] ; Save old task's coprocessor state.

; *****
; * [4] Now set fptss to this task. If needed, load up the
; * prior coprocessor state of this task. Interrupts
; * must be disabled throughout.
; *****
DNA_Restor:
    CLI
    ; This byte indicates that this task had prior
    ; coprocessor state.
    CMP byte ptr [ECX + (TSS_Size + FP_Save - 1)],1
    JNE DNA_Init
    FRSTOR [ECX + TSS_Size]
    JMP DNA_Done
DNA_Init:
    FNINIT
DNA_Done:
    MOV fptss, SI     ; Store this task's TSS selector into
    ; fptss, set byte indicating coprocessor has been used
    ; by this task, clear TS, and set IF.
    MOV byte ptr [ECX + (TSS_SIZE + FP_Save - 1)],1
    CLTS
    STI
    IRET
```

► **Listing 7.2:** Device not available exception handler (continued)

Debugging Support

Chapter 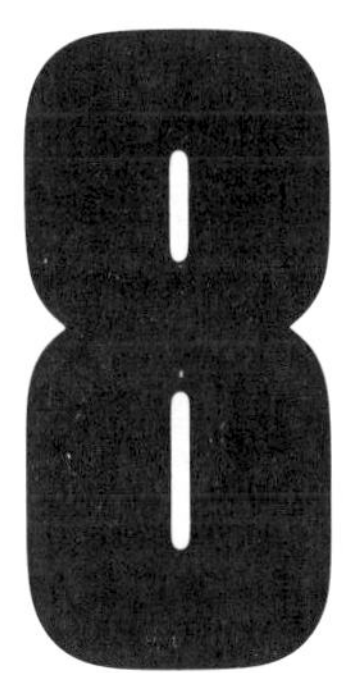

AS ALL PROGRAMMERS ARE AWARE, PROGRAMS need to be debugged. Debugging has traditionally been more art than science. To take some of the magic out of debugging, software debuggers have been developed to assist programmers in finding the exact location of their bug(s—we all know there is more than one!). Software debuggers have such features as stepping through code one instruction at a time, setting breakpoints at certain locations in the program (stop at the start of this statement), and stopping when variable xyz becomes the value 0FA445h. Software debuggers have played no small part in getting many major programs functioning correctly.

In this chapter, we do not present a specific 80386 software debugger. Instead, we present the basic debug facilities the 80386 supports. These basic features can have a software debugger built on top of them to develop a full software debugging facility.

The debugging facilities of the 80386 include a one-byte trap intruction (INT 3), trap on task switch, single-step by instruction, and detection of four simultaneous breakpoint conditions for instruction fetch, data write, and data read or write. The remainder of this chapter describes these facilities in more detail. The breakpoint facilities of the 80386 provide a significant extension to the debug facilities found in prior 86 family members.

► Terminology

Before beginning our description, we need to clarify the terminology used in this chapter.

Chapter 6 has described the possible exceptions of the 80386 in some detail. This chapter will describe in more detail the *debug exception,* which is detected as part of executing an instruction. A *debug handler* is the routine that receives control when a debug interrupt or an enabled debug exception is detected.

A debug exception is classified as a fault or a trap, depending on when the exception is raised. A *debug fault* is raised at the instruction boundary immediately before the execution of the instruction raising the exception. Thus, the exception handler is entered with the saved CS:EIP pointing to the instruction that raised the fault. A *debug trap* is raised at the instruction boundary immediately after the execution of the instruction causing the exception. Therefore, the CS:EIP value stored at entry to the exception handler points to the instruction after the one causing the exception. Faults occur "before," and traps occur "after" the instruction raising the exception. The following list summarizes which exception types are traps and which are faults.

1. Traps

   Task switch

   Single-step

   Data breakpoints

2. Faults

   Debug register protection

   Instruction breakpoints

► Debug Breakpoints

A breakpoint allows the programmer to set a specific condition at a particular linear address that causes program execution to jump into the exception handler. The 80386 supports four simultaneous breakpoint conditions. Thus, the programmer can set up to four locations in a program for which the 80386 will jump to the exception handler. The four breakpoints can each be of three different types:

- Instruction execution only
- Data writes
- Data reads or writes (but not instruction execution)

Debug Registers

To support the four breakpoints, eight additional registers are added to the 80386. These registers can only be read or written at privilege level 0. Attempted access at any other privilege level will raise an invalid opcode exception. Additionally, the registers can be further protected from reading or writing even at level 0 by the BD and GD bits in DR6 and DR7, which are described below. Access to these registers is provided by the move to/from debug register instructions

```
MOV reg,DRi
MOV DRi,reg
```

where DRi may be any of DR0, DR1, DR2, DR3, DR6, or DR7. These instructions are described in more detail in the operating-system section of Chapter 3.

Figure 8.1 displays the eight debug registers. The subsequent paragraphs explain these registers in detail.

DR0–DR3 — Registers DR0 through DR3 contain the linear address associated with each of the four breakpoint conditions. Additional breakpoint qualifiers are given in DR7. Since the linear address is used, the breakpoint facilities operate the same (and correctly) whether paging is enabled or not.

DR4–DR5 — The DR4 and DR5 registers are reserved for future use by Intel.

DR6 — The DR6 register is the debug status register. When a debug exception is raised, the processor sets DR6 to indicate the exception type and/or breakpoints that raised the exception.

DR7 — DR7 is the debug control register. The bits in this register allow each breakpoint register to be enabled, as well as the type of breakpoint (instruction, data write, and data read or write) to be selected. The protection of all breakpoint registers is specified in this register.

DR6

Upon entry to the debug handler, the DR6 register indicates what exception was detected. Note that the bits of DR6 do not indicate whether the breakpoint condition was enabled (which is indicated by DR7). The bits simply indicate that the condition was detected. Thus,

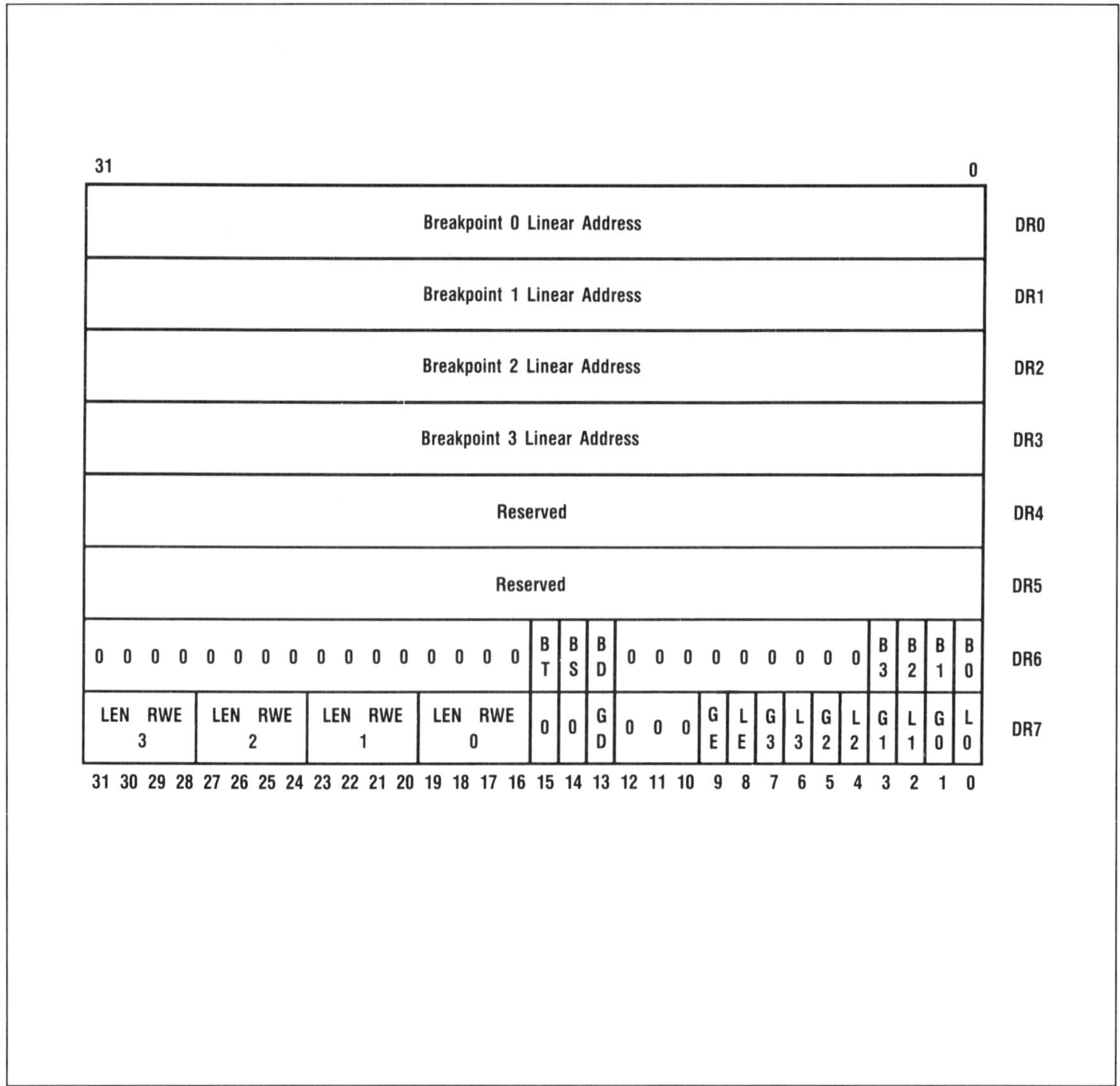

► **Figure 8.1:** Debug registers

the programmer needs to verify that the condition was detected as indicated in DR6, and the condition was enabled as specified in DR7.

Debug exceptions for two different instructions can be reported simultaneously. A fault on one instruction may be reported at the same time as a trap on the previous instruction. For example, an instruction breakpoint detected in one instruction may be reported at the same time as a data breakpoint on the previous instruction. The debug handler can examine the status bits in DR6 to determine which condition, or combination of conditions, were detected at the instruction boundary where a debug exception is raised.

B0–B3 The B0 through B3 bits indicate that the breakpoint condition specified by the corresponding breakpoint linear address register was detected. Note that these bits are set even if the breakpoint condition has not been enabled by DR7.

BD The BD bit is set at an instruction boundary if the next instruction will read or write to one of the eight debug registers (debug register protection). BD will be set whenever a read or write to the debug registers is about to occur. The condition need not be enabled by the GD bit of DR7.

BS The BS bit is set if a single-step exception occurs. The single-step condition is enabled by the TF bit in the EFLAGS register, as described in Chapter 2. The BS bit in DR6 is set if the program enters the debug handler because of a single-step condition. Unlike the other bits in DR6, the BS bit is set only if a single-step trap actually occurs, not if a single-step condition (enabled or not) was detected.

BT The BT bit indicates that the cause for the debug exception was a task switch into a task where the debug trap bit in the TSS is enabled. There is not an enable bit for this condition in DR7.

Note that the bits of DR6 are never cleared by the processor. Thus, the debug exception handler, before returning, should clear DR6 to avoid false interpretation of DR6 when the next exception condition is detected.

DR7

The bit definitions of the various fields of DR7, the debug control register, are given below.

LEN — The four 2-bit LEN fields indicate the length of the breakpoint for each of the four breakpoint registers. The encoding is

LEN	Description
00	One-byte length
01	Two-byte length
10	Reserved
11	Four-byte length

Note that the breakpoint linear address needs to be aligned on a multiple of the length field. If the corresponding breakpoint is an instruction execution breakpoint (denoted by RWE = 00), LEN must be 00.

RWE — The four 2-bit RWE fields indicate the type of access that will cause a breakpoint exception to be raised. The encoding is

RWE	Description
00	Instruction execution only
01	Data writes only
10	Reserved
11	Data reads or writes

GE/LE — The GE/LE bits indicate exact data breakpoints (global and local, respectively). If GE or LE is set, the processor will slow execution such that data breakpoints are reported on exactly the instruction that causes them. If these bits are not set, the processor may get slightly ahead of the reporting of the breakpoint conditions on instructions that perform data writes near the end of their execution. We recommend that either LE or GE be enabled whenever data breakpoints are enabled. Slowing processor execution in this way should not cause any problems besides a slight performance loss, except for regions of code

	where speed is critical. In such speed-critical portions of code, GE and LE will need to be disabled and some minor inaccuracies in debug exception reporting will have to be tolerated.
L0–L3/G0–G3	The L0 through L3 and G0 through G3 bits are the local and global enable signals for the four debug breakpoint registers. If either the local or global enable (L*i* or G*i*) is set, the breakpoint specified by the corresponding breakpoint register DR*i* is enabled.
GD	The GD bit enables the debug register protection condition that is flagged by BD of DR6. Note that GD is cleared at entry to the debug exception handler by the processor. This allows the handler free access to the debug registers.

Note that the L bits (LE, L0, L1, L2, L3) are local bits to a task. They allow debug conditions to be enabled for a particular task, whereas the G bits (GD, GE, G0, G1, G2, G3) are global and should be used for debug conditions that are true for all tasks in the system. The L bits are automatically cleared at each task switch by the processor, as described in Chapter 5.

Breakpoint Address Recognition

The combination of the LEN field and the breakpoint linear address specify the four linear address ranges that are checked for debug exceptions. As mentioned above, the breakpoint linear address must be aligned at addresses that are multiples of the length specified in LEN. In fact, the processor ignores low-order linear address bits when checking for breakpoints, depending on the LEN specification. For example, if LEN = 11 (length of 4), the low 2 bits of the linear address are ignored. If LEN = 01 (length of 2), the low bit of the linear address is ignored.

An access of the correct type of any byte in the address range specified by the breakpoint linear address and LEN will cause an exception. Every data access and instruction fetch is checked against all four breakpoint address ranges. If any byte of the breakpoint address range matches and the type of access matches (for instance, data read), a breakpoint exception is reported.

Table 8.1 gives several examples of data breakpoint recognition. Assume that all breakpoints are enabled and set for the correct type of access.

To set a breakpoint on an unaligned address, you must define two breakpoint conditions such that the combination of the two correctly covers the desired range of addresses. For instance, if there is a four-byte data item that you want to break on at address 00FFFEh, you will need to set a breakpoint at address 00FFFEh with LEN = 01 (two bytes) and a second breakpoint at address 010000h with LEN = 01.

Code vs. Data Breakpoints

There are several differences between instruction access breakpoints (code) and data reference breakpoints. First, and most obvious, is the different settings in the RWE field for each. Second, the only valid LEN setting for

		ADDRESS	LENGTH	BREAKPOINT
REGISTER CONTENTS	DR0	00FF02	1, LEN = 00	
	DR1	00CC32	2, LEN = 01	
	DR2	0D0004	4, LEN = 11	
	DR3	01FF00	4, LEN = 11	
ACCESSES THAT CAUSE EXCEPTIONS		00FF02	1	B0 = 1
		00CC33	1	B1 = 1
		0D0007	2	B2 = 1
		00FEFF	4	B0 = 1
		01FF00	4	B3 = 1
		01FF03	4	B3 = 1
ACCESSES NOT CAUSING EXCEPTIONS		00FF01	1	—
		00FF00	2	—
		00CC34	1	—
		01FEFF	1	—
		0D0000	4	—

► **Table 8.1:** Examples of breakpoint recognition

instruction breakpoints is 00 (or one byte). Instruction breakpoints must be set on the first byte of the instruction (instructions may be from 1 byte to 15 bytes in length). The *first byte* includes any prefix bytes that may be present with this instruction.

The third and most significant difference is that instruction breakpoints are classified as faults, whereas data breakpoints are traps. Recalling the discussion at the beginning of this chapter, this means that instruction breakpoint faults are detected and reported prior to the execution of the instruction, and data breakpoint traps are reported after they read or write to the breakpoint location. This difference has two important points. First, a data breakpoint does not protect the data location from writes. If you want to protect the data location from writes, the debug handler can save a copy of the old data, since a data write occurs before the debug handler is invoked.

Since instruction breakpoints are reported prior to instruction execution, it is obvious that the instruction cannot simply be "restarted"; on its second (or more) execution it will simply fault again. This sounds like an infinite loop unless the debug handler disables the breakpoint. But the debug handler need not disable the breakpoint because the 80386 has the RF bit of the EFLAGS register, described in Chapter 2. The RF bit, when set, causes any instruction breakpoint fault to be ignored. Note that nondebug faults will still be reported, however. The RF bit is automatically cleared by the processor at the successful completion of any instruction. Thus, the RF bit will allow the processor to not report an instruction breakpoint fault on the second (or more) execution of the instruction causing the instruction breakpoint fault, but will begin reporting instruction breakpoint faults on any subsequent instruction. RF also allows the second execution of the instruction to report other kinds of faults that may occur on this instruction. Note that RF will remain set until the instruction successfully completes, at which time it is automatically cleared by the processor.

But how does RF get set? It must be set by the debug handler before it returns, but it is also set for all other faults by the processor. Whenever a fault handler, not only a debug fault handler, is entered, the processor sets this bit in the image of the flags that is pushed onto the stack. Thus, when the fault handler exits, normally with the IRET instruction, the flags image is popped off the stack and placed into the EFLAGS register with RF set.

Also note that the RF bit, when set, inhibits the setting of any of the debug status bits in DR6 for instruction breakpoints.

Other Debug Capabilities

The breakpoint facility is not the only resource the 80386 provides for the debugger, even though it is probably the most important. The remainder of the 80386 debug features are summarized below.

Debug Trap in TSS

The T bit in the TSS described in Chapter 5 causes the debug handler to be invoked whenever a task switch through this TSS occurs. This provides a convenient way for the debugger to monitor the activities of certain tasks. The BT bit of DR6 notes that this condition was detected. There is no specific enable bit for this condition in DR7.

If the debug handler (interrupt 1) is serviced by a task gate (which is a valid thing to do) it is important that the debug trap flag of the corresponding TSS not be set, as an infinite loop of attempts to invoke the debug handler will occur.

INT 3

The one-byte breakpoint instruction INT 3 provides another means to debug programs. The first byte of the instruction where a break is desired can be replaced with the INT 3 instruction. Thus, when the INT 3 instruction is encountered, the interrupt 3 handler is entered.

There are several cases where INT 3 is not sufficient and the breakpoint registers are preferable.

1. You cannot insert an INT 3 instruction into code that is present in ROM.
2. When INT 3 is used, the code area is modified, and thus *any* task executing this code is interrupted. With the breakpoint facilities, you can have a particular task break on an instruction in shared code.
3. INT 3 cannot, of course, perform any data breakpointing.

INT 3 is quite useful in several situations.

1. Single-stepping and breakpoints enter the debug handler, which is interrupt 1. How can the debug handler be debugged? The INT 3 instruction provides the only convenient way to debug it.
2. You can insert an unlimited number of INT 3 instructions into the code, whereas there are only four breakpoint registers.
3. Earlier 86 family members did not contain the breakpoint register facilities the 80386 does. Thus, the INT 3 instruction played

a very important role in these processors, since it provided the only way to perform any breakpointing.

In summary, except for the special cases noted above, we recommend the unlimited use of the INT 3 instruction to perform breakpointing in code. We also recommend that the limited debug registers be saved for data breakpoints.

Single-Stepping

Single-stepping provides a convenient means for debuggers to slowly step through a section of a program. The single-step trap is enabled by the setting of the TF bit of the EFLAGS register, described in Chapter 2. If TF = 1 at the start of the instruction, a debug exception is taken at the end of the instruction (a trap), and the debug handler is entered.

Note that TF must be set when execution of the instruction begins for the trap to be taken. Thus, the trap is not taken on the instruction that sets the TF flag. The TF bit is cleared prior to entering the debug handler. TF is also cleared when an interrupt or exception is taken. If an external interrupt occurs at the same time a single-step interrupt occurs, the single step is processed first, which clears the TF bit. Before the first instruction of the debug handler is executed, the interrupt, if still pending, is taken. Thus, interrupt processing is done without single-stepping enabled. If you wanted to single-step through an interrupt handler, you could set a breakpoint at the first instruction of the interrupt handler, and then enable single-stepping after that break occured.

Executing 8086 and 80286 Programs

Chapter 9

THE FIRST EIGHT CHAPTERS OF THIS BOOK have described the 80386 as a 32-bit processor. This chapter looks at the compatibility features of the 80386 that let it execute programs written for the earlier 16-bit processors: the 8086, 8088, 80186, 80188, and 80286.

As described in Chapter 1, the 8086, 8088, 80186, and 80188 share a common architecture. The 80286 added a complete memory-management and protection model to this architecture. The 80286 has two modes of operation distinguished by the use of the new protection facilities. It is possible to use the 80286 without using the new protection features. In this mode, called real mode, the 80286 behaves just like an 8086. When the protection features are turned on, the 80286 behaves quite differently. This mode of execution is called protected mode.

Because the 8086, 8088, 80186, 80188, and the 80286 in real mode look alike to a programmer, we describe these processors in this chapter by taking the 8086 as representative of the group. The minor differences between these processors are summarized in Appendix A. Since the use of the 80286 in protected mode results in a very different programming model, this is treated separately.

First, we describe the basic machine registers and addressing modes available to 16-bit programs. This provides a brief equivalent of Chapter 2 for the 16-bit registers and address modes. Next, we describe how 8086 programs can be run on the 80386. There are two processor modes available for running 8086 programs: real mode and virtual-8086 mode. Real mode on the 80386, as with the 80286, is the mode of execution when the protection mechanism described in Chapter 5 is not used. Virtual-8086 mode is a new mode on the 80386 that supports execution of 8086 programs within the protection model. Finally, we discuss the execution of 80286 programs.

► Sixteen-bit Registers and Addressing Modes

Sixteen-bit programs use the low-order 16 bits of the registers defined in Chapter 2. Figure 9.1 illustrates these registers. There are eight 16-bit registers: AX, CX, DX, BX, SP, BP, SI, and DI. These are the low-order 16 bits of the 32-bit general registers described in Chapter 2. The high and low halves of the AX, CX, DX, and BX registers can be accessed as 8-bit registers. There are two 16-bit processor-control registers: IP and FLAGS. These are simply the low-order 16 bits of the EIP and EFLAGS registers described in detail in Chapter 2. The same six 16-bit segment registers described in Chapter 2 are available to 16-bit programs. The FS and GS registers are new on the 80386, so 16-bit programs written to execute on an 8086 or 80286 will not use these registers.

Memory addressing is similar to the memory addressing mechanism discussed in Chapter 2. Each memory reference specifies a segment part and an offset part. Since 16-bit programs use 16-bit offsets, the maximum segment size is 64K. Table 9.1 lists the address modes available to 16-bit programs for generating segment offsets. A 16-bit offset is formed by adding together a 16-bit base register, a 16-bit index register, and an 8- or 16-bit displacement. These additions use 16-bit arithmetic, so that carries out of bit 15 are ignored. Appendix G describes the encoding of the 16-bit address modes.

The 16-bit address modes are less general than the 32-bit address modes, although they have almost the same components. Index scaling is not available. Only the BX and BP registers can be used as base registers, and only the SI and DI registers can be used as index registers. When BP is used as a base register, the default segment register is SS. Otherwise the default is DS.

Use of 16-bit registers is controlled by the operand size of an instruction. Use of 16-bit address modes is controlled by the address size of an instruction. Recall from Chapter 5 that the D bit in a code segment descriptor sets the default size for both operands and addresses. A 16-bit default size is used for 16-bit 80286 programs by clearing the D bit to 0 in the descriptors of all 16-bit code segments. Programs executing in real

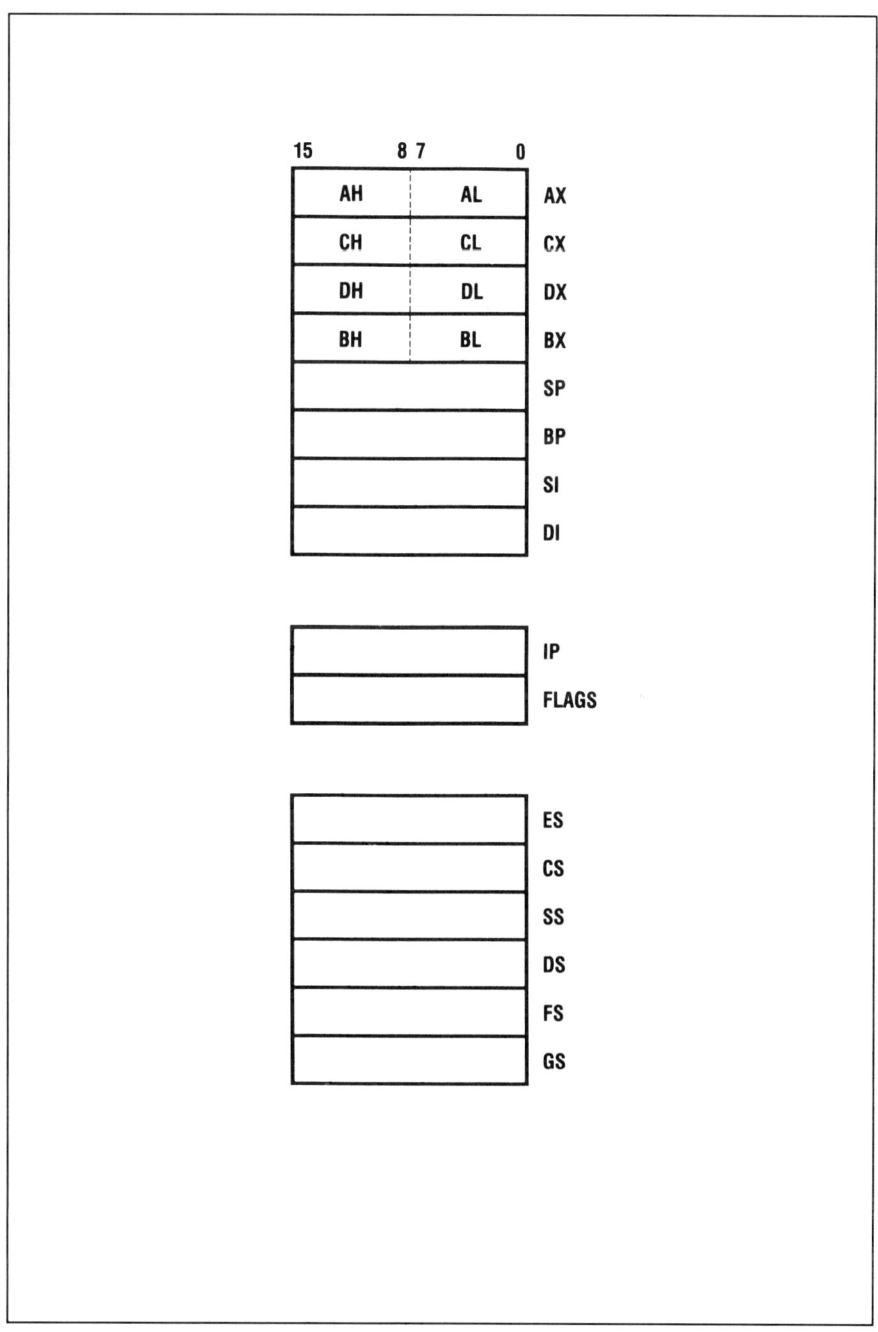

► **Figure 9.1:** 16-bit registers

BASE	+	INDEX	+	DISPLACEMENT
None		None		None
BX	+	SI	+	8 bits
BP[1]		DI		16 bits

[1] SS is the default segment register if BP is the base register.

► **Table 9.1:** 16-bit address modes

mode or virtual-8086 mode have a 16-bit default size. As described in Appendix G, an instruction prefix can be used to override the default size for either operands or addresses on any instruction.

The floating-point registers are the same on the 80387 as on the 8087 and 80287. Any 16-bit programs written for the 8086/8087 or 80286/80287 will use the floating-point register set described in Chapter 2.

► Executing 8086 Programs

Two execution modes are available on the 80386 for executing 8086 (and 8088, 80186, 80188, and real mode 80286) programs: real mode and virtual-8086 mode. When executing in these modes, the 80386 supports the same programming model as the 8086, except for some minor differences listed in Appendix A.

Real mode on the 80386 is the same as real mode on the 80286. When executing in real mode, the 80386 behaves just like an 8086, directly supporting the execution of 8086 programs. The 80386 executes in real mode when the memory-management, protection, and task mechanisms described in Chapter 5 are disabled by clearing the PE bit in register CR0 to 0. Because the protection mechanism is disabled in real mode, the 80386 executes as if it were at privilege level 0, the innermost or most privileged level. When the 80386 is executing in real mode, interrupts and exceptions are handled with a different mechanism than that described in Chapter 6. This interrupt mechanism is described later in this chapter, in the section on interrupt handling in real mode.

When the 80386 is initialized by a hardware reset, it begins execution in real mode, as described in a later section on 80386 state at initialization. This allows bootstrap code to initialize system tables before enabling protection, as shown in Chapter 7.

Virtual-8086 mode is new to the 80386. It supports the execution of 8086 programs within the context of the memory-management, protection, and task mechanisms described in Chapter 5. Special operating-system software known as a virtual-machine monitor can create a task that executes an 8086 program in virtual-8086 mode to support the illusion that the program is executing on an 8086 with full access to all 8086 resources. It is possible to execute an 8086 program in one task in virtual-8086 mode, a 16-bit protected mode 80286 program in another task, and a 32-bit protected mode 80386 program in a third task. The 80386 tasking mechanism described in Chapter 5 supports this flexibility in program execution.

A program executing in virtual-8086 mode runs at privilege level 3, the outermost or least privileged level. Paging can be used to allocate and protect memory for programs executing in virtual-8086 mode. If an interrupt is received, or if an exception is generated when a program is executing in virtual-8086 mode, the interrupt or exception is handled by switching to the normal protected mode described in Chapter 5, and then handling the interrupt or exception with the mechanism described in Chapter 6. The switch from virtual-8086 mode to protected mode is described in detail in a later section on entering and leaving virtual-8086 mode.

A virtual-machine monitor can support the execution of several 8086 programs "at once" by creating several tasks that execute in virtual-8086 mode, and running an 8086 program in each task. Because of the illusion presented by the combination of the virtual-machine monitor software and the virtual-8086 hardware facilities, each of these 8086 programs executes as if it had access to a full 8086. Other tasks in the system can execute protected mode 16-bit 80286 programs, or 32-bit protected mode 80386 programs, and ordinary task switches used to suspend one task and resume another. This makes it possible for the 80386 to run a diverse collection of tasks, some in virtual-8086 mode and others in protected mode, and smoothly task-switch between them. This is a powerful mechanism that combines the large base of 16-bit PC (8086 and 80286) programs with more sophisticated 32-bit applications originally written for minicomputers and mainframe computers. Virtual-8086 mode, in conjunction with the 80386's task-management facilities described in Chapter 5, provides the key hardware facilities to support this powerful software model.

In contrast to the powerful multitasking model supported in protected mode and virtual-8086 mode, real mode has no task support, and so can only support one 8086 program. This 8086 program will have direct access to the 80386 processor, with no protection, no memory management, and no multitasking support.

The next several sections discuss the mechanisms that are common to real mode and virtual-8086 mode. After the common features are covered, we will discuss the facilities unique to virtual-8086 mode and then real mode.

Segmentation and Addressing

The 8086 programming model uses segmentation to support a two-dimensional memory addressing model that is the same as the model described in Chapter 2. 8086 programs use the same two-part memory addresses as protected mode programs. These two-part addresses consist of a segment part and an offset part. The offset part is generated using one of the 16-bit address modes given in Table 9.1. The segment part of an address is taken from a segment register that must have been previously loaded to address the desired segment. Although the segment part of an address is taken from a segment register as in protected mode, segment parts of addresses are handled quite differently in 8086 programs.

8086 memory addressing does not use the segment descriptor tables described in Chapter 5 to define the base address, limit, and attributes of segments. Instead, segments are fixed in size at 64K bytes, and allow read, write, or execute access. Segments in real mode implicitly have a DPL of 0, since real mode programs execute as if they were at privilege level 0. Segments in virtual-8086 mode have a DPL of 3, since virtual-8086 mode programs execute at privilege level 3. Segments addressed by CS implicitly have their D (*Default*) bit 0, so that 8086 programs have the default operand and address size set to 16. Segments addressed by SS implicitly have their D bit 0, so that stack references use the 16-bit ESP register.

The segment register value is used to specify the base address of the segment in the linear address space as the numeric value of the segment register multiplied by 16 (or shifted left 4 bit positions). Because the 16-bit segment register holds a number up to 2^{16}, the largest segment base address is 2^{20} after multiplying by 16 (2^4). This means that a segment can start at any 16-byte boundary within the first megabyte of the linear address space.

The segment base address is added to the offset specified in the address mode of an instruction to obtain the linear address of the specified memory location. As illustrated in Figure 9.2, 32-bit arithmetic is used. This addition yields a 21-bit result on the 80386, where the twenty-first bit is the carry out of bit 20. Since segment limits are fixed at 64K, the largest offset that can be generated is 0FFFFh, and the segment offset is shown as 16 bits in Figure 9.2.

Because segment register values are treated simply as 16-bit numbers, it is not possible to get an exception when loading a value into a segment register. There is no check made on the value loaded into a segment register, so any 16-bit number can be used. For example, the value 0 can be used, which would be treated as a null selector when protection is enabled.

For example, suppose a memory reference specifies a segment register that contains the value 1234h, and specifies a 16-bit address mode that gives an offset of 5. The resulting linear address is computed as

	12340h	segment register value multiplied by 16
+	5h	offset given by address mode
	12345h	resulting linear address

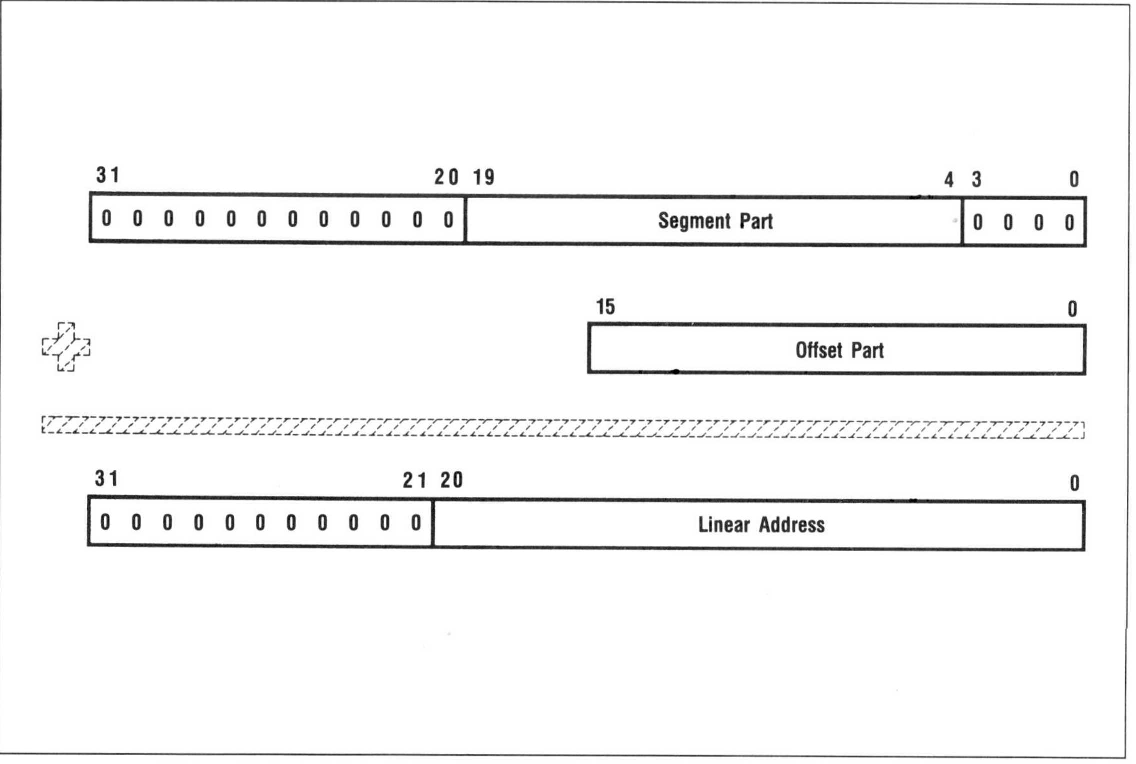

► **Figure 9.2:** Real and virtual-8086 linear address formation

As another example, the largest linear address that can be generated results when a memory address is formed using a segment register value of 0FFFFh, and an offset of 0FFFFh. The resulting linear address is computed as

```
    FFFF0h   segment register value multiplied by 16
+    FFFFh   offset given by address mode
  --------
   10FFEFh   resulting linear address
```

The segment base addition yields the linear address of a memory operand. In real mode this is also the physical address, since paging cannot be used in real mode. In virtual-8086 mode, paging can be used to translate this linear address to a physical address, or if paging is disabled this linear address is passed through as the physical address. In real mode, or in virtual-8086 mode when paging is disabled, the largest physical address that can be generated is 10FFEFh, or slightly above 1 megabyte. If paging is used in virtual-8086 mode, any page in the 1-megabyte linear address range can be mapped to any page in the 4G physical address space.

Exceptions When Referencing Memory

When the 80386 is executing in real mode or virtual-8086 mode, stack segment and general protection exceptions can be reported for references to memory operands that are outside the fixed 64K segment limits. An offset generated using a 32-bit address mode can exceed 64K. Use of a 32-bit address mode requires use of an address size prefix. 8086 programs use only 16-bit address modes. These can generate a reference that is outside the fixed 64K limit if the offset is close to 64K and a two- or four-byte operand is referenced. For example, a four-byte operand at offset 0FFFEh will generate an exception, since the last two bytes are beyond 64K. Note that the 8086 does not generate exceptions in these cases. Instead, the address wraps around the segment limit to reference part of the operand at offset 0.

The exception reported when a memory reference exceeds the fixed 64K limit depends on the segment register used in the reference. If SS is the segment register, a stack segment exception is reported. Otherwise a general protection exception is reported.

If paging is enabled, a program executing in virtual-8086 mode can also generate a paging exception if it generates a linear address that is invalid or violates the protection model. Chapter 5 details the causes of paging exceptions.

Other exceptions can also occur when executing in real mode or virtual-8086 mode. For example, a divide error will be reported if a DIV or IDIV instruction is executed with a divisor of 0. Most of the exceptions described in Chapter 6 can occur when executing an 8086 program. Only the exceptions that occur when loading segment registers cannot occur in real mode or virtual-8086 mode, since segment registers are treated simply as 16-bit values.

Memory References in Real and Virtual-8086 Modes

The instructions that load segment registers execute differently in real mode and virtual-8086 mode than in protected mode. Instead of the semantics described in Chapter 5 for these instructions, the simpler descriptions given in Chapter 3 suffice to describe the actions of the instructions that load segment registers.

The routine AccessVirtual( ) described in Chapter 5 is changed to the routine Access8086Virtual( ) shown in Listing 9.1 when the processor is executing in real mode or virtual-8086 mode. In these modes, no references are made to the shadow descriptor registers. Instead, the segment base is obtained by multiplying the value in the visible segment selector register by 16. Also, the segment offset and length are checked to ensure

```
/* Access data in a segment addressed by a Segment Register SReg */
/* 8086 mode version for real and virtual-8086 modes.            */
Access8086Virtual(SReg, Offset, Length, RW, IntNumber, Data)
   SegmentRegister SReg;
   int Offset, Length, /* offset in segment, and length of data  */
       RW,             /* 0 if read, 1 if write                   */
       IntNumber,      /* $SS for SS access, $GP for other registers */
       *Data;          /* Pointer to Data to read or write        */
{
   /* Check to ensure access is within 64K segment boundary.     */
   if  (Offset+Length > 10000h)
        SegmentException(IntNumber, 0);

    /* If Offset is within limit, access in linear space.        */
    AccessLinear(SReg.Selector*16 + Offset, Length, CPL, RW, Data);

} /* end Access8086Virtual */
```

► **Listing 9.1:** Access8086Virtual( ) subroutine

that the reference lies totally within the 64K segment limit. In these modes, all segments are readable, writable, and executable.

Emulating the 8086 20-bit Address Arithmetic

The 8086 supports a 20-bit physical address space, but the 80386 uses 32-bit arithmetic when computing linear addresses. 8086 programs may not work properly unless the carry into the twenty-first bit is handled properly. If executing in real mode, or in virtual-8086 mode with paging disabled, the 21-bit linear address is used directly as the physical address driven to external hardware by the 80386. In this case, external hardware is required to simulate the 20-bit address space of the 8086. The simplest hardware solution is to use only the low 20 address pins, ignoring the upper 12 address bits to support only a megabyte of physical memory. Another solution involves using external logic to force a 0 onto address bit 20 (the twenty-first address bit) when executing 8086 programs.

Paging can be used in virtual-8086 mode to simulate the 20-bit linear address wraparound by mapping the pages in the linear address range from 100000h to 10FFEFh to the same physical addresses as the pages in the linear address range from 0 to FFEFh. This technique simulates 20-bit address arithmetic by mapping the addresses in pages above 1 megabyte to the corresponding pages that have the same linear address modulo 2^{20}. This technique supports the 20-bit address arithmetic needed by 8086 programs without requiring any external hardware.

This use of paging to simulate 20-bit addressing is illustrated in Figure 9.3. For simplicity, the identity page map is used in the lower 1 megabyte of the linear address space. This is illustrated by having the linear address range from 0 to 00FFFFh map to the physical address range from 0 to 00FFFFh, as well as mapping the linear address range 010000h to 0FFFFFh to the physical address range 010000 to 0FFFFFh. The linear address range from 100000h to 10FFFFh is mapped to the physical address range 0 to 00FFFFh to simulate the 20-bit address arithmetic required by 8086 programs.

Invalid Instructions

The instructions listed in Table 9.2 are not supported in real mode or virtual-8086 mode. If one of these instructions is used in these modes, an invalid opcode exception (Chapter 6) occurs. None of these instructions are supported by the 8086. Furthermore, they manipulate protected mode segment selectors and descriptors that have no meaning in real or virtual-8086 modes.

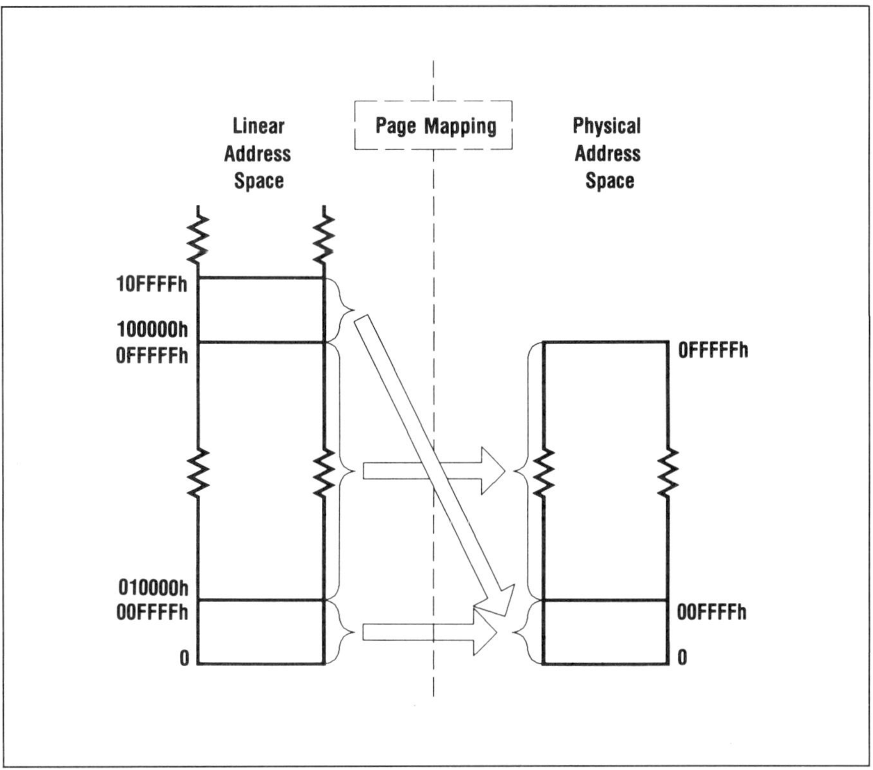

► **Figure 9.3:** Paging simulates 20-bit address arithmetic

ARPL
LAR
LLDT
LSL
LTR
SLDT
STR
VERR
VERW

► **Table 9.2:** Invalid instructions in real mode and virtual-8086 mode

8086 Format for FLDENV, FSTENV, and FNSTENV

The FLDENV, FSTENV, and FNSTENV instructions described in Chapter 3 load or store the control-word, status-word, tag-word, and error-pointer registers from memory. Chapter 2 described the memory format used by these instructions when executed in protected mode. Figure 9.4 illustrates the format used if these instructions are executed with an operand size of 16 (the default size) in real mode or virtual-8086 mode. Programs that execute on an 8086 specify a 16-bit operand size for these instructions. A 32-bit operand size can be used on the 80386 but is neither useful nor recommended.

The format of the control-word, status-word, and tag-word register values is unchanged from the format given in Chapter 2, but the error pointers are stored in a different form. Instead of providing a two-part address for the error pointers, they are provided as 20-bit linear addresses. Refer to Chapter 2 for the format of the opcode.

The FRSTOR, FSAVE, and FNSAVE instructions load and store the

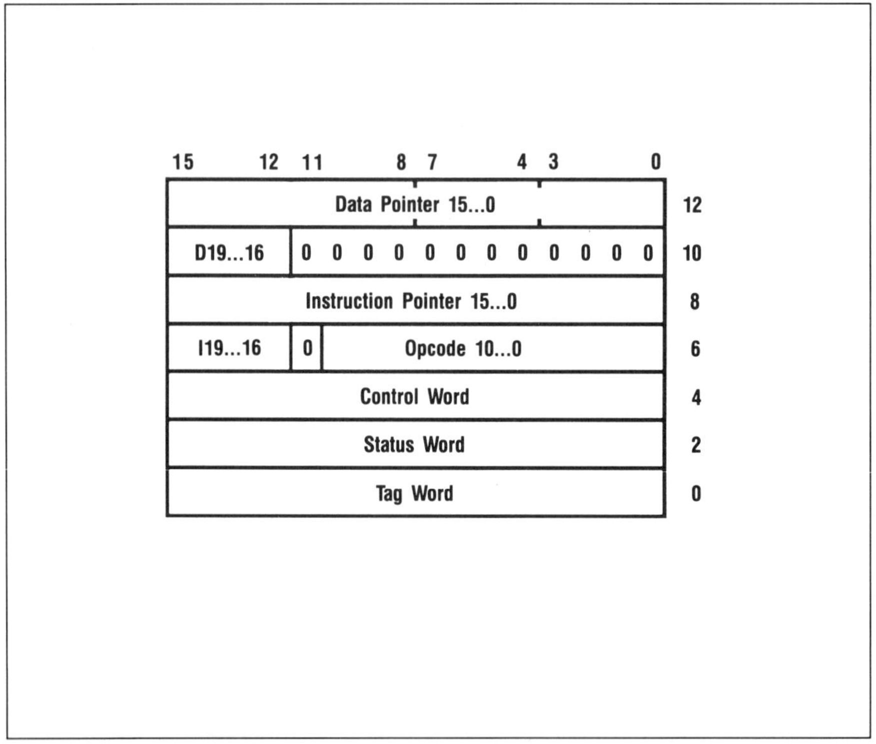

► **Figure 9.4:** 8086 format for FLDENV, FSTENV, and FNSTENV

floating-point accumulators in addition to the registers handled by FLDENV, FSTENV, and FNSTENV. If executed with the 16-bit operand size used by 8086 programs, the control-word, status-word, tag-word, and error-pointer registers are stored in the format given in Figure 9.4. Then ST(0) is loaded or stored from offset 14, ST(1) from offset 24, ST(2) from offset 34, up through ST(7), which is loaded or stored from offset 84. ST(0) through ST(7) are stored in 80-bit temporary real format in all modes.

Virtual-8086 Mode Considerations

The following sections describe the features that are specific to virtual-8086 mode. As described in a later section on entering and leaving virtual-8086 mode, the processor executes in virtual-8086 mode when the VM bit in the EFLAGS register is 1. First, the changes to instructions that are sensitive to the I/O privilege level are described. Then, the methods used to switch between protected mode and virtual-8086 mode are described, to complete the treatment of virtual-8086 mode.

IOPL in Virtual-8086 Mode

When the 80386 is in virtual-8086 mode, instructions that access the EFLAGS register are sensitive to the I/O privilege level (IOPL) described in Chapter 5. The CLI and STI instructions are sensitive to IOPL in all modes (real, virtual-8086, and protected) of the 80386. The PUSHF, POPF, INT n, and IRET instructions are changed to cause a general protection exception with an error code of 0 if executed in virtual-8086 mode when IOPL is less than 3, the privilege level of virtual-8086 mode programs. This ensures that all instructions that can change or store the IF bit in EFLAGS will be sensitive to IOPL. As described in the next section, this allows operating-system software to support a "virtual EFLAGS" register.

When the I/O instructions IN, OUT, INS, or OUTS are executed in virtual-8086 mode, they do not check IOPL before testing the I/O bitmap, as described in Chapter 5 for protected mode programs. Instead, these I/O instructions always reference the I/O permission bitmap stored in the current TSS to determine whether to allow the I/O reference (permission bits are 0) or to generate a general protection exception (one or more permission bits are 1 or beyond the TSS limit). The I/O instructions ignore the IOPL field when executed in virtual-8086 mode.

Because the I/O instructions do not check IOPL when executing in virtual-8086 mode, and the PUSHF, POPF, INT n, and IRET instructions do check IOPL (as do CLI and STI), the IOPL field is interpreted quite differently in virtual-8086 mode than in protected mode. In virtual-8086 mode, IOPL is used to protect the IF bit in the EFLAGS register, and has nothing to do with the I/O instructions. In protected mode, IOPL affects the I/O instructions as well as some of the instructions that can change IF (CLI and STI).

Virtual-8086 Mode with IOPL<3 Operating-system software can set IOPL to a value less than 3 so that a virtual-8086 mode program will generate an exception whenever it executes an instruction that might modify or store the IF bit. The general protection exception handler can then support a virtual EFLAGS register that is different from the actual EFLAGS register in the 80386. The virtual EFLAGS register has IF set as directed by the virtual-8086 mode program, while typically the actual EFLAGS register would have IF = 1 (interrupts enabled) when executing the virtual-8086 program. Operating-system software can use the IF bit in the virtual EFLAGS register to determine if interrupts should be reported to a virtual-8086 task (virtual IF = 1), or held pending (virtual IF = 0). The PUSHF instruction generates an exception so that the exception handler can emulate it by pushing the virtual EFLAGS register on the stack, rather than the actual EFLAGS register.

Virtual-8086 Mode with IOPL = 3 You can execute a program in virtual-8086 mode with IOPL set to 3. This allows the instructions that access the IF bit to execute without raising an exception, giving the virtual-8086 program direct control over INTR interrupt masking. This supports full-speed execution of an 8086 program that executes a large number of instructions sensitive to IOPL. If such a program is executed with IOPL less than 3, many general protection exceptions will be generated, causing a great deal of overhead in repeatedly executing the general protection exception handler to emulate these instructions. With IOPL set to 3, these instructions execute at full speed.

One danger of this approach is that an erroneous or malicious virtual-8086 program could then mask INTR interrupts for a long period of time. This could cause the operating system to fail because it could not service interrupts in time.

To avoid this failure, you could use a watchdog timer to generate an NMI if INTR interrupts are disabled for too long. For example, the NMI timer could be set to interrupt on a period that is twice the length of the normal system timer tied to an INTR interrupt. The system timer handler would reinitialize the NMI watchdog timer every time it executed in response to an INTR interrupt. In this configuration, the NMI watchdog timer would generate an NMI only if the normal system timer INTR did not get serviced for a dangerously long period of time.

Another problem with executing a virtual-8086 program with IOPL set to 3 is that the INT *n* software trap instruction will not generate a general protection exception. Instead, a trap will occur with the given vector number n unless the DPL of the IDT gate is less than 3, in which case a general protection exception will be generated. For vector numbers that must have their IDT gates set to 3, the use of an INT *n* instruction in virtual-8086 mode to enter the handler can be detected simply by looking at the VM bit in the EFLAGS image saved when the handler is entered.

Entering and Leaving Virtual-8086 Mode

The 80386 can switch between protected mode and virtual-8086 mode using the mechanisms described in the next several sections. As with interrupts and exceptions, these mode transfers can occur within a single task, or as part of a task-switch operation. A switch from protected mode to virtual-8086 mode occurs under the following circumstances:

1. An IRET executed in protected mode with NT = 0 in the EFLAGS register will pop EIP, CS, and EFLAGS values from the stack to return to an interrupted procedure within the same task. If the VM bit is 1 in the popped EFLAGS value, and if the IRET is executed with CPL = 0, the interrupted procedure is resumed in virtual-8086 mode. As described in Chapter 5, if the IRET is executed with CPL other than 0, the VM bit is not changed, and so the return is to a protected mode program. Also note that the operand size for the IRET must be 32. An IRET with an operand size of 16 will only restore the lower 16 bits of EFLAGS, and will set (leave) VM = 0.
2. A task switch to a task described by a 386 TSS will resume the new task in virtual-8086 mode if the EFLAGS image loaded from the new TSS has VM = 1. A JMP or CALL instruction to a task gate or TSS, an interrupt through a task gate, or an IRET with NT = 1 in the EFLAGS register can cause a task switch. Since a 286 TSS only stores the low-order 16 bits of EFLAGS, the VM bit is loaded as a 0 during a task switch that uses a 286 TSS.

A switch from virtual-8086 mode to protected mode occurs when an interrupt is signaled or an exception occurs. The interrupt or exception is handled by switching from virtual-8086 mode to protected mode, and then handling the interrupt or exception in protected mode using the interrupt mechanism described in Chapter 6. This mechanism uses the

IDT (Interrupt Descriptor Table) to vector to the handler for the interrupt or exception using one of two methods:

1. The interrupt or exception can be handled in the same task if the IDT entry for the interrupt or exception contains a 386 trap gate or a 386 interrupt gate. The 386 gate types must be used so that the full 32-bit EFLAGS register is saved (which will have VM = 1) to be restored by the matching IRET. The interrupt or exception handler must be at privilege level 0, or else a general protection exception is raised with the new CS selector in the error code. This implies that the matching IRET will be executed at privilege level 0 to allow the VM bit to be changed back to 1.
2. The interrupt or exception is handled in a separate task if the IDT entry contains a task gate. In this case, the current TSS must have the 386 TSS format to ensure that the full 32-bit EFLAGS value can be saved. The new task can be of any type. The new task might contain a 16-bit protected mode program described by a 286 TSS, or a 32-bit protected mode program described by a 386 TSS with VM = 0, or even another virtual-8086 task described by a 386 TSS with VM = 1.

Because the NT bit in the EFLAGS register is ignored when executing in virtual-8086 mode, it is not possible to use IRET to perform a task switch out of a virtual-8086 mode task. An IRET executed in virtual-8086 mode will pop the saved IP, CS, and FLAGS registers to resume an interrupted program, regardless of the value in the NT bit.

Mode Transitions within a Task If an interrupt or exception handled by a 386 trap or interrupt gate is received when the processor is executing in virtual-8086 mode, the 80386 changes modes within the same task from virtual-8086 mode to protected mode. The matching IRET instruction will resume the interrupted virtual-8086 mode program by switching modes from protected mode back to virtual-8086 mode. As noted above, these mode transitions also involve a privilege-level transition. The virtual-8086 mode program executes at privilege level 3, and the handler must execute at level 0.

Interrupt/Exception through a 386 Trap or Interrupt Gate The transfer to the handler uses the same mechanism detailed in Chapter 6 for transitions through trap and interrupt gates, except that the virtual-8086 program's GS, FS, DS, and ES segment registers are pushed onto the new (level 0) stack before the normal interrupt processing begins. To keep the stack aligned, these are pushed as 32-bit values with the segment register in the low-order 16 bits, and the high-order bits undefined. These segment registers are then loaded with null selectors before the interrupt or exception handler is entered.

The four data segment registers GS, FS, DS, and ES are saved on the stack and loaded with null selectors before entering the protected mode interrupt handler, to permit the handler to save and restore the segment registers as valid protected mode values, regardless of the mode of the program executing when the handler is entered. If the handler is entered from a protected mode program, the segment registers will contain valid selectors that can be pushed at entry to the handler and then popped before the IRET. However, if the handler is entered from a virtual-8086 mode program, the segment registers might contain values that are invalid selectors in protected mode. By saving the virtual-8086 segment values on the stack, and loading the data segment registers (GS, FS, DS, and ES) with null selectors, the segment registers will contain valid protected mode values when the interrupt handler is entered.

Figure 9.5 illustrates the stack-switch operation that occurs during an interrupt or exception through a 386 trap or interrupt gate from a virtual-8086 mode program at level 3 to a protected mode interrupt handler, which has to be at level 0. The outer-level stack is addressed by the SS and SP registers, where SS contains an 8086 segment register value, not a protected mode segment selector. The new stack for the inner level is shown on the left at entry to the handler. The GS, FS, DS, and ES registers are pushed onto the new stack, in that order. Then the pointer to the outer-level stack is saved by pushing SS and ESP. Next, the old EFLAGS value is pushed, which will have its VM bit set to 1. Then, the return address is saved by pushing CS and EIP. Finally, an error code is pushed.

At entry to the handler, SS addresses the inner stack segment, and ESP points to the error code. Because the handler executes in protected mode, the SS register contains a selector for the inner-level stack, and the SS shadow descriptor registers are loaded from the descriptor for this segment. Similarly, the new CS selector addresses a protected mode code segment, and the CS shadow descriptor registers are loaded from the descriptor for this segment.

The interrupt or exception handler can examine the EFLAGS image saved on the stack to determine the mode of the interrupted program. If the VM bit in this saved EFLAGS image is 1, the interrupted program was executing in virtual-8086 mode. Otherwise, it was executing in protected mode. The EFLAGS register is always at the same offset from the ESP register, regardless of the mode of the interrupted program. As shown in Figure 9.5, the EFLAGS image is located at offset 12 from ESP if an error code was pushed. Otherwise, EFLAGS is at offset 8.

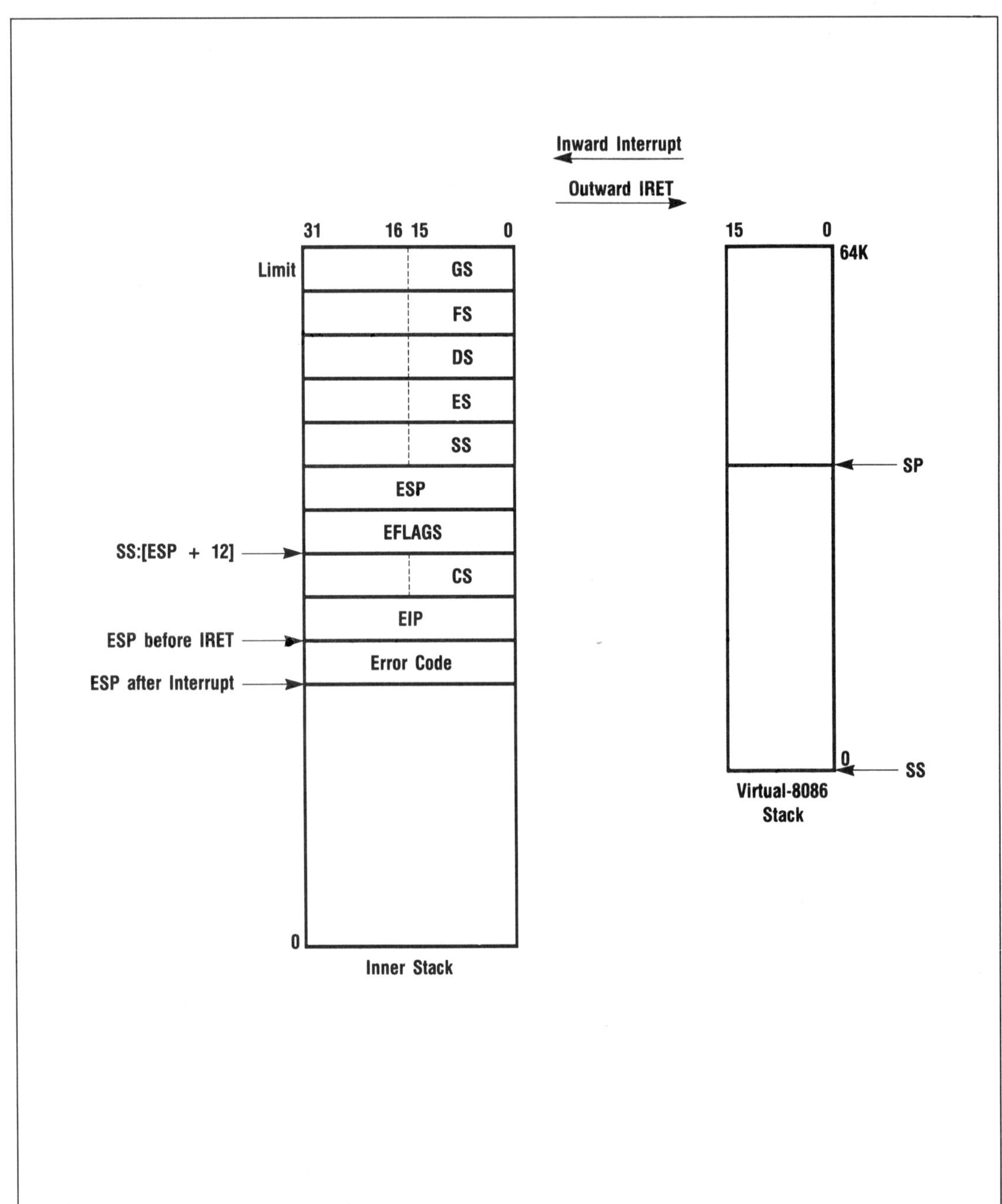

► **Figure 9.5:** Stack switch from virtual-8086 mode through trap or interrupt gate

The changes to the interrupt mechanism described in Chapter 6 to accommodate interrupts out of virtual-8086 mode are described in Listings 9.2 and 9.3. Listing 9.2 contains the modified version of the

```
/* Complete IntTrapGate routine, including virtual-8086 mode. */
/* Changes are highlighted. Original version is in Chapter 6. */
IntTrapGate'(Selector, Offset, ClearIF)
   SelectorType Selector;
   int Offset,
       ClearIF; /* if 1, clear IF before entering handler. */
                /* if 0, leave IF unchanged.               */
{
   SegAttributes Attributes;
   SelectorType GSelector;
   int Base, Limit, GOffset;

/* Selector test */
if ( (Selector & 0FFFCh) == 0) /* Null */
   SegmentException($GP, 0);

/* Read and test descriptor */
ReadDescriptor(Selector,&Attributes,&Base,&Limit,&GSelector,&GOffset);

if (Attributes.DType == 0) /* Can't be System segment or gate */
   SegmentException($GP, Selector);

/* Interrupt to inner-level nonconforming executable present       */
/* segment is OK, but requires switch to inner stack and inner CPL. */
if ( (Attributes.Type>=8) && (Attributes.Type<=11)
     && (Attributes.DPL < CPL) && (Attributes.P == 1) )
          InnerStack(Attributes.DPL, 0, Selector);

/* If coming from virtual-8086 mode, transition must be to level 0. */
if ( (CPL != 0) && (EFLAGS.VM == 1) )
   SegmentException($GP, Selector);

/* Call common routine to finish CS descriptor load. */
Selector.RPL = 0; /* Ignore RPL in selector read from gate. */
CSDescriptorLoad(Selector, Attributes, Base, Limit, $GP);

/* Verify target is within segment limit. */
if (Offset > CS.Limit)
   SegmentException($GP, 0);

/* Get to here only if all protection checks pass.  */
/* Push EFLAGS and return pointer,                  */
/* then modify EFLAGS and load CS selector and EIP. */
ESP = ESP-4;
AccessVirtual(SS, ESP, 4, 1 /* Write */, $SS, &EFLAGS);
ESP = ESP-4;
/* Push 4 bytes, with CS selector in low-order 2 bytes. */
AccessVirtual(SS, ESP, 4, 1 /* Write */, $SS, &CS.Selector);
ESP = ESP-4;
AccessVirtual(SS, ESP, 4, 1 /* Write */, $SS, &EIP);
```

► **Listing 9.2:** IntTrapGate'( ) subroutine

```
EFLAGS.VM = 0; /* Handler executes in protected mode.     */
EFLAGS.TF = 0; /* Turn off single stepping (Chapter 8). */
EFLAGS.NT = 0; /* Interrupt not handled by nested task. */
if (ClearIF == 1)
   EFLAGS.IF = 0;

CS.Selector     = Selector;
CS.Selector.RPL = CPL;
EIP             = Offset;
} /* end IntTrapGate' */
```

► **Listing 9.2:** IntTrapGate'( ) subroutine (continued)

IntTrapGate( ) routine given in Chapter 6. The changes for virtual-8086 mode are highlighted. The first change is to check the value of CPL just after the normal test for an inter-level transition. The handler must execute at level 0 if it can be entered from a virtual-8086 program. At the point where this test is inserted, CPL has been adjusted in the routine InnerStack( ) if necessary, so this is the place to test the CPL of the handler. If it is not at level 0, a $GP exception is raised with the CS selector of the handler as the error code.

The other change to IntTrapGate( ) is to set the VM bit in EFLAGS to 0 before entering the handler. This makes the handler execute in protected mode, even if entered from a virtual-8086 program.

Listing 9.3 shows the InnerStack( ) subroutine modified for interrupts out of virtual-8086 mode, with the changes highlighted. In this routine, the GS, FS, DS, and ES registers are pushed after the new stack is addressed by the SS and ESP registers, but before the old stack pointer is pushed. As the segment registers are pushed, they are loaded with null selectors.

IRET with NT = 0 to a Virtual-8086 Program The IRET instruction, if executed with NT = 0 in the EFLAGS register, will pop information from the stack to return to the interrupted program in the same task. If the IRET returns to a virtual-8086 mode program, the ES, DS, FS, and GS registers are popped off the stack after the normal IRET processing is complete. These values, along with the values loaded into SS and CS, are loaded as 8086 values, not as protected mode selectors.

Figure 9.5 also illustrates the stack before and after an inter-level IRET back to a virtual-8086 program in the same task. The current stack is the inner-level stack shown on the left, addressed as a protected

```
/* Routine to switch stacks for inter-level transitions. */
/* Changed from original version in Chapter 5 to include */
/* virtual-8086 actions, which are highlighted.          */
InnerStack'(NewCPL, DwordCount, NewCSSelector)
   int NewCPL,     /* Switch to stack for this privilege level       */
       DwordCount;/* Count of parameter dwords to copy to new stack */
   SelectorType NewCSSelector; /* need CS selector for error code.  */
{
   SelectorType NewSSSelector;
   SegmentRegister OldSS;
   int TSSOffset, NewESP, tempESP, OldCPL, Dword1;

/* Read new SS and ESP from TSS. */
TSSOffset = NewCPL*8 + 4;
if ( (TSSOffset + 7) > TR.Limit)
   SegmentException($TS, NewCSSelector);
AccessLinear(TR.Base+TSSOffset,   0 /* PL 0 */, 0 /* Read */, &NewESP);
AccessLinear(TR.Base+TSSOffset+4, 0 /* PL 0 */, 0 /* Read */,
                                                      &NewSSSelector);

/* Save old SS and CPL to use during parameter copy loop. */
OldSS = SS;
OldCPL = CPL;

/* Load SS with selector for new stack after changing to new CPL */
/* and loading descriptor into shadow registers.                 */
CPL = NewCPL;
SRegLoad(SS, NewSSSelector, $TS);
/* return if SS load was successful. */
SS.Selector = NewSSSelector;

/* Push data segment registers and load with null selectors, */
/* if coming from virtual-8086 mode. */
if (EFLAGS.VM == 1)
   {NewESP = NewESP-4;
    AccessVirtual(SS, NewESP, 4, 1 /* Write */, $SS, &GS.Selector);
    GS.Selector = 0; GS.Attributes.P = 0;
    NewESP = NewESP-4;
    AccessVirtual(SS, NewESP, 4, 1 /* Write */, $SS, &FS.Selector);
    FS.Selector = 0; FS.Attributes.P = 0;
    NewESP = NewESP-4;
    AccessVirtual(SS, NewESP, 4, 1 /* Write */, $SS, &DS.Selector);
    DS.Selector = 0; DS.Attributes.P = 0;
    NewESP = NewESP-4;
    AccessVirtual(SS, NewESP, 4, 1 /* Write */, $SS, &ES.Selector);
    ES.Selector = 0; ES.Attributes.P = 0;
   }

/* Push old SS and ESP.      */
NewESP = NewESP - 4;
AccessVirtual(SS, NewESP, 4, 1 /* Write */, $SS, &OldSS.Selector);
NewESP = NewESP - 4;
AccessVirtual(SS, NewESP, 4, 1 /* Write */, $SS, &ESP);
```

► **Listing 9.3:** InnerStack'( ) subroutine

```
/* Copy parameters. Writing to new stack uses new CPL.              */
/* Reading from old stack uses old CPL.                             */
/* Order of parameter copying is irrelevant, but is illustrated    */
/* as the same order as originally pushed on the outer stack by    */
/* pointing tempESP at the opposite end of the parameter block     */
/* from ESP.  With this order, we exit from the loop with  NewESP*/
/* pointing to the top of the new stack.                            */
tempESP = ESP + DwordCount*4;
for (i=1; i<=DwordCount; i++){
    CPL = OldCPL;
    tempESP = tempESP - 4;
    AccessVirtual(OldSS, tempESP, 4, 0 /* Read */,  $SS, &Dword1);
    CPL = NewCPL;
    NewESP = NewESP - 4;
    AccessVirtual(SS,      NewESP, 4, 1 /* Write */, $SS, &Dword1);
    } /* end parameter copy loop */

ESP = NewESP; /* exit loop with NewESP pointing to new stack top */
} /* end InnerStack' */
```

► **Listing 9.3:** InnerStack'( ) subroutine (continued)

mode segment with a selector in SS. Before executing the IRET instruction, the handler must adjust the stack by popping the error code so that ESP points to the return pointer. The IRET instruction pops EIP, CS, and EFLAGS from the inner stack. If VM = 1 in the EFLAGS value popped, and the IRET is executed at privilege level 0, the return is to a virtual-8086 program and CS is loaded as an 8086 segment register value. Since a return to virtual-8086 mode is a privilege-level transition (to level 3), and requires a change of stacks, the outer stack pointer is restored by popping ESP and then SS as an 8086 segment value. Finally, the ES, DS, FS, and GS registers are popped as 8086 segment values to complete the IRET.

Listing 9.4 contains the detailed description of IRET, modified to include a return to a virtual-8086 mode program. If the IRET is executed at level 0, and the VM bit is 1 in the new EFLAGS image popped from the stack, the return is to virtual-8086 mode. Instead of loading CS and SS as protected mode segments, only the visible segment selector registers are loaded. In addition, the ES, DS, FS, and GS registers are popped off the stack as 8086 segment register values.

Transfers to Different Tasks An interrupt or exception received in virtual-8086 mode will transfer to a different task if the IDT entry contains a

```
/* Detailed description of the IRET instruction, modified to   */
/* include returning to a virtual-8086 mode program.            */
/* Changes from original version in Chapter 6 are highlighted. */
IRET'()
{
   SelectorType Selector, GSelector;
   SegAttributes Attributes;
   EFLAGSType NewEFLAGS;
   int Base, Limit, Offset, GOffset, NewESP, NewSS;

/* Test NT bit to see if we do a Task return. */
if (EFLAGS.NT == 1)
   {/* Return through Task identified in link of current TSS.*/
    AccessLinear(TR.Base, 2, 0 /* PL 0 */, 0 /* Read */, &Selector);
    TaskGate(Selector, -1 /* Unlink */); /* see Chapter 5. */
   }

else {
   /* Otherwise pop interrupt return information from the stack. */
   AccessVirtual(SS, ESP, 4, 0 /* Read */, $SS, &Offset);
   ESP = ESP + 4;
   AccessVirtual(SS, ESP, 4, 0 /* Read */, $SS, &Selector);
   ESP = ESP + 4;
   AccessVirtual(SS, ESP, 4, 0 /* Read */, $SS, &NewEFLAGS);
   ESP = ESP + 4;

 if ( (NewEFLAGS.VM == 1) && (CPL == 0) )
  {/* Return to a virtual-8086 program. */
   /* Pop old stack pointer from stack, load to SS:ESP below. */
   AccessVirtual(SS, ESP, 4, 0 /* Read */, $SS, &NewESP);
   ESP = ESP - 4;
   AccessVirtual(SS, ESP, 4, 0 /* Read */, $SS, &NewSS);
   ESP = ESP - 4;

   /* Pop 8086 ES, DS, FS, and GS segment values from stack. */
   AccessVirtual(SS, ESP, 4, 0 /* Read */, $SS, &ES.Selector);
   ESP = ESP - 4;
   AccessVirtual(SS, ESP, 4, 0 /* Read */, $SS, &DS.Selector);
   ESP = ESP - 4;
   AccessVirtual(SS, ESP, 4, 0 /* Read */, $SS, &FS.Selector);
   ESP = ESP - 4;
   AccessVirtual(SS, ESP, 4, 0 /* Read */, $SS, &GS.Selector);

   /* Point to outer-level virtual-8086 stack, resume at CPL=3 */
   ESP = NewESP;
   SS.Selector  = NewSS; /* 8086 segment value */
   CPL = 3; /* Virtual-8086 program resumes at level 3. */
  } /* end virtual-8086 mode IRET. */
 else {
   /* Selector tests for IRET to protected mode */
   if ( ((Selector & 0FFFCh) == 0) || (Selector.RPL < CPL))
      SegmentException($GP, 0);
   if (Selector.RPL > CPL) {
```

► **Listing 9.4:** Detailed description of IRET'

```
        /* Inter-level IRET is required if Selector.RPL > CPL.      */
        /* Call subroutine to restore (outer level) stack from      */
        /* SS:ESP stack pointer now at top of (inner-level) stack. */
        OuterStack(Selector.RPL, 0);
        }

     /* Read and test CS descriptor */
     ReadDescriptor(Selector,&Attributes,&Base,&Limit,&GSelector,&GOffset);
     if (Attributes.DType == 0) /* Can't be System segment or gate */
        SegmentException($GP, Selector);

     /* Call common routine to complete CS descriptor load. */
     CSDescriptorLoad(Selector, Attributes, Base, Limit, $GP);

     /* Verify target is within segment limit. */
     if (Offset > CS.Limit)
        SegmentException($GP, 0);
  } /* end protected mode IRET. */

     /* Get to here if all protection tests pass.  Complete visible  */
     /* part of instruction by loading EFLAGS, CS selector, and EIP. */
     EFLAGS = NewEFLAGS;
     CS.Selector = Selector;
     EIP = Offset;
     } /* end NT=0 */
} /* end IRET' */
```

► **Listing 9.4:** Detailed description of IRET' (continued)

task gate. Also, a JMP, CALL, or IRET (with NT = 1) instruction executed in protected mode can perform a task switch. A task switch can be from a virtual-8086 mode program to a protected mode program or to another virtual-8086 program. Or a protected mode task can switch to another protected mode task or to a virtual-8086 mode task. If a task switch out of a virtual-8086 mode task occurs, the EFLAGS image saved in the old TSS will have a 1 in the VM bit position. A task switch to a task that has a 1 in the VM bit position in the EFLAGS image in the new TSS will switch to a virtual-8086 task.

A switch to or from a virtual-8086 task is the same as a switch to a protected mode task, except for the loading of the segment registers. A switch to a virtual-8086 mode task will load the segment registers (CS, SS, DS, ES, FS, and GS) as 8086 segment registers, not as protected mode selectors. Otherwise, the task switch is the same, including the loading of the LDTR with a protected mode selector for the task's LDT segment.

Listing 9.5 contains the TaskSwitch( ) routine introduced in Chapter 5, modified to include task switches to tasks containing a virtual-8086

```
/* TaskSwitch routine from Chapter 5 modified to include */
/* virtual-8086 mode tasks. Changes are highlighted.     */
TaskSwitch'(Selector, Attributes, Base, Limit, Linkage)
   SelectorType Selector;
   SegAttributes Attributes;
   int    Base, Limit,
          Linkage;       /* 0=NoLink, 1=Link, -1=UnLink on chain */
                         /* of nested tasks.                     */
{
if (Limit < 103)
   SegmentException($TS, Selector);

/* Save current machine state in old task's TSS */
AccessTSSState(1 /* Write */);

/* Point TR and Shadow registers to new TSS */
TR.Base       = Base;
TR.Limit      = Limit;
TR.Attributes = Attributes;
OldTSS        = TR.Selector; /* Save old task's TSS selector for link*/
TR.Selector   = Selector;

 /* Load machine state from new task's TSS */
AccessTSSState(0 /* Read */);

/* Handle differences in Linkage */
if (Linkage == 1 /* Link */) {
   /* Save old TSS selector in new TSS, set NT bit.  Leave old */
   /* TSS descriptor marked as busy. */
   AccessLinear(TR.Base, 2, 0 /* Level 0 */, 1 /* Write */, &OldTSS);
   EFLAGS.NT = 1;
   SetTSSBusy(Selector, 1);    /* Mark new TSS descriptor busy    */
   } /* end Link */
else if (Linkage == -1 /* UnLink */) {
   SetTSSBusy(OldTSS, 0);     /* Mark old TSS descriptor not busy */
   } /* end UnLink */
else if (Linkage == 0 /* NoLink */) {
   SetTSSBusy(OldTSS, 0);     /* Mark old TSS descriptor not busy */
   SetTSSBusy(Selector, 1);   /* Mark new TSS descriptor busy     */
   } /* end NoLink */

CR0.TS = 1; /* Set Task-Switched bit */

if (EFLAGS.VM == 1)
   CPL = 3; /* virtual-8086 mode runs at level 3. */
   else CPL = CS.Selector.RPL; /* CPL from RPL field of CS selector */

/* Visible state now restored.  Load descriptors into shadow */
/* registers for LDTR and segment registers.                 */
/* Mark all descriptors invalid for fault handling.          */
/* Present Attribute is ignored in virtual-8086 mode.        */
LDTR.Attributes.Present = 0;
CS.Attributes.Present = 0;
```

► **Listing 9.5:** TaskSwitch'( ) subroutine

```
SS.Attributes.Present = 0;
DS.Attributes.Present = 0;
ES.Attributes.Present = 0;
FS.Attributes.Present = 0;
GS.Attributes.Present = 0;

/* Must load LDTR first. LDTR loaded even in virtual-8086 mode. */
if (LDTR.Selector.TI == 1 /* in LDT */)
   SegmentException($TS, LDTR.Selector);
if ((LDTR.Selector & 0FFFCh) = 0 /* Null */) {
   /* OK if LDTR is null. */
   LDTR.Attributes.P = 0;
   }
else {/* Read and test descriptor if selector is not null */
   ReadDescriptor(LDTR.Selector,&Attributes,&Base,&Limit,
                  &GSelector,&GOffset);
   if ( (Attributes.DType == 1)
        || (Attributes.Type != 2 /* LDT */)
        || (Attributes.Present == 0) )
      SegmentException($TS, LDTR.Selector);
   /* Load LDTR shadow registers if all checks pass */
   SetAccessed(LDTR.Selector);
   LDTR.Attributes = Attributes;
   LDTR.Base       = Base;
   LDTR.Limit      = Limit;
   } /* end LDTR.Selector not Null */

if (EFLAGS.VM == 0) {
/* Load remaining descriptor shadow registers if in protected */
/* mode. CS load is same as a jump through a call gate.       */
JumpGate(CS.Selector, EIP, $TS);

SRegLoad(SS, SS.Selector, $TS);
SRegLoad(DS, DS.Selector, $TS);
SRegLoad(ES, ES.Selector, $TS);
SRegLoad(FS, FS.Selector, $TS);
SRegLoad(GS, GS.Selector, $TS);
} /* end protected mode descriptor shadow register loads. */

/* Clear LE bits in DR7. See Chapter 8 */
DR7.LE0 = 0;
DR7.LE1 = 0;
DR7.LE2 = 0;
DR7.LE3 = 0;

} /* end TaskSwitch' */
```

► **Listing 9.5:** TaskSwitch'( ) subroutine (continued)

mode program. The first change is that the privilege level of the new task is 3 if it is in virtual-8086 mode, instead of coming from the RPL field of the CS selector. A new LDT is addressed even if the task is executing in virtual-8086 mode. This is necessary since the task may switch out of virtual-8086 mode, for example, to handle an interrupt or exception through a trap or interrupt gate. These interrupt or exception handlers can expect to address segments mapped by the LDT.

The other change to the TaskSwitch( ) routine is that the descriptor shadow registers are not loaded if the new task is in virtual-8086 mode. Instead, only the segment selectors are needed, as loaded by the Access TSSState( ) routine.

Real Mode Considerations

The following sections describe features specific to programs that execute in real mode. First, the machine state at initialization is described. The 80386 is in real mode when it is turned on. A short bootstrap program, such as that shown in Chapter 7, is required to initialize the system segments and control registers before entering protected mode. Next, the methods available to transfer from real mode to protected mode and back to real mode are described. The third aspect of real mode is the difference in interrupt handling. A different interrupt mechanism is used when the processor is in real mode.

80386 State at Initialization

When the 80386 is reset, the processor begins execution in real mode, with the registers initialized with the values given in Table 9.3. Registers not listed in Table 9.3 are undefined after reset, and must be initialized by software. The *80386 Data Sheet* from Intel (cited in the Introduction) details the process of resetting the processor.

The EAX register contains a self-test signature if a self-test was selected as part of the reset process. This signature is 0 if the self-test passed. The value in EAX is undefined if the self-test was not selected at reset (and probably will not be 0). Refer to the *80386 Data Sheet* for details of how to select self-test at reset, and what is tested.

The EDX register is initialized with a component/revision ID. The component ID is in the DH register and is 3 for the 80386. Future processors in the 386 family will use different component IDs. Previous 86 family processors do not support this component/revision ID. Instead, they initialize DX to an undefined (random) value. The revision ID is in the DL register. This is a unique number for each major revision of the processor.

REGISTER	INITIAL VALUE
EAX	Self-test signature
ECX	Undefined
EDX	Component/revision ID
EBX	Undefined
ESP	Undefined
EBP	Undefined
ESI	Undefined
EDI	Undefined
EFLAGS	00000002h
EIP	0FFF0h
ES	0
CS	F000h
SS	0
DS	0
FS	0
GS	0
IDTR	Base = 0, limit = 3FFh
CR0	0 or 10h
DR7	0

► **Table 9.3:** Initial register values

The CS and EIP registers are initialized to 0F000h and 0FFF0h. Also, until the first intersegment control transfer occurs, references to the CS register go to a physical address that has 1s in the upper 12 address bits (A31 to A20). This means that after reset, the first instruction is fetched from physical address 0FFFFFFF0h, and intrasegment jumps can be used to execute code from the upper 64K (addresses 0FFFF0000h to 0FFFFFFFFh) of the physical address space. If the processor is still in real mode when the first intersegment transfer occurs (an intersegment CALL, JMP, RET, or IRET instruction, or an interrupt or exception), the transfer will reload the CS register and clear the upper 12 address bits to 0. Most 80386 systems will include a bootstrap ROM at the high end of memory, which will contain the bootstrap code as well as parts of the operating system.

The data segment registers SS, DS, ES, FS, and GS are initialized to 0, to address data in the lower 64K of memory (addresses 0 to 0FFFFh).

The EFLAGS register is initialized to 2, so that interrupts (IF = 0) and single-stepping (TF = 0) are disabled. IDTR is initialized to have a base address of 0 and a limit of 3FFh. This is compatible with the 8086, which stores its interrupt table at address 0. The interrupt table contains 256 four-byte entries, as described later in this chapter in the section on interrupt handling in real mode. CR0 is initialized to 0 or 10h, with all bits but the ET bit cleared to 0. ET is set to 1 if an 80387 is sensed by the 80386 at reset. Otherwise, if an 80287 or no coprocessor is present, the ET bit is 0. The initial value of CR0 has PE = 0 (protection disabled) and PG = 0 (paging disabled), so the processor is executing in real mode. DR7 is initialized to 0 to disable all debug breakpoints.

Software must initialize the stack by loading SS and SP with initial values before executing any instructions (or interrupts) that use the stack. Also, before interrupts are enabled, the interrupt table must be initialized. Although the 80386 is reset with interrupts disabled, NMIs are always enabled and might occur immediately after reset unless external hardware is provided to mask NMI.

Transfers from Real Mode to Protected Mode

After reset, a bootstrap program can be used to initialize system segments and control registers, and to set the PE bit in CR0 to 1 to begin execution in protected mode. Refer to Chapter 7 for a complete example of a transfer from real mode to protected mode. Immediately after you load CR0 with a 1 in the PE bit position, an intrasegment jump must be executed to flush the execution pipe of instructions that may have been fetched and decoded in real mode. This jump is typically to the next instruction.

After you enter protected mode, the segment registers should be reloaded with valid protected mode selectors (or null selectors). CS can be "reloaded" with an intersegment control transfer such as a JMP or CALL instruction. The TR register must be loaded with a selector for a system segment of type available TSS, and the LDTR must be loaded with a null selector or a system segment of type LDT.

The GDTR and IDTR must be loaded with the base and limit addresses of the GDT and IDT. Unlike the segment registers and the LDTR and TR registers, these registers can be loaded before entering protected mode. The IDT must be in the format used by protected mode interrupts, described in Chapter 6.

Transfers from Protected Mode to Real Mode

It is possible to transfer from protected mode to real mode in two ways:

1. Use external hardware to reset the 80386.
2. Load CR0 with a value that has a 0 in the PE bit position.

The first method is described in an earlier section of this chapter on machine state at initialization. The second method provides a software mode switch, but you must follow these guidelines:

1. The transfer must occur from a program executing in a code segment that is exactly 64K in size (limit = 0FFFFh).
2. Before loading CR0 to set PE to 0, the SS, DS, ES, FS, and GS segment registers must be loaded with selectors for a present read/write expand-up data segment, with DPL = 0, that is exactly 64K in size.
3. CR0 must be loaded with a value that has a 0 in the PE bit position.
4. Finally, a direct intersegment JMP instruction must be executed immediately after loading CR0. This JMP will flush the processor pipeline and transfer to the real mode program in the lower megabyte of physical memory.

During this mode transition, interrupts (including NMI) should be disabled until the IDTR is reloaded to point to an interrupt table in the format used in real mode. An alternative to switching back to real mode is to use virtual-8086 mode to execute 8086 programs.

Before you make the transition from protected mode to real mode, paging must be turned off. This is best done by executing in a code segment that is identity-mapped (has the same address in both the linear and physical address spaces), and using data that is also identity-mapped. Within this context, paging can be disabled by loading CR0 with a value that has a 0 in the PG bit position, executing an intra-segment jump to flush the processor pipeline, and finally, loading CR3 to flush the paging cache.

Interrupt Handling in Real Mode

Interrupts and exceptions that occur when the processor is executing in real mode are handled with a mechanism different from the method used in protected mode, which was described in Chapter 6. In real mode, interrupts and exceptions are handled using the simpler method from the 8086. The IDT has a different format in real mode, and interrupts and exceptions are handled using a method that is somewhat similar to the use of interrupt gates as described in Chapter 6.

In real mode, the interrupt descriptor table is an array of four-byte entries addressed by the IDTR register. Each entry contains a 32-bit pointer to the first instruction of the interrupt handler. As illustrated in Figure 9.6, each pointer contains an offset in the low-order 16 bits, and a segment register value in the upper 16 bits. This pointer gives the values to load into IP and CS to begin execution of the real mode interrupt handler.

In real mode, interrupts and exceptions are handled using a 16-bit version of the semantics given in Chapter 3 for the INT instruction. First, the 16-bit FLAGS register is pushed onto the stack, followed by the CS and IP registers. Then, the interrupt table is consulted to find the pointer to load into CS and IP to begin execution of the handler.

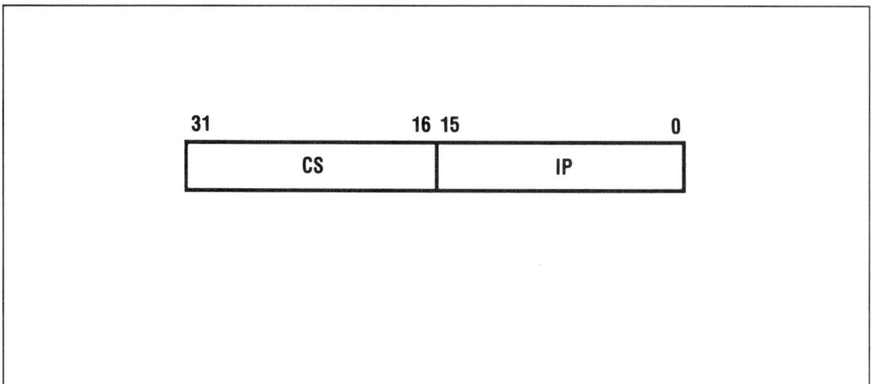

► **Figure 9.6:** Real mode interrupt table entry format

Finally, the TF and IF bits in EFLAGS are set to 0 to disable single-stepping and interrupts at entry to the handler. No error code is pushed for exceptions that occur in real mode.

The IRET instruction described in Chapter 3 can be used to return from real mode interrupt and exception processing. When executed in real mode, IRET uses the semantics detailed in Chapter 3, not the extended semantics described in Chapter 6 for protected mode IRET. IRET pops the IP, CS, and FLAGS values from the stack to resume the interrupted real mode program.

Figure 9.7 illustrates the values pushed during a real mode interrupt, and popped during a real mode IRET. The stack is illustrated as 16 bits wide to match the 8086 stack. The FLAGS register is pushed first, at the highest address. Then, the CS and IP registers are pushed. At entry to the interrupt or exception handler, SP points to the pushed IP image. No error code is pushed when handling real mode exceptions. The matching IRET will pop the IP, CS, and FLAGS values from the stack to resume execution, with SP restored to the value it had before the interrupt or exception.

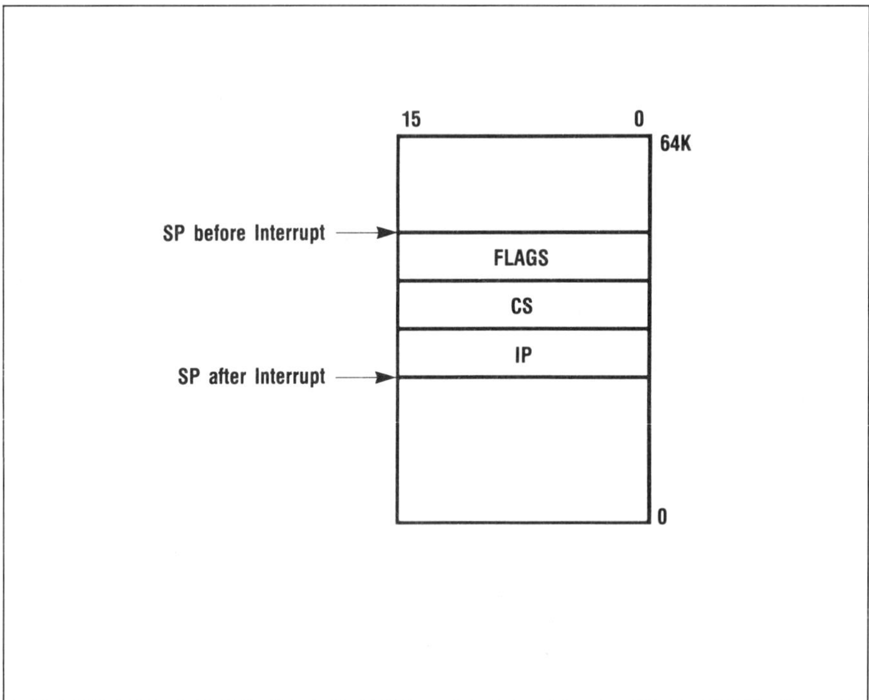

► **Figure 9.7:** Stack usage by real mode interrupts/exceptions, and IRET

Listing 9.6 details the handling of interrupts and exceptions in real mode. Note that the routine Access8086Virtual is used to access memory in the real mode stack. If the interrupt table entry for the given interrupt or exception is beyond the IDTR limit value, a general protection exception is raised. Double faults can occur if the IDTR limit value is smaller than required to access the interrupt table entry for the exception. If the IDTR limit is less than 35, the double fault entry cannot be accessed and the processor enters the shutdown state described in Chapter 6.

► Executing 80286 Protected Mode Programs

Programs that execute in protected mode on the 80286 will also execute on the 80386. You can run both 80286 application programs and

```
/* Process an Interrupt or Exception in real mode. */
InterruptREAL(VecNumber)

int VecNumber; /* Vector Number */

{
/* Push 16-bit FLAGS, CS, and IP. */
SP = SP-2;
Access8086Virtual(SS, SP, 2, 1 /* Write */, $SS, &FLAGS);
SP = SP-2;
Access8086Virtual(SS, SP, 2, 1 /* Write */, $SS, &CS.Selector);
SP = SP-2;
Access8086Virtual(SS, SP, 2, 1 /* Write */, $SS, &IP);

EFLAGS.TF = 0; /* Turn off single-stepping (Chapter 8). */
EFLAGS.IF = 0; /* Disable INTR interrupts. */

/* Read interrupt table entry for indicated vector number, */
/* and load CS and IP with the pointer to the handler.     */
if (VecNumber*4+3 > IDTR.Limit)
   SegmentException($GP, 0);

AccessLinear(IDTR.Base+VecNumber*4,   2, 0 /* PL 0 */, 0 /* Read */,
             &IP);
AccessLinear(IDTR.Base+VecNumber*4+2, 2, 0 /* PL 0 */, 0 /* Read */,
             &CS.Selector);

} /* end InterruptREAL */
```

► **Listing 9.6:** Interrupt and exception handling in real mode

operating systems on the 80386 with no change. There are two options for running 80286 application programs:

1. Run an 80286 operating system on the 80386, and run the 80286 application on this operating system. This method uses only the 16-bit subset of the 80386, in effect using the 80386 as a fast 80286.
2. Run a 32-bit operating system on the 80386, and run the 80286 application by interposing a 16-bit interface library between the application and the 32-bit operating system. This library translates the calls to 16-bit operating-system functions used by the 80286 application into calls to the 32-bit functions in the 80386 operating system.

The 80386 can run 80286 operating systems because the memory-management, protection, and tasking model of the 80286 is a subset of the 80386 model described in Chapter 5, just as the 80286 registers, address modes, and instructions are a subset of those on the 80386. The 80286 supports the same memory segments as the 80386, but with a smaller range of base addresses and segment limits. The 80286 supports system segments and gates with types less than 8 (available 286 TSS, LDT, busy 286 TSS, 286 call gate, task gate, 286 trap gate, and 286 interrupt gate).

The 80286 supports memory segments using descriptors of the same format as the 80386 descriptors shown in Figure 5.10, except that the high-order 16 bits are 0. This provides the following subset of 80386 memory segments.

1. The upper 8 bits of the base address are 0s, limiting the physical address space to 24 bits.
2. The G bit is 0, specifying a byte-granular limit.
3. The D bit is 0, providing a 16-bit default for code segments, stack segments, and expand-down segments.
4. The upper 4 bits of the limit are 0. Combined with the restriction to byte granularity, this provides a maximum segment limit of 0FFFFh to support a 64K segment size.

System segment descriptors (shown in Figure 5.11) share the same restrictions as memory segments. Gates (shown in Figure 5.12) are similarly restricted to have their high-order 16 bits equal to 0, limiting the offset field to 64K. 286 call gates also interpret the DwordCount field as a word count, not a dword count, so that use of a 286 call gate in an interlevel CALL will copy 2*DwordCount bytes of parameters.

The 286 call, trap, and interrupt gates push 16-bit data that is the lower 16 bits of the 32-bit data pushed by the 386 call, trap, and interrupt gates. Otherwise, they operate the same as the 386 gates, described in Chapter 5. The RET and IRET instructions can be used with a 16-bit operand size to return from procedures entered with these 286 gates.

The 286 task mechanism is the same as the 386 mechanism, except that only the 16-bit register state is saved and restored when switching from or to a task described by a 286 TSS. The 286 TSS format provides the low-order 16 bits of the fields in the 386 TSS, and also omits the CR3 field and the I/O permission bitmap.

The FLDENV, FRSTOR, FSTENV, FNSTENV, FSAVE, and FNSAVE instructions described in Chapter 3 load or store the control-word, status-word, tag-word, and error-pointer registers from memory. If these instructions are executed with a 16-bit operand size, the format used to save or restore this data is simply the lower 16 bits of each dword in the 32-bit format shown in Figure 2.22. This limits the offset parts of the error pointers to 16 bits, and omits the opcode field.

Comparison of 80386,
80286, and 8086

Appendix 

THIS APPENDIX DETAILS THE DIFFERENCES between the 8086, 80286, and 80386. The contents of this appendix do not repeat the details of register set, memory addressing, instruction encoding, 80286 segmentation, real mode segmentation, and real mode interrupt handling differences between the 80386 and 80286/8086, which were described in Chapter 9.

► 8086 Compared to the 80386

Table A.1 summarizes the instructions in the 80386 that are not in the 8086.

The entire protection model (four levels of protection, descriptors and their tables, tasks, and gates) and paging, and the instructions to support them, are not in the 8086 and are in the 80386. Table A.2 summarizes the protection model instructions in the 80386 that are not in the 8086.

In addition to these new instructions, the semantics of all instructions that affect segment registers (PUSH, POP, MOV, LES, LDS) and all instructions that alter control flow (CALL, INT, INTO, IRET, JMP, RET) are significantly different on the 80386 when in protected mode than they are in the 8086.

Below are differences in execution between the 8086 and 80386 of certain instructions.

Divide Exceptions

The CS:IP value for a divide error points to the next instruction on the 8086. The CS:EIP points to the instruction that caused the exception on the 80386.

INSTRUCTION	DESCRIPTION
PUSH imm	Push immediate data onto the stack
PUSHA and POPA	Push and pop all eight general registers
IMUL reg,imm	Signed multiply with immediate
IMUL reg,reg/mem,imm	Signed multiply with immediate
IMUL reg,reg/mem	Uncharacterized signed multiply
RCR/RCL reg/mem,imm	Rotate by an immediate
ROR/ROL reg/mem,imm	Rotate by an immediate
SAL/SAR reg/mem,imm	Shift by an immediate
SHL/SHR reg/mem,imm	Shift by an immediate
INS/OUTS	String input and output to a port
ENTER/LEAVE	Procedure entry and exit
BOUND	Array bounds checking
LSS/LFS/LGS	Segment load instructions
Jcc 32-bit displacement	Long-displacement conditional jumps
BT/BTC/BTR/BTS	Bit operations
BSF/BSR	Bit scan
SHRD/SHLD	Double shift instructions
SETcc	Set byte on condition
MOVSX/MOVZX	Move and sign/zero extend
MOV DRx,reg;reg,DRx	Move to/from debug register
MOV CRx,reg;reg,CRx	Move to/from control register
FS and GS prefixes	Segment prefixes for FS and GS

► **Table A.1:** 80386 application instructions not in the 8086

Undefined Opcodes

Opcodes that are not defined in the 8086 either cause invalid opcode exceptions (exception 6) in the 80386 or execute one of the new instructions.

Value of PUSH SP

The value pushed by PUSH SP is the post-incremented version for the 8086 and the pre-incremented version for the 80386.

Shifts and Rotates

The shift count of the 8086 for all shift and rotate instructions is 8 bits. The shift count is 5 bits on the 80386 (that is, counts are truncated modulo 32 on the 80386).

INSTRUCTION	DESCRIPTION
ARPL	Adjust requested privilege level
CLTS	Clear the task-switched flag
LAR	Load access rights
LGDT	Load global descriptor table
LIDT	Load interrupt descriptor table
LLDT	Load local descriptor table
LMSW	Load machine status word
LSL	Load segment limit
LTR	Load task register
SGDT	Store global descriptor table
SIDT	Store interrupt descriptor table
SLDT	Store local descriptor table
SMSW	Store machine status word
STR	Store task register
VERR	Verify segment for reading
VERW	Verify segment for writing

► **Table A.2:** 80386 protection model instructions not in the 8086

Redundant Prefixes

The 8086 has no instruction length limit. The 80386 limits the instruction length to 15 bytes. Thus, redundant prefixes may result in invalid opcode exceptions.

Accesses above 64K

The 8086 wraps around at 64K segment boundaries to address 0. This causes a limit violation if the segment is 64K, as it is in real address mode, in the 80386. This is true for memory operand accesses and sequential code accesses.

LOCK

LOCK is restricted to certain instructions on the 80386, as described in Chapter 3. The use of LOCK is not limited in the 8086.

Single-Stepping

The priority of the single-step exception is higher than external interrupts. Thus, an external interrupt handler will not be single-stepped.

FLAGS Register

The FLAGS register is different in bits 12 to 15, as detailed in Chapter 2.

NMI Interrupt

NMI cannot interrupt an NMI handler on the 80386 as it can on the 8086.

Coprocessor Error

Coprocessor errors use vector number 16 on the 80386. Any vector number can be used by the 8086.

Prefixes on Coprocessor Instructions

When a coprocessor exception handler is called, the value saved for CS:IP by the 8086 does not include prefixes, if there were any. The 80386 points to the start of the coprocessor instruction, including prefixes, if present.

One-Megabyte Wraparound

The 8086 has only 20 bits of physical address space. Segment + offset physical addresses that exceed 1 megabyte would wrap around (be truncated) to a 20-bit address. The 80386, having 32 bits of physical addresses, does not wrap around in this manner.

Repeated String Instructions

The CS:IP saved by the 8086 for repeated string instructions does not include prefixes, if there were any. The 80386 points to the start of the repeated string instruction, including prefixes.

► 80286 Compared to the 80386

The most significant differences between the 80286 and the 80386 are the 32-bit addresses and data types, and paging and memory management. To support these items, several instructions have been added to the 80386. In addition, several other application instructions have been added to the 80386. The differences in segmentation support and operand addressing were detailed in Chapter 9. Table A.3 summarizes the 80386 instructions that are not in the 80286.

INSTRUCTION	DESCRIPTION
LSS/LFS/LGS	Segment load instructions
Jcc 32-bit displacement	Long-displacement conditional jumps
BT/BTC/BTR/BTS	Bit operations
BSF/BSR	Bit scan
SHRD/SHLD	Double shift instructions
SETcc	Set byte on condition
MOVSX/MOVZX	Move and sign/zero extend
IMUL reg,reg/mem	Uncharacterized signed multiply
MOV DRx,reg;reg,DRx	Move to/from debug register
MOV CRx,reg;reg,CRx	Move to/from control register
FS and GS prefixes	Segment prefixes for FS and GS

► **Table A.3:** 80386 instructions not in the 80286

Below are differences in execution between the 80286 and 80386 of certain instructions.

LOCK

LOCK is restricted to certain instructions on the 80386, as described in Chapter 3. The use of LOCK is not limited in the 80286.

Comparison of 80387, 80287, and 8087

Appendix 

THIS APPENDIX DETAILS THE DIFFERENCES between the 8087, 80287, and 80387.

► 80287 (and 8087) Compared to the 80387

This section lists the differences between the 80387 and the 80287. The same differences also exist between the 80387 and the 8087. The next section details additional differences between the 80387 and the 8087 that do not exist between the 80387 and the 80287. Table B.1 summarizes the instructions in the 80387 that are not in the 80287/8087.

INSTRUCTION	DESCRIPTION
FPREM1	Partial remainder—IEEE
FUCOM/FUCOMP/FUCOMPP	Unordered compare
FSIN	Sine
FCOS	Cosine
FSINCOS	Sine and cosine

► **Table B.1:** 80387 application instructions not in the 80287/8087

Instruction Execution

In addition to the new instructions in Table B.1 are the following changes in certain instruction execution.

Extended Ranges

The ranges of the FSCALE, FPTAN, FPATAN, and F2XM1 instructions have been increased. The details of the new (and old) instruction ranges are given with the detailed instruction descriptions in Chapter 3.

FPTAN

Bit 10 of the status word (C2) is set to indicate incomplete FPTAN, where this bit is undefined for the 80287/8087.

Denormal Operations

FBSTP, FDIV, FIST, FISTP, FPREM, and FSQRT can operate on denormal operands on the 80387, where they cannot on the 80287/8087.

FPREM Condition Codes

The condition codes (CC3-CC0) are not reliably set on the 80287/8087, where they are on the 80387.

FLD Extended-Real Denormal

A denormal does not generate a denormal exception on the 80387, where it does on the 80287/8087.

FXTRACT

An operand of 0 generates the zero divide exception and sets ST(1) to minus infinity on the 80387, where the 80287/8087 sets ST(1) to 0 and no exception is reported. An operand of plus infinity generates no exception on the 80387, where an invalid operation exception is generated on the 80287/8087.

FLD Constant

The rounding control is in effect on the 80387, where it is not on the 80287/8087.

FLD Short Real/Long Real

Loading a denormal causes the number to be converted to extended precision on the 80387, where it is converted to an unnormal on the 80287/8087. When loading a signaling NaN, an invalid operation exception is raised on the 80387, where none is raised on the 80287/8087.

FSETPM

FSETPM is an 80287 instruction that is a FNOP on the 80387.

Transcendentals

The round-up bit of the status word is generated by the 80387, where it is undefined on the 80287/8087.

Other Differences

The following list summarizes other differences that do not deal with particular instructions but rather with initialization, data types, exception reporting, and the tag, status, and control words.

RESET

At reset, the IE and ES bits of the status word are set and the IM bit of the control word is reset to indicate that an 80387 is present, thus allowing the 80386 to determine whether an 80387 or the 80287 is present.

Quiet NaN

The 80287 has only one kind of NaN, a signaling NaN. The 80387 also supports a quiet NaN, which does not generate an exception.

Unsupported Formats

The 80387 generates an invalid operation exception whenever one of the unsupported formats is encountered (Table 1.7): pseudo-NaN, pseudo-zero, pseudo-infinity, and unnormal. The 80287/8087 supports these and does not generate an exception when encountered. Also, the 80287 defines pseudo-zero and unnormal as valid (00b in the tag word), where all are classified as special data (10b in the tag word) on the 80387.

Invalid Operation

An FSQRT, FDIV, and FPREM or conversion to BCD or integer will not raise an invalid operation exception on the 80387, as it does on the 80287/8087.

Denormal Exception

Transcendental instructions and FXTRACT will flag a denormal exception on the 80387, where they did not on the 80287.

Overflow Exception

When rounding mode is set to chop, the masked response to an overflow exception is the most positive or negative valid number on the 80387, where it is plus or minus infinity on the 80287/8087. If the overflow exception is not masked, the precision error will be flagged on the 80387, where it is not on the 80287. Also when unmasked, the result stored on the stack is rounded per precision control or opcode on the 80387, where it is not rounded on the 80287/8087.

Underflow Exception

When the underflow exception is masked, the 80387 will flag the underflow exception only when the underflow causes a loss in accuracy. The 80287 will flag the underflow exception on underflow when the rounding control is set to round-to-zero even if no loss of accuracy occurs. When the underflow exception is unmasked and the result is to be stored on the stack, the result is rounded per the precision control or opcode on the 80387, where it is not rounded on the 80287/8087.

Exception Precedence

The denormalization exception has the same precedence if masked or unmasked on the 80387, whereas it takes precedence over all other exceptions when unmasked on the 80287/8087. This saves unneeded normalizing of a denormal on the 80387.

Infinity Control

The 80387 supports only the affine interpretation of infinity, where the 80287/8087 supports both the affine and projective.

Stack Overflow/Underflow

In the case of a stack fault, bit 6 of the status word is set and bit 10 is set to denote stack underflow in addition to the invalid exception (bit 0) on the 80387. The 80287/8087 only signals invalid exception.

Status-Word Condition Bits

The status-word condition bits are set to 0 by FINIT, incomplete FPREM, and hardware reset on the 80387. The 80287 does not modify these bits by these operations.

Tag Word

It is possible to load tag values that are inconsistent with the contents in the register with the FLDENV and FRSTOR instructions. The 80387 only relies on the empty/non-empty bits (value 11 for empty and 00, 01, and 10 for non-empty) of the tag word and analyzes the non-empty register contents for all other cases. The 80287/8087 relies on the tag value to determine the operand class and does not analyze the register contents.

► 8087 Compared to the 80387

In addition to the changes between the 80287/8087 and the 80387 described above, the 8087 has additional differences compared to the 80387. Exception processing between the 80387 and the 8087 is the most significant area of change. 8087 exception handlers will, most likely, have to be rewritten to execute on the 80387. The applications code of the 8087 can, most likely, execute without change on the 80387.

FENI/FNENI and FDISI/FNDISI

The FENI/FNENI and FDISI/FNDISI instructions are ignored by the

80387 (no 80387 state is altered). 8087 exception handling code making use of these instructions is probably not compatible on the 80387.

Numeric Exceptions

As noted in Appendix A, the means of exception processing in the 8087 and the 80387 is quite different. The 8087 can process interrupts via any interrupt vector, where interrupts must be processed as interrupt vector 16 on the 80387. Additionally, the 8087 interrupts are processed via a separate interrupt controller device. This means of processing numeric exceptions is not valid on the 80387.

Exception Pointer

As detailed in Chapter 9, the format for the saved instruction and data pointers is different on the 8087 and 80387.

Segmentation

It is possible to generate a segmentation fault on the 80387 if the instruction lies outside the bounds of the segment (exception 13) or if the operand lies outside the segment (exception 9 or 13). Neither of these are possible on the 8087.

Exception 7

When executing a floating-point instruction, it is possible to generate an exception indicating emulation or task-switched (EM and TS bits of the 80386 CR0) on the 80387. Neither of these are possible on the 8087.

Prefixes on Coprocessor Instructions

When a coprocessor exception handler is called, the value saved for CS:IP by the 8087 does not include prefixes, if there are any. The 80387 points to the start of the coprocessor instruction, including prefixes if present.

WAIT Instruction

As discussed in Chapter 3, the 80387 and 80386 are automatically synchronized and do not require the programmer to include explicit WAIT instructions to force synchronization except after instructions that store data from the 80387 into memory. Programs including unnecessary WAITs execute properly, but are wasteful in code space and execution time, on the 80387.

Binary, Hexadecimal, and Decimal Table

Appendix C

HEX	BINARY	DECIMAL
0	0	0
1	1	1
2	10	2
3	11	3
4	100	4
5	101	5
6	110	6
7	111	7
8	1000	8
9	1001	9
A	1010	10
B	1011	11
C	1100	12
D	1101	13
E	1110	14
F	1111	15
10	10000	16
11	10001	17
⋮	⋮	⋮

Powers of Two

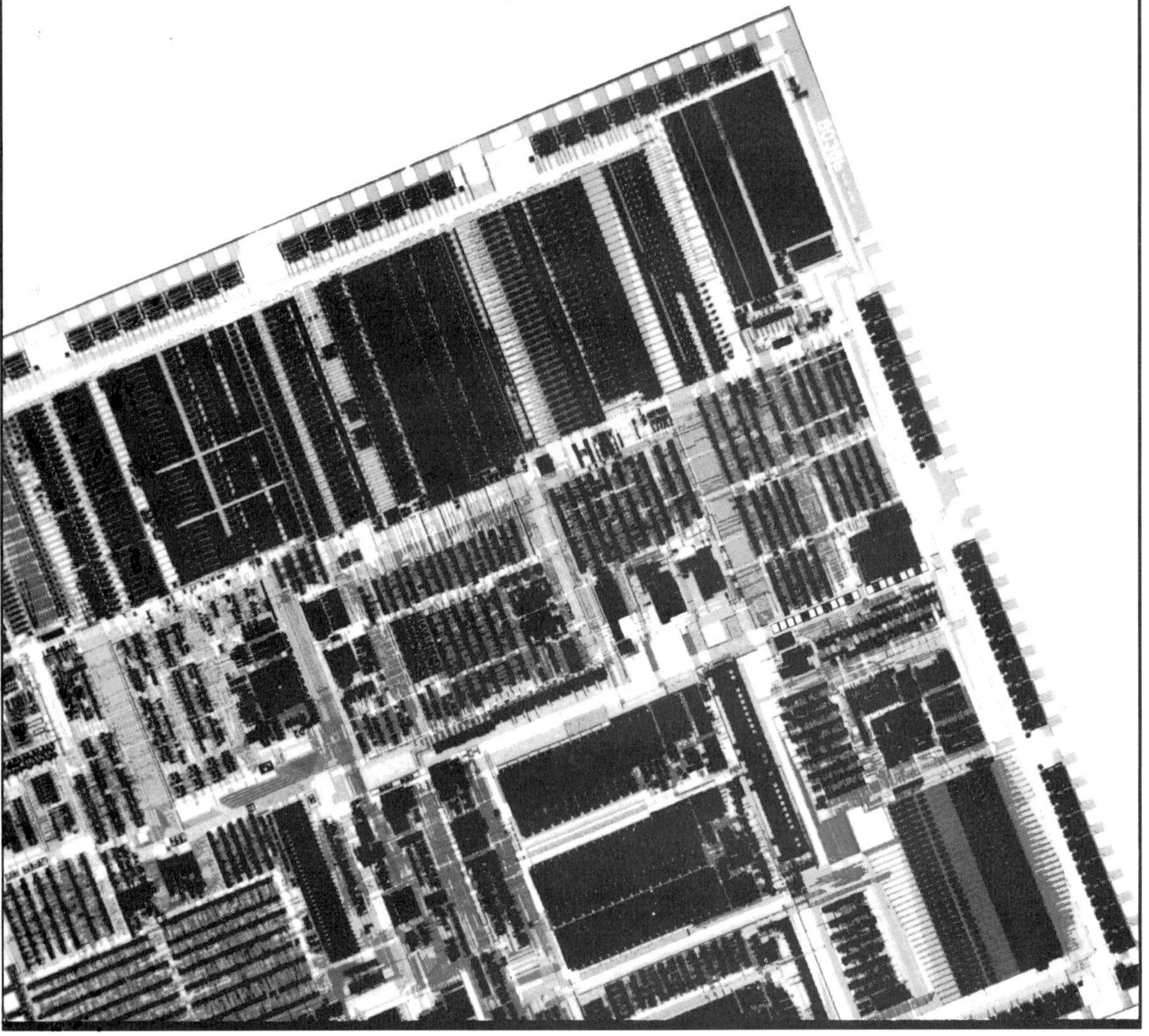

Appendix 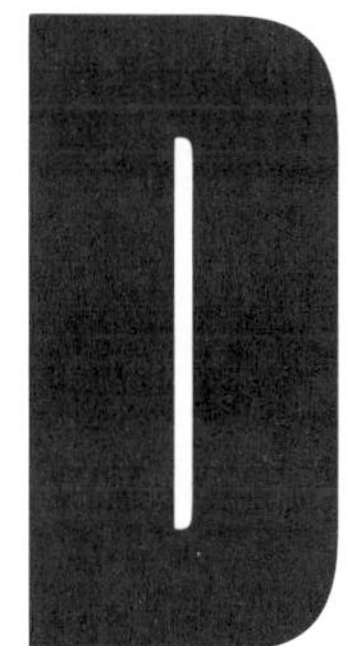

POWER	DECIMAL VALUE
2^0	1
2^1	2
2^2	4
2^3	8
2^4	16
2^5	32
2^6	64
2^7	128
2^8	256
2^9	512
2^{10}	1,024
2^{11}	2,048
2^{12}	4,096
2^{13}	8,192

POWER	DECIMAL VALUE
2^{14}	16,384
2^{15}	32,768
2^{16}	65,536
2^{17}	131,072
2^{18}	262,144
2^{19}	524,288
2^{20}	1,048,576
2^{21}	2,097,152
2^{22}	4,194,304
2^{23}	8,388,608
2^{24}	16,777,216
2^{25}	33,554,432
2^{26}	67,108,864
2^{27}	134,217,728
2^{28}	268,435,456
2^{29}	536,870,912
2^{30}	1,073,741,824
2^{31}	2,147,483,648
2^{32}	4,294,967,296

ASCII Table

Appendix 

	HIGH 3 BITS							
LOW 4 BITS	**000**	**001**	**010**	**011**	**100**	**101**	**110**	**111**
0000	NUL	DLE	SP	0	@	P	’	p
0001	SOH	DC1	!	1	A	Q	a	q
0010	STX	DC2	”	2	B	R	b	r
0011	ETX	DC3	#	3	C	S	c	s
0100	EOT	DC4	$	4	D	T	d	t
0101	ENQ	NAK	%	5	E	U	e	u
0110	ACK	SYN	&	6	F	V	f	v
0111	BEL	ETB	’	7	G	W	g	w
1000	BS	CAN	(	8	H	X	h	x
1001	HT	EM	)	9	I	Y	i	y
1010	LF	SUB	*	:	J	Z	j	z
1011	VT	ESC	+	;	K	[	k	{
1100	FF	FS	,	<	L	\	l	¦
1101	CR	GS	-	=	M	]	m	}
1110	SO	RS	.	>	N	^	n	~
1111	SI	US	/	?	O	_	o	DEL

Key

NUL	Null	DLE	Data Link Escape
SOH	Start of Heading	DC1	Device Control 1
STX	Start of Text	DC2	Device Control 2
ETX	End of Text	DC3	Device Control 3
EOT	End of Transmission	DC4	Device Control 4
ENG	Enquiry	NAK	Negative Acknowledge
ACK	Acknowledge	SYN	Synchronous Idle
BEL	BELL (audible)	ETB	End of Transmission Block
BS	Backspace	EM	End of Medium
HT	Horizontal Tabulation	SUB	Substitute
LF	Line Feed	ESC	Escape
VT	Vertical Tabulation	FS	File Separator
FF	Form Feed	GS	Group Separator
CR	Carriage Return	RS	Record Separator
SO	Shift Out	US	Unit Separator
SI	Shift In	DEL	Delete

80386
Opcode Map

Appendix F

THE OPCODE TABLES IN THIS APPENDIX AID IN interpreting 80386 object code. Use the high-order 4 bits of the opcode as an index to a row of the opcode table; use the low-order 4 bits as an index to a column of the table. If the opcode is 0FH, refer to the two-byte opcode table and use the second byte of the opcode to index the rows and columns of that table.

Keys to Abbreviations

Operands are identified by a two-character code of the form Zz. The first character, an uppercase letter, specifies the addressing method. The second character, a lowercase letter, specifies the type of operand.

Codes for Addressing Method

A Direct address; the instruction has no MODRM field; the address of the operand is encoded in the instruction; no base register, index register, or scaling factor can be applied; e.g., far JMP (EA).

C The reg field of the MODRM field selects a control register; e.g., MOV (0F20, 0F22).

D The reg field of the MODRM field selects a debug register; e.g., MOV (0F21, 0F23).

E A MODRM field follows the opcode and specifies the operand. The operand is either a general register or a memory address. If it is a memory address, the address is computed from a segment register and any of the following values: a base register, an index register, a scaling factor, a displacement.

F Flags register.

G The reg field of the MODRM field selects a general register; e.g., ADD (00).

I Immediate data. The value of the operand is encoded in subsequent bytes of the instruction.

J The instruction contains a relative offset to be added to the instruction-pointer register; e.g., JMP short, LOOP.

M The MODRM field may refer only to memory; e.g., BOUND, LES, LDS, LSS, LFS, LGS.

O The instruction has no MODRM field; the offset of the operand is coded as a word or dword (depending on address size attribute) in the instruction. No base register, index register, or scaling factor can be applied; e.g., MOV (A0–A3).

R The mod field of the MODRM field may refer only to a general register; e.g., MOV(0F20–0F24, 0F26).

S The reg field of the MODRM field selects a segment register; e.g., MOV (8C, 8E).

T The reg field of the MODRM field selects a test register; e.g., MOV (0F24, 0F26).

X Memory addressed by DS:SI; e.g., MOVS, COMPS, OUTS, LODS, SCAS.

Y Memory addressed by ES:DI; e.g., MOVS, CMPS, INS, STOS.

Codes for Operand Type

a Two one-word operands in memory or two dword operands in memory, depending on operand size attribute (used only by BOUND).

b Byte (regardless of operand size attribute).

c Byte or word, depending on operand size attribute.

d Dword (regardless of operand size attribute).

p 32-bit or 48-bit pointer, depending on operand size attribute.

s Six-byte pseudo-descriptor.

v Word or dword, depending on operand size attribute.

w Word (regardless of operand size attribute).

Register Codes

When an operand is a specific register encoded in the opcode, the register is identified by its name; e.g., AX, CL, or ESI. The name of the register indicates whether the register is 32, 16, or 8 bits wide. A register identifier of the form eXX is used when the width of the register depends on the operand size attribute. For example, eAX indicates that the AX register is used when the operand size attribute is 16, and the EAX register is used when the operand size attribute is 32.

One-Byte Opcode Map

	0	1	2	3	4	5	6	7
0	ADD						PUSH ES	POP ES
	Eb,Gb	Ev,Gv	Gb,Eb	Gv,Ev	AL,Ib	eAX,Iv		
1	ADC						PUSH SS	POP SS
	Eb,Gb	Ev,Gv	Gb,Eb	Gv,Ev	AL,Ib	eAX,Iv		
2	AND						SEG =ES	DAA
	Eb,Gb	Ev,Gv	Gb,Eb	Gv,Ev	AL,Ib	eAX,Iv		
3	XOR						SEG =SS	AAA
	Eb,Gb	Ev,Gv	Gb,Eb	Gv,Ev	AL,Ib	eAX,Iv		
4	INC general register							
	eAX	eCX	eDX	eBX	eSP	eBP	eSI	eDI
5	PUSH general register							
	eAX	eCX	eDX	eBX	eSP	eBP	eSI	eDI
6	PUSHA	POPA	BOUND Gv,Ma	ARPL Ew,Rw	SEG =FS	SEG =GS	Operand Size	Address Size
7	Short-displacement jump on condition (Jb)							
	JO	JNO	JB	JNB	JZ	JNZ	JBE	JNBE
8	Immediate Grpl			Grpl Ev,Ib	TEST		XCHG	
	Eb,Ib	Ev,Iv			Eb,Gb	Ev,Gv	Eb,Gb	Ev,Gv
9	NOP	XCHG word or double-word register with eAX						
		eCX	eDX	eBX	eSP	eBP	eSI	eDI
A	MOV				MOVSB Xb,Yb	MOVSW/D Xv,Yv	CMPSB Xb,Yb	CMPSW/D Xv,Yv
	AL,Ob	eAX,Ov	Ob,AL	Ov,eAX				
B	MOV immediate byte into byte register							
	AL	CL	DL	BL	AH	CH	DH	BH
C	Shift Grp2		RET near		LES Gv,Mp	LDS Gv,Mp	MOV	
	Eb,Ib	Ev,Ib	Iw				Eb,Ib	Ev,Iv
D	Shift Grp2				AAM	AAD		XLAT
	Eb,1	Ev,1	Eb,CL	Ev,CL				
E	LOOPNE Jb	LOOPE Jb	LOOP Jb	JCXZ Jb	IN		OUT	
					AL,Ib	eAX,Ib	Ib,AL	Ib,eAX
F	LOCK		REPNE	REP REPE	HLT	CMC	Unary Grp3	
							Eb	Ev

One-Byte Opcode Map

	8	9	A	B	C	D	E	F
0	OR						PUSH CS	2-byte escape
	Eb,Gb	Ev,Gv	Gb,Eb	Gv,Ev	AL,Ib	eAX,Iv		
1	SBB						PUSH DS	POP DS
	Eb,Gb	Ev,Gv	Gb,Eb	Gv,Ev	AL,Ib	eAX,Iv		
2	SUB						SEG =CS	DAS
	Eb,Gb	Ev,Gv	Gb,Eb	Gv,Ev	AL,Ib	eAX,Iv		
3	CMP						SEG =CS	AAS
	Eb,Gb	Ev,Gv	Gb,Eb	Gv,Ev	AL,Ib	eAX,Iv		
4	DEC general register							
	eAX	eCX	eDX	eBX	eSP	eBP	eSI	eDI
5	POP into general register							
	eAX	eCX	eDX	eBX	eSP	eBP	eSI	eDI
6	PUSH Ib	IMUL GvEvIv	PUSH Ib	IMUL GvEvIb	INSB Yb,DX	INSW/D Yv,DX	OUTSB DX,Xb	OUTSW/D DX,Xv
7	Short-displacement jump on condition (Jb)							
	JS	JNS	JP	JNP	JL	JNL	JLE	JNLE
8	MOV				MOV Ew,Sw	LEA Gv,M	MOV Sw,Ew	POP Ev
	Eb,Gb	Ev,Gv	Gb,Eb	Gv,Ev				
9	CBW	CWD	CALL Ap	WAIT	PUSHF Fv	POPF Fv	SAHF	LAHF
A	TEST		STOSB Yb,AL	STOSW/D Yv,eAX	LODSB AL,Xb	LODSW/D eAX,Xv	SCASB AL,Xb	SCASW/D eAX,Xv
	AL,Ib	eAX,Iv						
B	MOV immediate word or double into word or double register							
	eAX	eCX	eDX	eBX	eSP	eBP	eSI	eDI
C	ENTER Iw,Ib	LEAVE	RET far		INT 3	INT Ib	INTO	IRET
			Iw					
D	ESC (Escape to coprocessor instruction set)							
E	CALL Av	JMP			IN		OUT	
		Jv	Ap	Jb	AL,DX	eAX,DX	DX,AL	DX,eAX
F	CLC	STC	CLI	STI	CLD	STD	INC/DEC Grp4	Indirct Grp5

Two-Byte Opcode Map (First Byte Is 0FH)

	0	1	2	3	4	5	6	7
0	Grp6	Grp7	LAR Gv,Ew	LSL Gv,Ew			CLTS	
1								
2	MOV Cd,Rd	MOV Dd,Rd	MOV Rd,Cd	MOV Rd,Dd	MOV Td,Rd		MOV Rd,Td	
3								
4								
5								
6								
7								
8	Long-displacement jump on condition (Jv)							
	JO	JNO	JB	JNB	JZ	JNZ	JBE	JNBE
9	Byte Set on condition (Eb)							
	SETO	SETNO	SETB	SETNB	SETZ	SETNZ	SETBE	SETNBE
A	PUSH FS	POP FS		BT Ev,Gv	SHLD EvGvIb	SHLD EvGvCL		
B			LSS Mp	BTR Ev,Gv	LFS Mp	LGS Mp	MOVZX	
							Gv,Eb	Gv,Ew
C								
D								
E								
F								

Two-Byte Opcode Map (First Byte Is 0FH)

	8	9	A	B	C	D	E	F
0								
1								
2								
3								
4								
5								
6								
7								
8	Long-displacement jump on condition (Jv)							
	JS	JNS	JP	JNP	JL	JNL	JLE	JNLE
9	SETS	SETNS	SETP	SETNP	SETL	SETNL	SETLE	SETNLE
A	PUSH GS	POP GS		BTS Ev,Gv	SHRD EvGvIb	SHRD EvGvCL		IMUL Gv,Ev
B			Grp-8 Ev,Ib	BTC Ev,Gv	BSF Gv,Ev	BSR Gv,Ev	MOVSX	
							Gv,Eb	Gv,Ew
C								
D								
E								
F								

Opcodes Determined By Bits 5,4,3 OF MODRM Field

mod	nnn	R/M

Group	000	001	010	011	100	101	110	111
1	ADD	OR	ADC	SBB	AND	SUB	XOR	CMP
2	ROL	ROR	RCL	RCR	SHL	SHR		SAR
3	TEST Ib/Iv		NOT	NEG	MUL AL/eAX	IMUL AL/eAX	DIV AL/eAX	IDIV AL/eAX
4	INC Eb	DEC Eb						
5	INC Ev	DEC Ev	CALL Ev	CALL eP	JMP Ev	JMP Ep	PUSH Ev	

Opcodes Determined By Bits 5,4,3 OF MODRM Field

mod	nnn	R/M

Group	000	001	010	011	100	101	110	111
6	SLDT Ew	STR Ew	LLDT Ew	LTR Ew	VERR Ew	VERW Ew		
7	SGDT Ms	SIDT Ms	LGDT Ms	LIDT Ms	SMSW Ew		LMSW Ew	
8					BT	BTS	BTR	BTC

80386 Instruction Format and Timing

Appendix 

THIS APPENDIX DESCRIBES THE 80386 INSTRUCTION set. Table G.1 lists all instructions along with instruction encoding diagrams and clock counts. Further details of the instruction encoding are then provided in the following sections, which completely describe the encoding structure and the definition of all fields occurring within 80386 instructions.

80386 Instruction Encoding and Clock Count Summary

To calculate elapsed time for an instruction, multiply the instruction clock count, as listed in Table G.1, by the processor clock period (e.g., 62.5 ns for an 80386-16 operating at 16 MHz CLK signal).

For more detailed information on the encodings of instructions, refer to the section on Instruction Encodings.

Table G.1: 80386 Instruction Set Clock Count Summary

INSTRUCTION	FORMAT			Clk Count Virtual 8086 Mode	CLOCK COUNT: Real Address Mode or Virtual 8086 Mode	CLOCK COUNT: Protected Virtual Address Mode	NOTES: Real Address Mode or Virtual 8086 Mode	NOTES: Protected Virtual Address Mode
GENERAL DATA TRANSFER								
MOV = Move:								
Register to Register/Memory	1000100w	mod reg r/m			2/2	2/2	b	h
Register/Memory to Register	1000101w	mod reg r/m			2/4	2/4	b	h
Immediate to Register/Memory	1100011w	mod 000 r/m	immediate data		2/2	2/2	b	h
Immediate to Register (short form)	1011 w reg	immediate data			2	2		
Memory to Accumulator (short form)	1010000w	full displacement			4	4	b	h
Accumulator to Memory (short form)	1010001w	full displacement			2	2	b	h
Register Memory to Segment Register	10001110	mod sreg3 r/m			2/5	18/19	b	h, i, j
Segment Register to Register/Memory	10001100	mod sreg3 r/m			2/2	2/2	b	h
MOVSX = Move With Sign Extension								
Register From Register/Memory	00001111	1011111w	mod reg r/m		3/6	3/6	b	h
MOVZX = Move With Zero Extension								
Register From Register/Memory	00001111	1011011w	mod reg r/m		3/6	3/6	b	h
PUSH = Push:								
Register/Memory	11111111	mod 110 r/m			5	5	b	h
Register (short form)	01010 reg				2	2	b	h
Segment Register (ES, CS, SS or DS) (short form)	000 sreg2 110				2	2	b	h
Segment Register (ES, CS, SS, DS, FS or GS)	00001111	10 sreg3 000			2	2	b	h
Immediate	011010s0	immediate data			2	2	b	h
PUSHA = Push All	01100000				18	18	b	h
POP = Pop								
Register/Memory	10001111	mod 000 r/m			5	5	b	h
Register (short form)	01011 reg				4	4	b	h
Segment Register (ES, CS, SS or DS) (short form)	000 sreg 2 111				7	21	b	h, i, j
Segment Register (ES, CS, SS or DS FS or GS)	00001111	10 sreg 3 001			7	21	b	h, i, j
POPA = Pop All	01100001				24	24	b	h
XCHG = Exchange								
Register/Memory With Register	1000011w	mod reg r/m			3/5	3/5	b, f	f, h
Register With Accumulator (short form)	10010 reg				3	3		
IN = Input from:								
Fixed Port	1110010w	port number		†26	12	6*/26**		m
Variable Port	1110110w			†27	13	7*/27**		m
OUT = Output to:								
Fixed Port	1110011w	port number		†24	10	4*/24**		m
Variable Port	1110111w			†25	11	5*/25**		m
LEA = Load EA to Register	10001101	mod reg r/m			2	2		

* If CPL ≤ IOPL   ** If CPL > IOPL

Table G.1: 80386 Instruction Set Clock Count Summary (continued)

INSTRUCTION	FORMAT	CLOCK COUNT		NOTES	
		Real Address Mode or Virtual 8086 Mode	Protected Virtual Address Mode	Real Address Mode or Virtual 8086 Mode	Protected Virtual Address Mode
SEGMENT CONTROL					
LDS = Load Pointer to DS	11000101 / mod reg r/m	7	22	b	h, i, j
LES = Load Pointer to ES	11000100 / mod reg r/m	7	22	b	h, i, j
LFS = Load Pointer to FS	00001111 / 10110100 / mod rog r/m	7	25	b	h, i, j
LGS = Load Pointer to GS	00001111 / 10110101 / mod reg r/m	7	25	b	h, i, j
LSS = Load Pointer to SS	00001111 / 10110010 / mod reg r/m	7	22	b	h, i, j
FLAG CONTROL					
CLC = Clear Carry Flag	11111000	2	2		
CLD = Clear Direction Flag	11111100	2	2		
CLI = Clear Interrupt Enable Flag	11111010	3	3		m
CLTS = Clear Task Switched Flag	00001111 / 00000110	5	5	c	l
CMC = Complement Carry Flag	11110101	2	2		
LAHF = Load AH into Flag	10011111	2	2		
POPF = Pop Flags	10011101	5	5	b	h, n
PUSHF = Push Flags	10011100	4	4	b	h
SAHF = Store AH into Flags	10011110	3	3		
STC = Set Carry Flag	11111001	2	2		
STD = Set Direction Flag	11111001	2	2		
STI = Set Interrupt Enable Flag	11111011	3	3		m
ARITHMETIC					
ADD = Add					
Register to Register	000000dw / mod reg r/m	2	2		
Register to Memory	0000000w / mod reg r/m	7	7	b	h
Memory to Register	0000001w / mod reg r/m	6	6	b	h
Immediate to Register/Memory	100000sw / mod 000 r/m / immediate data	2/7	2/7	b	h
Immediate to Accumulator (short form)	0000010w / immediate data	2	2		
ADC = Add With Carry					
Register to Register	000100dw / mod reg r/m	2	2		
Register to Memory	0001000w / mod reg r/m	7	7	b	h
Memory to Register	0001001w / mod reg r/m	6	6	b	h
Immediate to Register/Memory	100000sw / mod 010 r/m / immediate data	2/7	2/7	b	h
Immediate to Accumulator (short form)	0001010w / immediate data	2	2		
INC = Increment					
Register/Memory	1111111w / mod 000 r/m	2/6	2/6	b	h
Register (short form)	01000 reg	2	2		
SUB = Subtract					
Register from Register	001010dw / mod reg r/m	2	2		

Table G.1: 80386 Instruction Set Clock Count Summary (continued)

INSTRUCTION	FORMAT	CLOCK COUNT: Real Address Mode or Virtual 8086 Mode	CLOCK COUNT: Protected Virtual Address Mode	NOTES: Real Address Mode or Virtual 8086 Mode	NOTES: Protected Virtual Address Mode
ARITHMETIC (Continued)					
Register from Memory	0010100w | mod reg r/m	7	7	b	h
Memory from Register	0010101w | mod reg r/m	6	6	b	h
Immediate from Register/Memory	100000sw | mod 101 r/m | immediate data	2/7	2/7	b	h
Immediate from Accumulator (short form)	0010110w | immediate data	2	2		
SBB = Subtract with Borrow					
Register from Register	000110dw | mod reg r/m	2	2		
Register from Memory	0001100w | mod reg r/m	7	7	b	h
Memory from Register	0001101w | mod reg r/m	6	6	b	h
Immediate from Register/Memory	100000sw | mod 011 r/m | immediate data	2/7	2/7	b	h
Immediate from Accumulator (short form)	0001110w | immediate data	2	2		
DEC = Decrement					
Register/Memory	1111111w | reg 001 r/m	2/6	2/6	b	h
Register (short form)	01001 reg	2	2		
CMP = Compare					
Register with Register	001110dw | mod reg r/m	2	2		
Memory with Register	0011100w | mod reg r/m	5	5	b	h
Register with Memory	0011101w | mod reg r/m	6	6	b	h
Immediate with Register/Memory	100000sw | mod 111 r/m | immediate data	2/5	2/5	b	h
Immediate with Accumulator (short form)	0011110w | immediate data	2	2		
NEG = Change Sign	1111011w | mod 011 r/m	2/6	2/6	b	h
AAA = ASCII Adjust for Add	00110111	4	4		
AAS = ASCII Adjust for Subtract	00111111	4	4		
DAA = Decimal Adjust for Add	00100111	4	4		
DAS = Decimal Adjust for Subtract	00101111	4	4		
MUL = Multiply (unsigned)					
Accumulator with Register/Memory	1111011w | mod 100 r/m				
Multiplier-Byte		9-14/12-17	9-14/12-17	b, d	d, h
-Word		9-22/12-25	9-22/12-25	b, d	d, h
-Doubleword		9-38/12-41	9-38/12-41	b, d	d, h
IMUL = Integer Multiply (signed)					
Accumulator with Register/Memory	1111011w | mod 100 r/m				
Multiplier-Byte		9-14/12-17	9-14/12-17	b, d	d, h
-Word		9-22/12-25	9-22/12-25	b, d	d, h
-Doubleword		9-38/12-41	9-38/12-41	b, d	d, h
Register with Register/Memory	00001111 | 10101111 | mod reg r/m				
-Word		9-22/12-25	9-22/12-25	b, d	d, h
-Doubleword		9-38/12-41	9-38/12-41	b, d	d, h
Register/Memory with Immediate to Register	011010s1 | mod reg r/m | immediate data				
-Word		9-22/12-25	9-22/12-25	b, d	d, h
-Doubleword		9-38/12-41	9-38/12-41	b, d	d, h

Table G.1: 80386 Instruction Set Clock Count Summary (continued)

INSTRUCTION	FORMAT	CLOCK COUNT: Real Address Mode or Virtual 8086 Mode	CLOCK COUNT: Protected Virtual Address Mode	NOTES: Real Address Mode or Virtual 8086 Mode	NOTES: Protected Virtual Address Mode
ARITHMETIC (Continued)					
DIV = Divide (Unsigned)					
Accumulator by Register/Memory	1 1 1 1 0 1 1 w | mod 1 1 0 r/m				
Divisor—Byte		14/17	14/17	b,e	e,h
—Word		22/25	22/25	b,e	e,h
—Doubleword		38/41	38/41	b,e	e,h
IDIV = Integer Divide (Signed)					
Accumulator By Register/Memory	1 1 1 1 0 1 1 w | mod 1 1 1 r/m				
Divisor—Byte		19/22	19/22	b,e	e,h
—Word		27/30	27/30	b,e	e,h
—Doubleword		43/46	43/46	b,e	e,h
AAD = ASCII Adjust for Divide	1 1 0 1 0 1 0 1 | 0 0 0 0 1 0 1 0	19	19		
AAM = ASCII Adjust for Multiply	1 1 0 1 0 1 0 0 | 0 0 0 0 1 0 1 0	17	17		
CBW = Convert Byte to Word	1 0 0 1 1 0 0 0	3	3		
CWD = Convert Word to Double Word	1 0 0 1 1 0 0 1	2	2		
LOGIC					
Shift Rotate Instructions					
Not Through Carry **(ROL, ROR, SAL, SAR, SHL, and SHR)**					
Register/Memory by 1	1 1 0 1 0 0 0 w | mod TTT r/m	3/7	3/7	b	h
Register/Memory by CL	1 1 0 1 0 0 1 w | mod TTT r/m	3/7	3/7	b	h
Register/Memory by Immediate Count	1 1 0 0 0 0 0 w | mod TTT r/m | immed 8-bit data	3/7	3/7	b	h
Through Carry **(RCL and RCR)**					
Register/Memory by 1	1 1 0 1 0 0 0 w | mod TTT r/m	9/10	9/10	b	h
Register/Memory by CL	1 1 0 1 0 0 1 w | mod TTT r/m	9/10	9/10	b	h
Register/Memory by Immediate Count	1 1 0 0 0 0 0 w | mod TTT r/m | immed 8-bit data	9/10	9/10	b	h
	T T T Instruction				
	0 0 0 ROL				
	0 0 1 ROR				
	0 1 0 RCL				
	0 1 1 RCR				
	1 0 0 SHL/SAL				
	1 0 1 SHR				
	1 1 1 SAR				
SHLD = Shift Left Double					
Register/Memory by Immediate	0 0 0 0 1 1 1 1 | 1 0 1 0 0 1 0 0 | mod reg r/m | immed 8-bit data	3/7	3/7		
Register/Memory by CL	0 0 0 0 1 1 1 1 | 1 0 1 0 0 1 0 1 | mod reg r/m	3/7	3/7		
SHRD = Shift Right Double					
Register/Memory by Immediate	0 0 0 0 1 1 1 1 | 1 0 1 0 1 1 0 0 | mod reg r/m | immed 8-bit data	3/7	3/7		
Register/Memory by CL	0 0 0 0 1 1 1 1 | 1 0 1 0 1 1 0 1 | mod reg r/m	3/7	3/7		
AND = And					
Register to Register	0 0 1 0 0 0 d w | mod reg r/m	2	2		

Table G.1: 80386 Instruction Set Clock Count Summary (continued)

INSTRUCTION	FORMAT	Clk Count Virtual 8086 Mode	CLOCK COUNT: Real Address Mode or Virtual 8086 Mode	CLOCK COUNT: Protected Virtual Address Mode	NOTES: Real Address Mode or Virtual 8086 Mode	NOTES: Protected Virtual Address Mode
LOGIC (Continued)						
Register to Memory	0010000w, mod reg r/m		7	7	b	h
Memory to Register	0010001w, mod reg r/m		6	6	b	h
Immediate to Register/Memory	1000000w, mod 100 r/m, immediate data		2/7	2/7	b	h
Immediate to Accumulator (Short Form)	0010010w, immediate data		2	2		
TEST = And Function to Flags, No Result						
Register/Memory and Register	1000010w, mod reg r/m		2/5	2/5	b	h
Immediate Data and Register/Memory	1111011w, mod 000 r/m, immediate data		2/5	2/5	b	h
Immediate Data and Accumulator (Short Form)	1010100w, immediate data		2	2		
OR = Or						
Register to Register	000010dw, mod reg r/m		2	2		
Register to Memory	0000100w, mod reg r/m		7	7	b	h
Memory to Register	0000101w, mod reg r/m		6	6	b	h
Immediate to Register/Memory	1000000w, mod 001 r/m, immediate data		2/7	2/7	b	h
Immediate to Accumulator (Short Form)	0000110w, immediate data		2	2		
XOR = Exclusive Or						
Register to Register	001100dw, mod reg r/m		2	2		
Register to Memory	0011000w, mod reg r/m		7	7	b	h
Memory to Register	0011001w, mod reg r/m		6	6	b	h
Immediate to Register/Memory	1000000w, mod 110 r/m, immediate data		2/7	2/7	b	h
Immediate to Accumulator (Short Form)	0011010w, immediate data		2	2		
NOT = Invert Register/Memory	1111011w, mod 010 r/m		2/6	2/6	b	h
STRING MANIPULATION						
CMPS = Compare Byte Word	1010011w		10	10	b	h
INS = Input Byte/Word from DX Port	0110110w	†29	15	9*/29**	b	h, m
LODS = Load Byte/Word to AL/AX/EAX	1010110w		5	5	b	h
MOVS = Move Byte Word	1010010w		7	7	b	h
OUTS = Output Byte/Word to DX Port	0110111w	†28	14	8*/28**	b	h, m
SCAS = Scan Byte Word	1010111w		7	7	b	h
STOS = Store Byte/Word from AL/AX/EX	1010101w		4	4	b	h
XLAT = Translate String	11010111		5	5		h
REPEATED STRING MANIPULATION Repeated by Count in CX or ECX						
REPE CMPS = Compare String (Find Non-Match)	11110011, 1010011w		5+9n	5+9n	b	h

* If CPL ≤ IOPL   ** If CPL > IOPL

Table G.1: 80386 Instruction Set Clock Count Summary (continued)

INSTRUCTION	FORMAT	Clock Count: Real Address Mode or Virtual 8086 Mode	Clock Count: Protected Virtual Address Mode	Notes: Real Address Mode or Virtual 8086 Mode	Notes: Protected Virtual Address Mode
REPEATED STRING MANIPULATION (Continued)					
REPNE CMPS = Compare String					
(Find Match)	11110010 | 1010011w — (Clk Count Virtual 8086 Mode)	5+9n	5+9n	b	h
REP INS = Input String	11110010 | 0110110w — †27+6n	13+6n	7+6n*/27+6n**	b	h, m
REP LODS = Load String	11110010 | 1010110w	5+6n	5+6n	b	h
REP MOVS = Move String	11110010 | 1010010w	7+4n	7+4n	b	h
REP OUTS = Output String	11110010 | 0110111w — †26+5n	12+5n	6+5n*/26+5n**	b	h, m
REPE SCAS = Scan String					
(Find Non-AL/AX/EAX)	11110011 | 1010111w	5+8n	5+8n	b	h
REPNE SCAS = Scan String					
(Find AL/AX/EAX)	11110010 | 1010111w	5+8n	5+8n	b	h
REP STOS = Store String	11110010 | 1010101w	5+5n	5+5n	b	h
BIT MANIPULATION					
BSF = Scan Bit Forward	00001111 | 10111100 | mod reg r/m	10+3n	10+3n	b	h
BSR = Scan Bit Reverse	00001111 | 10111101 | mod reg r/m	10+3n	10+3n	b	h
BT = Test Bit					
Register/Memory, Immediate	00001111 | 10111010 | mod 100 r/m | immed 8-bit data	3/6	3/6	b	h
Register/Memory, Register	00001111 | 10100011 | mod reg r/m	3/12	3/12	b	h
BTC = Test Bit and Complement					
Register/Memory, Immediate	00001111 | 10111010 | mod 111 r/m | immed 8-bit data	6/8	6/8	b	h
Register/Memory, Register	00001111 | 10111011 | mod reg r/m	6/13	6/13	b	h
BTR = Test Bit and Reset					
Register/Memory, Immediate	00001111 | 10111010 | mod 110 r/m | immed 8-bit data	6/8	6/8	b	h
Register/Memory, Register	00001111 | 10110011 | mod reg r/m	6/13	6/13	b	h
BTS = Test Bit and Set					
Register/Memory, Immediate	00001111 | 10111010 | mod 101 r/m | immed 8-bit data	6/8	6/8	b	h
Register/Memory, Register	00001111 | 10101011 | mod reg r/m	6/13	6/13	b	h
CONTROL TRANSFER					
CALL = Call					
Direct Within Segment	11101000 | full displacement	7+m	7+m	b	r
Register/Memory					
Indirect Within Segment	11111111 | mod 010 r/m	7+m/ 10+m	7+m/ 10+m	b	h, r
Direct Intersegment	10011010 | unsigned full offset, selector	17+m	34+m	b	j,k,r

Notes

† Clock count shown applies if I/O permission allows I/O to the port in virtual 8086 mode. If I/O bit map denies permission exception 13 fault occurs; refer to clock counts for INT 3 instruction.

* If CPL ≤ IOPL   ** If CPL > IOPL

Table G.1: 80386 Instruction Set Clock Count Summary (continued)

INSTRUCTION	FORMAT	CLOCK COUNT: Real Address Mode or Virtual 8086 Mode	CLOCK COUNT: Protected Virtual Address Mode	NOTES: Real Address Mode or Virtual 8086 Mode	NOTES: Protected Virtual Address Mode
CONTROL TRANSFER (Continued)					
Protected Mode Only (Direct Intersegment)					
Via Call Gate to Same Privilege Level			52+m		h,j,k,r
Via Call Gate to Different Privilege Level, (No Parameters)			86+m		h,j,k,r
Via Call Gate to Different Privilege Level, (x Parameters)			94+4x+m		h,j,k,r
From 286 Task to 286 TSS			273		h,j,k,r
From 286 Task to 386 TSS			298		h,j,k,r
From 286 Task to Virtual 8086 Task (386 TSS)			217		h,j,k,r
From 386 Task to 286 TSS			273		h,j,k,r
From 386 Task to 386 TSS			300		h,j,k,r
From 386 Task to Virtual 8086 Task (386 TSS)			217		h,j,k,r
Indirect Intersegment	11111111 | mod 011 r/m	22+m	38+m	b	h,j,k,r
Protected Mode Only (Indirect Intersegment)					
Via Call Gate to Same Privilege Level			56+m		h,j,k,r
Via Call Gate to Different Privilege Level, (No Parameters)			90+m		h,j,k,r
Via Call Gate to Different Privilege Level, (x Parameters)			98+4x+m		h,j,k,r
From 286 Task to 286 TSS			278		h,j,k,r
From 286 Task to 386 TSS			303		h,j,k,r
From 286 Task to Virtual 8086 Task (386 TSS)			221		h,j,k,r
From 386 Task to 286 TSS			278		h,j,k,r
From 386 Task to 386 TSS			305		h,j,k,r
From 386 Task to Virtual 8086 Task (386 TSS)			221		h,j,k,r
JMP = Unconditional Jump					
Short	11101001 | 8-bit displacement	7+m	7+m		r
Direct within Segment	11101001 | full displacement	7+m	7+m		r
Register/Memory Indirect within Segment	11111111 | mod 100 r/m	7+m/ 10+m	7+m/ 10+m	b	h,r
Direct Intersegment	11101010 | unsigned full offset, selector	12+m	27+m		j,k,r
Protected Mode Only (Direct Intersegment)					
Via Call Gate to Same Privilege Level			45+m		h,j,k,r
From 286 Task to 286 TSS			274		h,j,k,r
From 286 Task to 386 TSS			301		h,j,k,r
From 286 Task to Virtual 8086 Task (386 TSS)			218		h,j,k,r
From 386 Task to 286 TSS			270		h,j,k,r
From 386 Task to 386 TSS			303		h,j,k,r
From 386 Task to Virtual 8086 Task (386 TSS)			220		h,j,k,r
Indirect Intersegment	11111111 | mod 101 r/m	17+m	31+m	b	h,j,k,r
Protected Mode Only (Indirect Intersegment)					
Via Call Gate to Same Privilege Level			49+m		h,j,k,r
From 286 Task to 286 TSS			279		h,j,k,r
From 286 Task to 386 TSS			306		h,j,k,r
From 286 Task to Virtual 8086 Task (386 TSS)			222		h,j,k,r
From 386 Task to 286 TSS			275		h,j,k,r
From 386 Task to 386 TSS			308		h,j,k,r
From 386 Task to Virtual 8086 Task (386 TSS)			224		h,j,k,r

Table G.1: 80386 Instruction Set Clock Count Summary (continued)

INSTRUCTION	FORMAT	CLOCK COUNT: Real Address Mode or Virtual 8086 Mode	CLOCK COUNT: Protected Virtual Address Mode	NOTES: Real Address Mode or Virtual 8086 Mode	NOTES: Protected Virtual Address Mode
CONTROL TRANSFER (Continued)					
RET = Return from CALL:					
Within Segment	11000011	10 + m	10 + m	b	g, h, r
Within Segment Adding Immediate to SP	11000010 16-bit displ	10 + m	10 + m	b	g, h, r
Intersegment	11001011	18 + m	32 + m	b	g, h, j, k, r
Intersegment Adding Immediate to SP	11001010 16-bit displ	18 + m	32 + m	b	g, h, j, k, r
Protected Mode Only (RET):					
to Different Privilege Level					
Intersegment			68		h, j, k, r
Intersegment Adding Immediate to SP			68		h, j, k, r
CONDITIONAL JUMPS					
NOTE: Times Are Jump "Taken or Not Taken"					
JO = Jump on Overflow					
8-Bit Displacement	01110000 8-bit displ	7 + m or 3	7 + m or 3		r
Full Displacement	00001111 10000000 full displacement	7 + m or 3	7 + m or 3		r
JNO = Jump on Not Overflow					
8-Bit Displacement	01110001 8-bit displ	7 + m or 3	7 + m or 3		r
Full Displacement	00001111 10000001 full displacement	7 + m or 3	7 + m or 3		r
JB/JNAE = Jump on Below/Not Above or Equal					
8-Bit Displacement	01110010 8-bit displ	7 + m or 3	7 + m or 3		r
Full Displacement	00001111 10000010 full displacement	7 + m or 3	7 + m or 3		r
JNB/JAE = Jump on Not Below/Above or Equal					
8-Bit Displacement	01110011 8-bit displ	7 + m or 3	7 + m or 3		r
Full Displacement	00001111 10000011 full displacement	7 + m or 3	7 + m or 3		r
JE/JZ = Jump on Equal/Zero					
8-Bit Displacement	01110100 8-bit displ	7 + m or 3	7 + m or 3		r
Full Displacement	00001111 10000100 full displacement	7 + m or 3	7 + m or 3		r
JNE/JNZ = Jump on Not Equal/Not Zero					
8-Bit Displacement	01110101 8-bit displ	7 + m or 3	7 + m or 3		r
Full Displacement	00001111 10000101 full displacement	7 + m or 3	7 + m or 3		r
JBE/JNA = Jump on Below or Equal/Not Above					
8-Bit Displacement	01110110 8-bit displ	7 + m or 3	7 + m or 3		r
Full Displacement	00001111 10000110 full displacement	7 + m or 3	7 + m or 3		r
JNBE/JA = Jump on Not Below or Equal/Above					
8-Bit Displacement	01110111 8-bit displ	7 + m or 3	7 + m or 3		r
Full Displacement	00001111 10000111 full displacement	7 + m or 3	7 + m or 3		r
JS = Jump on Sign					
8-Bit Displacement	01111000 8-bit displ	7 + m or 3	7 + m or 3		r
Full Displacement	00001111 10001000 full displacement	7 + m or 3	7 + m or 3		r

Table G.1: 80386 Instruction Set Clock Count Summary (continued)

INSTRUCTION	FORMAT			Clock Count: Real Address Mode or Virtual 8086 Mode	Clock Count: Protected Virtual Address Mode	Notes: Real Address Mode or Virtual 8086 Mode	Notes: Protected Virtual Address Mode
CONDITIONAL JUMPS (Continued)							
JNS = Jump on Not Sign							
8-Bit Displacement	01111001	8-bit displ		7 + m or 3	7 + m or 3		r
Full Displacement	00001111	10001001	full displacement	7 + m or 3	7 + m or 3		r
JP/JPE = Jump on Parity/Parity Even							
8-Bit Displacement	01111010	8-bit displ		7 + m or 3	7 + m or 3		r
Full Displacement	00001111	10001010	full displacement	7 + m or 3	7 + m or 3		r
JNP/JPO = Jump on Not Parity/Parity Odd							
8-Bit Displacement	01111011	8-bit displ		7 + m or 3	7 + m or 3		r
Full Displacement	00001111	10001011	full displacement	7 + m or 3	7 + m or 3		r
JL/JNGE = Jump on Less/Not Greater or Equal							
8-Bit Displacement	01111100	8-bit displ		7 + m or 3	7 + m or 3		r
Full Displacement	00001111	10001100	full displacement	7 + m or 3	7 + m or 3		r
JNL/JGE = Jump on Not Less/Greater or Equal							
8-Bit Displacement	01111101	8-bit displ		7 + m or 3	7 + m or 3		r
Full Displacement	00001111	10001101	full displacement	7 + m or 3	7 + m or 3		r
JLE/JNG = Jump on Less or Equal/Not Greater							
8-Bit Displacement	01111110	8-bit displ		7 + m or 3	7 + m or 3		r
Full Displacement	00001111	10001110	full displacement	7 + m or 3	7 + m or 3		r
JNLE/JG = Jump on Not Less or Equal/Greater							
8-Bit Displacement	01111111	8-bit displ		7 + m or 3	7 + m or 3		r
Full Displacement	00001111	10001111	full displacement	7 + m or 3	7 + m or 3		r
JCXZ = Jump on CX Zero	11100011	8-bit displ		9 + m or 5	9 + m or 5		r
JECXZ = Jump on ECX Zero	11100011	8-bit displ		9 + m or 5	9 + m or 5		r
(Address Size Prefix Differentiates JCXZ from JECXZ)							
LOOP = Loop CX Times	11100010	8-bit displ		11 + m	11 + m		r
LOOPZ/LOOPE = Loop with Zero/Equal	11100001	8-bit displ		11 + m	11 + m		r
LOOPNZ/LOOPNE = Loop While Not Zero	11100000	8-bit displ		11 + m	11 + m		r
CONDITIONAL BYTE SET							
NOTE: Times Are Register/Memory							
SETO = Set Byte on Overflow							
To Register/Memory	00001111	10010000	mod 000 r/m	4/5	4/5		h
SETNO = Set Byte on Not Overflow							
To Register/Memory	00001111	10010001	mod 000 r/m	4/5	4/5		h
SETB/SETNAE = Set Byte on Below/Not Above or Equal							
To Register/Memory	00001111	10010010	mod 000 r/m	4/5	4/5		h

Table G.1: 80386 Instruction Set Clock Count Summary (continued)

INSTRUCTION	FORMAT			Clock Count: Real Address Mode or Virtual 8086 Mode	Clock Count: Protected Virtual Address Mode	Notes: Real Address Mode or Virtual 8086 Mode	Notes: Protected Virtual Address Mode
CONDITIONAL BYTE SET (Continued)							
SETNB = Set Byte on Not Below/Above or Equal							
To Register/Memory	00001111	10010011	mod 000 r/m	4/5	4/5		h
SETE/SETZ = Set Byte on Equal/Zero							
To Register/Memory	00001111	10010100	mod 000 r/m	4/5	4/5		h
SETNE/SETNZ = Set Byte on Not Equal/Not Zero							
To Register/Memory	00001111	10010101	mod 000 r/m	4/5	4/5		h
SETBE/SETNA = Set Byte on Below or Equal/Not Above							
To Register/Memory	00001111	10010110	mod 000 r/m	4/5	4/5		h
SETNBE/SETA = Set Byte on Not Below or Equal/Above							
To Register/Memory	00001111	10010111	mod 000 r/m	4/5	4/5		h
SETS = Set Byte on Sign							
To Register/Memory	00001111	10011000	mod 000 r/m	4/5	4/5		h
SETNS = Set Byte on Not Sign							
To Register/Memory	00001111	10011001	mod 000 r/m	4/5	4/5		h
SETP/SETPE = Set Byte on Parity/Parity Even							
To Register/Memory	00001111	10011010	mod 000 r/m	4/5	4/5		h
SETNP/SETPO = Set Byte on Not Parity/Parity Odd							
To Register/Memory	00001111	10011011	mod 000 r/m	4/5	4/5		h
SETL/SETNGE = Set Byte on Less/Not Greater or Equal							
To Register/Memory	00001111	10011100	mod 000 r/m	4/5	4/5		h
SETNL/SETGE = Set Byte on Not Less/Greater or Equal							
To Register/Memory	00001111	01111101	mod 000 r/m	4/5	4/5		h
SETLE/SETNG = Set Byte on Less or Equal/Not Greater							
To Register/Memory	00001111	10011110	mod 000 r/m	4/5	4/5		h
SETNLE/SETG = Set Byte on Not Less or Equal/Greater							
To Register/Memory	00001111	10011111	mod 000 r/m	4/5	4/5		h
ENTER = Enter Procedure	11001000	16-bit displacement, 8-bit level					
L = 0				10	10	b	h
L = 1				12	12	b	h
L > 1				15 + 4(n − 1)	15 + 4(n − 1)	b	h
LEAVE = Leave Procedure	11001001			4	4	b	h

Table G.1: 80386 Instruction Set Clock Count Summary (continued)

INSTRUCTION	FORMAT	CLOCK COUNT: Real Address Mode or Virtual 8086 Mode	CLOCK COUNT: Protected Virtual Address Mode	NOTES: Real Address Mode or Virtual 8086 Mode	NOTES: Protected Virtual Address Mode
INTERRUPT INSTRUCTIONS					
INT = Interrupt:					
Type Specified	11001101 | type	37		b	
Type 3	11001100	33		b	
INTO = Interrupt 4 If Overflow Flag Set	11001110				
If OF = 1		35		b, e	
If OF = 0		3	3	b, e	
Bound = Interrupt 5 If Detect Value Out of Range	01100010 | mod reg r/m				
If Out of Range		44		b, e	e, g, h, j, k, r
If In Range		10	10	b, e	e, g, h, j, k, r
Protected Mode Only (INT)					
INT: Type Specified					
Via Interrupt or Trap Gate to Same Privilege Level			59		g, j, k, r
Via Interrupt or Trap Gate to Different Privilege Level			99		g, j, k, r
From 286 Task to 286 TSS via Task Gate			282		g, j, k, r
From 286 Task to 386 TSS via Task Gate			309		g, j, k, r
From 268 Task to virt 8086 md via Task Gate			226		g, j, k, r
From 386 Task to 286 TSS via Task Gate			284		g, j, k, r
From 386 Task to 386 TSS via Task Gate			311		g, j, k, r
From 368 Task to virt 8086 md via Task Gate			228		g, j, k, r
From virt 8086 md to 286 TSS via Task Gate			289		g, j, k, r
From virt 8086 md to 386 TSS via Task Gate			316		g, j, k, r
From virt 8086 md to priv level 0 via Trap Gate or Interrupt Gate			119		
INT: TYPE 3					
Via Interrupt or Trap Gate to Same Privilege Level			59		g, j, k, r
Via Interrupt or Trap Gate to Different Privilege Level			99		g, j, k, r
From 286 Task to 286 TSS via Task Gate			278		g, j, k, r
From 286 Task to 386 TSS via Task Gate			305		g, j, k, r
From 268 Task to Virt 8086 md via Task Gate			222		g, j, k, r
From 386 Task to 286 TSS via Task Gate			280		g, j, k, r
From 386 Task to 386 TSS via Task Gate			307		g, j, k, r
From 368 Task to Virt 8086 md via Task Gate			224		g, j, k, r
From virt 8086 md to 286 TSS via Task Gate			285		g, j, k, r
From virt 8086 md to 386 TSS via Task Gate			312		g, j, k, r
From virt 8086 md to priv level 0 via Trap Gate or Interrupt Gate			119		
INTO:					
Via Interrupt or Trap Grate to Same Privilege Level			59		g, j, k, r
Via Interrupt or Trap Gate to Different Privilege Level			99		g, j, k, r
From 286 Task to 286 TSS via Task Gate			280		g, j, k, r
From 286 Task to 386 TSS via Task Gate			307		g, j, k, r
From 268 Task to virt 8086 md via Task Gate			224		g, j, k, r
From 386 Task to 286 TSS via Task Gate			282		g, j, k, r
From 386 Task to 386 TSS via Task Gate			309		g, j, k, r
From 368 Task to virt 8086 md via Task Gate			226		g, j, k, r
From virt 8086 md to 286 TSS via Task Gate			287		g, j, k, r
From virt 8086 md to 386 TSS via Task Gate			314		g, j, k, r
From virt 8086 md to priv level 0 via Trap Gate or Interrupt Gate			119		

Table G.1: 80386 Instruction Set Clock Count Summary (continued)

INSTRUCTION	FORMAT			CLOCK COUNT		NOTES	
				Real Address Mode or Virtual 8086 Mode	Protected Virtual Address Mode	Real Address Mode or Virtual 8086 Mode	Protected Virtual Address Mode
INTERRUPT INSTRUCTIONS (Continued)							
BOUND:							
Via Interrupt or Trap Gate to Same Privilege Level					59		g, j, k, r
Via Interrupt or Trap Gate to Different Privilege Level					99		g, j, k, r
From 286 Task to 286 TSS via Task Gate					254		g, j, k, r
From 286 Task to 386 TSS via Task Gate					284		g, j, k, r
From 268 Task to virt 8086 Mode via Task Gate					231		g, j, k, r
From 386 Task to 286 TSS via Task Gate					264		g, j, k, r
From 386 Task to 386 TSS via Task Gate					294		g, j, k, r
From 368 Task to virt 8086 Mode via Task Gate					243		g, j, k, r,
From virt 8086 Mode to 286 TSS via Task Gate					264		g, j, k, r
From virt 8086 Mode to 386 TSS via Task Gate					294		g, j, k, r
From virt 8086 md to priv level 0 via Trap Gate or Interrupt Gate					119		
INTERRUPT RETURN							
IRET = Interrupt Return	11001111			22			g, h, j, k, r
Protected Mode Only (IRET)							
To the Same Privilege Level (within task)					38		g, h, j, k, r
To Different Privilege Level (within task)					82		g, h, j, k, r
From 286 Task to 286 TSS					232		h, j, k, r
From 286 Task to 386 TSS					265		h, j, k, r
From 286 Task to Virtual 8086 Task					214		h, j, k, r
From 286 Task to Virtual 8086 Mode (within task)					60		
From 386 Task to 286 TSS					271		h, j, k, r
From 386 Task to 386 TSS					275		h, j, k, r
From 386 Task to Virtual 8086 Task					224		h, j, k, r
From 386 Task to Virtual 8086 Mode (within task)					60		
PROCESSOR CONTROL							
HLT = HALT	11110100			5	5		l
MOV = Move to and From Control/Debug/Test Registers							
CR0/CR2/CR3 from register	00001111	00100010	11 eee reg	10/4/5	10/4/5		l
Register From CR0–3	00001111	00100000	11 eee reg	6	6		l
DR0–3 From Register	00001111	00100011	11 eee reg	22	22		l
DR6–7 From Register	00001111	00100011	11 eee reg	16	16		l
Register from DR6–7	00001111	00100001	11 eee reg	14	14		l
Register from DR0–3	00001111	00100001	11 eee reg	22	22		l
TR6–7 from Register	00001111	00100110	11 eee reg	12	12		l
Register from TR6–7	00001111	00100100	11 eee reg	12	12		l
NOP = No Operation	10010000			3	3		
WAIT = Wait until BUSY# pin is negated	10011011			6	6		

Table G.1: 80386 Instruction Set Clock Count Summary (continued)

INSTRUCTION	FORMAT	CLOCK COUNT: Real Address Mode or Virtual 8086 Mode	CLOCK COUNT: Protected Virtual Address Mode	NOTES: Real Address Mode or Virtual 8086 Mode	NOTES: Protected Virtual Address Mode
PROCESSOR EXTENSION INSTRUCTIONS					
Processor Extension Escape	11011TTT | mod LLL r/m TTT and LLL bits are opcode information for coprocessor.	See 80287/80387 data sheets for clock counts			h
PREFIX BYTES					
Address Size Prefix	01100111	0	0		
LOCK = Bus Lock Prefix	11110000	0	0		m
Operand Size Prefix	01100110	0	0		
Segment Override Prefix					
CS:	00101110	0	0		
DS:	00111110	0	0		
ES:	00100110	0	0		
FS:	01100100	0	0		
GS:	01100101	0	0		
SS:	00110110	0	0		
PROTECTION CONTROL					
ARPL = Adjust Requested Privilege Level					
From Register/Memory	01100011 | mod reg r/m	N/A	20/21	a	h
LAR = Load Access Rights					
From Register/Memory	00001111 | 00000010 | mod reg r/m	N/A	15/16	a	g, h, j, p
LGDT = Load Global Descriptor					
Table Register	00001111 | 00000001 | mod 010 r/m	11	11	b, c	h, l
LIDT = Load Interrupt Descriptor					
Table Register	00001111 | 00000001 | mod 011 r/m	11	11	b, c	h, l
LLDT = Load Local Descriptor					
Table Register to Register/Memory	00001111 | 00000000 | mod 010 r/m	N/A	20/24	a	g, h, j, l
LMSW = Load Machine Status Word					
From Register/Memory	00001111 | 00000001 | mod 110 r/m	10/13	10/13	b, c	h, l
LSL = Load Segment Limit					
From Register/Memory	00001111 | 00000011 | mod reg r/m				
Byte-Granular Limit		N/A	20/21	a	g, h, j, p
Page-Granular Limit		N/A	25/26	a	g, h, j, p
LTR = Load Task Register					
From Register/Memory	00001111 | 00000000 | mod 001 r/m	N/A	23/27	a	g, h, j, l
SGDT = Store Global Descriptor					
Table Register	00001111 | 00000001 | mod 000 r/m	9	9	b, c	h

Table G.1: 80386 Instruction Set Clock Count Summary (continued)

INSTRUCTION		FORMAT			CLOCK COUNT		NOTES	
					Real Address Mode or Virtual 8086 Mode	Protected Virtual Address Mode	Real Address Mode or Virtual 8086 Mode	Protected Virtual Address Mode
SIDT	= Store Interrupt Descriptor Table Register	00001111	00000001	mod 001 r/m	9	9	b, c	h
SLDT	= Store Local Descriptor Table Register To Register/Memory	00001111	00000000	mod 000 r/m	N/A	2/2	a	h
SMSW	= Store Machine Status Word	00001111	00000001	mod 100 r/m	10/13	10/13	b, c	h, l
STR	= Store Task Register To Register/Memory	00001111	00000000	mod 001 r/m	N/A	2/2	a	h
VERR	= Verify Read Access Register/Memory	00001111	00000000	mod 100 r/m	N/A	10/11	a	g, h, j, p
VERW	= Verify Write Accesss	00001111	00000000	mod 101 r/m	N/A	15/16	a	g, h, j, p

NOTES

Notes a through c apply to 80386 real address mode only:

a. This is a protected mode instruction. Attempted execution in real mode will result in exception 6 (invalid opcode).

b. Exception 13 fault (general protection violation) will occur in real mode if an operand reference is made that partially or fully extends beyond the maximum CS, DS, ES, FS or GS limit, FFFFh. Exception 12 fault (stack segment limit violation or not present) will occur in real mode if an operand reference is made that partially or fully extends beyond the maximum SS limit.

c. This instruction may be executed in real mode. In real mode, its purpose is primarily to initialize the CPU for protected mode.

Notes d through g apply to 80386 real address mode and 80386 protected virtual address mode:

d. The 80386 uses an early-out multiply algorithm. The actual number of clocks depends on the position of the most significant bit in the operand (multiplier).

Clock counts given are minimum to maximum. To calculate actual clocks, use the formula

Actual Clock = if m <> 0 then max ([$\log_2$ | m |],3) + 6 clocks:

if m = 0 then 9 clocks

where m is the multiplier.

e. An exception may occur, depending on the value of the operand.

f. LOCK# is automatically asserted, regardless of the presence or absence of the LOCK# prefix.

g. LOCK# is asserted during descriptor table accesses.

Notes h through r apply to 80386 protected virtual address mode only:

h. Exception 13 fault (general protection violation) will occur if the memory operand in CS, DS, ES, FS, or GS cannot be used due to either a segment limit violation or access rights violation. If a stack limit is violated, an exception 12 (stack segment limit violation or not present) occurs.

i. For segment load operations, the CPL, RPL, and DPL must agree with the privilege rules to avoid an exception 13 fault (general protection violation). The segment's descriptor must indicate "present" or exception 11 (CS, DS, ES, FS, GS not present) will occur. If the SS register is loaded and a stack segment not present is detected, an exception 12 (stack segment limit violation or not present) occurs.

j. All segment descriptor accesses in the GDT or LDT made by this instruction will automatically assert LOCK# to maintain descriptor integrity in multiprocessor systems.

k. JMP, CALL, INT, RET, and IRET instructions referring to another code segment will cause an exception 13 (general protection violation) if an applicable privilege rule is violated.

l. An exception 13 fault occurs if CPL is greater than 0 (0 is the most privileged level).

m. An exception 13 fault occurs if CPL is greater than IOPL.

n. The IF bit of the flag register is not updated if CPL is greater than IOPL. The IOPL and VM fields of the flag register are updated only if CPL = 0.
o. The PE bit of the MSW (CR0) cannot be reset by this instruction. Use MOV into CR0 if desiring to reset the PE bit.
p. Any violation of privilege rules as applied to the selector operand does not cause a protection exception; rather, the zero flag is cleared.
q. If the coprocessor's memory operand violates a segment limit or segment access rights, an exception 13 fault (general protection violation) will occur before the ESC instruction is executed. An exception 12 fault (stack segment limit violation or not present) will occur if the stack limit if violated by the operand's starting address.
r. The destination of a JMP, CALL, INT, RET, or IRET must be in the defined limit of a code segment, or an exception 13 (general protection violation) will occur.

The instruction clock count assumptions are as follows:

1. The instruction has been prefetched and decoded, and is ready for execution.
2. Bus cycles do not require wait states.
3. There are no local bus HOLD requests delaying processor access to the bus.
4. No exceptions are detected during instruction execution.
5. If an effective address is calculated, it does not use two general register components. One register, scaling, and displacement can be used within the clock counts shown. However, if the effective address calculation uses two general register components, add 1 clock to the clock count shown.

Conventions for instruction clock count notation are as follows:

1. If two clock counts are given, the smaller refers to a register operand and the larger refers to a memory operand.
2. n = number of times repeated.
3. m = number of components in the next instruction executed, where the entire displacement (if any) counts as one component, the entire immediate data (if any) counts as one component, and each of the *other* bytes of the instruction and prefix(es) each count as one component.

► Instruction Encoding

All instruction encodings are subsets of the general instruction format shown in Figure G.1. Instructions consist of one or two primary opcode

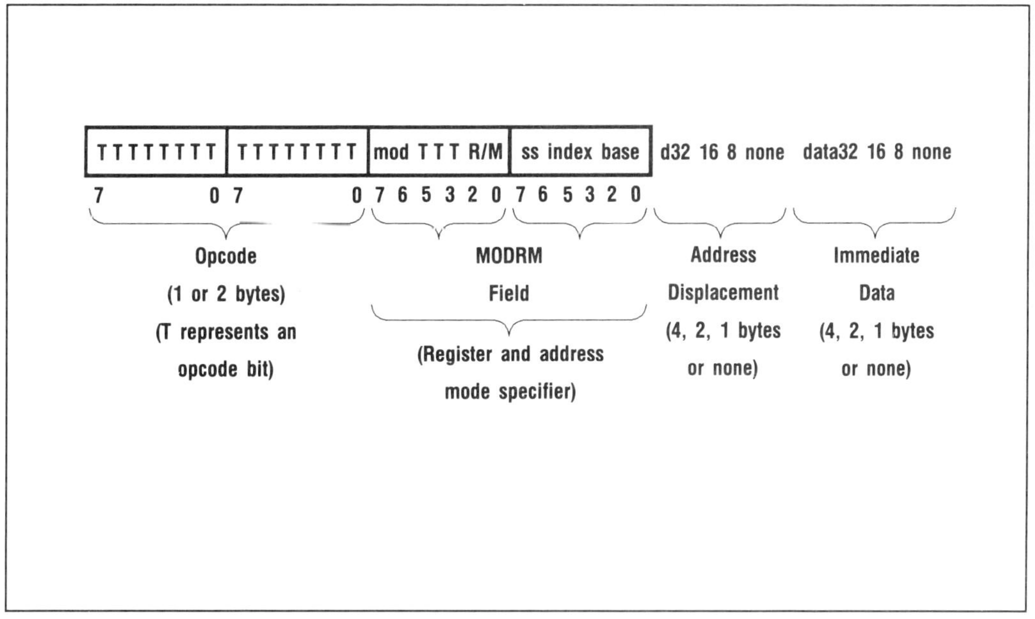

► **Figure G.1:** General instruction format

bytes, possibly an address specifier consisting of the one- or two-byte MODRM field and a displacement if required, and possibly an immediate data field.

Within the primary opcode or opcodes, smaller encoding fields may be defined. These fields vary according to the class of operation. The fields define such information as direction of the operation, size of the displacements, register encoding, or sign extension.

Almost all instructions referring to an operand in memory have a one- or two-byte MODRM field following the primary opcode byte(s).

Addressing modes can include a displacement immediately following the MODRM field. If a displacement is present, the possible sizes are 8, 16, or 32 bits.

If the instruction specifies an immediate operand, the immediate operand follows any displacement bytes. The immediate operand, if specified, is always the last field of the instruction.

Figure G.1 illustrates several of the fields that can appear in an instruction, such as the mod field and the R/M field, but the figure does not show all fields. Several smaller fields also appear in certain instructions, sometimes within the opcode bytes themselves. Table G.2 is a complete list of all fields appearing in the 80386 instruction set. Following Table G.2 are detailed tables for each field.

FIELD NAME	DESCRIPTION	NUMBER OF BITS
w	Specifies if data is byte or full size (full size is either 16 or 32 bits)	1
d	Specifies direction of data operation	1
s	Specifies if an immediate data field must be sign-extended	1
reg	General register specifier	3
MODRM	Address mode specifier (effective address can be a general register)	2 for mod; 3 for R/M
ss	Scale factor for scaled index address mode	2
base	General register to be used as base register	3
index	General register to be used as index register	3
sreg2	Segment register specifier for CS, SS, DS, ES	2
sreg3	Segment register specifier for CS, SS, DS, ES, FS, GS	3
tttn	For conditional instructions, specifies a condition asserted or a condition negated	4

Note: Table G.1 shows encoding of individual instructions.

► **Table G.2:** Fields within 80386 instructions

32-Bit Extensions of the Instruction Set

With the 80386, the 86/186/286 instruction set is extended in two orthogonal directions: 32-bit forms of all 16-bit instructions are added to support the 32-bit data types, and 32-bit addressing modes are made available for all instructions referencing memory. This orthogonal instruction set extension is accomplished by having a default (D) bit in the code segment descriptor, and two instruction prefixes.

Whether the instruction defaults to operations of 16 bits or 32 bits depends on the setting of the D bit in the code segment descriptor, which gives the default length (either 32 bits or 16 bits) for both operands and effective addresses when executing that code segment. In real mode or virtual 8086 mode, no code segment descriptors are used, but a D value of 0 is assumed internally by the 80386 when operating in those modes (for 16-bit default sizes compatible with the 8086/80186/80286).

Two prefixes, the operand size prefix and the effective address size prefix, allow overriding individually the default selection of operand size and effective address size. These prefixes may precede any opcode bytes and affect only the instruction they precede. If necessary, one or both of the prefixes may be placed before the opcode bytes. The presence of the operand size prefix and the effective address prefix will toggle the operand size or the effective address size, respectively, to the value "opposite" from the default setting. For example, if the default operand size is for 32-bit data operations, then presence of the operand size prefix toggles the instruction to 16-bit operation. As another example, if the default effective address size is 16 bits, presence of the effective address size prefix toggles the instruction to use 32-bit effective address computations.

These 32-bit extensions are available in all 80386 modes, including real mode or virtual 8086 mode. In these modes, the default is always 16 bits, so prefixes are needed to specify 32-bit operands or addresses.

Unless specified otherwise, instructions with 8-bit and 16-bit operands do not affect the contents of the high-order bits of the extended registers.

Encoding of Instruction Fields

Within the instruction are several fields indicating register selection, addressing mode, and so on. The exact encodings of these fields are defined here.

Encoding of Operand Length (w) Field

For any given instruction performing a data operation, the instruction is executing a 32-bit operation or a 16-bit operation. Within the constraints of the operation size, the w field encodes the operand size as either one byte or the full operation size, as shown in the table below.

w Field	Operand Size during 16-bit Data Operations	Operand Size during 32-bit Data Operations
0	8 bits	8 bits
1	16 bits	32 bits

Encoding of the General Register (reg) Field

The general register is specified by the reg field, which may appear in the primary opcode bytes, or as the reg field of the MODRM byte, or as the R/M field of the MODRM byte. Table G.3 shows the encoding of the reg field when the w field is not present in the instruction, and Table G.4 shows the reg-field encoding when w is present.

REG FIELD	REGISTER SELECTED DURING 16-BIT DATA OPERATIONS	REGISTER SELECTED DURING 32-BIT DATA OPERATIONS
000	AX	EAX
001	CX	ECX
010	DX	EDX
011	BX	EBX
100	SP	ESP
101	BP	EBP
110	SI	ESI
111	DI	EDI

► **Table G.3:** Encoding of reg field when w field is not present in instruction

REG FIELD	REGISTER SPECIFIED BY REG FIELD DURING 16-BIT DATA OPERATIONS: FUNCTION OF w FIELD (WHEN w = 0)	(WHEN w = 1)
000	AL	AX
001	CL	CX
010	DL	DX
011	BL	BX
100	AH	SP
101	CH	BP
110	DH	SI
111	BH	DI

REG FIELD	REGISTER SPECIFIED BY REG FIELD DURING 32-BIT DATA OPERATIONS: FUNCTION OF w FIELD (WHEN w = 0)	(WHEN w = 1)
000	AL	EAX
001	CL	ECX
010	DL	EDX
011	BL	EBX
100	AH	ESP
101	CH	EBP
110	DH	ESI
111	BH	EDI

► **Table G.4:** Encoding of reg field when w field is present in instruction

Encoding of the Segment Register (sreg) Field

The sreg field in certain instructions is a 2-bit field allowing one of the four 80286 segment registers to be specified (see Table G.5). The sreg field in other instructions is a 3-bit field, allowing the 80386 FS and GS segment registers to be specified (see Table G.6).

2-BIT sreg2 FIELD	SEGMENT REGISTER SELECTED
00	ES
01	CS
10	SS
11	DS

► **Table G.5:** 2-bit sreg2 field

3-BIT sreg3 FIELD	SEGMENT REGISTER SELECTED
000	ES
001	CS
010	SS
011	DS
100	FS
101	GS
110	do not use
111	do not use

► **Table G.6:** 3-bit sreg3 field

Encoding of Address Mode

Except for special instructions, such as PUSH or POP, where the addressing mode is predetermined, the addressing mode for the current instruction is specified by a one- or two-byte MODRM field, which follows the opcode byte(s).

A two-byte MODRM field is specified when using 32-bit addressing mode and the MODRM field has R/M = 100 and mod = 00, 01, or 10. The 32-bit addressing mode is then a function of the mod, ss, index, and base fields.

The MODRM field also contains 3 bits (shown as TTT in Figure G.1) sometimes used as an extension of the primary opcode. The 3 bits, however, may also be used as a register field (reg).

When calculating an effective address, either 16-bit addressing or 32-bit addressing is used. The 16-bit addressing uses 16-bit address components to calculate the effective address, whereas 32-bit addressing uses 32-bit address components to calculate the effective address. When 16-bit addressing is used, the MODRM byte is interpreted as a 16-bit addressing mode specifier. When 32-bit addressing is used, the MODRM byte is interpreted as a 32-bit addressing mode specifier.

Table G.7 defines all encodings of all 16-bit addressing modes, and Tables G.8 and G.9 define all encodings of 32-bit addressing modes.

MODRM	EFFECTIVE ADDRESS	MODRM	EFFECTIVE ADDRESS
00 000	DS:[BX + SI]	10 000	DS:[BX + SI + d16]
00 001	DS:[BX + DI]	10 001	DS:[BX + DI + d16]
00 010	SS:[BP + SI]	10 010	SS:[BP + SI + d16]
00 011	SS:[BP + DI]	10 011	SS:[BP + DI + d16]
00 100	DS:[SI]	10 100	DS:[SI + d16]
00 101	DS:[DI]	10 101	DS:[DI + d16]
00 110	DS:d16	10 110	SS:[BP + d16]
00 111	DS:[BX]	10 111	DS:[BX + d16]
01 000	DS:[BX + SI + d8]	11 000	register—see below
01 001	DS:[BX + DI + d8]	11 001	register—see below
01 010	SS:[BP + SI + d8]	11 010	register—see below
01 011	SS:[BP + DI + d8]	11 011	register—see below
01 100	DS:[SI + d8]	11 100	register—see below
01 101	DS:[DI + d8]	11 101	register—see below
01 110	SS:[BP + d8]	11 110	register—see below
01 111	DS:[BX + d8]	11 111	register—see below

► **Table G.7:** Encoding of 16-bit address mode with MODRM byte

MODRM	REGISTER SPECIFIED BY R/M DURING 16-BIT DATA OPERATIONS: FUNCTION OF w FIELD (WHEN w = 0)	(WHEN w = 1)
11 000	AL	AX
11 001	CL	CX
11 010	DL	DX
11 011	BL	BX
11 100	AH	SP
11 101	CH	BP
11 110	DH	SI
11 111	BH	DI

MODRM	REGISTER SPECIFIED BY R/M DURING 32-BIT DATA OPERATIONS: FUNCTION OF w FIELD (WHEN w = 0)	(WHEN w = 1)
11 000	AL	EAX
11 001	CL	ECX
11 010	DL	EDX
11 011	BL	EBX
11 100	AH	ESP
11 101	CH	EBP
11 110	DH	ESI
11 111	BH	EDI

► **Table G.7:** Encoding of 16-bit address mode with MODRM byte (continued)

MODRM	EFFECTIVE ADDRESS	MODRM	EFFECTIVE ADDRESS
00 000	DS:[EAX]	10 000	DS:[EAX + d32]
00 001	DS:[ECX]	10 001	DS:[ECX + d32]
00 010	DS:[EDX]	10 010	DS:[EDX + d32]
00 011	DS:[EBX]	10 011	DS:[EBX + d32]
00 100	escape to two-byte	10 100	escape to two-byte
00 101	DS:d32	10 101	SS:[EBP + d32]
00 110	DS:[ESI]	10 110	DS:[ESI + d32]
00 111	DS:[EDI]	10 111	DS:[EDI + d32]
01 000	DS:[EAX + d8]	11 000	register—see below
01 001	DS:[ECX + d8]	11 001	register—see below
01 010	DS:[EDX + d8]	11 010	register—see below
01 011	DS:[EBX + d8]	11 011	register—see below
01 100	escape to two-byte	11 100	register—see below
01 101	SS:[EBP + d8]	11 101	register—see below
01 110	DS:[ESI + d8]	11 110	register—see below
01 111	DS:[EDI + d8]	11 111	register—see below

MODRM	REGISTER SPECIFIED BY REG OR R/M DURING 16-BIT DATA OPERATIONS: FUNCTION OF w FIELD	
	(WHEN w = 0)	(WHEN w = 1)
11 000	AL	AX
11 001	CL	CX
11 010	DL	DX
11 011	BL	BX
11 100	AH	SP
11 101	CH	BP
11 110	DH	SI
11 111	BH	DI

► **Table G.8:** Encoding of 32-bit address mode with one-byte MODRM field

MODRM	REGISTER SPECIFIED BY REG OR R/M DURING 32-BIT DATA OPERATIONS: FUNCTION OF w FIELD (WHEN w = 0)	(WHEN w = 1)
11 000	AL	EAX
11 001	CL	ECX
11 010	DL	EDX
11 011	BL	EBX
11 100	AH	ESP
11 101	CH	EBP
11 110	DH	ESI
11 111	BH	EDI

► **Table G.8:** Encoding of 32-bit address mode with one-byte MODRM field (continued)

MOD BASE	EFFECTIVE ADDRESS
00 000	DS:[EAX +(scaled index)]
00 001	DS:[ECX +(scaled index)]
00 010	DS:[EDX +(scaled index)]
00 011	DS:[EBX +(scaled index)]
00 100	SS:[ESP +(scaled index)]
00 101	DS:[d32 +(scaled index)]
00 110	DS:[ESI +(scaled index)]
00 111	DS:[EDI +(scaled index)]
01 000	DS:[EAX +(scaled index) +d8]
01 001	DS:[ECX +(scaled index) +d8]
01 010	DS:[EDX +(scaled index) +d8]
01 011	DS:[EBX +(scaled index) +d8]
01 100	SS:[ESP +(scaled index) +d8]
01 101	DS:[EBP +(scaled index) +d8]
01 110	DS:[ESI +(scaled index) +d8]
01 111	DS:[EDI +(scaled index) +d8]

► **Table G.9:** Encoding of 32-bit address mode with two-byte MODRM field

10 000	DS:[EAX + (scaled index) + d32]
10 001	DS:[ECX + (scaled index) + d32]
10 010	DS:[EDX + (scaled index) + d32]
10 011	DS:[EBX + (scaled index) + d32]
10 100	SS:[ESP + (scaled index) + d32]
10 101	DS:[EBP + (scaled index) + d32]
10 110	DS:[ESI + (scaled index) + d32]
10 111	DS:[EDI + (scaled index) + d32]

SS	SCALE FACTOR
00	×1
01	×2
10	×4
11	×8

INDEX	INDEX REGISTER
000	EAX
001	ECX
010	EDX
011	EBX
100	no index reg**
101	EBP
110	ESI
111	EDI

***Important Note:*
When index field is 100, indicating "no index register," then ss field MUST equal 00. If index is 100 and ss does not equal 00, the effective address is undefined.

► **Table G.9:** Encoding of 32-bit address mode with two-byte MODRM field (continued)

Encoding of Operation Direction (d) Field

In many two-operand instructions, the d field is present to indicate which operand is considered the source and which is the destination.

d	Direction of Operation
0	Register/Memory←Register "reg" field indicates source operand; "mod R/M" or "mod ss index base" indicates destination operand
1	Register←Register/Memory "reg" field indicates destination operand; "mod R/M" or "mod ss index base" indicates source operand

Encoding of Sign-Extend (s) Field

The s field occurs primarily in instructions with immediate data fields. The s field has an effect only if the size of the immediate data is 8 bits and is being placed in a 16-bit or 32-bit destination.

s	Effect on Immediate Data8	Effect on Immediate Data 16/32
0	None	None
1	Sign-extend Data8 to fill 16-bit or 32-bit destination	None

Encoding of Conditional Test (tttn) Field

For the conditional instructions (conditional jumps and set on condition), tttn is encoded where n means use the condition (n = 0) or its negation (n = 1), and ttt gives the condition to test, as shown in Table G.10.

Encoding of Control or Debug Register (eee) Field

For the loading and storing of the control, debug, and test registers, the encoding is as follows:

1. When interpreted as a control register field

eee Code	Reg Name
000	CR0
010	CR2
011	CR3

2. When interpreted as a debug register field

eee Code	Reg Name
000	DR0
001	DR1
010	DR2
011	DR3
110	DR6
111	DR7

3. When interpreted as a test register field

eee Code	Reg Name
110	TR6
111	TR7

Do not use any other encoding.

MNEMONIC	CONDITION	tttn
O	Overflow	0000
NO	No Overflow	0001
B/NAE	Below/Not Above or Equal	0010
NB/AE	Not Below/Above or Equal	0011
E/Z	Equal/Zero	0100
NE/NZ	Not Equal/Not Zero	0101
BE/NA	Below or Equal/Not Above	0110
NBE/A	Not Below or Equal/Above	0111
S	Sign	1000
NS	Not Sign	1001
P/PE	Parity/Parity Even	1010
NP/PO	Not Parity/Parity Odd	1011
L/NGE	Less Than/Not Greater or Equal	1100
NL/GE	Not Less Than/Greater or Equal	1101
LE/NG	Less Than or Equal/Not Greater Than	1110
NLE/G	Not Less Than or Equal/Greater Than	1111

► **Table G.10:** Encoding of conditional test field

Machine Instruction Decoding Guide

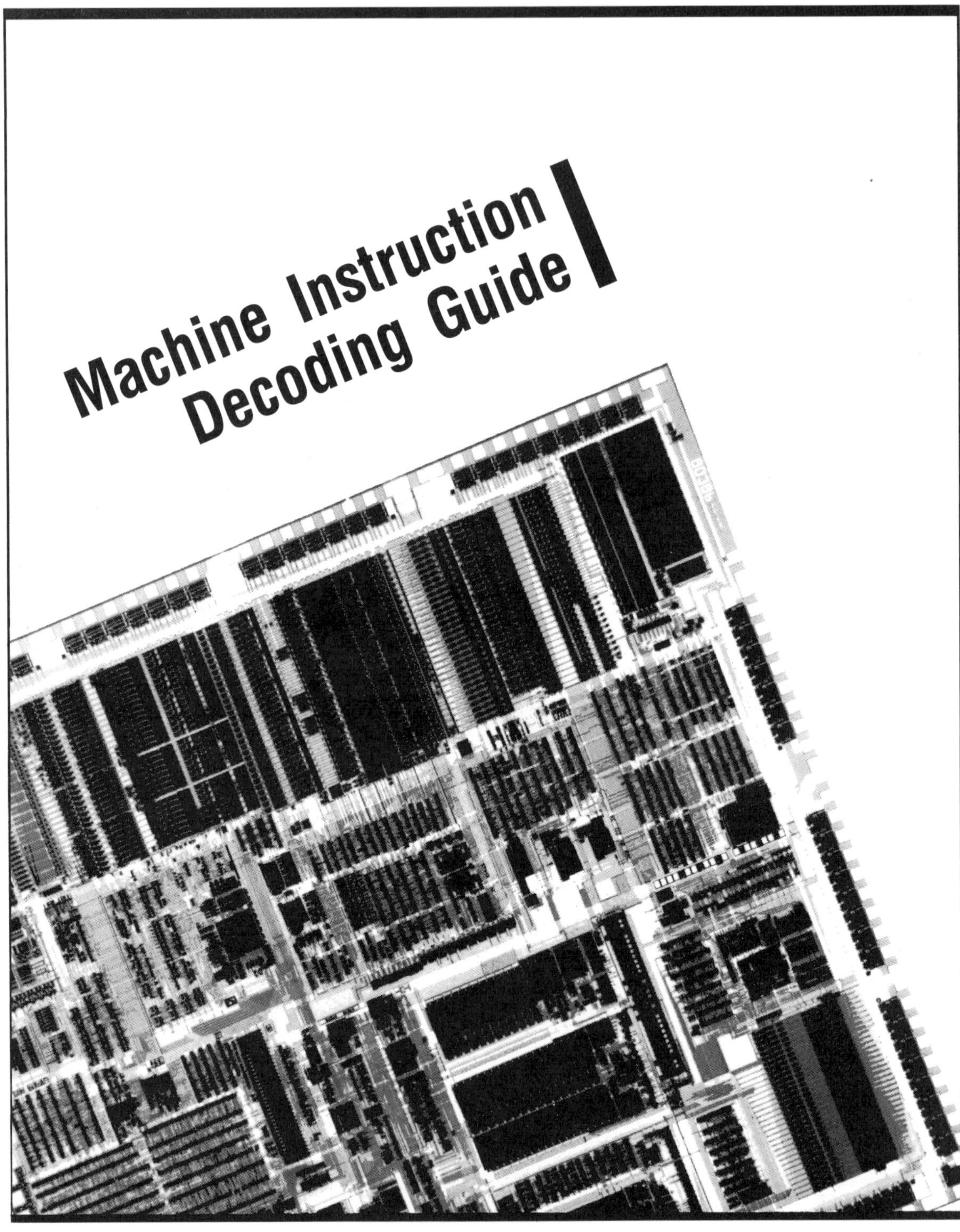

Appendix H

1st Byte		2nd Byte	Bytes 3-7	ASM386 Instruction Format	
Hex	Binary				
D8	1101 1000	MOD 000 R/M	SIB, displ	FADD	single-real
D8	1101 1000	MOD 001 R/M	SIB, displ	FMUL	single-real
D8	1101 1000	MOD 010 R/M	SIB, displ	FCOM	single-real
D8	1101 1000	MOD 011 R/M	SIB, displ	FCOMP	single-real
D8	1101 1000	MOD 100 R/M	SIB, displ	FSUB	single-real
D8	1101 1000	MOD 101 R/M	SIB, displ	FSUBR	single-real
D8	1101 1000	MOD 110 R/M	SIB, displ	FDIV	single-real
D8	1101 1000	MOD 111 R/M	SIB, displ	FDIVR	single-real
D8	1101 1000	1100 0 REG		FADD	ST,ST(i)
D8	1101 1000	1100 1 REG		FMUL	ST,ST(i)
D8	1101 1000	1101 0 REG		FCOM	ST(i)
D8	1101 1000	1101 1 REG		FCOMP	ST(i)
D8	1101 1000	1110 0 REG		FSUB	ST,ST(i)
D8	1101 1000	1110 1 REG		FSUBR	ST,ST(i)
D8	1101 1000	1111 0 REG		FDIV	ST,ST(i)
D8	1101 1000	1111 1 REG		FDIVR	ST,ST(i)
D9	1101 1001	MOD 000 R/M	SIB, displ	FLD	single-real
D9	1101 1001	MOD 001 R/M		reserved	
D9	1101 1001	MOD 010 R/M	SIB, displ	FST	single-real
D9	1101 1001	MOD 011 R/M	SIB, displ	FSTP	single-real
D9	1101 1001	MOD 100 R/M	SIB, displ	FLDENV	14 or 28 bytes***
D9	1101 1001	MOD 101 R/M	SIB, displ	FLDCW	2 bytes
D9	1101 1001	MOD 110 R/M	SIB, displ	FSTENV	14 or 28 bytes***
D9	1101 1001	MOD 111 R/M	SIB, displ	FSTCW	2 bytes
D9	1101 1001	1100 0 REG		FLD	ST(i)

1st Byte		2nd Byte	Bytes 3-7	ASM386 Instruction Format
Hex	Binary			
D9	1101 1001	1100 1 REG		FXCH ST(i)
D9	1101 1001	1101 0000		FNOP
D9	1101 1001	1101 0001		reserved
D9	1101 1001	1101 001–		reserved
D9	1101 1001	1101 01––		reserved
D9	1101 1001	1101 1 REG		*(1)
D9	1101 1001	1110 0000		FCHS
D9	1101 1001	1110 0001		FABS
D9	1101 1001	1110 001–		reserved
D9	1101 1001	1110 0100		FTST
D9	1101 1001	1110 0101		FXAM
D9	1101 1001	1110 011–		reserved
D9	1101 1001	1110 1000		FLD1
D9	1101 1001	1110 1001		FLDL2T
D9	1101 1001	1110 1010		FLDL2E
D9	1101 1001	1110 1011		FLDPI
D9	1101 1001	1110 1100		FLDLG2
D9	1101 1001	1110 1101		FLDLN2
D9	1101 1001	1110 1110		FLDZ
D9	1101 1001	1110 1111		reserved
D9	1101 1001	1111 0000		F2XM1
D9	1101 1001	1111 0001		FYL2X
D9	1101 1001	1111 0010		FPTAN
D9	1101 1001	1111 0011		FPATAN
D9	1101 1001	1111 0100		FXTRACT
D9	1101 1001	1111 0101		FPREM1
D9	1101 1001	1111 0110		FDECSTP
D9	1101 1001	1111 0111		FINCSTP
D9	1101 1001	1111 1000		FPREM
D9	1101 1001	1111 1001		FYL2XP1
D9	1101 1001	1111 1010		FSQRT

1st Byte		2nd Byte	Bytes 3-7	ASM386 Instruction Format	
Hex	Binary				
D9	1101 1001	1111 1011		FSINCOS	
D9	1101 1001	1111 1100		FRNDINT	
D9	1101 1001	1111 1101		FSCALE	
D9	1101 1001	1111 1110		FSIN	
D9	1101 1001	1111 1111		FCOS	
DA	1101 1010	MOD 000 R/M	SIB, displ	FIADD	short-integer
DA	1101 1010	MOD 001 R/M	SIB, displ	FIMUL	short-integer
DA	1101 1010	MOD 010 R/M	SIB, displ	FICOM	short-integer
DA	1101 1010	MOD 011 R/M	SIB, displ	FICOMP	short-integer
DA	1101 1010	MOD 100 R/M	SIB, displ	FISUB	short-integer
DA	1101 1010	MOD 101 R/M	SIB, displ	FISUBR	short-integer
DA	1101 1010	MOD 110 R/M	SIB, displ	FIDIV	short-integer
DA	1101 1010	MOD 111 R/M	SIB, displ	FIDIVR	short-integer
DA	1101 1010	110- ----		reserved	
DA	1101 1010	1110 0---		reserved	
DA	1101 1010	1110 1000		reserved	
DA	1010 1010	1110 1001		FUCOMPP	
DA	1101 1010	1110 101-		reserved	
DA	1101 1010	1110 11--		reserved	
DA	1101 1010	1111 ----		reserved	
DB	1101 1011	MOD 000 R/M	SIB, displ	FILD	short-integer
DB	1101 1011	MOD 001 R/M	SIB, displ	reserved	
DB	1101 1011	MOD 010 R/M	SIB, displ	FIST	short-integer
DB	1101 1011	MOD 011 R/M	SIB, displ	FISTP	short-integer
DB	1101 1011	MOD 100 R/M	SIB, displ	reserved	
DB	1101 1011	MOD 101 R/M	SIB, displ	FLD	extended-real
DB	1101 1011	MOD 110 R/M	SIB, displ	reserved	
DB	1101 1011	MOD 111 R/M	SIB, displ	FSTP	extended-real
DB	1101 1011	110- ----		reserved	
DB	1101 1011	1110 0000		**(1)	
DB	1101 1011	1110 0001		**(2)	

1st Byte		2nd Byte	Bytes 3-7	ASM386 Instruction Format
Hex	Binary			
DB	1101 1011	1110 0010		FCLEX
DB	1101 1011	1110 0011		FINIT
DB	1101 1011	1110 0100		**(3)
DB	1101 1011	1110 0101		reserved
DB	1101 1011	1110 011–		reserved
DB	1101 1011	1110 1–––		reserved
DB	1101 1011	1111 ––––		reserved
DC	1101 1100	MOD 000 R/M	SIB, displ	FADD double-real
DC	1101 1100	MOD 001 R/M	SIB, displ	FMUL double-real
DC	1101 1100	MOD 010 R/M	SIB, displ	FCOM double-real
DC	1101 1100	MOD 011 R/M	SIB, displ	FCOMP double-real
DC	1101 1100	MOD 100 R/M	SIB, displ	FSUB double-real
DC	1101 1100	MOD 101 R/M	SIB, displ	FSUBR double-real
DC	1101 1100	MOD 110 R/M	SIB, displ	FDIV double-real
DC	1101 1100	MOD 111 R/M	SIB, displ	FDIVR double-real
DC	1101 1100	1100 0 REG		FADD ST(i),ST
DC	1101 1100	1100 1 REG		FMUL ST(i),ST
DC	1101 1100	1101 0 REG		*(2)
DC	1101 100	1101 1 REG		*(3)
DC	1101 1100	1110 0 REG		FSUBR ST(i),ST
DC	1101 1100	1110 1 REG		FSUB ST(i),ST
DC	1101 1100	1111 0 REG		FDIVR ST(i),ST
DC	1101 1100	1111 1 REG		FDIV ST(i),ST
DD	1101 1101	MOD 000 R/M	SIB, displ	FLD double-real
DD	1101 1101	MOD 001 R/M		reserved
DD	1101 1101	MOD 010 R/M	SIB, displ	FST double-real
DD	1101 1101	MOD 011 R/M	SIB, displ	FSTP double-real
DD	1101 1101	MOD 100 R/M	SIB, displ	FRSTOR 94 or 108 bytes***
DD	1101 1101	MOD 101 R/M	SIB, displ	reserved
DD	1101 1101	MOD 110 R/M	SIB, displ	FSAVE 94 or 108 bytes***
DD	1101 1101	MOD 111 R/M	SIB, displ	FSTSW 2 bytes

1st Byte		2nd Byte	Bytes 3-7	ASM386 Instruction Format	
Hex	Binary				
DD	1101 1101	1100 0 REG		FFREE	ST(i)
DD	1101 1101	1100 1 REG		*(4)	
DD	1101 1101	1101 0 REG		FST	ST(i)
DD	1101 1101	1101 1 REG		FSTP	ST(i)
DD	1101 1101	1110 0 REG		FUCOM	ST(i)
DD	1101 1101	1110 1 REG		FUCOMP	ST(i)
DD	1101 1101	1111 ----		reserved	
DE	1101 1110	MOD 000 R/M	SIB, displ	FIADD	word-integer
DE	1101 1110	MOD 001 R/M	SIB, displ	FIMUL	word-integer
DE	1101 1110	MOD 010 R/M	SIB, displ	FICOM	word-integer
DE	1101 1110	MOD 011 R/M	SIB, displ	FICOMP	word-integer
DE	1101 1110	MOD 100 R/M	SIB, displ	FISUB	word-integer
DE	1101 1110	MOD 101 R/M	SIB, displ	FISUBR	word-integer
DE	1101 1110	MOD 110 R/M	SIB, displ	FIDIV	word-integer
DE	1101 1110	MOD 111 R/M	SIB, displ	FIDIVR	word-integer
DE	1101 1110	1100 0 REG		FADDP	ST(i),ST
DE	1101 1110	1100 1 REG		FMULP	ST(i),ST
DE	1101 1110	1101 0---		*(5)	
DE	1101 1110	1101 1000		reserved	
DE	1101 1110	1101 1001		FCOMPP	
DE	1101 1110	1101 101-		reserved	
DE	1101 1110	1101 11--		reserved	
DE	1101 1110	1110 0 REG		FSUBRP	ST(i),ST
DE	1101 1110	1110 1 REG		FSUBP	ST(i),ST
DE	1101 1110	1111 0 REG		FDIVRP	ST(i),ST
DE	1101 1110	1111 1 REG		FDIVP	ST(i),ST
DF	1101 1111	MOD 000 R/M	SIB, displ	FILD	word-integer
DF	1101 1111	MOD 001 R/M	SIB, displ	reserved	
DF	1101 1111	MOD 010 R/M	SIB, displ	FIST	word-integer
DF	1101 1111	MOD 011 R/M	SIB, displ	FISTP	word-integer
DF	1101 1111	MOD 100 R/M	SIB, displ	FBLD	packed-decimal

1st Byte		2nd Byte	Bytes 3-7	ASM386 Instruction Format	
Hex	Binary				
DF	1101 1111	MOD 101 R/M	SIB, displ	FILD	long-integer
DF	1101 1111	MOD 110 R/M	SIB, displ	FBSTP	packed-decimal
DF	1101 1111	MOD 111 R/M	SIB, displ	FISTP	long-integer
DF	1101 1111	1100 0 REG		*(6)	
DF	1101 1111	1100 1 REG		*(7)	
DF	1101 1111	1101 0 REG		*(8)	
DF	1101 1111	1101 1 REG		*(9)	
DF	1101 1111	1110 0000		FSTSW AX	
DF	1101 1111	1110 0001		reserved	
DF	1101 1111	1110 001–		reserved	
DF	1101 1111	1110 01––		reserved	
DF	1101 1111	1110 1–––		reserved	
DF	1101 1111	1111 ––––		reserved	

NOTES

* The marked encodings are ***not*** generated by the language translators. If, however, the 80387 encounters one of these encodings in the instruction stream, it will execute it as follows:

(1) FSTP ST(i)
(2) FCOM ST(i)
(3) FCOMP ST(i)
(4) FXCH ST(i)
(5) FCOMP ST(i)
(6) FFREE ST(i) and pop stack
(7) FXCH ST(i)
(8) FSTP ST(i)
(9) FSTP ST(i)

** The marked encodings can be generated by the language translators; however, the 80387 treats them as FNOP. They correspond to the following 8087 or 80287 instructions:

(1) FENI
(2) FDISI
(3) FSETPM

*** The size of operand transferred depends on the 80386 operand size attribute in effect for the instruction.

80387 Extensions to the 80386 Instruction Set

Appendix 

INSTRUCTIONS FOR THE 80387 ASSUME ONE OF the five forms shown in Table I.1. In all cases, instructions are at least two bytes long and begin with the bit pattern 11011b, which identifies the floating-point instructions. Instructions that refer to memory operands specify addresses using the 80386 addressing modes.

The instruction summaries in Table I.2 assume the following:

1. The instruction has been prefetched and decoded, and is ready for execution.
2. Bus cycles do not require wait states.
3. There are no local bus HOLD requests delaying processor access to the bus.
4. No exceptions are detected during instruction execution.
5. If an effective address is calculated, it does not use two general register components. One register, scaling, and displacement can be used within the clock counts shown. However, if the effective address calculation uses two general register components, add 1 clock to the clock count shown.

Table I.1 80387 Instruction Forms

<table>
<tr><th rowspan="2"></th><th colspan="9">Instruction</th><th colspan="2" rowspan="2">Optional Fields</th></tr>
<tr><th colspan="4">First Byte</th><th colspan="5">Second Byte</th></tr>
<tr><td>1</td><td>11011</td><td colspan="2">OPA</td><td>1</td><td colspan="2">MOD</td><td>1</td><td>OPB</td><td>R/M</td><td>SIB</td><td>DISP</td></tr>
<tr><td>2</td><td>11011</td><td colspan="2">MF</td><td>OPA</td><td colspan="2">MOD</td><td colspan="2">OPB</td><td>R/M</td><td>SIB</td><td>DISP</td></tr>
<tr><td>3</td><td>11011</td><td>d</td><td>P</td><td>OPA</td><td>1</td><td>1</td><td colspan="2">OPB</td><td>ST(i)</td><td></td><td></td></tr>
<tr><td>4</td><td>11011</td><td>0</td><td>0</td><td>1</td><td>1</td><td>1</td><td>1</td><td colspan="2">OP</td><td></td><td></td></tr>
<tr><td>5</td><td>11011</td><td>0</td><td>1</td><td>1</td><td>1</td><td>1</td><td>1</td><td colspan="2">OP</td><td></td><td></td></tr>
<tr><td></td><td>15–11</td><td>10</td><td>9</td><td>8</td><td>7</td><td>6</td><td>5</td><td>4 3</td><td>2 1 0</td><td></td><td></td></tr>
</table>

NOTES

OP = Instruction opcode, possibly split into two fields, OPA and OPB

MF = Memory Format
00—32-bit real
01—32-bit integer
10—64-bit real
11—64-bit integer

P = Pop
0—Do not pop stack
1—Pop stack after operation

ESC = 11011

d = Destination
0—Destination is ST(0)
1—Destination is ST(i)

R XOR d = 0—Destination (op) Source

R XOR d = 1—Source (op) Destination

ST(i) = Register stack element *i*
000 = Stack top
001 = Second stack element
:
111 = Eighth stack element

MOD (mode field) and R/M (register/memory specifier) have the same interpretation as the corresponding fields of 80386 instructions (refer to Appendix G).

SIB (Scale Index Base) byte and DISP (displacement) are optionally present in instructions that have MOD and R/M fields. Their presence depends on the values of MOD and R/M, as for 80386 instructions.

Table I.2 80387 Extensions to the 80386 Instruction Set

Instruction	Encoding			Clock Count Range			
	Byte 0	Byte 1	Optional Bytes 2–6	32-Bit Real	32-Bit Integer	64-Bit Real	16-Bit Integer
DATA TRANSFER							
FLD = Load[a]							
Integer/real memory to ST(0)	ESC MF 1	MOD 000 R/M	SIB/DISP	20	45–52	25	61–65
Long integer memory to ST(0)	ESC 111	MOD 101 R/M	SIB/DISP	56–67			
Extended real memory to ST(0)	ESC 011	MOD 101 R/M	SIB/DISP	44			
BCD memory to ST(0)	ESC 111	MOD 100 R/M	SIB/DISP	266–275			
ST(i) to ST(0)	ESC 001	11000 ST(i)		14			
FST = Store							
ST(0) to integer/real memory	ESC MF 1	MOD 010 R/M	SIB/DISP	44	79–93	45	82–95
ST(0) to ST(i)	ESC 101	11010 ST(i)		11			
FSTP = Store and Pop							
ST(0) to integer/real memory	ESC MF 1	MOD 011 R/M	SIB/DISP	44	79–93	45	82–95
ST(0) to long integer memory	ESC 111	MOD 111 R/M	SIB/DISP	80–97			
ST(0) to extended real	ESC 011	MOD 111 R/M	SIB/DISP	53			
ST(0) to BCD memory	ESC 111	MOD 110 R/M	SIB/DISP	512–534			
ST(0) to ST(i)	ESC 101	11001 ST (i)		12			
FXCH = Exchange							
ST(i) and ST(0)	ESC 001	11001 ST(i)		18			
COMPARISON							
FCOM = Compare							
Integer/real memory to ST(0)	ESC MF 0	MOD 010 R/M	SIB/DISP	26	56–63	31	71–75
ST(i) to ST(0)	ESC 000	11010 ST(i)		24			
FCOMP = Compare and pop							
Integer/real memory to ST	ESC MF 0	MOD 011 R/M	SIB/DISP	26	56–63	31	71–75
ST(i) to ST(0)	ESC 000	11011 ST(i)		26			
FCOMPP = Compare and pop twice							
ST(1) to ST(0)	ESC 110	1101 1001		26			
FTST = Test ST(0)	ESC 001	1110 0100		28			
FUCOM = Unordered compare	ESC 101	11100 ST(i)		24			
FUCOMP = Unordered compare and pop	ESC 101	11101 ST(i)		26			
FUCOMPP = Unordered compare and pop twice	ESC 010	1110 1001		26			
FXAM = Examine ST(0)	ESC 001	11100101		30-38			
CONSTANTS							
FLDZ = Load +0.0 into ST(0)	ESC 001	1110 1110		20			
FLD1 = Load +1.0 into ST(0)	ESC 001	1110 1000		24			
FLDPI = Load pi into ST(0)	ESC 001	1110 1011		40			
FLDL2T = Load $\log_2(10)$ into ST(0)	ESC 001	1110 1001		40			

Shaded areas indicate instructions not available in 80287/8087.

NOTE

a. When loading single- or double-precision zero from memory, add 5 clocks.

80387 Extensions to the 80386 Instruction Set (Continued)

Instruction	Encoding			Clock Count Range			
	Byte 0	Byte 1	Optional Bytes 2–6	32-Bit Real	32-Bit Integer	64-Bit Real	16-Bit Integer
CONSTANTS (Continued)							
FLDL2E = Load $\log_2(e)$ into ST(0)	ESC 001	1110 1010		40			
FLDLG2 = Load $\log_{10}(2)$ into ST(0)	ESC 001	1110 1100		41			
FLDLN2 = Load $\log_e(2)$ into ST(0)	ESC 001	1110 1101		41			
ARITHMETIC							
FADD = Add							
Integer/real memory with ST(0)	ESC MF 0	MOD 000 R/M	SIB/DISP	24–32	57–72	29–37	71–85
ST(i) and ST(0)	ESC d P 0	11000 ST(i)		23–31[b]			
FSUB = Subtract							
Integer/real memory with ST(0)	ESC MF 0	MOD 10 R R/M	SIB/DISP	24–32	57–82	28–36	71–83[c]
ST(i) and ST(0)	ESC d P 0	1110 R R/M		26–34[d]			
FMUL = Multiply							
Integer/real memory with ST(0)	ESC MF 0	MOD 001 R/M	SIB/DISP	27–35	61–82	32–57	76–87
ST(i) and ST(0)	ESC d P 0	1100 1 R/M		29–57[e]			
FDIV = Divide							
Integer/real memory with ST(0)	ESC MF 0	MOD 11 R R/M	SIB/DISP	89	120–127[f]	94	136–140[g]
ST(i) and ST(0)	ESC d P 0	1111 R R/M		88[h]			
FSQRT[i] = Square root	ESC 001	1111 1010		122–129			
FSCALE = Scale ST(0) by ST(1)	ESC 001	1111 1101		67–86			
FPREM = Partial remainder	ESC 001	1111 1000		74–155			
FPREM1 = Partial remainder (IEEE)	ESC 001	1111 0101		95–185			
FRNDINT = Round ST(0) to integer	ESC 001	1111 1100		66–80			
FXTRACT = Extract components of ST(0)	ESC 001	1111 0100		70–76			
FABS = Absolute value of ST(0)	ESC 001	1110 0001		22			
FCHS = Change sign of ST(0)	ESC 001	1110 0000		24–25			

Shaded areas indicate instructions not available in 80287/8087.

NOTES

b. Add 3 clocks to the range when d = 1.
c. Add 1 clock to *each* range when R = 1.
d. Add 3 clocks to the range when d = 0.
e. typical = 52 (When d = 0, 46–54, typical = 49).
f. Add 1 clock to the range when R = 1.
g. 135–141 when R = 1.
h. Add 3 clocks to the range when d = 1.
i. $-0 \leqslant ST(0) \leqslant +\infty$.

80387 Extensions to the 80386 Instruction Set (Continued)

Instruction	Encoding			Clock Count Range
	Byte 0	Byte 1	Optional Bytes 2–6	
TRANSCENDENTAL				
FCOS[k] = Cosine of ST(0)	ESC 001	1111 1111		123–772j
FPTAN[k] = Partial tangent of ST(0)	ESC 001	1111 0010		191–497j
FPATAN = Partial arctangent	ESC 001	1111 0011		314–487
FSIN[k] = Sine of ST(0)	ESC 001	1111 1110		122–771j
FSINCOS[k] = Sine and cosine of ST(0)	ESC 001	1111 1011		194–809j
F2XM1[l] = $2^{ST(0)} - 1$	ESC 001	1111 0000		211–476
FYL2X[m] = ST(1) * $\log_2$(ST(0))	ESC 001	1111 0001		120–538
FYL2XP1[n] = ST(1) * $\log_2$(ST(0) + 1.0)	ESC 001	1111 1001		257–547
PROCESSOR CONTROL				
FINIT = Initialize NPX	ESC 011	1110 0011		33
FSTSW AX = Store status word	ESC 111	1110 0000		13
FLDCW = Load control word	ESC 001	MOD 101 R/M	SIB/DISP	19
FSTCW = Store control word	ESC 101	MOD 111 R/M	SIB/DISP	15
FSTSW = Store status word	ESC 101	MOD 111 R/M	SIB/DISP	15
FCLEX = Clear exceptions	ESC 011	1110 0010		11
FSTENV = Store environment	ESC 001	MOD 110 R/M	SIB/DISP	103–104
FLDENV = Load environment	ESC 001	MOD 100 R/M	SIB/DISP	71
FSAVE = Save state	ESC 101	MOD 110 R/M	SIB/DISP	375–376
FRSTOR = Restore state	ESC 101	MOD 100 R/M	SIB/DISP	308
FINCSTP = Increment stack pointer	ESC 001	1111 0111		21
FDECSTP = Decrement stack pointer	ESC 001	1111 0110		22
FFREE = Free ST(i)	ESC 101	1100 0 ST(i)		18
FNOP = No operations	ESC 001	1101 0000		12

Shaded areas indicate instructions not available in 80287/8087.

NOTES

j. These timings hold for operands in the range $|x| < \pi/4$. For operands not in this range, up to 76 additional clocks may be needed to reduce the operand.
k. $0 \leq |ST(0)| < 2^{63}$.
l. $-1.0 \leq ST(0) \leq 1.0$.
m. $0 \leq ST(0) < -\infty$, $-\infty < ST(1) < +\infty$
n. $0 \leq |ST(0)| < (2 - SQRT(2))/2$, $-\infty < ST(1) < +\infty$.

Index

TO JOIN THE SYBEX MAILING LIST OR ORDER BOOKS
PLEASE COMPLETE THIS FORM

NAME ______________________ COMPANY ______________________

STREET ______________________ CITY ______________________

STATE ______________________ ZIP ______________________

☐ PLEASE MAIL ME MORE INFORMATION ABOUT **SYBEX** TITLES

ORDER FORM (There is no obligation to order)

PLEASE SEND ME THE FOLLOWING:

TITLE	QTY	PRICE
______________	_____	_____
______________	_____	_____
______________	_____	_____
______________	_____	_____
TOTAL BOOK ORDER	_____	$_____

SHIPPING AND HANDLING PLEASE ADD $2.00 PER BOOK VIA UPS _____

FOR OVERSEAS SURFACE ADD $5.25 PER BOOK PLUS $4.40 REGISTRATION FEE _____

FOR OVERSEAS AIRMAIL ADD $18.25 PER BOOK PLUS $4.40 REGISTRATION FEE _____

CALIFORNIA RESIDENTS PLEASE ADD APPLICABLE SALES TAX _____

TOTAL AMOUNT PAYABLE _____

☐ CHECK ENCLOSED ☐ VISA
☐ MASTERCARD ☐ AMERICAN EXPRESS

ACCOUNT NUMBER ______________________

EXPIR. DATE _______ DAYTIME PHONE ______________

CUSTOMER SIGNATURE ______________________________________

CHECK AREA OF COMPUTER INTEREST:

☐ BUSINESS SOFTWARE

☐ TECHNICAL PROGRAMMING

☐ OTHER: ______________________

OTHER COMPUTER TITLES YOU WOULD LIKE TO SEE IN PRINT:

____

____

THE FACTOR THAT WAS MOST IMPORTANT IN YOUR SELECTION:

☐ THE SYBEX NAME

☐ QUALITY

☐ PRICE

☐ EXTRA FEATURES

☐ COMPREHENSIVENESS

☐ CLEAR WRITING

☐ OTHER ______________________

OCCUPATION

☐ PROGRAMMER

☐ SENIOR EXECUTIVE

☐ COMPUTER CONSULTANT

☐ SUPERVISOR

☐ MIDDLE MANAGEMENT

☐ ENGINEER/TECHNICAL

☐ CLERICAL/SERVICE

☐ BUSINESS OWNER/SELF EMPLOYED

☐ TEACHER

☐ HOMEMAKER

☐ RETIRED

☐ STUDENT

☐ OTHER: ______________

CHECK YOUR LEVEL OF COMPUTER USE

☐ NEW TO COMPUTERS

☐ INFREQUENT COMPUTER USER

☐ FREQUENT USER OF ONE SOFTWARE PACKAGE:

NAME ____________________

☐ FREQUENT USER OF MANY SOFTWARE PACKAGES

☐ PROFESSIONAL PROGRAMMER

OTHER COMMENTS:

____

____

____

____

____

____

____

PLEASE FOLD, SEAL, AND MAIL TO SYBEX

SYBEX, INC.
2021 CHALLENGER DR. #100
ALAMEDA, CALIFORNIA USA
94501

SEAL

One-Byte 80386 Opcode Map

	0	1	2	3	4	5	6	7	8	9	A	B	C	D	E	F
0	ADD						PUSH ES	POP ES	OR						PUSH CS	2-byte escape
	Eb,Gb	Ev,Gv	Gb,Eb	Gv,Ev	AL,Ib	eAX,Iv			Eb,Gb	Ev,Gv	Gb,Eb	Gv,Ev	AL,Ib	eAX,Iv		
1	ADC						PUSH SS	POP SS	SBB						PUSH DS	POP DS
	Eb,Gb	Ev,Gv	Gb,Eb	Gv,Ev	AL,Ib	eAX,Iv			Eb,Gb	Ev,Gv	Gb,Eb	Gv,Ev	AL,Ib	eAX,Iv		
2	AND						SEG =ES	DAA	SUB						SEG =CS	DAS
	Eb,Gb	Ev,Gv	Gb,Eb	Gv,Ev	AL,Ib	eAX,Iv			Eb,Gb	Ev,Gv	Gb,Eb	Gv,Ev	AL,Ib	eAX,Iv		
3	XOR						SEG =SS	AAA	CMP						SEG =CS	AAS
	Eb,Gb	Ev,Gv	Gb,Eb	Gv,Ev	AL,Ib	eAX,Iv			Eb,Gb	Ev,Gv	Gb,Eb	Gv,Ev	AL,Ib	eAX,Iv		
4	INC general register								DEC general register							
	eAX	eCX	eDX	eBX	eSP	eBP	eSI	eDI	eAX	eCX	eDX	eBX	eSP	eBP	eSI	eDI
5	PUSH general register								POP into general register							
	eAX	eCX	eDX	eBX	eSP	eBP	eSI	eDI	eAX	eCX	eDX	eBX	eSP	eBP	eSI	eDI
6	PUSHA	POPA	BOUND Gv,Ma	ARPL Ew,Rw	SEG =FS	SEG =GS	Operand Size	Address Size	PUSH Ib	IMUL GvEvIv	PUSH Ib	IMUL GvEvIb	INSB Yb,DX	INSW/D Yv,DX	OUTSB DX,Xb	OUTSW/D DX,Xv
7	Short-displacement jump on condition (Jb)															
	JO	JNO	JB	JNB	JZ	JNZ	JBE	JNBE	JS	JNS	JP	JNP	JL	JNL	JLE	JNLE
8	Immediate Grpl			Grpl Ev,Ib	TEST		XCHG		MOV				MOV Ew,Sw	LEA Gv,M	MOV Sw,Ew	POP Ev
	Eb,Ib	Ev,Iv			Eb,Gb	Ev,Gv	Eb,Gb	Ev,Gv	Eb,Gb	Ev,Gv	Gb,Eb	Gv,Ev				
9	NOP	XCHG word or double-word register with eAX							CBW	CWD	CALL Ap	WAIT	PUSHF Fv	POPF Fv	SAHF	LAHF
		eCX	eDX	eBX	eSP	eBP	eSI	eDI								
A	MOV				MOVSB Xb,Yb	MOVSW/D Xv,Yv	CMPSB Xb,Yb	CMPSW/D Xv,Yv	TEST		STOSB Yb,AL	STOSW/D Yv,eAX	LODSB AL,Xb	LODSW/D eAX,Xv	SCASB AL,Xb	SCASW/D eAX,Xv
	AL,Ob	eAX,Ov	Ob,AL	Ov,eAX					AL,Ib	eAX,Iv						
B	MOV immediate byte into byte register								MOV immediate word or double into word or double register							
	AL	CL	DL	BL	AH	CH	DH	BH	eAX	eCX	eDX	eBX	eSP	eBP	eSI	eDI
C	Shift Grp2		RET near		LES Gv,Mp	LDS Gv,Mp	MOV		ENTER Iw,Ib	LEAVE	RET far		INT 3	INT Ib	INTO	IRET
	Eb,Ib	Ev,Ib	Iw				Eb,Ib	Ev,Iv			Iw					
D	Shift Grp2				AAM	AAD		XLAT	ESC (Escape to coprocessor instruction set)							
	Eb,1	Ev,1	Eb,CL	Ev,CL												
E	LOOPNE Jb	LOOPE Jb	LOOP Jb	JCXZ Jb	IN		OUT		CALL Av	JMP			IN		OUT	
					AL,Ib	eAX,Ib	Ib,AL	Ib,eAX		Jv	Ap	Jb	AL,DX	eAX,DX	DX,AL	DX,eAX
F	LOCK		REPNE	REP REPE	HLT	CMC	Unary Grp3		CLC	STC	CLI	STI	CLD	STD	INC/DEC Grp4	Indirct Grp5
							Eb	Ev								